Latin American Macroeconomic Reforms

Center for Research on Economic Development and Policy Reform

Latin American Macroeconomic Reforms
The Second Stage

Edited by **José Antonio González, Vittorio Corbo, Anne O. Krueger, and Aaron Tornell**

The University of Chicago Press

Chicago and London

José Antonio González is a senior research associate and Latin American project coordinator at the Center for Research on Economic Development and Policy Reform (CREDPR). Vittorio Corbo is professor of economics at Pontificia Universidad Católica de Chile. Anne O. Krueger is the Herald L. and Caroline L. Ritch Professor in Humanities and Sciences, director of CREDPR, and senior fellow by courtesy at Hoover Institution. Aaron Tornell is a nonresident senior fellow of CREDPR and professor of economics at University of California–Los Angeles.

The University of Chicago Press, Chicago 60637
The University of Chicago Press, Ltd., London

Printed in the United States of America
12 11 10 09 08 07 06 05 04 03   1 2 3 4 5
ISBN: 0-226-30267-9 (cloth)

Library of Congress Cataloging-in-Publication Data

Latin American macroeconomic reforms : the second stage / edited by
José Antonio González . . . [et al.]
p. cm.
Papers prepared for a conference held by Stanford University's Center for Research on Economic Development and Policy Reform in Nov. 2000.
Includes bibliographical references (p.) and index.
ISBN 0-226-30267-9 (cloth : alk. paper)
1. Monetary policy—Latin America—Congresses. 2. Latin America—Commercial policy—Congresses. 3. Fiscal policy—Latin America—Congresses. I. González Anaya, José Antonio, 1967–
II. Stanford University. Center for Research on Economic Development and Policy Reform.

HG660.5 .L38 2003
339.5′098—dc21

2002032046

∞ The paper used in this publication meets the minimum requirements of the American National Standard for Information Sciences—Permanence of Paper for Printed Library Materials, ANSI Z39.48-1992.

Contents

II. Financial Policies

III. Fiscal Policies

Foreword

Arnold C. Harberger

Nearly half a century has passed since I first set foot on Latin American soil on July 1, 1955, but I can say without fear of exaggeration that I have been a watchful and interested observer of that area's economic events and policies ever since. Under these circumstances it is quite natural for me to call attention in this foreword to what Latin America was like back then, and to how substantial have been the economic changes, reforms, even transformations that have taken place over the intervening decades.

The first thing I think of when the "old regime" comes to mind is inflation—inflation that had its roots, more than 90 percent of the time, in fiscal deficits financed either directly by the central bank, or indirectly by the banking system through monetary expansion engendered by the central bank. There are stories to tell about these inflations. In the beginning we were still operating under the Bretton Woods system, which envisioned fixed exchange rates as the norm, punctuated by occasional devaluations to correct for so-called fundamental disequilibria. In the inflationary countries of the time—principally Argentina, Brazil, Chile, and Uruguay—these fundamental disequilibria were, of course, man-made. Something we were not fully aware of then is that inflation comes about only reluctantly in a true fixed exchange rate system. What happens first is a rapid draining of a country's international reserves as a large fraction of the newly printed money is inevitably spent on tradable goods. We learned this lesson in the late 1960s and early 1970s, as the so-called monetary approach to the balance of payments was conceived and elaborated. This caused us to take a second look at the inflations of the 1950s and 1960s, and some from even

Arnold C. Harberger is professor of economics at the University of California, Los Angeles, and professor emeritus at the University of Chicago.

later. What we found was that, yes, there was printing of money to finance fiscal deficits, and yes, this provided the fuel for inflationary rises in the price level. The new insight, however, was that there was an intervening step between these two stages, namely, the imposition of trade restrictions to prevent, or at least stem, the loss of international reserves. These restrictions took on all sorts of forms—tariffs, import licenses, lists of prohibited imports, lists of permitted imports (with all others being prohibited), special surcharges levied on top of tariffs and other applicable taxes, mandatory delays between the receipt of imports and the payment for them, prior deposits by which importers were required to deposit and hold large multiples of (even up to ten times) the value of expected imports at the central bank (at zero interest and for extended periods) before permission to import was granted. Then there were multiple exchange rates, which always fascinated me because they set widely different prices for something (like the U.S. dollar) that is more homogenous than almost any other tangible real-world commodity. When I first saw multiple rates in Chile in the 1950s, they differed by a factor of up to three. The culmination was during the Allende period, when at one point in early 1973 there were about a dozen *official* rates of exchange, ranging from a low of 25 escudos to a high of more than 1, 200 escudos to the dollar!

The experiences just cited created a link between the problems of inflation and protectionism, which was the second dominant characteristic of Latin American economic policies in my early decades of observing. Of course, there were other sources of protectionism besides simply protecting the countries' reserves during inflationary episodes. There was also a sort of chronic protectionism, pursued actively by policymakers. The intellectual father of that protectionism was Raul Prebisch, an Argentine economist and long-time head of the United Nations' Economic Commission for Latin America, whose experts actually "helped" countries design protectionist schemes of "import-substituting industrialization."

Thus we had a sort of permanent protectionism, motivated by a desire for self-sufficiency and a very suspicious and defensive attitude toward world markets, side by side with an ad hoc protectionism motivated primarily by balance-of-payments considerations in the face of inflationary monetary and fiscal policies. The worst of the ad hoc protectionist measures were rarely permanent—they so disrupted ordinary business dealings that they could hardly be so. The typical pattern here was an inflationary spurt bolstered by a series of ad hoc import restrictions. This went on until the complaints (about both the inflation itself and its consequent trade interventions) became so loud that the government simply had to listen. Then there would be a general reform, usually entailing a fiscal package, a promise of monetary discipline, and a major devaluation, plus the release of many of the ad hoc restrictions.

This pattern led to another characteristic of several Latin American economies in those years, namely, a sawtooth pattern of the real exchange rate. Each nominal devaluation would lead to a sharp jump in the real price of the dollar, which then would be eroded as further internal inflation ensued (because the reform package did not "stick"). This up-and-down movement of the real exchange rate proved to be an additional type of protectionism, as business leaders soon learned how precarious it was to invest in export-oriented activities. An investment that promised a real rate of return of 20 percent per year could easily be turned into a serious money loser, merely through the inflation-induced upward drift of costs while revenues remained essentially unchanged, deriving from world prices converted at a fixed exchange rate.

One of the first steps in the direction of reform was the introduction in a few countries (first Brazil, then Chile, then Colombia) of the concept of *minidevaluations.* This was a sort of managed float, designed to keep the real exchange rate from bouncing back and forth in the old sawtooth pattern. There are really two variants of the minidevaluation story. One is very close to a flexible exchange rate, in which the policy, while aiming to keep the nominal exchange rate moving more or less with the price level, nonetheless allows the real exchange rate to move up or down in the process, seeking its own equilibrium. The second variant, pursued in Brazil (1968–79) and in Chile (1985–98) includes also trying to fix (Brazil) or seriously influence (Chile) the equilibrium value of the real exchange rate. This is much more difficult than just smoothing fluctuations, but it proved possible to do. Brazil achieved near-stability of the real exchange rate for nearly eleven years using a combination of international reserve accumulation and modification of trade restrictions as the main policy instruments. Chile managed to substantially influence the time path of the real exchange rate, using first the early payment of international debts, and later the accumulation of international assets as its main instruments.

The final characteristic of the old policy regime in Latin America was a proliferation of state enterprises on the one hand and of arbitrary, typically ill-conceived regulations of private enterprises on the other. State enterprises fell prey to all of their innate vulnerabilities—keeping their product prices so low that they needed perennial subsidies to stay alive, being cut off from credit markets because of their financial weakness, paying above-market wages to low-skilled workers and below-market salaries to executives, refusing to abandon unprofitable products or production lines, and so on.

Regulations on many private-sector activities presented similar problems—public utility rates too low to permit the economic viability of enterprises; many arbitrary controls on investments, whether domestic or foreign in origin; huge amounts of red tape involved in starting new businesses; enormously heavy-handed efforts at "directing" the lending operations of banks; and interest rate regulations that fostered negative real rates during many of the inflation episodes, and generated huge disincentives to saving as well as a complete abdication of market forces in controlling the allocation of investments.

It is difficult to exaggerate how much Latin America has changed since those days. It was by no means, however, a smooth trajectory from bad to good. Two major blots stand out along the path from then to now. The first is a commentary on our human frailty. Somewhere along the line, starting in the early 1960s and carrying through to the 1970s, the "old" inflationary countries—Argentina, Brazil, Chile, and Uruguay, plus (to a degree) Bolivia and Peru—learned that they should try to avoid highly volatile real exchange rates, negative real interest rates, and the like. In short, the lesson was, if you're going to have inflation, learn to live with it. This was good advice, and by and large it led to periods when, in spite of inflation, savers could earn positive real interest rates on their savings and real exchange rates were less volatile than before. Broadly speaking, Chile and Uruguay by 1975 or so had learned this lesson well, and gained significantly as a result. In the other countries, however, the law of unanticipated consequences prevailed. Yes, they institutionalized inflationary adjustments in various sectors of their economies—but instead of resulting in lower economic cost for the same or similar inflation rates, their actions seem to have resulted in much higher inflation rates. It is as if in the earliest period, when there were basically no mechanisms in place for living with inflation, the most that countries could stand was an inflation rate of around 100 percent. Then, as the mechanisms of living with inflation were being introduced, this breaking point moved up to about 400 percent. Finally, as the mechanisms became more refined and more widespread, the breaking point went up to something like 20 or 30 percent per month, reaching in some cases over 20,000 percent over the span of a year. All of which goes to show that economic science holds no cure for irresponsibility in government!

The other blot on the record in the last quarter of the century was the emergence of inflation in a number of previously stable countries, notably Mexico and countries in Central America. Many Mexicans believe that the untimely death of Rodrigo Gomez, longtime governor of the Banco de México, had a lot to do with that country's loss of fiscal and ultimately monetary discipline. I do not have a strong opinion here, but am certain that, had Gomez continued as central bank governor, the level of antieconomic populism in Mexico's economic policy would have been greatly reduced.

In the cases of the Central American countries, I find it difficult to pinpoint a cause for their fall from grace. The period 1960–78 represented almost an economic paradise for the region as a whole, with real growth rates averaging about 6 percent per year under successfully operated, fixed exchange rate systems. Then, however, the dam broke, and one by one these countries drifted into inflationary phases that ultimately led to the abandonment of their long-time exchange rate stability.

I offer here only two possible explanations, which could well have worked in tandem to produce this result. The first was the negative shock of the sharp drop in coffee prices combined with the great rise of petroleum prices at the end of the 1970s. Were these shocks strong enough to strain their fixed exchange rates to the breaking point? I do not know, but it is a worthy topic for study. One thing that we do know is that fixed exchange rate systems can successfully manage real exchange rate adjustment in response to small shocks in either direction, and in response to large shocks when they are positive (such as export price booms or big inflows of capital). The Achilles heel of fixed exchange rate systems, however, is the large negative shock (an export price bust or a sudden major flight of capital).

My second explanation for the collapse of discipline in the Central American economies was their succumbing to temptation. The story is this: As world inflation accelerated in the late 1970s, the interest rates at which the Central American countries could borrow became (temporarily) negative in real terms. This caused a number of them to actively seek foreign loans, only to have their expectations betrayed when real price interest rates turned sharply positive in the early 1980s.

By now, however, economic policy seems to be more on track in Latin America as a whole than it has been at any time in the past half century. This is why this volume takes for granted the so-called first stage reforms, and focuses on the second stage.

Certainly, the tone of the papers is generally upbeat, sometimes perhaps bordering on triumphalism. My own belief is that the Latin American economies have indeed entered a new stage, but also that they will continue to be hit by shocks and vicissitudes, old and new.

I would urge readers to be wary of formulas that have the flavor of panaceas. One such formula of which we have heard much in recent years is currency boards or dollarization. These represent an extreme form of a fixed exchange rate system, in which the central bank essentially abandons the role of lender of last resort. This may work well when there are no major negative shocks, and perhaps if some other lender of last resort enters the picture when needed. However, recent experience shows that the rules of this game are indeed very hard to follow in times of serious adversity. In the most prominent case of a so-called currency board, Argentina saved its system by seriously deviating from the rules of the game in both of its recent moments of major strain—1995 and 2001. This was done both by modifying the reserve requirements to which commercial banks were subject, and by defining certain dollar-denominated Argentine government bonds as foreign currency that could serve as part of the central bank's international reserves. My judgment is that this breaking of the rules was a vital element in dealing with these crises. So I take this experience not as a complaint about Argentine policy but as a warning against thinking that a strict currency board (or dollarization) represents a sensible "corner solution" for countries subject to major negative shocks.

The second panacea against which I would like to warn is the idea that central bank policy is at its best when it is concentrated on a single objective, most often price stability, or a stable and low rate of inflation. The story here is much like the previous one. It is wonderful to think of Costa Rica's central bank faithfully following a price-level target, or one of a 2–5 percent annual inflation rate. This can work well for years, even decades, and can yield great positive dividends—but then think of the troubles that could come: a president assassinated, an earthquake destroying half the buildings in San Jose, a total collapse of coffee and banana prices, an "unreliable" government reaching power and causing a major flight of capital. All these shocks are ones that call for a devaluation of the equilibrium real exchange rate and a rise on the local real interest rate. My judgment would be that the least costly solution would typically entail using all three shock absorbers—a modest deflationary pressure on the prices of nontradables, a rise in the nominal exchange rate sufficient to bring the real exchange rate into equilibrium, and a rise in real interest rates sufficient to avert major capital flight and to equilibrate the internal capital market. Note that keeping the exchange rate fixed would require a much higher interest rate and a much more forceful deflation than this combined package. Note, too, that a rigid inflation or price-level target essentially entails a deflation of nontradables prices sufficient to fully offset the upward impact of any devaluation on the price level of tradables.

I do not want to be misunderstood. I am not arguing against a country's adopting a fixed exchange rate, or against a central bank's pursuing a price level or inflation target. However, I do want to argue against making these objectives so dominant that they are asked to prevail, no matter what the shock, no matter how adverse the circumstances. Reason and common sense should prevail in economic policy, as in other aspects of life. In the end, policy should be based on a sober and professional weighing of costs and benefits, not on arbitrary rules, even if they are, most of the time, very good rules.

I hope this brief foreword gives readers of this book something of the flavor of Latin America's recent economic history. Readers will see many topics explored and many fruitful suggestions for the remaining tasks that the countries of the Western Hemisphere face as they adjust their policies for the twenty-first century. Readers will perceive, too, that the authors of this volume do not sing in unison. There are rich tonalities to be appreciated, and interesting juxtapositions of counterpoint. What readers can be sure of is an excellent sampling of the best professional thinking that can be found today, on the problems of economic policy facing the countries of Latin America.

Acknowledgments

The papers in this volume were initially prepared for the first Latin American Conference held by Stanford's Center for Research on Economic Development and Policy Reform (CREDPR). Given Latin America's long history of macroeconomic instability, it seemed appropriate to make the first conference in the subject of macroeconomic reforms: monetary, fiscal, and financial.

The most important debts are to the contributors to this volume. All of the authors delivered excellent papers in a timely fashion. Their contributions and cooperation made the editing of this volume a relatively simple and pleasant task.

Funds for the conference and the editing of the volume came from the President's Fund of Stanford University, the William and Flora Hewlett Foundation, the Lynde and Harry Bradley Foundation, the Becthel Foundation, Banco Santander, CEMEX, and Veritas. We are grateful to them all.

Cosima A. Schneider, of the Stanford economics department, and Grecia Marrufo, a postdoctoral fellow at CREDPR, provided expert and conscientious research assistance in the preparation of this volume.

Last but not least we would like to thank Nicholas Hope, deputy director for the center, who has been a key contributor to its success; the administrative staff, particularly Helen McMahon, Nichelle Sevier, and Dafna Baldwin, for their work in overseeing conference arrangements; and John Shoven, director of the Stanford Institute for Economic Policy Research (SIEPR), Deborah Carvalho, institute administrator, and their colleagues at SIEPR for their support of CREDPR and the conference.

Introduction

José Antonio González and Anne O. Krueger

If this volume had been written ten years ago, the dominant macroeconomic policy themes would have been inflation stabilization, fiscal discipline, and trade and financial liberalization.[1] Latin America was regarded as a region in the world with endemic inflation and macroeconomic instability. The region's economic performance had generally been poor, and the conventional wisdom was that it would remain so unless macroeconomic stability was reestablished through fiscal discipline, financial liberalization, and greater openness to the rest of the world.

Remarkable changes occurred in the region during the 1990s. Figure 1 shows that the median inflation rate in Latin America has fallen dramatically (and the average even more so), public-sector deficits have shrunk remarkably, and macroeconomic imbalances are generally smaller or even absent. Most Latin American economies are considerably more open than they were a decade ago, and their economic policies in general are less distorted.

Nonetheless, issues remain. As with other areas of economic policy reform, success in getting through the first stage only opens the way for needed second-stage reforms to complete the process and take full advantage of the effort previously made. Progress in macroeconomic reforms has made countries more stable, but they are still vulnerable to internal and ex-

José Antonio González is a senior research associate and Latin American project coordinator at the Center for Research on Economic Development and Policy Reform (CREDPR). Anne O. Krueger is the Herald L. and Caroline L. Ritch Professor in Humanities and Sciences, director of CREDPR, and senior fellow by courtesy at Hoover Institution.

1. See Bruno et al. (1990) and Bruno et al. (1992) for good examples of the major macroeconomic policy issues at the end of the 1980s.

ternal shocks, and it is important to continue to improve macroeconomic management in order to avoid the probability of a crisis. To assess progress to date and analyze the need for further reforms with respect to macroeconomic policy and financial issues, a conference was held at Stanford University's Center for Research on Economic Development and Policy Reform (CREDPR) in November 2000. Academics, policymakers, and others concerned with the nature of these issues met for two days. The papers presented in this volume are revised versions of those presented at the conference, and they provide many examples of the need to continue to move the reform process forward and the manner in which to do so.

The papers and discussion at the conference focused on what we have arbitrarily labeled "second-stage macroeconomic reforms." In the literature, attaining macroeconomic stability is usually considered the first and most crucial "first-generation reform, " whereas second-generation reforms are usually thought to be microeconomic and institutional in nature—regulation for newly privatized industries, education and health reforms to address income distribution and poverty issues, improvement of the rule of law to operate better markets, and the creation of institutions to support first-generation changes. However, the evolution of macroeconomic policies in Latin America shows us that one can think of second-stage macroeconomic reforms that are needed if the full benefits of first-stage reforms are to be realized. The papers contained in this volume present a few—it is to be hoped, the most important—of these second-stage reforms that countries need to address.

Monetary policy in Latin America shifted away from the elimination of fiscal dominance during the first macroeconomic reform stage to the elimination of financial-sector dominance in this second stage. The emphasis is not on inflation stabilization from close to or actually hyperinflationary levels, as it was in the late 1980s, but on inflation targeting to lower inflation from high to low single digits. The implications for interest and exchange rate policy are key and need to be reevaluated. Finally, the emphasis today is on developing institutional arrangements for responsible monetary policies. Countries found that independent central banks with exchange rate targets could not conduct independent monetary policy. The changes today include establishing truly independent central banks with clear mandates and public monetary rules.

The financial-sector reform agenda shifted away from interest rate and capital account liberalization to sustainable increases in financial-sector depth, improvements in competition, improvements in regulation and supervision, and implementation of institutional mechanisms to manage national liquidity in an environment of volatile capital flows while at the same time eliminating the "umbilical cord" between the financial sector and the central bank. The changes look to reduce the probability of financial crisis and better manage the renewed and expanded access to world capital markets.

Finally, fiscal discipline has been accepted as a sine qua non for macroeconomic stability. In the first-stage macroeconomic reforms, fiscal policy discussions centered on the importance of fiscal discipline and the dangers of depending on inflation tax for revenues. Today, the second-stage challenges look to institutionalize fiscal discipline through constitutional fiscal responsibility laws, improving the efficiency of already existing tax systems, improving the allocative efficiency and equity of expenditures, and modifying institutional arrangements to deal with increasingly decentralized federal systems.

Figures 1–4 indicate that the cautious optimism and shift in emphasis reflect the success of Latin American countries in achieving greater macroeconomic stability but, at the same time, highlight the region's remaining vulnerability. Latin American countries need to continue to reform macroeconomic policies in order to reap the full benefits of macroeconomic stability.

Figure 2 gives the median inflation rates in Latin America from 1980 to 2000. The median inflation rate fell from over 100 percent per year to less than 10 percent by 1999 (the average inflation rate in the 1980s was even higher because of some triple-digit hyperinflationary countries). Much of the reason for this reduction in inflation originated in the wholehearted adoption of fiscal discipline shown in figure 1. Nonfinancial public-sector deficits went from a median of more than 4 percent in the early 1980s to less than 2 percent by 2000. Monetary policy is no longer hamstrung by the need to support fiscal imbalances.

Figure 3 gives annual data on the median real gross domestic product

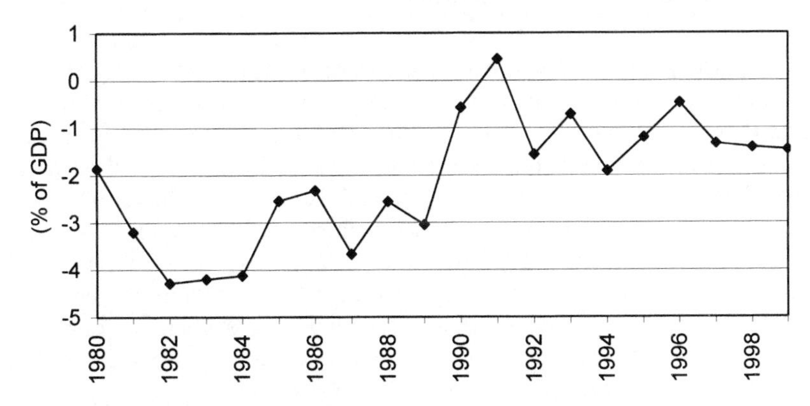

Fig. 1 Median nonfinancial public-sector deficits in Latin America
Notes: The sample of Latin American countries includes: Argentina, Bolivia, Brazil, Chile, Colombia, Ecuador, Mexico, Peru, Uruguay, and Venezuela. The source for inflation rates, current account balances, and GDP growth rates is the *International Financial Statistics*. The fiscal balances come from the *Government Financial Statistics*.

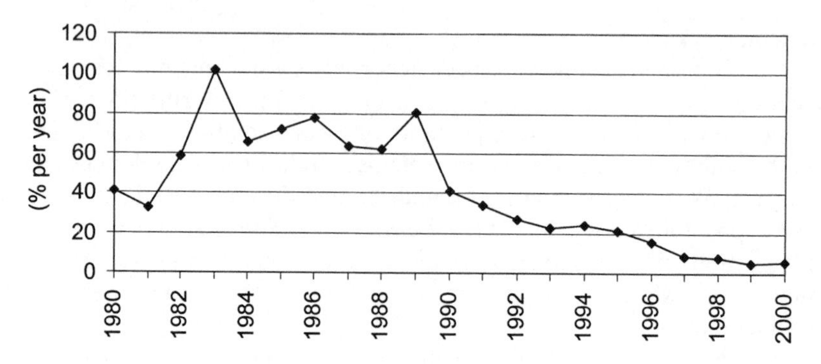

Fig. 2 Latin America median inflation rates

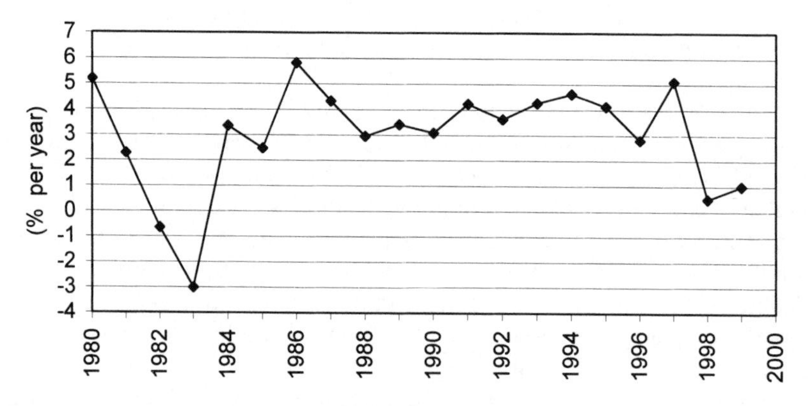

Fig. 3 Median GDP growth in Latin America

(GDP) growth rate for Latin America over the same period. After a dismal economic performance in the early 1980s, Latin American economic growth accelerated to a rate of over 3 percent annually from 1986 through 1997. Since then, however, growth has once again fallen. The decline in the growth rate reflects some of Latin America's continuing vulnerability. Figure 4 sheds further light on this issue by showing the median current account deficits experienced by Latin American countries over the same two decades. Latin America ran large current account deficits in the early 1980s (leading up to the debt crisis). The deficits almost disappeared by the late 1980s and then reemerged in the 1990s as capital inflows increased in response to more satisfactory economic growth rates.

A significant share of these fluctuations results from external shocks even though Latin American fiscal and monetary policies have generally improved. Current account balances fluctuate significantly with the supply of capital inflows from abroad, and terms-of-trade shocks affect an

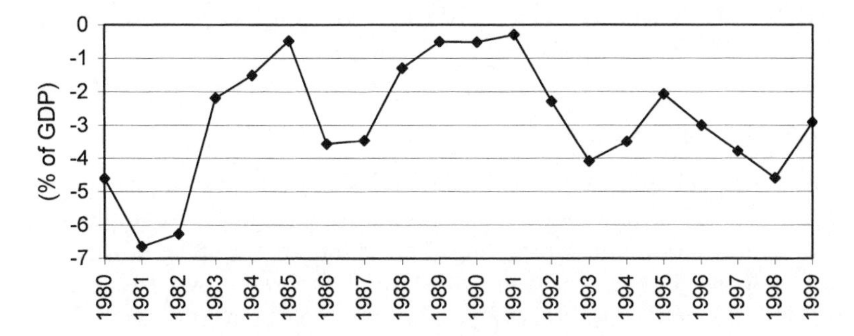

Fig. 4 Median current account balances in Latin America

export base that, although diversifying, is still concentrated with a heavy share of primary products. The dramatic drop in growth rates following the 1997 crises is evidence that Latin America was vulnerable to the Asian, Russian, and Brazilian crises because macroeconomic stability does not eliminate vulnerability to external or internal shocks.

A more drastic example of this vulnerability is the recent experience in Argentina. The conference predated the Argentinean crisis by a little over a year. None of the papers addresses the Argentinean crisis directly, but four of the five papers on the financial sector deal with measures to abate vulnerability. The consensus among Latin American economists even as early as November 2000 was that some sort of correction was inevitable. The issue was not whether there was going to be a financial crisis but when and exactly how it was going to play out. Contagion was not perceived to be a major concern, because other countries in the region appeared to have solid macroeconomic fundamentals. However, it is fair to say that most in the profession greatly underestimated the magnitude of the economic meltdown and the degree of social unrest that actually took place. We have chosen not to superficially revise the papers or provide a premature assessment of events; instead, we opted to capture the status of macroeconomic policymaking in Latin America as of November 2000, which we think remains true even after Argentina: macroeconomic reforms have come a long way, but they are still far from complete.

The papers in this volume address many of the issues associated with second-stage macroeconomic reforms in greater depth. The papers fall into three broad categories—monetary, financial, and fiscal policies—and they emphasize the second-stage nature described earlier. The content of the papers shows that monetary and financial policies have become increasingly linked, and the division between financial and monetary policy is blurring. Part I starts with the papers that focus primarily on monetary policy. The papers in Part II are concerned primarily with financial policies. Part III then covers aspects of fiscal policy designed to improve the efficiency of government expenditures and revenues.

Part I: Monetary Policies

In the first chapter, Vittorio Corbo and Klaus Schmidt-Hebbel provide an overview of the perils and challenges that Latin American countries face as they move to inflation targeting. This is the first instance of a second-stage reform. The region made substantial progress toward eradicating high inflation in the first stage (figure 1 shows that the average is now below 10 percent), and the issue in this second stage is to achieve and maintain low one-digit inflation levels. The Corbo and Schmidt-Hebbel paper assesses the implementation and results of inflation targeting. The authors start by reviewing the issues relevant for the choice of exchange rate regimes and monetary rules, documenting the evolution of exchange rate and monetary policy over the past two decades. Their starting point is the recognition that there are three options open to policymakers: an exchange rate anchor for policy, a monetary anchor, or an inflation target. They believe that Latin American countries are moving to "corner solutions" with either a fully pegged regime (with a currency board or currency union) or a freely floating exchange rate complemented with inflation targeting.

Corbo and Schmidt-Hebbel then contrast the experience of different groups of countries. Brazil and Chile are full-fledged inflation-targeting regimes, whereas Colombia, Mexico, and Peru are found to be partial inflation-targeting regimes. Output sacrifices in moving to low inflation generally appear to have been relatively low, and even negative in some cases, and output volatility has decreased.

The authors conclude by focusing on the dynamics of inflation reduction in Chile, the country with the longest experience. They find that initial progress in reducing inflation toward the target rate was slow as the public was learning about the true commitment of the central bank; that the gradual phasing-in of inflation targeting helped in reducing inflationary expectations and thereby contributed to reducing inflation directly and indirectly through changes in wage and price dynamics; and that a "cold-turkey" implementation of inflation targeting would have resulted in a significantly larger output sacrifice in the short run.

In addition to the papers presented in this volume, panel discussions were held at the conference. Fortunately some panelists consented to write up their remarks. In his panel intervention, Alejandro Werner provides a pragmatic view of Mexico's gradual and piecemeal adoption of inflation targeting as a comment to Corbo and Schmidt-Hebbel's paper. He argues that Mexico adopted an inflation-targeting framework in a gradual and piecemeal way out of the commitment to price stability, the breakdown of a stable relationship between money growth and inflation, the adoption of a floating exchange rate, and the need for a transparent framework to improve the credibility of the monetary authority. He addresses four issues. First, he describes the preconditions for the preconditions for the transition to inflation targeting, highlighting the importance of fiscal discipline, central bank independence, and the adoption of floating regimes with limited intervention. Second, he highlights the pragmatic advantages of inflation targeting as a monetary policy, which rest on establishing a transparent framework for the conduct of monetary policy that is useful as a marketing device, a communication tool, and a mechanism of accountability to the public at large. Specifically, he notes that (1) establishing a clear set of short- and medium-run objectives, and setting up the channels through which central banks communicate what actions are being undertaken to accomplish these goals, increases the efficiency of monetary policy; (2) providing a structure and choosing instruments that allow short-term deviations from the target while maintaining the long-run inflation objective creates a credible nominal anchor; (3) forcing the central bank to be explicit about the risks associated with its inflation projections justifies the central bank's continuous monitoring and policy reactions; and (4) by establishing clear mechanisms of accountability, the inflation-targeting framework provides a useful technology to discipline the monetary authority. Third, Werner also documents Mexico's gradual transition to inflation targeting after it abandoned the crawling band exchange rate regime in 1994.

Finally, Werner addresses some future challenges faced by inflation-targeting countries in Latin America. Due to a chronically inflationary past, Werner sees the extreme sensitivity of inflation expectations and inflation itself (due to the history of inflation) to exchange rate movements as limiting the scope of the exchange rate to function as a shock absorber. The challenge is to turn the exchange rate into one more relative price, rather than a signal of future changes in the rate of inflation. Moreover, there exists a potential conflict if a rise in interest rates in response to increased aggregate demand results in an increased current account deficit that increases external vulnerability. Werner sees the best solution as lying in improved coordination of monetary and fiscal policy.

In the next chapter, José Antonio González examines the way dollarization affects the transmission channel of nominal exchange rate fluctuations into domestic inflation for thirteen countries in Latin America between 1980 and 2000. To this end, he estimates both long-run and annual pass-through of nominal exchange rate changes to the price level. Over the longer term, he finds a relatively constant relationship between the exchange rate and the domestic price level with purchasing power parity (PPP) holding, so that there is full exchange rate pass-through to domestic prices, thus confirming Werner's concern in this regard.

González notes that the experience differs somewhat for different groups of countries and that higher pass-through is not associated with higher dollarization. The monetary policy implications are that partially dollarized economies can still adjust their real exchange rate through nominal devaluations and that increases in dollarization do not hinder the functioning of exchange rate changes: a nominal devaluation leads to changes in relative prices of tradables versus nontradables by about the same proportion regardless of the degree of dollarization in a country. The result indicates that even if the unit of account is the U.S. dollar, the price of nontradables is determined by local supply and demand conditions rather than by indexation. However, he does find a consistent, albeit insignificant, relationship between a higher speed of adjustment and the degree of dollarization both within and across countries.

In chapter 3, Márcio G. P. Garcia and Tatiana Didier review the arguments in the finance and open macroeconomics literature relevant for the central bank to set the level of interest rates in an open economy. There are two risks: currency and country. However, those risks share some common causes. Thus, if those common causes are successfully addressed, domestic interest rates can fall substantially.

Garcia and Didier then provide estimates of the factors that entered into country and currency risk for Brazil, and analyze the determinants of those risks. Fiscal deficits and domestic and international financial market conditions all play a role. Convertibility risk, defined as the risk that one might not be able to convert local into foreign currency, was important in Brazil during the period of international financial crises but no longer appears significant. After the change in the exchange rate regime, the country risk associated with Brazil appears to have diminished substantially, but currency risk has remained, according to their estimates. Garcia and Didier conclude by noting that high domestic interest rates seem to reflect uncertainty about the future behavior of the balance of payments, and that if vigorous export growth could be achieved without devaluation, it would do much to lower domestic interest rates.

The epilogue to the monetary policy section is by Gustavo H. B. Franco and originated from his panel discussion. He traced some of the salient characteristics of Brazil's monetary experience. It serves as a somber reminder that fiscal dominance of monetary policy was a reality in Brazil until the mid-1990s. Franco's exposition provides an excellent summary of the institutional difficulties that the Banco Central do Brasil has endured as it has evolved from an institution subjugated to the excesses of fiscal policy to a well-functioning but not yet solidly established independent central bank. In Brazil, monetary policy prior to the start of the Real plan in 1994 was guided by two objectives: (1) to finance government through the lowest-cost combination of money, indexed debt issuance, and an open "window" for state development banks for sectoral funds; and (2) to prevent dollarization by making well-remunerated indexed instruments that could out-compete the foreign currency instruments that were abundantly available. The end of fiscal dominance of monetary policy only appeared when the treasury provided hard budget constraints through measures "below the line, " restricting the borrowing needs of the federal and subnational governments (as opposed to budgetary control). Once inflation abated, the Brazilian central bank was able to change its objectives to the pursuit of price stability and the avoidance of financial crises.

Franco proceeds to analyze the efficacy of the current institutional arrangements and monetary policy in Brazil. He believes that fiscal dominance has continued to diminish, that the banking system is sound, and that the central bank is operating by inflation targeting. Although monetary policy in Brazil has progressed remarkably, Franco ends with a precautionary note about the legal fragility of the independence of the central bank.

Part II: Financial Policies

Throughout the world, the distinction between banks and other financial institutions is increasingly blurred, and this creates challenges for monetary policy. As mentioned earlier, the discussion on financial-sector policies is not centered on interest and capital account liberalization but on improving regulation and supervision, creating institutions to improve the depth and efficiency of the financial system, and setting up mechanisms to lower fragility and decrease the probability of financial crisis.

The first paper in this section is by Francisco Gil Díaz. He argues that central banks should take a narrow view of their mandate to lower inflation, making every effort to reduce links to the financial sector in order to avoid moral hazard in the financial system, and pursue a "corner" exchange rate policy: either a pure float or a fixed (through a currency board) exchange rate. He uses the 1995 Mexican financial crisis as a case from which these lessons can be learned. He traces the origins of Mexico's crisis back to the 1982 nationalization of the Mexican banks and thereafter when appropriate liberalization policies were undermined by both a defective privatization and the flawed decisions of the incoming Zedillo administration. In addition, dysfunctional institutional arrangements placed the responsibility both for conducting exchange rate policy and for providing lender-of-last-resort facilities on the Banco de México, which led many to see the bank's open purse as making its exchange rate policy pronouncements less than fully credible.

Gil Díaz dismisses his preferred solution, to eliminate independent domestic currencies and lenders of last resort altogether, as politically infeasible. Instead, he concludes that the best alternative is to improve institutional arrangements, making sure that exchange rate policy is at one polar extreme or the other, and cutting the umbilical cord between the banking sector and the central bank by carefully defining what the Banco de México will and will not do with regard to the commercial banks during financial crisis. For example, he argues that after the Mexican crisis in 1995, the bailout should have been handled in a "once-and-for-all" single swoop, not in the piecemeal series of actions that were adopted to prevent banks from continuing to make bad loans in the expectation that their entire portfolio would benefit from any bailout package.

In his panel intervention, Roberto Zahler takes issue with Gil Díaz's view and elaborates on the difficulties and conflicts of pursuing too narrowly the objective of price stability, which without question should be the primary objective of monetary policy. His exposition elaborates on some of the nuances of this apparently simple objective. The first consideration is that monetary and financial policies are quite interrelated through the central bank's roles as lender of last resort and, in many cases, financial supervisor and regulator.

The author argues that the central bank's anti-inflation policies must not generate any major imbalances in other key areas of the economy, like unemployment, imbalances in financial markets, or an untenable deterioration of external accounts. Moreover, it should play an active role in avoiding bubbles in "key macro prices" like the real exchange rate and "voluntary" foreign capital inflows, which increase the fragility of the financial sector and decrease the efficiency of monetary policy. Zahler concludes with reflections on the institutional arrangements of central banks, emphasizing that autonomy and independence should be accompanied by increased accountability, transparency, and coordination with fiscal and financial policies.

In chapter 5, Ricardo J. Caballero argues that Latin American countries need to design better international liquidity management because the region still experiences terms-of-trade shocks and capital flow sudden stops. The author addresses three sequential questions: Is there a need for decentralized or centralized international liquidity management? What are the macroeconomic policies the public sector should follow even while the private sector is facing the socially efficient prices in deciding its international liquidity position? And when and how should the government attempt to force the private sector to increase its international liquidity position? He argues that weak links to international financial markets can trigger excess volatility through sudden withdrawals of international liquidity and that underdeveloped financial markets make the economy too vulnerable to external shocks as investors do not value international liquidity enough, creating less international collateral than is socially optimal.

Two sets of policy recommendations are put forth. If the private sector is already facing the socially efficient prices when deciding on its international liquidity position, the decentralized equilibrium is efficient, given structural constraints, and the government should limit its actions to alleviate these constraints. There are two generic strategies: (1) structural reforms in financial markets and the contractual environment; and (2) use of any commitment capability that the government may have (and the private sector does not) that is valuable to international investors and lenders. The second set of policies concentrates on the time and manner in which the government should attempt to force the private sector to increase its international liquidity position.

In chapter 6, Philip L. Brock uses the trade liberalization experiences of Chile in the 1970s and 1980s and the United States in the 1830s and 1840s to argue that trade liberalizations create conditions conducive to a financial crisis. Rather than following the sudden stop literature and argumentation, Brock emphasizes the importance of time-to-build considerations and moral hazard in the creation of lending booms that lead to financial fragility following a trade liberalization. His proposition contrasts with the view that trade liberalization and crises have no connection and that government deposit insurance causes crises following trade liberalization. The similarities between the two countries' experiences are remarkable. Trade liberalization was followed by capital inflows, exchange rate appreciation, and a massive expansion of banking credit, all of which left the country vulnerable to external shocks.

Brock argues that an economy that is growing slowly with a protective trade regime has few investments and requires little liquidity. Trade liberalization results in a new set of investment opportunities, and the economy moves from a self-financing structure to one with a need for financing a time-to-build export production capacity. This results in increased demand for longer-term credit. Financial liberalization leads to large capital inflows that fit into the time-to-build view of adjustment to trade liberalization, trade deficits, and diminished supplies of liquid assets by banks. The control of bank moral hazard becomes politically difficult as traditional instruments, which rely on constraining the growth of banks, come into conflict with the increased credit demands of a high-growth economy. In the aftermath of financial crises, second-stage reforms in both the United States and Chile focused on debt adjustment, the elimination of special privilege from banking, and constitutional reform to limit state intervention in banking.

In chapter 7, Stephen Haber investigates two current financial-sector questions using the contrasting concurrent historical episodes of the textile industry in Mexico and Brazil at the turn of the nineteenth century. What impact do small and concentrated banking systems have on the competitive structure and performance of the manufacturing industry? Why do financial markets not serve as a substitute for banks? In Mexico during the *Porfiriato*, government policies constrained the number of banks in any market while capital markets and foreign investment did not serve as substitutes. As a result, only a small group of entrepreneurs was able to benefit from bank finance, and most had to rely upon retained earnings and their informal network of business associates for funds. In Brazil the banking system was similar to Mexico's, but bond and equity markets replaced the banking system quite effectively. The reason is that, with the fall of the Brazilian monarchy, there was banking deregulation that included new general incorporation and disclosure laws that were advanced and unusual for the time. As a result, there was a fourfold increase in the capitalization of the stock market in just three years.

The rates of total factor productivity (TFP) growth in Brazilian textile manufacturing were twice that of Mexico. Brazil's textile industry outgrew Mexico's by a factor of five at a time when Mexican income per capita growth exceeded that of Brazil. The level of concentration fell in Brazil while it actually increased in Mexico to a level much greater than that which could be explained by economies of scale. Moreover, Mexican firms were large by international comparisons. Haber concludes that, compared to their Brazilian counterparts, Mexican firms were capital-constrained, and financial markets and banks in Mexico were not choosing winners: they were choosing insiders.

In chapter 8, Pablo E. Guidotti uses the Argentine experience in the last decade to argue that because of the increasing frequency, damage, and contagion effects of recent financial and balance-of-payments crises, the challenge for emerging markets is to better manage capital market disruptions. The strategy to encourage sustainable international capital flows and reduce volatility should focus on three areas. The first broad area is three elements of liquidity risk management in the financial sector: transparency, the need for minimum liquidity requirements (because banks manage their individual liquidity without internalizing systemic risk and because they prevent evergreening), and an effective resolution of problem banks (because no credible banking supervision and regulation can be enforced without a strong signal that banks need to manage risk effectively).

The second broad area is that public and private debt management prior to the crisis is a key element in determining the success or failure of dealing with an external shock. He argues that stocks have more explanatory power than flows and that the maturity structure of the debt is as important as its size because liquidity crises occur despite solvency. Finally, the third broad area is the implications of the recommendations outlined above on different exchange rate regimes. Rather than advocating fixed versus flexible exchange rate regimes a priori, Guidotti argues that with an adequate risk and liquidity management strategy and a commitment to price stability, the choice of exchange rate regime becomes irrelevant. He finds that a fixed exchange rate requires more (international) liquidity, whereas a flexible exchange rate regime requires more institutional strength to attain credibility and deeper financial markets. He points out that part of the reason for the crisis is that the liquidity management strategy was inconsistent or insufficient given the exchange rate regime.

Part III: Fiscal Policies

Part III includes three papers on fiscal policy, and tax policy in particular. Most of the countries in the region have achieved the desired level of fiscal stability. The fiscal issues today are to improve tax collection efficiency, equity, and institutional arrangements to better function in increasingly decentralized governments.

In chapter 9, Vito Tanzi presents a broad view of progress and challenges in tax policy in Latin America, which, in the last decade, experienced a high degree of activism and several reforms and reform attempts. The most influential tax developments in the region were (1) the debt crisis of the early 1980s, which reduced the ability to finance public spending through foreign borrowing and increased the costs of servicing the debt, forcing countries to increase tax revenues; (2) high inflation throughout the 1980s and early 1990s, which eroded real tax revenues due to the collection lag, also known as the *Tanzi effect*; (3) trade liberalization, which lowered tariff revenues; and (4) capital account liberalization, which forced reductions in tax rates to maintain competitiveness.

The author discusses two major tax policy developments in the region. First, trade and cascading domestic sales taxes were replaced with the value-added tax (VAT). The VAT has become the workhorse tax in Latin America, but there is still heterogeneity in its collection efficiency due to exemptions and special regimes. Second, with few exceptions, Latin American countries continue to be resistant to income taxes, especially those levied on personal income. As a result, fiscal needs have introduced interesting experimentation with new taxes and new approaches to taxation. Finally, he concludes that although tax systems in Latin America have made important headway, attention now needs to be turned to improvements in tax equity and efficiency, through improvements in tax administration rather than tax policy.

In chapter 10, Enrique Dávila and Santiago Levy describe a clearly second-stage tax reform to improve collection efficiency. They argue for the elimination of all special regimes and for establishing a uniform 15 percent VAT rate for every good and service. The most important goods and services affected are food, medicines, and books. The argument for the reform is that using the VAT exceptions as redistributive measures is far from efficient because most of the benefits go to the top quintiles of the population. Their proposal has become the centerpiece of Gil Díaz's tax reform proposal in Mexico's current administration.

The measure would generate additional fiscal resources of, at least, 81.3 billion pesos. At the same time, the authors recognize that the poorest segments of the population would be adversely affected and would need to be compensated in order to avoid further hardship. They estimate that the cost of granting an "exact" (Slutsky) compensation for the poorest 75 percent of the population, under the pessimistic assumption that 75 percent of the increase in VAT is transferred to prices, would amount to 32.5 billion pesos. The measure would therefore generate 48.8 billion pesos' worth of net resources for the three levels of government (federal, state, and municipal). In fact, it is possible to overcompensate part of the low-income population and generate available net resources, making the VAT reform simultaneously revenue raising and redistributive. If at least some of those resources are channeled toward social programs, the redistributive impact of the reform is strengthened.

In his comments to Dávila and Levy's paper, Ricardo Fenochietto notes that although the paper concentrates on the Mexican case, the issue is universal and a classic dilemma in Latin America and other emerging economies because the VAT is the most popular consumption tax. Fenochietto argues that the authors are too benevolent in singling out targeting as the only disadvantage of using VAT exemptions as poverty-alleviating mechanisms. First, the exemptions are limited by the income of the household, which is a paradox because their purpose is poverty alleviation. Moreover, exemptions are limited by a poor tax administration, which cannot reimburse to the last stage of transformation, the taxes collected in the previous stages. Second, productive distortions arise as goods are artificially modified to qualify for exemption. Third, the exemptions give rise to rent-seeking by producers who want their products to be included in the exemption basket. Fenochietto provides some shortcomings of the direct transfer programs analyzed in the paper but concludes that the paper takes the right approach.

In chapter 11, Rogério L. F. Werneck reviews the progress and the challenges for indirect taxation in Brazil. Brazil's tax burden had fluctuated at around one-fourth of GDP in the twenty years leading to 1990. The fiscal adjustment necessary to attain a stable macroeconomic scenario came from increases in revenue, not from expenditures cuts, as was the case in most of the countries in Latin America. Few imagined that at the end of the 1990s the tax burden would reach 32 percent of GDP through the introduction of inefficient and distortionary indirect taxes.

Werneck first traces the historical roots of Brazil's tax system. He argues that, as resources were transferred to subnational levels of the government, the federal government devised exotic taxation schemes that would not be shared with lower-level governments. In a simple consistency model, Werneck shows that by introducing a VAT, an excise tax, and a retail sales tax with broad bases it is possible to eliminate all existent indirect and cascading taxes and still have acceptable levels of tax rates. The paper concludes by highlighting the additional difficulties that the Brazilian fiscal federalism imposes on successful tax reforms.

In her comment to Werneck's paper, Carola Pessino stresses three issues. First, she discusses the need to solve the vertical fiscal imbalance problems that exist in many federal countries. Using evidence from Argentina, she argues that tax reform will not occur without "share-revenue" reforms because subnational governments spend a large share of total expenditure but raise a small share of total revenue. Second, she notes that the ideal tax to replace the Brazilian state origin VAT (the ICMS) and other turnover taxes is the shared value-added tax (SVAT), which is in effect a dual VAT. The SVAT is a destination consumption tax that does not distort location of firms, does not allow for tax wars, is practical for countries with high tax evasion, and allows for further decentralization. Third, Pessino indicates that the political difficulty of replacing origin taxation with destination taxation can be solved through the Canadian-like equalization transfer.

Finally, Michael Michaely presents an innovative diagrammatic representation of Werneck's tax reform proposition that could be applied to other countries more generally.

As these papers show, Latin America has come a long way in its fiscal and financial policies. Overall, macroeconomic policymaking has shifted away from stabilization and achieving more rapid economic growth to reducing the volatility of growth rates and economic vulnerability. Labeling this change in emphasis and in the nature of reforms as second-generation macroeconomic reforms is arbitrary, but it seems appropriate. One can only hope that policymakers in the next decade will be able to build on progress to date, reforming along the lines suggested here and in other ways to foster further improvements in the economic performance of the Latin American economies.

I

Monetary Policies

1

Inflation Targeting
The Latin American Experience

Vittorio Corbo and Klaus Schmidt-Hebbel

1.1 Introduction

Latin America was the region with the highest inflation in the world until the early 1990s. High inflation was the result of many decades of massive neglect of macroeconomic stability.[1] Fiscal dominance, in the sense that monetary policy was primarily dictated by fiscal financing needs, was the rule rather than the exception.

However, following the industrial countries' lead in their pursuit of price stability beginning in the 1980s, the region implemented a substantial departure from past policies around 1990. By then, most countries in Latin America launched stabilization efforts aimed at reducing inflation toward one-digit annual levels. The results have been dramatic. In the 1980s, four countries recorded inflation rates above 200 percent per annum and the average annual regional inflation rate stood at 145 percent; by the end of the 1990s, only two large countries (Mexico and Venezuela) had annual inflation rates above 10 percent and the region's average rate was below 10 percent. Currently many countries have attained low, single-digit inflation levels similar to industrial-country levels. Many factors have been behind the decision to make a frontal attack on inflation. First, the poor inflation record of the 1980s and the high political and economic costs that it entailed

Vittorio Corbo is professor of economics at Pontificia Universidad Católica de Chile. Klaus Schmidt-Hebbel is chief of research at the Central Bank of Chile.

We thank Agustín Carstens, Ronald McKinnon, Alejandro Werner, and other conference participants for their comments, and Oscar Facusse, Verónica Mies, Matías Tapia, and José Antonio Tessada for excellent discussion and outstanding assistance.

1. This was not all, however; during this period economic policies were characterized by having a distrust of markets, and by promoting heavy government intervention and isolation from foreign trade.

raised the public's demand for price stability. Second, a large improvement in the quality of the debate and economic policies was achieved due to the critical mass of policymakers and academics trained at top U.S. and European graduate schools. Many of these students returned to their own countries upon graduation to upgrade the quality of training and public policy. They convinced policymakers and the public at large that inflation is costly, the main contribution of monetary policy lies in delivering low inflation, monetary policy does not have permanent effects on employment, and the cost of reducing inflation is much lower under rational expectations and credible policies. Third, the introduction of market-oriented reforms reflected a growing understanding that macroeconomic stability facilitates the functioning of markets and contributes to better resource allocation.

Stabilization has been achieved under different monetary and exchange regimes in Latin America, ranging from dollarization to inflation targeting (IT) under floating exchange rates. This paper focuses on the experience stabilization under inflation targeting. It does so by assessing the implementation and results of inflation targeting in Latin America from a broad perspective. The paper starts by reviewing the issues considered in the choice of exchange rate regimes and monetary frameworks in section 1.2, in the light of recent theory and policy experience. The next section documents the evolution of exchange rate and monetary regimes in Latin America during the last two decades. Section 1.4 describes the Latin American and world samples of inflation targeters and compares their performance to that of non–inflation targeters, focusing on their success in meeting inflation targets, their output sacrifice in achieving low inflation, and their output volatility.

The subject of section 1.5 is how monetary policy is carried out in five inflation-targeting countries in the region (Brazil, Chile, Colombia, Mexico, and Peru), with reference to the design of IT in the world sample of inflation targeters. Section 1.6 focuses on the longest inflation-targeting experience in the region (the 1991–2000 case of Chile), evaluating how IT has affected inflation expectations and hence the effectiveness of monetary policy, using a battery of alternative model estimations and simulations. The main conclusions in section 1.7 close the paper.

1.2 Alternative Exchange Rate and Monetary Policy Regimes

What determines the choice of currencies and exchange rate regimes? In choosing an exchange rate regime, initial conditions are important. In particular, for countries in which, due to a long history of high inflation and currency crises a substantial part of asset and liabilities are foreign-currency denominated, the advantages of flexible exchange rates would be more limited because the room for an independent monetary policy would be restricted by its exchange rate effects. In contrast, for countries that have in place a monetary and institutional framework capable of delivering low inflation, exchange rate flexibility could be advantageous.

Historically, the literature on the choice of exchange rate regime was based on other structural country features. However, after the early work on exchange rate choices and optimum currency areas (or OCAs; Mundell 1961; McKinnon 1963), this literature fell into oblivion for three decades. Motivated by the experience of the European Monetary Union (EMU) and the abandonment of intermediate regimes by emerging countries in the wake of financial turmoil in the late 1990s, a spate of new work is looking at the issue of optimal exchange regimes.[2]

For countries that can make a choice, today's consensus view holds that the potential benefits from monetary union or dollarization (or a 100 percent credible currency board) stem from lower inflation, elimination of currency risk and its associated premium, elimination of currency transaction costs, and elimination of currency mismatch in foreign assets and liabilities. These benefits could be particularly important in countries without much room to run an independent monetary policy. At the other extreme, maintaining a domestic currency under a free float offers potential benefits derived from allowing for nominal (and hence more real) exchange rate flexibility, an independent monetary policy employed for stabilization purposes, direct access to seigniorage revenue, and direct central-bank exercise in providing lender-of-last-resort services on a temporary basis.

A host of structural and policy conditions determines the extent of the previous gains and losses associated with each regime choice. Traditional OCA factors to be considered consist of the degree of international factor mobility and correlations of factor prices; the extent of domestic price and wage flexibility; the degree of foreign trade openness and integration; the degree of symmetry of domestic and external shocks and business cycles; and the extent of domestic output, export, and portfolio diversification. Other important factors, mostly in the realm of policies and financial markets, have been added recently: completeness and depth of domestic financial markets and their integration into world markets (particularly in their ability to hedge exchange risk and to accept domestic-currency-denominated issues of foreign debt); and coordination of monetary union or dollarization with overall economic and political union, transfer payments, and adoption of similar regulatory and tax codes.

It is far easier to list the latter costs, benefits, and determining factors in choosing exchange regimes than it is to put numbers to such choices. In fact, an overall evaluation of the relation between regime choice and welfare is hampered by three serious limitations: there is no well-established

2. Among recent work on exchange rate regimes are Obstfeld (1995), Ghosh et al. (1997), Edwards and Savastano (2000), Frankel (1999), and Mussa et al. (2000).

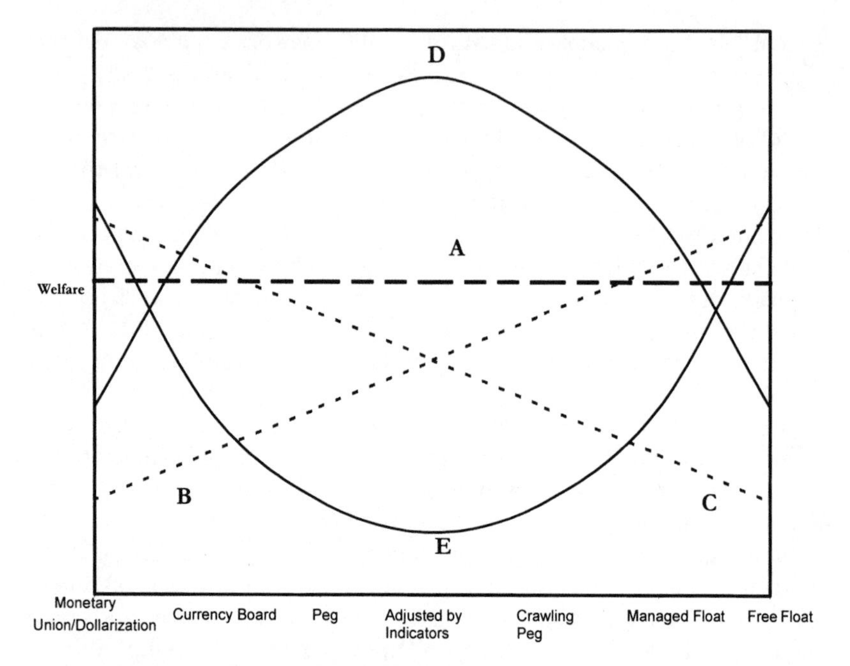

Fig. 1.1 Exchange rate regimes and welfare

encompassing framework that takes account of the various dimensions and variables that determine regime choice, there is little agreement on the empirical weight of different costs and benefits that entail such a decision, and the costs and benefits may change over time in response to regime changes. Hence, regional or country-specific evaluations of exchange regimes tend to be partial, emphasizing each factor separately.[3]

Having this difficulty in mind, we may still discuss the possible relations between overall country welfare and its choice of exchange regime, using the schedules drawn in figure 1.1. Schedule A reflects the textbook case under which regime choice has no bearing on country welfare, as a result of instantaneous clearing in all domestic markets and their perfect integration into complete international goods and capital markets. In the absence of any market friction there is no gain from exchange rate flexibility, independent monetary policy, or provision of lender-of-last-resort services when adopting a domestic currency and choosing any degree of exchange

3. In addition to various studies on the costs and benefits of EMU, some country evaluations outside Europe include Coleman (1999) and Hargreaves and McDermott (1999) for New Zealand, and Morandé and Schmidt-Hebbel (2000a) for Chile. The latter authors conclude that, among various Southern Hemisphere countries, Chile would gain the least (or lose the most) if it gave up its currency. Subject to large idiosyncratic shocks and significant temporary wage and price rigidity, and a conservative monetary policy, it is argued that Chile has the most to gain from a floating exchange rate and an independent monetary policy.

rate flexibility—the only residual issue is a minor one, related to the international distribution of seigniorage revenue. At the same time, nothing is gained by giving up the domestic currency, because currency transaction costs are nil and perfect financial markets hedge the currency-risk premiums and currency mismatch.

A monotonic positive (negative) schedule between exchange rate flexibility and welfare arises when the net benefits (costs) of flexibility are positive and grow (decline) with flexibility. Countries that exhibit features like significant lack of factor mobility; domestic wage and price sluggishness; low trade integration; low (or negative) correlation of shocks and business cycles with the rest of the world; large concentration of output, exports, and portfolios; lack of policy and regulatory coordination with other countries; low exchange-risk premiums; high access to foreign markets for exchange rate hedges and domestic-currency-denominated debt; low inflation; a stabilizing monetary policy; and low currency transaction costs are reflected by schedule B. The opposite is true for countries reflected by schedule C.

What about intermediate regimes? In their heyday a decade ago, adjustable pegs seemed to provide a perfect compromise between credibility (due to the nominal anchor provided by the exchange rate peg or band) and flexibility (to allow for limited and gradual adjustment of the real exchange rate in response to shocks). Both academics and policymakers had in mind a nonmonotonic relation such as schedule and arguing for and adopting variants of crawling pegs, fixed bands, or crawling bands. After a decade of growing disappointment with intermediate arrangements—caused by a spate of currency misalignment, speculative attacks, and single or twin crises in Europe, Asia, and Latin America—the current consensus for countries that are well integrated to capital markets has shifted toward schedule E, consistent with the *corners hypothesis* (as espoused by Obstfeld 1995; Summers 2000; Mussa et al. 2000; Edwards and Savastano 2000; and Fischer 2001). Although this view is not unanimous (see Williamson 1996; Frankel 1999, for arguments in favor of intermediate regimes), the growing country migration toward the extreme arrangements provides policy support to the corners hypothesis. Furthermore, the disappointment about intermediate regimes is becoming broader, encompassing fixed regimes and currency boards on one side and managed floats on the other. Financial turmoil and contagion in open economies that have adopted currency boards (e.g., Argentina and Hong Kong), and protracted high exchange-rate risk premiums after nine years of Argentina's currency board (reflected both directly and indirectly through large country-risk premiums; see Powell and Sturzenegger 2000), mark disillusion with currency boards and may explain Ecuador's outright dollarization and the recent shift of El Salvador toward dollarization. At the same time, a growing view that foreign exchange interventions are costly and, at best, yield only temporary effects (as illustrated recently by the coordinated intervention in support of the euro) has led Latin American countries such as Chile, Colombia, and Brazil to adopt clean floats.

With respect to monetary regimes, once a country decides to pursue a low inflation objective it needs to decide about the monetary regime to be used to anchor the evolution of the price level. Three fundamental options can be considered: an exchange rate anchor, a monetary anchor, and an inflation target.[4]

An exchange rate anchor uses an exogenously determined trajectory of the exchange rate as a nominal anchor. A money anchor relies on a precommitted path for the money supply to anchor inflation. In IT, the anchor for inflation is the publicly announced inflation target itself. The credibility of this policy relies both on the power given to the central bank to orient monetary policy toward achieving the target and on its willingness to use its power for this purpose.

When using an exchange rate target, a central bank knows precisely what it has to do; the public knows at every moment whether the central bank is succeeding; and the exchange rate affects import prices and the prices of other tradables directly. An exchange rate peg can quickly garner credibility, at least for the short term; in the long term, credibility can be retained only by success in maintaining the exchange rate peg. As we saw above, however, a fixed exchange rate is very costly for a government to maintain when its promises not to devalue lack credibility. In particular, credibility suffers when unemployment is high or the health of the banking system is in jeopardy.

This is not all. The use of the exchange rate as an anchor also requires that the appropriate institutional structure be developed to prevent the financial system from becoming too vulnerable to an eventual exchange rate correction. The latter could be developed through appropriate financial sector regulation. This vulnerability—which develops as exchange rate fixing, with an open capital account and weak financial regulation—usually results in undue risk-taking and, as a consequence, in an unsustainable expansion of credit that could result in a financial bubble (increasing financial fragility in the process; Corbo and Fischer 1995; Edwards and Végh 1997; and Mishkin 1997). This problem is illustrated by the experience of Chile in the early 1980s and Mexico in the first half of the 1990s, and in the recent experience of Asia (Thailand, Korea, Malaysia, and Indonesia). In all these cases, after the fixing of the exchange rate, the initial spread between the domestic and the foreign interest rate—adjusted for the expected rate of devaluation—rose sharply, providing substantial encouragement for capital inflows and credit expansion. The result was a

4. On monetary anchors, see Calvo and Végh (1999), Bernanke and Mishkin (1997), and Bernanke et al. (1999).

combination of large capital inflows, an expenditure boom, and a sharp real appreciation. In these cases, a sudden reversal of capital flows was all it took to set the stage for a major crisis.

For countries that are not ready or willing to go the avenue of currency boards or full dollarization and that decide instead to use a flexible exchange rate system, the question about the choice of a monetary framework is still open. For a monetary framework to be successful, it must provide sufficient independence to the central bank that it can focus its monetary policy toward the ultimate objective of achieving low inflation. Leaving out the use of an exchange rate peg, the remaining options are the use of a monetary aggregate or an inflation target.

The effectiveness of the use of a monetary aggregate as a nominal anchor for inflation depends, first of all, on the authority and capacity of the central bank to carry out an independent monetary policy aimed at achieving and maintaining low inflation. At a more technical level, however, the effectiveness of a monetary anchor depends on the stability of the demand for the monetary aggregate that is used as an anchor. It is the stability of the demand for the monetary aggregate that provides a link between the monetary anchor and the inflation rate. The stability of the demand for money presents a problem when there is considerable financial innovation, or when there is a sudden change in the level of inflation.

In particular, in an economy that has experienced a period of high and variable inflation, the demand for money becomes very unstable as economic agents develop ways to economize in the use of domestic money balances. Therefore, when the rate of inflation is reduced, *hysteresis effects* emerge, generating a breakdown in the old demand-for-money relationship. That is, when the inflation rate returns to previously observed lower values, the quantity of money demanded is lower than it was before the outburst of inflation. In cases like these, predicting the quantity of money demanded becomes very difficult and the use of a money target could be a very ineffective way to achieve a given inflation objective. Thus, it is not surprising that as countries have moved to flexible exchange rate regimes they have searched for new monetary anchors. Here, a third type of anchor is becoming increasingly popular: inflation targeting.

Inflation targeting was initially introduced by industrial countries with the objective of keeping inflation close to a long-run low level. New Zealand introduced the system with this purpose first, in March 1990. Since then IT has been introduced in Canada (February 1991), the United Kingdom (October 1992), Sweden (January 1993), Australia (1993), and the European Central Bank (October 1998).

Under IT, the target rate of inflation provides a monetary anchor and monetary and fiscal policies are geared toward achieving the inflation target. The attractiveness of this framework is that its effectiveness does not rely on a stable relationship between a monetary aggregate and inflation, while at the same time it avoids the problems associated with fixing the exchange rate. An additional advantage for emerging countries is that the trajectory of the market exchange rate provides important information on market evaluation of present and future monetary policy, such as the information provided by nominal and real yields on long-term government papers in industrial countries (Bernanke et al. 1999).

A well-defined IT framework requires the satisfaction of a set of conditions (Svensson 2000; King 2000): (1) public announcement of a strategy of medium-term price stability and an intermediate target level for inflation for a period into the future over which monetary policy could affect inflation, (2) an institutional commitment to price stability in the form of rules of operations for the monetary authority, and (3) a clear strategy for how monetary policy will operate to bring inflation close to the announced target, usually beginning with conditional forecast of inflation for the period for which the target is set. This strategy requires specifying operational procedures of what the central bank will undertake when the inflation forecast differs from the target. The procedures should be transparent and the monetary authority should be accountable for attaining the objective that has been set.

Given the lags in the operation of monetary policy, the inflation target must be set for a period far enough into the future to ensure that the monetary policy could have a role in determining future inflation. In practice, central banks announce a target for the next twelve or twenty-four months. For this time frame they develop a conditional forecast of inflation—based on the existing monetary policy stance and a forecast of the relevant exogenous variables—and set a strategy, and then communicate to the public the policy actions they would take in response to deviations of inflation from target levels.

Under IT, the official inflation target is the ultimate objective of policy, and an inflation forecast (not always made public) is the intermediate objective.[5] Monetary policy, with appropriate fiscal underpinnings, is the main instrument used to pursue the target. When the conditional inflation forecast is above the inflation target, the level of the intervention interest rate is raised with the purpose of bringing inflation close to the target. One advantage of IT is that inflation itself is made the target, committing monetary policy to achieve an explicit inflation objective and thus helping to shape inflation expectations. However, herein also resides its main disadvantage. Because inflation is not directly under control of the central bank, it becomes difficult to evaluate the monetary stance on the basis of the observed path of inflation. Furthermore, because monetary policy operates with substantial lags, it could be costly to precommit an uncondi-

5. Sometimes the rate of growth of a monetary aggregate is used as an intermediate objective.

tional inflation target—independently of changes in external factors that affect inflation—and to change monetary policy to bring inflation back to the target. Aiming at the inflation target when a shock causes a temporary rise in inflation could be very costly in terms of a severe slowdown in growth or increased output volatility (Cecchetti 1998).

To address some of these problems, several options have been proposed: setting the inflation target in terms of a range rather than a point; setting a target for core inflation rather than observed inflation; excluding indirect taxes, interest payments, and energy prices from the targeted price index; or setting the target for periods long enough so that short-term shocks to inflation do not require a monetary response.[6]

Emerging markets that have adopted inflation targets that begin at inflation levels well above their long-run objectives have had to deal with the problem of inflation convergence. Usually these countries have begun to reduce inflation without full-fledged IT frameworks in place. Once they have made enough progress in reducing inflation, they have announced annual targets and gradually put into place the components of full-fledged IT regimes on their way to low and stationary inflation.

1.3 Exchange Rate and Monetary Regimes in Latin America

The recent evolution of exchange rate and monetary regimes in Latin America has been conditioned by the region's increasing integration into world capital markets. Thus Latin America has been moving lately toward two extremes: credible fixed exchange rate systems (currency boards or full dollarization) and floating exchange rate systems. As a result, the once popular exchange rate target regimes of the 1980s and 1990s—difficult to sustain because of increasing capital mobility—are being abandoned in the region (Obstfeld and Rogoff 1995; IMF 2000).

Indeed, Latin America shows a strong and continuing trend from pegged exchange rate regimes toward more flexible arrangements during the last two decades. According to the International Monetary Fund (IMF) classification of exchange rate regimes, the share of countries with pegs, among eighteen Latin American countries, has fallen from 67 percent in 1979 to only 23 percent in 2000 (fig. 1.2). The share of countries with freely floating rates has increased from zero in 1979 to 32 percent in 2000. Intermediate regimes (such as those where the exchange rate is adjusted by various indicators) have remained stable at 27 percent, while managed floats have increased from 27 percent to 37 percent. As compared to the 1999 world distribution of exchange rate regimes, Latin America has relatively more flexible exchange rate arrangements.

6. For a review of the costs and benefits of these alternative options see Bernanke et al. (1999, chap. 3).

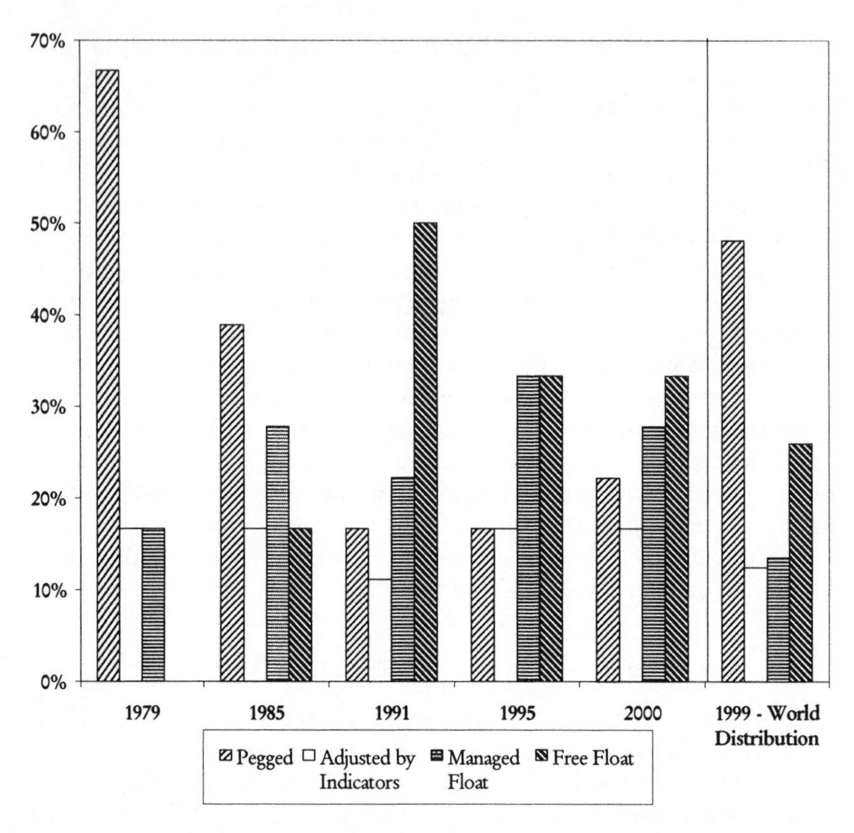

Fig. 1.2 Country distribution of exchange rate regimes in Latin America: IMF classification (1979–2000)

Sources: For years 1979, 1985, 1991 and 1995 for Latin America and 1999 for World Distribution: IMF (*International Financial Statistics,* 2000). For the year 2000 for Latin America: authors' classification based on central banks' statements and Web pages.

Notes: Eighteen countries are included in Latin America's distribution: Argentina, Bolivia, Brazil, Chile, Colombia, Costa Rica, Dominican Republic, Ecuador, El Salvador, Guatemala, Honduras, Mexico, Nicaragua, Panama, Paraguay, Peru, Uruguay, and Venezuela. World distribution includes 185 countries.

In a recent paper (Fischer 2001), exchange rate regimes are classified using the judgment of IMF staff as reported in the IMF's annual report (2000, 141–143), and not the regimes declared by the countries. A comparison between the distribution of exchange rate arrangements in 1991 and 1999 shows that the share of countries with intermediate regimes have been reduced substantially (from 62 to 34 percent) while the share of the extreme cases have increased, from 16 to 25 percent for hard pegs (including the European countries that entered the monetary union) and from 23 to 42 percent for the floaters. For emerging markets (i.e., those developing markets that are more integrated into world capital markets), the change in the share of floaters is even more pronounced, from 30 percent in 1991 to 48 percent in 1999. In the case of nine Latin American countries in 1999, Fischer classifies five as independent floaters (Brazil, Chile, Colombia, Mexico, and Peru), two as having hard pegs (Argentina and Panama), one with a crawling band (Venezuela), and one in the transition to dollarization (Ecuador). This stands in striking contrast with 1991, when only Peru was an independent floater, while Argentina was in transition to a currency board and Panama was dollarized. The other six countries had some variant sort of a soft peg (including crawling pegs) or a crawling band in place.

Levy-Yeyati and Sturzenegger (2000) provide another classification of exchange rate regimes, in which exchange rate regimes are inferred from the actual behavior of nominal exchange rates and foreign reserves (fig. 1.3). In their classification, "de facto" pegs are shown to decline from 20 percent in 1979 to 6 percent in 1999. Moreover, de facto free floats represent the dominant share (60 percent) of regimes in Latin America—a figure that is almost twice the "de jure" share of floats in the IMF classification.

Hence, on average, Latin America shows an unambiguous decline of pegs and an increase in floating regimes, whereas intermediate regimes do not show much of a trend (except in Fischer 2001). Considering the regime shifts that have taken place during the last two years (not all of them reflected in the data in figs. 1.2 and 1.3), various medium-sized and large countries have adopted free floats, including Brazil, Chile, and Colombia. It is sometimes claimed that countries that declare themselves to have a flexible exchange rate act, in practice, as if their exchange rate were fixed or semi-fixed. According to this view they would exhibit "fear of floating" (Calvo and Reinhart 2000). Not making use of exchange rate flexibility could be due to the central bank's fear of large pass-through effects from devaluation to inflation or large risks of exchange rate adjustment when private agents exhibit a currency mismatch of their assets and liabilities.[7] Following Calvo and Reinhart, we now analyze how close to real floating these regimes are by comparing the volatility of exchange rates and international reserves before and after the formal announcement of a free float. We also compare these measures of volatility with the ones for four other countries that are used as a control group.

The degree of volatility is approximated by the probability that the monthly changes in exchange rates and foreign reserves fall within ranges of 1.0 percent and 2.5 percent, respectively. When carrying out this exercise, we do not control for the fundamentals or shocks that could affect the

7. However, recent analytical and empirical work shows convincingly that pass-through effects are much weaker than was initially thought (Obstfeld and Rogoff 2001; Goldfajn and Werlang 2000).

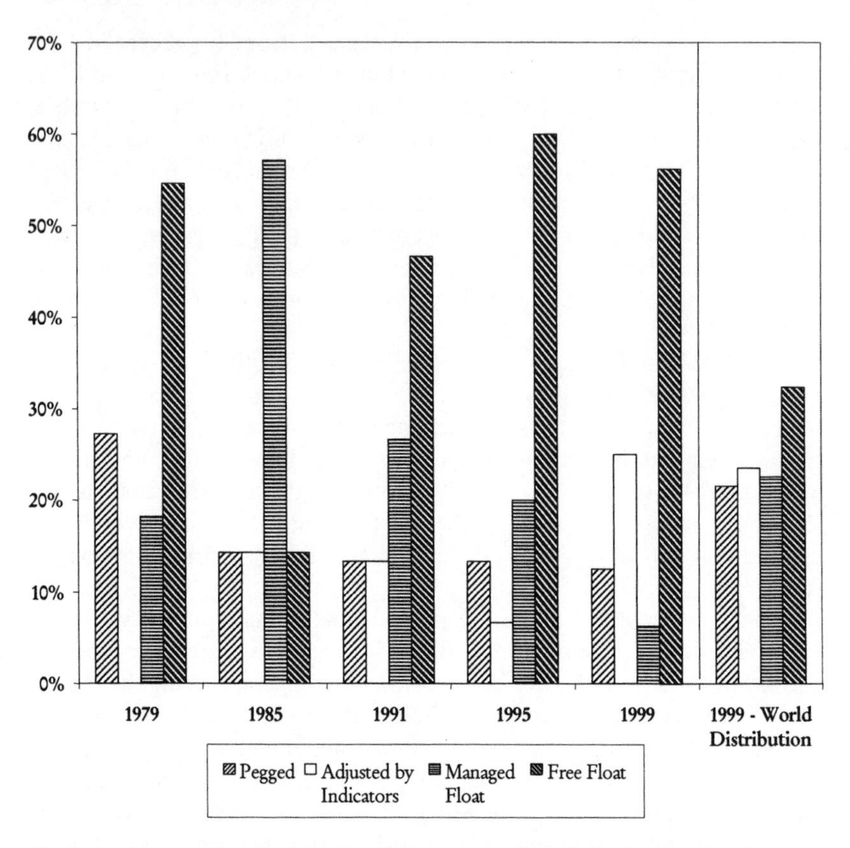

Fig. 1.3 Country distribution of exchange rate regimes in Latin America: Levy-Yeyati and Sturzenegger classification based on cluster analysis (1979–99)

Sources: Levy-Yeyati and Sturzenegger (2000).

Notes: Latin America: Same countries as in figure 1.2. However, sample size varies in time, as some country regimes are deemed inconclusive under this analysis. Those regimes are not included in the distribution. Inconclusive countries are as follows: 1979, Ecuador, Guatemala, Mexico, Paraguay, and Venezuela; no information available for Nicaragua and Uruguay. 1985, El Salvador and Venezuela. No information available for Colombia, Nicaragua, and Uruguay. 1991, Chile and El Salvador. No information available for Nicaragua. 1995, El Salvador and Paraguay. No information available for Nicaragua. 1999, El Salvador. World distribution includes 102 countries (after eliminating 23 inconclusive countries).

exchange-rate and foreign-reserve trajectories, so our conclusions are conditional on this assumption.[8]

The results are reported in table 1.1. If the exchange regime has not changed much, then the probabilities that the percentage changes in the two variables fall within the given ranges should not change. However, if official adoption of a float is for real, then the probabilities should be lower

8. Our monthly frequency is determined by data availability for foreign reserves, for which daily data are not available.

Table 1.1 **Exchange Rate and Foreign Reserves Volatility**

		Probability That Monthly % Change Falls Within Certain Range			
		Nominal Exchange Rate		Foreign Exchange Reserve	
Country	Period	±1%	±2.5%	±1%	±2.5%
Brazil	Jan. 1995–Dec. 1998	58.8	97.3	9.7	24.0
	Jan. 1999–July 2000	4.9	14.4	6.8	16.9
Chile	Jan. 1985–Dec. 1989	29.8	67.0	10.4	25.5
	Feb. 1990–Aug. 1999	46.2	87.7	20.3	48.1
	Sept. 1999–Sept. 2000	34.9	74.6	46.2	86.3
Colombia	Feb. 1990–Aug. 1999	30.9	68.5	25.8	58.9
	Sept. 1999–Sept. 2000	30.7	66.1	31.4	68.0
Mexico	Feb. 1990–Nov. 1994	65.7	98.2	5.9	14.7
	Dec. 1994–Sept. 2000	12.4	30.4	3.6	9.0
Peru	Feb. 1992–Sept. 2000	29.8	66.3	13.8	33.7
Austria	Jan. 1990–Dec. 1998	100	100	15.2	36.8
Canada	Jan. 1990–May 2000	63.4	97.5	1.1	2.8
The Netherlands	Jan. 1990–Dec. 1998	100	100	15.7	37.9
New Zealand	Feb. 1993–Sept. 2000	36.7	76.5	12.0	29.3

Sources: Authors' calculations based on each country's central bank's information, except for Austria, Canada, and the Netherlands, which are based on the IMF's *International Financial Statistics* (various issues).

(higher) in the floating period for the variation in the exchange rate (foreign reserves). In Brazil and Mexico this is indeed the case for the nominal exchange rate but not for foreign reserves. In the case of Brazil, this result could be due to the deliberate decision to use foreign reserves to pay its foreign debt after the start of floating.[9] For Mexico, there was a deliberate policy to avoid large jumps in the nominal exchange rate through explicit exchange rate market interventions through the use of foreign reserves.[10] In

9. More generally, one observes many changes in central bank holdings of foreign reserves in countries that float freely, for reasons that are unrelated to foreign exchange intervention purposes. Two of the main reasons are deliberate portfolio swaps by central banks and changes in cross-currency valuations that affect the value of foreign reserve holdings. Moreover, after adopting a free float, some countries reduce over time their initial levels of foreign reserves that are excessive under a float. However, in the absence of detailed information of portfolio shifts and valuation changes, we are unable to adjust our volatility measures for these factors. Hence our measures of reserve volatility under floats exhibit a generally upward bias.

10. We divide the second period into two subsamples (December 1994–December 1997, and January 1998–September 2000) to test whether the high volatility of foreign reserves was observed during the full floating period. Our results confirm that from January 1998 onward, foreign reserves were more stable than in the previous period (61.7 percent probability that the percentage change falls within the 2.5 percent band). So it appears that Mexico is really floating today.

particular, the central bank sells put option rights to buy dollars. Every day the central bank auctions $200 million at a minimum exchange rate that is 2 percent above the preceding day's market level.

In the case of Chile, although the two measures of volatility change in the right direction, the differences are not large. Although there has been no intervention since February 1999 in the foreign exchange market, the exchange rate volatility has increased by only a little. This can be attributed to the fact that much volatility was already observed under the preceding regime of a wide exchange rate band. Levy-Yeyati and Sturzenegger (2000), who found that the Chilean exchange rate regime was de facto flexible during most of the 1990s, confirm this. In Peru, exchange rate volatility is similar to that during the floating period of Chile, but the volatility of foreign reserves is larger. The latter result indicates that Chile gained more stability with less intervention.

The measures of volatility for the two industrial countries with free floats (Canada and New Zealand) show that they are not really free floaters in the limited sense of our unconditional tests: they exhibit significant volatility in foreign reserves and not much in the exchange rate. By contrast, the two industrial countries that were pegging their currencies to the deutsche Mark (Austria and the Netherlands) exhibit very low volatility in their exchange rates and high volatility in their foreign reserves. When comparing the volatility of the Latin American declared free floaters with that of New Zealand, we conclude that Chile and Colombia exhibit similar exchange rate volatility but lower foreign-reserve volatility. In contrast, Brazil has larger exchange rate volatility.

At the other extreme of exchange rate regimes, in early 2000 Ecuador joined Panama in choosing a credible fixed exchange rate regime by adopting the U.S. dollar. El Salvador adopted a similar step toward this direction in late 2000, declaring the U.S. dollar legal tender on an equal footing with the Salvadoran currency.

Hence a very recent shift (not yet reflected in the data) away from the intermediate arrangements and toward the extremes is taking place in the region, consistent with the corners hypothesis.

Now let us focus on the country distribution of nominal targets (or nominal anchors) chosen by central banks in their conduct of monetary policy (fig. 1.4). According to the IMF survey of 185 countries in the world for 1999, half of them have exchange rate anchors in place, while 8 percent use monetary aggregates, and 9 percent use inflation targets. A 32 percent share of countries either has no explicit target or uses a combination of targets. In an alternative study by Mahadeva and Sterne (2000) for ninety-three countries (where countries that choose more than one target appear more than once), the country distribution among the three anchors is much more balanced. Moreover, more than half of the countries in their group target inflation, either exclusively or among other nominal targets.

Our own measures of country distribution for Latin America (also with

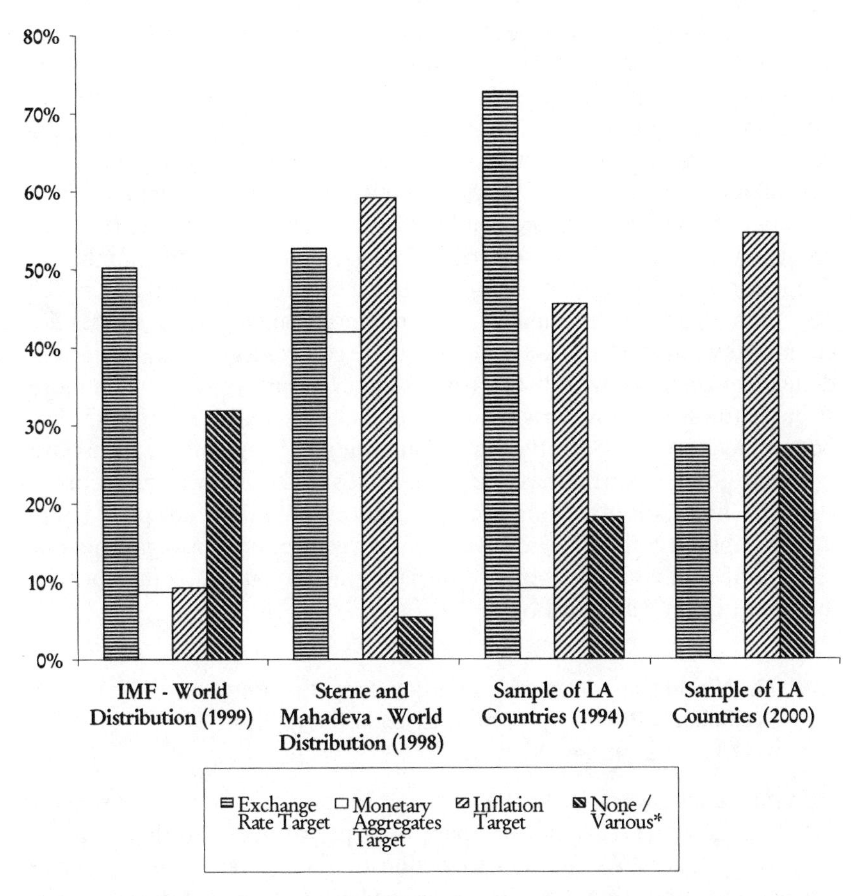

Fig. 1.4 Country distribution of nominal targets for monetary policy: World and Latin American samples

Sources: IMF (*International Financial Statistics,* 2000) and Mahadeva and Sterne (2000) for world distribution. Mishkin and Savastano (2001) and central banks' statements and Web pages for Latin American countries.

Notes: IMF classifies 185 countries. Mahadeva and Sterne include 93 countries. Latin American sample: Argentina, Bolivia, Brazil, Chile, Colombia, Ecuador, Panama, Peru, Mexico, Uruguay, and Venezuela. Countries with more than one nominal anchor or explicit targets are classified by the IMF in the None/Various group, the same as countries with no explicit targets. Mahadeva and Sterne separately account for each possible target, so countries appear in more than one category. Hence, only countries with no explicit nominal target are included under None/Various in their classification. The same applies to the sample of Latin American countries (Bolivia's credit target is classified as None/Various).

double-counting) show a distinct shift away from exchange rate targets in Latin America. Of eleven Latin American countries representing more than 90 percent of Latin American gross domestic product (GDP), eight countries targeted the exchange rate in 1994 (under a peg, a band, or a managed float) whereas only three countries continued doing so in 2000 (Argentina, Uruguay, and Venezuela). At the same time, those targeting monetary aggregates increased from one in 1994 to two in 2000 (Mexico and Peru). However, in Mexico monetary aggregates have been used increasingly as an intermediate objective with the final objective of targeting inflation. Inflation targeters increased from five in 1994 to six in 2000 (Brazil, Chile, Colombia, Mexico, Peru, and Uruguay). Among the latter, full inflation targeters (as of October 2000) are Brazil, Chile, and Mexico.

Finally, let us consider the combined time trend of exchange rate and monetary regimes in Latin America. Table 1.2 shows how the number of countries with intermediate combinations (currency boards to adjustable pegs, combined with exchange rate or monetary-aggregate targets) is declining between 1994 and 2000. In fact, there is a trend away from intermediate arrangements, weakly toward the upper left corner and much more strongly toward the lower right corner. In fact, one additional country has been added to the upper left corner (Ecuador adopting dollarization) and four additional countries have positioned closely to the lower right corner (Brazil, Chile, Colombia, and Mexico, in addition to Peru, adopting a free float combined with IT). The lower right corner dominates, regarding not only number of countries but also the combined weight of its members as a share of Latin America's GDP.

1.4 The World Experience with Inflation-Targeting Regimes: Preliminary Results in Latin America in Comparison to Other Regions and Regimes

In this section we describe the Latin American and world samples of inflation targeters (ITers) and compare their performance to that of non–inflation targeters. We focus in particular on their inflation performance and success in meeting their targets, as well as on their output sacrifice in achieving lower inflation and their output volatility.[11]

Inflation targeting began in 1990 with public announcements of inflation targets in New Zealand and Chile. According to Schaechter, Stone, and Zelmer (2000), there had been thirteen full-fledged IT experiences in the world up to February 2000: Australia, Brazil, Canada, Chile, the Czech Republic, Finland, Israel, New Zealand, Poland, South Africa, Spain, Sweden, and United Kingdom. Of these, Finland and Spain had abandoned IT in January 1999 when they joined the European Monetary Union (EMU). In our count, seventeen full-fledged IT country experiences began during or before October 2000, as we add Korea, Mexico, Thailand, and Switzerland to the thirteen above-mentioned countries.

11. Recent books and articles describe the design features and general results of IT in the small but quickly growing number of countries that have adopted IT since 1990. See, in particular, Leiderman and Svensson (1995), Mishkin and Posen (1997), Bernanke et al. (1999), Kuttner and Posen (1999), Haldane (1999), Mishkin (2000), Mishkin and Savastano (2001), and Schaechter et al. (2000).

Table 1.2 **Exchange Rate Regimes and Nominal Targets in 11 Latin American Countries, 1994 and 2000**

	Dollarization/ Monetary Union	Currency Board	Peg	Adjustable Peg/ Exchange Rate Band	Managed Float	Free Float
1994						
No explicit target/other targets	Panama			Bolivia (credit target)		
Exchange rate target		Argentina	Venezuela	Bolivia Brazil Chile Ecuador Mexico Uruguay		
Monetary aggregates target				Colombia	Peru	
Inflation target				Chile Colombia Ecuador Uruguay (1995)	Peru	
2000						
No explicit target/other targets	Ecuador Panama			Bolivia (credit target)		
Exchange rate target		Argentina		Uruguay Venezuela		
Monetary aggregates target					Mexico Peru	
Inflation target				Uruguay	Mexico Peru	Brazil Chile Colombia

Sources: Mishkin and Savastano (2001), Mahadeva and Sterne (2000), and central banks' statements and Web pages.

Table 1.3 **Regional Samples of Full, Partial, and Non–Inflation Targeting Countries**

Country Sample	Full ITers	Partial ITers	Non-ITers
Latin America	Brazil	Colombia	
	Chile	Mexico	
		Peru	
Rest of world	*Old*		
	Australia		Denmark
	Canada		France
	Finland		Germany
	Israel		Italy
	New Zealand		Japan
	Spain		The Netherlands
	Sweden		Norway
	United Kingdom		Portugal
	Recent		Switzerland
	Czech Republic		United States
	Poland		
	South Africa		
	Korea		
	Thailand		

However, in order to conduct our empirical analysis for the 1986–99 period, we consider a sample of eighteen countries, subdivided into three main groups according to the extent of IT adoption (table 1.3). The first is composed of fifteen full-fledged ITers subdivided into two Latin American full ITers (Brazil and Chile), eight "old" full ITers from other regions (countries that have had IT in place dating back at least to 1995), and five "recent" full ITers (countries that adopted IT during the last two years). The second group is composed of three "partial" ITers in Latin America (Colombia, Mexico, and Peru), which do have officially announced targets in place but lack some of the components of a full-fledged IT framework.[12] Our third set is a control group of ten industrial economies that either target the exchange rate or monetary aggregates, or have no explicit target in place; or, in the case of EMU members, that have adopted the euro after targeting their exchange rates for most of the 1990s to the deutsche mark. We label this control group as *non-inflation targeters* (non-ITers).[13]

Figure 1.5 depicts adoption dates and inflation rates at adoption for fifteen full ITers and three Latin American partial ITers.[14] The following styl-

12. Mexico became a full ITer in October 2000 but is considered a partial ITer for the purpose of the historical analysis.

13. Switzerland fully adopted IT in February 2000 but is considered a non-ITer for the purpose of the historical analysis.

14. Starting dates are defined by the first month of the first period for which inflation targets have been announced previously. For example, the starting date for Chile is January 1991 (the first month of calendar year 1991, for which the first inflation target was announced in

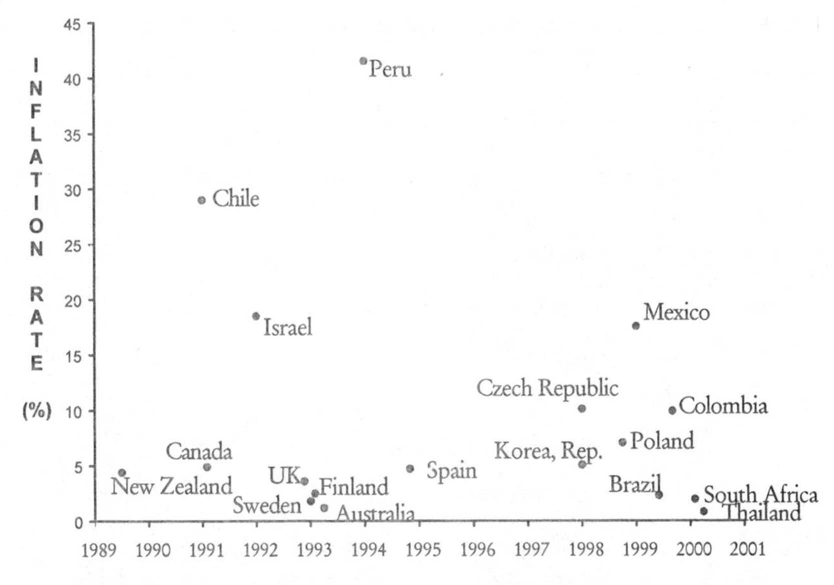

Fig. 1.5 Inflation at adoption of inflation-targeting framework in 18 countries (1988–2000)

Sources: Authors' calculations based on data from the IMF's *IFS* (various issues), country sources, and Schaechter et al. (2000).

Note: Inflation attained one quarter before adopting IT.

ized facts are apparent from inspection. Only five industrial countries had IT in place in 1999. Among emerging economies, Chile, Israel, and Peru adopted IT in the early 1990s. However, eight additional emerging countries have been added since 1998.

One salient feature of these international IT experiences is that many emerging countries adopted IT while their inflation levels were still well above stationary inflation rates. In Chile and Israel inflation stood at 25 percent and 17 percent, respectively, when they adopted IT in the early 1990s. In Peru inflation was 42 percent when adopting IT in early 1994. Among the newcomers, Colombia, the Czech Republic, and Mexico had inflation rates of 10 percent at adoption, Korea and Poland had initial inflation rates in the 5–7 percent range, and Brazil, South Africa, and Thailand had inflation levels below 3 percent. The subsequent success of emerging countries in bringing inflation toward low stationary levels is prima facie evidence that IT can be successfully adopted to reduce inflation from (low) double-digit levels toward low single-digit rates.

How successful have countries been in reducing inflation and meeting their targets under IT? We measure IT success in three simple dimensions:

September 1990). The initial inflation level is defined as the year-on-year consumer price index inflation rate of the last quarter before the first month of inflation targeting (e.g., the fourth quarter of 1990, in the case of Chile).

Table 1.4 **Disinflation around Year of Adoption of Inflation Targeting, 18 Countries**

Country Sample	Full ITers	% Change	Partial ITers	% Change
Latin America	Brazil	–15.8	Colombia	–10.9
	Chile	0.8	Mexico	–24.9
			Peru	–398.4
	Average (all Latin America)	–7.5		
Rest of world	*Old*			
	Australia	–5.4		
	Canada	–2.5		
	Finland	–5.0		
	Israel	–9.3		
	New Zealand	–14.1		
	Spain	–2.4		
	Sweden	–8.3		
	United Kingdom	–7.0		
	Recent			
	Czech Republic	–7.0		
	Poland	–20.2		
	South Africa	–3.7		
	Korea	–3.7		
	Thailand	–2.6		
	Average	–7.4		

Sources: Authors' calculations based on data from the IMF's *International Financial Statistics* (various issues) country sources, and Schaechter et al. (2000).

Notes: Disinflation measured as change in annual inflation rate between three years before and one year after IT adoption year.

the reduction of inflation shortly before and after adopting IT, the speed at which inflation was brought down from the start of IT through the attainment of stationary inflation, and the average deviation of inflation outcomes from target levels.

A general feature of IT is that countries prepare for adopting IT by reducing inflation around the date of IT adoption (year t). This feature is generally observed in industrial and emerging, transitional and stationary, full and partial ITers (table 1.4). All eighteen countries, with the exception of Chile, have reduced their inflation rates between years $t - 3$ and $t + 1$.[15] The range of inflation reduction scores is very wide because it includes massive stabilization cases that brought inflation down from high inflation levels (at the extreme, from triple-digit levels in Peru) as well as cases in which inflation was close to low stationary levels (e.g., in Canada, Spain, and Thailand).

Now consider the speed of convergence to stationary inflation among ITers (table 1.5). Average convergence time of inflation to stationary

15. This result is not sensitive to the choice of period around IT adoption.

Table 1.5 **Convergence to Stationary Inflation under Inflation Targeting in 18 Countries, 1989–2000**

	Initial Inflation	Date	Final Inflation	Date	Quarters of Convergence	Inflation Change	Average Inflation per Quarter
			Latin America				
Full ITers							
Brazil[a]	8.3	Apr. 1999	7.9	Jan. 2000	1	–0.4	–0.4
Chile	29.0	Apr. 1990	3.8	Jan. 1999	33	–25.2	–0.8
Average	18.7		5.9		17	–12.8	–0.6
Partial ITers							
Colombia	10.0	Feb. 1999	10.6	Feb. 2000	4	0.6	0.2
Mexico	17.6	Apr. 1998	10.6	Jan. 2000	5	–7.0	–1.4
Peru	41.5	Apr. 1993	2.8	Mar. 1999	23	–38.7	–1.7
Average	23.0		8.0		11	–15.0	–1.0
			Rest of World				
Old Full ITers							
Australia	1.2	Jan. 1993	1.2	Jan. 1993	0	0.0	0.0
Canada	4.9	Apr. 1990	1.6	Feb. 1992	5	–3.3	–0.7
Finland	2.5	Apr. 1992	2.0	Mar. 1993	3	–0.5	–0.2
Israel	18.5	Apr. 1991	1.9	Apr. 1999	24	–16.7	–0.7
New Zealand	4.4	Feb. 1989	2.8	Feb. 1991	8	–1.6	–0.2
Spain	4.7	Mar. 1994	1.6	Feb. 1997	11	–3.1	–0.3
Sweden	1.8	Apr. 1992	1.8	Apr. 1992	0	0.0	0.0
United Kingdom	3.6	Mar. 1992	1.8	Jan. 1993	2	–1.8	–0.9
Average	5.2		1.8		7	–3.4	–0.5
Recent Full ITers							
Czech Republic	10.1	Apr. 1997	2.9	Jan. 1999	5	–7.2	–1.8
Poland	7.0	Mar. 1998	10.3	Jan. 2000	6	3.3	0.6
South Africa	2.0	Apr. 1999	2.0	Apr. 1999	0	0.0	0.0
Korea	5.1	Apr. 1997	0.7	Jan. 1999	5	–2.4	–0.5
Thailand	0.8	Jan. 2000	0.8	Jan. 2000	0	0.0	0.0
Average	5.0		3.3		3	–1.3	–0.6
Overall average	9.6		3.7		8	–5.8	–0.6

Sources: Authors' calculations based on data from the IMF's *IFS* (various issues), country sources, and Schaechter et al. (2000).

Notes: Convergence refers to most recent available observation. Stationary inflation for countries that do not explicitly announce a long-term inflation target is calculated as inflation attained by industrial countries (2–3 percent).

[a]Initial Inflation is calculated two quarters ahead, in order to adjust for the extraordinarily low inflation in January 1999.

inflation (or to current inflation in the case of ITers that have not yet converged) has been eight quarters, at an average disinflation rate of 0.6 percent per quarter.[16] Among the countries that have completed transition to their long-term stationary target levels, Chile and Israel had the longest transition periods (around eight years)—perhaps not surprising, considering their high initial inflation rates. Australia and Sweden, at the other extreme, adopted IT when they had already attained stationary inflation.

Inflation targeters have been generally very successful in meeting their inflation targets. Performance is measured here as each country's average annual absolute or relative inflation deviation from its officially announced point or range target. We express these figures both in percentage points and relative to inflation (table 1.6).

The overall record of the eighteen IT experiences in the world is an annual average absolute deviation of 1.04 percentage points (or 0.50 per percentage point of inflation). However, the dispersion of individual country records is large. Among old full ITers—those countries that have had at least four years of IT experience—the average annual absolute miss of the inflation target is lowest in Canada (at 0.20 percentage points), followed by Chile and New Zealand (at 0.40 percentage points) and is highest in Israel (at 1.67). Relative to inflation, the best target performance among old full ITers is achieved by Chile and the United Kingdom (at a 0.12 deviation relative to inflation), followed closely by Israel (at 0.14), while the largest misses are recorded by Australia (1.44) and Finland (2.12). At a regional level, the record of full and partial ITers in Latin America—with the exception of Colombia—is comparable to the attainment of inflation targets in other regions.

It is straightforward to compute sacrifice ratios (i.e., percentage GDP losses per percentage units of inflation reduction) as measures of the costs of disinflation under IT. Sacrifice ratios are computed for eighteen ITers and for the inflation stabilization from three years before to one year after IT adoption (see table 1.7)—the strong stabilization period identified in table 1.4.

Among Latin American IT experiences, GDP sacrifice ratios have been very low, even negative in three of the five countries. The same is true for the five recent full ITers outside the region. In contrast, sacrifice ratios have been positive and relatively large for the eight full and old ITers outside the region, with an average sacrifice of 0.88 percentage points of GDP per percentage point of inflation reduction. (The only exemption was Canada, with a large negative sacrifice ratio.)

An alternative method is to compare sacrifice ratios for disinflation periods under IT to sacrifice ratios before adoption of IT, and to comparable

16. When considering only the fourteen countries that have achieved convergence to their stationary inflation targets by early 2000, roughly the same averages are obtained.

Table 1.6 **Annual Average Deviation of Actual from Target Inflation under Inflation Targeting in 18 Countries, 1989–2000 (various subperiods)**

	Percentage Points		As Ratio to Current Inflation	
	Relative	Absolute	Relative	Absolute
		Latin America		
Full ITers				
Brazil	0.00	0.00	0.00	0.00
Chile	–0.12	0.40	–0.08	0.12
Average	–0.06	0.20	–0.04	0.06
Partial ITers				
Colombia	–5.23	5.23	–0.54	0.54
Mexico	–0.68	0.68	–0.06	0.06
Peru	–0.67	0.77	–0.05	0.14
Average	–2.19	2.23	–0.22	0.25
		Rest of World		
Old Full ITers				
Australia	–0.18	1.13	1.25	1.44
Canada	–0.15	0.20	–0.60	0.67
Finland	–0.69	0.69	–2.12	2.12
Israel	0.46	1.62	0.02	0.14
New Zealand	0.06	0.40	–0.08	0.25
Spain	0.15	0.45	–0.01	0.21
Sweden	–0.71	0.71	1.05	1.05
United Kingdom	0.09	0.31	0.00	0.12
Average	–0.12	0.69	–0.06	0.75
Recent Full ITers				
Czech Republic	–0.60	0.82	–0.26	0.29
Poland	1.00	1.00	0.10	0.10
South Africa	0.00	0.00	0.00	0.00
Korea	–2.30	2.30	–0.71	0.71
Thailand	0.00	0.00	0.00	0.00
Average	–0.63	1.37	–0.29	0.37
Overall average	–0.60	1.04	–0.13	0.50

Sources: Authors' calculations based on data from the IMF's *IFS* (various issues), country sources, and Schaechter et al. (2000).

Notes: Relative (absolute) deviation: sum of relative deviations divided by number of periods. Relative (absolute) deviation as a ratio to current inflation: sum of relative (absolute) deviations as ratios to inflation divided by number of periods. Depending on the IT framework, inflation target is defined as a range or as a point.

sacrifice ratios among non-ITers (table 1.8). Sacrifice ratios for ITers before IT adoption are computed for the period from 1980 to the year of adoption, and afterward through 1999. For the control group of ten non-ITers, sacrifice ratios are calculated for the decade of the 1990s. In both Chile and Peru—the longest IT experiences in Latin America—sacrifice ratios turned from positive before IT to negative afterward. This stands in

Table 1.7 Sacrifice Ratios during Inflation Stabilization with Inflation Targeting in 18 Countries, 1998–2000

	Full ITers	Ratio	Partial ITers	Ratio
Latin America	Brazil	–0.15	Colombia	0.15
	Chile	–0.40	Mexico	–0.03
			Peru	–0.06
	Average	–0.28	Average	0.06
Rest of world	*Old*			
	Australia	1.14		
	Canada	–2.25		
	Finland	2.44		
	Israel	0.60		
	New Zealand	0.16		
	Spain	2.50		
	Sweden	0.64		
	United Kingdom	0.89		
	Average	0.77		
	Recent			
	Czech Republic	–0.66		
	Poland	–1.07		
	South Africa	–2.27		
	Korea	0.39		
	Thailand	1.89		
	Average	–0.87		

Sources: Authors' calculations based on data from the *IFS* (various issues) and country sources.

Notes: Based on annual GDP data (various subperiods). Sacrifice ratios are calculated as cumulative GDP variation (to a trend calculated by a Hodrick-Prescott filter) divided by inflation change between three years before and one year after *IT* adoption year.

contrast to the group of eight full old ITers outside the region, where sacrifice ratios changed, on average, from –0.32 to +0.19 after IT adoption. Here, too, are two exceptions, however: in Israel and Finland sacrifice ratios turned negative after IT adoption.

Among non-ITers, sacrifice ratios have been larger during the 1990s, on average, than among IT countries after their IT adoption. The average sacrifice ratio among ten industrial-country non-ITers is 0.30 for the last decade, with a dispersion that includes countries with positive and negative ratios.

The results suggest that IT does not necessarily reduce sacrifice ratios in industrial countries that already had relatively low inflation before adopting IT, and does not necessarily improve their performance in comparison to other non-IT industrial countries. However, there is some evidence that IT reduces the cost of stabilization in emerging economies that start at moderate or high levels of inflation—possibly a double bonus earned from the reduction of inflation, per se, and the gain in credibility from guiding inflation expectations by announcing (and attaining) official inflation targets.

Table 1.8 **Sacrifice Ratios during Inflation Stabilization in 18 IT Countries and 10 Non-IT Countries, 1980 (1990)–2000**

	Full ITers			Partial ITers			Non-ITers	
	Country	Before	After	Country	Before	After	Country	During 1990s
Latin America	Brazil	0.42	—	Colombia	–0.06	—		
	Chile	0.37	–0.7	Mexico	–0.11	—		
	Average	0.40	–0.7	Peru	0.84	–0.75		
				Average	–0.09	–0.75		
Rest of world	*Old*						Denmark	0.90
	Australia	–1.41	0.01				France	–0.45
	Canada	–6.84	0.64				Germany	–0.12
	Finland	0.03	–4.74				Italy	0.25
	New Zealand	–0.67	0.22				Japan	1.46
	Spain	–0.85	0.82				The Netherlands	1.47
	Sweden	0.08	0.22				Norway	–0.87
	United Kingdom	0.75	0.02				Portugal	–0.39
	Israel	0.17	–0.14				Switzerland	0.87
	Average	–0.32[a]	–0.19[a]				United States	0.78
	Recent						Average	0.39
	Czech Republic	–5.69	0.36					
	Poland	0.04	—					
	South Africa	–0.17	—					
	Korea	–1.92	0.59					
	Thailand	–1.72	—					
	Average	–2.83	0.48					

Sources: Authors' calculations based on data from the IMF's *IFS* (various issues) and country sources.

Notes: Based on annual GDP data (various subperiods). Sacrifice ratios are calculated as the cumulative GDP variation (to a trend calculated by a Hodrick-Prescott filter) divided by inflation change in any disinflation period. Sacrifice ratios of ITers are calculated before (since 1980) and after adopting IT framework. A dash indicates that the time span after IT adoption is too short to compute a sacrifice ratio.

[a]Excluding Canada and Finland.

Finally, we report volatility of industrial output before and after IT adoption, and compare it to output volatility among industrial-country non-ITers (table 1.9). Volatility—measured as the standard deviation of quarterly industrial output from its Hodrick-Prescott trend—fell in ten of eleven IT countries after adoption of IT, in comparison to their pre-IT volatility. Output volatility was cut by half or more in four IT countries: Chile, Peru, Australia, and Canada. Average post-IT volatility in the ten IT countries is 2.4, a figure that is somewhat lower than the 3.3 average volatility in the control group of ten non-IT industrial countries. In sum, adoption of IT by emerging and industrial countries is correlated with a large decline in their output volatility to levels that are similar to (or somewhat smaller than) those observed in non-IT economies in the Organization for Economic Cooperation and Development (OECD).

1.5 The Recent Shift toward Inflation Targeting in Latin America

Different varieties of IT are applied today in five Latin American countries: Brazil, Chile, Colombia, Mexico, and Peru. What prompted their central banks to adopt this particular monetary regime? As in other regions, early IT adopters in the region began this new regime in an evolutionary way, by announcing public inflation objectives and learning only over time—from other countries' and their own experience—about the necessary prerequisites and components of what now is viewed as a full-fledged IT regime (see Bernanke et al. 1999 and Schaechter et al. 2000).

As elsewhere in the world, four main factors have prompted Latin American countries to adopt IT. First, public announcement of central bank inflation targets makes those targets both the economy's nominal anchor and the main monetary policy objective. Second, forward-looking, numerical inflation targets complement public information about monetary policy objectives and implementation to make monetary policy more effective in a world of forward-looking, rational private agents. Third, publicly announced inflation targets are an easy way to make central banks accountable to society at large and to their political representatives—a major prerequisite imposed on newly independent central banks. The latter factor can explain IT adoption in countries that have long democratic traditions but that have recently granted operational independence to central banks (like many industrial-country ITers) and others that have embraced democracy only recently (e.g., the Latin Americans in the 1990s).[17] Finally, disappointment of alternative monetary and exchange

17. Among industrial countries, the United Kingdom is an outlier of the general case of independence-to-IT sequencing: IT adoption in 1992 preceded operational independence granted by the Blair government in 1997 to the Bank of England. Among developing-country targeters, the Central Bank of Brazil adopted full IT in 1999 but still has not been granted full operational independence.

Table 1.9 **Output Volatility in 18 IT Countries and 10 Non-IT Countries, 1980–2000**

	Full ITers			Partial ITers			Non-ITers	
	Country	Before	After	Country	Before	After	Country	During 1990s
Latin America	Brazil	4.8	—	Colombia	4.5	—		
	Chile	6.2	3.1	Mexico	4.0	—		
	Average	5.5	—	Peru	11.5	5.1		
				Average	6.7	—		
Rest of world	*Old*						Denmark	2.8
	Australia	2.8	1.2				France	1.6
	Canada	4.4	2.2				Germany	2.4
	Finland	3.1	2.5				Italy	2.3
	Israel	2.9	1.7				Japan	3.3
	New Zealand	3.4	3.1				The Netherlands	2.2
	Spain	2.4	1.7				Norway	2.8
	Sweden	3.1	3.4				Portugal	10.8
	United Kingdom	2.4	1.3				Switzerland	2.8
	Average	2.6	2.1				United States	2.3
	Recent						Average	3.3
	Czech Republic	9.4	4.3					
	Poland	8.5	—					
	South Africa	3.2	—					
	Korea	3.6	—					
	Thailand	5.5	—					
	Average	6.0	—					

Sources: Authors' calculations based on data from the IMF's *IFS* (various issues) and country sources.

Notes: Based on quarterly industrial production data (various subperiods). Volatility calculated as standard deviation of industrial production variation (to a trend calculated by a Hodrick-Prescott filter). A dash indicates that the time span after IT adoption is too short to compute a sacrifice ratio.

rate regimes—ranging from true disappointment with money growth targets to abandonment of fixed exchange rate regimes after full-fledged balance-of-payments crises—led many countries to adopt IT as the only remaining alternative.

The main design and implementation features of IT in Latin America are summarized in table 1.10. For comparison, the features of IT are summarized for IT countries in other regions, divided into newcomers (table 1.11) and old-timers (table 1.12).

The third and fourth columns of table 1.10 report announced target levels and actual inflation rates for the five Latin American targeters. The last two columns of the table report the exchange rate system and the target index considered. The five countries have adopted a floating exchange rate system after using currency bands in the 1980s or 1990s (with the exception of Peru). The first country to abandon the currency band was Mexico, after its late 1994 crisis. The three other countries abandoned their exchange rate bands in 1999, when they faced high costs in interest rates and activity when defending the exchange rate bands.

Chile began to build up IT in 1990, following the announcement of an inflation objective introduced in the first report to the senate by the then–newly independent central bank. The second country that announced inflation targets, although without a formal IT system, was Peru in 1991. At the time the announced inflation objective was part of a broader stabilization program supported by the IMF. Then Colombia, Brazil, and finally Mexico moved toward announcing targets. As of today, only Brazil (since June 1999) and Chile (since May 2000) have full-fledged IT regimes in place. Among other features, both countries have fully relinquished use of any monetary growth and exchange rate targets and issue regular inflation reports with numerical inflation forecasts over the relevant projection horizons.

In October 2000 Mexico announced inflation targets for the next three years in a system that it is quickly converging toward a full-fledged IT framework. Colombia has been struggling with the introduction of IT since the early 1990s. The country had trouble pursuing the inflation objective with sufficient strength due to persistent problems of fiscal dominance and the simultaneous pursuit of a real exchange rate objective. As a result, its stabilization program lacked full credibility and, not surprisingly, inflation performance has suffered as well. It was only after Colombia abandoned its exchange rate band and adopted a float (September 1999) that the central bank could focus its attention more closely on reducing inflation. In Peru a strong stabilization commitment of the Ministry of the Economy and the central bank is in place, even in the absence of a full-fledged IT system. Rather, the central bank pursues monetary targets, usually in conjunction with IMF programs. As progress has been made in reducing inflation, however, the country has been moving toward the adoption of more formal IT.

Table 1.10 **Latin American Inflation Targeters**

Country	Date Introduced	Target Inflation Rate (%)	Effective Inflation Rate (%)	Exchange Rate Regime	Target Index	Target Setter	Monetary Policy Operating Target	Inflation Report	Central Bank Legal Framework
Brazil	June 1999	1999: 8.0 (±2%) 2000: 6.0 (±2%) 2001: 4.0 (±2%)	1999: 8.9 2000: 7.9[a]	Floating since 1999. Crawling exchange rate band used before	IPCA (national CPI)	Joint, government and central bank	Overnight interest rate	Yes	• Instrument independence. • Loans to national treasury prohibited. • If the target is failed, the central bank must send a public letter to the minister of finance explaining the reasons of the failure and the actions necessaryto return to the correct path. • Currency stability and price stability as objectives.
Chile	1991	1991: 15.0–20.0 1992: 15.0 1993: 10.0–12.0 1994: 9.0–11.0 1995: 9.0 1996: 6.5 1997: 5.5 1998: 4.5 1999: 4.3 2000: 3.5 2001 onward: 2.0–4.0	1991: 18.7 1992: 12.7 1993: 12.2 1994: 8.9 1995: 8.2 1996: 6.6 1997: 6.0 1998: 4.7 1999: 2.3 2000: 4.2[b]	Floating since September 1999. Exchange rate band used before.	Total CPI	Central bank in consultation with minister of finance	Overnight interest rate (real terms)	Yes	• Instrument independence, but finance minister can suspend board decisions for two weeks except for decisions unanimously taken by the board. • Loans to government prohibited. • Price stability as primary objective. Normal functioning of the internal and external payment systems as secondary objectives.
Colombia	September 1999	1999: 15.0 2000: 10.0 2001: 8.0 2002: 6.0	1999: 9.2 2000: 9.2[b]	Floating since September 1999. Crawling exchange rate band used before and led to conflicts between exchange rate and inflation objectives. Intervention can be used to smooth fluctuations.	Total CPI	Joint, government and central bank	Monetary base (daily)	Yes	• Minister of finance is the president of the board. • Loans to the government prohibited. • Price stability and finance system's strength as objectives.

(*continued*)

Table 1.10 continued

Country	Date Introduced	Target Inflation Rate (%)	Effective Inflation Rate (%)	Exchange Rate Regime	Target Index	Target Setter	Monetary Policy Operating Target	Inflation Report	Central Bank Legal Framework
Mexico	1999	1999: 13.0 2000: < 10.0 2001: 6.5 2002: 4.5 2003: similar to principal trade partners' inflation (3%)	1999: 12.3 2000.8.9[b]	Floating with intervention since financial crisis in 1994.	Total CPI	Central bank	Monetary base (daily)	Yes	• Instrument independence. • Loans to government prohibited. • Price stability as objective.
Peru	1994	1994: 15.0–20.0 1995: 9.0–11.0 1996: 9.5–11.5 1997: 8.0–10.0 1998: 7.5–9.0 1999: 5.0–6.0 2000: 3.5–4.0 2001: 2.5–3.5 2002: 1.5–2.5 2003: 1.5–2.5	1994: 15.4 1995: 10.2 1996: 11.8 1997: 6.5 1998: 6.0 1999: 3.7 2000: 3.7	Floating since 1994. Intervention can be used to smooth fluctuations.	Total CPI	Central bank in consultation with minister of finance	Monetary base (daily)	No	• Instrument independence. • Loans to government or state institutions prohibited. • Restrictions to loan portfolio composition prohibited. • Multiple exchange rates prohibited. • Price stability as objective.

Source: Authors' elaboration.

[a]Twelve months to August.

[b]Twelve months to September.

Table 1.11 **Recent Inflation-Targeting Countries**

Country	Date Introduced	Target Inflation Rate (%)	Current Exchange Rate Regime	Target Index
Czech Republic	December 1997	1998: 5.5–6.5 1999: 4.0–5.0 2000: 3.5–5.5 2001: 2.0–4.0 2005: 1.0–3.0	Floating	Underlying CPI (except regulated prices and indirect taxes).
Korea	1998	1998: 9.0 (±1% band) 1999: 3.0 (±1% band) 2000: 2.5 (±1% band) From 2001 onward: 2.5	Floating. In exceptional cases, if there is a large discrepancy in the exchange market, which increases volatility, central bank can intervene.	Underlying CPI (except noncereal agricultural products and petroleom-based-product prices). In 1999 and 1998, the target was total CPI.
Poland	October 1998	1998: <9.5 1999: 6.6–7.8 2000: 5.4–6.8 2003: <4	Floating.	Total CPI.
South Africa	February 2000	2002: 3.0–6.0	Floating.	Underlying CPI (except interest costs).
Thailand	April 2000	From 2000 onward: 0.0–3.5	Floating. Short interest rates can be adjusted in the case of pressures over the exchange rate.	Average quarterly underlying CPI (except raw food and energy prices).

Source: Authors' elaboration.

Table 1.12 Old Inflation-Targeting Countries

Country	Date Introduced	Target Inflation Rate (%)	Exchange Rate Regime	Target Index	Escape Clauses	Target Setter(s)	Monetary Policy Operating Target	Central Bank Legal Framework
Australia	1993	2.0–3.0% on average over business cycle	Floating	Since September 1998, a revised CPI; before, treasury underlying CPI[a]	None	Joint, government and central bank	Overnight cash interest rate	• Instrument independence. • The RBA is required to consult with the government. There is a formal dispute resolution mechanism. • Multiple objectives.
Canada	Feb. 1991	Dec. 91: 3.0–5.0 Dec. 92: 2.0–4.0 June 94: 1.5–3.5 Since Dec. 95: 1.0–3.0 (in effect until Dec. 2001)	Floating	Underlying CPI (except food, energy, and indirect taxes)	Aim to get back on track over two years in the event of a temporary price shock affecting inflation by more than 0.5%	Joint, government and central bank	Overnight interest rate	• Instrument independence, but minister of finance can, in exceptional cases, issue a formal directive to the central bank governor. • Loans to government restricted. • Multiple objectives.
Finland[b]	Feb. 1993–June 1998	Annual average of 2.0 by 1995	EMU	Underlying CPI (except indirect taxes, subsidies, housing prices, and mortgage interest)				
Israel	1992	1992: 14.0–15.0 1993: 10 1994: 8 1995: 8.0–11.0 1996: 8.0–10.0 1997: 7.0–10.0 1998: 7.0–10.0 1999: 4 2000: 3.0–4.0 2001: 3.0–4.0	Crawling exchange rate band	Total CPI	None	Government in consultation with central bank	Short-term interest rate	• Instrument independence. • Loans to government prohibited. • Multiple objectives (currency stability and real objectives).

New Zealand	July 1989	1990: 3.0–5.0 1991: 2.5–4.5 1992: 1.5–3.5 1993–1996: 0.0–2.0 Since 1997: 0.0–3.0	Floating	Total CPI[c]	Unusual events tolerated provided they do not generate general inflationary pressures	Joint, government and central bank	Overnight interest rate	• Instrument independence subject to a requirement that monetary actions be taken with regard to financial-system soundness. • Price stability as primary objective (central bank governor may be dismissed in case the target is not achieved).
Spain[b]	Nov. 1994–June 1998	June 1996: 3.5–4.0 Dec. 1997: 2.5 1998: 2	EMU	Total CPI				
Sweden	Jan. 1993	Since 1995: 2 (±1%)	Floating	Total CPI	None	Central bank	One-week interest rate	• The board is appointed by the parliament. • Instrument independence. • Loans to government prohibited. • Price stability as primary objective.
United Kingdom	Oct. 1992	1992–1995: 1.0–4.0 Since 1995: 2.5	Floating	RPIX (except mortgage interest)	None	Government	Short-term repo rate	• Instrument independence. • Price stability as primary objective.

[a]Treasury underlying CPI in Australia excludes roughly half of CPI basket. Since September 1998, authorities decided to set the target in terms of a revised total CPI index that is more ample and well known by the public.

[b]Spain and Finland fixed their currencies to the euro in January 1999.

[c]In 1999 the New Zealand Statistical Agency removed interest charges from the CPI. Prior to then the inflation targets where defined in terms of the total CPI less interest charges and other first-round effect prices.

On paper, central banks' legal objectives differ widely among countries. In Mexico and Peru the official central-bank objective is defined as the attainment of price stability, whereas in Brazil it is a dual objective of currency and price stability. In Chile and Colombia there are multiple official objectives: price stability and the stability of the domestic and foreign payments systems. However, in all countries the primary objective governing monetary policy has become price stability. Progress in reducing inflation and formalization of inflation targets has been made possible by institutional developments that have provided larger degrees of independence to central banks. The central banks of the five countries have been provided substantial degrees of independence in the 1990s and central bank loans to the government are prohibited. Legal independence is observed in the five countries. However, full independence in setting inflation targets is observed only in Mexico, whose central bank alone sets the target. In Chile and Peru the target is set by the central bank in consultation with the government, whereas in Brazil and Colombia it is set jointly by the government and the central bank. With respect to the use of instruments, the central banks of Brazil, Mexico, and Peru enjoy full operational independence in using their monetary instruments (the interest rate or monetary base). In the case of Brazil, the monetary instrument is the overnight nominal rate of short-term government debt. In Chile it is the overnight real interest rate. In Colombia, Mexico, and Peru the monetary instrument is the daily monetary base. In these five countries, open-market operations are used to attain target levels for the monetary instrument. They are conducted on central bank bonds (in Chile, Colombia, and Peru) or on treasury bonds (in Brazil and Mexico).

In Chile, the minister of finance is a nonvoting member of the central bank board and is entitled to suspend board decisions for up to two weeks, for decisions that have not been approved unanimously by the board. However, governments have yet to exercise this option since central bank independence was granted in 1990. In Colombia the minister of finance is the president of the central bank board and one of seven members. The rationale for this arrangement is that it purportedly contributes to raise coordination between fiscal and monetary policymakers. However, this has not always been the case—indeed, many times the arrangement has been a source of friction between monetary and fiscal authorities.

Finally, all countries other than Peru issue regular inflation reports that differ significantly in scope and coverage from country to country.

1.6 The Inflation-Targeting Experience of Chile: Does the Introduction of a Target Make a Difference?

Chile was the first country to embrace IT in Latin America and is the first to complete both its transition toward a full-fledged IT framework and convergence to stationary inflation. Hence this country's experience is of special interest, particularly with regard to whether IT has contributed to reduce inflation and whether it made a difference in the speed and cost of price stabilization.

In their study of IT in industrial countries, Bernanke et al. (1999) found inconclusive evidence on the latter questions. Thus, although IT made a difference in the behavior of variables related to inflation, they found no evidence that countries that applied IT benefited from lower stabilization costs. However, they did find that the introduction of IT made a difference in the trajectory of macroeconomic variables related to inflation.

Here we analyze the role played by the introduction of IT on the reduction of Chilean inflation, as well as the costs associated with this reduction. The main question to be addressed is whether the setting of IT had an effect on the structure of the economy and on inflation dynamics in particular.

In our model below, the main channel through which IT affects inflation dynamics is its effect on inflation expectations, which in turn affect price and wage inflation. Inflation expectations, an endogenous variable in our model, are measured in two alternative ways: first, by comparing nominal and real interest rates of similar instruments, and second, by using exogenous inflation forecasts published by Consensus Economics (*Latin American Consensus Forecasts,* various issues). One may expect that announced inflation targets were not fully credible at early stages and thus their effects on inflation expectations should become more important only over time. This learning period should show up in the results.

1.6.1 The Effects of Inflation Targeting on Expected Inflation

First, we ask whether IT adoption in late 1990 made a difference for inflation dynamics. We start by generating inflation forecasts for the 1990s from single-equation inflation models estimated for the period before IT adoption. We use three models: (1) a Phillips curve, (2) a reduced-form inflation equation, and (3) an autoregressive integrated moving average (ARIMA) time-series model.[18] In all models we use a measure of core inflation that excludes perishable products from the headline Consumer Price Index (CPI). The models are estimated with monthly data (twelve-month rates of change) and quarterly data (quarter-on-quarter rates of change), from the mid-1980s through late 1999.

Model-based, out-of-sample inflation forecasts are reported in figures 1.6 and 1.7. The results are informative and consistent, showing that forecasts based on the three models are well above actual declining inflation levels.[19] This provides some prima facie evidence that something occurred after the introduction of IT that contributed to reducing inflation.

However, the simple comparison of forecasts does not address the ques-

18. After the model selection procedures, we estimate an autoregressive moving average (ARMA) model for core inflation, with quarterly and monthly data.

19. The difference between the forecasts and the actual values becomes very large after 1993.

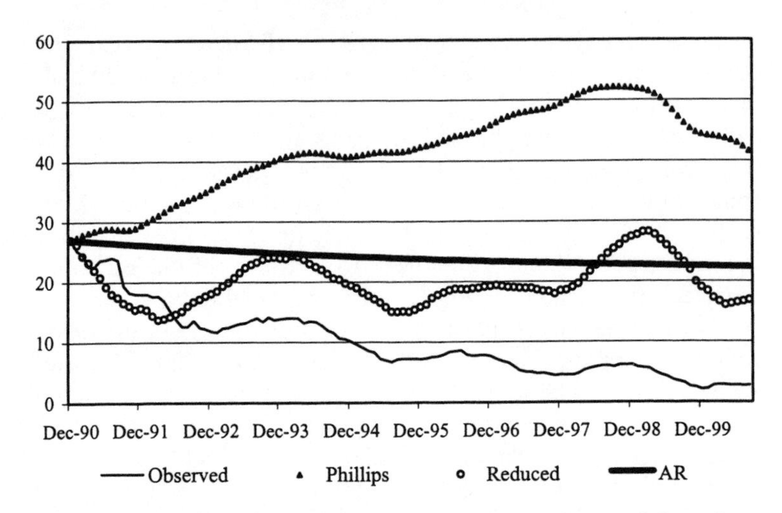

Fig. 1.6 Out-of-sample forecasts: Monthly data (12-month rate of change)

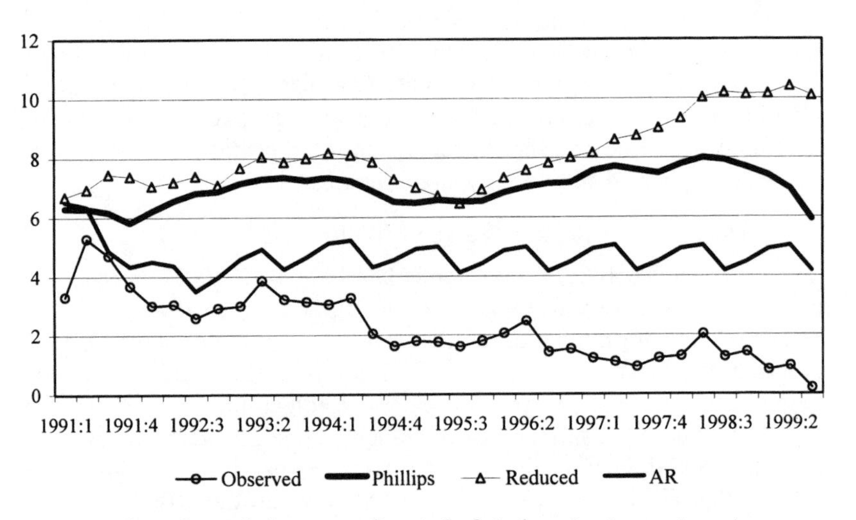

Fig. 1.7 Out-of-sample forecasts: Quarterly data (quarter-to-quarter rate of change)

tion about what was behind the success in achieving inflation rates below the forecasts. One could argue that inflation reduction was not a result of introducing IT but of other factors such as the payoff from earlier structural reforms, fiscal orthodoxy, or the sharp appreciation in the wake of large capital inflows during the early 1990s.

To take into account possible changes in the structure of the economy but short of specifying a complete structural model (which is our task below), we estimate an unrestricted vector autoregression (VAR) model. The VAR system comprises endogenous variables such as core inflation, the

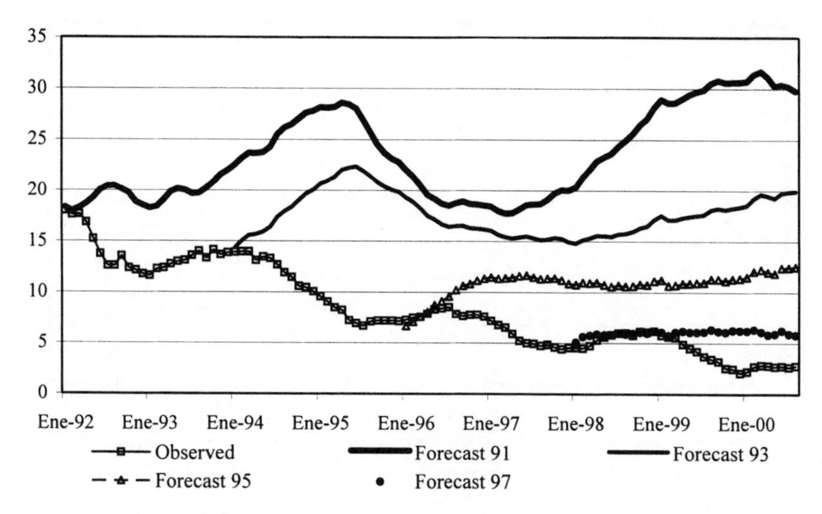

Fig. 1.8 Out-of-sample forecasts from rolling VARs: First set of VARs, odd years (12-month rate of change)

rate of change of the monthly index of aggregate economic activity, the rate of change of nominal money (M1), the rate of change of the nominal exchange rate, and the policy interest rate. Foreign inflation is taken as an exogenous variable.[20] All variables are expressed as twelve-month rates of change. We estimate this VAR model using rolling regressions, leaving out the first year of the sample and adding one year at a time, starting with data through December 1991. The inflation forecasts obtained from these VAR models are reported in figures 1.8 and 1.9. Although forecasts became closer to actual inflation rates when adding more recent years (and leaving out earlier ones), the ratio between the forecast errors and actual inflation levels remained fairly constant over time.

Now we want to investigate whether the announced inflation targets played a role in the path of inflation reduction. An obvious hypothesis to analyze is whether the target affected inflation expectations, providing through this channel an anchor for the inflation process. If this were the case, then the unemployment cost of reducing inflation would be lower under IT than under a conventional stabilization strategy not based on IT.

In order to analyze the effects of the targets on inflation expectations, we start with the most direct measure of inflation expectations: inflation expectations published in *Latin American Consensus Forecasts* (*CF*) by Consensus Economics.[21] First we compare the *CF* expectations measure with two measures derived from VAR models and with actual inflation. The

20. We also used the terms of trade as an additional exogenous variable, but the results were not much affected by their inclusion.

21. We thank Consensus Economics for providing this data series.

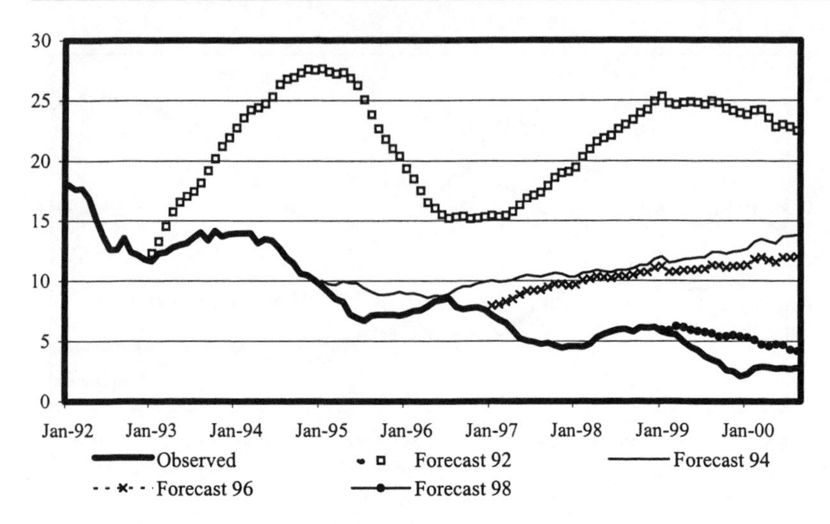

Fig. 1.9 Out-of-sample forecasts from rolling VARs: Second set of VARs, even years (12-month rate of change)

first VAR model (VAR1) comprises the variables defined for the previous VAR model, except for replacing core inflation with headline (total) CPI inflation.[22] The second VAR model (VAR2) adds the inflation target as an exogenous variable additional to those included in VAR1. Both VAR models are estimated with monthly data of twelve-month variations of the variables by rolling regressions, with data through December of each preceding year.

The results of these comparisons for December-to-December inflation are reported in table 1.13. They show that *CF* market inflation expectations are quite different from the values estimated from the VAR models and from announced target levels. Moreover, the discrepancy between *CF* inflation expectations and the inflation targets becomes smaller over time. This result provides evidence that inflation targets became more credible with the passing of time and the attainment of annual inflation rates close to announced target levels. Hence the use of IT, along with an appropriate institutional support allowing the public to understand that the main objective of the monetary policy is to bring inflation close to target levels, facilitated Chile's process of price stabilization. Furthermore, inflation itself is less sensitive to nominal shocks than it is in a system without the IT anchor. In addition, the existence of the target and a clear central bank commitment to its achievement also provides some insurance against conventional time-inconsistency problems of macroeconomic policies.

22. We replaced core inflation by headline (total) CPI inflation because the targets are defined as December-to-December changes of the headline CPI.

Table 1.13 Inflation Forecasts and Expected Inflation (Dec.-to-Dec. rate of change)

	Observed	Consensus	VAR1	VAR2	Target
1991	18.7	n.a.	—	—	17.5
1992	12.7	n.a.	19.4	—	15.0
1993	12.2	15.4	23.1	—	11.0
1994	8.9	11.3	18.5	—	10.0
1995	8.2	8.7	8.2	—	9.0
1996	6.6	7.1	9.4	9.1	6.5
1997	6.0	5.7	6.6	6.7	5.5
1998	4.7	4.8	6.7	5.2	4.5
1999	2.3	4.2	3.9	4.5	4.3

Source: Authors' calculations. n.a. = not available. Dashes indicate that VAR was not computed due to data length.

1.6.2 The Effects of Targeting Inflation

In order to learn more about the process by which IT introduction helped reduce inflation, we now specify and estimate a small econometric model for Chilean inflation. The literature on the structural modeling of inflation in Chile is extensive.[23] We will concentrate on open-economy-type models studied during the last fifteen years. Corbo (1985) built a model of Chilean inflation to study inflation dynamics up to the early 1980s, using a reduced form of the Salter-Swan-Dornbusch dependent economy model. Corbo and Solimano (1991) investigated the dynamics of Chilean inflation up to the late 1980s, using a small structural model. Edwards (1995) examined the question of Chilean inflation dynamics and inertia in the context of the use of the exchange rate as a nominal anchor for the 1974 to 1982 period.

Corbo and Fischer (1994) estimated a small structural model similar to that used in Bruno (1978, 1991) and Corbo (1985). In their solution of the structural model, they found that substantial inertia characterized inflation during the 1980s. Finally, Corbo (1998) estimates a model in which inflation expectations enter in the wage equation but not in the price equation. Also in his model, the policy interest rate and the output gap are taken as exogenous; hence they are not solved within the model.

The model that we use is an extension of the model used in Corbo (1998), whereby inflation expectations, measured by the comparison of nominal and real interest rates of similar instruments, enters explicitly into the wage and inflation equation. Furthermore, inflation expectations are determined by a four-quarter moving average of the previous inflation, the inflation target, and an expectation error.

23. For earlier models of Chilean inflation see Harberger (1963). For a review of inflation models for countries with moderate inflation see Dornbusch and Fischer (1993).

The full model is reflected by the following equations:

(1) $$\pi_t^S = \alpha_0 + \alpha_1\omega_t + \alpha_2\hat{e}4_t + \alpha_3 \text{gap}_{t-1} + \alpha_4 D2 + \alpha_5 D3 + \alpha_6 D4 + \alpha_7 \pi_{t+1}^E + \alpha_8 \pi_t^*$$

(2) $$\omega_t = \beta_0 + \beta_1 \pi_t^E + \beta_2 \pi_{t-2} + \beta_3 D2 + \beta_4 D3$$

(3) $$\text{gap}_t = \gamma_0 + \gamma_1 \text{gap}_{t-1} + \gamma_2 \text{tot}_t + \gamma_3 \text{prbc}_{t-2} + \gamma_4 \text{KPIB}_t \times D96$$

(4) $$\text{desem}_t = \delta_0 + \delta_1 \text{gap}_t + \delta_2 \text{desem}_{t-1} + \delta_3 D2 + \delta_4 D3 + \delta_5 D4$$

(5) $$\text{gdcc}_t = \chi_0 + \chi_1 \text{gap}_t + \chi_2 \text{gdcc}_{t-1}$$

(6) $$\hat{e}_t = \phi_0 + \phi_1 \pi_{t-1} + \phi_2 \pi_{t-1}^* + \phi_3 \Delta \text{RIN}_t + \phi_4 \text{DESV}_t + \phi_5 \text{KPIB}_t \times D96$$

(7) $$\pi_{t+1}^E = \mu_0 + \mu_1 Tar_{t+4} + \mu_2 \frac{\pi_t + \pi_{t-1} + \pi_{t-2} + \pi_{t-3}}{4} + \mu_3 \frac{\pi_t + \pi_{t-1} + \pi_{t-2} + \pi_{t-3}}{4} - \pi_{t-4}^E$$

(8) $$\pi_t = \lambda_0 + \lambda_1 \pi_t^S + \lambda_2 D3 + \lambda_3 D4 + \lambda_4 A93 + \lambda_5 A94 + \lambda_6 A96 + \lambda_7 A98$$

where

π_t^S = core inflation, quarterly rate of change;
π_t = headline CPI inflation, quarterly rate of change;
π_{t+1}^E = expected rate of inflation, quarterly, for period $t + 1$ based on information available at period t;
ω_t = quarterly rate of change of the wage rate;
$\hat{e}_t$ = quarterly rate of change of the nominal exchange rate, in pesos per dollar;
$\hat{e}4_t$ = four-quarter moving average of $\hat{e}_t$;
π_t^* = external inflation in dollars, quarterly rate of change;
gap_t = gap between the seasonally adjusted quarterly GDP and its trend, as a percentage of the trend (trend is measured using a Hodrick-Prescott filter);
tot_t = four-quarter moving average of the log of the terms of trade;
prbc_t = real interest rate of central bank debt paper with ninety days of maturity (PRBC-90), annual rate;
KPIB_t = capital inflows as percentage of nominal GDP;

desem_t = quarterly unemployment rate;
gdcc_t = current account deficit of the year ending in quarter t, as percentage of nominal GDP;
ΔRIN_t = quarterly change in central bank foreign reserves, in U.S. dollars;
DESV_t = difference between the log of the market nominal exchange rate and the log of the central parity of the exchange rate band, both in period t;
Tar_t = quarterly inflation rate implicit in the inflation target announced by the central bank;[24]
$D2, D3, D4$ = seasonal dummies for the second, third, and fourth quarters, respectively;
$D96$ = dummy variable that takes the value of 1 from the first quarter of 1996 until the end of the sample (third quarter of 2000) to reflect the sharp increase in capital inflows; and
$A93, A94, A96, A98$ = dummy variables that take the value of 1 for 1993, 1994, 1996, and 1998, respectively, for irregular supply shocks that could affect the difference between core and headline CPI inflation.

Equation (1) for core inflation is specified as a weighted average of inflation for tradable and nontradable goods and services, and includes expected inflation. Equation (2) for wage inflation includes lagged inflation (reflecting explicit indexation schemes in wage contracts) and expected inflation (reflecting forward-looking wage contracts). Equation (3) specifies the output gap as a function of its own lag, the terms of trade, the lagged value of the real interest rate, and capital inflows. Equation (4) relates the unemployment rate to the output gap (Okun's law). Equation (5) specifies the current account deficit ratio to GDP as a function of the output gap and its lagged value. Equation (6) describes the evolution of the nominal exchange rate within the exchange-rate band that was in place until late 1999. Equation (7) relates expected inflation to the forward-looking inflation target, a moving average of lagged inflation levels, and an inflation forecast error term. Equation (8) relates actual inflation to core inflation, and introduces seasonal dummies and annual dummies for particular weather- and oil-related shocks.

Model estimation results are reported in the appendix. We now proceed to compare simulated values (obtained from the model's dynamic simulation) and actual values for core inflation. In the first simulation we take the actual real interest rate as given. The comparison of simulated and actual

24. Computed by the authors linearizing the target expressed as a December-to-December rate of change.

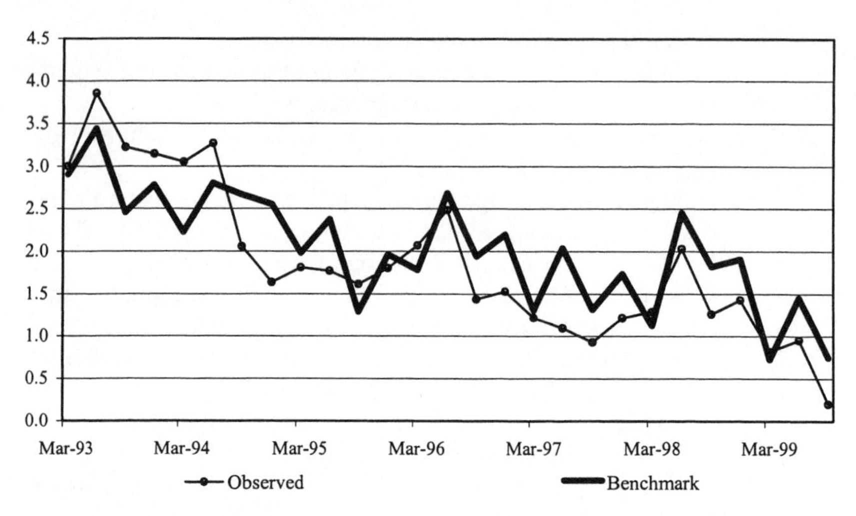

Fig. 1.10 Observed and benchmark values of the core inflation (quarterly rate of change)

values for core inflation is shown in figure 1.10. It can be observed that model forecasts are quite close to actual values, except for 1997. Using these simulated values as a benchmark (Benchmark 1), we proceed now with the first counterfactual simulation. Here we analyze (Simulation 1) what would have happened if the target had not been made public and therefore had not affected expectations.[25] That is, in Simulation 1 we simulate the dynamic response of the Chilean economy if inflation expectations in the 1990s had been formed in the way they were formed in the 1980s.

The comparison of simulated values with those from the benchmark model is presented in figure 1.11. Simulated values are above benchmark values, particularly at the end of 1996. These results are consistent with the hypothesis that the introduction of explicit inflation targets helped in reducing inflation. The mechanism at work is the effect of the inflation target on inflation expectations, and of the latter on wage inflation and core price inflation. A clearer picture emerges when we compare the cumulative sum over four quarters of quarterly inflation simulated by Simulation 1 to the benchmark values (table 1.14). The comparison again suggests a clear break since late 1996, showing that the effect of the target on actual inflation became important only some time after the introduction of IT. This is not surprising, because in the early stages the public was probably uncertain about the central bank's commitment to attain the inflation target. It

25. For this purpose, we first estimate an equation for inflation expectations for the period before the introduction of IT (until the fourth quarter of 1990) and use this equation to model inflation expectations in the 1990s.

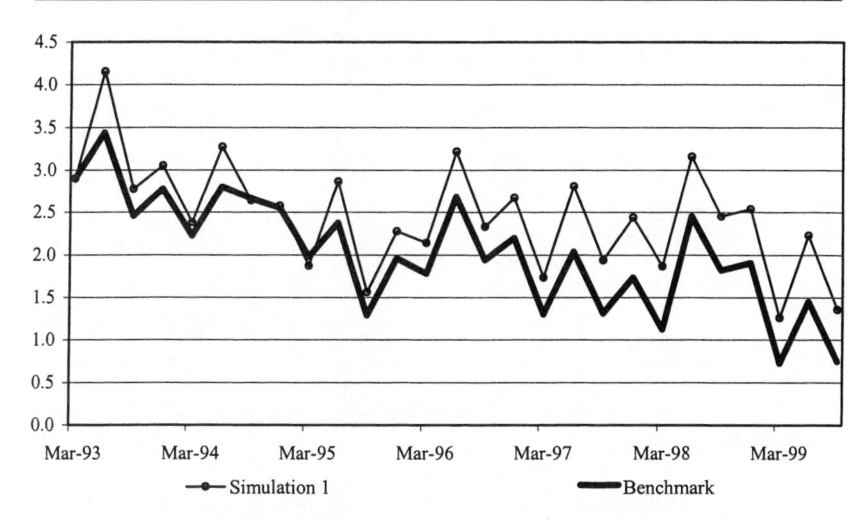

Fig. 1.11 Core inflation: Counterfactual 1 (quarterly rate of change)

Table 1.14 Core Inflation: Benchmark and Simulation 1 (four-quarter accumulated sum of quarterly rates)

	Benchmark	Simulation 1
Dec. 1993	11.6	12.9
June 1994	10.3	11.5
Dec. 1994	10.2	10.9
June 1995	9.6	10.0
Dec. 1995	7.6	8.6
June 1996	7.7	9.2
Dec. 1996	8.6	10.4
June 1997	7.5	9.5
Dec. 1997	6.4	8.9
June 1998	6.6	9.4
Dec. 1998	7.3	10.0
June 1999	5.9	8.5

Source: Authors' calculation in base of the estimated model.

was also for 1996 that the central bank announced (in September 1995) a more aggressive target of 6.5 percent, whereas the target for the 1995 had been set at 9 percent and actual inflation had reached 8.2 percent.

A final issue that we address is regarding the likely macroeconomic effects of alternative stabilization paths. Here we run two counterfactual simulations for the speed and intensity of price stabilization in the 1990s: a more gradualist disinflation path (Simulation 2) and a more aggressive path (Simulation 3). The gradualist strategy considers a reduction in target inflation by only 0.5 percentage points per year, beginning in 1994. The

Table 1.15 Alternative Paths for the Inflation Targets (Dec.-to-Dec. rate of change)

	Effective	Soft	Aggressive
Dec. 1991	17.5	17.5	17.5
Dec. 1992	15.0	15.0	15.0
Dec. 1993	11.0	11.0	11.0
Dec. 1994	10.0	8.0	10.5
Dec. 1995	9.0	5.0	10.0
Dec. 1996	6.5	3.0	9.5
Dec. 1997	5.5	3.0	9.0
Dec. 1998	4.5	3.0	8.5
Dec. 1999	4.3	3.0	8.0
Dec. 2000	3.5	3.0	7.5

Source: Authors' elaboration.

cold-turkey stabilization assumes a target inflation of 3 percent for 1996 and beyond (table 1.15).

When the targets are altered, the policy interest rate must be changed accordingly. Hence the structural model presented above must be extended to include the following policy reaction function for the central bank:

$$(9)\qquad \text{prbc}_t = (1-\rho)\times[\psi_0 + \psi_1(\pi 4^S_{t+3} - \text{Tar4}_{t+3}) + \psi_2 \text{gdcc}_{t+2}] + \rho\text{prbc}_{t-1} + \psi_3 D983^{26}$$

This policy reaction function is consistent with Corbo (2002), which extends previous work by Taylor (1993) and Clarida, Gali, and Gertler (1998) for countries that follow a target of gradual inflation reduction. In this equation, the policy interest rate is specified as a function of the gap between expected inflation and target inflation, the gap between the current account deficit ratio to GDP and a target ratio (which is set at 4.5 percent of GDP), and the lagged value of the policy rate.[27]

The amended model (which now includes the policy reaction function) is run to provide a new set of benchmark results (Benchmark 2). The results for simulated core inflation and actual core inflation are compared in figure 1.12. Now the simulated values are closer to the actual values than the ones obtained by the Benchmark 1 model results. Hence, by the endogenizing of the policy interest rate, the interest rate is adjusted when the inflation forecast differs from the target level, helping to bring actual inflation closer to the target.

26. In this equation, $\pi 4^S_t$ is the four-quarter cumulative sum of quarterly core inflation rates, Tar4_t is the four-quarter cumulative sum of quarterly target inflation rates, and $D983$ is a dummy variable (equal to 1 in the third quarter of 1998).

27. Because the right-hand-side variables of this equation are endogenous variables, we estimate this equation using generalized method of moments (GMM) in order to obtain consistent and efficient coefficient estimates.

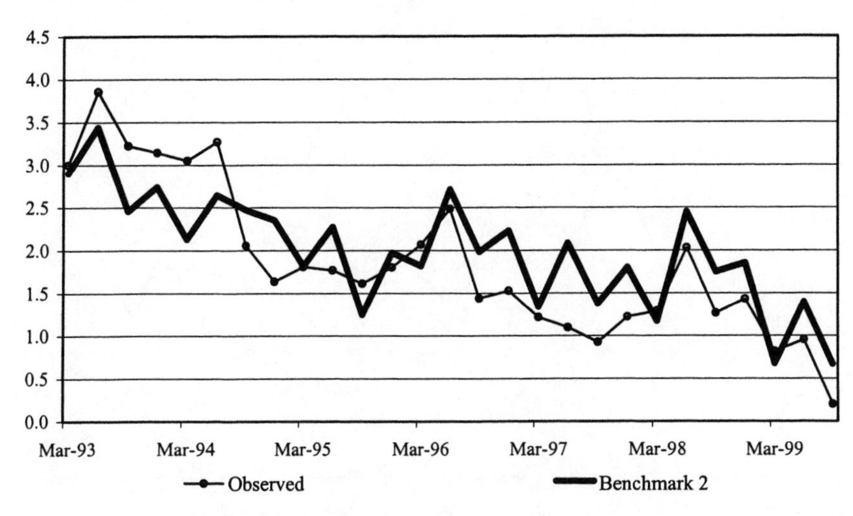

Fig. 1.12 Observed and Benchmark 2 values of the core inflation (quarterly rate of change)

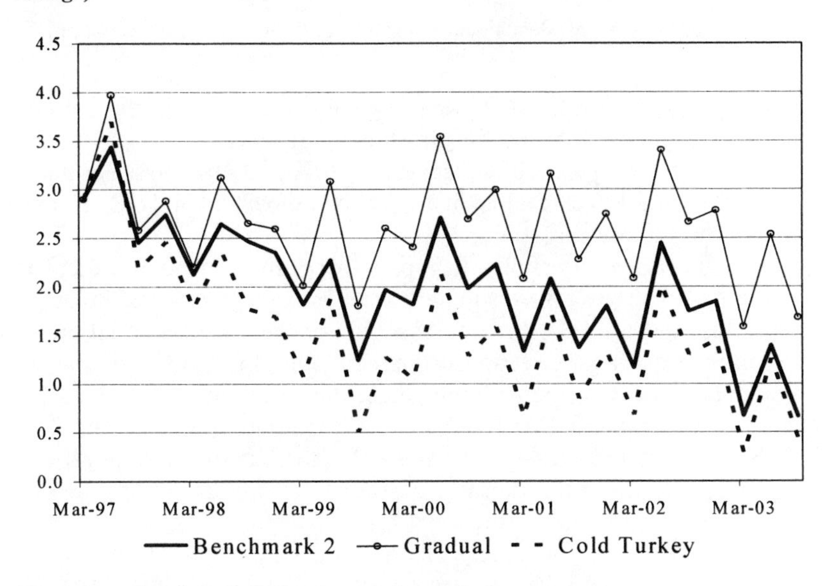

Fig. 1.13 Core inflation: Benchmark 2 and alternative targets

The counterfactual simulation results for core inflation under the gradualist strategy (Gradual), the cold-turkey approach (Cold Turkey), and the benchmark case (Benchmark 2) are reported in figure 1.13. Unsurprisingly, core inflation under the gradualist (cold-turkey) approach is well above (below) the Benchmark 2 path. However the differences between the gradualist and benchmark simulations start declining toward the end of

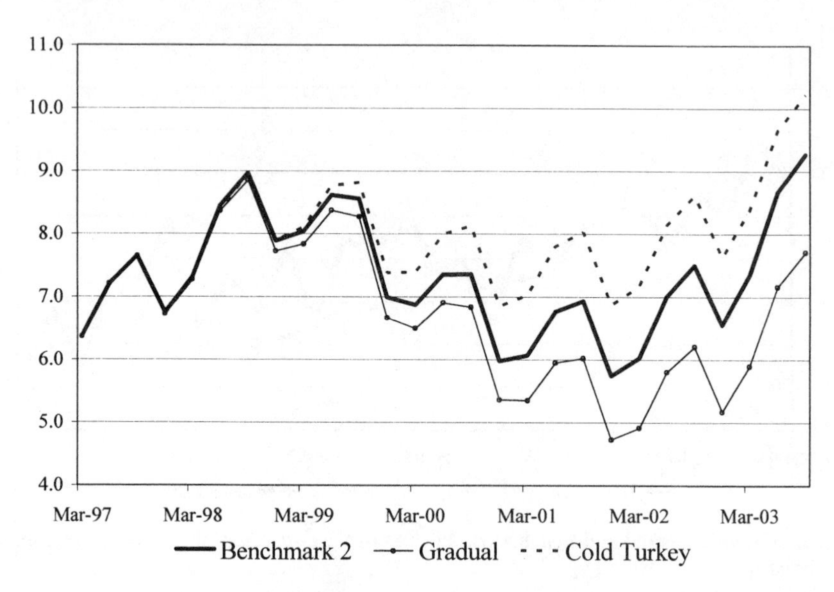

Fig. 1.14 Unemployment: Benchmark 2 and alternative targets (quarterly rate)

the simulation period. In the case of the cold-turkey target, the convergence of the simulated values toward target values is much slower, confirming that inflation exhibits substantial inertia and that the selection of a hard target could have resulted in higher unemployment and only a small gain in terms of lower inflation.

The comparison of unemployment paths for both strategies is presented in figure 1.14. The latter is a result of slow adjustment of expected inflation toward the target level. To throw further light on the cost of disinflation we also compute the sacrifice ratio for the reduction of inflation, comparing the cumulative sum of the unemployment increases with the cumulative sum of the gains in inflation reduction. The computed sacrifice ratio is –1.26. By contrast, in the case of the gradualist strategy the sacrifice ratio is only –0.95, showing that alternative disinflation speeds entail different costs of employment and output.

Now we check the robustness of our results by using an alternative definition of expected inflation—that is, the *CF* measured instead of the difference between nominal and real interest rates. For this purpose, we reestimate equations (1), (2), and (7), using the alternative measure of inflation expectations. Then, after introducing these new equations in the model, we again run the benchmark and the two counterfactual simulations. The results, reported in figures 1.15 and 1.16, are fairly similar to the ones discussed above. The sacrifice ratios are –1.26 for the cold-turkey strategy and –0.99 for the gradualist approach. This confirms the robustness of our results to alternative measures for inflation expectations.

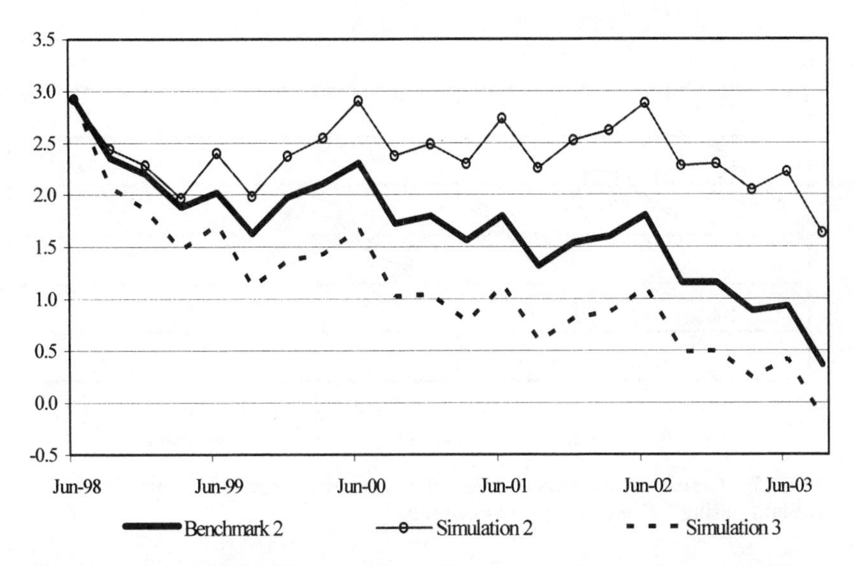

Fig. 1.15 Core inflation: Benchmark 2, soft targets, and aggressive targets using *CF* (quarterly rate of change)

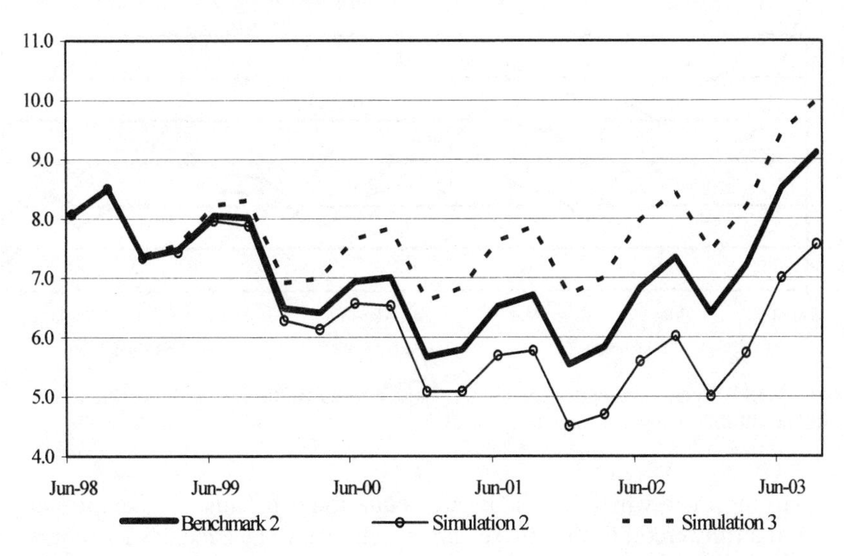

Fig. 1.16 Unemployment: Benchmark 2, soft targets, and aggressive targets using *CF* (quarterly rate)

It could be claimed that the comparison between the cold-turkey and gradual approaches to disinflation conducted above does not properly represent the cold-turkey case because expected inflation does not adjust at once to the target level.[28] That is, it does not assume full credibility of the

28. We thank Alejandro Werner for this point.

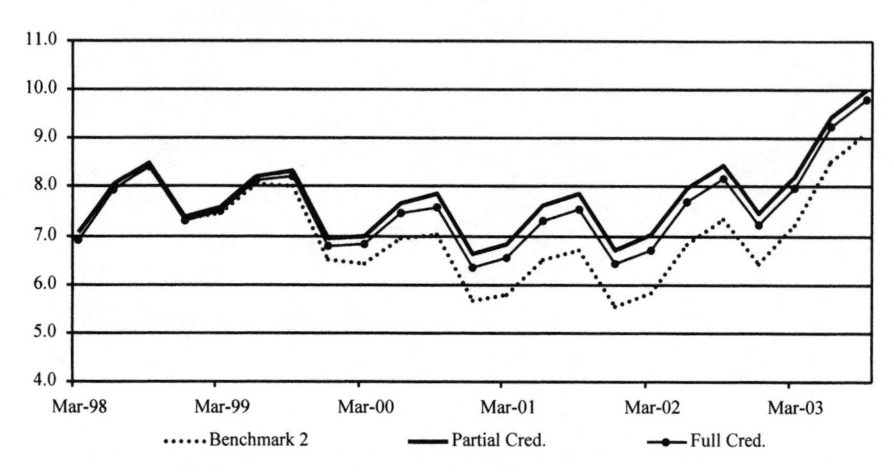

Fig. 1.17 Core inflation: Benchmark 2 and aggressive targets with partial and full credibility using *CF* (quarterly rate of change)

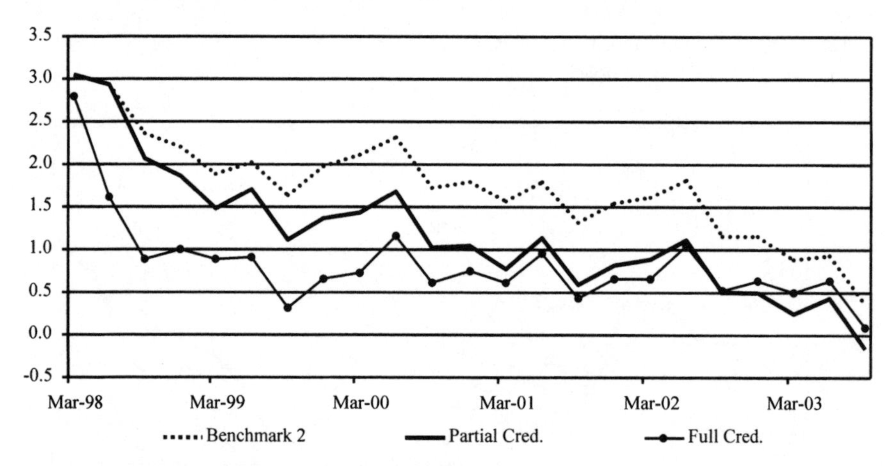

Fig. 1.18 Unemployment: Benchmark 2 and aggressive targets with partial and full credibility using *CF* (quarterly rate)

inflation target, which is still given by equation (7). Thus, to take into account a fully credible cold-turkey approach (using the *CF* measure of inflation expectations), we impose in equation (7) the restrictions $\mu_0 = \mu_2 = \mu_3 = 0$ and $\mu_1 = 1$. The result of the simulation for this restricted version of equation (7) is reported in figures 1.17 and 1.18. As can be seen, the reduction of inflation would have been quicker at the beginning than in the case without full credibility, while the unemployment cost is not so much different in both cases. The sacrifice ratio for this case is –0.529 instead of the –1.26 obtained for the case with partial credibility, and it is even lower than in the case of the gradualist approach. Therefore we conclude that the actual sacrifice ratio of the cold-turkey approach is bounded between –1.26 and –0.529.[29]

1.7 Conclusions

After forty years of high and variable inflation, during the last decade Latin America has made major progress toward eradicating inflation. As a result, at the beginning of the twenty-first century, average inflation is below 10 percent and several countries are well on the way toward achieving and maintaining low, one-digit inflation levels. Inflation reduction was made possible by a frontal attack on public-sector deficits and by a deliberate effort to break the historical inflation dynamics that resulted in high inertia. The recent experience of industrial countries in their pursuit of price stability played an important role by providing a technology to accommodate exchange rate flexibility with monetary discipline: inflation targeting. Ultimately, it has been the combination of progress in achieving fiscal discipline and the restricted discretion embedded in IT that made possible the success in inflation reduction.

This paper has examined the recent experience of inflation targeting in Latin America. A review of alternative exchange rate and monetary policy regimes set the stage by analyzing different arrangements and their pros and cons, in the light of theory and recent international experience. Then a brief review of the empirical evidence on the distribution of regimes during the last two decades in the world at large and Latin America in particular was conducted. A clear, recent shift away from intermediate exchange regimes is noted, particularly in Latin America, where a few countries have adopted currency boards or outright dollarization and many more countries have adopted free floats, typically in conjunction with IT.

A worldwide comparison of implementation and performance of IT provides various preliminary results of interest for the five Latin American ITers. Most ITers brought inflation significantly down around the year of adoption of IT, were successful in attaining their target levels, and exhibit sacrifice ratios and output volatility that are lower after than before adopting IT and comparable to (or sometimes lower than) the levels observed in non-IT industrial economies. Among ITers, the Latin Americans have performed comparatively well. Fiscal discipline and institutional developments that have provided more independence to central banks have supported the adoption of IT and the progress in reducing inflation.

Chile is the country that has used IT for the longest period and is where inflation has already converged to the steady-state, long-term target.

29. It should be mentioned that in the price and wage equations, the actual values of the coefficients also depend on the degree of credibility of the inflation target; therefore, with full credibility, the coefficients of expected inflation in both equations could be higher—resulting in an even lower sacrifice ratio.

Hence it is of much interest to draw the lessons from this experience. Three main lessons emerge: First, the initial progress in reducing inflation toward the target is slow because the public is learning about the true commitment of the central bank to attain the target. Second, the gradual phasing in of IT helped in reducing inflation expectations, contributing to reduce inflation directly by lowering inflation expectations and indirectly by changing wage and price dynamics. Third, with respect to the speed of inflation reduction, a cold-turkey approach would have resulted in a larger sacrifice ratio stemming from higher unemployment during the early years of IT when credibility was gradually built up.

Appendix

Estimated Model Used in Simulations

$$\text{(A.1)} \quad \pi_t^s = -0.632 + 0.432\omega_t + 0.141\hat{e}4_t + 0.105\text{gap}_{t-1} + 1.394D2 + 0.686D3 + 0.517D + 0.285\pi_t^E + 0.141\pi_t^*$$

$$\text{(A.2)} \quad \omega_t = 1.378 + 0.826\pi_t^E + (1 - 0.826)\pi_{t-2} - 1.221D2 - 1.249D3$$

$$\text{(A.3)} \quad \text{gap}_t = 1.621 + 0.675\text{gap}_{t-1} + 0.059\text{tot}_t + 0.427\text{prbc}_{t-2} + 0.055\text{KPIB}_t \times D96$$

$$\text{(A.4)} \quad \text{desem}_t = 1.292 - 0.126\text{gap}_t + 0.843\text{desem}_{t-1} + 0.604D2 + 0.207D3 - 1.214D4$$

$$\text{(A.5)} \quad \text{gdcc}_t = -0.278 + 0.220\text{gap}_t + 0.850\text{gdcc}_{t-1}$$

$$\text{(A.6)} \quad \hat{e}_t = -0.326 + 0.379\pi_{t-1} - 0.70\pi_{t-1}^* - 0.002\Delta\text{RIN}_t - 0.245\text{DESV}_t - 0.079\text{KPIB}_t \times D96$$

$$\text{(A.7)} \quad \pi_{t+1}^E = 0.426 + 1 \times \text{Tar}_{t+4} + 0 \times \frac{\pi_t + \pi_{t-1} + \pi_{t-2} + \pi_{t-3}}{4} + 0.125 \times \frac{\pi_t + \pi_{t-1} + \pi_{t-2} + \pi_{t-3}}{4} - \pi_{t-4}^E$$

$$\text{(A.8)} \quad \pi_t = -0.347 + 1.078\pi_t^S + 0.982D3 + 1.093D4 - 0.711A93 - 0.762A94 - 0.617A96 - 0.702A98$$

This is the version used for the simulations and the counterfactuals. All the restriction over the coefficients were tested before they were imposed, including the homogeneity of degree 1 for the price and wage equations, equations (1) and (2).

References

Bernanke, B., T. Laubach, F. Mishkin, and A. Posen. 1999. *Inflation targeting.* Princeton: Princeton University Press.

Bernanke, B., and F. Mishkin. 1997. Inflation targeting: A new framework for monetary policy? *Journal of Economic Perspectives* 11 (2): 97–116.

Bruno, M. 1978. Exchange rates, import costs, and wage-price dynamics. *Journal of Political Economy* 86 (June): 379–403.

———. 1991. High inflation and the nominal anchors of an open economy. *Princeton Essays in International Finance* no. 183. Princeton University, Department of Economics, International Finance Section.

Calvo, G., and C. Reinhart. 2000. Fear of floating. *Quarterly Journal of Economics* 117 (2): 379–408.

Calvo, G., and C. Végh. 1999. Inflation stabilization and BOP crises in developing countries. Chap. 24 in *Handbook of macroeconomics,* vol. 1C, ed. J. Taylor and M. Woodford. Amsterdam: Elsevier Science.

Carstens, A., and A. Werner. 1999. Mexico's monetary policy framework under a floating exchange rate regime. *Documento de Investigación* no. 9905. Mexico City: Banco de México.

Cecchetti, S. 1998. Policy rules and targets: Framing the central banker's problem. *FRBNY Economic Policy Review* 4 (2): 1–14.

Clarida, R., J. Gali, and M. Gertler. 1998. Monetary policy rules in practice: Some international evidence. *European Economic Review* 42:1033–68.

Coleman, A. 1999. Economic integration and monetary union. Treasury Working Paper no. 99/6. New Zealand: Treasury Department, June.

Corbo, V. 1985. International prices, wages, and inflation in open economy. *Review of Economics and Statistics* 67:564–73.

———. 1998. Reaching one-digit inflation: The Chilean experience. *Journal of Applied Economics* 1 (1): 123–63.

———. 2002. Monetary policy in Latin America in the 90s. In *Monetary policy rules and transmission mechanisms,* ed. N. Loayza and K. Schmidt-Hebbel, Santiago: Central Bank of Chile.

Corbo, V., and S. Fischer. 1994. Lessons from the Chilean stabilization and recovery. In *The Chilean economy: Policy lessons and challenges,* ed. B. Bosworth, R. Dornbusch, and R. Laban, 29–68. Washington, D.C.: Brookings Institution.

———. 1995. Structural adjustment, stabilization, and policy reform: Domestic and international finance. In *Handbook of development economics,* vol. 3, ed. J. Behrman and T. Srinivasan, 2845–2924. Amsterdam: Elsevier.

Corbo, V., and A. Solimano. 1991. Chile's experience with stabilization revisited. In *Lessons of economic stabilization and its aftermath,* ed. M. Bruno, S. Fischer, E. Helpman, and N. Liviatan, with L. (Rubin) Meridor, 57–91. Cambridge: MIT Press.

Dornbusch, R., and S. Fischer. 1993. Moderate inflation. *World Bank Economic Review* 7 (1): 1–44.

Edwards, S. 1995. Exchange rates, inflation, and disinflation: Latin American experience. Chap. 12 in *Capital controls, exchange rates, and monetary policy in the world economy.* Cambridge: Cambridge University Press.

Edwards, S., and M. Savastano. 2000. Exchange rates in emerging economies: What do we know? What do we need to know? In *Economic policy reform: The second stage,* ed. A. O. Krueger, 453–510. Chicago: University of Chicago Press.

Edwards, S., and C. Végh. 1997. Banks and macroeconomic disturbances under predetermined exchange rates. *Journal of Monetary Economics* 40:239–78.

Enders, W. 1995. *Applied econometric time series.* New York: Wiley.

Fischer, S. 2001. Exchange rate regimes: Is the bipolar view correct? *Journal of Economic Perspectives* 15 (2): 3–24.

Frankel, J. 1999. No single currency regime is right for all countries or at all times. NBER Working Paper no. 7338. Cambridge, Mass.: National Bureau of Economic Research, September.

Gosh, A., A. Gulde, J. Ostry, and H. Wolf. 1997. Does the nominal exchange rate regime matter? NBER Working Paper no. 5874. Cambridge, Mass.: National Bureau of Economic Research, January.

Goldfajn, I., and S. Werlang. 2000. The pass-through from depreciation to inflation: A panel study. Working Paper no. 5. Brasilia: Banco Central Do Brazil.

Greene, W. 2000. *Econometric analysis.* New York: Prentice Hall.

Haldane, A. 1999. *Targeting inflation.* London: Bank of England.

Harberger, A. 1963. The dynamics of inflation in Chile. In *Measurement in economics: Studies in mathematical economics and econometrics in memory of Yehuda Grunfeld,* ed. C. Christ, 219–50. Stanford, Calif.: Stanford University Press.

Hargreaves, D., and J. McDermott. 1999. Issues relating to optimal currency areas: Theory and implications for New Zealand. *Reserve Bank of New Zealand Bulletin* 62 (3): 16–29.

International Monetary Fund (IMF). 2000. Annual report. Washington, D.C.: IMF.

———. Various issues. *Exchange arrangements and exchange restrictions.* Washington, D.C.: IMF.

———. Various issues. *International financial statistics.* Washington, D.C.: IMF.

King, M. 2000. Monetary policy: Theory in practice. Presentation to the joint luncheon of the American Economic Association and the American Finance Association. ASSA Meetings, January, Boston, Mass.

Kuttner, K., and A. Posen. 1999. Does talk matter after all? Inflation targeting and central bank behavior. *Federal Reserve Bank of New York Staff Reports* 88.

Leiderman, L., and L. Svensson. 1995. *Inflation targeting.* London: Center for Economic Policy Research.

Levy-Yeyati, E., and F. Sturzenegger. 2000. Classifying exchange rate regimes: Deeds vs. words. Economic Department, Universidad Torcuatto Di Tella. Mimeograph.

Mahadeva, L., and G. Sterne, eds. 2000. *Monetary policy frameworks in a global context.* London: Routledge.

Mátyás, L. 1998. *Generalized method of moments estimation.* Cambridge: Cambridge University Press.

McKinnon, R. 1963. Optimal currency areas. *American Economic Review* 53:717–24.

Mishkin, F. 2000. Inflation targeting for emerging-market countries. *American Economic Review* 90 (2): 105–09.

———. 1997. Strategies for controlling inflation. In *Monetary policy and inflation targeting,* ed. Phillip Lowe, 7–38. Sydney: Reserve Bank of Australia.

Mishkin, F., and A. Posen. 1997. Inflation targeting: Lessons from four countries. *Federal Reserve Bank of New York Economic Policy Review* 3:9–117.
Mishkin, F., and M. Savastano. 2001. Monetary policy strategies for Latin America. *Journal of Development Economics* 66 (October): 415–44.
Morandé, F., and K. Schmidt-Hebbel. 2000a. Chile's peso: Better than (just) living with the dollar? *Cuadernos de Economía* 110 (April): 117–226.
———. 2000b. Monetary policy and inflation targeting in Chile. In *Inflation targeting in practice: Strategic and operational issues and application to emerging market economies,* ed. M. I. Bléjer, A. Ize, A. M. Leone, and S. Werlang. Washington, D.C.: International Monetary Fund.
Mundell, R. 1961. A theory of optimum currency areas. *American Economic Review* 51 (4): 657–65.
Mussa, M., P. Masson, A. Swoboda, E. Jadresic, P. Mauro, and A. Berg. 2000. Exchange rate regimes in an increasingly integrated world economy. IMF Occasional Paper no. 193. Washington, D.C.: International Monetary Fund.
Obstfeld, M. 1995. International currency experience: New lessons and lessons relearned. *Brookings Papers on Economic Activity* 1:119–211.
Obstfeld, M., and K. Rogoff. 1995. The mirage of fixed exchange rates. *Journal of Economic Perspectives* 9 (fall).
———. 2001. Perspectives on OECD economic integration: Implications for U.S. current account adjustment. In *Global economic integration: Opportunities and challenges.* Kansas City, Missouri: Federal Reserve Bank of Kansas City.
Powell, A., and F. Sturzenegger. 2000. Dollarization: The link between devaluation and default risk. Economics Department, Universidad Torcuato Di Tella. Manuscript.
Schaechter, A., M. Stone, and M. Zelmer. 2000. Practical issues in the adoption of inflation targeting by emerging market countries. IMF Occasional Paper no. 202. Washington, D.C.: International Monetary Fund, December.
Summers, L. H. 2000. International financial crises, causes, prevention, and cures. *American Economic Review* 90 (2): 1–16.
Svensson, L. E. O. 2000. Open-economy inflation targeting. *Journal of International Economics* 50 (February): 155–83.
Taylor, J. 1993. Discretion versus policy rules in practice. *Carnegie-Rochester Conference Series on Public Policy* 39:195–214.
Williamson, J. 1996. *The crawling band as an exchange rate regime: Lessons from Chile, Colombia, and Israel.* Washington, D.C.: Institute for International Economics.

Comment Alejandro Werner

Mexico adopted an inflation-targeting framework in a gradual and piecemeal way. Inflation targeting (IT) emerged out of the commitment to price stability, the breakdown of a stable relationship between money growth and inflation, the adoption of a floating exchange rate, and the need for a transparent framework to improve the credibility of the monetary author-

Alejandro Werner is director of economic studies at the Bank of Mexico.

ity. This short commentary on IT in Latin America from a Mexican perspective addresses four issues: (1) preconditions for the transition to IT; (2) some practical advantages of IT as a framework for conducting monetary policy, emphasizing the improvement in communication and transparency; (3) a few comments on Mexico's transitions toward IT; and (4) the main challenges faced by monetary policy in the region as a whole.

Preconditions for the Transition to Inflation Targeting

In the 1970s and early 1980s, institutional and structural problems in many Latin American countries led to severe macroeconomic imbalances that prevented central banks from accomplishing their primary goal of price stability. The debt crisis that began in 1982 signaled a shift away from decades of import substitution, state intervention, and cycles of macroeconomic populism.[1] By the late 1980s, it became clear that macroeconomic stability was a sine qua non condition for sustainable growth. The overall reform effort had the establishment of macroeconomic stability as one of its major components and, therefore, it shaped the evolution of monetary policy.

The first of the main factors influencing the transformation of monetary policy and central banks in Latin America was the mounting evidence from the region's experience with high rates of inflation (in some cases, hyperinflation), which showed the large costs of inflation in terms of output growth, income distribution, and financial-sector deepening. This situation temporarily closed the door to any short-term benefit associated with discretionary monetary policy and increased the awareness regarding the high costs and limited benefits of the monetary authority's failure to focus on price stability.

Second, after years of fiscal mismanagement, stabilization efforts were anchored on a significant strengthening of public finances and a trend toward improving fiscal institutions, eliminating the pressure to monetize public-sector deficits.[2]

These first two factors led, in the late 1980s and early 1990s, to a move toward granting independence to some central banks. The independence gained by the regional central banks gave incentives for a further consolidation of public finances, given that such a move would forbid the monetary authority to finance public-sector deficits. This was no small achievement, given that several inflationary episodes in Latin America were rooted in the monetization of fiscal deficits. Central-bank independence was a signal that Latin America was committed to institutionalizing the

1. As defined by Dornbusch and Edwards (1991).

2. See Aspe (1993) for a complete account of the Mexican stabilization program of the early 1990s.

initial move toward responsible fiscal and monetary policies.[3] In many cases—of which Mexico is a notable example—the independence was granted during a period when predetermined exchange rate regimes were in place. This last element severely curtailed monetary independence. In other words, the mandate of newly independent central banks was not really price stability but a monetary policy that was consistent with the exchange rate targets.

Constituting the third and last element that shaped the recent evolution of monetary policy in the region were the balance-of-payments-cum-financial crises of the mid 1990s that highlighted the difficulties of fixing the exchange rates in a world of highly mobile capital. The European Monetary System (EMS) collapse in 1992, the Mexican crisis of 1994–95, and the subsequent Asian, Russian, and Brazilian crises moved several countries in the region to abandon their predetermined crawling exchange rate systems and to adopt a regime at one of the extremes of the policy spectrum: a free-floating regime (Mexico, Brazil, and Chile) or a fixed exchange rate supported by a currency board (Argentina and Ecuador).[4] I should highlight that floating regimes in the region have major differences between them, as evidenced by the volatility of exchange rates, interest rates, and international reserves; the degree of intervention by the central banks; and the degree of attention paid to the exchange rate in the implementation of monetary policies. However, the major coincidence is that these regimes avoid explicit commitments regarding the level of the nominal exchange rate and therefore eliminate the possibility of costly games' being played between market participants and the monetary authority.[5]

The adoption of floating regimes with limited intervention proved to be the other major turning point for monetary policy in the region. Central-bank independence eliminated fiscal dependence of monetary policies, and a free-floating exchange rate gave them the autonomy to pursue independent monetary policies with price stability as their primary objective.

With these elements in place, several countries in the region began to move toward IT. Chile underwent a gradual transition in which an IT framework coincided with a crawling exchange rate band. In 1999, once the effects of the 1998 international financial crisis had receded, Chilean authorities decided to abandon the exchange rate target zone and let their currency float. Mexico also underwent a gradual transition toward IT

3. See Franco's intervention (this volume's Part I Epilogue) for a more complete elaboration of the dangers of fiscal dependence and the fragility of institutional arrangements in Brazil to make sure there are no relapses.

4. This was the case in November 2000, when these comments were written. However, at the time these comments are being published, Argentina's currency board has already collapsed and a dirty float has been adopted.

5. Gil Díaz (chap. 4 in this volume) elaborates thoroughly on the moral hazard created by perverse exchange rate regimes.

since the adoption of the floating exchange rate in December 1994. On the other hand, Brazil embraced a full-fledged IT framework immediately after the devaluation of the real, as a way to generate confidence in the new regime sufficient to avoid the inflationary effects of the devaluation of the real in 1999. Until now, these experiences have been positive for these countries.

Inflation Targeting as a Pragmatic Approach to Monetary Policy in Mexico

Instead of focusing on the more technical details of inflation targets, I would like to highlight what, in my view, are the main advantages of the framework and provide a few details on the evolution of Mexico's monetary policy framework as it is converging toward IT. On the technical side, I do not think that it prescribes anything new, given that, in a world of floating exchange rates and unstable relationships between monetary aggregates and prices, the only alternative is forward-looking monetary policy, which is the way policy is conducted by inflation targeters and non–inflation targeters alike.[6] Therefore, the strengths of IT rest on establishing a transparent framework for the conduct of monetary policy that is useful as a marketing device, a communication tool, and a mechanism of accountability to the public at large. Specifically:

1. Establishing a clear set of short- and medium-run objectives, and setting up the channels through which central banks communicate what actions are being undertaken to accomplish these goals, increases the efficiency of monetary policy. This is the case because the effects of monetary policy actions on the whole yield curve and other asset prices hinge heavily on expectations. Therefore, if the actions undertaken by the monetary authority are interpreted clearly by market participants, their effect on inflation expectations, price- and wage-setting behavior, long-term interest rates, and other asset prices will be closer to the one desired by the authorities.

2. By providing a structure and choosing instruments that allow short-term deviations from the target when negative shocks appear, while maintaining the long-run inflation objective, this long-run target plays the role of a successful nominal anchor.

3. By explicitly talking about the balance of risks in the inflation projection, and in some cases even quantifying it, the monetary authority is able to convey the message that constant monitoring and quick reactions are needed in case a negative shock arises, by specifying clearly what would happen in the absence of a policy response.

4. By establishing clear mechanisms of accountability, the IT framework provides a useful technology to discipline the monetary authority, to

6. The emphasis on transparency and communication has been made by several other authors, most notably Bernanke et al. (1999).

increase society's awareness of the benefits of price stability, to raise the visibility of the goals of monetary policy, and to influence other macroeconomic policies so that they are consistent with the inflation targets.

The Transition toward Inflation Targeting in Mexico

The twin balance-of-payments and financial crises that hit Mexico in 1994–95 forced the Bank of Mexico to abandon a narrow exchange rate band and led to adoption of a floating regime. As a result of the peso devaluation and subsequent inflation surge, the credibility of the bank was severely damaged. Public criticism focused on the lack of transparency regarding the conduct of the monetary policy, the dissemination of information, and the monetary laxity before, during, and immediately after the crisis.

In response to its credibility crisis, in 1995 the bank adopted as its nominal anchor a monetary growth target, defined as a growth ceiling on net domestic credit. Facing large uncertainty, the bank decided to let the markets determine both the exchange rate and the interest rate; therefore, the bank established borrowed reserves (BR)[7] as its instrument of monetary policy. As in preceding years, the bank determined an annual inflation target of 42 percent for 1995, 20.5 percent for 1996, and 15 percent for 1997.

This monetary policy framework was maintained in 1996 and 1997. Inflation fell from 52 percent in 1995 to 16 percent in 1997. Although the inflation targets were not attained in 1995 and 1996, inflation was close to target in 1997.

Since 1998, the monetary policy framework began a gradual transition toward an explicit, full-fledged IT regime, reinforcing the role of the inflation target and raising policy transparency. The monetary base has become less relevant and the inflation target is more important in the conduct of policy. The bank set multiannual inflation targets in 1999: a target ceiling of 13 percent for that year and a goal of gradual convergence of inflation to the level prevalent in Mexico's main trading partners, set at a stationary annual inflation target of 3 percent for 2003. Target ceilings were set at 10 percent for 2000, 6.5 percent for 2001, and 4.5 percent for 2002. Since 1999, inflation has been below these ceilings. In 2000, the bank began publishing its quarterly inflation report, which analyzes inflation prospects, the conduct of monetary policy, and the balance of risks for future inflation.

Thus, Mexico's transition toward IT has been gradual, like Chile's. As of now, Mexico, like Brazil and Chile, has in place the main components of a full-fledged IT framework: a floating exchange rate, an independent monetary authority that sets inflation as the main goal of monetary pol-

7. See Carstens and Werner (1999) for a detailed description of the details of monetary policy implementation in Mexico.

icy, the absence of other nominal anchors and of fiscal dominance, and the implementation of monetary policy within a transparent framework in which communication with the public plays a key role. A future challenge is to consider substituting a more traditional interest rate instrument for the current quantitative instrument of monetary policy (the borrowed reserves target, or *corto*).

Future Challenges Faced by Inflation-Targeting Countries

Let me now turn to the challenges faced by the inflation-targeting central banks in the region. First of all, although Chile, Mexico, and Brazil have had successful experiences to date, the latter two countries still need to bring inflation down to the level observed in developed countries, a phenomenon that has not been seen in our economies for quite some time. A broad recommendation to help achieve this goal is to have sound public finances.

Second, due to our history of unsound fiscal policy, high inflation, and drastic devaluations accompanied by financial crisis, inflation expectations and inflation itself are extremely sensitive to exchange rate movements. Although the macroeconomic situation has changed, expectations are still heavily influenced by too many years of instability, forcing the monetary-policy reaction function to be very responsive to developments in the foreign exchange market. This necessary response reduces the advantages of the flexible exchange rate as a shock absorber, while the solid macroeconomic framework forces a change in the way expectations are formed, credibility is built up, and the pass-through is reduced. Once this is accomplished, the exchange rate will play a larger role as a relative price and will stop being a signal of future inflation. Therefore, the full benefits of the regime will come into effect.

There is a final point that I would like to address. In an open economy, when the central bank raises interest rates in response to an acceleration of aggregate demand, it runs the risk of increasing the current account deficit, in turn augmenting the vulnerability of the economy to shifts in investors' confidence. This happens because the increase in real interest rates, in addition to reducing aggregate demand, appreciates the real exchange rate, biasing expenditures toward tradable goods. Thus, for open emerging markets there is a serious trade-off between following restrictive monetary policies and current account vulnerability. To improve the results of this trade-off it is imperative to have an extremely good coordination between fiscal and monetary policies. The current situation in Mexico is a perfect example of this policy dilemma. During the first half of 2000, aggregate demand and gross domestic product have been growing at annual rates above 10 and 7 percent, respectively. Due to the threat to long-term inflation targets represented by this growth above potential, the Bank of Mexico remained in a tightening mode throughout 2000. This led to high real interest rates and contributed to the appreciation of the currency. The increase in aggregate demand, and to a lesser extent the appreciation of the currency, generated a doubling of the non–oil trade balance deficit between the first half of 2000 and the same period in 1999. These developments highlight the importance of supporting the monetary policy restriction with a fiscal adjustment to reduce aggregate demand without increasing the vulnerability of our external accounts.

I think that the success or failure of the IT strategy will shape the future of central banks in the region. The currency and financial crises experienced by the EMS in 1992 and by Mexico in 1994–95, and the international financial crisis of 1997–99 have convinced me that there is no middle ground between some kind of floating exchange rate with an independent monetary policy and the adoption of a common currency with the abandonment of monetary autonomy. The recent experiences with IT in emerging markets and the common currency in Europe will provide important references for the consolidation of central banks around the globe or their eventual concentration into a few regional monetary authorities.

References

Aspe, P. 1993. *Economic transformation the Mexican way.* Cambridge: MIT Press.

Bernanke, B., T. Laubach, F. Mishkin, and A. Posen. 1999. *Inflation targeting: Lessons from the international experience.* Princeton, N.J.: Princeton University Press.

Carstens, A., and A. Werner. 1999. *Mexico's monetary policy framework under a floating exchange rate regime.* Working Paper no. 9905. Mexico City: Banco de México.

Dornbusch, R., and S. Edwards, eds. 1991. *The macroeconomics of populism in Latin America.* Chicago: University of Chicago Press.

2

Exchange Rate Pass-Through and Partial Dollarization
Is There a Link?

José Antonio González

2.1 Introduction

Perhaps as a result of the international capital markets turmoil, academics and policymakers have revived the old debate of fixed versus flexible rates for developing countries, with a new variation: the desirability of relinquishing one's own domestic currency altogether and adopting a hard currency instead, namely the dollar. The consensus is that the choice of exchange rate regime involves converging to either one of two polar-opposite solutions: a free-floating or a fixed exchange rate (see Gil Díaz' chap. 4 and Werner's comment to chap. 1 in this volume for two examples). This paper takes the view that, independent of the exchange rate regime, the choice of currency by economic agents in a country is not, in practice, a discrete one. There is a continuum of possibilities, at the extreme ends of which a country can use only its national currency or fully adopt the dollar. In Latin America alone, at one extreme end of the continuum we find Panama, where the dollar is legal tender and it is the only currency available; Ecuador is in the process of dollarizing; and Argentina has a currency board. At the other extreme we find such countries as Brazil and Venezuela, where dollar bank accounts are not allowed. Along the middle of the continuum there has emerged a whole series of ad hoc regimes, each of which varies in

José Antonio González is a senior research associate and Latin American coordinator at the Center for Research on Economic Development and Policy Reform, Stanford University.

The author would like to thank participants at the World Bank Conference on Dollarization in Latin America, held at the Universidad Torcuato di Tella in Buenos Aires, Argentina, 5–7 June 2000, and seminar participants at the Econometric Society meetings in Universidad de San Andress, Argentina, August 2001, for many useful comments. Remaining errors are mine.

its degree of dollarization:[1] Bolivia, Peru, Nicaragua, and Uruguay maintain their own currencies, in which most transactions are denominated; a large proportion of bank savings, however, is in dollars.

The purpose of this paper is not to advocate or even evaluate the welfare implications of a higher or lower degree of dollarization, but rather to investigate macroeconomic policymaking under these partially dollarized regimes—in particular, whether dollarization affects the degree and speed of transmission of nominal exchange rate movements into domestic inflation (i.e., the degree and speed of exchange rate pass-through of the nominal exchange rate into domestic inflation).[2]

The study of exchange rate pass-through in Latin America is important to policymakers for two reasons:

1. Monetary policy affects only the nominal exchange rate directly. The effects on the real exchange rate depend on the degree to which movements in the nominal exchange rate translate into inflation. A firm tenet of the monetary approach is that, in the long run, a nominal devaluation translates one-for-one into an increase in the domestic price level, eliminating any changes in the real exchange rate. In practice, a nominal devaluation will translate into a real depreciation if wages and prices are less than fully flexible and there is not an accommodating monetary policy.

2. When faced with an external balance, policymakers in partially dollarized economies have been reluctant to devalue the nominal exchange rate (or to increase the crawl, depending on the regime), based on the argument that because of a high degree of dollarization, nominal exchange rate movements translate entirely and quickly into inflation (i.e., a higher degree of dollarization implies a higher and faster exchange rate pass-through).

The effects and presence of dollar indexation are well known: "An economy that is strongly indexed—and in particular, with exchange rate influences on indexation—an attempt at creating employment via easy money would be frustrated and an exchange rate depreciation precipitates offsetting wage and price inflation."[3] In an economy that is perfectly dollar indexed, a nominal devaluation translates instantaneously into a rise in

1. The definition of *dollarization* used in this work is the proportion of banking liabilities denominated in dollars. See section 1.2 for a short discussion on the implications of using this definition.

2. The definition of *pass-through* in this work is given by $_{fi} = (\Delta P_i/P_i)/(\Delta[EP^*]/EP^*)$ and is interpreted as the degree to which changes in the nominal exchange rate translate into domestic prices. The clarification is important because, during the late-1980s revival of the study of pass-through in the United States, the focus was on the effects of exchange rate movements on import and export prices (see Baldwin 1988a, b; Baldwin and Krugman 1987, 1989; and Krugman 1986 for the original arguments).

3. In a paper describing the Mexican stabilization experience, Córdoba (1991) highlights the lack of indexation to past inflation or the nominal exchange rate in Mexico and warns of the effects in countries with indexation.

all prices and wages, barring any real effects. In a high-inflation regime in which prices are revised often, the nominal exchange rate is often used as a benchmark, and "studies of high inflation show close cumulative movements of internal prices and the exchange rate" (i.e., dollar indexation; Dornbusch 1988, 68).[4]

The argument in partially dollarized economies arises because most of them experienced high inflation (and, in many cases, hyperinflation) in the 1980s, during which time the consumer price index tracked the nominal exchange rate quite closely becoming heavily dollar indexed. In fact, many prices were quoted in dollars on a day-to-day basis in countries such as Argentina, Bolivia, and Peru. As inflation abated, dollarization ratios increased, and many prices continued to be quoted in dollars; conventional wisdom simply assumed that high dollarization ratios implied that the level of dollar indexation remained high.[5] The issue has seldom been contested, to the point that even International Monetary Fund (IMF) country documents justify the policy almost as a matter of fact: "The real effects of a nominal devaluation in country . . . are limited due to the high degree of dollarization."[6]

Using price and dollarization data for thirteen countries in Latin America, I found no significant cross-country or within-country relationship between dollarization and pass-through, contradicting the conventional wisdom that predicts a positive relationship between the level of exchange rate pass-through and the degree of dollarization. The policy implications are (1) that countries with a higher degree of dollarization do not have less ability to adjust the real exchange rate through nominal exchange rate fluctuations, and (2) that as a country's degree of dollarization increases, it does not loose its channel to adjust the real exchange rate through nominal devaluations. I did find a positive (but not significant) cross-country relationship between the speed of adjustment and dollarization and the level of inflation. In addition, in a very long time period of twenty years, pass-through estimates for an expanded sample of Latin American countries are close to 1 (although only three out of sixteen are statistically insignificant different from 1), making purchasing power parity (PPP) a surprisingly reasonable benchmark.

The results of this paper suggest that the degree of dollarization and the degree of dollar indexation (measured as the degree of exchange rate pass-through) are not necessarily the same, or even correlated. The reasoning behind this apparently counterintuitive result lies in the existence of a nontradables sector, and in the role of money as a unit of account. In an open

4. Although the same studies were quick to point out that relative prices showed large deviations.

5. Where the author was part of this "conventional" wisdom.

6. The quote above is one of many examples from missions to partially dollarized countries, but these IMF reports are confidential, precluding making country-specific references.

economy one would expect the exchange rate pass-through of tradables to be close to 1 because of arbitrage, regardless of the currency used. However, there is no possibility for arbitrage in nontradables and therefore movements in the exchange rate do not have to be fully reflected. The prices of nontradables are set by supply and demand inside the country regardless of the currency used because the latter is working as a unit of account. An example may clarify the issue: Prices in the high-end real estate market in Mexico are quoted in dollars, yet the value of houses in dollars varies according to the supply and demand inside the country regardless of fluctuations in the exchange rate. In fact, when a devaluation occurs and economic activity in the country falls, property prices in dollars are adjusted downward to clear demand. Thus, even a perfectly dollarized market will not adjust fully and instantaneously.

The rest of the paper is organized as follows. Section 1.2 discusses some basic theory and the transmission mechanisms of nominal exchange rate movements into the domestic price level. Section 1.3 discusses the data, the estimation process, and the results, and section 1.4 presents some conclusions.

2.2 Basic Definitions and Transmission Mechanisms

The theory for the determination of exchange rate pass-through is not new; this section merely cites the most relevant work. The point of departure for the study of pass-through is the law of one price and the PPP literature. Dornbusch (1988), in *The New Palgrave: A Dictionary of Economics,* presents an excellent definition and a review of the literature. From the beginning it was clear that there were various reasons that PPP and the law of one price would not hold. "Most of the time, PPP does not hold in any interesting sense. Certainly the notion that the equilibrium exchange rate is such that a dollar should buy the same basket of goods in the United States and Japan would only hold in an extraordinary world. What is really interesting about PPP is the systematic directions in which the literature has documented divergences from PPP (Dornbusch 1987, 214). The purpose of this section is briefly to (re-)state the transmission mechanisms and the theoretical reasons for deviations from PPP.

The strong version of PPP states that their price levels determine the exchange rate between two countries in any period of time. Therefore, if PPP holds, exchange rate fluctuations translate into proportional movements in the domestic price level; i.e., pass-through is equal to 1. Purchasing power parity requires two restrictive assumptions: (1) that there is instantaneous costless, and frictionless arbitrage, and (2) that the same goods enter the basket of goods with the same weight in every country. Surely neither of these can hold all the time, leading to the weak or relative version of PPP under which the law of one price holds up to a constant. It has also come to be known as the *inflation theory of exchange rates,* suggesting that changes in the exchange rate between two countries are determined by the difference of their inflation levels (i.e., $\hat{e} = \hat{P} - \hat{P}^*$). The weak version eliminates the requirement that arbitrage is costless but it does require that it occur at a constant cost. This clearly will not be the case if there are quantitative restrictions in place or if there are modifications in trade policy. More important, the determination of domestic inflation may use different shares of goods in their respective baskets, and certainly nontraded groups are not the same and cannot be arbitraged.

The literature has identified different types of structural and transitory deviations from PPP, although pinpointing the source of the deviations has proved difficult. A key element in structural deviations is that they hinge on the existence of nontradable goods, for which the law of one price does not have to hold. The proposition of this paper is that nontradable prices will differ across countries even if they have the same currency. If supply and demand conditions differ, the resulting price will be different. The most important structural deviation from strong and weak versions of PPP arises from differences in productivity or differences in productivity changes, respectively. The phenomenon was discovered by Ricardo, who noted that real prices of home goods are high "in countries where manufactures flourish."[7] The mechanism, now called the Balassa-Samuelson effect, assumes the law of one price applies to tradables. An increase in productivity in the traded sector puts upward pressure on the nominal wage. Without a commensurate increase in productivity in the home goods sector, nontradable prices increase.[8] Thus a country that is catching up because it has greater increases in productivity will observe a rise in its domestic price level when measured in a common currency; i.e., its real exchange rate will appreciate. The phenomenon has been documented in country cross-sections and long-term time series. Other structural deviations from PPP can arise because of supply shocks, permanent terms of trade (TOT) shocks, changes in tastes between traded and nontraded goods, or changes in commercial policy.[9] Countries in Latin America were subject to most, if not all, of the above.

Transitory deviations from PPP beyond those caused by transportation and information costs (which make arbitrage difficult on a continuous basis) arise because of sticky prices and wages compared to exchange rates. The literature has theoretically justified slowly adjusting domestic prices and wages for many reasons. The implications have been explored extensively. Indeed, slowly adjusting prices are implicit in the standard

7. As quoted in Dornbusch (1988, 73).

8. The result was restated by Harrod in the 1930s, Balassa in the 1960s, and Samuelson (who formalized it) in the 1960s, and more recently in the Dornbusch, Fischer, and Samuelson (1977) framework.

9. A good reference for a formal exposition of the mechanisms is Dornbusch (1980).

Mundell-Fleming model of international macroeconomics. The question that the empirical section addresses is the size and duration of these temporary deviations.

There is one notable type of shock that does create a deviation from PPP even if the domestic price indexes have different shares and goods in their baskets: namely, a monetary shock when the conditions for the homogeneity postulate of monetary theory exist. In this case, a change in the money supply will lead to a proportionate change in all prices, including the exchange rate. This type of shock is important because of the high inflation levels in Latin America. During high inflation, pronounced spiral increases in the money supply and the price level can dwarf real shocks and offer support for PPP.

There is a long history of empirical evidence on PPP, both in support of and against it. Dornbusch (1988) presents a review of the empirical evidence until that date. Most developments since then have concentrated on expanding the data set using more narrowly defined goods and improving the econometric techniques. The evidence from looking both at inflation differentials and at narrowly defined manufactured goods leaves little doubt that they have been large and persistent.

If the evidence for PPP has been so time dependent and inconclusive, why is this exercise relevant for Latin American countries at this point? The answer has to do with investigating the way the transmission mechanisms of monetary policy have changed with dollarization. Monetary policy can have real effects by changing relative prices of tradables and nontradables and by changing the cost of money in the asset markets. Moreover, the approach is to estimate the degree of exchange rate pass-through without attempting to pass judgment on the theory of PPP. In particular, the empirical estimates test whether this transmission mechanism has been affected by the dollarization of financial assets. Looking at pass-through rather than at a version of PPP (or even at the real exchange rate) is the right approach of looking at the transmission mechanisms of nominal devaluations into the price level, because one needs not be concerned about the factors that can upset PPP.

2.2.1 Transmission Mechanisms

The transmission mechanisms of fluctuations of the nominal exchange rate into the domestic price level are standard ones and will not be formally developed here. First, fluctuations in the nominal exchange rate change the price of imports, which directly affects the overall price index. For a small country with perfect competition at home and abroad, the change in the price of imports should be one-for-one. However, Dornbusch (1987) showed that if there is oligopolistic competition, or if imported and domestic goods are imperfect substitutes, exchange rate pass-through can be less than 1 as firms strategically modify their pricing behavior and consumers change their pattern of consumption to increase or decrease imported goods.[10] Although the market-structure models are in partial equilibrium, they provide insight into the way segmented markets of traded goods can systematically deviate from PPP. Using a Cournot setting, Dornbusch finds that import share and lower concentration increase the degree of pass-through. In two types of models of imperfect substitutes he shows that pass-through falls as product differentiation increases. A body of literature arose in the 1980s to explain the pricing-to-market behavior during the pronounced dollar appreciation and depreciations. The arguments centered on imperfect competition in the form of sunk costs to entry (Baldwin 1988a, b; Baldwin and Krugman 1987, 1989; Krugman 1986), and market share (Froot and Klemperer 1989; see Knetter 1989, 1992, 1993 for a good review of this literature). Although Latin American countries are becoming more important to the United States, I assume these affects are small and temporary.

Second, besides the direct effect that fluctuations of import prices have on the domestic consumption basket, imports have an indirect effect on the domestic price level when they are used as inputs. The higher the use of imported goods as inputs or intermediate goods, the higher the effect on the domestic price level.

A third way in which nominal exchange rate fluctuations can affect the price level is through dollar indexation, as discussed before. The higher the proportion of contracts denominated in dollars, the higher the degree of pass-through into the domestic price level. Specifically, this work will estimate whether dollarization has affected the degree of dollar indexation in partially dollarized economies.

The main factor affecting the speed of adjustment of the domestic price index is the level of inflation. The higher the level of inflation, the more often economic agents will change their prices. Therefore, a nominal exchange rate shock will be transmitted faster through the channels outlined above. The extreme case is hyperinflation, when prices are adjusted daily or even more often.

2.2.2 Dollarization in Eleven Countries in Latin America

The paper opts to use the share of deposits denominated in dollars. Given the efforts to eliminate exchange rate risk in banking, plotting the share of banking assets denominated in dollars presents similar results. The measure is imperfect, but there are few alternatives. The ideal measure is the share of transactions that are conducted in dollars or the share of prices that are denominated or indexed to the dollar. However, these are difficult to construct. Hopefully, the share of deposits denominated in dollars is an indication of the degree of dollar usage in the country.

10. See Dornbusch (1987) for a formal presentation.

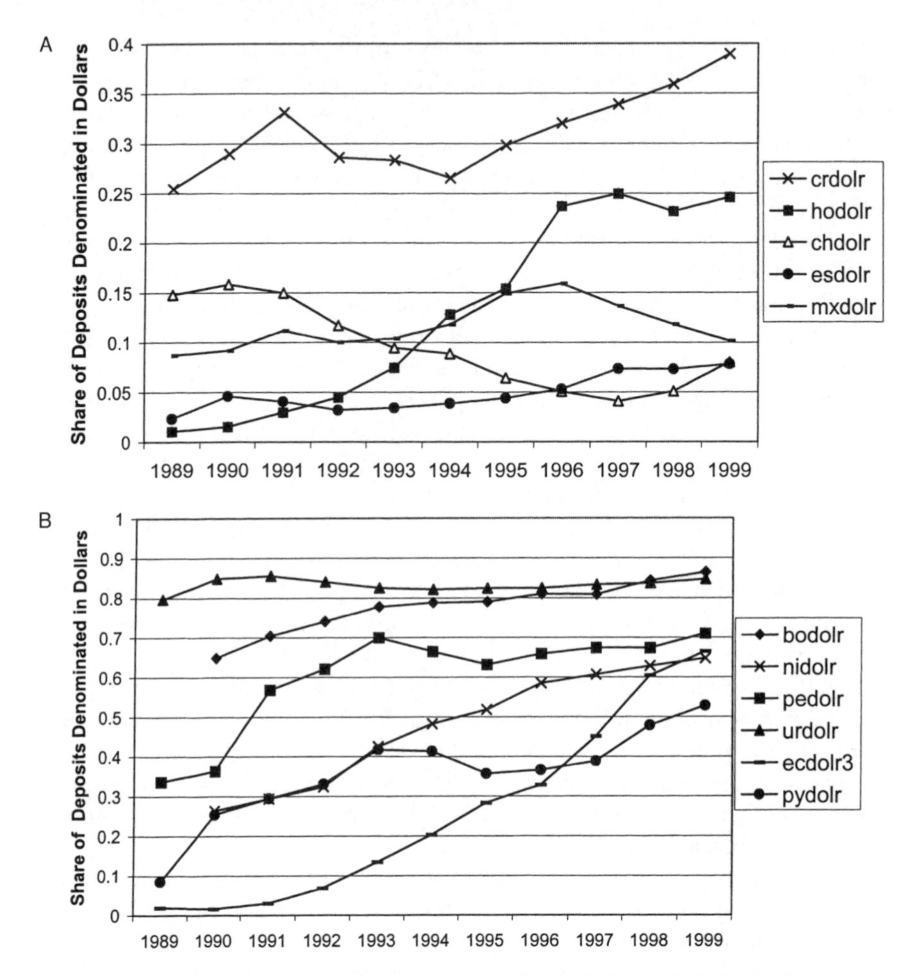

Fig. 2.1 Latin American economies: *A*, less dollarized; *B*, highly dollarized

Panels A and B of figure 2.1 present plots for the degree of dollarization in eleven countries in Latin America. For expositional purposes only, the sample was divided into high- and low-dollarization countries. On one end, Bolivia and Uruguay exhibit dollarization ratios of more than 80 percent by the end of the decade. Peru and Nicaragua increased their dollarization ratios from about 30 percent in 1990 to about 70 percent by the end of the decade. On the other end, Mexico and other Central American countries had low, fairly constant dollarization ratios, whereas Brazil and Venezuela have a zero degree of dollarization by this definition.

Modeling the driving forces behind dollarization is left as a future venue of research, but there are two casual observations: First, the degree of dollarization presents a high degree of stationarity, and apparent irreversibility. Only Mexico and Chile exhibit sustained reductions (albeit small declines at low levels) in the dollarization ratio. Thus, once a country's banking or monetary aggregates become dollarized, it appears to be difficult to reverse the dollarization process. It may be that authorities have not actively tried to reverse the situation; if they have, efforts have been unsuccessful. The result is interesting because the spreads between peso and dollar deposits even within the same bank are substantial and have been so for a long time. In other words, economic agents are willing to forgo a substantial interest payment in exchange for avoiding exchange rate risk.

Second, dollarization appears to increase as a result of both extreme price instability and a stabilization program that liberalized the financial sector enough to permit savings in dollars. Unfortunately, the data for Bolivia were not available since 1986, when dollar bank accounts were first allowed—but the fact remains that by 1990 the dollarization ratio was 80 percent. Moreover, the pattern in the early 1990s for Peru suggests that dollarization increases after extreme price instability but only after liberalization in the financial sector. The result makes sense because, despite price instability, if bank accounts in dollars are forbidden the degree of dollarization is restricted to currency holdings. Ecuador's meteoric rise since the middle 1990s also arises from the instability in the price level at first, and then because of the deliberate move toward dollarization. It is interesting that as of 1999 a significant proportion of savings was still in the domestic currency. The rise in the dollarization ratio in Paraguay coincides first with the opening of the capital account and the financial sector, and second with the loss in price stability and banking failures.

2.3 Data, Estimation Process, and Results

2.3.1 Data

I collected data for sixteen countries in Latin America. The data set for each country consists of monthly series of the consumer price index (CPI) from 1980 to 2000 as a measure of the domestic price level; the nominal dollar exchange rate; and the United States producer price index (PPI) and the Group of Seven (G7) PPI as measures of international prices. The exchange rate data came from the International Monetary Fund's *International Financial Statistics* (*IFS*). The consumer price indexes were obtained either from the *IFS* or directly from national sources. Monthly data provided the appropriate time frame to look at price fluctuations and eliminate the high variance that typically accompanies more frequent observations of the exchange rate.

The domestic price series for most countries during this period reflect a high degree of instability, to the point that many countries resorted to eliminating zeros from their currencies to make transactions easier. In general, at the beginning of the 1980s, the inflation was moderate but rising for most countries in the sample. Inflation typically rose out of control at some point during the 1980s. Finally, some type of stabilization plan was implemented as soon as the early 1980s (e.g., in Chile and Bolivia) and as late as 1994 (in Brazil). The international price series exhibited a relatively steady upward trend. Thus, most of the variance of the explanatory variables comes from fluctuations in the nominal exchange rate.

Although conceptually one would want to use the nominal effective exchange rate instead of the dollar exchange rate, using the nominal exchange rate makes the process considerably more cumbersome, the data are less reliable, and it is unclear whether much is gained. For Central American countries and Mexico, the dollar nominal exchange rate and the nominal effective exchange rate are very close. The issue is relevant only for South American countries for which the United States is not the main trading partner. The process is cumbersome because the weights of the nominal effective exchange rate change with trade patterns. More important, instead of using the U.S. or G7 PPI as an index of international prices, one would have to construct an index of international export prices using the price levels of trading partners.[11] For example, if Peru and Bolivia devalued their currencies concurrently with respect to the dollar, then the nominal effective exchange rate would not be affected for this bilateral trade relationship. The international price level faced by either of these countries would change as their export prices changed due to the bilateral devaluation. The problem is that most countries do not have export prices, forcing the use of an imperfect measure such as the wholesale price index (WPI). Three additional reasons justify using the nominal dollar exchange rate and the U.S. or G7 PPI. First, doing so gives all the countries a common world price, which is what one would expect from traded commodities. Given that all of these countries are small, their influence on the price of tradables should be small. Second, following McKinnon's (1999, 2001, 2002) argument for Asia, a case could be made that countries in Latin America use the dollar as a standard and that international trade in this region is heavily dollar indexed. Third, in the very long run, dollar exchange rate devaluations for most countries in the sample translated into almost full pass-through of the domestic price level, indicating that in the end the price of tradables in dollars can be assumed to be given.

The measure of dollarization used in this study is the amount of banking liabilities that are in dollars, as a share of total banking assets (or M4) between 1990 and 2000—i.e., the percentage of savings in dollars. Given the large efforts to prevent exchange rate exposure in banks, using banking assets or liabilities as a percentage of a broad measure of money does

11. Obviously the weights to construct the international price index for country X must be the same as those used for the nominal effective exchange rate.

not make a difference. For the purposes of this study, the appropriate measure is the level of dollar indexation in the form of the share of contracts that are conducted in dollars. However, those data are unavailable. Moreover, this is the conventional measure of dollarization, and a primary purpose of this work is to evaluate whether dollarization (as defined by policymakers) indeed implies that a nominal exchange rate fluctuation translates into a faster and closer-to-proportional increase of the domestic prices.

The reason for choosing the 1980–2000 time period is that it was important to have a long enough time horizon. Many countries in this Latin American sample experienced pronounced appreciations and reversals that lasted a few years. For example, Mexico's appreciation and reversal cycles lasted six years; and Chile experienced a continuous depreciation from the outset of the debt cycle in 1982 until roughly the middle of 1988, before a steady appreciation since then. Ignoring the 1980s might lead to the wrong conclusions.

2.3.2 Estimation Process

The point of departure for the estimation process is the weak version of PPP. In logs, this translates into

$$p_{i,t} = \alpha_i + \phi_i(e_{i,t}p_t^*) \tag{1}$$

where $p_{i,t}$ is the domestic price level for country i at time t, α_i is the markup constant for country i, $e_{i,t}$ is the nominal exchange rate of country i in pesos per dollar, p_t^* is the international price level, and ϕ_i is the estimated coefficient of pass-through for country i.

The first estimation problem encountered is that, not surprisingly, all of the series were nonstationary and contained a unit root, making conventional estimation methods inappropriate.[12] The simplest alternative is to difference the data and test for stationarity. The problem is that the regression estimates lose long-term memory and the long-run equilibrium properties embedded in the original series.

In this case, the long-run equilibrium properties of series are exactly the law of one price and PPP. The earlier discussion suggests that temporary deviations are expected for various reasons but that there should be a stable underlying long-run relationship between the domestic and international price levels when measured in a common currency. Therefore, the theory behind the joint behavior of the series naturally suggests a cointegration framework to estimate equation (1). The estimation method does not impose PPP or the law of one price. Rather, it allows temporary devi-

12. Nelson and Plosser (1982) first put forth the argument. See Gonzalez (1998) for a brief, nontechnical description of the issues.

ations while it estimates a long-run relationship (if one exists) between the variables, which may or may not be consistent with PPP and the law of one price (see the discussion below).

For all the countries, the series of domestic and international prices measured in domestic currency failed to reject a cointegration vector at the 5 percent significance level using a Johansen test for both the 1980–2000 and the 1990–2000 periods. (The results of the tests are available upon request.) The cointegration relation allowed for trends in the series and a constant because nominal variables were used, but it did not allow a trend in the cointegration relationship.

From an economic standpoint, the failure to reject this simple form of the cointegration merely states that there is in fact a long-term, stable relationship between the domestic and the international price levels when measured in a common currency. The result is conceptually consistent but does not impose or by itself imply PPP. However, the stable long-run relationship does imply that temporary deviations cancel out,[13] and hence that only the permanent structural deviations from PPP (i.e., permanent or secular TOT shocks, trade liberalization, and most important, productivity differentials) discussed in section 1.2 need to be considered.

Econometrically, the existence of cointegration implies that the errors from the cointegrating regression are stationary, that there will be no spurious regression results, and that one can use an error correction model (ECM) of the form

$$(2) \qquad \Delta p_{i,t} = \mu_i + \phi_i \Delta f + (1 - \delta)(p_{i,t-1} - f_{i,t-1}) + \text{lagdiff} + \varepsilon_{i,t},$$

where $f_{i,t} = e_{i,t} p_t^*$, ϕ_i is the long-run pass-through coefficient for country i, and $(1 - \delta)$ is the speed of adjustment. The speed-of-adjustment term is the coefficient of the error correction term and can be interpreted as the disequilibrium response to shocks. The ECM described above is the appropriate estimation tool for various reasons. First, it provides an out-of-equilibrium response of the series that reveals how quickly the series return to equilibrium. Because all of these countries are small and will not affect the world price (measured as the U.S. or G7 PPI), the speed of adjustment really does measure how quickly the domestic price level of each country returns to its long-term stable relationship with the international price level.

Second, this ECM estimates the long-term stable relationship between the domestic and the international price levels without imposing PPP or any other relationship on the data.[14] The ECM allows the long-term stable relationship to be one in which the existence of PPP is corroborated or the

13. This is not to say that each type of temporary shock cancels itself out, but that the set of temporary shocks cancel each other out in the aggregate.

14. The existence of a stable long-term relationship was already established through the cointegration test.

long-term coefficient can be different from 1 due to any of the structural theoretical arguments put forth in section 1.2. The estimation process allows long-term appreciating or depreciating trends due to permanent changes in the determinants of the real exchange rate: productivity differentials working through the Balassa-Samuelson effect, secular TOT shocks, and permanent trade liberalizations. In fact, I argue that in general an ECM is a better way to obtain relevant information from the PPP relationship. The literature has concentrated on testing whether PPP holds in the strictest sense; yet there are many theoretically sound and practical realities that cause this relationship to fail to hold in predictable ways. This estimation process allows for these real shocks to occur but at the same time preserves the fact that there is an underlying reason for the domestic and international price series to return to their long-run relationship.

One can say PPP holds only when the pass-through coefficient ϕ_i is equal to 1. The result implies that, at least in the long run, nominal exchange rate movements[15] are reflected in proportional increases in the domestic price levels. Given the restrictive theoretical assumptions discussed previously, the emergence of PPP is quite remarkable. It implies that aggregation issues do not play a systematic role. Moreover, it implies that the structural reasons for deviations from PPP in the aggregate cancelled each other out. For example, it is possible for a country to have a positive productivity differential (to be catching up) that was offset by adverse TOT shocks and trade liberalization. The estimation process in this paper cannot discern whether either of the underlying issues is at work and the estimate is simply consistent with PPP.

A pass-through coefficient ϕ_i lower than 1 implies movements in the nominal exchange rate (times the international price level) translated, on average, into less than proportional increases in the domestic price level (i.e., on average, the real exchange rate depreciated during the period). Permanent equilibrium real depreciations in the real exchange rate arise because of trade liberalization and a permanent and adverse TOT shock, and because (most importantly) productivity in the home country increased at a slower pace than in the reference country. As discussed before, because these effects are not being studied separately, one can only conclude that in the aggregate the result was that the domestic price index depreciated, even though it is quite possible that the one or more of the determinants of the real exchange rate had an appreciating pressure. An exercise involving England versus the United States since 1930 would exhibit this result.

Conversely, a pass-through coefficient ϕ larger than 1 implies that country i experienced a real appreciation of its currency, on average. The rea-

15. Strictly speaking, movements in the international price level. However, as discussed before, most of the variance comes from fluctuations in the nominal exchange rate.

soning is exactly as above, and it would arise in a world where convergence dominated the other effects. A postwar exercise for Japan would show this result strongly.

The out-of-equilibrium coefficient δ_i allows us to calculate the speed at which the domestic price level of each country returns to its stable long-term relationship with the world price level. A lower speed of adjustment in country *i* implies that the domestic price level in that country takes a longer time to return to its long-term relationship with the price level and that the relationship between the domestic and international price levels is not as tight. A slow speed of adjustment also makes the estimated long-term relationship a poor predictor of the nominal exchange rate in the short term. Long periods of adjustment can also result in changes to the real economy if there are nonconvexities such as the ones explored in the 1980s U.S. pass-through literature.

2.3.3 Results

The first step was to estimate pass-through in the very long run using equation (2). A likelihood ratio test was performed to determine the optimal lag length. Although for some of the cases two lags were enough to render the residuals white noise, for some of the countries the dynamics were not completely captured by a two-lag vector error correction (VEC). For uniformity, all of the VECs were estimated with three lags.

Table 2.1 shows the long-run pass-through coefficients from 1980 to 2000. The results show that in the very long run (twenty years), PPP is not a bad benchmark to predict exchange rates in Latin America. On one hand, out of sixteen countries, only Chile, Colombia, the Dominican Re-

Table 2.1 Long-Run Pass-Through, 1980–2000

	Pass-through Coefficient	Standard Error
Bolivia	0.96	0.01
Brazil	1.00	0.01
Chile	0.68	0.05
Colombia	0.75	0.06
Costa Rica	0.93	0.02
Dominican Republic	1.37	0.06
Ecuador	0.93	0.01
El Salvador	1.07	0.07
Guatemala	0.87	0.05
Honduras	0.87	0.05
Mexico	0.94	0.01
Nicaragua	1.01	0.02
Paraguay	0.78	0.01
Peru	1.06	0.01
Uruguay	0.99	0.01
Venezuela	1.13	0.07
Region average	0.97	0.03

public, and Paraguay have coefficients that are more than 20 percent off the PPP benchmark of 1. On the other hand, in strict terms, only Brazil, El Salvador, and Nicaragua follow PPP with estimates that are not statistically significantly different from 1. Part of the reason is that estimates are very precise, with an average standard error of 3 percent of the value of the coefficient.

Casual inspection of real exchange rates in Latin America indicate that despite this apparent convergence toward PPP, the real exchange rates ostensibly fluctuate in the region. The first point to note is that during the early 1980s most Latin American countries observed large real depreciations of their currencies. Most countries have not seen that level of appreciation of the exchange rate since then. The second gross generalization is that real exchange rates tend to appreciate gradually and with abrupt reversions. The time periods between corrections vary by country, with some lasting a few years. Thus it is important to insure that the estimation period includes at least a complete cycle.

For most of the countries in the sample, pass-through was less than 1, indicating that the domestic basket of goods lost value compared to the international basket when measured in a common currency. Only the Dominican Republic, El Salvador, and Venezuela observed sustained appreciations of their currencies during this time period. The overall depreciation can be explained by the large unsustainable collective appreciation leading up to the debt crisis, or by any of the structural arguments put forth above. However, as the regression results argue below, poststabilization performance has been dominated by a catch-up reflected in sustained (albeit gradual) real appreciations.

Table 2.2 shows pass-through coefficients using the same methodology, splitting the time period into two (from 1980 to 1990 and from 1990 to 2000).[16] Ideally, one would like to choose the time periods individually for each country to insure that a complete appreciation and reversal cycle was included. For uniformity, a decade was deemed long enough.

Estimates are more dispersed than in the 1980–2000 regressions and there is heterogeneity in the point estimates both within and across countries. The average standard error of the 1980s and the 1990s is 5 and 10 times larger, respectively, than in the twenty-year regression. Econometrically, cutting the time period in half had a strong detrimental effect on the precision of the estimates. Economically, the larger standard error in the 1990s implies that the variance of the real exchange rates increased. On one hand, the result is counterintuitive, given the number of countries that

16. It is reassuring to know that the estimates of pass-through obtained here coincide with estimates elsewhere in the literature. Hausmann, Panizza, and Stein (2000) find estimates of pass-through for Colombia, Mexico, and Peru that are remarkably close and estimates for Paraguay and Guatemala that are within 10 percent. Moreover, the Mexican estimate is consistent with an exercise performed by Garces-Díaz (1999) when the same time period was used.

Table 2.2 **Decade Pass-Through**

	1980–90		1990–2000	
	Coefficient	Standard Error	Coefficient	Standard Error
Bolivia	0.95	0.01	0.92	0.55
Brazil	0.82	0.05	0.92	0.04
Chile	0.64	0.03	1.27	0.30
Colombia	0.72	0.12	1.10	2.20
Costa Rica	1.09	0.08	1.19	0.52
Dominican Republic	1.34	0.18	1.35	0.16
Ecuador	1.16	0.15	1.20	0.04
El Salvador	1.30	0.17	4.08	1.75
Guatemala	0.71	0.02	1.01	0.13
Honduras	1.67	0.28	1.08	0.05
Mexico	0.93	0.01	0.94	0.02
Nicaragua[a]	0.72	0.12	0.48	0.52
Paraguay	0.69	0.04	0.71	0.11
Peru	1.19	1.16	0.49	0.30
Uruguay	0.91	0.10	1.10	0.23
Venezuela	0.44	0.09	1.20	0.02
Average[b]	0.97	0.16	0.95	0.34

[a]Since 1992.
[b]Not including El Salvador.

implemented price-stabilization plans. On the other, it implies that pure monetary disturbances, which are the only ones for which PPP holds with fewer restrictions, played a smaller role in the 1990s.

Surprisingly, even for as long a time period as a decade, pass-through coefficients are quite different from 1. Looking at the evidence across countries, only Colombia in the first decade is consistent with PPP.[17] During the 1990s, seven countries—Bolivia, Chile, Colombia, Costa Rica, Guatemala, Nicaragua, and Uruguay—are consistent with PPP, while Brazil and Mexico have point estimates that are close to 1. However, in half of the sample, the point estimates differ from 1 by more than 20 percent. Had there not been convergence to 1 in the twenty-year sample, the evidence would be interpreted as simply another example that PPP does not hold. However, given the twenty-year result, the dispersion-decade results combined with the speed-of-adjustment discussion below indicate that temporary deviations from the long-run relationship between the domestic and the international prices can take a long time.

For within-country estimates, five countries in the sample (Chile, Venezuela, Guatemala, El Salvador, and Honduras) have statistically different

17. Although the 95 percent confidence intervals of Costa Rica, Ecuador, and Peru are within 0.01 of including the PPP benchmark value of 1.

pass-through estimates for the 1980s versus the 1990s; for the first three of these, the pattern follows a deep depreciation in the aftermath of the debt crisis and a sustained recovery in the 1990s. Within-country estimates for the remaining six countries are not statistically different from each other. The result could mean stability in the exchange real exchange rate, but most of the time it simply means that the reversal took place within the estimation period, as in Mexico.

The results for Mexico and Brazil present an interesting contrast. Mexico exhibited a constant coefficient in both decades that is close to 1. Brazil's pass-through estimate increased from 0.82 to 0.92, reaching a level similar to Mexico's despite drastically different measures of openness. Part of the explanation is that although both countries had important departures from PPP, the reversals occurred within a decade, making the pass-through estimate converge. Furthermore, pass-through estimates remained constant despite the fact that the inflation average was substantially different between countries and decades, indicating that inflation does not affect the degree of pass-through into domestic prices (although, as argued before and documented below, it may affect the speed of adjustment).

The results for the Central American countries are a puzzle. Pass-through estimates deviate wildly from PPP. On one hand, this is not what one would expect from small countries most of whose trade is with the United States. On the other, most of these countries are primarily commodity-producing countries subject to large TOT shocks and with restricted access to capital markets to smooth out the shocks. In addition, their tradables sector is small, making the transmission channel into domestic prices small.

Table 2.3 shows "half-life" duration of shocks (i.e., the amount of time it takes for the domestic price level to absorb half of the shock). The adjustment process slowed down in the 1990s compared to the 1980s. The average half-life increased from twenty-one months to thirty-five months. As argued in section 1.2, higher rates of inflation are associated with more frequent price changes, and the average inflation rate in the region during the 1980s was higher.

The alternate presentation in table 2.4 shows the tremendous heterogeneity in the estimates of the speed of adjustment. On one hand, in Peru half of the shock is transmitted to the domestic price level in four or five months, whereas in Honduras it takes eight years. Although they are not entirely convincing, these results are consistent with other results in the literature.[18] Nevertheless, an avenue for further research is to refine the estimation process and investigate whether the speed-of-adjustment results

18. Hausmann et al. (2000) estimated half-lives that were consistent with those estimated here for the countries that overlapped. For example, they found that in Germany, the half-life was 130 months—i.e., more than ten years.

Table 2.3 **Pass-Through "Half-Lives" (months)**

	1980s	1990s
Bolivia	9	34
Brazil	19	14
Chile	13	48
Colombia	30	85
Costa Rica	11	69
Dominican Republic	46	24
Ecuador	30	69
El Salvador	80	73
Guatemala	14	17
Honduras	100	80
Mexico	13	22
Nicaragua	25	10
Paraguay	17	23
Peru	4	5
Uruguay	34	23
Venezuela	19	75
Region average	21	35

Note: Region average excludes El Salvador and Honduras.

Table 2.4 **Distribution of Duration of Exchange Rate Shocks**

Pass-Through Half-Life	1980s	1990s
Less than six months	Peru	Peru
Six months to one year	Bolivia, Costa Rica	Nicaragua
One–two years	Brazil, Chile, Guatemala, Mexico, Paraguay, Venezuela	Brazil, Dominican Republic, Guatemala, Mexico, Nicaragua, Paraguay, Uruguay
Two–three years	Colombia, Ecuador, Nicaragua, Uruguay	Bolivia
More than three years	Dominican Republic, El Salvador, Honduras	Chile, Colombia, Costa Rica, Ecuador, El Salvador, Honduras, Venezuela

are robust because the cross-country results are not intuitive. For example, Peru's quick translation of exchange rate movements into the domestic price level is contrasted with Bolivia's two- to three-year half-life despite the fact that both countries have similar degrees of openness, similar levels of inflation in the 1990s, and, as will be discussed below, similar dollarization ratios. The main difference could be explained only by the fact that the end of the hyperinflation in Peru came in 1992, whereas for Bolivia it came in 1986, and the dollar-indexation memory in Peru has maintained a

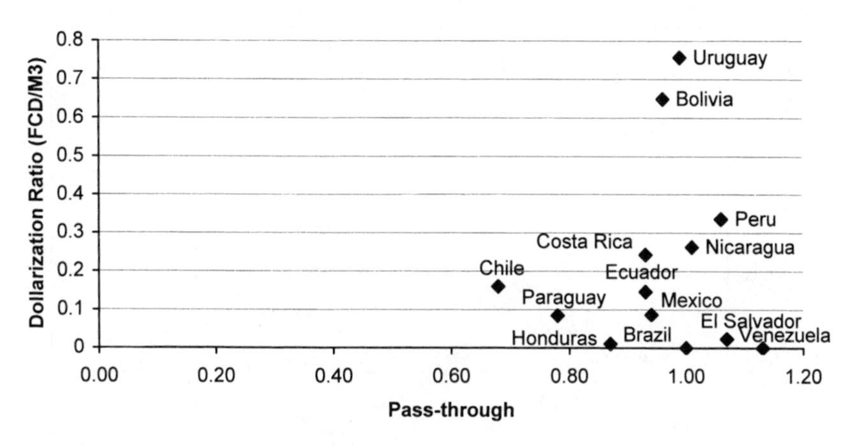

Fig. 2.2 Long-run exchange rate pass-through (1980–2000) versus 1990 dollarization ratio

quick transmission mechanism. If this is the case one may expect the speed of adjustment in Peru to fall in the future.

Once again the Central American countries present a puzzle. On one hand, Guatemala and Nicaragua have half-lives between one and two years; on the other, Costa Rica, El Salvador, and Honduras have half-lives of more than three years. A possible explanation is that most disturbances to the price level are not monetary but due to TOT shocks.

2.3.4 Exchange Rate Pass-Through and Dollarization within and across Countries

Figure 2.2 shows long-run (1980–2000) exchange rate pass-through versus the dollarization ratio in 1990, the middle of the period. As discussed above, long-run pass-through tends to center around 1, and from the plot, the degree of pass-through appears to be independent of the degree of dollarization. There appears to be more pass-through variance in countries with lower dollarization ratios, but that may be due to the fact that the country sample has few highly dollarized economies at the beginning of the 1990s.

Panels A and B of figure 2.3 present estimates of pass-through in the 1980s and in the 1990s versus the dollarization ratio at the end of each respective decade. In both time periods the relationship between dollarization and pass-through is not significant. During the 1980s, there is no obvious pattern. During the 1990s, if the plot suggests anything it is a negative relationship between pass-through and dollarization because highly dollarized economies tended to have lower pass-through. Moreover, the dollarization ratio explains very little of the variance of pass-through evident in low *R*-squareds. The plots suggest that the degree of dollarization as measured here does not play a significant role in the

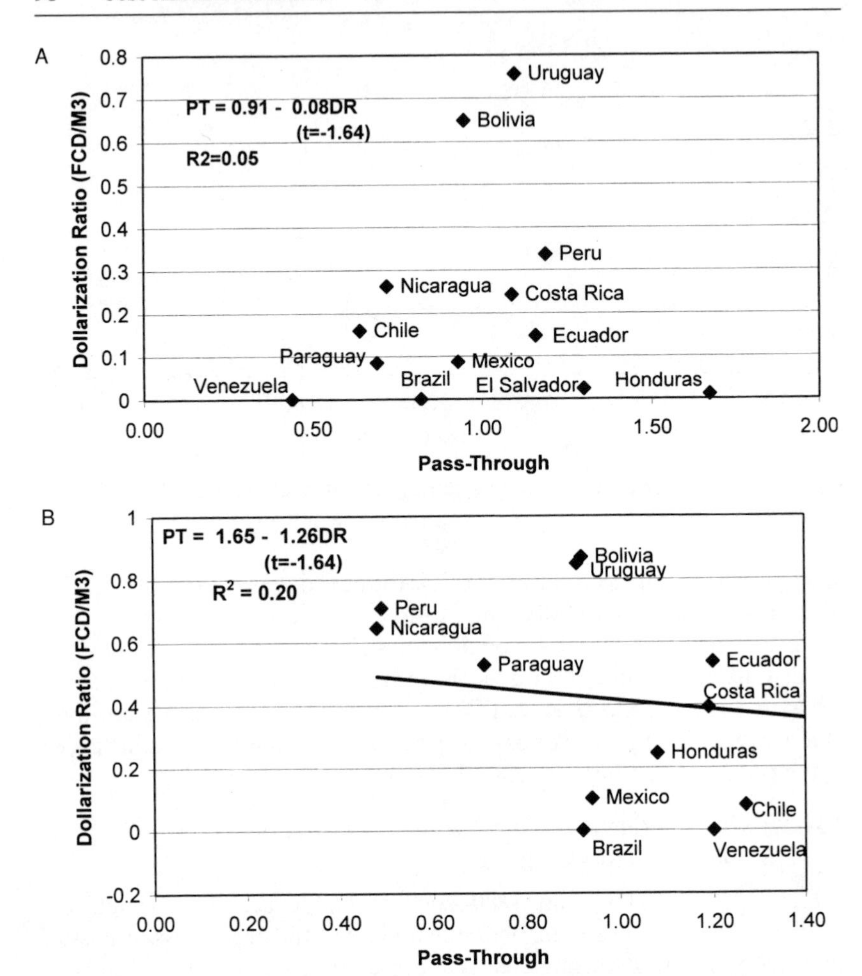

Fig. 2.3 Pass-through versus dollarization ratio: *A*, 1980–90 pass-through, 1990 dollarization ratio; *B*, 1990–2000 pass-through, 2000 dollarization ratio

transmission mechanism of nominal exchange rate fluctuations into the price level; i.e., dollarization as conventionally measured is not the same as the dollar-indexation phenomenon that occurred in many of these countries during high inflation.

In short, in countries with higher degrees of dollarization a nominal devaluation does not necessarily translate more fully into an increase in the price level. Therefore, a more dollarized economy does not have a lesser ability to adjust its exchange rate through nominal devaluations than does a less dollarized economy. The important question is whether, as a country becomes increasingly dollarized, its exchange rate pass-through increases and the authorities lose their ability to adjust the real

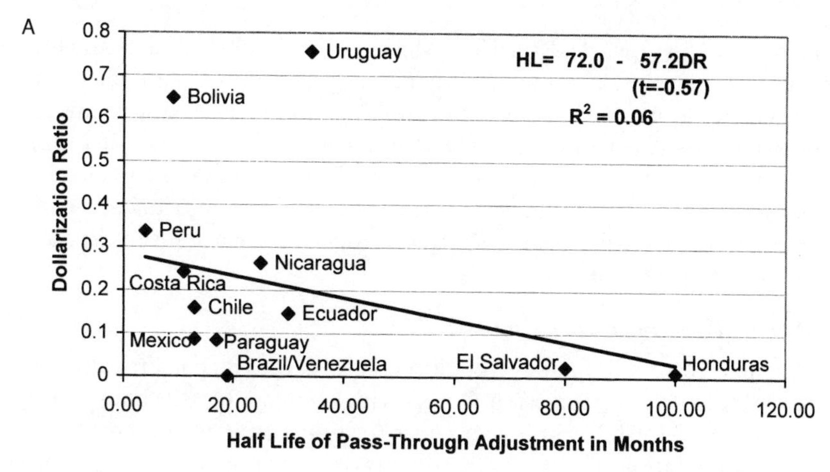

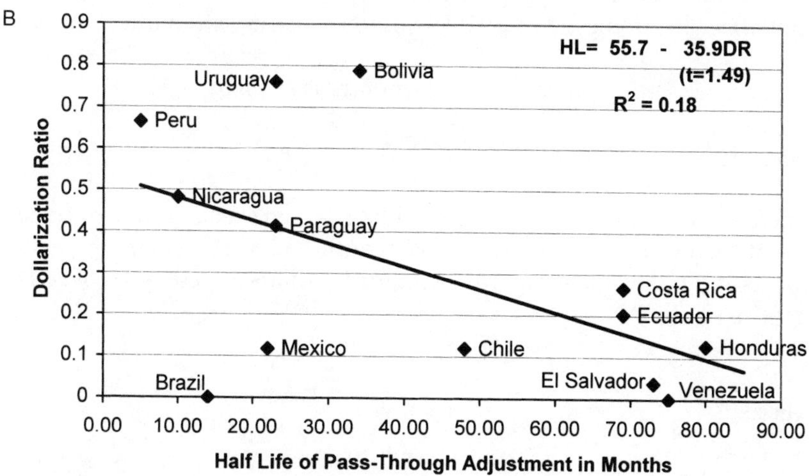

Fig. 2.4 Speed of adjustment and the dollarization ratio: ***A*****, 1980–90;** ***B*****, 1990–2000**

exchange rate through nominal exchange rate devaluations. The answer cannot be derived from the plots but it will be dealt with in the regression analysis.

Panels A and B of figure 2.4 plot the speed of adjustment versus the dollarization ratio. The relationship is positive but not significant.[19] Again, the dollarization ratio explains a small fraction of the variance of the speed of adjustment. The bipolar distribution of the speed of adjustment is odd, and as discussed before, the slow speed of adjustment for Central Ameri-

19. The negative slopes indicate that a higher dollarization ratio is (weakly) correlated with a faster speed of adjustment.

can countries is a puzzle. Brazil and Mexico, with quick responses and low dollarization ratios, are notable outliers. The explanation, particularly for Mexico, could be that the degree of dollarization measured here understates the prevalence of dollar indexation, which arises because of strong links with (and the fact that anecdotal evidence suggests many citizens hold accounts in) the United States. The faster speed of adjustment means that nominal disturbances are shorter lived, but does not mean they are different in magnitude.

A Simple Panel Regression Analysis

I constructed yearly pass-through coefficients with a geometric distributed lag/vector autoregression (VAR) with one lag. This technique was chosen over the VEC technique because the time period is too short to assume cointegration. Using a VAR permits one to ignore the other factors that affect the domestic price level without creating an omitted-variable bias.

The price setting process for each country is given by

$$p_{i,t} = \lambda_i + \phi_i \sum_{j=0}^{\infty} \delta_i f_{i,t-1} + \varepsilon_{i,t}, \tag{3}$$

where $1 - \delta_i$ is the factor by which the impact of an exchange rate (international price) shock diminishes every month and λ_i is a country-specific constant. I follow the standard procedure to estimate these types of equations to obtain[20]

$$p_{it} = \alpha_i + \phi_i f_{i,t} + \delta_i p_{i,t-1} + \upsilon_{it}, \tag{4}$$

where

$$\alpha_i = \lambda_i(1 - \delta_i) \quad \text{and} \quad \upsilon_{it} = \varepsilon_{it} - \delta\varepsilon_{it}.$$

I estimated equation (4) for each country between 1990 and 2000 to obtain ten yearly pass-through coefficients for each of the eleven countries. The pass-through coefficients from equation (5) can be interpreted as the effects of a nominal exchange rate fluctuation on the domestic price level in any given year. The coefficient is not the long-run relationship of the domestic and international price levels but the yearly contemporary effect. Therefore, to some degree the yearly pass-through coefficient embodies both the level and the speed of adjustment; i.e., a country with high pass-through but a slow speed of adjustment will be estimated as having a low coefficient.

The conceptual discussion and the graphical discussion above suggested that exchange rate pass-through could depend on the degree of dol-

20. One multiplies an expression for $p_{i,t-1}$ times δ and subtracts it from the $p_{i,t}$ expression. In the resulting equation I ignored the second-order term.

lar indexation (measured by the dollarization ratio) and the level of inflation. Therefore, the next step was to use the estimated exchange rate pass-through coefficients from equation (5) as dependent variables to construct a balanced panel of eleven countries for ten years from 1990 to 2000, resulting in a total of 109 observations. The panel regression took the form

$$\phi_{i,t} = \mu_i + \beta_{i,t}\text{Dollr}_{i,t} + \theta_i\pi_{i,t} + \zeta_{i,t} \tag{5}$$

where $\text{Dollr}_{i,t}$ and $\pi_{i,t}$ are the yearly dollarization ratios and the inflation rates, respectively.

Table 2.5 presents the pooled and within-country estimators of the panel regression. The pooled, cross-country results corroborate the plots in figures 2.3 and 2.4. There is no significant relationship between dollarization and exchange rate pass-through across countries. With and without yearly inflation the coefficient is positive but insignificant. Thus countries with higher degrees of dollarization do not necessarily have higher rates of pass-through, and they can still influence their real exchange rates through nominal devaluations.

Table 2.5 Panel Regressions of Yearly Pass-Through

	Dollarization	Inflation	R^2	No. of Obs.
Pooled results	0.199	–1.53	0.19	99
	(1.27)	(2.12)		
	0.050		0.18	99
	(1.22)			
Bolivia	–0.55	10.60		
	(2.99)	(14.4)		
Costa Rica	–4.32	4.10		
	(3.90)	(12.70)		
Ecuador	–2.87	–11.90		
	(2.34)	(26.00)		
El Salvador	–8.80*	6.82		
	(2.90)	(5.50)		
Honduras	4.54	–4.20		
	(3.36)	(3.80)		
Mexico	0.20	–2.10		
	(1.60)	(1.60)		
Nicaragua	0.72	–0.18		
	(0.87)	(0.92)		
Paraguay	0.62	1.37		
	(4.21)	(8.70)		
Peru	–0.92	11.70		
	(1.48)	(11.40)		
Uruguay	10.20	2.82		
	(12.8)	(8.21)		

Note: Standard errors in parenthesis. Within-country estimators: $R^2 = 0.36$.
*Significant at the 95 percent confidence level.

The discussion suggested that inflation should increase the speed of adjustment and thus the yearly pass-through coefficients. With more frequent price revisions, higher inflation would be expected to be associated with a faster speed of adjustment of the domestic price level to nominal exchange rate shocks. However, the point estimate was negative although insignificant. As a whole, both of the explanatory variables explain only a fifth of the variance of the pass-through coefficients, indicating that there are other, more important variables.

The within-country dollarization estimators similarly present ambiguous results. Except for El Salvador, all of the coefficients are insignificant at the 95 percent confidence level. For half of the countries—Bolivia, Costa Rica, Ecuador, El Salvador, and Peru—greater dollarization is associated with lower pass-through. For the other half—Honduras, Mexico, Nicaragua, Paraguay, and Uruguay—increased dollarization is associated with higher pass-through, supporting the hypothesis that higher dollarization increases dollar indexation.

The ambiguity of the within-country estimates indicates that as a country becomes more dollarized pass-through does not increase, and thus the country does not systematically loose its ability to adjust its real exchange rate through nominal devaluations.

The within-country inflation results also yield insignificant coefficients. Six of the ten countries (Bolivia, Costa Rica, El Salvador, Paraguay, Peru, and Uruguay) have positive coefficients, giving support to the hypothesis that higher inflation implies higher dollar indexation. However, four (Ecuador, Honduras, Nicaragua, and Mexico) have a negative relationship. The drawback of having dollarization data only for the 1990s is that most of the countries in the sample were not experiencing high inflation. The ambiguous results suggest that for moderate levels of inflation, dollar indexation does not play a major role. However, one cannot reject the hypothesis that for high levels of inflation, the mechanism does not play a more prominent role.

This is a case in which the lack of a relationship is an important result. It would have been surprising to find a significant relation in the regression analysis after the graphical motivation presented before. The evidence suggests that the degree to which nominal exchange rate movements translate into proportional fluctuations in the domestic price level is independent of the dollarization ratio and the inflation level for moderate levels of inflation.

2.4 Conclusion

The purpose of this paper is to test the "conventional wisdom" that, as a country becomes more dollarized, nominal exchange rate devaluations translate more fully and quickly into increases in the domestic price level. The question is important for partially dollarized economies because the answer may shed light on their ability to influence the real exchange rate through nominal exchange rate fluctuations.

The study finds no relationship between the level of dollarization and the degree of pass-through of the nominal exchange rate into domestic inflation for a wide sample of Latin American countries. I use the ratio of dollar deposits in the banking system as a measure of dollarization, and an ECM to estimate exchange rate pass-through. The relationship is ambiguous both in the 1980s and in the 1990s. In a simple regression analysis, yearly pass-through coefficients were constructed to create a panel regression of pass-through on dollarization and inflation. The cross-country coefficient was positive but insignificant; similarly, the cross-country inflation coefficient was negative and insignificant. Within-country estimates were always insignificant and split between positive and negative.

The plots and the panel results point toward two important results: (1) A higher degree of dollarization between countries does not lead to higher pass-through. Therefore, more dollarized economies do not necessarily have less ability to influence their real exchange rates through nominal exchange rate movements. (2) Within the same country, an increase in dollarization does not hinder a country's ability to adjust its exchange rate through nominal fluctuations. Higher dollarization does not necessarily mean higher dollar-indexation, as is commonly believed. The price index is not determined by the unit of accounting but by internal market conditions. Perhaps the reason the belief has been perpetuated is that there is no good measure of dollar indexation.

The result can be reconciled with existing models if one recalls that domestic inflation has an important component of nontradable prices whereby the law of one price does not have to hold at all. The prices of nontradables are determined by domestic supply and demand. The unit of account, peso or dollar, does not affect them. Changes in the nominal exchange rate will affect the prices of nontradables only through their real substitution and income effects; whether transactions are carried out in dollars or not should not make a difference. Dollarization will affect the prices of nontradables only to the degree that the share of deposits affects the income and substitution effects of a nominal devaluation.

The paper finds a more consistent (although not statistically significant) positive relationship between dollarization and the speed of adjustment. In more dollarized economies, the domestic price level tends to adjust faster to nominal exchange rate fluctuations even though, as discussed above, the magnitude of the pass-through is unaffected by the degree of dollarization (i.e., the faster speed of adjustment means that nominal disturbances are shorter lived, but not that they differ in magnitude).

In the course of the estimation process, I found that for many Latin American countries in the very long run (twenty years), pass-through is close to 1, implying that PPP is not a bad benchmark in the determination of the real and therefore the nominal exchange rate. Nevertheless, there have been pronounced and long-lived deviations from this arbitrarily chosen twenty-year average. Surprisingly, decade-long pass-through can be different from 1 and can differ from decade to decade for some of these countries, corroborating the idea that the deviations from the stable, long-term relationship between the domestic and the international price indexes can be substantial in magnitude and duration. The fact that PPP is a good benchmark simply states that, in the aggregate, the structural disturbances canceled each other out—not that PPP was a dominant force.

There are two venues for further research on this topic. One is to formalize the exchange rate pass-through in an economy in which agents' savings are in dollars—thus the substitution effects of a nominal devaluation are as in the standard model, but the income effects of a devaluation work in the opposite direction. The other is to expand the empirical effort to use tradable and nontradable price indexes, and to include other variables suggested by the theory to explain pass-through both within and across countries.

References

Baldwin, R. 1988a. Hysterisis in import prices: The beachhead effect. *American Economic Review* 78 (September): 773–85.

———. 1988b. Some empirical evidence on hysterisis in aggregate U.S. import prices. NBER Working Paper no. 2483. Cambridge, Mass.: National Bureau of Economic Research, January.

Baldwin, R., and P. Krugman. 1987. The persistence of the U.S. trade deficit. *Brookings Papers on Economic Activity,* issue no. 1:1–55. Washington, D.C.: Brookings Institution.

———. 1989. Persistent trade effects of large exchange rate shocks. *Quarterly Journal of Economics* 104 (November): 635–54.

Córdoba, J. 1991. Diez lecciones de la reforma económica de México (Ten lessons from the Mexican economic reforms). In *Nexos.*

Dornbusch, R. 1980. *Open economy and macroeconomics.* New York: Basic Books.

———. 1987. Exchange rates and prices. *American Economic Review* 77 (1): 93–106. Reproduced in R. Dornbusch, *Exchange rates and inflation,* Cambridge: MIT Press.

———. 1988. Purchasing power parity. *The new Palgrave: A dictionary of economics.* New York: Stockton Press. Reproduced in R. Dornbusch, *Exchange rates and inflation,* 70–103, Cambridge, MIT Press.

Dornbusch, R., with S. Fischer and P. Samuelson. 1977. Comparative advantage, trade, and payments in a Ricardian model with a continuum of goods. *American Economic Review* 67 (5): 904–81.

Froot, K., and P. Klemperer. 1989. Exchange rate pass-through when market share matters. *American Economic Review* 79 (September): 637–54.

Garcés-Diaz, Daniel. 1999. Determinacion del nivel de precios y la dinámica inflacionari en México. Documento de Investigacion. Mexico City: Banco de México.

González, J. A. 1998 Regímines comerciales y el traspaso del tipo de cambio: Hay un enigma Mexicano? (Trade regimes and exchange rate pass-through: Is there a Mexican puzzle?). *El Trimestre Económico* 65 (257).

Hausmann, R., U. Panizza, and E. Stein. 2000. Why do countries float the way they float? Research Department, Interamerican Development Bank. Mimeograph, March.

Knetter, M. 1989. Price discrimination by U.S. and German exporters. *American Economic Review* 79 (March): 198–210.

———. 1992. Exchange rates and corporate pricing strategies. NBER Working Paper no. 4151. Cambridge, Mass.: National Bureau of Economic Research, August.

———. 1993. International comparisons of pricing-to-market behavior. *American Economic Review* 83 (June): 473–86.

Krugman, P. 1986. Pricing to market when exchange rate matters. NBER Working Paper no. 1926. Cambridge, Mass.: National Bureau of Economic Research, May.

McKinnon, R. 1999. The East Asian dollar standard: Life after death? *Economic Notes* 29 (1).

———. 2001. After the crisis, the East Asian dollar standard resurrected: An interpretation of high-frequency exchange rate pegging. In *Rethinking the East Asian miracle,* ed. J. Stiglitz and S. Yusuf. Washington, D.C.: World Bank.

———. 2002. The East Asian exchange rate dilemma and the world dollar standard. Stanford University. Mimeograph, February.

Nelson, C. R., and C. Plosser. 1982. Trends and random walks in macroeconomic time series. *Journal of Monetary Economics.*

Vegh, C. A. 1992. Stopping high inflation: An analytical overview. *IMF Staff Papers* 39 (September): 626–95. Reprinted in *Great inflations of the twentieth century: Theories, policies, and evidence,* ed. P. Sklos, Hampshire, U.K.: Edward Elgar, 1995.

3

Very High Interest Rates and the Cousin Risks
Brazil During the Real Plan

Márcio G. P. Garcia and Tatiana Didier

3.1 Introduction

The interest rate constitutes one of the most important macroeconomic variables responsible for an economy's good performance. It is essential to have a well-calibrated interest rate, because interest rates play an important role in the determination of several economic variables—e.g., output and employment levels, the exchange rate, and others. Not surprisingly, it is almost impossible to obtain a consensus about the ideal interest rate level. The fact that Alan Greenspan has a high degree of respectability is a recent phenomenon in the United States. In the beginning of the Volcker era, less than twenty years ago, the unemployment associated with the anti-inflationary effort led people to print "Wanted" posters with pictures of Volcker and the Fed board of governors! Recently, in Brazil, it is not unusual to read complaints in the newspaper about the high level of interest rates.

Figure 3.1 shows the monthly evolution of Brazilian real interest rates in the last twenty-five years. The thinner line represents the monthly real interest rate (RIR, expressed in percent per year) and the thicker line is the respective twelve-month moving average RIR (also expressed in percent per year). The horizontal line segments show the RIR averages in three periods: the second half of the 1970s, the 1980s plus a few months, and the opening up of domestic financial markets to international investors (since

Márcio G. P. Garcia is associate professor in the department of economics, PUC-Rio, Brazil. Tatiana Didier is a consultant at the World Bank.

We would like to thank the research assistance provided by Bernardo Carvalho, Tiago Berriel, Bruno Ferman, and Igor Abdalla. All errors are our own.

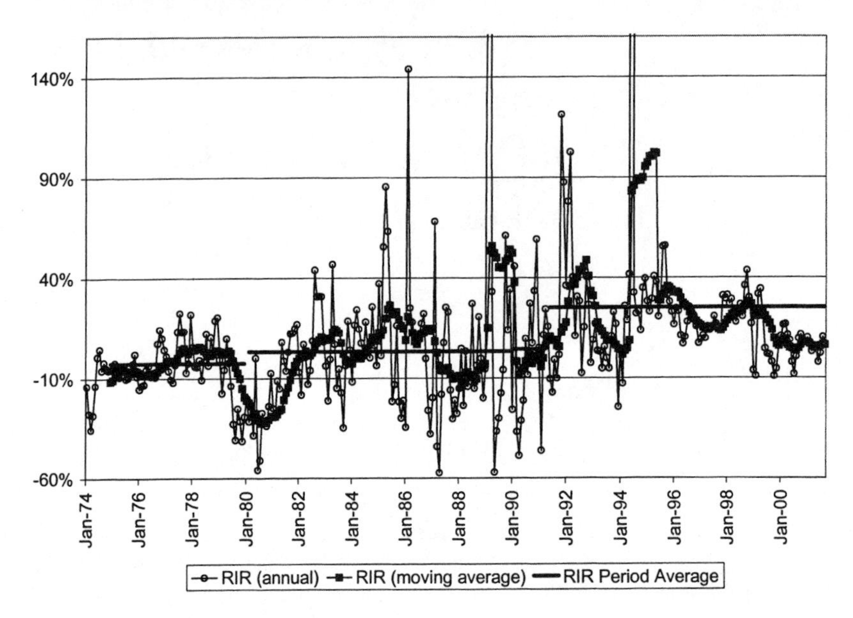

Fig. 3.1 Real interest rates
Source: Banco Central do Brasil.

May 1991). The huge jump in interest rates during the recent financial liberalization period is clear.[1]

Two key characteristics of the nineties in Brazil were the inflation stabilization that came with the Real Plan in July 1994, and the trade and financial openness of the Brazilian economy. We adopted May 1991 as the reference date of the financial liberalization because it coincides with the edition of the famous Annex IV that opened the Brazilian economy to the possibility of external portfolio investments.

When an economy liberalizes its capital account, it loses one degree of freedom to fix its own interest rate. This is due to capital flows. Under a fixed exchange rate regime (or a controlled one), a low interest rate could bring about capital outflows, which cause monetary contraction and a consequent rise in interest rates. Under a flexible exchange rate regime, a low interest rate would cause an incipient capital flight that would depreciate the exchange rate. Between these two polar-opposite regimes, there are several other possibilities, such as a crawling peg–cum–controls over

1. We use here the Selic rate (the analogue of the Fed funds rate) deflated by the centered general price index (IGP-DI). Therefore, we refer to the very high real interest rates that enter the liability side of the government and of financial institutions. Active interest rates are even higher, given the very high bank spread in Brazil, a phenomenon that is pervasive in Latin America (see Brock and Rojas-Suárez 2000). However, we do not analyze the active interest rates behavior in this paper.

the capital flows. Since the financial liberalization in the beginning of the nineties, Brazil has adopted several different exchange rate regimes and forms of capital controls.

We aim at studying the determinants of interest rates in Brazil since it became a financially open economy. Based on the interest parity conditions, we study the behavior of what we call the cousin risks: the currency risk and the country (Brazil) risk. These two risks are fundamental in the determination of a floor for the domestic interest rate, and reducing them is the main objective if one aims at achieving interest rates compatible with sustained economic growth.

Section 3.2 of this paper deals with theoretical derivations as well as measurement and estimation issues pertaining to country and currency risks. Section 3.3 applies the developments of section 3.2 to generate several country-risk measures and one currency-risk estimate. Section 3.4 uses the country- and currency-risk measures to analyze (decompose) the domestic interest rate. Finally, Section 3.5 discusses the determinants of the very high real interest rates in Brazil, as well as the policy actions that should be taken in order to achieve lower real interest rates without compromising inflation stability, thereby fostering higher growth.

3.2 Country Risk and Currency Risk: What Are They?

3.2.1 Country Risk

At present, developed countries are considered financially integrated. The financial integration, however, was achieved only in the last decades (see, e.g., Frankel 1991). Even the developed economies had severe restrictions on international capital flows in the beginning of the seventies.

For many emerging markets, these restrictions to the international capital flows just began to be withdrawn in the beginning of the nineties, together with the implementation of the Brady Plan. In spite of this increasing financial integration, it cannot be said that there is perfect capital mobility among these countries, as we are going to see next.

Among the several possible measures of perfect capital mobility, Frankel (1991) concludes that the most appropriate is the covered parity of interest rates, in which "capital flows equalize interest rates among countries when denominated in the same currency" (229). The covered interest parity differential (CID) is usually known as country risk, because it affects the yields of all financial assets in a certain country. The developed countries do not have CID (i.e., the CID among them is negligible). This means that if a large multinational enterprise wants to make a loan in U.S. dollars, the interest rate would be the same whether the commercial paper is issued in England or in the United States. However, had the bond been floated in an emerging market (without a foreign collateral), the interest rate (in U.S. dollars) would have been higher. This difference is one possible measure of the country risk.

Because it contaminates all financial assets in a certain country, the country risk cannot be hedged within that country—i.e., it will not be eliminated with investment diversification among the assets in that country. Being a systemic risk, the country risk increases the yield required for all the assets in the country, or, equivalently, it reduces the price of the assets if compared to the identical ones issued in the developed countries.[2]

The differential (or deviation) of the covered interest rate parity[3] is the best measure of the lack of perfect capital mobility "because it captures all barriers to integration of financial markets across national boundaries: transactions costs, information costs, capital controls, tax laws that discriminate by country of residence, default risk, and risk of future capital controls" (Frankel 1991, 240).

Thus, the country risk is a portrait of the economic and financial situation of a certain country, also showing the political stability and the historic performance in fulfilling its financial obligations.

3.2.2 Currency Risk

The risk aversion that usually characterizes the behavior of investors in financial markets may drive the price of some financial assets away from the relevant expectations. Risk-averse investors do not enter in fair gambles (gambles with zero expected value). They require some compensation, which generates a positive expected value for most investments.

In emerging markets, investors in currency futures require something more than the expected currency depreciation to sell their hard currency in the future. There is a currency risk that creates a wedge between the expected price of the hard currency (typically the U.S. dollar) in the future and the price of that currency in the currency futures or forward market.

Unfortunately, in contrast with what occurs with the country risk, the currency risk is not measurable directly through the existing assets' yields. This impossibility of direct measurement is due to the inability of observing the expected depreciation. Here we will use one econometric technique to uncover the currency risk.

3.2.3 Measurement Methods of the Cousin Risks

We will use several securities, especially derivatives, to measure the country and currency risks. Through the U.S.-dollar (USD) futures mar-

2. We acknowledge the fact that the country risk is usually considered a diversifiable risk from the point of view of foreign investors. However, the empirical evidence that we will show demonstrates very clearly that the country risk is priced. It is possible that this apparent puzzle is related to another one: the enormous home bias prevalent in many economies (see, e.g., Obstfeld and Rogoff 1996, 305).

3. We will define *covered interest parity* formally in the next sections.

ket, at BM&F (from the Portuguese Bolsa de Mercadorias e Futuros),[4] it is possible to measure the country risk through the arbitrage concept. The USD futures contracts[5] are contracts between two market players, in which the player with the long position commits to buy from the player with the short position a predetermined amount of U.S. dollars at a given date in the future, paying the agreed delivery price (in Brazilian reaies). Conversely, the institution with the short position commits to sell at that future date for that predetermined delivery price the amount of U.S. dollars previously agreed.[6] Thus, on the futures contract settlement date, if the spot U.S. dollar costs more than the futures price, the player with the long position wins (because he or she bought the same dollar for a lower price than the market price), and the player with the short position loses.

Under perfect capital mobility, the USD futures market allows for arbitrage transactions between the domestic and international interest rates. Through that arbitrage transaction, we are going to extract one measure of Brazil risk.

In finance theory, an *arbitrage opportunity* is a financial transaction in which it is possible to obtain some positive gain without any risk from a zero initial capital investment. In practice, the arbitrage concept is used to describe low-risk transactions, such as buy (cheaply) in a market and resell (more expensively) in another market. Thus, the description of that arbitrage transaction requires an analysis of two cases: The first one is when the USD futures contract is expensive, and the second one is when it is cheap. As we will see, we are more interested in the second case, which will originate a positive Brazil risk.

1. *First case:* The USD futures contract is expensive ($f > s[1 + i]/[1 + i^*]$).

a. Buy US$1 in the spot exchange rate market, paying BR$$s$ (s is the USD spot price).

b. To pay for that purchase of US$1, a loan of BR$$s$ is needed in the domestic market, accruing interest at rate i (i.e., in the expiry date of the loan, BR$$s(1 + i)$ will be paid back).

c. Invest the US$1 bought in the international market, receiving interest of i^* (i.e., in the expiry date of the investment, US$ $(1 + i^*)$ will be received).

d. Sell in the USD futures market at the prevailing price f the amount that is going to be received for the international investment, US$ $(1 + i^*)$;

4. BM&F is the Commodities and Futures Exchange in São Paulo, Brazil, and is the main exchange where derivative securities are traded.

5. This subsection draws heavily from Garcia (1997).

6. This description is incomplete because we are omitting important operational details such as the collaterals required by BM&F, and daily margin settlements. Introducing them in the analysis, however, makes the analysis much more complicated without adding further insights.

i.e., BR$$f(1 + i^*)$ is going to be received for the sale of U.S. dollars in the futures market at the settlement date of the futures contract, which coincides with the loan expiry date.

Transactions 1(a) through 1(d) give a profit of BR$ $(f[1 + i^*] - s[1 + i])$ at the settlement date of the USD futures contract without the need of any initial capital. Note that there is no risk at all in this whole transaction, because all the prices are known at the present time. If the profit is positive, it is said that there is an arbitrage opportunity. If this occurs, it is possible to make a profit following steps 1(a) through 1(d) without incurring in any risk at all and without any initial capital.

2. *Second case:* The USD futures contract is cheap $(f < s[1 + i]/[1 + i^*])$.

a. Sell US$1 in today's market, receiving BR$$s$ (s is the USD spot price).

b. To obtain the US$1 sold in transaction 2(a) a loan of US$1 is necessary in the international market, paying for that the interest of i^* (i.e., at the expiry date of the loan, US$ $(1 + i^*)$ will be paid back).

c. BR$$s$ obtained in transaction 2(a) should be invested in the domestic market, accruing the interest rate i (i.e., in the expiry date of the investment, BR$$s(1 + i)$ will be received).

d. The US$$(1 + i^*)$ will be bought in the USD futures market at the prevailing price f; i.e., the amount that is known that will be paid to the international creditor should be bought and the final price for that purchase is BR$$f(1 + i^*)$.

Transactions 2(a) through 2(d) result in a profit of BR$ $(s[1 + i] - f[1 + i^*])$ at the settlement date of the USD futures contract, without the need of any initial capital. As this is a riskless transaction, because all prices are known at the present time, if the profit is positive, it is said that there is an arbitrage opportunity. If that occurs, it is possible to have a profit following steps 2(a) through 2(d) without incurring any risk at all and without any initial capital. It should be noted that cases 1 and 2 are mutually exclusive.

In practice, financial markets are aware of those arbitrage opportunities; thus we can expect that neither of the cases above will last for long. Therefore, the very existence of arbitrageurs in financial markets means that there will be a lack of arbitrage opportunities like the two cases described above. The only case in which neither arbitrage opportunity occurs is when BR$$(f[1 + i^*] - s[1 + i])$ = BR$$(s[1 + i] - f[1 + i^*])$ = BR$0, i.e.,

$$f = \frac{s \cdot (1 + i)}{(1 + i^*)}. \quad (1)$$

However, in practice, the USD futures price almost always lies below the value of f in equation (1), as seen in figure 3.2, which portrays the typical behavior of a USD futures contract. The lowermost horizontal graph

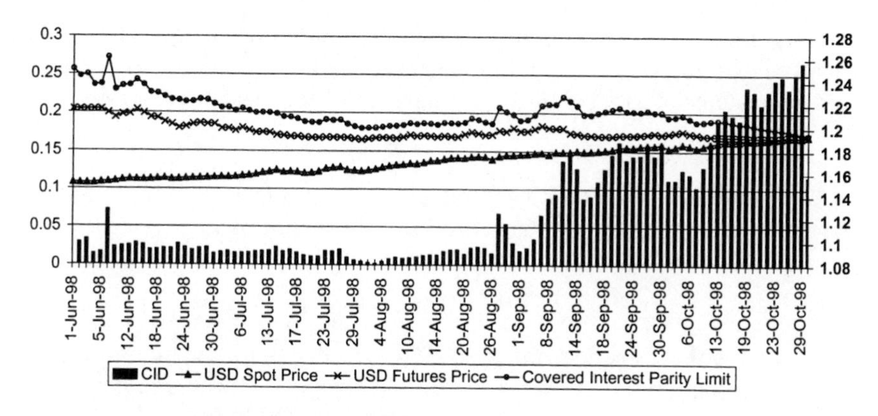

Fig. 3.2 Covered interest parity differential
Sources: Banco Central do Brasil, BM&F, and Federal Reserve System.

(marked with triangles) is the exchange rate (BRL/USD), from 1 June 1998 to 3 November 1998 (right-hand-side scale). The middle horizontal graph (marked with crosses) is the futures price for the November futures contract (maturing on the first business day of November 1998). The uppermost horizontal graph (marked with circles) is the theoretical limit established by covered interest parity (i.e., what the futures price would have been had covered interest parity been held). The wedge between the actual futures price and the theoretical one is the CID, which is represented by the vertical bars in percentage per year (left-hand-side scale).[7] That wedge is the *country risk*.

When the USD future rate lies below limit f, established in equation (1), there is an arbitrage opportunity like the one described in the second case of the last section (when the USD futures contract is cheap). In such an environment, a foreign investor may resort to a loan in the United States, transfer the funds to Brazil, and invest them at a fixed interest rate. Simultaneously, the foreign investor hedges against currency devaluation in the USD futures market and can still have a net gain after the repayment of the loan in the United States. In theory, it is possible for the foreign investor to have a positive profit with a zero initial investment without assuming any risk at all—i.e., there would be an arbitrage profit. Indeed, that has been the source of immense profits for many players in the Brazilian financial market in the nineties until the start of the international financial crises.

When that arbitrage profit is zero, then the covered interest parity condition holds. Covered interest parity is equivalent to equation (1). However, figure 3.2 shows that, in Brazil, that condition was usually violated.

7. One should not be very impressed by the increase in the CID a few days before the contract settlement date, because, as maturity approaches, the contract loses liquidity and the price is no longer very informative.

There was a covered interest parity differential, described before as a good measure for the country risk. In the next section, we are going to use the covered interest parity condition to analyze the domestic interest rate.

3.2.4 Analysis of the Domestic Interest Rate

For emerging markets such as Brazil's, the domestic interest rate can be analyzed in the following way, according to the definition of covered interest parity and adding the country risk:[8]

$$i = i^* + (f - s) + cor \tag{2}$$

Following the same notation used before, i is the domestic interest rate; i^*, the international interest rate; f (in logs) the USD futures price; s (in logs) the USD spot price; and cor, the country risk.

The second term of the equation above is called the *forward premium*, and it is observable through the futures market.[9] The forward premium can be analyzed in the following way:

$$(f - s) = E_t(s_T - s_t) + cur \tag{3}$$

The first term on the right side of the equation $E_t(s_T - s_t)$, is the expected depreciation measured today, i.e., the difference between the (log of) spot U.S. dollar today, t, and the value of the (log of) spot U.S. dollar at the end of the period, T. The second term, cur, is the currency-risk premium, i.e., the difference between the USD futures price and the expectation of the spot U.S. dollar at the settlement date (the first term usually being higher than the second one). As we shall see, at times of uncertainty, this difference increases, then decreases in less turbulent periods.

The problem faced is that currency risk is not measurable in a direct way, because there are no direct measures of expectations. What is registered is the USD futures price, but USD futures are distinct (usually higher) than the expectations of the USD spot in the future.

Therefore, for countries with floating exchange rate regimes, it is interesting to decompose the domestic interest rate according to the following equation:

$$i = i^* + E_t(s_T - s_t) + cor + cur \tag{4}$$

Based on equation (2), it is possible to obtain the country risk from the residual:

8. This subsection is strongly based on Garcia and Olivares Leandro (2001). Here, the meaning of the word *analysis* is *breakdown*. Note also that, from this section on, we begin to use continuous compounding. We do this to ensure, in the following interest-rate decomposition exercises, that the parts add up to the total. As is well known, only in continuous compounding and simple compounding are equivalent rates proportional (e.g., 1 percent per month corresponds to 12 percent per year).

9. As we will explain later (subsection 3.4.2), the measure of the forward premium also depends on where the contract is traded.

$$cor = i - i^* - (f - s)$$

It is also possible to obtain another measure for the country risk, again by residual, through the yield (usually referred to as *coupon* in the Brazilian market) of U.S. dollar–linked bonds, which is the rate of return, in foreign currency, of a domestic investment (in Brazil) in a U.S. dollar–indexed bond.[10] It is possible to analyze the yield of this coupon on U.S. dollar–linked bonds (cc):

$$cc = i^* + cor \tag{5}$$

In the following section we will use financial instruments (including derivatives) available in domestic and international financial markets to measure the components of the right side of equation (4), and proceed to the analysis of domestic interest rates.

3.3 Measurement of Currency Risk and Country Risk

In this section, we generate the measures for the country risk and the estimates for the currency risk. Those measures will be used in the analysis of domestic interest rates in the next section.

3.3.1 Brazil Risk

We developed several measures of Brazil risk, computed in different ways for the period January 1995 to June 2001.[11] These different measures come from several securities, including derivatives. The country-risk measures will vary according to the securities used in their computation. We will now describe the different financial instruments used in the analysis.

Swaps

The first approach for the CID for the Brazilian case was made using data from the Brazilian fixed income markets, which capture all the variables involved in this analysis. The following two swap contracts were used: DI × Dol, which is a currency swap, and DI × Pre, which is an interest rate swap. Swaps may be interpreted as a collection of forward agreements. Each of the swaps used here is akin to only one forward agreement, since each involves only one settlement; and since forward contracts are quite similar to futures contracts, our approach will be based on the arbitrage conditions developed in section 3.2.3 for the futures contracts.

The raw data used in this analysis are one-year contracts, thereby cap-

10. This rate is traded in BM&F through both a futures contract (DDI) and a swap contract (Dol × Pre) for different maturities (the swap is longer). The reader should consult the description of BM&F contracts at [www.bmf.com.br]. For the validity of equation (5), it is necessary that the rate traded in BM&F be converted to continuous compounding.

11. For data on the early nineties, see Garcia and Valpassos (2000).

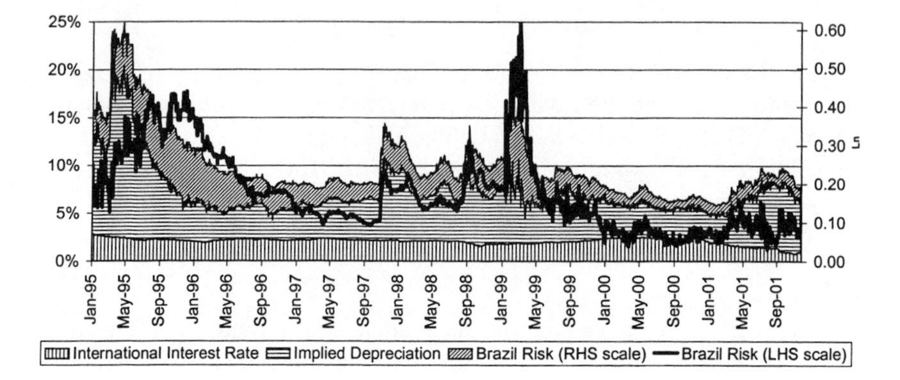

Fig. 3.3 Brazil-risk swaps
Sources: Banco Central do Brasil, BM&F, and Federal Reserve System.

turing one-year-ahead expectations. Thus, they should reflect one-year expectations for currency depreciation and for domestic and international interest rates.[12] We also conducted the same analysis with the other (shorter) time spans available, but opted for the one-year-ahead period (the longest available) because it is less volatile.[13]

The results are displayed in figure 3.3. The different areas show the behavior of each of the components analyzed (left-hand-side scale) and the thick line represents the Brazil risk (right-hand-side scale).[14] The sum of all areas is the one-year-ahead domestic interest rate, measured by the Swaps DI × Pre contracts (right-hand-side scale; see appendix A for a description of Swaps contracts).

Bonds Issued Abroad (foreign debt)

Another way to measure the Brazil risk is through the Brazilian foreign debt, the majority of which is denominated in U.S. dollars. Therefore, the measure of Brazil risk is the difference between the secondary market yield of these bonds and the yield of a risk-free bond, typically a U.S. Treasury bond with the same expiry date of swap contracts (i.e., the bond's spread-over-treasury).

C-Bonds and IDUs are the Brazilian bonds considered in this analysis. The IDU (Interest Due and Unpaid) is a sovereign bond issued on 20 November 1992 (US$7, 100 million) with expiry date on 1 January 2001, under the terms of the Brady agreement. A C-Bond (Brazil Capitalization [C] Bond) is a sovereign bond issued on 15 April 1994 (US$7, 387 million), and has a longer life, expiring on 15 April 2014. Therefore, the difference in yields between these two bonds reflects, among other effects, the slope

12. A detailed description of the data set is in appendix A.
13. See appendix B for a comparison between Brazil risk in the short and medium run.
14. The upper area is the same as the line, only in different scales.

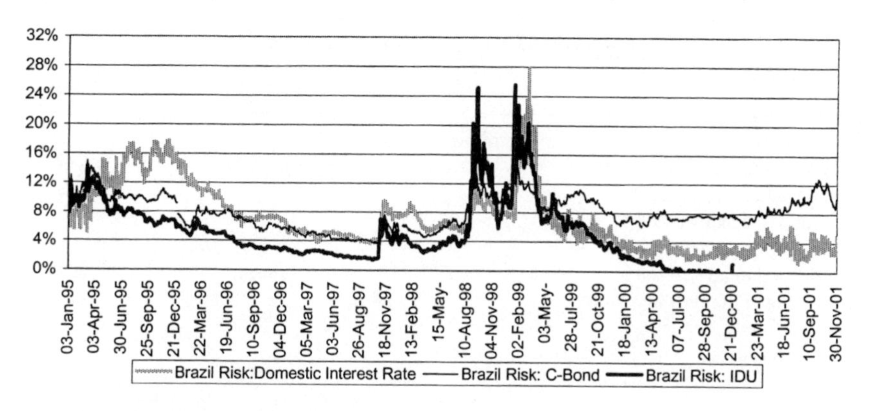

Fig. 3.4 Brazil-risk bonds
Sources: Bloomberg, BM&F, and Federal Reserve System.

of the yield curve. In the beginning of the period analyzed here, IDU bonds were the most traded Brazilian bonds in foreign markets. However, they began to lose liquidity in the market as they approached maturity, and in the last few years, the C-Bond became the most liquid Brady bond. Figure 3.4 shows all the measures of Brazil risk together, allowing a comparative analysis.

As it can be seen from figure 3.4, the measures of Brazil risk move together. After the Mexican crisis (December 1994), all of the measures were decreasing until the Asian crisis in October 1997. After that event, all of them began a decreasing trend, although at a level higher than before the Asian crisis, until the start of the Russian crisis and the collapse of hedge fund Long-Term Capital Management (LTCM) in August 1998. The Brazil risk increased substantially during that period (by all measures) and, again, decreased after the crisis. However, it remained at an even higher level than before the Russian crisis, which was already higher than before the Asian crisis. The downward trend ended with Brazilian devaluation in January 1999. When it happened, all the three measures exploded and began a soft decline only in the second quarter of 1999. In summary, all these measures show a very high correlation, strongly reacting to the local and international crises. Table 3.1 shows both first and second statistical moments of the different measures of the Brazil risk.

Although they are extremely positively correlated, the differences among the different measures are not negligible. Some of the reasons for these differences are the existence of different kind of risks inherent to any of the financial instruments used in the analysis, different tax treatments among them, and the fact that these instruments have different maturities and durations (they are at different points of the yield curve).

Another important reason to explain the difference between the Brazil-risk measure derived from the domestic interest rate and the others derived from the secondary market yields of the foreign debt (Stripped Spread

Table 3.1 **Statistics of Brazil Risk's Different Measures**

	BR: C-Bond	BR: IDU	IDU: C-Bond
	Correlations		
Precrises (until October 1997)	0.70235	0.64840	0.96563
Controlled exchange rate (until December 1998)	0.63865	0.49838	0.90309
Floating exchange rate (since January 1999)	0.76184	0.86569	0.88780
Floating exchange rate (since June 1999)	0.76010	0.85229	0.79566
Crises (controlled exchange rate) (until December 1998)	0.67948	0.75570	0.91039
	Swaps	C-Bond	IDU
	Means		
Precrises (until October 1997)	0.09047	0.07455	0.05077
Controlled exchange rate (until December 1998)	0.08564	0.07484	0.05512
Floating exchange rate (since January 1999)	0.05302	0.08421	0.04342
Floating exchange rate (since June 1999)	0.03736	0.08001	0.02328
Crises (controlled exchange rate) (until December 1998)	0.07166	0.07320	0.06279
	Volatilities (standard deviations)		
Precrises (until October 1997)	0.04061	0.02637	0.02903
Controlled exchange rate (until December 1998)	0.03581	0.02601	0.03516
Floating exchange rate (since January 1999)	0.04408	0.01576	0.05183
Floating exchange rate (since June 1999)	0.01387	0.01148	0.02545
Crises (controlled exchange rate) (until December 1998)	0.01562	0.02574	0.04507

Note: See text for abbreviations. BR is the Brazil risk measured with swaps contracts.

C-Bond and IDU/London Interbank Offered Rate, or IDU/LIBOR) is the fact that domestic interest rates in the short run are somewhat under the central bank's control. The others merely reflect expectations of agents expressed by the secondary market yield of these bonds. For example, the central bank might fix the domestic interest rate at a higher level than the risk perception of foreign investors would require to maintain their funds in domestic bonds. In this case—which actually occurred from mid-1995 until the Asian crisis, and again during the first four months of 1998—there were huge capital inflows, causing large accumulations of foreign reserves (which seemed to be one of the central bank's policy objectives during those periods).

Therefore, the Brazil risk measured through domestic interest rates (swaps) measures how much yield the domestic fixed-return assets *offer* to cover the Brazil risk. The Brazil risk measured through the yields of external debt bonds (Stripped Spread C-Bond and IDU/LIBOR) measures the yield investors *require* to cover the Brazil risk. When the former measure was greater than the latter one, there was a capital inflow. In the same way, when the former was smaller, there was a capital outflow.

This situation, however, seems to have changed recently. As shown in figure 3.4, the Swaps line (domestic interest rate) has been systematically below the Stripped Spread C-Bond line without causing further depreciation.[15] Probably, this new dynamic is associated with more inflow of direct investments in Brazil, which are much less sensitive to the interest rates than the short-run capital that has entered (and left) until the Brazilian real's devaluation of January 1999. Now, we turn to the currency-risk estimation.

3.3.2 Currency Risk

As noted before, the currency risk cannot be measured directly through financial instruments: currency risk is unobservable. In a classic paper, Fama (1984) derived and tested a model for the joint measurement of the currency-risk premium variation and the expected depreciation variation of forward rates. He used data from nine of the most internationally traded currencies in the period of August 1973–December 1982, and he found evidence that both components of forward rates vary with time. The two main conclusions of Fama's paper are the following:

1. The currency-risk premium and the forward market's expected depreciation rates are negatively correlated.
2. Movements in the forward rates are mostly due to risk premium variations.

Garcia and Olivares Leandro (2001) check the validity of these "fundamentals" conclusions of Fama for Brazil, using data of the USD futures market of BM&F from April 1995 to December 1998, a period in which a controlled exchange rate regime was adopted. The first of Fama's conclusions—that the expected depreciation covaries negatively with the risk premium—was refuted, with the estimates indicating a positive correlation between them. The second of Fama's conclusions—that the larger part of futures price variations is due to risk premium variations—was corroborated by the point estimates, although it has not been possible to reject the hypothesis that the variance of risk premium was equal to the variance of expected depreciation rate. Therefore, Fama's (1984) frame-

15. For the recent period, IDU has become less relevant because it lost liquidity due to its short maturity.

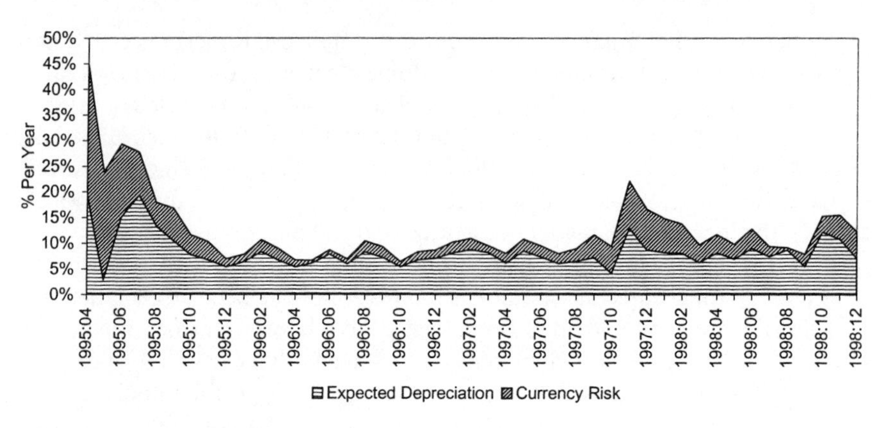

Fig. 3.5 Forward premium analysis

work corroborated the importance of the currency risk in the determination of USD futures price in Brazil, and consequently, as a component of domestic interest rates.

The same analysis was undertaken with another data set. This alternative data set contains daily data for one-month-ahead currency swap contracts traded in BM&F (akin to one-month-ahead forward contracts). The available data cover 10 December 1997 to 19 November 1999. The results obtained show that, before the floating of the Brazilian real in January 1999, the estimates of the slope coefficient of Fama's regression were not usually negative; however, they were close to zero. When the turbulent period of January–February of 1999 was included in the regression, that slope coefficient drastically increased, and after that period, it decreased and oscillated around the (positive) value of 1. This change in level can be explained by change in the exchange rate regime. Brazil abandoned the crawling-peg regime—where the variance in the risk premium was at least as important as (if not even more important than) the variance of the expected devaluation rate—for the floating exchange rate, in which the variance of the expected depreciation became higher than the variance of risk premium.

Garcia and Olivares Leandro (2001) go beyond the indirect measurement of the expected depreciation and currency-risk premium shares allowed for by Fama's framework, and use an econometric technique aimed at estimating a nonobservable variable—the Kalman filter—to estimate the currency risk and the expected depreciation (these two add up to the forward premium).

The resulting estimates for the currency risk and for the expected depreciation obtained by Garcia and Olivares Leandro (2001) are shown in figure 3.5. After estimating the currency risk, the expected depreciation is obtained by subtracting the currency risk from the forward premium. Figure 3.5 shows the analysis of forward premium. This analysis is very use-

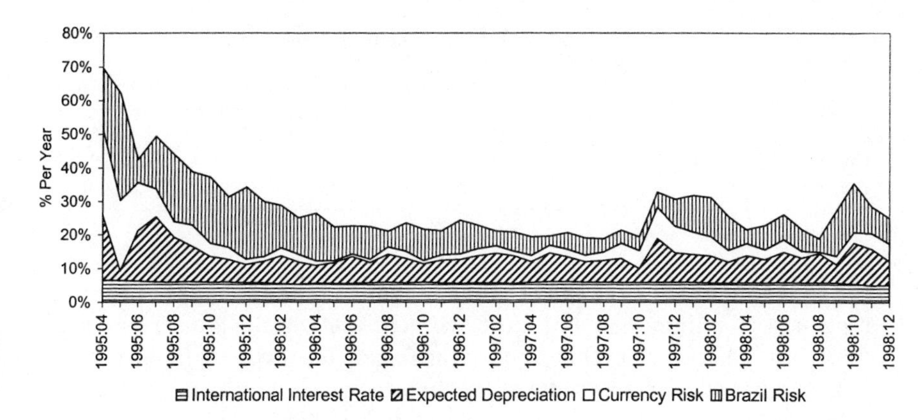

Fig. 3.6 Analysis of domestic interest rate

ful in examining the domestic interest rate, which is the subject of the next section.

3.4 Analysis of the Domestic Interest Rate

3.4.1 Breakdown of the Domestic Interest Rate

From the results obtained by Garcia and Olivares Leandro (2001), it is possible to analyze the domestic interest rate. Based on what was seen earlier (see equation [4]), the domestic interest rate can be decomposed as the sum of the following components:[16]

- International interest rate
- Expected currency depreciation
- Currency risk
- Country risk

Figure 3.6 shows this analysis. To understand the joint behavior of those components, it is interesting to study the correlation among our estimates of currency risk, expected depreciation rate, and the CID (the Brazil risk). Table 3.2 shows the correlation among the variables. Observe that there is a positive correlation between the currency-risk premium and expected depreciation rate, which is consistent with the results of Garcia and Olivares Leandro (2001) using the Fama methodology.[17] On the other side,

16. It should be remembered that the adoption of continuous compounding allows us to express the domestic interest rate as sum of its components.

17. Remember that the so-called *forward premium puzzle* (negative slope coefficient in Fama's regression) is implied by the existence of a negative correlation between the risk premium and the expected depreciation rate, but Garcia and Olivares Leandro (2001) have not found a negative coefficient to Brazil.

Table 3.2 Correlation between Estimates (April 1994–December 1998)

	Expected Depreciation	Currency Risk	Brazil Risk
Expected depreciation	1.000	0.505	0.066
Currency risk		1.000	0.499
Brazil risk			1.000

the CID (the Brazil risk) shows a much higher correlation with the currency-risk premium than with expected depreciation, the latter being almost null. This indicates that some of the factors that explain the currency risk could be the same as some of the factors that explain the Brazil risk. (This is why we call those two risks the *cousin risks*.)

In summary, when using the estimate for the currency-risk premium obtained via the Kalman filter, it was possible to estimate the expected depreciation rate. Garcia and Olivares Leandro (2001) thus calculated the CID, or Brazil risk. The interest rate decomposition exercise showed not only that the covered interest parity cannot be verified in the Brazilian case, but also that CID constitutes a sizeable component of the domestic interest rate. There is a positive correlation between the currency risk and the expected depreciation rate. The Brazil risk shows a high correlation with the currency risk and is almost orthogonal to the expected depreciation, which is an indication that both risks could mostly be explained by common macroeconomic factors. In the next section, some preliminary attempts are made at identifying some macroeconomic factors that lie behind the cousin risks.[18]

3.4.2 Determinants of the Cousin Risks

In this section, a preliminary analysis will be undertaken to identify some of the determinants of Brazil risk and currency risk. It could be argued that the currency-risk premium is due to the fact that it is a systemic risk associated with the inability to diversify relative to the exchange rate. This risk is associated, as is Brazil risk, with the domestic macroeconomic fundamentals and with the external shocks.

An interesting political economy question considers which factors among the macroeconomic fundamentals that affect both currency and Brazil risks are more important, because it is exactly these that should be confronted to allow a more effective fall in interest rates. For example, if Brazil risk and currency risk are both determined by fragile fiscal fundamentals, an improvement in these conditions would bring about a sub-

18. The purpose is to investigate the determinants of both the Brazil Risk and the currency risk. However, we still do not have any reliable estimate of currency risk for the period after the devaluation of the Brazilian real, restricting subsection 3.4.2.

stantial fall in interest rates. If these risks are determined mainly by doubts about balance-of-payments sustainability, however, it will not be an improvement in the fiscal situation that could bring a significant decrease in interest rates. We now turn to the study of these determinants.

One of the main determinants of a country's (say, Brazil's) risk is the convertibility risk—i.e., the risk associated with the possibility of being unable to convert Brazilian reaies into foreign currency. This risk encompasses the possibility that capital controls may be introduced preventing the international transfer of funds, but that they do not include the default risk (which is included in the country risk).

To obtain one measure of this convertibility risk, a data set of implied currency depreciation in Brazilian reaies' nondeliverable forwards (NDFs) contracts traded in New York was used, subtracting the expected depreciation measured by swap contracts from the NDFs as it was done to calculate one of the measures of Brazil risk. Hence the difference between these expected depreciations is a proxy for the convertibility risk.[19]

In other words, an NDF contract is essentially the same as the currency swap (or futures) contract traded in BM&F in São Paulo, except for the fact that the contract traded in New York is settled in U.S. dollars and the contract traded in São Paulo is settled in Brazilian reaies. For example, an investor who had bet on the Brazilian real devaluation before January 1999 would have made a lot of money, but the gain would have been paid in dollars in New York and in reaies in Brazil. Under free convertibility, both gains would be the same, because it would be possible to obtain U.S. dollars with the equivalent sum of Brazilian reaies. However, if any controls were imposed on the remittance of U.S. dollars to the foreign country after the devaluation, the two amounts would not be the same. The investor who traded in São Paulo would receive Brazilian reaies (nominally) equivalent to the U.S. dollar, but would be unable to receive the equivalent amount in dollars. In the past, when this kind of situation happened, the so-called black market of U.S. dollars traded at a huge premium. It is because of this convertibility risk that the price of the U.S. dollar in the NDFs (measured by the inverse of the price of Brazilian real NDF) is higher than the USD futures traded in the BM&F in São Paulo. The difference between prices is transformed into annual yields, with the results shown in panel A of figure 3.7.

In this figure, it is possible to observe that a learning process concerning the pricing of the convertibility risk occurred. Until the Asian crisis, the convertibility risk was around zero (i.e., the markets were not pricing the convertibility risk). Therefore, during this period until the first crisis (the Asian crisis), the *convenience yield*—the yield that reflects the differences

19. All data are daily and relative to the one-year period from December 1995 to June 2001.

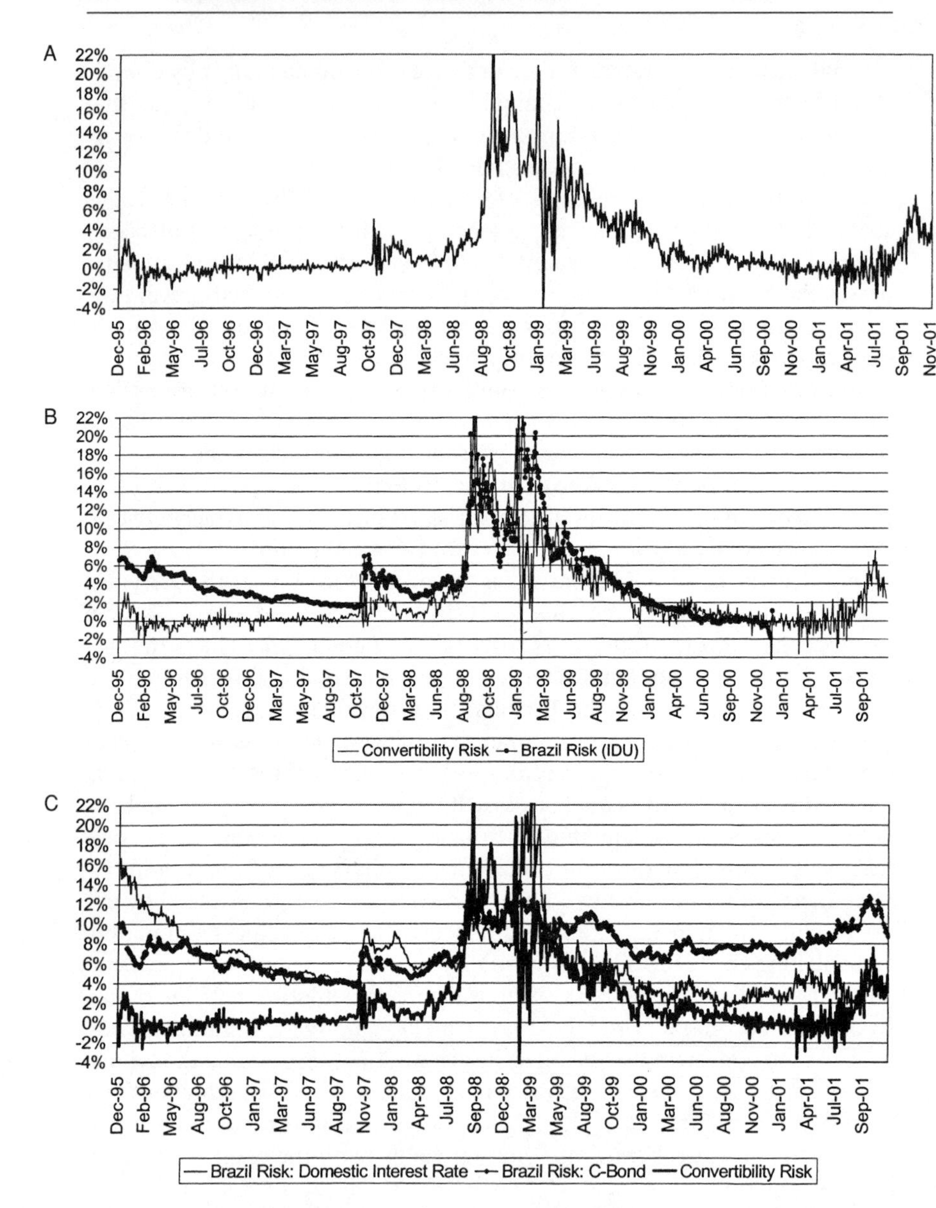

Fig. 3.7 Convertibility risk: *A,* convertibility risk only; *B,* convertibility risk and country risk; *C,* convertibility risk in Brazil

Sources: Bloomberg (panels A, B, and C); BM&F and Federal Reserve System (panel C).

between the prices of contracts traded in New York and those traded in São Paulo—did not reflect the convertibility risk.

When the Asian crisis erupted in October 1997, the market suddenly learned that those two contracts were not equal, i.e., that the contracts traded in São Paulo had a higher risk than the NDFs traded in New

York—namely, the convertibility risk. At that time, stories were flying about arbitrageurs who sold USD futures in New York and bought them in São Paulo, thinking that they were completely hedged in their investments. When the Asian crisis happened and the arbitrageurs found out they were carrying risks and not arbitraging, they rushed to close out their positions, selling in São Paulo and buying in New York, which might have instigated the sudden jump in the convertibility risk that is seen in panel A of figure 3.7.[20]

Since the convertibility risk is one of the components of the country (Brazil) risk, it is interesting to compare the behavior of the two risks. In panel B of figure 3.7, the Brazil risk is measured by the Brazil risk (IDU) measure, whose duration is shorter than that of the C-Bond. In panel C, the Brazil risk is measured by the stripped spread of the C-Bond (Brazil Risk: C-Bond) and by Brazil Risk: Domestic Interest Rate.

Note that after the Asian crisis, the convertibility risk became closer to the country risk, but now at a positive level, in contrast with the earlier period. Thus, after the Asian crisis, convertibility risk and country risk began to move together.

During the Russian crisis (August 1998) and the fall of LTCM, the convertibility risk jumped again, rising to extremely high levels in comparison to the preceding periods. Then it became of similar magnitude of the country risk, and in the subsequent very turbulent periods, it became even higher than the latter.

Thus, after the Asian crisis, markets learned to price convertibility risk, which then became an important component of the country (Brazil) risk, and both risks began to exhibit similar behavior. The worse the crisis, the more important the convertibility risk became in explaining country risk. When the economic environment improved after the devaluation, the convertibility risk began a soft fall, although it has not returned to negligible levels previous to the Asian crisis, remaining at a positive (although lower) level.

Now we will analyze another determinant of Brazil risk: the situation of the external fixed-return market. Different kinds of financial instruments have different kinds of credit risk, with U.S. Treasury bonds having zero credit risk. The appetite of international markets for credit risk (inversely related to the degree of risk aversion for credit risk) varies over time. For example, the collapse of LTCM started a process of flight to quality, in which the investors suddenly became more risk averse and tried to sell all their riskier assets to invest the funds in safe U.S. Treasury bonds. This movement affected Brazilian bonds in a negative way, despite the remarkable improvements in domestic fundamentals that followed the International Monetary Fund (IMF) agreement in the last quarter of 1998.

20. Brazilian tax laws could have played a role, as well as fears that a possible bankruptcy of many institutions could threaten the clearinghouse solvency.

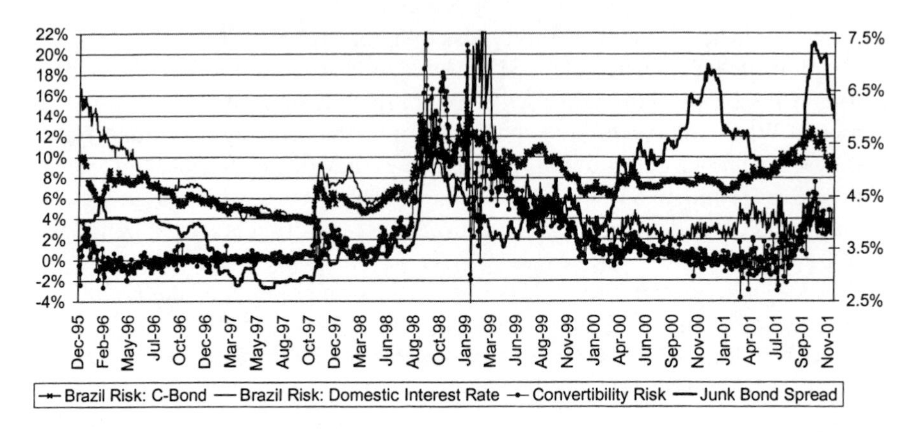

Fig. 3.8 Brazil-risk components
Sources: Bloomberg, BM&F, and Federal Reserve System.

To measure the demand side for the Brazilian bonds, or the degree of risk aversion, the U.S. Ten-Year Junk Bond Spread[21] was used. In this spread, all U.S. junk bonds whose credit ratings are the same as those for Brazilian sovereign debt are included, i.e., bonds that have lower ratings, below Baa (or BBB or B2, in the case of private bonds), according to credit rating agencies such as Standard and Poor's and Moody's.[22]

Therefore, the U.S. Ten-Year Junk Bond Spread measures the appetite for risk of the U.S. fixed-rate market; the higher the spread, the lower the appetite for risk. Figure 3.8 shows the U.S. Ten-Year Junk Bond Spread data (on the right-hand-side scale) together with the other measures of country risk and convertibility risk (on the left-hand-side scale). Observe that the demand for riskier bonds in the United States worsened when LTCM collapsed after the Russian crisis, improved after that and worsened again in 2000, reaching the same levels as during the 1998 crisis. This is a factor of utmost importance affecting Brazilian bond prices and, through capital flows, domestic interest rates as well. Needless to say, it is impossible to have any control over that important demand-side variable.

To improve the comparison, we calculated the correlations between the Stripped Spread of C-Bond (C-Bond), Brazil Risk measured with Swaps (BR), Convertibility Risk (RC), Junk-Bond Spread (JBS), and implied depreciation present in swap contracts (called the forward premium, or FP). These correlations were computed for different subsamples, with the results displayed in table 3.3.

Table 3.3 corroborates our previous conclusion that the market did not

21. Data are obtained from Bloomberg.
22. For a detailed analysis of the relation between the ratings of these agencies and country risk, see appendix C.

Table 3.3 **Correlations**

	C-Bond: RC	RC: FP	C-Bond: FP	BR: JBS	C-Bond: JBS	BR: RC
Precrises (until October 1997)	–0.1302	0.1619	–0.3946	0.7835	0.8327	0.0766
Controlled exchange rate (until December 1998)	0.7399	0.4399	0.2467	0.6409	0.8626	0.1689
Floating exchange rate (since January 1999)	0.68227	0.4193	0.79327	–0.45289	–0.40608	0.70091
Floating exchange rate (since June 99)	0.77216	0.67391	0.75058	–0.51784	–0.31865	0.87168
Crises (controlled exchange rate) (until December 1998)	0.8984	0.0303	0.1595	0.6633	0.8848	0.6186

Note: See text for abbreviations.

price the convertibility risk until the Asian crisis, since its correlation with Brazil risk (in both measures used) was very small. However, as the period increases (including the period until December 1998), this correlation becomes stronger, especially when the correlation between the Convertibility Risk and Stripped Spread of C-Bond is considered. The strong correlation between Convertibility Risk and Brazil Risk is maintained (and it becomes even higher with RB) in the period when the Brazilian economy was under a floating exchange rate regime, after the crisis period (since June 1999). In the crisis periods, the strong positive correlation with Brazil Risk is maintained. However, observing the correlation between convertibility risk and one-year expected depreciation measured by swaps contracts traded on BM&F, it can be seen that this increases with time. The correlation, with a maximum value of 0.67, however, does not become stronger.

Thus, two important results associated with the relevance of convertibility risk can be observed through these comparisons. The first one is related to the learning process that has occurred with NDF Brazilian real contracts traded in New York. The second result is related to changes in the composition of Brazil risk in crisis periods, during which the convertibility risk becomes the most important component.

Another important and interesting result is the increase in the correlation between the forward premium and Brazil risk measured through C-Bonds after the adoption of a floating exchange rate. One possible conjecture is that, with a floating exchange rate regime, the increase in country risk affects not only currency risk, as occurred in the controlled exchange rate period, but also the expected currency depreciation, resulting in a higher correlation with the forward premium (which is the sum of expected depreciation and currency risk).

However, it is clear that these are not the only determinants of currency and Brazil risks. Truly, these are only two of the determinants of them. Variables that reflect the expected future behavior of fiscal and balance-of-

Table 3.4 Regressions

Independent Variable	OLS	2SLS	GMM
Constant	–0.226	–0.179	–0.726***
	(0.88)	(0.68)	(4.74)
CBOND_SPREAD (–1)	0.765***	0.784***	0.696***
	(14.36)	(14.63)	(17.78)
PSBR_EXP1Y	–3.493***	–3.320***	–5.284***
	(3.43)	(3.29)	(7.33)
CA_EXP1Y	0.121	0.101	0.273***
	(1.43)	(1.15)	(5.21)
JBS	0.110**	0.101**	0.163***
	(2.32)	(2.15)	(5.47)
IBOVESPA_USS	–0.587***	–0.664***	–0.477***
	(9.14)	(4.72)	(6.36)
Observations	107	103	103
R^2	0.94	0.94	0.93

Notes: This table shows the regressions of C-Bond spread on its lagged value, PSBR_EXP1Y, CA_EXP1Y, JBS, and IBOVESPA_USS using two different methods: 2SLS and GMM. They include as instruments five lags of each regressor. The standard errors and covariances are White-heterocedasticity consistent in 2SLS estimations. Absolute value of *t*-statistics in parentheses. See text for abbreviations.

***Significant at the 1 percent level.

**Significant at the 5 percent level.

payments accounts, as well as variables that reflect the degree of domestic financial market instability, should also be considered in an analysis of this kind.

Table 3.4 shows the results obtained from a regression analysis with the purpose of explaining Brazil risk measured by the Stripped Spread of C-Bonds. The sample period is the floating exchange rate period, from May 1999 to June 2001, with weekly data. The variables included in the regression are as follows:

- One-year-ahead expected domestic fiscal conditions (public-sector borrowing requirements, nominal public surplus, in percentage of gross domestic product, or PSBR_EXP1Y);
- One-year-ahead expected current account deficit (CA_EXP1Y);
- International financial market conditions, measured by the credit derivative that provides the spread between high-yield U.S. corporate bonds and the U.S. Treasury bond of equivalent duration (junk bond spread, or JBS); and
- Domestic financial market conditions, measured by the domestic stock exchange return in U.S. dollars (IBOVESPA_USS).

The expected signs are the following: negative for the expected nominal surplus (the greater the expected public deficit, the higher the country risk); positive for the expected current account deficit (the greater the ex-

Table 3.5 **Regressions: Alternative Specification**

Independent Variable	2SLS	GMM
Constant	–1.253***	–2.394***
	(3.52)	(5.54)
PSBR_EXP1Y	–16.409***	–16.528***
	(19.32)	(18.07)
CA_EXP1Y	0.578***	0.935***
	(3.52)	(7.49)
JBS	0.531***	0.488***
	(9.32)	(10.05)
IBOVESPA_USS	–0.756***	–0.320***
	(2.85)	(2.73)
Observations	103	103
R^2	0.80	0.80

Notes: This table shows the regressions of C-Bond Spread on PSBR_EXP1Y, CA_EXP1Y, JBS, and IBOVESPA_USS using two different methods: 2SLS and GMM. They include as instruments five lags of each regressor. The standard errors and covariances are White-heterocedasticity consistent in 2SLS estimations. Absolute value of *t*-statistics in parentheses. See text for abbreviations.

***Significant at the 1 percent level.

pected current account deficit, the higher the country risk); positive for the junk bond spread (the higher the credit-risk spread, the higher the country risk); and negative for the stock market returns (the higher the returns, the lower the country risk).

The one-year-ahead expected variables come from a weekly survey conducted by the Brazilian central bank with major Brazilian financial institutions.[23] Using them on the regression analysis, we try to capture the market expectations that are essential in the perception of a country risk. To take into account the endogeneity and simultaneity of the regressors, appropriate methods to estimate these regressions would be the two-stage least squares (2SLS) and generalized method of moments (GMM). Both methods were estimated using as instruments five lags of each regressor.

The results are quite good. All variables included in the regression have the right sign and become significant in the GMM analysis. The *R*-squared is quite high and the regression passed both autocorrelation and normality tests.[24]

An important thing to notice is the CBOND_SPREAD lagged component. If it is excluded from the regression, as in table 3.5, in spite of the fall on *R*-squared, all coefficients are still significant and all variables still have the right sign. Thus, not only this CBOND_SPREAD lagged component is relevant in the analysis but also all the other variables analyzed. Nevertheless, given the small sample (108 observations), further testing is needed.

23. These data are available at the central bank Web site [www.bcb.gov.br].

24. See appendix D for statistical tests on those variables to corroborate these estimations.

3.5 Conclusion: What Are the Determinants of Such High Real Interest Rates?

We reviewed the arguments in the finance and open macroeconomics literature that are relevant for the central bank to set the level of the interest rate in an open economy. Several relevant concepts were shown and analyzed through several financial instruments traded in domestic and international markets, especially financial derivatives. Country risk (Brazil risk) was measured with different financial instruments and currency risk was estimated through the Kalman filter.

We show that—besides the currency risk, which is also relevant in developed economies—the country risk (Brazil risk) is important to determine the domestic interest rates. Brazil risk and currency risk have a strong positive correlation (0.5) for the controlled exchange rate period of the Real Plan. This suggests that both risks might share common causes, which justifies their being called the cousin risks. Thus, when and if the common causes are confronted, the fall of domestic interest rates can be substantial, because both currency and Brazil risks may fall at the same time.

Although we have not yet been able to provide reliable estimates for currency risk from the floating exchange rate period, the fact is that the correlation between Brazil risk and the forward premium (which is the sum of currency risk and expected depreciation) significantly increased after the change in the exchange rate regime—i.e., in the current floating exchange rate regime, the determinants of Brazil risk seem to affect the exchange rate (via currency risk and via expected depreciation) and the domestic interest rates much more strongly.

Preliminary results identify the components of Brazil risk, e.g., the fiscal results, and the domestic and international financial markets conditions. The convertibility risk, defined as risk associated with the possibility of being unable to convert Brazilian reaies into foreign currency, showed up as an important cause of Brazil risk during the international financial crisis periods, but is no longer relevant.

If one assumes that the real exchange rate will remain constant, it is possible to make an educated guess of the currency-risk size, and to compare it to the Brazil risk. Although these measures have varied a lot in the floating rate period, it is clear that the currency risk remains quite high, despite the floating regime, whereas the country risk has been substantially reduced. Therefore, it seems that the main benefits of the battle for a fall in domestic real interest rates are in the determinants of currency risk, which should be associated with the sustainability of the balance of payments, especially the behavior of the current account and thus the behavior of imports and exports.

Noting that the expected future behavior of the current account deficits also showed up as an important determinant of the Brazil risk, we speculate that improvements on the sustainability of the current account are likely to produce a large fall in the domestic interest rate, since they will affect both the currency and the country risks. These improvements should come from stronger export growth, which must result much more from productivity gains than from further real depreciation, given the already historically high (depreciated) level of the real exchange rate. To achieve continued productivity gains in the future, the reforms that were all but paralyzed—labor, social security, tax, financial, privatization—must be pushed forward by the president who will take office in 2003.

The mirror image of improving the current account sustainability is the improvement of domestic saving. Recently, private saving has hovered around 19 percent of gross domestic product (GDP) while the public saving has been negative (around 3 percent of GDP), with external saving (the current account deficit) filling the gap for an investment rate a little over 20 percent of GDP. To achieve sustained growth rates on the order of 4 to 5 percent per year, investment will have to rise by a few percentage points of GDP, and so must the domestic saving rate, since the current account deficit is already believed to be as high as can be financed by international markets. The reforms mentioned above should help to improve domestic saving. Other measures, such as the rebuilding of a financial market for mortgages and programs for lower-income houses, should help increasing domestic saving and investment. Nevertheless, improvement of domestic saving will remain the key challenge to achieve sustainable growth in Brazil in the next decades. If we are able to improve domestic saving, that shall contribute to lower the country and currency risks substantially (through the current account sustainability effect explained before), thereby reducing real interest rates and fostering growth.

As highlighted in Caballero (chapter 5 in this volume), even if Brazil increases its domestic saving rate, the vagaries of international capital markets will continue to hurt economic growth. The high country and currency risks are in great measure a result of this state of affairs. The increasing integration of the Brazilian economy, both financial and through expanded trade, should help to lower the cousin risks. However, the road ahead may prove much bumpier than this optimistic scenario.

Appendix A
Data Set

Domestic Interest Rate

The domestic interest rate used is the swap DI × Pre for 360 days. Swap is an exchange of risk, without the transfer of principal, and what matters is the difference between the yields of each side of the contract traded. It is possible to say that they are really forward contracts. In an interest rate swap, which in this case is the swap DI × Pre, the investor who buys one contract is investing his or her money at a floating interest rate (CDI/CETIP – DI variation)[25] and paying a fixed interest rate (Pre side). The quotation of those contracts is given by the Pre rate (based on 360 days), which is used in the calculation of Brazil risk.

International Interest Rate

The country chosen as representative of the rest of the world was the United States. As a proxy for international interest rates that captures expectations for one year, we used the Treasury Constant Maturity Rate (one-year, published by the U.S. Board of Governors of the Federal Reserve). This one-year expected interest rate, composed of the yields of traded bonds in the U.S. financial market, is adjusted to reflect this constant maturity of one year. The adjustment used interpolations of daily yield curves, based on the yields (bid yields of end of the day, closed market) of U.S. Treasury securities traded in the so-called over-the-counter market (i.e., a contract that it is settled directly by traders and not through a financial institution, as when done by phone). These yields are calculated through the composition of prices obtained by the Federal Reserve Bank of New York. Therefore, even if there is no bond with this maturity, through this methodology it is possible to obtain a price for a bond with that maturity.

Expected Devaluation and Currency Risk Premium

To measure the expected devaluation in a certain period, the Dol × Pre currency swap rate would be the correct one to use. However, these contracts do not have enough liquidity to reflect economic agents' expectations accurately. Thus, the information in DI × Pre and DI × Dol interest rate swap contracts[26] are analyzed together and could give us the information in the Dol × Pre currency swaps. Swaps contracts were explained before, and because they are very similar to forward contracts, we can use them as a good indication of the market's expected devaluation. These two contracts are among the most liquid, if the period since 1999 is considered. Hence this calculation is not merely an abstract measurement of expected devaluation in the economy—it should be very close to the true measure

25. CDI/CETIP is an interest rate published by CETIP (Central de Custódia e de Liquidação Financeira de Títulos), which is an average of CDI market traded rates; CDI is a fixed-income bond representing credit operations among banks.

26. Considering, for example, the data set of May 2000, the number of opened Swap DI × Pre contracts was 4, 875, 496, reflecting a financial traded volume of US$24, 440, 704.00, with 893, 820 traded contracts. Of the DI × Dol Swaps contracts, 1, 304, 542 contracts were opened, reflecting a traded volume of US$7, 086, 790.00 with 259, 237 traded contracts, while only 1, 127 contracts were opened for Dol × Pre swap contracts and none of them was traded.

of it. One of the advantages of this data set could be the reduction of costs associated with this kind of transaction through the aggregate of all these costs (transaction costs, borrowing costs, and the cost of hedging) into two contracts.

In a DI × Dol currency swap contract, there is an exchange of two floating rates. Whoever takes the long position in this contract receives the yield of DI and pays USD depreciation in the period of the contract, plus a known fixed interest rate (known as the *coupon* on U.S. dollar–linked bonds). The price of that contract is given by that interest rate, which is linear and based on a 360-days basis.[27]

Thus, the USD expected devaluation was calculated through the difference between the quotations of DI × pre and cleaned coupon on U.S. dollar–linked bonds[28] of DI × Dol swap contracts. However, a risk premium is inherent in the expected devaluation measured through swaps contracts. That risk premium can give a biased estimate of expected devaluation if compared to what really is going to occur in the period.

Appendix B

Brazil Risk: Short Run 3 Medium Run

Figure 3B.1 shows Brazil risk as analyzed previously through swap contracts and a measure of the short run[29] (three months), calculated in the same way as the other measure, although it uses the USD futures market traded in BM&F. Thus the differences between these two measures of Brazil Risk reflect basic differences due to the short and medium run. One fact evident in this comparison in figure 3B.1 is the higher volatility of the short-run measure: for the period of January 1995–June 2001, it is 6.2 percent, higher than the volatility of the other measure (which reflects one-year Brazil Risk, at 4.2 percent). This reflects the fact that short-run expectations are more sensitive to daily changes in financial markets. Generally, these fluctuations are due to very specific factors that might have affected the expectations only on that specific day, but they are associated with very short-run expectations and are not supposed to affect the medium- and long-run economic conditions. Therefore, the analysis of Brazil Risk measured with Swaps is much more interesting and adequate relative to the other measure with USD futures contracts.

27. For a detailed description of these contracts, see BM&F's Web site [www.bmf.com.br].

28. Cumpom Cambial data were cleaned through the methodology described in Lemgruber (1999).

29. This Brazil risk measure was used in Garcia and Valpassos (2000).

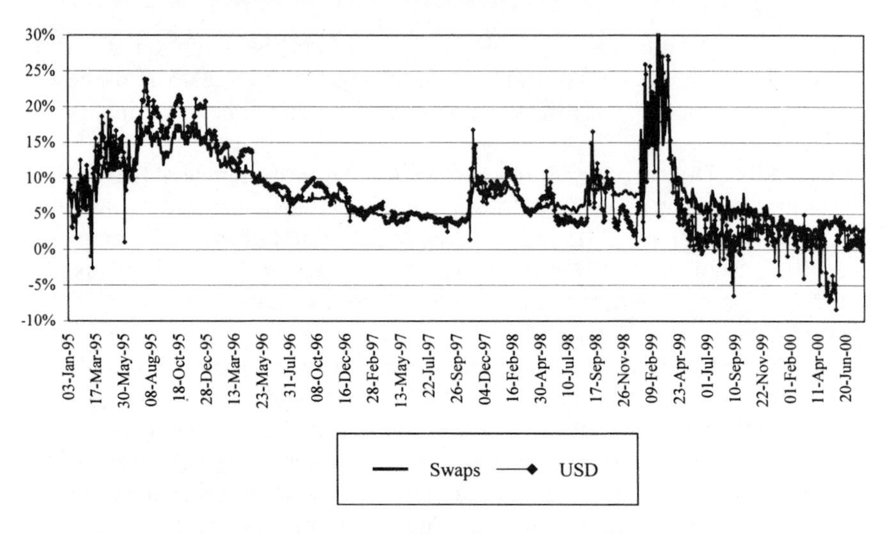

Fig. 3B.1 Brazil risk: short run × medium run
Sources: Banco Central do Brasil, BM&F, and Federal Reserve System.

Appendix C
Credit Rating Agencies

The risk of a bond issued by any government in a foreign currency is related to the fact that this government could possibly be unable to issue money to pay its debt. Therefore, the role of a credit rating agency is to try to analyze the ability and willingness of the government to generate enough foreign exchange to pay back its obligations. In this way, the sovereign rating should be the highest in a certain country, and any other private issuance should not be able to receive a higher classification than that sovereign ceiling. This is due to the fact that the government has the legal power to intervene through currency controls in the capacity of all private firms to meet their obligations denominated in foreign currency. Fitch IBCA Ratings, for example, considers in its analysis not only public obligations, but also private ones denominated in foreign currencies to analyze the need of a certain country to generate foreign exchanges. This is due to the fact that in the 1980s there was a renegotiation of external debts by several governments that took responsibility for the private-sector debt as well.

To Moody's and Standard and Poor's, the credit rating is an opinion about the future ability, legal obligation, and willingness of the issuer to make all the payments. Therefore, its objective is strictly to analyze the credit conditions of the issuer and the possibilities of default, considering the guarantees given by the issuer and the size of the possible losses for

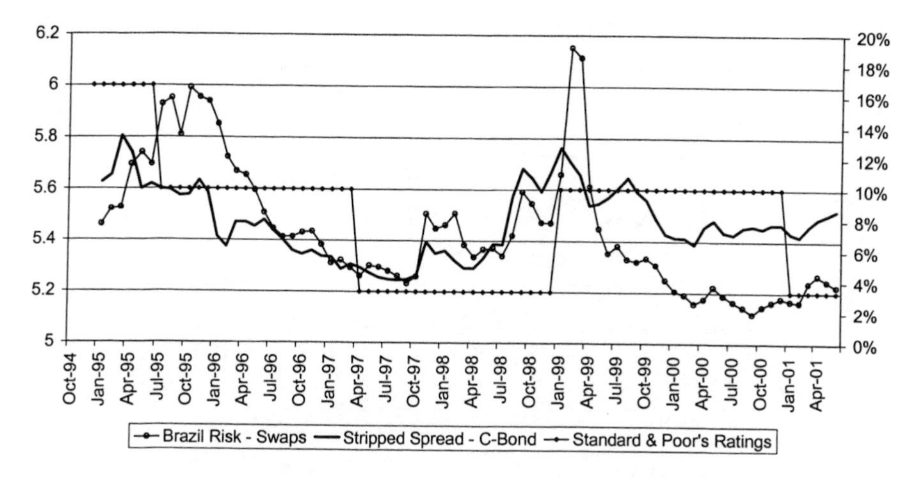

Fig. 3C.1 Rating: Standard and Poor's
Sources: Bloomberg, BM&F, and Federal Reserve System.

someone who buys that credit instrument. To analyze the so-called sovereign ceiling, the agencies consider the macroeconomic fundamentals of a certain economy, including implied volatility in the economy. To do that, they consider variables that could in some way foresee possible problems; these variables include growth, inflation, current account, and unemployment level as well as other, less evident variables such as the flexibility of an economy and its openness. However, these credit ratings do not measure, for example, risks related to the lost of market value of these credit instruments and risks related to bilateral conflicts between the issuer's country and the institution's country, where the issue took place. Another risk that is not incorporated in these ratings is convertibility risk, i.e., whether the payment of a certain obligation would be affected by any kind of control adopted by the government in relation to the currency of denomination.

Observe in figures 3C.1–3C.3 the actions related to Brazilian long-term debt (denominated in foreign currency) of the three credit rating agencies: Standard and Poor's, Moody's, and Fitch IBCA, for the period of the Real Plan. Observe in particular the lagged behavior[30] of these agencies in comparison to the behavior of Brazil risk, measured by swaps (defined earlier) and the stripped spread of the C-Bond.

30. Credit rating agencies classify in a very similar way long-run debts denominated in foreign currency of countries. To transform these ratings into values that could be observed in a figure, a scale from zero to 10 was created, with 10 being the worst possible classification. That is, the values were arbitrary in such a way that when there is an improvement in credit rating of the country, it would be shown in the figure by a decline in the relative values of this classification. In that way, there will be a positive correlation between country risk and these ratings.

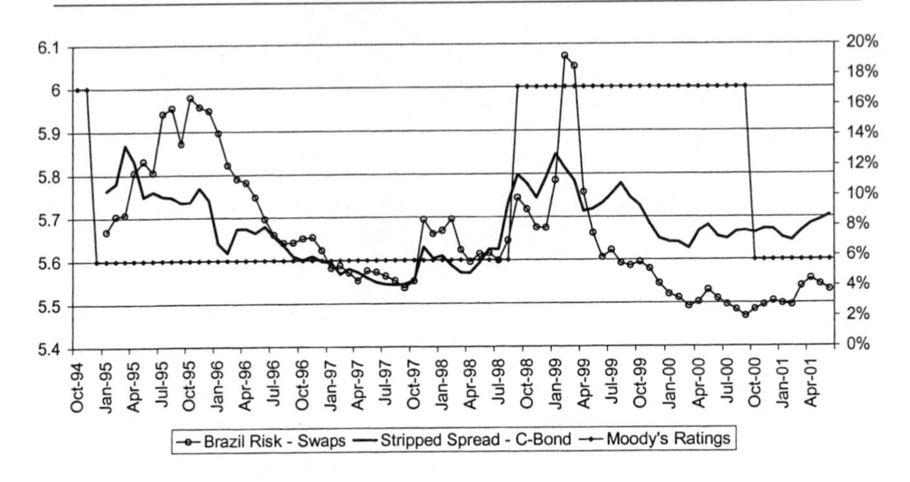

Fig. 3C.2 Rating: Moody's
Sources: Bloomberg, BM&F, and Federal Reserve System.

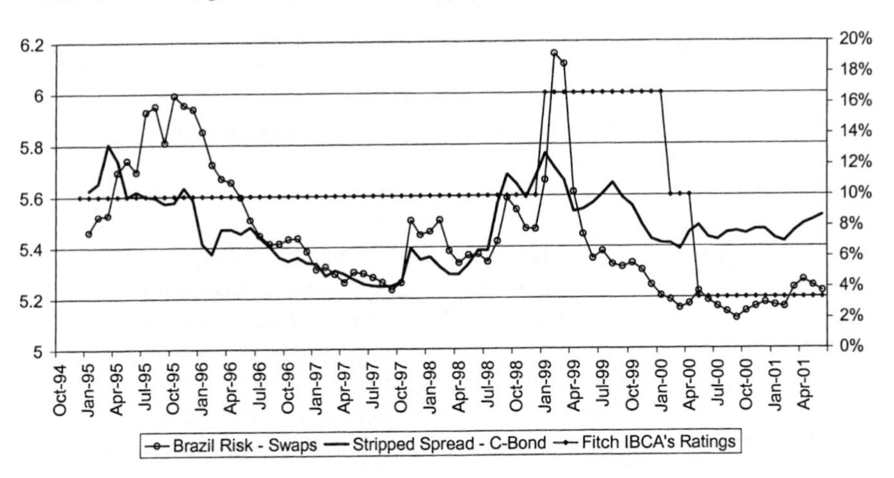

Fig. 3C.3 Rating: Fitch IBCA
Sources: Bloomberg, BM&F, and Federal Reserve System.

Throughout figures 3C.1–3C.3, it is possible to see the conservative behavior of certain agencies such as Moody's. Eighteen months after the adoption of a floating exchange rate regime in Brazil, in January of 1999, Moody's still had not changed its B2 rating of Brazilian long-term debt denominated in foreign currency. However, Fitch IBCA changed its rating twice in the same period, improving its rating from B in January 1999 to BB+.

Appendix D
Statistical Tests

In this appendix we analyze causality, unit roots, and possible cointegration relationships among those variables used in the regression analysis. Figure 3D.1 graphs those time-series data, from May 1999 to June 2001.

To test the existence of a unit root on those variables we performed augmented Dickey-Fuller tests using four lags, without a constant or a trend (DF), with a constant but without a trend (DFc), and with a constant and a trend (DFc, t). The results are in tables 3D.1–3D.5.

Some of these variables have a unit root; thus, it is essential to test cointegration with the dependent variable CBOND_SPREAD. We proceed using the Johansen cointegration test with four lags and with the test assumption of a linear deterministic trend in the data (tables 3D.6–3D.8). As seen the tables, none of the variables is cointegrated with CBOND_SPREAD. We then go a step further, testing cointegration among all variables (see table 3D.9).

Now, considering IBOVESPA_USS as an exogenous variable, the results change. However, one should consider the fact that these results are shown to be extremely sensitive to changes in test specifications (table 3D.10). To analyze causality in that data set, we use Granger causality tests, as seen in table 3D.11. These Granger causality tests did not indicate any bivariate causality in this data set. However, this test does not entirely fit our analysis. Thus, it follows an analysis of restricted and unrestricted vector autoregressions (VARs). Table 3D.12 shows the unrestricted system (VARs) and table 3D.13 shows the restricted one vector error correction, or VEC). The restricted system has cointegration restrictions and should be used with nonstationary series that are known to be cointegrated. The VEC specification restricts the long-run behavior of endogenous variables to converge to their cointegration relationships, while allowing for a wide range of short-run dynamics. The cointegration term is known as the *error correction term* because the deviation from the long-run equilibrium is corrected gradually through a series of partial, short-run adjustments.

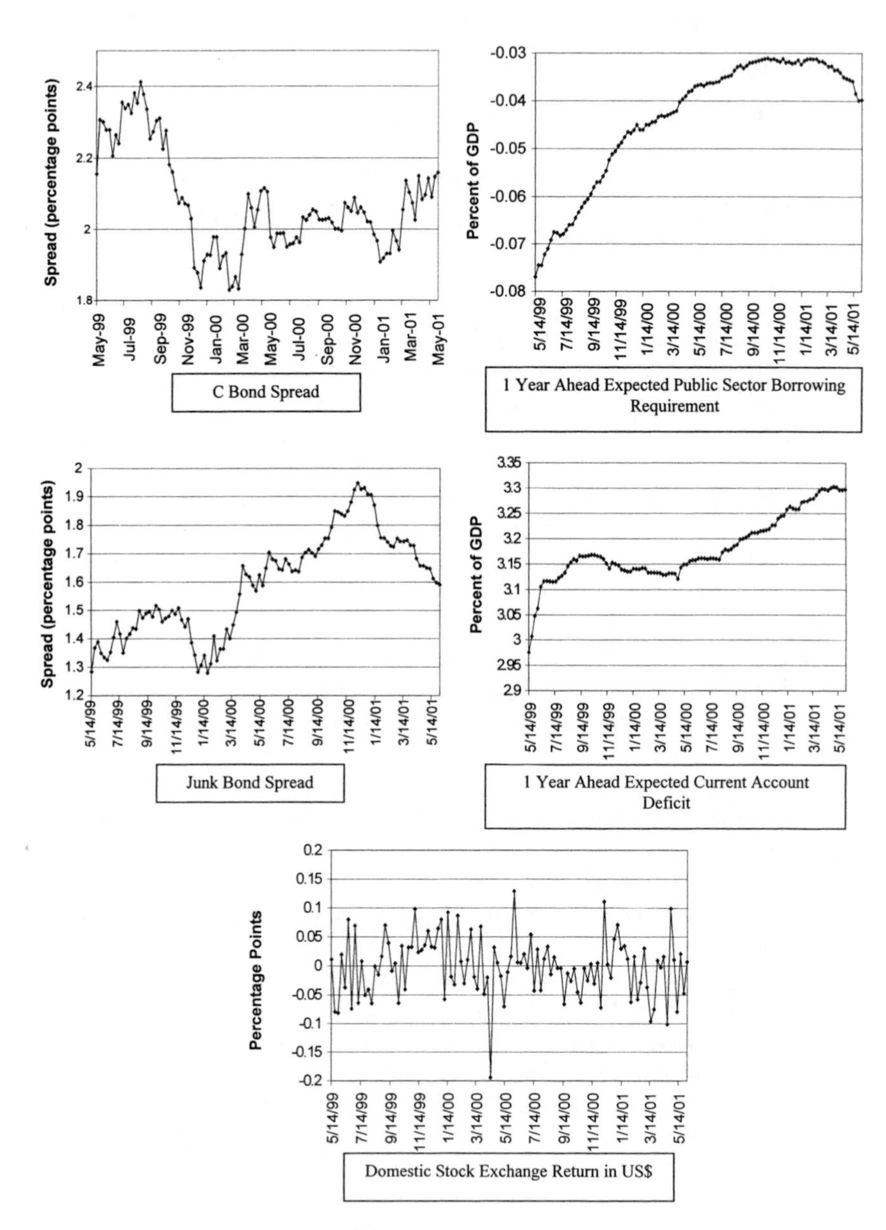

Fig. 3D.1 Macroeconomic variables time-series charts

Sources: Banco Central do Brasil and Bloomberg.

Table 3D.1 **Unit Root Test on CBOND_SPREAD**

	Test Statistics	Critical Value[a]
DF	–0.4067	–1.9432
DFc	–1.8008	–2.8895
DFc, t	–1.3113	–3.4535

Note: See text for abbreviations.

[a]MacKinnon critical values for rejection of hypothesis of a unit root.

Table 3D.2 **Unit Root Test on PSBR_EXP1Y**

	Test Statistics	Critical Value[a]
DF	–0.9949	–1.9432
DFc	–2.2712	–2.8895
DFc, t	1.0982	–3.4535

Note: See text for abbreviations.

[a]MacKinnon critical values for rejection of hypothesis of a unit root.

Table 3D.3 **Unit Root Test on CA_EXP1Y**

	Test Statistics	Critical Value[a]
DF	2.4719[a]	–1.9432
DFc	0.6896	–2.8895
DFc, t	–1.1640	–3.4535

Note: See text for abbreviations.

[a]MacKinnon critical values for rejection of hypothesis of a unit root.

Table 3D.4 **Unit Root Test on IBOVESPA_USS**

	Test Statistics	Critical Value[a]
DF	–3.4747*	–1.9432
DFc	–3.4558*	–2.8897
DFc, t	–3.6570*	–3.4535

Note: See text for abbreviations.

[a]MacKinnon critical values for rejection of hypothesis of a unit root.

*Statistically significant.

Table 3D.5 **Unit Root Test on JBS**

	Test Statistics	Critical Value[a]
DF	0.4487	–1.9432
DFc	–1.6515	–2.8895
DFc, t	–1.0975	–3.4535

Note: See text for abbreviations.

[a]MacKinnon critical values for rejection of hypothesis of a unit root.

Table 3D.6 **Johansen Cointegration Test on CBOND_SPREAD and PSBR_EXP1Y**

Eigenvalue	Likelihood Ratio	5% Critical Value	1% Critical Value	Hypothesized No. of Cointegrating Equations
0.86386	11.41116	15.41	20.04	None
0.020233	2.105354	3.76	6.65	At most, 1

Unnormalized cointegrating coefficients

CBOND_SPREAD	PSBR_EXP1Y	
0.762842	15.42873	
0.841066	0.118837	

Normalized cointegrating coefficients: 1 cointegrating equation[a]

CBOND_SPREAD	PSBR_EXP1Y	C
1.000000	20.22533	–1.209678
	(7.09556)	
Log-likelihood	790.4427	

Notes: Test assumption: linear deterministic trend in the data. Likelihood ratio rejects any cointegration at the 5 percent significance level. See text for explanation of abbreviations.

[a]Asymptotic standard errors in parentheses.

Table 3D.7 **Johansen Cointegration Test on CBOND_SPREAD and CA_EXP1Y**

Eigenvalue	Likelihood Ratio	5% Critical Value	1% Critical Value	Hypothesized No. of Cointegrating Equations
0.040800	4.533449	15.41	20.04	None
0.002356	0.242905	3.76	6.65	At most, 1

Unnormalized cointegrating coefficients		
CBOND_SPREAD	CA_EXP1Y	
0.792176	–0.071595	
0.166946	1.768379	
Normalized cointegrating coefficients: 1 cointegrating equation[a]		
CBOND_SPREAD	CA_EXP1Y	C
1.000000	–0.090378	–1.777256
	(1.07559)	
Log-likelihood	571.4778	

Notes: Test assumption: linear deterministic trend in the data. Likelihood ratio rejects any cointegration at the 5 percent significance level. See text for explanation of abbreviations.
[a]Asymptotic standard errors in parentheses.

Table 3D.8 **Johansen Cointegration Test on CBOND_SPREAD and JBS**

Eigenvalue	Likelihood Ratio	5% Critical Value	1% Critical Value	Hypothesized No. of Cointegrating Equations
0.036625	7.151501	15.41	20.04	None
0.031609	3.308274	3.76	6.65	At most, 1

Unnormalized cointegrating coefficients		
CBOND_SPREAD	JBS	
0.082485	0.587684	
0.766989	0.104562	
Normalized cointegrating coefficients: 1 cointegrating equation[a]		
CBOND_SPREAD	JBS	C
1.000000	7.124756	–13.46704
	(32.8385)	
Log-likelihood	369.4658	

Notes: Test assumption: linear deterministic trend in the data. Likelihood ratio rejects any cointegration at the 5 percent significance level. See text for explanation of abbreviations.
[a]Asymptotic standard errors in parentheses.

Table 3D.9 **Johansen Cointegration Test on CBOND_SPREAD and All Nonstationary Variables**

Eigenvalue	Likelihood Ratio	5% Critical Value	1% Critical Value	Hypothesized No. of Cointegrating Equations
0.188756	55.35344	47.21	54.46	None***
0.155371	33.80721	29.68	35.65	At most, 1**
0.131520	16.41488	15.41	20.04	At most, 2**
0.018189	1.890741	3.76	6.65	At most, 3
Unnormalized cointegrating coefficients				
CBOND_SPREAD	PSBR_EXP1Y	CA_EXP1Y	JBS	
–1.294544	–16.12693	3.134402	–0.177473	
–1.006411	–27.70021	–1.505606	1.192773	
0.707320	17.14818	–1.624548	–1.017857	
0.936122	4.388785	0.775442	–0.491296	
Normalized cointegrating coefficients: 1 cointegrating equation[a]				
CBOND_SPREAD	PSBR_EXP1Y	CA_EXP1Y	JBS	C
1.000000	12.45761	–2.421240	0.137093	5.953661
	(2.96176)	(0.78587)	(0.29086)	
Log-likelihood	1435.729			
Normalized cointegrating coefficients: 2 cointegrating equations[a]				
CBOND_SPREAD	PSBR_EXP1Y	CA_EXP1Y	JBS	C
1.000000	0.000000	–5.660270	1.230425	13.99288
			(1.84461)	(0.45310)
0.000000	1.000000	0.260004	–0.087764	–0.645325
			(0.09860)	(0.02422)
Log-likelihood	1444.425			
Normalized cointegrating coefficients: 3 cointegrating equations[a]				
CBOND_SPREAD	PSBR_EXP1Y	CA-EXP1Y	JBS	C
1.000000	0.000000	0.000000	2.273365	–5.703225
			(1.71257)	
0.000000	1.000000	0.000000	–0.135672	0.259413
			(0.07460)	
0.000000	0.000000	1.000000	0.184256	–3.479711
			(0.29593)	
Log-likelihood	1451.687			

Notes: Series: CBOND_SPREAD PSBR_EXP1Y CA_EXP1Y JBS. Test assumption: Linear deterministic trend in the data. Likelihood ratio test indicates three cointegrating equations at the 5 percent significance level. See text for explanation of abbreviations.

[a]Asymptotic standard errors are in parentheses.

***Denotes rejection at the 1 percent level.

**Denotes rejection at the 5 percent level.

Table 3D.10 Johansen Cointegration Test on CBOND_SPREAD and All Nonstationary Variables

Eigenvalue	Likelihood Ratio	5% Critical Value	1% Critical Value	Hypothesized No. of Cointegrating Equations
0.193686	46.98539	47.21	54.46	None***
0.110699	25.02656	29.68	35.65	At most, 1**
0.098439	13.05996	15.41	20.04	At most, 2**
0.024116	2.489945	3.76	6.65	At most, 3

Unnormalized cointegrating coefficients

CBOND_SPREAD	PSBR_EXP1Y	CA_EXP1Y	JBS	
–0.422508	–21.21360	–1.095836	1.524325	
1.977097	34.35756	–1.690820	–0.760444	
–0.605164	–3.979539	3.599759	–0.011429	
–0.800673	–3.141669	–1.285331	0.594393	

Normalized cointegrating coefficients: 1 cointegrating equation[a]

CBOND_SPREAD	PSBR_EXP1Y	CA_EXP1Y	JBS	C
1.000000	50.20876	2.593646	–3.607802	–2.432886
	(37.9038)	(4.10887)	(3.40430)	
Log-likelihood	1467.769			

Normalized cointegrating coefficients: 2 cointegrating equations[a]

CBOND_SPREAD	PSBR_EXP1Y	CA_EXP1Y	JBS	C
1.000000	0.000000	–2.680716	1.321434	4.358563
		(1.30675)	(0.46733)	
0.000000	1.000000	0.105049	–0.098175	–0.135264
		(0.05954)	(0.02129)	
Log-likelihood	1473.753			

Normalized cointegrating coefficients: 3 cointegrating equations[a]

CBOND_SPREAD	PSBR_EXP1Y	CA-EXP1Y	JBS	C
1.000000	0.000000	0.000000	1.766327	–4.894315
			(1.11631)	
0.000000	1.000000	0.000000	–0.115609	0.227326
			(0.04594)	
0.000000	0.000000	1.000000	0.165961	–3.451644
			(0.25954)	
Log-likelihood	1479.038			

Notes: Series: CBOND_SPREAD PSBR_EXP1Y CA_EXP1Y JBS. Test assumption: Linear deterministic trend in the data. Likelihood ratio test indicates three cointegrating equations at the 5 percent significance level. See text for explanation of abbreviations.

[a]Asymptotic standard errors are in parentheses.

***Denotes rejection at the 1 percent level.

**Denotes rejection at the 5 percent level.

Table 3D.11 Granger Causality Tests

Null Hypothesis	1 Lag		2 Lags		3 Lags	
	F-Statistics	Probability	*F*-Statistics	Probability	*F*-Statistics	Probability
PSBR_EXP1Y does not Granger-cause	4.3133	**0.0403**	2.0968	0.1282	1.5335	0.2106
CBOND_SPREAD does not Granger-cause	2.4915	0.1175	1.7708	0.1754	0.5316	0.6617
JBS does not Granter-cause	0.5968	0.4415	0.0566	0.9451	0.9010	0.4436
CBOND_SPREAD does not Granger-cause	0.1704	0.6806	3.1713	**0.0462**	2.4096	0.0716
CA_EXP1Y does not Granger-cause	0.7729	0.3814	0.0036	0.9964	0.2195	0.8827
CBOND_SPREAD does not Granger-cause	6.0365	**0.0157**	3.1786	**0.0458**	1.1433	0.3356
IBOVESPA_USS does not Granger-cause	0.0053	0.9422	0.3187	0.7278	0.3157	0.8140
CBOND_SPREAD does not Granger-cause	0.0435	0.8351	0.2400	0.7871	0.5322	0.6613

Note: See text for abbreviations.

Table 3D.12 Vector Autoregression Estimates

	CBOND_SPREAD	PSBR_EXP1Y	JBS	IBOVESPA_USS	CA_EXP1Y
CBOND_SPREAD(–1)	0.703871	–0.000110	0.043853	0.118794	–0.008379
	(0.07634)	(0.00095)	(0.05603)	(0.08236)	(0.01113)
	(9.22060)	(–0.11532)	(0.78267)	(1.44233)	(–0.75268)
PSBR_EXP1Y(–1)	–4.361887	0.975192	1.374335	2.272939	–0.426761
	(1.32023)	(0.01651)	(0.96903)	(1.42444)	(0.19252)
	(–3.30387)	(59.0633)	(1.41826)	(1.59567)	(–2.21669)
JBS(–1)	0.137766	0.000931	0.938885	–0.107905	0.029231
	(0.05822)	(0.00073)	(0.04273)	(0.06282)	(0.00849)
	(2.36628)	(1.27818)	(21.9710)	(–1.71779)	(3.44294)
IBOVESPA_USS(–1)	–0.082399	0.001649	–0.129833	–0.029575	–0.026565
	(0.09634)	(0.00120)	(0.07071)	(0.10395)	(0.01405)
	(–0.85528)	(1.36835)	(–1.83606)	(–0.28453)	(–1.89089)
CA_EXP1Y(–1)	0.164463	–0.005362	–0.184405	–0.056495	0.958375
	(0.12198)	(0.00153)	(0.08953)	(0.13161)	(0.01779)
	(1.34827)	(–3.51482)	(–2.05966)	(–0.42927)	(53.8783)
C	–0.318114	0.015062	0.654957	0.202177	0.087589
	(0.36379)	(0.00455)	(0.26702)	(0.39251)	(0.05305)
	(–0.87444)	(3.31065)	(2.45286)	(0.51509)	(1.65108)
R^2	0.888529	0.997820	0.961066	0.035016	0.987604
Adjusted R^2	0.883011	0.997712	0.959138	–0.012755	0.986990
Sum sq. resids	0.239654	3.75E-05	0.129109	0.278980	0.005096
S.E. equation	0.048711	0.000609	0.035753	0.052556	0.007103
F-statistic	161.0129	9244.298	498.6257	0.732991	1609.374
Log-likelihood	174.5979	643.4226	207.6897	166.4689	380.6107
Akaike information criteria	–3.151362	–11.91444	–3.769901	–2.999419	–7.002069
Schwarz criteria	–3.001484	–11.76456	–3.620023	–2.849540	–6.852191
Mean dependent	2.072420	–0.043153	1.593734	–0.001709	3.181802
S.D. dependent	0.142416	0.012735	0.176872	0.052224	0.062277
Determinant residual covariance	5.62E-20				
Log-likelihood	1612.297				
Akaike information criteria	–29.57564				
Schwarz criteria	–28.82625				

Notes: Standard errors and *t*-statistics in parentheses. See text for explanation of abbreviations.

Table 3D.13 Vector Error Correction Estimates

Cointegrating Equation	CointEq1
CBOND_SPREAD(–1)	1.000000
PSBR_EXP1Y(–1)	20.01013
	(8.00168)
	(2.50074)
JBS(–1)	–0.642291
	(0.52773)
	(–1.21707)
IBOVESPA_USS(–1)	12.78519
	(10.5027)
	(1.21732)
CA_EXP1Y(–1)	1.675910
	(2.40669)
	(0.69636)
C	–5.491498

Error Correction	D(CBOND_SPREAD)	D(PSBR_EXP1Y)	D(JBS)	D(IBOVESPA_USS)	D(CA_EXP1Y)
CointEq1	–0.010477	–0.000244	–0.007553	–0.064499	–0.002484
	(0.01246)	(0.00017)	(0.00907)	(0.01344)	(0.00169)
	(–0.84087)	(–1.46892)	(–0.83240)	(–4.80035)	(–1.47161)
D(CBOND_SPREAD(–1))	–0.118460	–0.002959	0.113034	0.054974	0.028305
	(0.12505)	(0.00166)	(0.09107)	(0.13485)	(0.01694)
	(–0.094732)	(–1.77713)	(1.24118)	(0.40766)	(1.67060)
D(PSBR_EXP1Y(–1))	–9.703188	0.358455	4.360157	–9.753747	1.435692
	(6.37812)	(0.08492)	(4.64504)	(6.87829)	(0.86418)
	(–1.52132)	(4.22108)	(0.93867)	(–1.41805)	(1.66134)

D(JBS(–1))	–0.023747	–0.001776	–0.018655	–0.019148	–0.017223
	(0.13937)	(0.00186)	(0.10150)	(0.15030)	(0.01888)
	(–0.17039)	(–0.95716)	(–0.18380)	(–0.12740)	(–0.91206)
D(IBOVESPA_USS(–1))	0.049725	0.001890	0.006971	–0.188543	0.022820
	(0.09793)	(0.00130)	(0.07132)	(0.10561)	(0.01327)
	(0.50774)	(1.44941)	(0.09774)	(–1.78520)	(1.71974)
D(CA_EXP1Y(–1))	–0.383412	0.019937	–0.470655	–0.388544	0.314041
	(0.64371)	(0.00857)	(0.46880)	(0.69419)	(0.08722)
	(–0.59563)	(2.32619)	(–1.00396)	(–0.55971)	(3.60067)
C	0.003241	0.000147	0.002076	0.005349	0.001363
	(0.00554)	(7.4E-05)	(0.00404)	(0.00598)	(0.00075)
	(0.58479)	(1.99848)	(0.51448)	(0.89507)	(1.81477)
R^2	0.41020	0.267400	0.074135	0.536010	0.266713
Adjusted R^2	–0.017100	0.223000	0.018022	0.507889	0.222271
Sum sq. resids	0.243030	4.31E-05	0.128900	0.282641	0.004462
S.E. equation	0.049546	0.000660	0.036083	0.053432	0.006713
F-statistic	0.705784	6.022533	1.321169	19.06108	6.001409
Log-likelihood	171.7271	629.5324	205.3370	163.7245	383.6051
Akaike information criteria	–3.108058	–11.74589	–3.742208	–2.957065	–7.105756
Schwarz criteria	–2.932170	–11.57001	–3.566320	–2.781178	–6.929869
Mean dependent	–0.001395	0.000327	0.002102	0.000812	0.002750
S.D. dependent	0.049128	0.000748	0.036413	0.076167	0.007612
Determinant residual covariance	5.85E-20				
Log-likelihood	1595.071				
Akaike information criteria	–29.34096				
Schwarz criteria	–28.33589				

Notes: Standard errors and *t*-statistics in parentheses. See text for explanation of abbreviations.

References

Brock, P., and L. Rojas-Suárez. 2000. *Why so high? Understanding interest rate spreads in Latin America.* Washington, D.C.: Inter-American Development Bank.

Fama, E. 1984. Forward and spot rates. *Journal of Monetary Economics* 14:319–38.

Frankel, J. A. 1991. Quantifying international capital mobility in the 1980's. In *National saving and economic performance,* ed. B. D. Bernheim and J. B. Shovers, 227–60. Chicago: University of Chicago Press.

Garcia, M. G. P. 1997. A macroeconomia do dólar futuro (The macroeconomics of U.S. dollar futures). *Resenha BM&F* 118:37–45.

Garcia, M. G. P., and G. A. Olivares Leandro. 2001. O prêmio de risco da taxa de câmbio no Brasil durante o Plano Real (The exchange rate risk premium in Brazil during the Real Plan). *Revista Brasileira de Economia* 55 (2): 151–82.

Garcia, M. G. P., and M. V. F. Valpassos. 2000. Capital flows, capital controls, and currency crisis: The case of Brazil in the nineties. In *Capital flows, capital controls, and currency crises: Latin America in the 1990s,* ed. F. Larrain. Ann Arbor: University of Michigan Press.

Lemgruber, E. F. 1999. Cupom limpo, cupom sujo e assincronismo na coleta das informações. Universidad Federal do Rio de Janeiro. Mimeograph.

Obstfeld, M., and K. Rogoff. 1996. *Foundations of international macroeconomics.* Cambridge: MIT Press.

Epilogue to Part I: Circumstances and Institutions

Notes on Monetary Policy in Brazil in the Last Fourteen Years

Gustavo H. B. Franco

Looking back to the record of monetary policy in Brazil in the recent past, it occurred to me that Brazilian policymakers are entering into the seventh year of the Real Plan, an effort ending a hyperinflation process that, according to Bruno's criteria,[1] lasted a little more than seven years. It would be interesting, therefore, to go back in time for exactly fourteen years in order to observe as much time under hyperinflation as after its extermination.

In light of my experience at the central bank (Banco Central do Brasil) during the second half of that period, two elements seem to be key to Brazil's monetary policy during these turbulent fourteen years: circumstances and institutions. This may sound like somewhat of a platitude: On the one hand, after all, "money is not a mechanism; it is a human institution, one of the most remarkable human institutions, " according to Hicks (1967, 59), so that all questions of monetary policy could be seen ultimately as institutional in nature. On the other hand, is not public policy, and monetary policy more specifically, mostly an effort to respond to circumstances?

Gustavo Franco is associate professor of economics at Pontifical Catholic University (PUC), Rio de Janeiro, and partner to Securitas–Latin America and Rio Bravo Investments, LLC.

1. The classical hyperinflation definition is due to Philip Cagan's 1956 seminal contribution to Milton Friedman's *Studies in the Quantitative Theory of Money.* According to Cagan's (1987) original view, hyperinflation begins when inflation reaches 50 percent per month, and ends when it falls below this level for more than a year. Later, in his "hyperinflation" entry in the *New Palgrave Dictionary,* he favored a qualitative definition, with no threshold. Bruno (1993, 272) argued that 20 percent per month would be a better threshold because, on the one hand, 20 percent would be little different from 50 percent as regards the qualitative aspects of high inflation, and on the other, 20 percent would better signal the passage from chronic inflation to hyperinflation.

The problem with the Brazilian experience during these years was that actions and policies of the central bank seemed either overwhelmed by circumstances or severely constrained by existing institutions—so much so that policy choices always appeared exceedingly limited, or even minor, in view of available alternatives. On the one hand, emergencies seemed the rule rather than the exception, given the extraordinary times in which we were living; on the other, it was common to see second or third best (or even outright bad) policies being "traded for" institutional advances, or rules to preclude such policies in the future. Building institutions in order to be able to practice monetary policy along conventional lines was always a key consideration throughout these years even when it resulted in less than ideal short-term policy choices.

Indeed, fourteen years ago monetary policy in Brazil could hardly have deserved this designation. Brazil was entering hyperinflation as the Cruzado Plan, the first of the heterodox stabilization plans of the late 1980s, was bound to disaster. To be precise, and again using Bruno's definition, hyperinflation began in the summer of 1987 and ended in July 1994—seven years plus a couple of months. The record of monetary policy, or nonpolicy, during these years is very interesting, at least insofar as we learn how policies and practices are molded by a storm with which they are not meant to interfere. In addition, as commonly argued by those researching hyperinflation, there is much to learn about the nature of monetary phenomena from extreme cases in which distortion and abnormality appear in overgrown states not normally seen.

It is impossible to overstate what a serious pathology hyperinflation is, and how near this traumatic experience still is to Brazilians. There have been a little more than a dozen cases in history of such a phenomenon, almost always in the presence of wars, revolutions, and the like.[2] Invariably, the fiscal conditions are disastrous and political paralysis adds insult to injury. A detailed record of the evolution of Brazilian hyperinflation will not be presented here, where the focus will be on the key aspects of monetary policy.

It is very important to keep in mind that world-class inflation is a novel situation that many Brazilian adults have not experienced in their lifetimes. Histories of how amazingly the economy worked while inflation was running at 40 percent per month are not merely distant memories of old men barely recalling the 1920s. We have just celebrated the seventh anniversary of the *real*, the new currency that was introduced partly in February 1994 and fully in July of that year to eradicate the disease. Many of the practices, habits, and institutions (as well as the wounds and scars) of

2. This has always been the conventional wisdom as regards hyperinflations, but of the more recent Latin American cases—Brazil, Argentina, Peru, Bolivia, and Nicaragua—only the latter could possibly be included in such category. The Yugoslavian case may also be included among those in which military hostilities are paramount.

hyperinflation are very much alive. In fact, one can aptly describe the seven years beginning in July 1994 as being dedicated to the institutional reconstruction of the currency—that is, to the rebuilding of an institutional framework within which monetary policy in the conventional sense is increasingly possible. It is also important to stress that this process is far from complete.

This paper is divided into three sections. The first considers the 1986 landscape, the impact of the 1988 constitution, and the slide into hyperinflation. Considerable attention will be devoted to the workings of the central bank during these exceptional years. The second section deals with the stabilization and the changes introduced as regards practices and institutions by the 1994 monetary reform. The first years of stabilization were made especially sensitive by the very delicate situation of the banking system. Finally, the third section considers the monetary policy reaction to the external crises following the Thai devaluation and the switch to floating exchange rates with an inflation-targeting regime.

Monetary Practices during the Hyperinflation Years

As we recall key elements of the monetary policy that was in force in 1986, right before we entered the storm, we may indeed feel it was a long time ago, as if the conceptual distance were as tangible as the temporal one.

- State-owned Banco do Brasil, the largest commercial bank in the country, could lend with no limitations to both the government and the private sector, and then credit itself at Banco Central do Brasil for that same amount with a simple accounting entry in a device known as *conta movimento*; the central bank worked, therefore, as a discount window for Banco do Brasil.
- A parallel budget was drafted by a public body called Conselho Monetário Nacional (known by the acronym CMN), to which the central bank was subordinated and in which revenues were ultimately the issuance of money and the reserve requirements captured from private banks, and spending was composed of several credit programs conducted by the public banks (federal and state) and even directly by ministries. This budget was known as the "monetary budget" (*orçamento monetário*) and bore no relationship with the fiscal budget approved by the congress. It was like an autonomous budget to allocate credit from official institutions and seigniorage revenues.
- State (provincial) banks did not have such automatic access to central bank resources but over the years benefited from several ad hoc programs of capitalization and forced funding out of the resources of the central bank and out of reserve requirements imposed on private banks.

- CMN was the lawful monetary authority of the country, responsible for the conception of and guidelines for monetary policy. It was a council formed by several ministers (finance, planning, labor, social security, industry and commerce), the governor of Banco Central do Brasil, the presidents of the five federal banks, and five representatives of the private sector, including the president of the National Federation of Banks (*Febraban*) and a nominee of the unions.
- Financial repression was increasingly strong, and was understood as taxation (direct and disguised) of the banking system in order to capture part of the inflation tax banks were earning by the nonremuneration of demand deposits. Reserve requirements on demand deposits were incredibly high (never below 80 percent), and were imposed on savings deposits and even mutual funds. Funds held as reserves were then allocated to several uses, such as subsidized credit to agriculture. Savings deposits were, in addition, directed to compulsory housing lending at below-market rates. Several rounds of policy measures, creating mismatching between asset and liability indexation in savings deposits and housing loans, worked like forced loans to banks to be recognized as the treasury's obligations, and securitized (only years later).

There were several reasons, not to be detailed here, to explain why the fiscal situation in Brazil experienced a profound deterioration with the initiation of the first civilian government in two decades.[3] The seeds of hyperinflation were sown and the process exploded as the price freeze implemented during the Cruzado Plan collapsed late in 1986. It seems a paradox that it was precisely in this same year, as part of the attempt to save the otherwise doomed Cruzado Plan, that the accounting devices described above (the *conta movimento* and the *orçamento monetário*) were both extinct. Interestingly, what was intended to stimulate progress turned out to produce the opposite effect: public banks, both federal and state, all assumed a yet-unknown degree of autonomy, (most notably state banks) all practicing very aggressive development finance only to come to the central bank's window individually, on an ad hoc basis, when liquidity problems appeared. Rediscount loans were granted and consolidated afterward, or transferred to states or to the federal government, or capitalized in ways similar to what had been done to state banks. Mechanisms to finance states, the federal treasury, and development programs only became decentralized and less transparent.

It is easy to miss the important point that the *conta movimento* and the *orçamento monetário* were mechanisms through which the federal government concentrated all power to control the use of seigniorage and effec-

3. See Franco (1995) for a record of the fiscal crisis in institutional details.

tively controlled credit expansion on the part of Banco do Brasil. Such centralization of responsibilities was typical of the years of military rule that ended in 1985. One can interpret the abolition of these mechanisms at first as moving toward a more conventional form of relationship between the central bank and Banco do Brasil. It may also be seen as part of a movement of decentralization that "democratized" the use of seigniorage, especially among states and also by the federal development banks.[4]

The most diverse political constituencies (state banks, regionally focused federal banks, sectoral funds fed by budgetary allocations and Banco do Brasil loans and under the influence of private-sector federations, etc.) wanted to exercise money-issuing capabilities without the discipline imposed by the CMN and the ordinary budget. The result was that the deterioration of public finances seemed unprecedented as the discretionary control exercised by the finance ministry and by the central bank was altogether destroyed. In this connection, it is also interesting that 1986 was the year of the creation of the secretary of the treasury at the finance ministry. No doubt this was an advance as far as institutions are concerned, but for the first five years or so this secretary had no structure and staff. Institutions are crucial, but they need people to make them live.

It is difficult to precisely quantify the consequences of the deterioration of the quasi-fiscal deficit, because it was not until years later, when the Real Plan was in force and the central bank adopted an entirely different attitude toward official banks, that one could access the books of such institutions and determine the alarming proportion of loans of very bad quality. Strictly speaking, if these banks had consumed all their capital and more during the years preceding 1994, we should rightly allocate this spending to the previous years. This accounting, and assignment of responsibilities, proved very difficult to undertake.

The 1988 Constitution

Two years after these events, in 1988, a new constitution was promulgated, and its spirit was to reconstruct democracy by advancing the fragmentation of the central government, or the decentralization of the state. In many ways the result of the process was similar to the disaggregation of the Soviet Empire: the strong central power, the federal government, lost control over tax revenues (through revenue-sharing mechanisms) and spending (with earmarking of federal money to regional and sectoral uses)

4. It is useful to have in mind that federal banks, with the exception of Banco do Brasil (which was a general-purpose commercial bank, although with a strong focus on agriculture), had very specific regional or sectoral objectives: Caixa Econômica Federal soon to become larger than Banco do Brasil in assets, was a mortgage bank; Banco Nacional de Desenvolvimento Econômico e Social was an industry bank; Banco da Amazônia was focused on the Amazon region; and Banco do Nordeste do Brasil was focused on the northeast region.

and became the weak part of a diverse federation. In addition, the resentment against the military produced an urge toward "redeeming the social debt" that considerably amplified social spending, especially social security, health benefits, and small regional investments of local interest.

The most common descriptions of the fiscal consequences of the 1988 constitution were "disaster" or "catastrophe." Under the new constitutional rules, and adopting an upscale political-economy view of the problem, one could easily see a huge mismatch between aspirations (seen as obligations to spend that were imposed on the state, most notably on the federal government) and possibilities (which were limited to the amount of taxes that society would agree to transfer to all levels of government). Again, a revealing paradox was visible: together with all the directives condemning Brazil to fiscal disaster, the 1988 constitution would introduce the prohibition to the central bank to finance the treasury directly and indirectly in any form. No doubt the measure should be seen as progress, yet it came with two caveats. First, like the extinction of the *orçamento monetário*, the new measure would decentralize access to seigniorage at the central bank, so that state and federal banks could continue to work as unfunded development banks seeking finance ultimately at the central bank on an ad hoc basis. Interestingly, no restriction existed that prevented federal and state banks from financing their controlling shareholders, although this prohibition had been established for private banks in 1986.

Second, the central bank had a sizable portfolio of treasury bonds; when they fell due, would the central bank be prohibited from renewing them? Could these bonds be exchanged for others with the same face value? Lawyers answered yes to both questions, so the new directives' effective result was to create a quota for the central bank's financing of the treasury and for the extent to which the treasury could exchange the existing bonds for others with longer tenors and lower rates, and renew them with no restriction. The difference in market value of such bonds was not relevant, according to the official attorneys.

The latter examples show only that even the most conventional measures toward fiscal discipline, and toward the separation of the central bank from the treasury, could have the opposite effect on public finances and monetary policy, at least in the short run. It is interesting to note that there was a considerable amount of pragmatism in this Faustian bargain through which fiscal and monetary laxity in the present was surrendered in exchange for the future austerity or for institutions that would narrow the options for fiscal irresponsibility.

The Workings of Hyperinflation

As hyperinflation progressed, new and interesting practices would develop in the field of monetary policy that, in fact, would mark a substantial difference between Brazil and most other countries in similar situations in which dollarization was a natural outcome. During the prehyperinflation years one could say that the only goal of monetary policy was to finance government. Now there was something else. As Brazil seemed to slide toward the wrong side of the inflation tax Laffer curve, higher and higher levels of inflation seemed necessary to finance the budget deficit. The issuance of indexed domestic debt assumed crucial importance in financing what could no longer be financed only with the revenues from printing money. Various indexed instruments were offered, but maturities were shortened to the very minimum because the rapidly deteriorating fiscal situation offered no confidence to savers on these new bonds, and indexation was never perfect (and the less efficient, the longer the tenor). As things turned out, the whole stock of domestic debt was bought and sold every day under repurchase ("repo") agreements by the central bank. Technically, the average maturity of the domestic debt was shortened to a single day and the yield was the overnight rate. This incredible phenomenon could never be duly captured in statistics.

In this context, high-powered money was shrunk to a meager 0.5 percent or less of gross domestic product (GDP), which evidently meant that money, or at least this form of unindexed money, was disappearing while "quasi money" or highly liquid indexed debt reached 20 percent of GDP or more. Since indexed debt was readily convertible by the central bank into the conventional unindexed means of payment, it was not inappropriate to say the indexed money replaced the conventional money. Many people sought unusual definitions of money to encompass these liquid instruments, in order to enforce the control of monetary aggregates in the conventional form. No such attempts ever progressed much because, for reasons to be explained, in order to prevent dollarization under the Brazilian hyperinflation environment it was necessary to target domestic interest rates.

Under this system of monetary policy the central bank would turn whatever portion of existing quasi money was desired by the public into conventional money in the morning and reverse the operation in the evening so that everyone could rightly use unindexed means of payments to complete transactions during the day, but sleep with their financial wealth protected from inflation. This regime was once aptly described as a "domestic currency substitution regime" (Carneiro and Garcia 1994). Its base was the abundance of quasi money, or debt instruments subject to daily indexation by the overnight interest rate, which was, ultimately, the carrying cost of all the repo operations made with all sorts of bonds in circulation.

The interest rate was fixed in a simple form: Because these were times in which a crawling peg was practiced to devalue the exchange rate, and interest rate parity was to be obeyed, the overnight rate was set equal to the international (federal funds) overnight rates, plus the devaluation (or the inflation rates differential) plus a sound margin to account for country risk. Monetary policy, insofar it was fixing interest rates according to the formula described above, accomplished two objectives: (1) providing fluid substitutability between conventional (unindexed) money and indexed bonds (quasi money), and (2) generously rewarding the holders of the indexed bonds for not dollarizing their wealth.

In every other hyperinflation case, it is normal for domestic financial wealth to seek foreign currencies for shelter, and the economy is said to dollarize. Inflations of this sort are basically driven by the exchange rate: As wealth holders fly toward the dollar, the exchange rate is pressured down, which accelerates inflation on the one hand and, on the other, creates the current account surplus necessary to transfer out the emigration of the national financial wealth. This is where the Brazilian hyperinflation differed from the Argentine, and most of the others. It is typical with the latter to see dollarization accompanied by current account surpluses of 3 percent of GDP or more, so that the difference between M4 and M1 is transferred into dollars in a few years. In Argentina, for example, in seven years, 20 percent or more of GDP could have migrated into dollar-denominated instruments; residents then would have transferred their financial wealth offshore, and might (and usually did) repatriate portions of it as foreign investment. The government could tap these resources as if it were contracting external debt, as was the case in Argentina. In fact, in dollarized economies the distinction between domestic and foreign debt loses its meaning because domestic wealth was transferred abroad in a clean Machlup-like way.

To summarize, monetary policy during the hyperinflation years was guided by two crucial considerations: (1) to finance government by the most efficient combination of money and indexed debt issuance, and by maintaining a window for state and development banks, for sectoral funds in the regular budget, and for special programs; and (2) to prevent dollarization by means of the abundance of well-remunerated indexed instruments to outcompete foreign currencies as defenses from inflation mostly by virtue of the easy substitutability between regular and indexed money. No doubt these policies were successful to prevent dollarization, but, as it is common to hear from the Argentine, the costs of the domestic debt under the domestic currency substitution regime were far superior to the costs of financing government-tapping resources from off-shore pools of previously exported savings of nationals. The comparison is interesting but needs much more elaboration: There are costs and benefits in preserving a national currency, both of which go beyond computations of seigniorage, as the later experience of Argentina would suggest.

Stabilization and the Reconstruction of Monetary Policy

It is also interesting to note that during these years (1987–93) four heterodox stabilization plans were attempted: *Plano Bresser, Plano Verão,*

Plano Collor 1, and *Plano Collor* 2. All involved price freezes, and some involved debt defaults (on three occasions, according to Standard & Poor's), *tablitas*, and the introduction of a new currency. All these plans failed, despite their capability of obtaining some temporary reduction of inflation at the cost of producing sometimes huge dislocations and losses to be claimed and recognized only years later. All these situations produced shocks in the demand for money in addition to departures from the domestic currency substitution regime, shocks that turned out to be only temporary but produced impacts (liabilities and damages) in the years to come.

Progress in the field of fiscal policies, and more specifically progress toward institutions and practices that could isolate monetary policy from fiscal considerations, was mostly conceptual, even though the elements for a better, if not a sound, monetary policy were slowly being built. With the right institutional constraints (at least partially) in place, the feasibility of fiscal and monetary policy in line with stabilization would become a matter of enforceability, or of political will, and also of opportunity.

However, despite the progress in previous years, in 1993, when preparations for the Real Plan started, one knew that the reconstruction of a national currency would require huge new steps toward the reinvention of institutions, practices, and mechanisms of monetary policy. Some bases were built, but there should be no illusions that money was to be reconstructed from scratch.

The policy mix responsible for defeating hyperinflation, of which monetary policy was a key component, was composed of several elements:

- A monetary reform consisting of the introduction of an interim money of account—the *Unidade Real de Valor* (URV)—with the purpose of accomplishing the deindexation, or the nominalization, of all prices, wages, and contracts, with extreme caution to prevent distributive effects from disturbing the equilibrium of contracts. Later, the unit of account was to be issued as a full currency, at which time its name would be changed to *Real*;[5]
- The enforcement in public banks of a disposition forgotten in a 1986 White-Collar Crime Act, mentioned above, through which banks were forbidden to lend to their controlling partners. That was to apply to state banks and to federal banks as of 1993. The measure was instantly effective, and lasting, for state banks. Later, however, federal banks received from the Brazilian equivalent of the attorney general a legal opinion that was approved by the president (and thus became binding, like a presidential decree), exempting federal banks from the prohibition. At this point, however, with the right appointments to key positions in these banks, they were put under strict control of the finance ministry.

5. For a detailed description of economic and legal aspects of the 1994 monetary reform, see Franco (1995).

- Very high nominal interest rates—in July 1994, the first month of the new currency, the overnight rate was fixed at 7 percent per month—combined with flexible exchange rates (a revolution, considering the many years under the crawling peg) and sound, or at least much better, fiscal policies. These were very powerful anchors to stabilization, even though little change was engineered in the mechanics of monetary policy at first;
- Taking political control of the CMN by reducing its membership to three (maintaining the finance minister as president and the central bank governor as secretary, with the third member now the planning minister);
- Ceilings on credit granted by private banks to public entities of any sort (known as *contingenciamento*), and preparations for large-scale intervention (both private and official) in banks in trouble; and
- A constitutional amendment to weaken earmarking of revenues and thus strengthen the secretary of the treasury's ability to undertake fiscal repression, or not to execute the budget;

This policy mix was very powerful and secured a good start for the Real Plan. Annual inflation rates in the last month of hyperinflation—June 1994—were at approximately 5, 500 percent. In 1995, the first full year under the new currency, inflation was slightly over 20 percent for the year on consumer prices and around 7 percent for wholesale prices, and GDP grew 4.2 percent after 5.9 percent in 1994. Interest rates had been lowered to around 25 percent per year.

It is crucial to note that the hard budget constraint resulted from measures taken "below the line"—that is, introducing restrictions to financing of deficits, either through the increased ability of the treasury to deny money to budget allocations, or through the closing of windows in public and private banks. For several reasons not to be detailed here it was impossible to enforce fiscal discipline through budgetary instruments; in fact, the budget was and to a certain extent still is a major source of *lack* of discipline. In consequence, the battle to be fought was in the financing area, both in the treasury and in connection to banks.

The Banking Crisis

One knows that banks would face turbulent times with the end of hyperinflation, because they would lose their ability to benefit from the inflation tax. Revenues from demand deposits and from what was called "the float" and "resources in transit" represented sizeable proportions (more than half, sometimes) of total bank revenues, and such revenues would disappear entirely. This, however, was only the surface, or what could be seen at a distance. Adaptation to stabilization would represent a much more serious blow to the system. Soon it would be clear that two different banking crises were latent. The first had to do with public banks—almost all of them, federal and state—with serious problems due to the serious erosion of their capital through the years under the guise of fiscal spending. The second, related to private banks, consisted both of the above-mentioned need to replace inflation as source of revenue, and a recasting of the several forms of taxation created over the years to capture the excess profits created by inflation, including reserve requirements and forced loans. Besides, for a banking system that was geared mostly to finance government, the degree of compliance with the Basel guidelines was almost zero even under the assumption that public banks should not be considered "true" banks.

In summary, the fiscal crisis that was part and parcel of hyperinflation was turned into a banking crisis, in the context of which the introduction of banking supervision and capital requirements was at the very least a large cultural shock with serious consequences. There was no question that monetary policy during these crucial years had to be conducted with a keen eye on their effects on a very fragile system. Interest rates should be kept high, but the banking system should be spared from the damages caused by wealth effects.

The years 1995 and 1996 were spent in a state of near emergency, as the central bank was trying to prevent bank failures from developing into an open crisis. After July 1994, 158 financial institutions suffered intervention or liquidation; 52 of these were banks and 69 were broker-dealers, nearly all private. Considering that the capital of all state and federal banks had been fully exhausted, it is fair to presume that, at the onset of the stabilization plan, more than half the capital of the system had vanished. Precise numbers have yet to be produced in support of this conjecture, but there was not a shade of doubt that a serious systemic crisis was fully ready to explode.

Two large government-sponsored programs to prevent such a crisis were created:

- The PROER program was designed to finance the sale of the "good part" of private banks that were in acute distress (i.e., that had negative net worth), provided that the buyer would take all liabilities with the public and would buy an equal amount of assets and liabilities. The loans were made to the "bad part, " or the "bad bank" that would buy heavily discounted government securities that would secure a zero net worth when taken at nominal value. Approximately US$10 billion would be disbursed under the program, and some part of the loans, possibly a substantial part, will most likely return. Three private banks that belonged to the top ten commercial banks in Brazil for many years were involved in this program: (1) Banco Econômico, eventually acquired by Banco Bilbao Vizcaya; (2) Banco Bamerindus,

part of which bought by Hong Kong and Shanghai Bank Corporation (HSBC); and (3) Banco Nacional, part of which absorbed by Unibanco.
- The PROES program was designed to privatize, capitalize, or liquidate state banks. Its concept was based on financing from the federal government for states to acquire "bad assets" and capitalize their banks provided that they sell or liquidate them. In case states want to retain the banks half of the amount necessary was to be provided by those states. To date, several such banks were privatized (including the largest ones from the states of São Paulo, Rio de Janeiro, Minas Gerais, and Paraná), seven were liquidated, and seven were taken over by the federal government to be sold. Only five subsist independently. The total amount disbursed may reach US$50 billion in loans from the federal government to the states. Estimates of the costs of past capitalization and forced funding programs could double this amount.

Other chapters in the effort to prevent a banking crisis should not be forgotten: the first is that the federal government capitalized Banco do Brasil twice, the first in approximately US$7 billion in 1996; the second was an acquisition of troubled credits of more or less that same size. Caixa Econômica Federal, the federal mortgage bank, was the object of a large-scale restructuring in 2001, including capitalization and acquisition of bad loans in values that could go over US$15 billion. Banco do Nordeste and Banco da Amazônia still need similar treatment and will be most likely transformed into development agencies after the recognition and assumption of their losses by the treasury. It is also noteworthy that during these crucial years the relaxing of restrictions on foreign direct investment in the banking industry was crucial to secure transactions under the PROER and PROES programs, and then to complete them. The share of assets owned by foreign banks rose to approximately 25 percent in 1999 from less than 10 percent in 1993. The total value of foreign direct investment into the banking industry during 1995–2000 reached US$17.5 billion.[6] Since these amounts refer solely to registered capital, they may represent only a part of foreign resources brought to Brazil as quasi capitalization or funding to newly established operations.

New Directions in Monetary Policy and the Exchange Rate Regime

While the banking crisis was being averted, considerable progress was being made in the field of monetary policy. One of the most important advances was the creation of a Monetary Policy Committee (COPOM) within the central bank in June 1996, following the example of countless

6. Of which US$481 million was in the insurance sector and US$1, 128 million was in "activities connected to financial intermediation."

other central banks around the world. Even though independence was simply not secured in law, the creation of such a popular institution with its accompanying rituals of prescheduled meetings and publication of minutes was key to protecting decisions on the interest rate from political influence.

Also of crucial importance to monetary policy was the fact that the central bank would discontinue the practice of granting repurchase of all domestic debt in circulation. In addition, the central bank and the treasury would jointly reduce the share of domestic debt indexed by the overnight rate (i.e., zero-duration debt) and increase the share of fixed interest bonds. In 1997, just before the Asian crisis, the share of overnight indexed debt in circulation had been reduced to less than 15 percent and the repo arrangements were altogether eliminated. There was no question that the power of monetary policy would substantially increased as wealth effects would begin to be relevant, nor that the financial system would no longer be fully immunized from variations in interest rates.

Interest rates had been falling gradually since April 1995, but as the Asian crisis brought the need of a tightening to defend the currency, the issue of the exchange rate regime, and in particular its implications to the interest rate, became more and more contentious. It turned out that exchange rate policy was intimately connected to the success of the stabilization plan. In the first six months of the Real Plan—in the second semester of 1994—the exchange rate was under a floating regime, which was as mentioned, extremely helpful to stabilization. In view of the buoyant external situation, however, the still-large fiscal deficit (which established a crowding-out situation, precluding interest rates from falling much without doing severe damage to the always delicate rolling-over of domestic debt), and the absolute priority given to stabilization, the exchange rate regime moved toward a crawling band system. Why?

In the early phase of the Real, the crucial problem faced by the central bank was a capital account bonanza that was taking place on top of a balanced current account, thanks to the undervalued currency left as a legacy of hyperinflation. The choice of a float under capital mobility would leave room for monetary policy autonomy—except for the fact that the overly large fiscal deficit would force interest rates up, which would attract far too much capital, on top of already buoyant conditions, and quickly appreciate the exchange rate. These circumstances were not entirely inconvenient, at least for a while, because the exchange rate appreciation would reduce the undervaluation (thus moving toward the recreation of normalcy as regards the current account) and would greatly help reduce inflation. Yet, the continuation of a large budget deficit would result in more and more appreciation, which could not go on much longer. The natural reactions were, at first, to intervene in the foreign exchange market in order to arrest the appreciation, to sterilize the accumulation of reserves, and to introduce selective restrictions on capital inflows.[7] The latter in particular faced criticism from the International Monetary Fund (IMF) for instance, even though influential studies from research associates of the IMF eventually help such restrictions gain respectability as instruments to deal with capital surges.[8]

In this context, with the mitigation of capital mobility (however imperfect) and the introduction of a target-zone system to intervene in the exchange rate, the central bank sought to prevent further appreciation of the exchange rate, and even to accomplish some depreciation, while maintaining a tough stance on monetary policy. The mix was far from the ideal, but the continued failure to address the budget deficit left no alternative; it was a matter of controlling the damage done by the lack of a proper fiscal policy and the continuation of the crowding-out or fiscal dominance situation.

Monetary and Exchange Rate Policies under Strained External Circumstances

After the Russian crisis one could safely argue that the conditions described above had changed. The external situation had changed for the worse and the fiscal situation for the better (especially after the agreement with the IMF), and deindexation had progressed to such an extent that one could be less concerned with the inflationary repercussions of a float that was likely to produce a sizeable depreciation. These new circumstances would seem to point toward a return to a float, and the central bank was effectively trying to move to this direction, yet in a gradual fashion. Leaving regimes with rigidities is no simple matter, especially under strained conditions.[9] Brazil had agreed with IMF in December 1998 that the gradual increase in flexibility was to continue. It was unfortunate that the central bank's strategy was interrupted by the president's decision to move more aggressively toward lowering interest rates in his second term, which would be made possible, it was argued, with a new exchange rate system: the "endogenous diagonal band, " as it was called by his proponent.[10] Many things would be changed and the original project of reconstructing economic development on entirely new bases would, as a result, be seriously compromised.[11]

The first quarter of 1999 was a time of great turmoil. The new exchange

7. For discussions on how to deal with a capital account bonanza, see Corbo and Hernández (1996) and Eichengreen and Fishlow (1998).

8. See, for instance, Calvo, et al. (1993).

9. See IMF (1997) for a comprehensive discussion.

10. See Franco (2000) for a description and a discussion of exchange rate policies under the Real Plan, and its abrupt modification in January 1999.

11. See Franco (1999) for a broader discussion of the development issues involved and choices available for the future.

rate policy was a failure and the central bank was forced into an uncontrolled float and a very large devaluation. Interest rates had to be raised above 40 percent for the third time in less than two years, the agreement with the IMF was reinforced, and the situation fell under control by midyear. The exchange rate moved from 1.22 Brazilian reales (BR$) to the dollar in December 1998 to BR$2.20 in February 1999, only to fall to BR$1.65 in July.

Monetary policy was crucial to tame the dislocations produced by the devaluation. Apart from simply increasing interest rates to 45 percent as normalcy was reestablished, however, a new system of inflation targets was introduced. As of mid-2000 one could describe the crucial aspects of monetary policy as follows:

- Fiscal dominance would seem to be less important than ever before, as the consolidated fiscal deficit finally reached levels close to 3.0 percent of GDP. Debt overhang and high country-risk spreads, however, would still constrain the central bank's ability to reduce interest rates. The share of domestic debt in zero-duration debt was kept at about half, with great market resistance to any move toward prefixed interest rates.
- Banks are now almost entirely in line with Basel discipline, except perhaps for the federal banks and the state banks in the privatization pipeline. Compliance is increasing and the system is in its best shape ever, although it is still plagued by fiscal repression (on a much smaller scale). Reserve requirements are about half today, at around 3 percent of GDP.
- A presidential decree established that the CMN would adopt an inflation-targeting system to be enforced by the central bank through the use of the instruments it would see fit. An inflation report would be offered by the central bank, along with the usual ritual of procedures and justifications typical of inflation-targeting regimes.
- Exchange rates were under a float, although the central bank intervened occasionally in a direct manner and more often indirectly through sales of domestic debt indexed by the exchange rate. There have been debates on whether the central bank should act on the market using foreign exchange derivatives, particularly nondeliverable instruments, futures, swaps, and options.

A long way had to be traveled and many obstacles overcome for Brazil to adopt what appears to be a simple and widely supported system for monetary policy. There is no question we had remarkable progress, but the institutional fragility of the existing situation raises concerns. Basically, central bank independence does not yet exist in Brazil. In the laws creating the Real, an imposition of then-president Itamar Franco had to be accepted: that the CMN would be "subject to directives from the President."

Since CMN is the monetary authority of the country, nothing really prevents a new president from revoking the inflation-targeting decree and establishing new, development-oriented missions to the central bank. Since central bank board members do not have fixed terms in office, all can replaceable *ad nutum* by the president; and since the privatization of public banks has been slow, many will survive at the end of the Cardoso presidency in 2002, ready to be relaunched in the old-fashioned way.

Indeed the accomplishments of the last few years should not be taken for granted. As a new presidential election looms large, concerns about a backlash in the field of monetary policy are rising. Institutional protection should be given to practices that now are based only on Cardoso's will and on the agreement with the IMF. The process, however, is quite cumbersome. As a matter of fact, a constitutional amendment would have to be approved in order to allow the regulation of central bank independence, and to supply the much-needed institutional bases for currency stability. In addition, a consolidation of monetary and banking laws would be necessary to cut the ties between the president and the CMN and establish the latter as the defender of the currency.

Times are different now with regard to Cardoso's approval rates and capacity to control the congressional agenda. Central bank independence is not an easy topic, and opposition parties are wary of the issue's being raised precisely when they have increased their chances of winning the 2002 election. This is not to say that a left-wing government would revert all developments described above and restore inflationist policies. It remains to be seen, however, whether the opposition has absorbed the notions of fiscal responsibility and sound money so painfully learned in the last fourteen years.

References

Bruno, Michael. 1993. *Crisis, stabilization, and economic reform: Therapy by consensus.* Oxford, U.K.: Clarendon Press.

Cagan, Phillip. 1987. Hyperinflation. In *The New Palgrave: A Dictionary of Economics,* ed. John Eatwell, Murray Milgate, and Peter Newman. London: Macmillan.

Calvo, Guillermo A., Leonardo Leiderman, and Carmen M. Reinhart. 1993. Capital inflows and real exchange rate appreciation in Latin America. *IMF Staff Papers* 40 (March): 109–51.

Carneiro, Dionisio Dias, and Marcio Garcia. 1994. Capital flows and monetary control under a domestic currency substitution regime: The recent Brazilian experience. In *Affluencia de capitales y estabilización en América Latina,* ed. Roberto Steiner. Bogota: Fedesarollo.

Corbo, Vittorio, and Leonardo Hernández. 1996. Macroeconomic adjustment to capital inflows: Lessons from recent Latin American and East Asian experience. *World Bank Research Observer* 11 (February):

Eichengreen, Barry, and Albert Fishlow. 1998. Contending with capital flows:

What is different about the 1990s? *Capital flows and financial crises,* ed. Miles Kahler, 23–68. New York: Cornell University Press.
Gustavo, Franco H. B. 1995. *O Plano Real e outros ensaios*. Rio de Janeiro: Francisco Alves.
———. 1999. *O desafio Brasileiro: Ensaios sobre estabilizacão, moeda e globlização*, São Paulo: Editora 34.
———. 2000. The Real Plan and the exchange rate. Princeton *Essays in International Finance* no. 217. Princeton University, Department of Economics, International Finance Section.
Hicks, John. 1967. *Critical essays in monetary theory.* Oxford, U.K.: Clarendon Press.
International Monetary Fund. 1997. Exit strategies: Policy options for countries seeking greater exchange rate flexibility. Washington, D.C.: IMF. Internal document, December.

II

Financial Policies

4

The China Syndrome or the Tequila Crisis

Francisco Gil Díaz

4.1 The Primary Sources of Moral Hazard

In just the last thirty years there have been 112 worldwide banking crises (three of them in Mexico: 1977, 1982, and 1995), affecting a total of ninety-three countries (Sánchez Santiago, "Las Momias del IPAB," in *El Economista,* 6 June 2000; and Klingebiel 2000). These economic breakdowns have been followed by salvage operations of bank depositors that involve considerable jumps in public debt. Besides the fiscal costs, there have been substantial capricious wealth transfers, personal and corporate bankruptcies, output contractions, inflation, and often a severe questioning of the efficacy of the market model for economic organization. A cause-and-effect confusion about some of these crises has led even reputable economists to recommend the temporary abandonment of features essential to the proper functioning of markets, such as freedom of capital movements[1] (Krugman 1998, 1999). Given the importance of the matter and the lack of consensus among economists and policymakers about the origins of these crises, a search for answers to this transcendental matter is imperative. Perhaps the query we ought to pose ourselves should be whether we have incurred policy failures or there is a deeper institutional root that will unavoidably keep encouraging the buildup of factors that contribute to a crisis.

As with many matters, the answer may have eluded us because we have

Francisco Gil Díaz was chief executive officer of Avantel when this paper was written. He is now minister of the treasury (Hacienda) in Mexico.

1. Although "Kono and Schuknecht (1998) find that the liberalization of financial services leads to less distorted and less volatile capital flows, not the contrary" (Hawkins and Turner 1999, note 44).

failed to pose the proper questions.[2] Money meltdowns (Shelton 1994), whether in the form of national banking collapses or international epidemic (systemic?) crises, are attributed to a wide diversity of causes, but seldom (Hayek 1978) to fundamental institutional flaws. Insufficient regulation and supervision of financial sectors—the horse most popularly flogged—may even be a source of moral hazard. Therefore, when we deal with regulation and supervision, it might prove fruitful to attempt to identify the ultimate roots of moral hazard. At the macro level, the primary source of financial shocks seems to be an erroneous choice of the exchange rate regime. At the original-sin level (Eichengreen and Hausmann 1999 apply this term to another phenomenon) the ultimate root of moral hazard is central bank credit. In this epistemological vein, exchange rate regimes owe their existence to central banks.

The large number of recent financial crises, their substantial contagion effects on emerging markets (the most recent viruses, in Mexico, Southeast Asia, and Russia, resulted from such contagion), and their potential to create destructive chain reactions even among developed markets have given rise to renewed research into their causes. The belief that lack of supervision of financial institutions is the primary cause has spawned proposals for a cosmopolitan approach to supervision, and considerable thought is being devoted to the design of new rules, with concentration on improving opaque and untimely information from some emerging markets.

The reason for the uniqueness of financial markets in this regard is the potential for fraudulent or careless behavior (moral hazard). Potential for fraud comes, of course, with every contract, but systemic potential for fraud has an ulterior source: central banks.[3] In any national economy the singularity of central banks originates in their ability to create unlimited quantities of domestic base money. In turn, when faced with liquidity problems national governments turn to the international community for international base money. The possibility of recourse to outside support is a source of moral hazard,[4] but the potential for abuse is enhanced because assistance does not have to come from real resources (savings); some central banks and the International Monetary Fund (IMF), as institutions

2. Other endeavors are not that different. On a recent Sunday one priest wove his sermon around a sign on a highway that had impressed him. The first line of the sign "Christ is the answer"; the line below, "But what is the question?"

3. Hayek's ideas concerning private banking have more empirical support than is generally acknowledged, as portrayed in the role the Suffolk bank performed in New England as a reliable lender of last resort, despite a generalized panic (Rolnick, Smith, and Weber 2000).

4. Aggarwal (1999) observes: "Although this IMF led rescue reduced the losses suffered by the Japanese, German, and U.S. banks that had made high risk, high margin, loans to Asian countries, it worsened the moral hazard problem in international banking and increased the likelihood of future imprudent bank lending sprees (like those in Latin America in the 1980s and in Asia in the 1990s)" (394).

with the power to issue special drawing rights (SDRs), have the wherewithal to issue internationally accepted means of payment.[5] These lines of credit are sometimes drawn upon automatically, often as a result of concerted international rescue efforts. Therefore, national moral hazard is compounded by the expectation of outside assistance, if the consequences of nonsupport are deemed to be systemic.

The fact that means of payment are connected, sometimes in seemingly interminable chains that would collapse and cause multiple reactions if one of their links were destroyed, is also a cause for concern and may even have originated the perceived need to have a lender of last resort. There is a generalized opinion that payment chains cannot be broken, that in a fix, liquidity must be provided at all costs. Under this assumption we have a rationale for the need for national and world central banks. Without a gold standard, growing economies constitute another justification for the need for central banks: If the fiduciary money required by the growth of transactions were not provided, the price level would have to fall continuously.

The causal chain is thus originated at central banking. Central banking is at the source of potential unlimited lending of last resort; in turn, commercial fractional reserve banking creates a daily need for such (intraday or end-of-day)[6] last-resort lending, and enhances the quantities that may eventually be required from the central bank. Fractional reserve banking also increases the asymmetry in returns that may be obtained from speculative or fraudulent banking investments: owners or administrators will benefit from leveraged investments but may bear only a fraction of the losses.

4.1.1 The Monetary-Policy Origins of Moral Hazard

First, as promised, I shall make some comments on the implications for moral hazard in exchange rate regimes.[7] Despite all the hoopla about exchange rate combinations, there are only two possible regimes: a fixed exchange rate at one extreme, and a freely floating one at the other. Combinations converge with time into the first regime or are equivalent to the

5. The dollar, the euro, and the yen are internationally accepted currencies that can be issued on a last-resort basis. The IMF, as a lender to "forestall or cope with an impairment of the international monetary system," or general agreement to borrow (GAB), feeds on lending from the eleven large industrial countries. The IMF also has an issuer role as a creator of supplementary reserves in the form of SDRs, although SDR issuance has been nonexistent since 1970 (Bordo and James 2000). The moral hazard that arises from the role of international institutions was not born out of the Tequila crisis, as Bordo and James suggest; witness the international and IMF support for France in 1968.

6. Intraday lending has been diminished or eliminated by payment systems that have evolved toward the instantaneous settlement of every transaction. End-of-day lending can also be reduced or eliminated, but with fractional reserve banking the central bank will always lurk in the background as a potential savior in desperate liquidity need.

7. This is the so-called *corners hypothesis.* Frankel, Schmukler, and Serven (2000) provide an out-of-the-oven theoretical and econometric discussion of this issue.

second one, even if disguised around some policy guidelines.[8] A lower or an upper exchange rate band, or both, as departures from the two extreme regimes to achieve some eclectic combination, implacably end up with the characteristics and vices of a fixed regime.

All recent international economic crises[9] had common elements: substantial capital inflows (i.e., large current account deficits) and a commitment to defend fixed exchange rates or exchange rate bands. An undue credit expansion into frequently unrecoverable loans was another shared feature. The official explanation of the Mexican crisis—low saving rates—is conspicuously absent in Asia. In the aftermath of these crises were banking collapses and rescues of depositors. These experiences raise the customary chicken-and-egg question: Did "good" economic policies attract net capital inflows, or did fixed nominal exchange rates due to the high yield implicit in one-sided bets lure "excessive" net capital inflows that were not necessarily well invested?

The first hypothesis is presented to defend these policies while they hold, but even if good economic policies are magnets for capital inflows, fixed exchange rates are to blame for speculative and ultimately destructive behavior. In this regard the performance of foreign capital inflows into Mexico[10] prior and after the December 1994 crisis is telling. Short-term capital flows were large and volatile during 1994 leading to the December 1994 crisis, while becoming small and stable after the beginning of 1996. The opposite is true of foreign exchange inflows to the Mexican money market prior to the crisis (prior to the flexible exchange rate), when, from 1990 to September 1994, $40 billion in short-term capital poured in.

The explanation for such a behavior reversal may lie in the moral hazard originated in an exchange rate commitment, the effects of which are accentuated by the speed and liquidity that characterize today's financial markets. To appreciate the above, consider the amounts invested by foreign residents in Mexico's money market (government securities and other money market instruments) as of two significant dates: end of December 1995 and end of December 1999.[11] At the end of 1995, the stock amount of these investments was $3.8 billion. One year later, in December 1996, it had barely edged up to $3.9 billion and to $4.1 billion by the end of 1999.

8. See Frankel, Schmukler, and Serven (2000) for a discussion of the Chilean experience with so-called real exchange rate targeting.

9. As much can be said of the Russian, Brazilian, Southeast Asian, and recent Mexican crises. The Scandinavian and U.K. crises of 1992 also fit the pattern.

10. The same can be said of the Asian crises in 1998.

11. The 1995 crisis year was left out because during that year the government decided to stop issuing and to liquidate the amount of *tesobonos* outstanding. The behavior of short-term capital from December 1995 up to the present has already been detailed above. The turbulence of that year's continuous crises, including some political ones, also justifies its exclusion.

Over the course of three years not only was the change in the number minimal; its ups and downs were also insignificant.

The shift in the exchange rate regime between the precrisis and postcrisis periods may explain the radical shift in the nature of foreign capital flows into Mexico. The current stability of short-term capital flows, to the extent that their variability reflects a lesser volatility of their stock demand, may hold the key to understanding the remarkable stability of the exchange rate over the recent period. In turn, the perilous situation into which the Mexican economy fell before 1995 was the outcome of pathological market behavior provoked by the fixed, or quasi-fixed, exchange rate that prevailed at the time, without the automatic self-adjusting processes of a currency board.

The performance described above is more remarkable given the large influx of other categories of foreign resident capital into Mexico: during the past three years the country has been one of the largest emerging-market recipients of foreign direct investment in the world. It has also received large equity investments as well as a resumption of foreign bank loans and floated private liabilities in international money markets. These flows that pour into more resilient stocks contributed to the financing of current account deficits that cumulated to $39.5 billion over four years (1996–99), plus an increase of international reserves of $15 billion.

Not only did the amount of foreign residents' money channeled to Mexican monetary instruments remain stationary over the latter period, but this money was also more impervious to shocks: its term to maturity was considerably longer than that of the forty-eight-hour investments that flowed in large quantities prior to the 1995 crisis. The instruments now being purchased by foreign residents tend to have a maturity of at least three months, with six months to one year being the favorites.[12]

The evidence weighs heavily in support of the notion that investors behave rationally whereas pathological market outcomes are a creature of government intervention. During the years under the peso-dollar band (1991–94), when the exchange rate veered toward the floor of its initially narrow interval, a combination of high peso yields and exchange rate appreciation attracted large volumes of short-term capital inflows. Once the exchange rate reached its floor, investors continued to obtain high yields under the understanding that exceptional returns were possibly transitory because the availability of hard currency (despite the implicit promise of convertibility) had as a limit a fraction of the country's international reserves. The interest rate required to bring capital in, given those uncertain-

12. Along this line of reasoning, Trigueros (1997) concludes that foreign direct investment, portfolio investment, and foreign currency deposits issued by commercial banks, as well as the direct credit they obtained, exhibited remarkable stability after the onset of the crisis.

ties, had therefore to include a premium; and the term for which money market investors were willing to commit their capital had to be extremely short, allowing them to keep one foot in and the other out, so to speak.

As long the central bank had sufficient international reserves the other extreme possibility was for the exchange rate to be at its peso-dollar ceiling. During the existence of the band, this phenomenon occurred only when radical political events[13] created confidence shocks. Each of those shocks drained international reserves. At some critical juncture the incentive for investors was to try to be the first out of the local currency, in a situation that corralled them into such a desperate corner that virtually no interest rate would have been sufficient to encourage them to stay.

The implications of a fixed regime for moral hazard are clear: it places the central bank at the mercy of short-term international money managers. At one of the two extreme possibilities for the exchange rate, an excess supply of foreign currency tends to cause it to appreciate. To hold onto the exchange rate, the central bank will have to purchase the excess supply of foreign currency, accumulate reserves, and issue internal domestic debt, and will end up subtracting credit from the economy.[14]

Mexico's experience is one more confirmation that an exchange rate commitment generates two polar possibilities. One is to attract vast foreign inflows invested in extremely short-term instruments; the other is to have investors fly away as quickly as possible. This is old news, of course—the idea that exchange rates tend to veer off to their allowable extremes and that, once there, the system has all the flaws and dangers of a fixed exchange rate, was pointed out several decades ago by Harry Johnson. Oth-

13. Notwithstanding the political shocks, sooner or later the vulnerability derived from enormous, instantly callable liabilities was going to create a run. There were several runs during the year that drained reserves to only $13 billion as of the end of November 1994. Then the die was cast when, at his December inauguration, Zedillo shook confidence by his failure to confirm outgoing treasury secretary Pedro Aspe (Barro 1996; Robert Bartley, opinion column, *Wall Street Journal,* July 2000; Sergio Sarmiento, editorial, *Reforma,* 21 September 2000) at the helm of the treasury: Hard currency resumed its exit instead of flowing back in, until the signal for the final attack was given by Zedillo's personal decision to overrule the Foreign Exchange Commission integrated by central bank governors, the treasury secretary, and one undersecretary that had recommended to float and thereby seal the scant remaining international reserves. Zedillo instructed them instead to set a new ceiling to the exchange rate (an ephemeral one, as it turned out) that opened a window for the near-exhaustion of reserves, leading, in a mere day and a half, to a forced float and the final death knell to confidence. The crisis was then deepened by the government's failure for several months to present a coherent program to meet the budgetary needs that the exchange rate collapse was going to create. Even then, only ample hard-currency backing from the U.S. Treasury and from international institutions explain the avoidance of a monetary (and political?) collapse.

14. This is a misnomer. The total amount of credit remains constant even if the central bank's credit is negative, just as there is no credit injection when, at the other end of the exchange rate band, the central bank ends up subtracting credit as it tries to prevent a depreciation of the exchange rate. In the latter case the central bank's balance sheet would record an "expansion of internal credit," with total credit, again, remaining constant.

erwise, if the exchange rate does not stick to either of its extremes, the system behaves as a floating exchange rate. So why contaminate it with bands? Unfortunately, it seems necessary to continue rebottling old wines for the consumption of some economists, as well as for policymakers.

The case study of Mexico is congruent with the hypothesis that one of the sources of moral hazard, in this case with substantial macroeconomic consequences, is the incentive provided to speculators to play the short-term capital Ponzi scheme created by fixed exchange rates. This behavior adds to whatever problems the commercial banking system may face from its own moral hazard roots and may be sufficient to create a banking crisis, without having government officers and banks engaged in irresponsible acts. However, the exchange rate regime was not the only economic policy flaw of the period under examination.

4.1.2 The Banking Original Sin (or homemade moral hazard)

With some important exceptions (Hayekians [Feito 1999] and followers of Henry Simons among others), economists tend to confuse bank demand deposits[15] with savings that can be tapped for long-term projects. A representative example from the literature is the following: "Banks issuing demand deposits can improve on a competitive market by providing better risk-sharing among people who need to consume at different random times" (Diamond and Dybvig 1983, 396).

In a Fisherian intertemporal model (Fisher 1930) there is room for intermediary institutions (McKinnon 1973) that select borrowers (or claims issued by negative savers) and diminish portfolio risk by bundling assets with negative risk covariance, and that in turn issue liabilities held by individual savers. There is no reason, however, for these institutions to be issuers of demand liabilities as well; they can issue consols or time-matched claims on themselves. In fact, whatever the time distribution of the consumption pattern of savers, demand deposits run the risk of being massively and instantly converted into cash and may lead to an unmanageable run with systemic and macroeconomic consequences. Given these risks, the only possible explanation for institutions with grossly mismatched balance sheets is the existence of someone willing to come to their rescue in case of need. Such is the source of original sin, which of course lays the foundation for the committing of venial sins such as credit to the private sector financed with sight deposits. Venial sins are transformed into mortal ones when the size and growth of such credit become excessive.

Among recent crises, the Mexican experience shares several traits with the almost immediately successive Asian ones. We know now that collapsed Asian countries also experienced vast credit expansions of dubious

15. Demand deposits are part of the definition of money or hoarding.

Table 4.1 **Price Index of Urban Land in Mexico City (end of period, 1980 = 100)**

Year	Price Index
1987, fourth quarter	1,930.29
1988, first-quarter	2,422.87
1989, first-quarter	7,814.56
1990, first-quarter	12,012.23
1991, first quarter	16,451.04
1992, first quarter	23,079.09
1993, first quarter	31,933.75
1994, fourth quarter	33,927.21

Source: Banco de México, Dirección General de Investigación Económica.

quality. The similarities between the Mexican and the Asian crises and others also include astronomical increases in real estate prices.[16] More fundamentally, because of their exchange rate systems, excessive amounts of short-term money[17] were fatally attracted. The similarities end there, however, because Asian countries' high export growth had petered out prior to their crises, while Mexico's non-oil exports were growing in 1994 at a pace of 20 percent, over an already high base.[18]

As we realize the nature of Mexico's and other recent crises, one of the key questions raised is, *what should economists watch?* Reflecting on the evidence reviewed and on recent developments,[19] it is becoming ever more evident that economists should discard the Freudian (anal?) obsession with the real exchange rate, or with the current account of the balance of payments.[20] As we shall see, however, a combination of an all-inclusive (well-measured) public budget, the growth in credit, and some market-oriented measurement parameters of the health of the financial system are the symptoms one should perhaps be aware of.

Another issue raised by recent crises is the appropriate exchange rate regime. Some economists or policymakers may opt for what I believe are the increasingly futile bands, others for flexible exchange rates. The argument presented above suggests that the answer is to be found at either of

16. In Mexico City, real estate prices (table 4.1) increased 17.6 times in the December 1987–December 1994 period, while the consumer price index over the same time span increased 3.6 times. These asset-price bubbles coincided with a large expansion of mortgage credit into housing and office building booms.

17. There were exceptions, such as Korea, which relied mostly on bank loans.

18. Contrary to some widely held perceptions. Information concerning the behavior of the Mexican economy was available to anyone who wanted to see it. Data on the balance of payments; the nature, size, and volatility of capital flows; the size and speed of expansion of credit; and the growth of the nonperforming portfolios of banks were there for anyone to observe, with a timeliness and quality equaled even then by few countries.

19. The real exchange rate was, at the end of 2000, back at its supposedly dangerous 1994 level.

20. The expression is paraphrased from Miller and Upton (1974), who used it in a similar context.

two extremes: either no autonomous issuing of currency at all—with the currency board as an approximation of this solution—or a flexible exchange rate. However, a well-functioning flexible exchange rate requires institutional buttresses; it is insufficient simply to let it run loose. Among other ingredients, coverage mechanisms are essential, but local institutions that allow for cover may be found wanting. At the end of a transaction investors must be assured of the delivery of hard currency. The importance of this ingredient was evident at the outset of the Mexican crisis. Despite a deep local market in forward contracts, the foreign exchange market did not contribute to the stabilization of the peso and of local interest rates until the appearance of futures transactions in the Chicago Mercantile Exchange guaranteed delivery (Gil Díaz 1999).

Having expanded on the pros and cons of alternative exchange rate regimes and their implications for the attraction of some particular capital flows, I believe I should pay tribute to the obvious—to the other institutional elements essential to a well-functioning economy and therefore to a well-behaved floating rate. Recent currency stability in Mexico was aided by the reforms detailed above, but it would not have been possible without a deep contraction in domestic credit to the private sector that compensated for the government deficit, without wage revisions that have not outstripped gains in productivity, nor without political stability.

4.2 A Leveraged Buyout, Complementary Regulatory Failures, and the Onset of the Tequila Crisis

The Tequila crisis did not gestate in one moment or in one year; its explanation should be sought in the tensions the economy, like a pressure cooker, accumulated during the six years prior to December 1994, and, more fundamentally, in the wounds inflicted upon the banking sector by their 1982 expropriation. Said pressures are closely related to banks, to their human capital losses after being expropriated, to the way they were privatized, and to the renewed favorable environment brought to Mexico through dexterous treasury budgetary management, privatization of sclerotic state enterprises, and market deregulation.

Prior to December 1994, credit expansion went haywire: credit increased 25 percent per year in real terms for six consecutive years. A substantial portion of the loans that the banking system churned out in this interval had a poor or nonexistent possibility of recovery even before the skyrocketing interest rates and the exchange rate depreciation that ensued in December 1994.

Several factors enhanced the intrinsic deposit-banking moral hazard responsible for this expansion: (1) after several years of government ownership the human capital of commercial banks had eroded considerably;[21]

21. To be fair one should point out at least two exceptions: Banorte and Banamex.

(2) the capitalization of some banks was thin or completely transparent; and (3) the financial system underwent a substantial liberalization.

The liberalization of the banking system released sudden copious resources that banks felt compelled to lend; the increase in lending induced an increase in aggregate demand that, with a fixed exchange rate and with readily available accommodating foreign capital would contribute in turn to widen the deficit on the current account of the balance of payments quickly and excessively. The new liberal measures included the disappearance of forced bank loans to some sectors, the freeing of interest rates, and the elimination of reserve requirements.

Having stated the above, not all bank privatizations were flawed. There were three kinds of banks, or three groups or tiers of purchasers of banks.

One tier of shareholders immediately started figuring out how to conduct fraudulent operations through their banks. It was not a question of bad loans; it was a question of black holes in their accounts, money whose final destination had not been found. The amounts irretrievable reached several billion dollars solely from these operations, involving large irrecoverable amounts that were not isolated cases of possibly imprudent loans or soured investment projects. Some of the small and medium-sized banks that comprised this tier were in the hands of people who are now being prosecuted or who are abroad facing extradition requests. Many of these funds were simply channeled to their owners' private uses.

The next tier is the thin capitalization tier. Purchasers raised the money needed to bid for the banks by convincing other investors that they would enjoy large capital gains, thus luring them into accepting loans to pay for the shares they were committing to buy as soon as they had control of the bank. (The first tier also used this capitalization ruse, but it was not the root of their failures.) Regarding this second tier, bidders paid too little or nothing for their banks, and a consolidation of assets and liabilities would have cancelled most of their apparent capital. In this tier and in the other two, the capital of some banks was subscribed with "cross-financing" that involved an understanding between different groups of bidders to lend from bank A to the purchasers of bank B in order to have bank B do the same with the purchasers of bank A. There were even instances of development-bank lending to buttress some acquisitions.

The third tier is where the two big banks are situated, as well as a few others (some very small ones, actually; Banorte is the prime example). In this tier, one finds that real capital was put in and that there were no fraudulent schemes; but even in this segment one finds cases in which there was some bad lending, although a substantial portion of this bad lending took place before the banks were privatized.

At the beginning of the Salinas presidential term commercial banks found themselves with a sudden gush of funds while the banks were still in government hands. The initial reason for this windfall is that there was a reduction of government debt. Internal government debt went down from 20 percent of gross domestic product (GDP) to 5 percent of GDP over a couple of years as the proceeds of the privatization of all kinds of firms (as well as some current government surpluses) went into a liquidation of that debt. Moreover, the successful renegotiation of the government's external debt was concluded just before the banks were privatized, putting Mexican banks again into the international borrowing market. These two developments propitiated rapid credit increases, and, under weak management and supervision, the bad loans began to be generated.

At the same time, far-reaching financial-sector liberalization was undertaken that introduced several desirable features that should provide for a more competitive banking sector. As will be seen throughout this section, however, since the reform was incomplete, some of its features encouraged an additional increase in the supply of credit of such magnitude and speed that it overwhelmed weak supervisors, the scant capital of the banks, and even borrowers.

Besides the two elements described above, several other factors contributed to the 1988–94 credit explosion: the improved economic expectations brought about the real estate and stock market boom (already mentioned above) and a strong private investment response. The latter was due in part to the need to adjust the capital stock to the substantial restructuring requirements that the trade opening and market deregulation placed on the economy. Besides the reduction of public debt, there was an abundance of loanable funds because of the phenomenal increase in the domestic and foreign availability of securitized paper (Hale 1996).

A balance sheet adjustment of the private sector underway by the second half of 1993 and the late adoption by some commercial banks of more prudent policies were signs that the nonperforming loan problem had exceeded manageable dimensions before 1994: "Wide insufficiency of capital was becoming perceptible, a phenomenon explained by the relatively high level of past due loans that had not been adequately provisioned. Moreover, some commercial banks were operating with serious problems that were not readily noticeable to the financial authorities. In some instances, bank administrators acted with disregard to existing regulations and proper banking standards" (Mancera 1997, 228–41). Consumer and housing credit increased because of natural causes but banks pushed even these loans beyond reasonable limits. There were poor borrower screenings and credit volume excesses, and then the 1993 economic growth slowdown made the net indebtedness of the private sector burdensome.

As of the second quarter of 1994 sharply higher real interest rates[22] and

22. The demand for peso assets has been shown to be highly sensitive to changes in the price of the thirty-year U.S. Treasury bond, which experienced a sharp rise in 1994. See Calvo, Leiderman, and Reinhart (1993).

a considerable but still orderly depreciation of the peso (prior to the December debacle), the aftermath of the assassination of a presidential candidate, and other unfortunate political events poured gasoline onto an already smoldering coal.

The devaluation of December 1994 had a limited immediate impact on the financial position of commercial banks.[23] Nonetheless, the devaluation prompted other damaging effects as inflation and interest rates skyrocketed, economic activity collapsed, the burden of servicing credits denominated in domestic and foreign currency increased, and banks' capitalization ratios plunged.

The financial situation of private firms evolved from an unprecedented net asset position at the end of 1988 to a substantial, quick, and fragile indebtedness by 1994. A remarkable coincidence of converging events and policy measures combined to produce this phenomenon. In fact, all the cards were stacked in favor of a collapse:

1. The financial sector was liberalized, lending and borrowing rates were freed, and the remaining indicative credit allotments to specific sectors were abolished.
2. Government surpluses drastically reduced public internal peso debt. The debt reduction freed the portfolios of banks and facilitated the elimination of reserve requirements.
3. To calculate nonperforming loans, banks applied a *due payments criterion:* the amount of payments due after ninety days was recorded as delinquent, instead of the value of the loans themselves.
4. Banks were hastily privatized, in many instances with no due respect to fit and proper criteria in the selection of shareholders, or of their top officers (Honohan 1997). It must be noted, however, that the banks remained in government hands for half of the expansionary period and that part of the sour loans had already been extended. (table 4.2).
5. Several banks were purchased without their new owners' proceeding to their proper capitalization, as required by their financial situation, since shareholders often leveraged their stock acquisitions, sometimes with loans provided by the very banks bought out or from other reciprocally collaborating institutions.

23. The banks' last effort to cover their positions contributed to the fast depletion of reserves prior to the float. The explanation lies in a foreign-currency liabilities-matching requirement that they had been allowed to satisfy in part through holdings of *ajustabonos,* securities linked to the consumer price index. Understandably, the *ajustabono* position was largely eliminated in the week prior to the devaluation: between December 15 and 23, the banks increased their dollar assets to the tune of US$3.2 billion. The amount was substantial and originated in an earlier speculation in *ajustabonos* that had led banks to hold inordinate amounts of them. Since banks could not issue matching liabilities, allowing them to fund these assets with dollar liabilities was considered an expedient way to prevent them from incurring losses. The regulator's bet would have worked under a smoothly depreciating exchange rate, but the expectation of a discontinuous devaluation, fueled by Zedillo's failure to act promptly, detonated a sooner and harsher crisis.

Table 4.2 **Privatization Dates of Commercial Banks**

Bank	Date
Multibanco Mercantil de México	August 1991
Banpaís	August 1991
Cremi	August 1991
Confía	September 1991
Banco de Oriente	September 1991
Bancrecer	September 1991
Banamex	September 1991
Bancomer	October 1991
BCH	November 1991
Serfin	January 1992
Comermex	February 1992
Somex	March 1992
Atlántico	March 1992
Promex	April 1992
Banoro	April 1992
Banorte	June 1992
Internacional Banco del Centro	July 1992

Source: Taken from Ortiz Martínez (1994).

6. Taxes on intercountry capital flows (dividends, interest, etc.) were drastically reduced or eliminated.

7. Foreigners were allowed to hold short-term domestic government debt as of December 1990.

8. Short-term, dollar-indexed, peso-denominated Mexican government securities, *tesobonos*, were issued at the end of 1991.

9. The higher echelons of banks lost a substantial amount of human capital during their government years. With these officers, institutional memory migrated as well. This experience is not unique to Mexico: "Formerly regulated banks may lack the necessary credit evaluation skills to use newly available resources effectively"[24] and "unless properly overseen, liberalization can result in too rapid growth of bank assets, over-indebtedness and price-asset bubbles" (Lindgren, Garcia, and Saal 1996, 107).

10. There was full government backing of bank deposits.

11. There were no capitalization rules based on portfolio market risk. This regulatory failure encouraged asset-liability mismatches that in turn led to a highly liquid liability structure, more than two-thirds overnight for the banks, with a potential to create huge strains on the lender of last resort capabilities of the central bank.

24. See Lindgren, García, and Saal (1996, 100). Moreover, according to Honohan (1997), "Often hailed as the panacea for banking weaknesses of one sort or another, privatization has all too often been the regime change which incubated more serious problems. This has been the case both in transition economies and in developing countries that had operated with state owned banks. The problem has generally lain in the lack of suitability or experience of the new owners, in the inadequate capitalization of the privatized banks or both."

12. Banking supervision was weak and was overwhelmed by the great increase in banks' portfolios.

13. Some commercial banks abused the unlimited supply of daylight overdraft facilities at the central bank and created vast amounts of deposits drawing on the interbank credit market and on the money market.

14. The banking sector did not have a consumer loan credit bureau, and it did not actively utilize the business bureau available.

15. The wide trade opening and deregulation that swept the economy altered relative prices and canceled opportunities in traditional sectors. Formerly privately "good" projects turned into bad ones and altered the relative ability to service debt of many sectors and types of enterprises (Lindgren, Garcia, and Saal 1996, 12).

16. There was a phenomenal expansion of credit from the development banks.

17. Enormous, unprecedented amounts of foreign capital became available worldwide, particularly to Mexico. One of the salient newcomers to these capital markets was securitized flows (table 4.3).

18. The banking sector faced procedural and judicial difficulties that enhanced the spread between lending and borrowing rates. This problem was considerably accentuated by the onset of inflation (in the former inflationary period banks did not have substantial amounts of credit outstanding) and the economic collapse of 1995.

These elements, combined with a greatly improved perception of the country's short- and long-term prospects, generated the conditions that would result in the Mexican crash. A paragraph from Lindgren, Garcia, and Saal (1996) portray well what went on. Referring to Mexico from 1994 to the present, they write: "After many years of nationalized banking [from

Table 4.3 **Dollar-denominated Obligations of the Financial System**

	US$ millions
November 1994	
Balance of the external debt of the commercial banks	25,966.00
Balance of the short-term foreign debt of the development banks	4,562.20
Tesobonos	24,690.70
Total liabilities of the commercial banks with Mexican residents (net of interbank operations)	112,902.00
Net international reserves	12,483.90
Cash in circulation	14,251.10
1995	
Interest on the foreign debt	11,715.90
Public sector and Banco de México	7,368.90
Private sector	4,347.00

Source: Comisión Nacional Bancaria y de Valóres.

1982 to mid-1992], commercial banks lacked the experience and organizational and information systems to adequately assess credit and other market risks and to monitor and collect loans. Accounting practices did not follow international standards. Concentration of loans and loans to related parties was a problem in those banks that were subsequently subject to intervention" (107). In relation to many countries the *Bank Soundness* book finds that "banks that are, or were recently, state-owned were a factor in most of the instances of unsoundness in the sample" (Lindgren, Garcia, and Saal 1996, 107) and "it becomes more difficult to distinguish good from bad borrowers when bank loans are growing rapidly" (110).

This combination of factors constitutes another experience[25] of how, despite important economic achievements, financial liberalization[26] can go astray in an environment that has no adequate safeguards against the predatory practices to which banks can be induced by full deposit protection. Thin or no capitalization was another key ingredient that combined with the other factors to induce imprudent credit growth.[27]

Fast credit growth and its aftermath are not exclusively features of Mexico's crisis. Chile, in its 1982 crisis, suffered from the same. Kaminski and Reinhart (1999) reviewed the experiences of twenty countries that experienced banking and balance-of-payments crises and found that in about half of these, the banking crisis preceded the balance-of-payments crisis. The causal pattern was reversed in only a few instances. Thus, there is support for the notion that unsound banks exert negative effects on the external balance and the exchange rate (Lindgren, Garcia, and Saal 1996, 77–78); moreover, "all the sampled countries except Venezuela experienced a sharp expansion of credit to the private sector prior to the crisis" (84).

The numbers related to the expansion of credit during the Salinas administration are impressive. From December 1988 to November 1994, the amount of credit outstanding from local commercial banks to the private sector rose in real terms from 90.3 billion pesos to 340 billion. Also in real terms, the relative increase in this credit over the six-year period was 277 percent, or about 25 percent per year.[28]

Some items of this expansion provide a better picture of the trends that characterized it: credit card liabilities rose 31 percent per year, direct credit

25. Chile's 1982–83 crisis has many parallels with Mexico's. See Gil Díaz (1995) and Velasco (1987).

26. Mancera (1997) discusses the causes of the increase in private debt and provides a full presentation of the diverse financial salvage operations required in the aftermath of the crisis.

27. "Unusual asset price movements, rapid growth of lending, especially for property transactions and for financing of stock market positions, capital inflows: these are some of the tell-tale signals of a credit financed asset-price boom which may prove to be unsustainable" Honohan (1997, 13).

28. All the figures quoted in this section were provided directly by the Economic Research Department of Banco de México.

Table 4.4 External Financial Flows to the Private Sector ($ millions)

Concept	1988	1989–94
Total	943	97,096
Loans	–1,548	23,984
Banks	1,380	16,209
Nonbanks	–2,928	7,775
Portfolio	–389	43,787
Shares	0	28,403
Bonds	–389	14,381
Direct investment	2,880	30,325

Source: Banco de México, balance-of-payments statistics.

for consumer durables rose at a yearly rate of 67 percent, and mortgage loans rose at an annual rate of 47 percent. All these rates of growth are in real terms.

External credit flows to the private sector went from negative $193 million in 1988 to $23.2 billion in 1993 and to $27.8 billion in 1994. The flow fell to $8.9 billion in 1994, but this decrease was more than compensated by the lower international reserves of Banco de México that year, which went down by $18.9 billion. Therefore, the total use of external resources was $27.8 billion in 1994.

The accumulated amounts related to external flows are also substantial (see table 4.4). A total of $97 billion over the six-year term that increases to $115.9 billion once the fall in reserves that occurred in 1994 is included.

These rates of growth are portentous. As Honohan (1997, p. 1 of annex) warns, "there are general indicators which apply whether or not there is a macroeconomic boom and bust cycle." Honohan lists, among others, the following telltale signs:

- "One measuring balance sheet change, namely the growth in aggregate lending (in real terms). This is the classic indicator of individual bank failure and may also serve for systems."
- "Two drawn from the structure of the balance sheet, namely the loan-deposit-ratio and reliance on foreign borrowing."

The story is not yet complete, however. Starting in 1993, the government decided to break with a long and healthy practice of including in the definition of its consolidated deficit the amounts channeled through government development banks, a concept known as the deficit (or surplus, as the case might be) due to "financial intermediation."

Financial intermediation had been included in the deficit to restrain overall budget expansion; to prevent the use of development banks to disguise public expenditures; because they expand credit based on central

Table 4.5 **Deficit Due to Financial Intermediation**

Year	% of GDP
1990	1.07
1991	2.80
1992	2.66
1993	3.33
1994	3.68

Source: Banco de México.

and not market decisions; and because their loans to the private sector were of dismal quality.

The abandonment of this deficit definition contributed to an additional expansion of credit and to careless lending: "During the past government *Nacional Financiera* extended 470,000 credits, of which half were not viable . . ." and "they were not viable even before the crisis."[29]

From the figures shown in table 4.5 it can be appreciated that the pressure from financial intermediation to GDP was not negligible and contributed therefore to the size of current account deficits that reached 3.0 percent, 5.1 percent, 7.4 percent, 6.5 percent, and 7.9 percent of GDP each year between 1990 and 1994.

The unseemly attraction of foreign resources and the liquidation of large amounts of government debt that crowded in low-quality bank lending, combined with the moral hazard cocktail concocted by the various measures already enumerated, nurtured an increase in private aggregate demand that contributed to the rapidly rising current account deficit. Furthermore, the deficit was financed in large part by short-term capital. This deficit was combined with the commitment, a pledge consecrated in the Pacts regularly convened among the government, the private sector, labor organizations, and farmer representatives, to contain the exchange rate within a widening but relatively tight band.

For most of the period the exchange rate stuck to its peso-dollar floor, as high interest rates attracted short-term capital, development banks and private firms borrowed abroad, and foreign money flowed into the stock market. The central bank essentially accommodated the demand for base money (i.e., currency) and in that endeavor sterilized foreign exchange inflows or outflows, allowing international reserve increases (or decreases, as the case might have been). Because of the predominant excess supply of dollars, the amount of reserves constantly increased up until the uncertain

29. Gilberto Borja was CEO of Nacional Financiera (the largest development bank) for a brief period that was interrupted when he made the statement quoted here (in *El Economista,* 9 September 1996, p. 20).

period prior to the U.S. Congressional vote on the North American Free Trade Agreement (NAFTA), when the increase was temporarily interrupted, only to resume after NAFTA was approved up to the start of 1994's political wobbles (table 4.6).

The deficit in the balance of trade rose by 5.83 percentage points of GDP over the period, explainable up to 81 percent (4.74 percent/5.83 percent) by the rise in private investment (see table 4.7). However, a substantial portion of this increased private investment went into unprofitable ventures, thus contributing to the unsustainability of the current account deficit. Some of these undertakings were highly leveraged toll roads, unrecoverable home mortgages, or credit unions that invested with low or negative returns and were financed with vast resources channeled through the development banks. Some of the credit, in turn, went to finance nonexistent enterprises, to the hugely levered acquisition of bank shares, to noncollateralized loans, and so on.

Thus financial disequilibria, a classic overindulgence in credit, a frenzy of spending, and a substantial short-term debt combined with the sitting-duck features of a fixed exchange rate linked up to set the stage for the initiation of the 1995 economic crisis.

The crisis had little or nothing to do with lower savings in spite of what has been argued by many (see table 4.8), but a lot to do with excessively

Table 4.6 **International Reserves**

	1988	1989	1990	1991	1992	1993	1994
US$ billions at end of each year	6.4	6.6	10.2	17.5	18.6	24.5	6.1

Source: Banco de México.

Table 4.7 **Current Account Deficit as a Proportion of GDP**

	1988	1989	1990	1991	1992	1993	1994
Percentage	–1.4	–2.8	–3.0	–5.1	–7.4	–6.5	–7.9

Source: Banco de México (1995).

Table 4.8 **Consumption and Investment Growth (changes as proportion of GDP in constant prices)**

		Consumption			Investment		
	Exports – Imports	Total	Private	Governmental	Total	Private	Governmental
Years 1989–94	5.83	1.4	1.76	–0.36	4.44	4.74	–0.30

Source: Banco de México, taken from the national accounts.

rapid spending and credit expansion, as McKinnon and Pill (1995), Calvo and Mendoza (1995), and Hale (1996) have pointed out.

The virtually fixed exchange rate exhibited both its virtues (by steadily stabilizing prices) and its dangers (particularly the fragility of the economy to a speculative attack) within the environment created.

Just as many European currencies collapsed in 1992 after unrelenting speculative attacks on their narrow bands, 1994 political events triggered what for one economist was a death foretold (Calvo and Mendoza 1995) but a surprise nonetheless:[30] a drain in international reserves until the exchange rate ceiling had to be abandoned on December 1994.

4.3 A Financial Interpretation of the Crisis

Are recent economic crises—the European in 1992 and the Mexican in 1994—the results of unsustainable policies given unexpected shocks, or a reflection of multiple equilibria not closely related to measured fundamentals (Bordo and Schwartz 1996; Gil Diaz and Carstens 1996b)?

The classic position related to misaligned fundamentals can be traced back to Johnson (1972), where an excess credit expansion is translated into a loss of international reserves and eventually into a balance-of-payments crisis. This position can also be found in Sargent and Wallace (1981), who provide a closed economy vision in which a persistent deficit and real interest rates above the rate of economic growth eventually relieve debt saturation. At this point private agents refuse to continue purchasing debt, the deficit is monetized, and inflation ensues. This chain of events is not very different from the open economy model. Finally, Krugman (1979), in a model reminiscent of Mundell (1968), follows on this tradition in a futile attempt to time the speculative attack, which will force an abandonment of the exchange rate and thereby propitiate a rise in inflation (Johnson; Sargent and Wallace; Krugman; Mundell).

In all these classic approaches, an excessive expansion of credit leads the public, whether national or foreign, into a refusal to continue purchasing debt; in all of them, a day of reckoning is finally forced upon the government and society.

Bordo and Schwartz (1996) scroll through the experiences of currency crises dating from the eighteenth century to Mexico's recent episode and find reassuring evidence to support the classical contention that currency crises stem from inconsistencies between currency commitments and in-

30. Some rumblings made a timely appearance in the literature: "In a February 1993 survey on México, *The Economist* alerted readers that the potential problems affecting the financial sector included an expansive growth rate in credit allocation, problems associated with high interest rates and currency risk, and rising past due loans. The article also noted that one analyst had forecast a banking crisis within eighteen months" (Mcquerry 1999). February 1993 plus 18 months takes us into August 1994, a near hit.

ternal prices, or impending wars. Literally, "the theory of self-fulfilling speculative attack may have intellectual merit but contributed nothing to our understanding of real-world events. In every crisis examined here, the fundamentals are more than adequate to account for the actions of speculators" (1996, 46).[31]

This account brings us back to the Mexican crisis. Which were its fundamental causes? All the factors listed above made some contribution, but the contention of this paper is that those that were truly essential or that had the greatest significance were the combination of the exchange rate regime (Bordo and Schwartz 1996) with a rapid expansion of credit, a substantial part of which was of poor quality to boot.[32] The surge of bad credits is in turn explained by flimsy bank capitalization and the failure to ensure that bankers met the fit and proper criteria to own or to manage the institutions.

The next few paragraphs will be dedicated to identifying the detonators of the 1995 economic implosion under a quasi-fixed exchange rate. One frequently cited is the U.S. Federal Reserve tightening of 1994. Fed tightening does matter; in the early 1980s Fed actions were an important part of the explanation of international economic behavior. Rates went up dramatically in the United States and worldwide. They had a big impact on the U.S. economy, the economic slowdown of which depressed Latin American export prices. But did the 1994 jacking-up of U.S. interest rates really matter that much to Mexico? Or were the political shocks of that year, together with the fact that Mexico's current account was getting far out of line (given banking mismatches and the overhang of a huge amount of liquid liabilities redeemable in dollars under declining international reserves), the trigger of the depletion of international reserves? How important are those (retrospectively) relatively small movements of U.S. interest rates in 1994 as drivers of what happened to the peso-dollar exchange rate? In the context of the accumulated pressures and the knife's edge the economy was traversing in 1994, the U.S. interest rate rise may have aggravated Mexico's travails but cannot be singled out as the cause of a crisis of the magnitude Mexico experienced in 1995.

It would be incorrect to isolate a single factor such as the proportion of short-term government debt held by foreigners whose holdings have been shown to be particularly volatile (Calvo 1996). Such volatility is probably derived from the ease with which, under a fixed or quasi-fixed exchange rate, peso demand fluctuations must be and are expected to be readily ac-

31. Honohan (1997, 2–3) reaches similar conclusions.

32. Many other such quotes—such as Honohan's in footnote 27—and additional evidence are found in the literature. Rapid growth in bank lending is considered "a classic leading indicator of individual bank failure, and may also serve for systems" (Honohan 1997, p. 1 of Annex. See also Gavin and Hausmann 1995). See also Honohan (1997, 3–6).

commodated.[33] Volatility and risk stem in part from the exchange rate regime. A floating rate presents speculators with currency uncertainty compounded by other risks, notably market value risks.

The lower risk that speculators confront under a fixed exchange rate is borne by the government—i.e., by society at large. The insurance premium paid by society to cover exchange rate risks is proportional to the size of the international reserves needed to reassure investors that potential claims will be satisfied. Mexico's reserves were insufficient even before December 1994 because of the size of the country's financial sector. Some authors, puzzled by the depth and virulence of the Mexican financial crisis, have tried to explain it (at least partly) by pointing out the financial vulnerabilities of the country (see Calvo 1996, 208). In this endeavor, Calvo compares Mexico's public debt service requirements for 1995, including amortizations, with those of Argentina, Brazil, and Chile and relates them to exports. The result is a rather high figure for Mexico, 160 percent, while the corresponding values for Argentina and Chile hover around 50 percent. Brazil had a ratio similar to Mexico's, but mostly non volatile investors—banks—held its debt.

This line of reasoning is insightful, but does not go far enough. Although Calvo does relate M2 to international reserves, the amounts involved at risk of a sudden demand shift refer to a concept much wider than M2.[34] All domestic and foreign liabilities, both peso and foreign-currency denominated, must be honored if there is a run on a country committed to a fixed exchange rate. The amounts involved according to Mexico's figures for 1994 are staggering: at the end of November 1994, US$30 billion in short-term bank debt; $25 billion in *tesobonos*; 100 percent of commercial banks' liabilities to resident claimants (or $113 billion); the interest on all private and public external debt due in 1995 (approximately $11.7 billion); and $14 billion in currency in circulation.

Thus, total amount that all potential claimants expected to collect under a run, at the prevailing exchange rate, equaled roughly $200 billion—45 percent of the country's GDP, or 15 times the international reserves held at the end of November 1994. The reason for adding up the concepts

33. Evidence of the ways different institutional arrangements condition market behavior can be found in the comparison of the 1988–89 adjustment period with the 1995–96 one (see Werner 1997). Werner found that the volatility of interest rates and the average value of the real interest rate were much lower in the latter period. Both intervals have several similarities, the most important one being that both were phases of adjustment to a crisis, but also a major difference: in the 1995–96 adjustment program a flexible exchange rate was adopted versus a predetermined rate in the 1988–89 program.

34. One could even counterargue that the lowest risk that convertibility entails regarding the possibility of a flight from the local currency is found in holdings that may be totally liquid but that are needed for transactions (M0 or M1) and, conversely, that the highest convertibility risk comes from those bank and government obligations not included in M2.

enumerated is that bank liabilities had full government backing. Therefore, there is no justification to include only *tesobonos*, or these plus M2, nor to exclude items belonging to bank liabilities or any other government bond. One must also take into account that about 70 percent of all bank liabilities were payable overnight and that the rest were extremely short term.

However, this situation of extreme liquidity was not new to Mexico or to most other countries. What was new was the coexistence of formidable growth in the volume and speed of international capital movements (see Hale 1996) with the persistence, in some countries, of a fixed exchange rate. In this regard Mexico's currency collapse was not much different from those of several European countries in 1992.

Hence, the combination of a fixed exchange rate (i.e., a commitment to convert to foreign exchange [a substantial amount of] domestic financial assets), the rise in U.S. interest rates, and the 1994 political shocks comprise the true measure of Mexico's financial vulnerability at the end of 1994.

Another thesis has to do solely or prominently with central bank behavior during 1994. It puts the burden of the blame for the crisis on an alleged central bank expansion of credit during that year. This outlook ignores the fact that fractional reserve banking requires a lender of last resort. Banks cannot liquidate loans when there is a run. Because of this simple but inescapable fact, all the lines that have been written about the so-called excessive expansion of the central bank's internal credit during 1994 are nonsensical. The logic of a fixed exchange rate is implacable. When there is a run banks are, all of the sudden, left with more loans than deposits. Hence, when the central bank lends to commercial banks to balance their positions, it is simply fulfilling its unavoidable obligation as lender of last resort. This chore is performed either by foreign creditors, which is unlikely when there is a run, or by the central bank. The critics ignore that the root problem was not the (unavoidable) behavior of the central bank during 1994, but rather the existence itself of a central bank with all the moral hazard consequences derived thereof plus the amplifying element of the quasi-fixed exchange rate regime prevailing at the time.

If commercial banks had had reserve requirements or large liquidity coefficients the qualitative nature of the argument would remain. In this case, the accounting result is that the central bank swaps dollars in exchange for the lower reserves held with it by commercial banks, instead of providing the dollars to the commercial banks in exchange for an increase of their liabilities at the central bank. Therefore, it makes no difference (except for different accounting conventions) whether there are no reserve or liquidity requirements; that in a run, banks run-down their reserves at the central bank; and that the latter increases its so-called internal credit. The fact that this operation is labeled *central bank credit* and the other is not is immaterial. In the case of commercial banks' reserves at the central bank, the central bank's liabilities decrease pari passu with its loss of international reserves, a result analogous to the so-called increase in central bank credit. Finally, if[35] the central bank requires other banks to hold part of their liabilities in liquid foreign assets, the central bank accounts may not even budge under a run; and yet the qualitative and economic result is the same, and the commercial banks lower simultaneously an asset and a liability. In this case part of the nation's international reserves are held by commercial banks. That is why, in this case, even though there is a loss of hard-currency reserves, the accounts of the central bank remain untouched.

To sum up the sequence of events amply described and documented elsewhere (see Mancera 1997; Gil Díaz and Carstens 1997), the chain reaction was initiated by an increase in the demand for dollars. This increase had a counterpart in a lower demand for peso assets, and was followed—as it turns out, simultaneously because of the implacable mechanics of the daily clearing of the payments system—by an increase in credit from the central bank to the commercial banks.

Therefore, in circumstances such as those described above, the increase in central bank credit is a fatal consequence of the fall in the demand for pesos, it is a passive reaction, and it is an unavoidable outcome of the lower demand for Mexican assets under a fixed exchange rate regime.

4.4 The Depositor's Bailout and Its Cost

The budgetary cost and the process itself have been the objects of numerous pieces in the literature, but the final cost will not be known before the banks reach the end of their loss-sharing period and FOBAPROA (Fondo Bancario de Protección al Ahorro, the entity in charge of safeguarding and disposing of the assets) realizes the last of the saleable ones. However, public debt will likely rise instead of experiencing a partial netting-out from asset realizations because the quality of most of the portfolio in the hands of the government is generally dismal, and because there are still some banks within the aegis of the National Banking Commission whose weak assets have not been transferred to FOBAPROA. Furthermore, some sizeable debt has been left to "float" around, with no apparent debtor, and will sooner or later end up booked as public debt. The preliminary estimate of the net increase in government debt as a result of the banking crisis is $64 billion, or 13 percent of 1999's GDP (Mackey 1999).[36]

The rescue of depositors successfully prevented a run on banks—no mean feat given the amount of economic and political uncertainty at the

35. The liquidity coefficient.

36. "Asian countries now have non-performing loans that are estimated to be between 30 and 40% of national GDP's whereas Japan's non-performing loans are estimated to be as much as a trillion dollars and over 30% of its GDP" (Aggarwal 1999, 397).

time. However, a rescue operation should ideally minimize moral hazard by operating with one fell swoop. In this regard a piecemeal rescue created lingering problems, increasing the amounts of debt covered and subsidizing borrowers of different kinds with the application of programs successively put forward in response to the demands of pressure groups.[37] Not creating a bad bank, not acting immediately to remove bankers and shareholders from failed institutions, and not putting the cleansed banks immediately under new ownership and different administrators contributed to the worsening of the quality of their portfolios and to magnify the amount of forbearance. The end cost and moral hazard were thus magnified.

Beyond the incrementalist (Mcquerry 1999, 19) approach, another major source of difficulty was the confusion of the roles of supervisor and rescuer into one agency, the National Banking Commission. The treasury was, in principle, directly responsible for conducting the rescuer role, but in its default it fell into the able hands of the president of the commission, who, however able, could not possibly have successfully reconciled the two contradictory functions.

4.5 Some Lessons

The perils of exchange rate policy have been amply discussed above. Exchange rates exist because there are currencies, and the latter, instead of being issued privately, are public monopolies.[38] All this is quite obvious; what is not so evident is that there is a need for a national currency and if there is one, the need for the central bank to be the lender of last resort.

Central banks avoid lending responsibilities and the related moral hazard under a currency board arrangement, but it is difficult to understand why anyone would want to have a currency board when the alternative of not having a national currency is available. Having a currency is clearly an inferior alternative to not having one at all if the choice is a currency board, because the public is never fully convinced that the board commitment is forever. As a consequence interest rates and growth suffer, and unions will forever attempt to test the authorities' resolve.

If national money exists, then a floating rate seems to be the preferred alternative. A floating rate, however, is only one element of a multidimensional basket of necessary policies. A floating rate will not be conducive by itself to a properly functioning financial system. Sound fiscal and monetary policies are, of course, part and parcel of the decalogue of the indispensable background of a healthy financial system. Even then, however, the financial system, being continuously under the centrifugal force of moral hazard, needs to thrive under a set of additional constraints.

37. A recent reliable reference on the rescue operations is Mcquerry (1999).

38. Gil Díaz (1999) discusses the Hayek (1978) proposal for the private issuance of money.

Supervision and reliable accounting practices are two of the constraints one cannot do without, and they go together—but the argument of this paper and the evidence it presents suggest that we should not go about these matters in the fashion to which we have been accustomed. Official supervision implies, at least in the public's perception, a responsibility shared by the government for the performance and integrity of bankers. A failed bank is a failed supervisor, notwithstanding deposit insurance (another of the multiple sources of moral hazard). Therefore, the public will inevitably pressure politically for government support after the collapse of a supervised bank.

A natural conclusion of this discussion would be to have a private agency perform supervision, in order to separate this function from the institution that controls the monetary base. However, the accounting practices and rigor of even international accounting firms is hostage to national interests when dealing with the private institutions of emerging markets. This leads us perhaps into international rating agencies, which still leaves open the question of what they ought to rate. The answer may lie more or less within the checklist of what national supervisors are already supposed to require: fit and proper criteria regarding controlling shareholders and officers, high minimum capital requirements, mark-to-market asset valuations, reserve ratios against nonperforming loans and criteria for identifying and classifying them, a publicly available database on the standing of borrowers, and so on—requirements that are well known in the literature and that have been well defined by the Basel Committee.

The IMF and the Basel Committee could provide specific guidelines for emerging market financial systems, but no supervisory role should be attached to such institutions as the IMF, given their need to find political middle ways (forbearance?) among their members when worrisome vital statistics begin to manifest themselves in any given economy. A market-oriented solution should rely to the extent possible on entities removed from governmental control or undue government influence.

Would there be a role for national regulatory institutions beyond the provision of a few general guidelines such as the ones suggested above? Since central banking is likely to remain a national prerogative, any solution will maintain a mixed character. Another desirable rule in this context would be to reduce moral hazard even more by requiring full liquidity coverage (not reserve requirements, as many nonmonetary economists tend to recommend) of sight deposits and of other quasi-liquid instruments, which would contribute to reducing the reliance on day-to-day and even (to some degree) on emergency lending of last resort. The same would be required of foreign exchange commitments by commercial banks. Local authorities should also require banks to publish information in a manner that is readily digestible by the general public. The purpose of such information would be to allow the public to easily discriminate risk among banks.

Within the same market-oriented spirit all commercial banks should be required to issue subordinated debt in international markets. This measure would make a strong contribution to attracting careful scrutiny from international investors and would ensure that only strong institutions are allowed to operate.[39] A minimum of 2 percent of deposits may be a sufficient amount as related (but not quite fully explicated) by Calomiris and Powell (2000) for Argentine banks.

Deposit insurance, one of the many sources of moral hazard, would have to be eliminated. It may be that its sudden elimination would create substantial short-term disintermediation, depending on the circumstances of any particular country, but a phased elimination would eventually put the system on a different standing.

The measures outlined in this final section have a dual motivation: first, to sever banking system as nearly as possible from the umbilical cord of central banking, and second, to eliminate the moral hazard that originates in indigenous regulatory agencies. Unfortunately, all these answers are second-best solutions because the ultimate source of moral hazard—the unlimited potential of additional liquidity—will always lurk in the background as long as central banks exist.

References

Aggarwal, Raj. 1999. Assessing the recent Asian economic crises: The role of virtuous and vicious cycles. *Journal of World Business* 34 (4): 392–408.

Banco de México. 1995. Annual report. Mexico City: Banco de México.

Barro, Robert. 1996. Monetary and financial policy. In *Getting it right: Markets and choice in a free society,* 49. Cambridge: MIT Press.

Bordo, Michael, and Harold James. 2000. The International Monetary Fund: Its present role in historical perspective. NBER Working Paper no. 7724. Cambridge, Mass.: National Bureau of Economic Research, June.

Bordo, Michael, and Anna J. Schwartz. 1996. Why clashes between internal and external stability goals end in currency crises, 1979–1994. *Open Economies Review* 7 (December): 437–68.

Calomiris, Charles, and Andrew Powell. 2000. Can emerging market bank regulators establish credible discipline? The case of Argentina, 1992–1999. NBER Working Paper no. 7715. Cambridge, Mass.: National Bureau of Economic Research, May.

39. Calomiris and Powell (2000) discuss the usefulness of this instrument for the case of Argentina. A relevant quote from their paper in this context is the following: "The market—if it has the correct information—may be more willing and able to discipline weak institutions than their supervisors."

Calvo, Guillermo. 1996. Capital flows and macroeconomic management: Tequila lessons. *International Journal of Finance Economics* 1:207–23.
Calvo, Guillermo, Leonard Leiderman, and Carmen M. Reinhart. 1993. Capital inflows and real exchange rate appreciation in Latin America. IMF Staff Papers 40:108–51.
Calvo, Guillermo, and Enrique Mendoza. 1995. Reflections on Mexico's balance-of-payments crisis: A chronicle of death foretold. *Journal of International Economics* 41 (3–4): 235–64.
Diamond, Douglas W., and Philip H. Dybvig. 1983. Bank runs, deposit insurance, and liquidity. *Journal of Political Economy* 91:401–19.
Eichengreen, Barry, and Ricardo Hausmann. 1999. Exchange rates and economic recovery in the 1930s. *Journal of Economic History* 45 (4): 925–46.
Feito, Jose Luis. 1999. Hayek y Keynes: El debate económico de entreguerras. La polémica sobre las causas y remedios de las recesiones (Hayek and Keynes: The economic debate of the interwar period. The debate about the causes and remedies of recessions). *Círculo de Empresarios,* Madrid, Spain.
Fisher, Irving. 1930. *The theory of interest.* New York: Macmillan.
Frankel, Jeffrey, Sergio Schmukler, and Luis Serven. 2000. Verifiability and the vanishing intermediate exchange rate regime. NBER Working Paper no. 7901. Cambridge, Mass.: National Bureau of Economic Research, September.
Gavin, M., and R. Hausman. 1995. The roots of banking crises: The macroeconomic context. Paper presented at the Conference on Banking Crises in Latin America, Washington, D.C.
Gil Díaz, Francisco. 1995. A comparison of economic crises: Chile 1982, Mexico in 1995. Paper presented at Forum 95 for Managed Futures and Derivatives. Managed Futures Association, July, Chicago, Ill.
———. 1999. Discussion summary to "Capital flows to Latin America." In *International capital flows,* ed. Martin Feldstein, 53–55. Chicago: University of Chicago Press.
Gil Díaz, Francisco, and Agustín Carstens. 1996a. One year of solitude: Some pilgrim tales about Mexico's 1994–95 crisis. *Papers and Proceedings of the American Economic Association* 86 (2): 6.
———. 1996b. Some hypotheses related to the Mexican 1994–95 crisis. Research paper no. 9601. Mexico City: Banco de México, January.
———. 1997. Pride and prejudice: The economics profession and Mexico's financial crisis, 1994–1995. Banco de México, mimeograph.
Hale, David. 1996. *Lessons from the Mexican crisis of 1995 for the post Cold War international order: The World Bank report on Mexico.* Chicago: Zurich-Kemper Investments.
Hawkins, John, and Philip Turner. 1999. Bank restructuring in practice: An overview. Policy Paper no. 6. Basel, Switzerland: Bank for International Settlements, August.
Hayek, Friedrich. 1978. *The denationalization of money: An analysis of the theory and practice of current currencies.* London: Institute of Economic Affairs.
Honohan, Patrick. 1997. *Banking system failures in developing and transition countries: Diagnosis and prediction.* Basel, Switzerland: Bank for International Settlements.
Johnson, Harry G. 1972. The monetary approach to the balance of payments. *Journal of Financial and Quantitative Analysis* 7.
Kaminski, Graciela, and Carmen Reinhart. 1999. The twin crises: The causes of banking and balance-of-payments problems. *American Economic Review* 89: 473–500.

Klingebiel, Daniella. 2000. The use of asset management in the resolution of banking crises: Cross-country experiences. World Bank Working Paper no. 2284. Washington, D.C.: World Bank.

Kono, Masamichi, and Ludger Schuknecht. 1998. *Financial services trade, capital flows, and financial stability.* World Trade Organization.

Krugman, Paul R. 1979. A model of balance of payments crisis. *Journal of Money, Credit, and Banking* 11:311–25.

———. 1998. Saving Asia: It's time to get radical. *Fortune,* 7 September.

———. 1999. Depression economics returns. *Foreign Affairs* 78 (1): 56–74.

Lindgren, Carl-Johan, Gillian Garcia, and Matthew I. Saal. 1996. *Bank soundness and macroeconomic policy.* Washington, D.C.: International Monetary Fund.

Mackey, Michael. 1999. Comprehensive evaluation of the operations and functions of the Fund for the Protection of Bank Savings (FOBAPROA) and quality supervision of the FOBAPROA program, 1995–98. Report to the Congress of Mexico, July.

Mancera, Miguel. 1997. Problems of bank soundness: Mexico's recent experience. In *Banking soundness and monetary policy: Issues and experiences in the global economy.* Washington, D.C.: International Monetary Fund.

McKinnon, Ronald I. 1973. *Money and capital in economic development.* Washington, D.C.: Brookings Institution Press.

McKinnon, Ronald I., and Huw Pill. 1995. Credible liberalizations and international capital flows: The overborrowing syndrome. Stanford University, Department of Economics, manuscript.

Mcquerry, Elizabeth. 1999. The banking sector rescur in Mexico. *Federal Reserve Bank of Atlanta Economic Review* 84 (3): 14–29.

Miller, Marton H., and Charles W. Upton. 1974. *Macroeconomics: A neoclassical introduction.* Homewood, Ill.: R. D. Irwin.

Mundell, Robert A. 1968. *International economics.* New York: Macmillan.

Ortiz Martinez, Guillermo. 1994. *La reforma financiera y la desincorporacion bancaria* (Financial reform and bank privatization). Mexico City: Fondo de Cultura Economica.

Rolnick, Arthur J., Bruce D. Smith, and Warren E. Weber. 2000. The Suffolk Bank and the panic of 1837. *Federal Reserve Bank of Minneapolis Quarterly Review* 24 (2): 3–13.

Sargent, Thomas J., and Neil Wallace. 1981. Some unpleasant monetarist arithmetic. *Federal Reserve Bank of Minneapolis Quarterly Review* 5 (3): 1–7.

Shelton, Judy. 1994. *Money meltdown: Restoring order to the global currency system.* New York: Free Press.

Trigueros, Ignatio. 1997. *Capital inflows and investment performance: Mexico.* Mexico City: Centro de Analisis e Investigacion Economica.

Velasco, Andres. 1987. Financial crises and balance of payments crises. *Journal of Development Economics* 27:263–83.

Werner, Alejandro. 1997. Un estudio estadistico sobre el comportamiento de la cotizacion del peso mexicano frente al dolar y de su volatilidad (A statistical study about the behavior of the peso-dollar exchange rate and its volatility). *Documento de Investigacion* no. 9701. Mexico City: Banco de Mexico.

Comment Roberto Zahler

Francisco Gil Díaz's paper is an interesting overview and a provocative interpretation of Mexico's macroeconomic crisis that erupted in late 1994, better known as the Tequila Crisis. In fact, it goes much further, suggesting policy options for the institutional setup of central banks and banking supervision in Latin America.

Gil Díaz's paper advocates quite extreme or polar solutions to recurrent emerging market economies' macroeconomic crises. They all coincide in minimizing the government's and central bank's role in economic policy design and implementation. Ideally, according to Gil Díaz, Latin American countries should have no domestic currency and the supervision should rest in the market, through the trading of banks' subordinated debt or an increasing role for private rating agencies, or both. He further argues that Latin American countries should try to avoid the existence of central banks. If that is not possible, the exchange rate regime should be freely floating. Furthermore, he discards completely the recommendation of "the temporary abandonment of features essential to the proper functioning of markets, such as freedom of capital movements."

Interesting and provoking as these points are, my main comment is that Gil Díaz's recommendations are excessively theoretical and quite out of touch with policymakers' real options and alternatives in any foreseeable future. Let me elaborate.

On financial-sector regulation and supervision, to assert that the elimination of deposit insurance and the reduction of the role of official supervisory agencies will seriously reduce moral hazard is unrealistic. Even the increasing role of foreign banks in most Latin American countries does not assure that their headquarters offices will play, de facto, a supervisory and regulatory role of Latin American countries' financial sectors.

In my opinion, the Latin American experience indicates that financial-sector liberalization can strongly contribute to saving and investment in a solvent, stable, sustainable, and efficient manner, but it requires key conditions: one is related to appropriate macroeconomic policy design and implementation (see below). The other is the establishment of an adequate preventive regulatory and supervisory framework, a policy challenge that remains at the top of the agenda for most of the region. The need for consolidated supervision is another major challenge for countries where conglomerates exist or are being created de facto, and where banking and financial operations are just one of their economic activities.

Countries where financial reforms and banking legislation are relatively

Roberto Zahler is president of Zahler and Co., and was governor of the Central Bank of Chile from 1991 to 1996.

advanced and where nonbank financial intermediaries, typically pension funds, have acquired an important dynamism and play a key role in the capital market face an additional challenge: to achieve integral financial-sector regulation and supervision, that is, to assure consistency regarding the norms that relate to different financial intermediaries. In other words, the process of disintermediation requires adapting financial (and not only bank) legislation and supervision. This adaptation should be oriented toward strengthening the institutional set-up of regulatory and supervisory agencies, as well as their intercoordination. This is necessary to incorporate changes as they appear (for example, corporate governance, minority shareholders' rights protection, and capacity to evaluate the risk involved in the rapid development of new financial techniques and instruments) and deepen the modernization, efficiency, and contribution of the overall financial system (and not only banks) to the ongoing process of saving and investment.

On the macroeconomic issue, Gil Díaz's optimum policy is the abolition of national central banks, which would also contribute decisively to reducing moral hazard. Gil Díaz does not propose to eliminate the Federal Reserve or the European Central Bank. Therefore, it implicitly considers that domestic monetary policy will be determined by some foreign central bank. However, there is no analysis in his paper regarding the requisites of optimum currency areas for particular countries in order to surrender, in an efficient manner, domestic monetary policy to some third country. Moreover, Gil Díaz does not discuss a major institutional change that has been taking place in Latin American countries, including Mexico, during the last ten years, which is that many central banks of the region have become independent.

Gil Díaz's proposals do not address one of the major challenges faced by most countries in the region: to reduce their macroeconomic instability. In fact, during the 1990s, Latin America was severely affected by three major crises, one related to the Tequila crisis, one to the Asian/Russian/Brazilian crisis, and the third to the slowdown in the United States and to the Argentine crisis. Reducing macroeconomic vulnerability remains one of the major tasks of overall macroeconomic policy design—including monetary and exchange rate policy—in the region. As is well known, such instability affects efficient resource allocation and, in particular, capital accumulation. Macroeconomic instability correlates positively with higher vulnerability of bank debtors, with inappropriate and erroneous risk evaluation by the financial sector and, consequently, with banking system fragility.

When we consider the initial conditions of an economy in terms of its structural, institutional, and cyclical features, experience shows that the attainment of stable and sustainable low rates of inflation in Latin American countries requires some basic criteria to guide monetary policy actions.

Medium- and Long-Term Horizon

A medium- and long-term perspective is the proper one for the central bank's decision-makers to take, because the ultimate aim is to ensure stability of the main macroeconomic variables and to avoid generating short-lived booms or busts that must be reversed later. The use of a short-term perspective in monetary policy implementation tends to take (at best) hasty and (at worst) ill-advised decisions whenever economic indicators deviate from desired values. This conflict between the short and long terms has prompted many countries to give their central banks the aforementioned independence, which contributes to placing the design and implementation of monetary policy on a longer time horizon perspective.

Overall Macroeconomic Equilibrium

A different approach to that of Gil Díaz is that the central bank's anti-inflation policy must attempt not to generate any major imbalances in other key areas of the economy. In other words, reductions in inflation must not be achieved at the cost of sharp increases in unemployment or idle capacity, imbalances in financial markets, or an untenable deterioration in external accounts. The recent experiences of the 1990s in Mexico (1994), Brazil (1999), and Argentina (2000) show that this approach is not being commonly implemented in the region and that low inflation in many occasions has been attained in an unsustainable way.

One key area relates to public finances. As is well known, controlling aggregate demand—the essence of macroeconomic stability—requires an adequate mix and coordination of fiscal and monetary policies. Although the prevention of fiscal deficit monetization is a necessary step in eliminating inflation, it is not sufficient because deficits can be financed, temporarily, by other means. To keep inflation down, the central bank's monetary policy needs to be backed up by an actively anti-inflationary fiscal policy. The latter requires sound debt management, no monetization of fiscal deficits, a tight control of the growth of public spending, and explicit countercyclical fiscal policies. If authorities attempt to counterbalance an expansionary fiscal policy with a restrictive monetary policy, the policy mix tends to push real interest rates to high levels, which in turn hurts investment. Therefore, high interest rates may end up triggering a recession, which usually puts political pressure on the central bank to abandon its price stability objective. Furthermore, high interest rates attract external capital, causing the domestic currency to appreciate. Although this diverts the pressure for greater expenditure toward the external economy, it undermines the competitive position of the tradables sector of the economy.

This latter effect contributes to what has traditionally been the Achilles heel of most Latin American economies, which was clearly present in the Mexican Tequila crisis, and which Gil Díaz dismisses: high and unsustainable current account deficits of their balance of payments.

Fiscal policy implication on monetary policy is also closely related to the soundness of domestic financial systems in Latin America. Banks typically have an explicit or widely recognized implicit government guarantee on many of their domestic and even on some foreign liabilities. Pension funds also have contingent fiscal resources compromised, especially in the form of minimum pensions. These transfers are usually excluded from the traditional accounting definition of fiscal spending and from parliamentary discussion and approval. However, they de facto increase private-sector wealth and spending. This market imperfection had a major impact in Latin America's foreign (and domestic) debt crisis of the early 1980s, in Mexico's crisis of 1994, and some of the countries in the Asian crisis of 1997. Gil Díaz refers extensively to this element of the crisis in his proposed institutional changes to minimize moral hazard.

In practice, the abovementioned contingent fiscal transfers should include an appropriate percentage of implicit and explicit banking deposit insurance schemes, and of exchange insurance and other contingent support typically given by governments, de jure or de facto, to banking system depositors, creditors, or borrowers when facing a banking-sector crisis. Similarly, the government, even when dealing with reformed and privatized social security capitalization schemes, usually guarantees minimum pension funds. If these contingent transfers were taken into account, public-sector liabilities, appropriately measured, would have been growing at a faster rate than what official statistics show. This transparency in information would have beneficial effects on the economic authorities' evaluation of the soundness and sustainability of macroeconomic policy and the consequent need for the adoption of proper and timely corrective measures.

Another key area of overall macroeconomic stability that crucially conditions the sustainability of monetary policy is the need to maintain external sector imbalances within a reasonable range. Experience suggests that, contrary to Gil Díaz's approach, Latin American policymakers should be aware that the current account of the balance of payments matters—a great deal. This is especially relevant if a country has large gross foreign financial requirements together with insufficient international reserves or a high stock of short-term foreign debt.

Special care should be taken if a country faces significant short-term voluntary foreign financial inflows, which usually take place during the expansive phase of the cycle. When faced with such inflows, and especially when the fiscal accounts are in equilibrium, authorities are tempted to rationalize the existence and persistence of large current account deficits based on the argument that those deficits do not originate in excessive (public) domestic spending but rather reflect a healthy and competitive economy, with plenty of profitable investment projects.

However, on most occasions it has been a combination of Latin American countries' high level of domestic interest rates, together with an improper evaluation by foreign creditors of country risk or exchange rate change risk, that attracts significant external short-term capital inflows. Under those conditions, in spite of an apparently adequate (i.e., restrictive) monetary policy, excessive domestic spending is not eliminated, because it is financed from abroad rather than from domestic money creation. In short, significant short-term capital inflows may disrupt monetary policy through the monetization of foreign debt, with the corresponding increase in money supply or lower domestic interest rates. This stimulates domestic spending over and above what was initially contemplated in the monetary and fiscal programming.

Short-term capital inflows may also disrupt the working of the foreign exchange markets. These inflows temporarily appreciate the domestic currency, generating a short-term equilibrium exchange rate of an unstable and unsustainable nature when compared to the long-run equilibrium value of the real exchange rate. This appreciation tends to trigger a relaxation of monetary and fiscal policy, due to its effect of (temporarily) reducing domestic inflation, while at the same time it stimulates a bigger balance-of-payments current account deficit.

Excessive short-term capital inflows may also disrupt the functioning of domestic financial markets because most of them are intermediated by the banking system. If the latter is not properly supervised and regulated, the increase in liabilities tends to be transferred in the form of excessive and risky domestic credit (related, concentrated, or mismatched). The outcome is to generate macroeconomic disequilibriums and a weakening of the banking sector. This occurs because of the increase in overall spending and because with abundant liquidity, domestic bankers tend to relax their credit and lending standards, deteriorating the quality of their loan portfolio.

In addition, Latin America nonbank financial markets are usually less developed than the banking sector and lack adequate depth, liquidity, and regulation and supervision. When a significant share of net short-term capital inflows are directed to the stock market or other (nontradable) markets, it usually translates into stock market and property price bubbles. This further stimulates domestic spending, due to (perceived although unrealized) wealth effects, which in turn lead to a higher current account deficit and higher odds of a currency crisis even if the banking sector is strong. As mentioned, the higher asset prices also bias upward banks' collateral valuation, and so they also contribute to banks' loan portfolio weakness.

In short, because of their size and speed, short-term financial inflows may contribute to creating or amplifying macroeconomic and financial disequilibriums, even when the recipient economies are well managed. This point is not analyzed in Gil Díaz's paper, which assumes that, by eliminating national central banks and minimizing governmental supervision, his proposed institutional setup would prevent these situations or would appropriately take care of them. In my opinion, experience and practice suggest that even when there is an adequate design and implementation of fiscal, monetary, exchange rate, international reserves, and financial-sector policies, if short-term foreign financing continues to flow into the country, measures should be taken to prevent that inflow from undermining the country's macroeconomic objectives.[1]

The Role of Key Macro Prices

Gil Díaz's paper assumes that prices, as long as they are market determined, are efficient and equilibrium prices. However, particular care should be taken when interest rates, exchange rates, and (in some cases) asset prices behave as outliers divorced from their fundamentals during a prolonged period of time, because this behavior may disrupt overall macroeconomic equilibrium. Macroeconomic policy, and especially monetary policy, may be extremely ineffective when some of these key prices are out of the norm. There are many examples in Latin America of situations in which distortions in key prices triggered severe crises. For example, under somewhat common situations a bubble of (usually nontradable) asset prices appears, stimulates credit growth and spending through a wealth effect, and complicates monetary policy. It also distorts the appropriate valuation of collateral in the bank lending process, increasing financial fragility. In addition, wide fluctuations of key macro relative prices transform dynamic and profitable sectors into problem sectors in short periods of time, and vice versa. Because banks share the losses but not the windfalls of their clients, defaults increase, on average, with the presence of unsustainable values of key macro prices. Therefore, a misalignment between those prices and their fundamentals generally has a harmful effect on the financial system.

Inadequate supervisory systems or regulations have led to moral hazard and agency risk situations that help to keep interest rates abnormally high. Although real interest rates should be positive, special care should be taken when they reach absurd high levels during a substantial period of time. In this case, although they are market-determined rates, they are not equilibrium rates, nor are they sustainable over time. These outlier rates will even-

1. One possible course of action is to financially open up to the rest of the world prudently, gradually, and at a pace that is coherent with the objective of overall macroeconomic equilibrium. Chile's liberalization and opening-up of the capital account of its balance of payments implemented in mid-1991 was carried forward with that strategy. A detailed analysis of the measures taken by Chile is found in Zahler (2000).

tually undermine the debtors' ability to pay to the financial system. Many financial crises in the region have been associated with extremely high real interest rates, which the economy could not tolerate indefinitely.

In practice, countries cannot wait for the development of a theoretical first best solution, such as the one suggested by Gil Díaz (and of which there are few, if any, concrete examples in the real world), to minimize, or eliminate, "the ultimate roots of moral hazard." In many occasions in Latin America when the authorities took no action, it was argued that high interest rates were not worrisome because they were market determined. However, because during a prolonged period of time those interest rates have been much higher than any reasonable rate of return in the nonfinancial sectors of the economy, such a situation usually reflects some hidden policy mistake and develops into a financial crisis.

In addition, under the aforementioned conditions monetary policy becomes extremely inefficient. If, for example, policy is designed to be contractionary, in fact it is not. This is because those high real rates of interest tend to be ineffective in moderating excessive spending. What happens is that those rates are not binding on bank debtors' behavior, given that borrowers expect to defer indefinitely the effective payment of those interest rates (rollover of loans) or to have their debt bailed out. Under those conditions extremely high interest rates do not contribute to rationing credit effectively and banks do not play their proper role in the transmission of monetary policy. The budget constraint is not operative, and therefore excessive spending takes place in spite of (and even because of) the presence of high real interest rates, thus impairing at the same time both macroeconomic conditions and the quality of banks' loan portfolios.

Another key macro price, which is intimately related to the effectiveness of monetary policy in Latin America, is the real exchange rate. Gil Díaz has a completely opposite view and states that "economists should discard the Freudian (anal?) obsession with the real exchange rate, or with the current account of the balance of payments." In some Latin American countries, one of Gil Díaz's "only two possible regimes," the fixed (nominal) exchange rate has been used, explicitly or implicitly, to fight inflation. In those cases inflation is usually brought down quickly, but only for a short period of time. Experience shows that using the exchange rate to reduce inflation faster will, in most cases, eventually backfire. Sooner or later the appreciation of the currency will no longer be sustainable, and costly side effects begin to be felt in other areas of the economy (e.g., declining competitiveness and a deterioration of the banking system), or a chaotic devaluation occurs, wiping out the progress made in reducing inflation.

Gil Díaz's other "only possible regime," a freely floating exchange rate, does not exist in practice, because central banks, both in industrial and in Latin American countries, do intervene in the spot or future foreign exchange market to reduce short-term excessive appreciations or depreciations of the currency. Allowing the domestic currency to appreciate excessively, even though this may happen because of market forces, often results in a ballooning foreign debt (usually short-term) and an unsustainable current account deficit, leaving the country highly vulnerable to external shocks or to changes in the expectations of international creditors and investors. When the situation has to be turned around—so that the country will be able to service that debt—the often traumatic effects include plummeting real wages, high unemployment, and sharp currency devaluations.

In general terms, Gil Díaz asserts, "investors behave rationally while pathological market outcomes are a creature of government intervention." There are many counterexamples of this assertion: herd behavior, contagion effects, short-term horizons, insufficient or untimely information, lack of transparency, and many other situations imply that market behavior, especially in the international financial sphere, is far from rational. To conclude that central banks should not exist (at least in Latin America) and that banking supervision and regulation should be based on "market-oriented parameters of the health of the financial system" (the latter having merit), and to imply that with those two major institutional innovations both balance-of-payments problems and moral hazard would be minimized is, in my opinion, an excessively ambitious proposition that requires much more grounding.

An alternative approach to enhancing macroeconomic and financial stability in Latin America, not analyzed in Gil Díaz's paper, is to strengthen central bank independence. This is a major institutional change that is still not well established in many countries of the region and requires, in open and democratic societies, central banks to be accountable and transparent. Together with its new charter, the central bank's policy objectives have narrowed to the control of inflation. Inflation targeting is becoming a unifying policy element that enables the central bank to control its ultimate objective and to take well-timed preventive action based on all the available information and to fine-tune in direct response to any changes in core inflation.

The trade-off associated with the flexibility afforded by the strategy of focusing on the ultimate target level of inflation and dispensing with intermediate monetary policy objectives is that the corresponding policies must have a high degree of credibility. This requires the monetary authority to make a firm commitment to its objective, and to elaborate its diagnosis, forecasts, and policy actions in a technically sound, responsible, and publicly transparent way.

It is not necessary, or even desirable, that inflation targeting should come up with any spectacular achievements in lowering inflation suddenly and abruptly. On the contrary, Latin America's successful experiences with lowering inflation in a stable and sustainable way indicates that the emphasis has been on persistence, systematic action, stability, and credibility in the fight against inflation. Due to this emphasis on a consistent, gradual decline in inflation, as the central bank continues to gain credibility, market behavior, contracts, and expectations increasingly incorporate the central bank's descending inflation targets into their decision-making process. In that gradual approach, the chances that strong imbalances will arise in labor, financial, and foreign exchange markets are minimized, and the advances achieved in controlling inflation will tend to consolidate themselves.

Reference

Zahler, Roberto. 2000. Policy options for capital importers. In *Reforming the international monetary and financial system,* ed. Peter B. Kenen and Alexander K. Swoboda, 161–74. Washington, D.C.: International Monetary Fund.

5

International Liquidity Management Problems in Modern Latin America
Their Origin and Policy Implications

Ricardo J. Caballero

5.1 Introduction

Despite the significant economic and institutional progress experienced by the main economies of the region over the last decade or so, Latin America still experiences substantial macroeconomic instability. Replacing the chronic domestic imbalances of the past, much of this instability stems from the occasional but sharp tightening of a country's access to international financial markets—what Guillermo Calvo (1998) has so appropriately dubbed the "sudden stop."

Facing this scenario, both the private and the public sectors are compelled to design an appropriate international liquidity management strategy. Unfortunately, although this is not a daunting task at the microeconomic level (i.e., given prices), there is still very limited understanding of its macroeconomic counterpart. In this paper I attempt to shed some light on this issue, drawing from some of my recent theoretical and applied work in this area. Since this is a policy conference, however, I go further and—somewhat "irresponsibly"—make a series of conjectures on the impact of international liquidity management considerations on the desirable features of macroeconomic policy.[1]

Ricardo J. Caballero is a Ford International Professor of Economics at Massachusetts Institute of Technology and a research associate at the National Bureau of Economic Research.

I am grateful to Anne O. Krueger, Aaron Tornell, and conference participants for their comments and suggestions.

1. The essence of the conceptual framework is an adaptation of that in Caballero and Krishnamurthy (2000, 2001, 2002b). The examples and applications are mostly from Caballero (2001); while some of the policy lessons owe to Caballero (2000), a background paper prepared for the report on "Dealing with Economic Insecurity in Latin America," by the Latin America Regional Studies Program of the World Bank. These papers can be downloaded from http://web.mit.edu/caball/www.

I develop the argument of the paper by addressing three sequential questions: (1) Why is there need for decentralized and centralized international liquidity management? (2) What are the types of structural and macroeconomic policies that a government should pursue, even if the private sector is using *socially* efficient prices in deciding its international liquidity position? (3) When and how should the government attempt to force the private sector to increase its international liquidity position?

Since the sudden-stop problem is primarily a financial one, the analysis in this paper builds on the presence of financial frictions. Although some of the latter are undoubtedly a part of the new global economy—in particular, the greater flexibility and options for capital as well as the highly leveraged nature of many of these investors—I chose to emphasize domestic weaknesses because these are probably easier to remedy and they account for a substantial part of the problem. Two of these weaknesses are widely observed in emerging economies and play a central role in my analysis: weak links with international financial markets, and underdeveloped domestic financial markets. Together, they justify and complicate the problem of international liquidity management.

5.2 Why Do We Need an International Liquidity Management Strategy?

The view portrayed in this paper links the answer to this question to the two financial deficiencies highlighted above. I build the story sequentially, one ingredient at a time, because this will clarify the different nature of the policy questions asked in sections 5.3 and 5.4, as well as the particular deficiencies that give rise to them. Let me begin with that which is most directly connected—it is indeed a necessary ingredient—to the need for international liquidity management: weak links with international financial markets.

5.2.1 Ingredient 1: Weak Links with International Financial Markets

These are simply financial constraints, possibly time varying, that limit the public and private international borrowing (as broadly understood) of emerging countries. The evidence for this is substantial. To highlight only a few dimensions of this problem, consider, for example, the path of an index of sovereign spreads for Latin America's largest economies over the second half of the 1990s, illustrated in figure 5.1. The large surge in these spreads around the Mexican and Russian crises starkly illustrates the massive withdrawal of much-needed foreign support for Latin American assets.

Moreover, while less-than-prime corporate assets in the United States also suffered during the Asian and Russian crises, the rise in their premiums was substantially smaller. This difference can also be appreciated over longer time intervals. Table 5.1, for example, compares the performance of several Argentine sovereign bonds with that of several U.S. corporate bonds

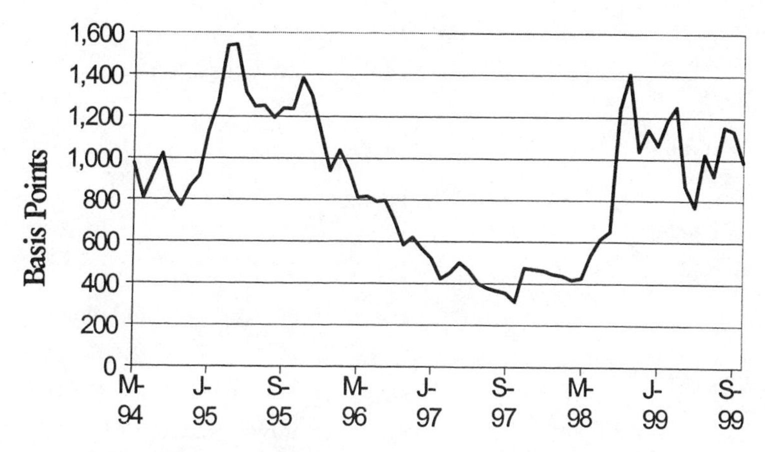

Fig. 5.1 Latin American sovereign spreads

Note: The time series is an average of Argentina, Brazil, Mexico, and Venezuela.

Table 5.1 The Volatility Premium

	S&P Rating	Moody's Rating	Spread Average	Spread Variance	Variance of Spread Changes
Argentina sovereign bonds	BB–	B1	4.28	2.25	0.36
	BB	Ba1	5.11	3.10	1.74
	BB		4.65	3.97	2.66
	BB	B1	4.59	4.12	1.76
Average			4.66	3.36	1.63
U.S. corporate bonds	BB		1.92	0.48	0.07
	BBB–	B1	3.38	0.62	0.41
	BB–	B1	4.50	0.49	0.23
	BB–	B1	4.49	0.44	0.15
	BB–		3.17	1.32	0.48
	BB		2.97	0.67	0.10
	BB–	B1	3.36	1.02	0.28
	BB–		4.91	6.51	2.13
Average			3.59	1.44	0.48

Source: Bond data from Datastream.

Notes: Spread Average means average over bond lifetime (or starting at earliest date available in Datastream). Argentine sovereign bonds: Argentina-Par G/R 93-23, Argentina 11 3/8% 97-17, Argentina 11% 96-06, Argentina 8 3/8% 93-03. U.S. corporate bonds: Fruit of the Loom 7% 81-11, Maxus Energy Corp. Deb 8 1/2% 89-08, Sea Containers 12 1/2% 93-04 (B). Sea Containers 12 1/2% 92-04 (A), AK Steel Holding Corp. 10 3/4% 94-04, Clark Oil Refining 9 1/2% 92-04, Bethlehem Steel Corp. Deb 8.45% 86-05, TRSP Maritima Mexico 9 1/4% 93-03.

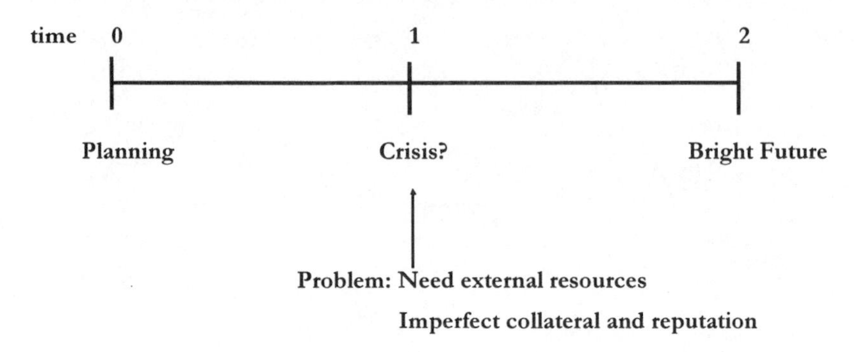

Fig. 5.2 Timing

of equivalent rating. The table reports the average spreads of these instruments over U.S. Treasury instruments, as well as the variance of these spreads and that of their changes. The evidence illustrates that, relative to U.S. corporate bonds, Latin American bonds pay a higher spread and their returns are substantially more volatile.[2] Moreover, the spread premium is probably a result of this excess volatility that mostly comes from episodes in which financial markets tighten for emerging markets. Latin American bonds appear illiquid from the point of view of spreads and volatility, despite the fact that their volume is often much larger than that of the specific U.S. corporate bonds described in the table.

A Simple Model

Connecting this ingredient to an external crisis due to international liquidity shortages is straightforward. I do this by sketching a model that is slightly richer than is needed at this point (for it explicitly considers a domestic financial market) but that will allow me to bring in the second ingredient later on with very little additional investment.

It is not too far-fetched to think about an emerging economy's time line in the terms described in figure 5.2. Date 0 corresponds to "normal" times, when investment, planning, and prevention are all very relevant. A significant part of this planning has to do with anticipating and preventing a crisis in the perhaps not too distant future at date 1.[3] Date 2 represents the future, always brighter than the present, but a significant obstacle is that the country—both its sovereignty and its corporations—often fails to persuade foreign financiers that they will share in that bright future if they help to avert the crisis (weak international financial links).

Figure 5.3 describes the elements that create a crisis as being driven entirely by insufficient external resources, but with a perfectly functioning do-

2. A similar pattern appears in other Latin American countries. See Caballero (2001) for evidence in Mexico.

3. Moreover, many of the business-cycle recessions as opposed to deep crisis episodes occur at date 0, when domestic policymakers attempt to prevent a deep crisis at date 1.

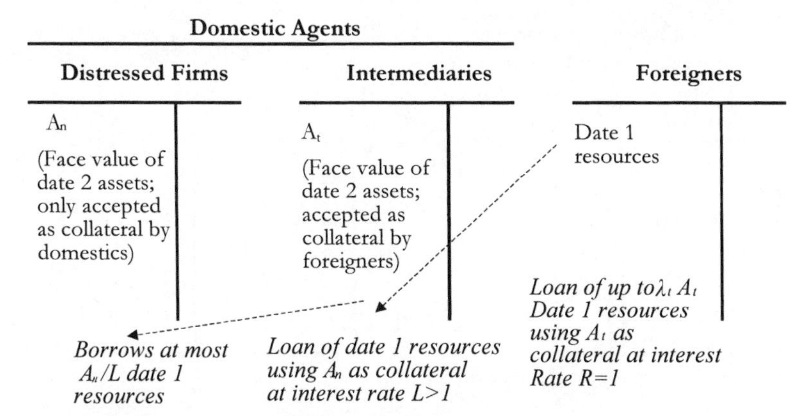

- Distressed firms have profitable projects but need date 1 resources
- Foreigners require collateral when lending date 1 resources at the international interest rate
- Only domestic intermediaries own internationally-accepted collateral

Fig. 5.3 Equilibrium in domestic financial markets

mestic financial system. We can think of a crisis as a time when (1) a significant fraction of firms or economic agents are in need of financing to either repay debt or implement new investments needed to save high-return projects, and (2) on net, the economy as a whole does not have enough assets and enough commitment to obtain the external resources it needs. Loosely, I refer to these assets and commitment as *collateral*, which needs not be interpreted literally as pledged assets but rather as the resources that are likely to be recouped by a lender. In order to make things as stark as possible, imagine that distressed firms have no assets of value to foreigners, but that the high date 2 return on their investment if successfully maintained, A_n, is fully pledgeable to other domestic agents. As a more concrete example, think of A_n as the value of a building (nontradable) delivered at date 2, and assume that absent a crisis the discount of future flows is simply zero, the international discount rate. The mass of these projects is 1.

Other domestic firms and investors (or foreign specialists) have assets, A_t, that are "good collateral" to foreigners—for example, U.S. Treasury bills, the present value of exports, and other domestic assets such as telecommunications companies that may be deemed more transparent and trustworthy by foreign investors. Because it is highly unlikely that foreigners would be willing to provide financing equivalent to the full value of these assets—due to a sovereign problem, for example—assume that one unit of A_t only secures a loan of λ_t date 1 resources.[4] Much of the policy discussion later in this paper has to do with increasing the value of this parameter.

4. Thus, in addition to binding microeconomic incentive problems, there may be sovereign risk associated with many of these assets, especially in the event of crises. The latter affects foreigners' valuation of these assets even when they acquire the private control rights.

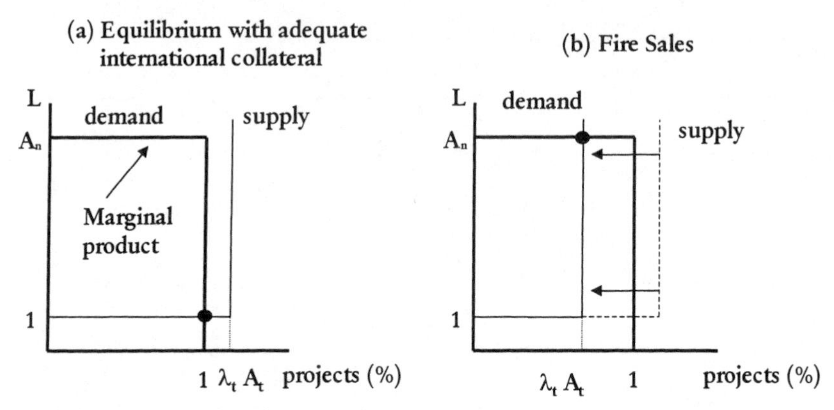

- Limited number of profitable projects
- Scarcity of international collateral limits the transfer of funds to distressed firms
- A decline in the quality of a country's international collateral can cause a fire sale

Fig. 5.4 Fire sales

Domestic financial markets are essentially the place where up to $\lambda_t A_t$ date 1 resources are made available to the distressed firms, which have date 2 assets A_n to pledge in exchange. When the economy's pledgeable resources are greater than the needs of distressed firms, arbitrage keeps the internal cost of funds L equal to the international interest rate (normalized to 1 here), all distressed firms are able to borrow funds, and only a fraction of domestic collateral A_n needs to be pledged. This is the case in panel A of figure 5.4. In this simple example, in which all projects have the same high return, the domestic demand for international liquidity by distressed firms is flat up to the point at which all projects are fully refinanced. The supply, on the other hand, is flat at the international interest rate until international collateral $\lambda_t A_t$ runs out, at which point it becomes vertical. When the aggregate needs of distressed firms are greater than pledgeable resources, competition among distressed firms transfers all of their private surplus (return above the international interest rate) to the domestic suppliers of international liquidity. Panel B illustrates this *fire sale* of domestic assets. The fraction of projects financed is $\lambda_t A_t < 1$, and the discount of domestic collateral jumps from 1 (the international level) to $L = A_n > 1$.

The most direct shock conducive to a fire sale and crisis is indeed a sudden loss in the international appeal of a country's assets. This can be due to country-specific factors as well as to changes and shocks in the segments of international financial markets relevant for the country. The turmoil after the Russian crisis in October 1998 is a prototypical example of the latter.

Shocks need not come directly from external financial factors to reflect the weakness of financial links, however. Panel A in figure 5.5 plots the

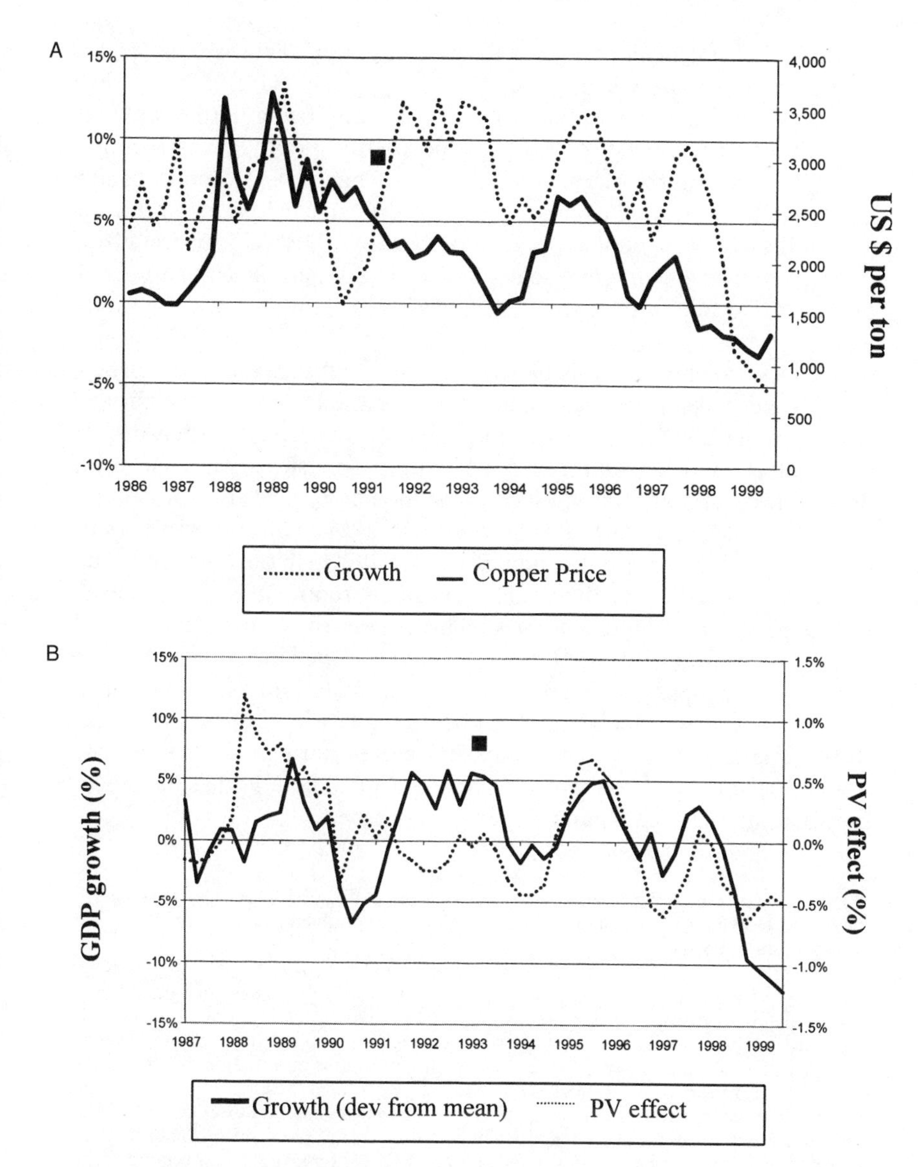

Fig. 5.5 Excess sensitivity and Chile: *A,* Growth and copper price; *B,* Present value effect of terms of trade shocks

Sources: Growth from the IMF's *International Financial Statistics;* copper prices (London Metal Exchange) from Datastream.

paths of the spot price of copper from the London Metal Exchange and Chile's quarterly growth in gross domestic product (GDP). The resemblance is stark, with the only important exception being the 1990 growth slowdown and its recovery episode, which had a purely domestic origin. Panel B documents the excessive sensitivity of Chile's GDP response to copper prices by plotting the annuity value of the expected present value impact of the decline in copper prices, as a share of GDP.[5] It is apparent from this figure (from the different scales in the axes, in particular) that fluctuations in GDP are an order of magnitude larger than a smoothing model would dictate.[6]

The view portrayed in this paper identifies the fundamental problem as one of weak links to international financial markets. Panel B of figure 5.6 reinforces this conclusion, illustrating the positive correlation between the current account deficit and the price of copper, opposite to what one would predict from standard smoothing arguments. The Tequila crisis of 1995 appears to be the exception that proves the rule, as the high copper price gave the Chilean economy enough liquidity to ride through the crisis and experience fast domestic growth despite the large international credit crunch experienced by emerging economies.[7] This is confirmed in panel B, which demonstrates that Chile used a large fraction of the liquidity given by the high price of copper to offset the decline in capital inflows as the current account deficit at normal prices reached its highest level during that year. Most importantly, exactly the opposite occurred during the 1998–99 crisis as the price of copper plummeted (erasing Chile's liquidity) at the precise time that international financial markets tightened.[8]

5. The present value effect is computed assuming an autoregressive (of order 4) process for the spot price of copper, a constant growth rate for copper production (7 percent), and a fixed discount rate (7.5 percent).

6. The price of copper has trends and cycles at different frequencies, some of which are persistent (see Marshall and Silva 1998). There seems to be no doubt, however, that the sharp decline in the price of copper during the current crisis was mostly the result of a transitory demand shock brought about by the Asian crisis. As the latter economies have begun recovering, so has the price of copper. I would argue that conditional on the information that the current shock was a transitory demand shock, the univariate process used to estimate the present value impact of the decline in the price of copper in figure 5.5 overestimates the extent of this decline. The lower decline in future prices is consistent with this view. The variance of the spot price is 6 times the variance of fifteen-months-ahead future prices. Moreover, the expectations computed from the AR process track reasonably well the expectations implicit in future markets but at the very end of the period, when liquidity-premium considerations may have come into play.

7. Capital flows were high, matching the high copper price, but the current account was not. The other exception reflects a domestically induced recession, which resulted from the monetary tightening implemented at the beginning of the new government to offset the inflationary pressures of the preceding political cycle. Capital flows remained high but ultimately led to the accumulation of international reserves rather than financing a current account deficit.

8. Note that terms of trade were also bad in 1993 and that, consistently, growth slowed down that year as well (see fig. 5.1). However, international financial markets were buoyant at the time, so this decline did not come together with a severe credit crunch.

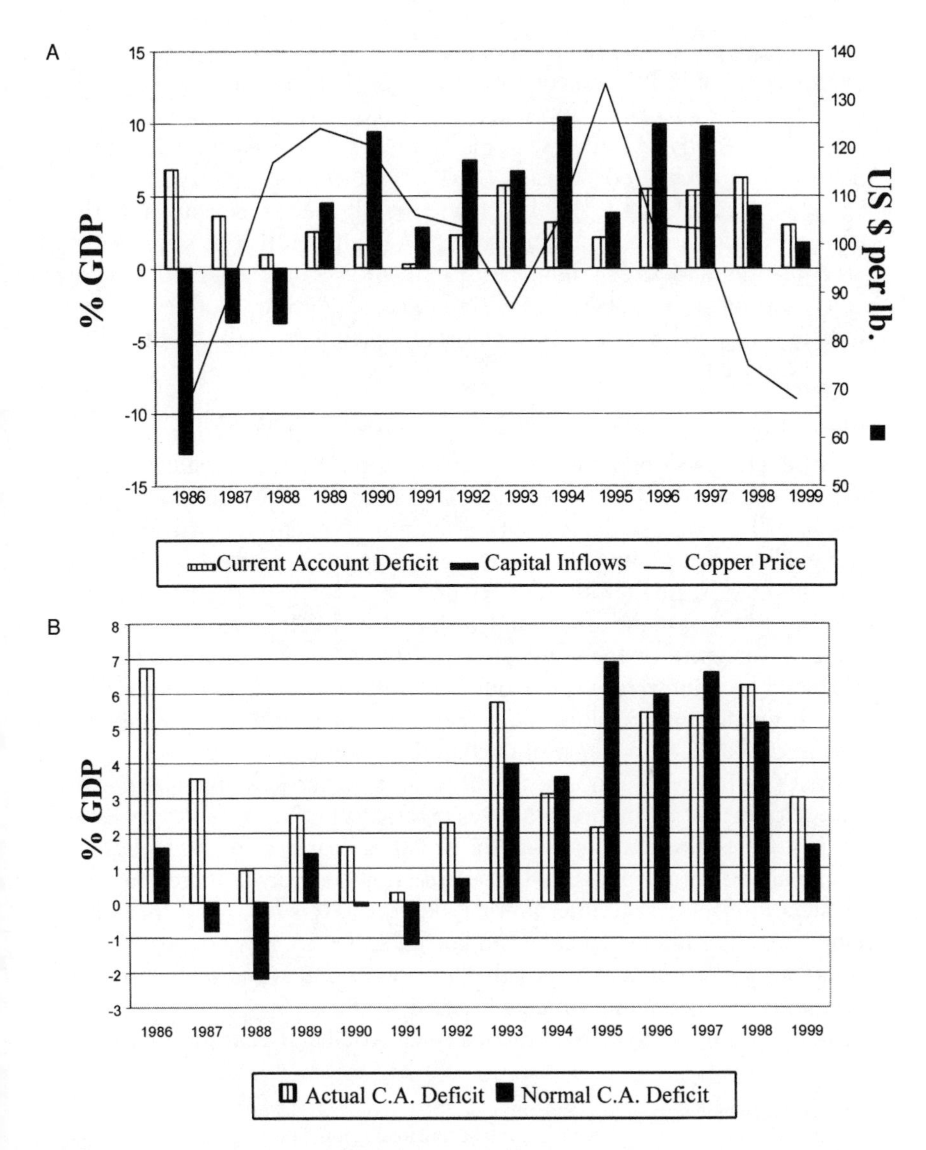

Fig. 5.6 Copper prices and Chile's current account: *A*, Balance of payments and copper price; *B*, Current account deficit

Sources: Data banks at Instituto Nacional de Estadisticas de Chile and Banco Central de Chile.

In order to place this scenario in the context of the model above, assume that international collateral consists primarily of claims on tradable goods while domestic collateral represents mostly assets issued by producers of nontradable goods.[9] An adverse terms-of-trade shock is simply a decline in the value of traded goods' assets, A_t, which reduces the country's borrowing capacity and shifts the supply curve to the left in a manner similar to the financial shocks above. A sufficiently large or sufficiently long sequence of terms-of-trade shocks can significantly reduce a country's international liquidity, causing a fire sale and corresponding real decline. Needless to say, the extent to which this is likely to happen depends critically on the tightness of external financial markets.[10]

5.2.2 Ingredient 2: Underdeveloped Domestic Financial Markets

Turning to the second ingredient, the development of domestic financial markets is instrumental not only in fostering investment and growth, but also in aggregating resources during distress. Underdeveloped financial markets limit the prompt reallocation of resources, creating wasteful contractions in those markets most affected by shocks or least plugged into the financial system. On the other hand, as financial development rises so does leverage—and with it the vulnerability of the financial system to shocks also increases. Many Latin American economies have suffered at both ends: chronic financial repression and underdevelopment and, when moving away from that, large collapse of the banking system.

Most significantly for the purpose at hand, however, it is this *domestic* underdevelopment that naturally creates externalities that justify macroeconomic policies aimed at changing the private sector's *international* liquidity management (as opposed to measures aimed simply at increasing the private sector's access to international liquidity). It is this point that I develop here, after briefly documenting the underdevelopment of most Latin American financial markets. For the latter, consider two basic features of these markets: their limited size and their illiquidity.

Figure 5.7 highlights Latin America's size problem. Regardless of how it

9. The international economics literature has long recognized the importance of international collateral and its relation with a country's tradables sector. Formal models of sovereign debt renegotiation are built around the question of what international lenders can use to threaten sovereign countries in the event of default. In this literature, international collateral is typically taken to be some fraction of exports. Cash revenues from exports can be seized before they make it back into the country. This feature was used by Mexico during the 1994–95 crisis when its oil revenues were made part of the collateral backing the liquidity package it received.

10. In isolation, these canonical shocks are not always large enough to justify the observed aggregate volatility created by a crisis, and at times crises occur even without their apparent presence. These features are not in contradiction to the basic premise, because both their presence and the high likelihood of their becoming a factor in the near future typically suffice to trigger public and private responses with recessionary consequences—and of course, these responses may indeed prevent larger crises in the near future. I will return to this discussion in the policy sections.

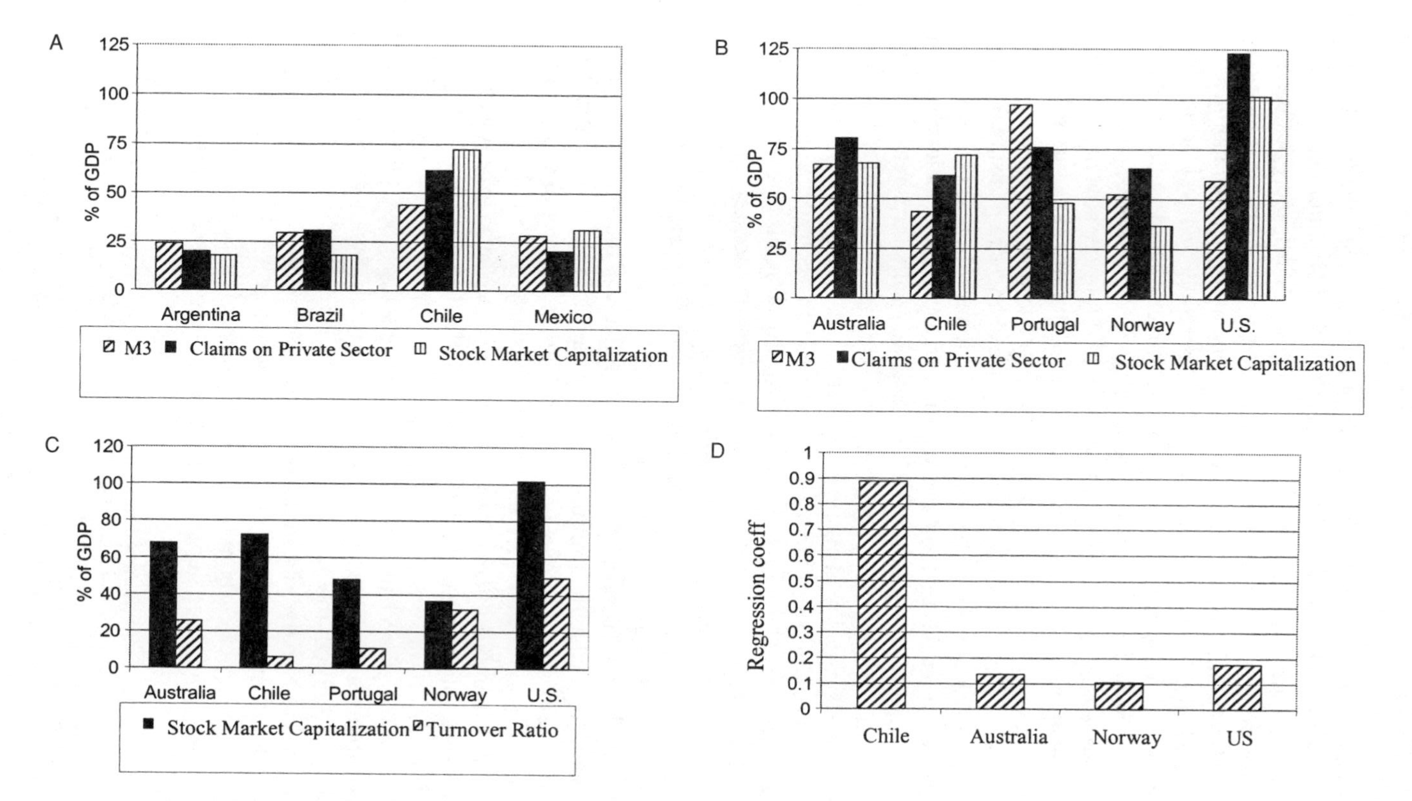

Fig. 5.7 Latin America's level problem

is measured, and despite significant improvements over the last decade, Latin America's financial markets and levels of financial intermediation are substandard. In panels A and B it is clear that M3, loans, and stock market capitalization, each relative to GDP, fare poorly with respect to Organization for Economic Cooperation and Development (OECD) economies.

Even when the standard measures of financial depth are at world-class levels, there is always evidence of underdevelopment. The dark bars in panel C confirm that in terms of stock market capitalization values, Chile is an outlier in the region and fares well when compared to more advanced economies. The light bars, on the other hand, reflect that Chile has a very substandard turnover ratio.[11] Panel D reports the results of running a simple regression of the absolute value of daily price changes (a measure of volatility) on the change in the fraction of total capitalization traded. Literally interpreted, it reveals that, on average, an increase in the volume traded (in terms of total capitalization value) is associated with an increase in price volatility that is about 10 times larger in Chile than in countries with presumably better developed financial markets.

We can now return to the model and enrich it to consider financial underdevelopment. The central point to be drawn from this extension is that unlike the case in which only ingredient 1 is present, domestic providers of international liquidity are not transferred all of the surplus during crises, and hence they are not given the right incentives to supply this liquidity. When domestic financial markets are imperfect in the sense that distressed firms without direct access to international financial markets do not have the means to pledge their returns fully to other domestics or informed investors, the ex ante incentive to hoard and supply international liquidity is weakened. Market-making is not a great business in a market with constrained demands. Imperfect domestic financial markets are captured here by the assumption that only a fraction $\lambda_n < 1$ of a distressed firm's value can be pledged.

Panel A in figure 5.8 illustrates the scenario just described. Given the date 0 allocations, a decline in λ_n reduces the effective demand for international liquidity. Although the marginal product curve (dashed line) remains unchanged, the effective demand curve (solid line) shifts down because the maximum payment per unit of investment is only $\lambda_n A_n$. As long as pledgeable assets are greater than the opportunity cost of funds (the international interest rate), however, domestic providers will make these loans.[12]

11. Although excessive churn can be wasteful, it is highly unlikely that Chile's depressed levels are enough to support a solid infrastructure of market makers able to provide optimal levels of immediacy and liquidity. Moreover, one could argue that the wastes associated with normal churn are a cost worth paying to reduce the extent of systemic liquidity crises when these arise. This is a theme worth researching further in the context of emerging economies.

12. Note that a decline in L does not necessarily imply that the domestic interest rate falls relative to the case with better developed domestic financial markets (for given international liquidity). It may imply instead that a larger share of the domestic "loan" becomes uncollateralized.

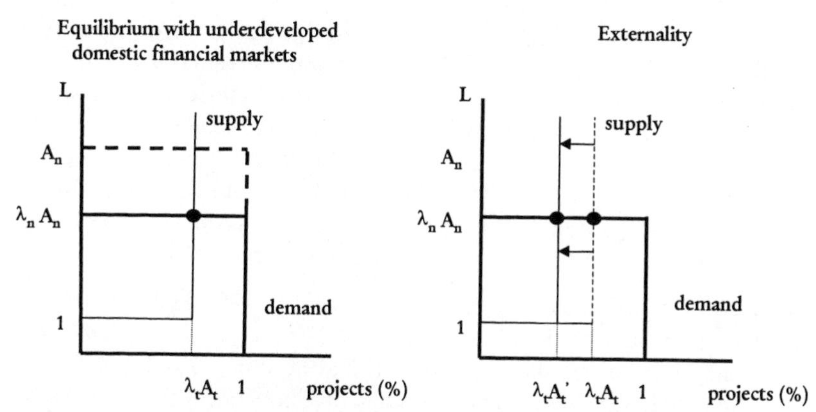

- Imperfect domestic collateral reduces the effective demand for funds
- Lower demand reduces intermediaries' expected returns for lending
- These lower returns reduce date 0 investment in international collateral
- Less international collateral increases the vulnerability of the economy to bad shocks

Fig. 5.8 Excess vulnerability

Domestic availability of international collateral will not remain unchanged, however. In this environment, friction in the market for domestic assets distorts the private returns of holding domestic and international collateral. The ex ante equilibrium response to such distortion at date 0 is captured in panel B, with an inward shift in the ex ante supply of international liquidity or collateral. Since domestic financial constraints limit the returns received by international liquidity providers below the full return of distressed projects, the incentive to provide such liquidity declines. In the process, the economy experiences more frequent fire sales and more severe distress in the event of an international squeeze on the country. The economy is, in the end, made too vulnerable to external shocks because domestic investors do not value international liquidity enough, creating less international collateral than is socially optimal.

In essence, this undervaluation of international liquidity corresponds to a reduced private-sector incentive to contract insurance against external aggregate shocks. This can take many forms aside from external overborrowing and distorted incentives to produce goods and assets appealing to foreign investors and lenders (international collateral). For example:

1. *Excessive dollarization of external liabilities.* When a country is exposed to sharp international liquidity shortages, it is socially desirable that the private sector contract its debt contingent on those shocks that generate such shortages. Denominating the external debt in local currency rather than "dollars" is one such contingency. The domestic borrower contracting in pesos trades off a higher interest rate for the insurance against aggregate shocks that depreciate the exchange rate. When international liquidity is un-

dervalued (relative to the second best—not the first best), borrowers will undervalue the latter hedge as well (see Caballero and Krishnamurthy 2002b).

2. *Distorted maturity structure*. Long-term external debt is like short-term debt plus rollover insurance. When domestic financial markets are underdeveloped, there is less incentive to buy this form of insurance as well, since the holders of the "insurance policy" that do not experience distress and financial needs at date 1 do not receive the full social return of their guaranteed debt-rollover (see Caballero and Krishnamurthy 2000).

Unfortunately, the harmful effects of these distorted decisions do not stop here because they are probably leveraged by supply factors. Once the size of the domestic market for international liquidity is reduced by domestic financial underdevelopment, foreign investors' incentives to become country specialists are reduced as well. If these specialists face liquidity risks themselves, they are likely to reduce their entry even further if few other specialists are willing to participate.[13]

Finally, while I have emphasized here the (dynamic) impact of domestic financial underdevelopment on international liquidity shortages, the reverse feedback is also present. International liquidity shortages can reduce effective domestic financial development by, for example, hurting the banking system. I will spend a few lines on the latter mechanism, as banks play a particularly important role in emerging markets and are especially fragile to international liquidity mismanagement.

Figure 5.9 illustrates two prototypes of the connection between external constraints and banking problems. Panel A shows the severe Mexican credit crunch that followed the Tequila crisis. Loans, particularly new loans, imploded early during the crisis, especially as the currency went into free fall and dragged the already weak balance sheets of Mexican banks with it. The Argentine case during the same episode started from the other side of the banks' balance sheets. Panel B illustrates the path of deposits and loans, indicating that it was not that the value of the loans imploded—perhaps because the exchange rate did not collapse—but that depositors ran for their deposits in order to convert them into dollars because they expected that the tight external conditions would make the convertibility system unsustainable.

The basic model is easily extended to include a banking sector that replaces the domestic credit chains discussed above. For example, in order to capture a Mexican-style credit crunch, let banks make loans to firms funded at date 0 by issuing debt to foreigners. At date 1, domestic holders of international assets mortgage them and deposit the proceeds in the banking system, which in turn intermediates new loans to distressed firms. Banks are subject to capital adequacy standards such that the ratio of the market

13. See Caballero and Krishnamurthy (2000) for a model of entry and thin markets in determining foreigners' reluctance to extend contingent credit lines.

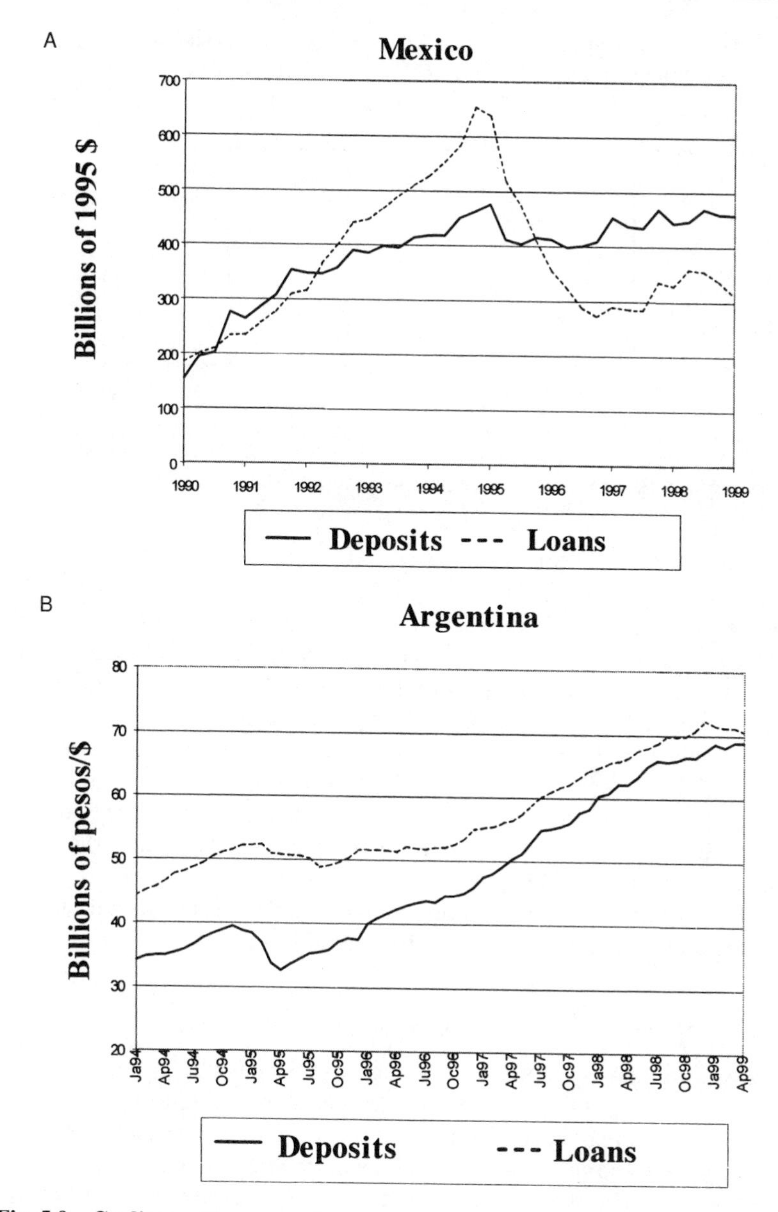

Fig. 5.9 Credit crunches

value of capital to loans must be at least α. When banks are unconstrained, the economy is equivalent to that described above with perfect domestic financial markets and weak financial links. Once adequacy standards bind, however, the supply curve for internal funds becomes backward bending as bank capital is eroded by higher interest rates that in turn lower asset prices.

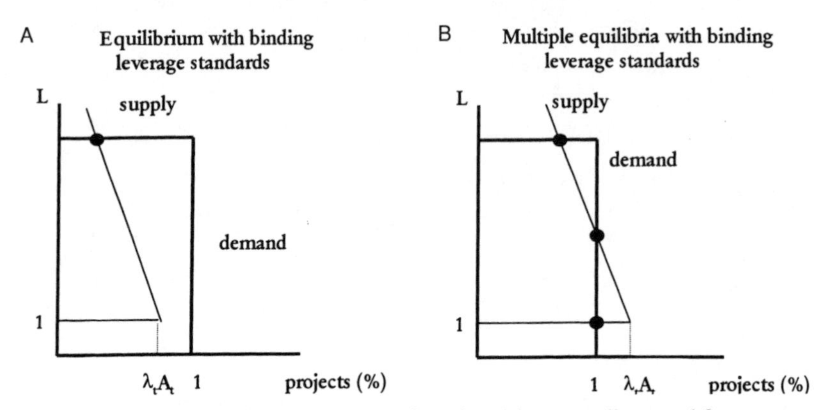

- Banks must hold sufficient capital against date 1 loans to distressed firms
- Higher interest rates reduce the value of date 0 loans, increasing market leverage
- Binding leverage standards require banks to reduce date 1 lending as interest rates

Fig. 5.10 Bank capital crunches

Panel A of figure 5.10 illustrates that this fire sale of assets may sharply reduce the banking sector's lending capacity, creating a credit crunch. Frictions in the banking sector are actually more serious than those described in undeveloped financial markets, above. Constrained banks cause a financial bottleneck as excess domestic resources are not properly channeled to distressed firms, wasting otherwise good international collateral. While the contraction in loan supply causes the increase in interest rates, the collapse in asset prices amplifies the impact of the crisis by deepening the credit crunch caused by distressed banks' balance sheets. Panel B demonstrates that the feedback between asset prices and feasible intermediation can easily bring about the possibility of multiple equilibria.

5.3 Policies for a Well-behaved Private Sector

Paralleling the sequential introduction of the central ingredients to justify an international liquidity management strategy, I discuss the policy aspects of this strategy in two steps. In the first one, which in its purest form corresponds to the case in which only the first ingredient (see section 5.2.1) is present, I address the following question: What are the types of structural and macroeconomic policies that a government should pursue, even if the private sector is using the socially efficient prices in deciding its international liquidity position?

If the private sector does as well as the social planner could do, facing identical collateral (financial) constraints, then effective policy would have to seek to relax these constraints. Technically, in this case the decentralized equilibrium is constrained efficient, and the government can improve things only if it can move the economy from the second toward its first best.

There are two generic strategies to attempt such improvement: (1) make structural reforms in financial markets and the contractual environment, and (2) use efficiently any commitment that the government may have (and the private sector does not) and that is valuable to international investors and lenders.

The following lists are not meant to be exhaustive but simply illustrative of the nature of the policies that are required in each instance. Beginning with the structural reforms and moving to the contractual environment and financial markets, it seems relevant to mention three complementary fronts:

1. *Institutions.* By now there is widespread consensus on a series of general recommendations to improve external financial links, which can be found in most "international financial architecture" pamphlets. These recommendations include norms of transparency and accountability; banks' sound practices for supervision, settlement, accounting, and disclosure; aggregate risk management; and a series of related measures and practices aimed at improving the country's contractual environment and corporate governance.[14]

2. *Fostering integration synergies.* It takes more than change in regulation and supervision to achieve the desired goal. A good example of this observation is the case of Chile. Although Chile has made and continues to make substantial progress in ensuring an appropriate legal environment as it relates to businesses, its limited size and very unequal wealth distribution make progress on the corporate-governance front difficult, especially when considering its natural or "structural" ownership concentration. This hints at an important synergy in fostering a much deeper integration with international financial markets: not only is good corporate governance needed to succeed on integration, but integration may be an essential ingredient to achieving good corporate governance, as well. It is for this reason that I find capital flows taxation, while justifiable on static second-best ground, potentially very harmful. A more reasonable recipe, I believe, is as follows: If

14. Teachers Insurance and Annuity Association College Retirement Equities Fund (TIAA-CREF), one of the largest institutional investors in the United States, has made public that it simply does not invest in claims issued by companies with poor corporate governance standards (see pp. 10–11 in the May 1999 issue of *Participant*, TIAA-CREF's quarterly news and performance magazine). Among its requirements are (1) that a company's board consist of a substantial majority of independent directors (i.e., no significant personal ties, current or past); (2) that a company's board must obtain shareholder approval for actions that could alter the fundamental relationship between shareholders and the board; and (3) that companies must base executive compensation on a pay-for-performance system, and should provide full and clear disclosure of all significant compensation arrangements. It does not take an in-depth knowledge of Latin American corporations to realize that very few of them would make it into TIAA-CREF's good corporate governance list.

the country's institutions are so far from ideal that the decentralized equilibrium is very unstable, taxing capital inflows contingently may be justified. If that is not the case, however, it may well pay off to bear the additional risk in exchange for more rapid development of financial links and markets.[15]

3. *Institutional investors.* Fostering and nurturing the development of well-supervised institutional investors is an efficient mechanism to delegate the enforcement of good corporate governance standards to the private sector, because these institutions often ponder such factors in their investment decisions.

As far as relaxing the private sector's international financial constraint during crises, consider three important—and quite different—areas of improvement:

1. *Fiscal policy.* Grounded on Keynesian mechanisms, *optimal* fiscal policy over the business cycle is traditionally thought of as being countercyclical. Latin American economies, unlike those of OECD nations, typically exhibit the opposite pattern; fiscal deficits are *pro*cyclical rather than countercyclical. This pattern has been interpreted as a seriously suboptimal policy, and most likely the result of the financial constraints faced by the governments themselves. This assessment may be true, but it misses an important point: If external financial shocks are an important source of fluctuations, the economy should distribute the scarce available international resources across domestic economic agents so as to smooth their differences in financial distress. It is highly unlikely that government expenditure, unless used very selectively to solve financial distress in the private sector, is the right place to allocate the marginal dollar.[16] Fiscal policy may need to be procyclical, after all.[17]

2. *Labor markets.* Most countries in the region are in need of a modern labor code, and the pervasive income inequality problem that affects them adds a series of additional complications to this task. For the purpose of this section, however, the main point to emphasize is the fact that—leveraged by financial problems—Latin American economies are exposed to

15. As of May 2000, Chile opted to permanently remove "taxation" of short-term capital inflows, as well as to implement a series of measures to facilitate both the participation of domestic firms in foreign financial markets and the participation of foreign investors in domestic markets. At the same time, several measures to improve corporate governance are being actively discussed. From the point of view adopted in this paper, these steps are significant steps forward.

16. This also suggests that fiscal adjustments during crises ought to be made on the expenditure rather than the taxes side. If the latter is unavoidable, they should probably be targeted away from the supply side of the economy.

17. This is an optimal policy argument, as opposed to the more standard one that explains the fiscal pattern in terms of the financial constraints faced by the government itself. Which effect dominates depends on whether the private sector (or perhaps a specific sector within it) or the government faces the tightest financial constraints during the crisis.

much larger short-term adjustment needs. These are highly unlikely to be accommodated fully—and to a different degree in different countries—by exchange rate movements. Thus the new labor code must allow for a more or less automatic recession-and-crisis package. I believe, for example, that to follow the advice of those who argue (as Argentina did in the recent past) that temporary contracts have not been effective in Europe is misguided.[18] The European problem is primarily one of lowering structural unemployment, whereas Latin American economies need also to deal with sharp short-term crises. Thus the Latin American solution should at the very least allow for a contingent relaxation of temporary contract constraints; this form of hiring should be fostered during crises.

3. *Sovereign risk and commitment.* A sovereign typically has access to policy options and decisions that may hurt or expand its private sector's international collateral. On one hand, a highly erratic and discretionary government will probably add sovereign risk to its private sector's assets. On the other hand, a government firmly and credibly committed to fostering foreign investment will probably expand the set of domestic assets that constitute good collateral—broadly understood—to foreigners. Similarly, macroeconomic policies should not be aimed at expropriating foreigners in a myopic fashion. This does not mean that there is no space for insurance from foreign investors to domestics, or that the states of the world under which this "insurance" pays can not be linked to (for example) the equilibrium exchange rate. The macroeconomic rules leading to such aggregate "insurance," however—including those which govern the exchange rate—must be made contingent on clearly verifiable observables that are outside the direct control of the country (e.g., the terms of trade and the Emerging Markets Bond Index Plus [EMBI+]).[19]

5.4 Policies to Offset the Private Sector's Underprovision

In addition to the previous policies, which aimed at moving the economy toward its first best, one ought to ask, *When and how should the government attempt to "force" the private sector to increase its international liquidity position?*

18. The argument against temporary contracts is not that they do not create employment, but separate insiders from outsiders even further by reducing the pressure on insiders and creating a class of temporary—and unskilled—workers.

19. Such clear rules not only facilitate risk sharing between foreigners and domestics but also help reduce uncertainties that further complicate the response of an economy to a shortage of international liquidity. For example, it is quite clear that a significant component of the recent Chilean recession had to do with the response of its central bank to several speculative attacks, which in turn were linked to the uncertainty about the central bank and treasury responses to the tight external scenario. Similarly, the very limited real exchange rate depreciation that was obtained from Mexico's sharp nominal depreciation during the Russian crisis may also have resulted from the uncertainty it triggered on future monetary policy.

From the perspective of the view portrayed in this paper, the answer to the "when" part of the question is *whenever the second ingredient—domestic financial development—is present in a significant manner.* In this case, the government will be trying to move the economy from a third to a second best. The main difficulty with the "how" part is that the government cannot count on the cooperation of the private sector, because the latter will often attempt to offset any centralized international liquidity holding that puts the aggregate of this liquidity beyond that of the decentralized equilibrium without intervention.

In what follows I give four examples—with some of their perils—of policies aimed at depressing the private sector's bias against international liquidity hoarding.

1. *Sterilization.* The quintessential monetary policy to deal with this international liquidity management problem is a *sterilized intervention* (essentially, a process in which the central bank sells public bonds for international reserves) during the capital flows boom. The counterpart ought to be the selling back of these reserves during external crises. Experience and theory suggest that the first half of this policy, the sterilized intervention, is difficult and expensive to implement for prolonged periods, and it may even backfire as the private sector reacts perversely to the quasi-fiscal deficit, appreciation, and reserves accumulation at the central bank.[20] Thus, this probably is not an instrument that can be used for medium-term prevention.

2. *Liquidity ratios.* A closely related measure that works mostly through controlling international liquidity aggregation within the country is active management of bank reserves and capital adequacy ratios, and possibly international liquidity ratios. The model sketched above hints that the levels of these ratios should be increasing with respect to the degree of underdevelopment of financial markets. In order to be effective in managing international liquidity intertemporally, these requirements must be procyclical. There are, however, two practical problems with such a recommendation that may make this strategy less useful. First, for those countries in which the health of the banking system is suspect, weakening standards at the time of crisis may make a run more likely—this was a concern in Argentina during the 1998–99 crisis. Second, in other cases, especially when the participation of foreign banks is great, the policy may be ineffective during crises because the constraint may not be binding. Figure 5.11 shows the capital adequacy ratios for different segments of the Chilean banking sector; it is

20. In Caballero and Krishnamurthy (2002b), a sterilization may backfire if the market for public bonds is illiquid. Essentially, in this case sterilization creates a liquidity mismatch in the central bank's balance sheet (it holds very liquid reserves against less liquid bonds), which acts as free liquidity insurance to the private sector. See Calvo (1991) for a model à la Sargent-Wallace whereby the quasi-fiscal deficit generated by the sterilization may hurt the credibility of the inflationary target.

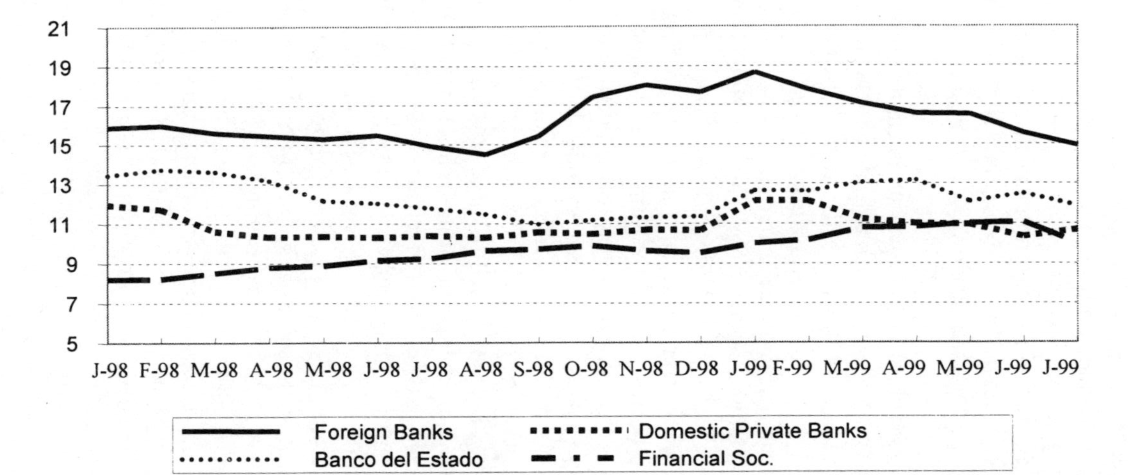

Fig. 5.11 Risk capital ratios of Chilean banks

apparent that foreign banks voluntarily withdrew. Although there is no doubt that fostering the arrival of solid international banks is a must, it is also important to understand the implications they may have for aggregate liquidity management.

3. *Capital controls*. Capital controls may supplement sterilization or, in principle, slow down capital inflows (perhaps of a targeted maturity) by themselves. However, there are at least four caveats to them:

a. If implemented, capital controls (to inflows) should be made contingent on the availability of external flows, lowering them during external crises.

b. Since an important part of the volatility in capital flows seems to be caused by suppliers' problems (e.g., hedge funds), it may be worthwhile to requiring liquidity ratios from them as well (although, as a practical matter, this seems rather difficult to implement and supervise).

c. The domestic "underinsurance" externality is likely to be more pronounced at the short end of the spectrum. Thus, controls should be biased toward reducing short-term capital flows.[21] Having said this, I must admit my concern with the emerging consensus that developing economies have excessive short-term borrowing relative to their international reserves. At some level the claim is trivially accurate—it is impossible to have a liquidity crisis if the country holds more reserves than short-term debt and renewals. At another, figure 5.12 shows that emerging economies are much more prudent than developed ones along this margin.[22] Running an economy with all the precautions that well-behaved emerging economies use is extremely expensive. Borrowing only long-term (expensive) and holding large amounts of reserves would most likely be considered very poor management for an average U.S. corporation. What is important here is to determine how large this ratio is relative to what the country's institutions and financial markets can support. Putting all emerging markets, regardless of financial development, in the same bag is likely to be unnecessarily burdensome for the most developed of these economies.

d. Most importantly, although the controls described above may be justifiable in terms of static second-best arguments, they are likely to hurt in the medium run once the endogenous arrival of international market-makers and corporate governance improvements are considered (see the discussion of this issue in the previous section).

4. *Monetary policy during crises.* Finally, all the measures above are preventive, but the policies expected to be implemented during crises also have an effect on ex ante precautionary decisions. For those emerging economies in which inflation expectations have already been stabilized, it is possible to

21. This argument is different from that which places the blame on "noisy" speculators who concentrate on short-term capital flows (see above).

22. The figure must be interpreted with caution, nonetheless, because an important difference between developed and developing economies is that the latter often must issue a larger share of their debt in foreign currency.

A

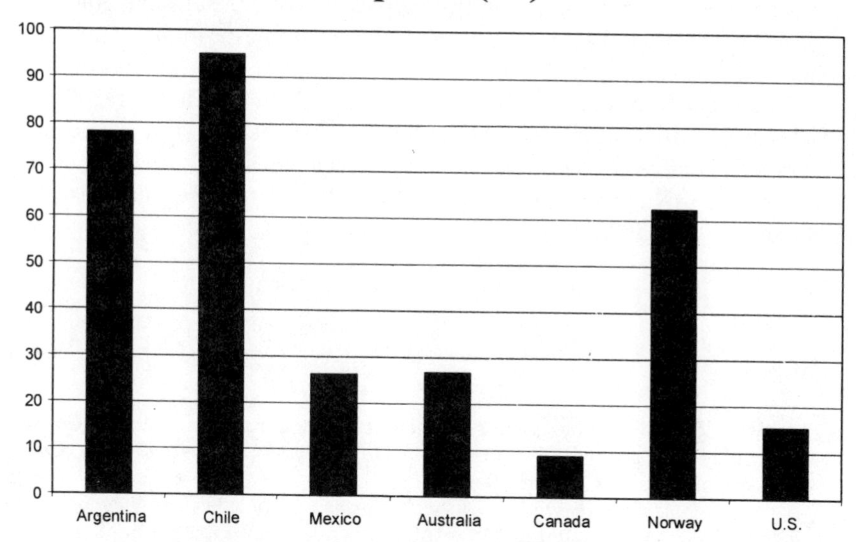

B

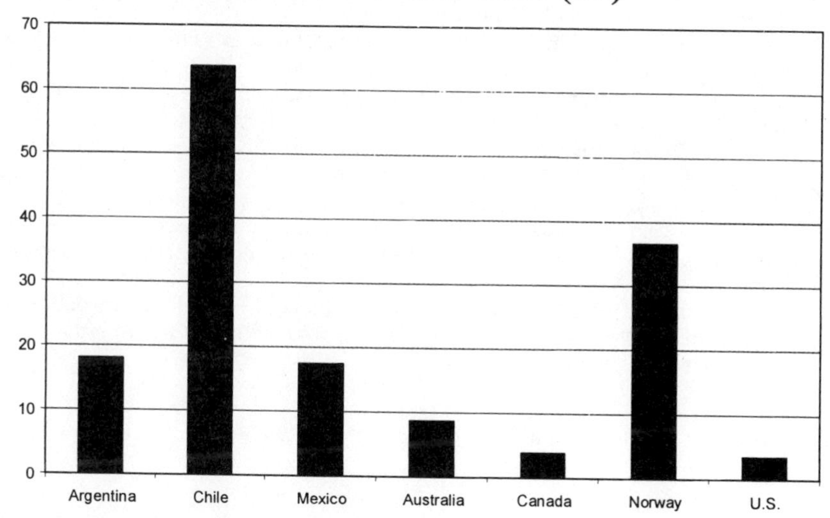

Fig. 5.12 Precautionary reserves

Sources: Reserves and Imports: IMF's *International Financial Statistics.* External Debt for developing countries: joint Bank for International Settlements, IMF, OECD, and World Bank statistics.

Notes: Data for 1997, except Norway data in panel B (1993). External debt for developed countries: the International Monetary Fund's (IMF's) *Balance-of-Payments Statistics.* External debt for emerging economies is the sum of debt securities issued abroad, Brady bonds, bank loans, trade credit, and multilateral claims. External debt for developed countries is the sum of debt securities and other investments (including loans, deposits, and trade credits) according to the IMF classification.

improve ex ante incentives by committing to an expansionary—or at least less contractionary than the central bank will be inclined to implement ex post—monetary policy during crises. Although domestic money cannot relax the main binding constraint, which is external, it does enhance domestic liquidity and in so doing moves equilibrium from than in figure 5.8 (fire sales and underinsurance) to that in figure 5.4 (fire sales without underinsurance). That is, if available, monetary policy can substitute for some of the more costly incentive mechanisms described above (see Caballero and Krishnamurthy 2002a).

References

Caballero, Ricardo J. 2000. Aggregate volatility in modern Latin America: Causes and cures. Background paper in *Dealing with economic insecurity in Latin America*. Washington, D.C.: World Bank, May.

———. 2001. *Macroeconomic volatility in reformed Latin America: Diagnosis and policy proposals*. Washington, D.C.: Inter-American Development Bank.

Caballero, Ricardo J., and Arvind Krishnamurthy. 2000. International liquidity management: Sterilization with illiquid financial markets. MIT, Department of Economics. Mimeograph, February.

———. 2001. International and domestic collateral constraints in a model of emerging market crises. *Journal of Monetary Economics* 48 (3): 513–48.

———. 2002a. A dual liquidity model of emerging markets. *American Economic Review, Papers and Proceedings* 92 (2): 33–37.

———. 2002b. Excessive dollar debt: Underinsurance and domestic financial underdevelopment. *Journal of Finance*, forthcoming.

Calvo, Guillermo. 1991. The perils of sterilization. *IMF Staff Papers* 38 (4): 921–26.

———. 1998. Capital flows and capital-market crises: The simple economics of sudden stops. University of Maryland, Department of Economics. Mimeograph, June.

Marshall, Isabel L., and Eduardo S. Silva. 1998. Fluctuaciones del precio del cobre (Fluctuations in the price of copper). *Informe Macroeconomico para la Empresa* 35 (September): 38–60.

6

Trade Liberalization and Financial Crisis
A Historical Comparison of Chile and the United States

Philip L. Brock

In truth, there has been a great deal of loose talk about tariffs and crises.
—Frank W. Taussig (1931)

6.1 Introduction

The conjunction of tariff changes and economic crises has fascinated economists for many years. Articles by Bates and Krueger (1993), Rodrik (1994), and Tornell (1995) suggest that economic crises may be required for trade liberalizations to become politically feasible. Other work, such as Krueger (1978), Little et al. (1993), and Corbo (1988), has emphasized the tightening of trade restrictions as a response to crises such as the Great Depression or the world fall in commodity prices in 1952–53.

The mainstream position on trade liberalization as a causal factor in economic crisis stresses the importance of pursuing appropriate macroeconomic policies to accompany trade reforms. Trade liberalization will lead to crisis only if inappropriate macro and financial-sector policies are followed. Two indirect channels have been suggested for the link between trade reform and financial crisis. The first one focuses on the credibility of trade reforms (Calvo 1987; Calvo and Mendoza 1994). Trade reforms that are perceived to be temporary will induce intertemporal substitution in consumption and investment that produces a worsening of the current account relative to a perceived permanent trade reform. A second channel stresses the role of moral hazard in bank regulation in open economies. McKinnon and Pill (1996) have emphasized the link between trade liberalization and moral hazard. Due to implicit or explicit government guarantees on domestic and foreign bank liabilities, bank financing of new investments resulting from a trade liberalization produces overborrowing and the increased likelihood of a government bailout of the banks.

Philip L. Brock is associate professor of economics at the University of Washington.

In this paper I explore another potentially important linkage between trade liberalization and financial crisis that emphasizes the supply of liquidity by the financial system. The paper's thesis is that a trade liberalization may create an especially fragile structure of long-term bank loans and short-term deposits that is conducive to a financial crisis. The analysis will emphasize the decisions played by central banks following trade liberalizations and leading up to financial crises.

To explore empirically the connection between trade liberalization and financial crisis, I examine the experience of the United States in the 1830s and Chile in the 1970s. These two cases necessarily provide a restricted comparison group. However, the two countries' experiences share a number of striking similarities as well as some important differences. Among the similarities are the following: gradual unilateral trade liberalization leading to a uniform tariff, fiscal surplus, large capital inflows followed by financial crisis, real exchange rate appreciation followed by depreciation, temporary reversal of liberalized trade policies following the crisis, and default on external debt. Among the important differences are those relating to 140 years of institutional structure: there was no International Monetary Fund (IMF) in the 1830s; central banking functions were rudimentary in the United States; and the U.S. monetary system functioned within the constraints of the gold standard, whereas Chile devalued its fixed exchange rate during the financial crisis. Examination of these two countries' experiences may therefore provide insights into behavior that bridges different historical periods and financial settings.

Section 6.2 develops the paper's conceptual framework regarding the role of central banks during the period following a trade liberalization. The section draws on a number of recent papers to highlight the importance of both "time-to-build" considerations and moral hazard when an economy shifts its production structure away from an inward-looking orientation and begins to undertake investments that, with time, will create an outward-oriented economy. Sections 6.3 and 6.4 compare the trade liberalizations in Chile during the 1970s and the United States during the 1830s, and examine explanations and evidence on the causes of the financial crises in the two countries. Section 6.5 turns to evidence from Chile and the United States regarding the time-to-build hypothesis of financial fragility. Section 6.6 examines the "second-generation" reforms that were implemented in the aftermath of the two financial crises. Section 6.7 concludes.

6.2 Trade Liberalization and Financial Crisis: A Conceptual Framework

At any given moment in time, most economies can be characterized as having some investments in the planning stage, some in the building stage, and some (perhaps many) in the production stage. If a viable project in the building stage needs financing beyond what was initially anticipated, a mature economy can generally provide financing to new investments so that they are not abandoned partway to completion because of lack of liquidity.

A major trade liberalization, however, alters an economy's production structure and firms' planned investments. At the time of the liberalization, the import-competing sector begins to contract so that cash flows from existing investments cannot be counted on as a source of liquidity for new exportable investments. Outside financing of new investments becomes more difficult, and there is a danger that creditors may restrict the amount of funds that are directed toward the exportable sector.

In the past several years a number of papers on financial crises have based their models on a three-period framework that in a general sense goes back to Diamond and Dybvig's (1983) model of bank runs. Although none of these papers discusses trade liberalization or trade policy, the three-period approach is useful for sorting out the financing issues that accompany the implementation of trade reforms. In a three-period world, a trade liberalization at period 0 creates opportunities for new investments, assuming that financing can be arranged. As the investments are being built in period 1 a financial crisis may occur (for several reasons related to liquidity shocks), and the new investments may end up partially abandoned in the absence of new funding. In period 2 a successful liberalization realizes the fruition of the new investments, but an unsuccessful liberalization must bear the costs of the abandoned projects. This stylized three-period time-to-build sequence seems to fit economies that are in the process of structural change, such as a trade liberalization.

To make these time-to-build models of financial crises work, there must be a random demand for liquidity in period 1. It is this liquidity demand that gives rise to financial intermediaries in these models. In the Diamond-Dybvig (1983) model—and in later extensions by Allen and Gale (1998, 2000), Gale and Vives (2002), and Chang and Velasco (2000)—liquidity management comes on the liability side of the banks, since some depositors have random liquidity needs in period 1. In the Holmström and Tirole (1998) model—as well as in the recent models by Diamond and Rajan (2001) and Caballero and Krishnamurthy (2001)—liquidity management occurs on the asset side of the banks, since firms have random additional financing requirements in period 1. Locating the source of the liquidity disturbance at the level of the firm following a trade liberalization is attractive, since firms may face random liquidity shocks as they adjust to the outward-oriented environment.

In these latter three models entrepreneurs cannot pledge the full value of the firms' output due to moral hazard and legal constraints. As a result, liquidity may be insufficiently supplied to firms that need it. In addition, a premium on liquidity will cause firms to invest too much in period 0 and liquidate too much in period 1, rather than making fewer investments in period 0 and arranging for a line of credit in period 1. Firms overinvest in period 0 as a way of self-insuring when liquidity is apt to be at a premium in period 1.

There are circumstances in these models in which projects will be liquidated when they should not be from a social point of view. Financial intermediaries can pool many borrowers and provide liquidity insurance (against idiosyncratic shocks) in the form of a credit line. When liquidity shocks are aggregate disturbances, financial intermediaries cannot provide liquidity insurance, since firms demand liquidity simultaneously in the event of a negative shock. Following an aggregate liquidity shock a government may be able to intervene in the supply of liquidity, but the intervention is not as simple as the introduction of deposit insurance into the Diamond and Dybvig (1983) model. In Holmström and Tirole (1998), the government can issue government bonds by virtue of its power to tax second-period consumption. These bonds provide liquid claims that act as a hedge against aggregate shocks in period 1.

The time-to-build literature on financial crises concentrates on moral hazard in firms' behavior as it relates to financial contracts and the structure of financial intermediaries. Liquidity provision by a central bank (or treasury) may prevent the inefficient liquidation of firms during a financial crisis. This is the "lender-of-last-resort" function, which may include the issue of liquid government debt as well as central bank credit. On the other hand, McKinnon and Pill (1996), Krugman (1998), Dooley and Shin (1999), and many others have expressed concern regarding the moral hazard created by the presence of implicit or explicit government guarantees on the banking system. Guarantees may create the incentive for banks to operate with an overly risky balance sheet. When the contracting constraints (stressed by liquidity models) on the asset side of banks create financial fragility and potentially inefficient liquidations of firms, and when implicit or explicit central bank guarantees simultaneously create a moral hazard, the central bank's role as lender of last resort becomes a balancing act.

The periods of tariff reduction in the United States during the 1830s and in Chile during the 1970s provide two similar episodes in which the increased demands for bank loans placed severe strains on the enforcement of prudential regulation. The next three sections sketch out the two tariff reductions, summarize the principal explanations that have been given for the resulting financial crises in each country, and then document the difficulties of enforcing prudential regulations in each case.

6.3 Trade Liberalization and Financial Crisis: Chile and the United States

On 11 September 1973 the military staged a coup in Chile and announced its intent to dismantle the excesses of state intervention in the economy. During the first three years following the coup, the average tariff was lowered from about 90 percent to about 27 percent. Equally significant, import licenses, prior import deposits, and import prohibitions were virtually eliminated. In the succeeding three years to mid-1979, tariffs were lowered to a uniform 10 percent rate (with the exception of automobiles). Within the next three years, however, the collapse of the Chilean financial system and a deep economic recession created pressure to reverse the liberalization.

Table 6.1 shows figures on the trade balance during the period of tariff reductions. After the average tariff fell to 14 percent in 1978, the trade balance turned negative for four years. This was the period of the economic boom in Chile following the opening of the economy. The trade deficit reflected an excess of investment over domestic saving, and by 1981that excess amounted to about 10 percent of Chile's gross domestic product (GDP). The deficit reverted to surplus in 1982 following the devaluation of the peso and the economy's slide into recession. The trade balance remained in surplus for the next five years as the economy dealt with the aftermath of a severe financial crisis.

A century and a half earlier, the United States had a trade liberalization and financial crisis that was strikingly similar to Chile's experience. The process began on 24 November 1832 when South Carolina announced (in the form of a decree law) its intention to nullify the federal tariff beginning in February and called up its militia to prepare for armed conflict. In the ensuing three months, Congress reached an agreement for the gradual dismantlement of the "American system" of import substitution that had reached its zenith in the late 1820s. Between 1833 and 1842 the Compromise Tariff set out a schedule of gradual tariff reductions and conversion of spe-

Table 6.1 **Chilean Trade Balance and Tariff Rates**

	Trade Balance (US$ millions)	Exports (US$ millions)	Imports (US$ millions)	Average Tariff Rate (%)
1974	357	2,151	1,794	67
1975	70	1,590	1,520	44
1976	643	2,116	1,473	33
1977	34	2,185	2,151	22
1978	–426	2,460	2,886	14
1979	–355	3,835	4,190	10
1980	–764	4,705	5,469	10
1981	–2,677	3,836	6,513	10
1982	63	3,706	3,643	10
1983	986	3,831	2,845	20
1984	363	3,651	3,288	35
1985	849	3,804	2,955	22
1986	1,100	4,199	3,099	22

Sources: Banco Central de Chile (1989), Edwards and Lederman (1998).

Table 6.2 U.S. Trade Balance and Implicit Tariff Rates, 1830–45

	Merchandise Trade Balance ($ millions)	Exports ($ millions)	Imports ($ millions)	Dutiable Imports ($ millions)	Free Imports ($ millions)	Ratio of Duties Calculated to Total Imports (%)	
						Dutiable	Free and Dutiable
1832	–13	62	75	68	7	43.0	30.0
1833	–13	70	83	63	20	38.3	29.0
1834	–6	81	87	47	40	40.2	21.8
1835	–22	100	122	64	58	40.4	21.3
1836	–52	107	159	89	70	34.9	19.5
1837	–19	94	113	62	51	29.2	16.1
1838	9	96	87	48	38	41.3	23.1
1839	–44	102	146	81	65	31.8	17.6
1840	25	112	86	44	42	34.4	17.6
1841	–11	104	115	58	57	34.6	17.4
1842	4	92	88	65	23	25.8	19.0
1843	40	78	37	26	12	29.2	20.1
1844	3	100	96	80	17	36.9	30.5

Source: U.S. Bureau of the Census (1975).

cific duties into tariff equivalents that resulted in a uniform 20 percent tariff in July 1842.

The United States entered into an economic boom during 1835 and 1836, with the trade deficit in 1836 representing approximately 5 percent of GDP. Financial panic in 1837 was followed by a pause in growth in 1838. Restored convertibility of the financial system permitted large capital inflows in 1839 prior to renewed financial distress that lasted from 1840 through 1844. The economy ran an overall large trade surplus between 1840 and 1844 in response to the financial distress and economic recession.

Table 6.2 shows the evolution of the tariff rates during the period. The Compromise Tariff initially lowered tariffs at the beginning of 1834 by one-tenth of the difference between their initial level and 20 percent. Additional tenths (each equal in size to the 1834 reduction) were taken off in 1836, 1838, and 1840. At the start of 1842 three-tenths were taken off, with the final three-tenths removed at the beginning of July 1842. During this period a number of goods, including especially iron rails for railroads, were admitted duty free. Consequently, average tariffs on all goods fell from 30 percent in 1832 to 16 percent in 1837, and average tariffs on dutiable goods fell from 43 percent to 29 percent.

There is no direct microeconomic evidence of the impact of the Compromise Tariff on various sectors of the U.S. economy. Henry Carey, a leading

Table 6.3 **Impact of Trade Liberalization on Chilean Manufacturing Production (1976–79)**

Subsector	Production Impact (% change)	Nominal Tariff, 1976 (%)	Production Impact Ranking	Tariff Ranking
Metal products	–64.7	45	1	2
Electrical and nonelectrical machinery	–58.7	40	2	4
Rubber products	–55.1	38	3	5
Basic metal industries	–53.9	60	4	9
Textiles	–44.7	46	5	1
Shoes and clothing	–44.6	44	5	3
Nonmetal mineral products	–27.9	33	7	7
Beverages	–20.6	29	8	10
Chemicals	–18.8	34	9	6
Tobacco	–15.5	23	10	15
Printing and publishing	–12.7	33	11	7
Paper and paper products	14.8	29	12	10
Food products	25.9	26	13	14
Wood and wood products	32.6	27	14	12
Furniture	61.7	27	15	12

Source: De la Cuadra and Hachette (1991, 258).
Note: Spearman rank correlation coefficient is 0.7821 (99 percent confidence level)

protectionist of the time, claimed that following 1833 "the building of furnaces and mills almost wholly ceased, the wealthy English capitalists having thus succeeded in regaining the desired control of the great American market for cloth and iron."[1] Taussig (1931) believed that the impact of the tariff was smaller, but he did concede that the Compromise Tariff had hurt manufacturers.

The evidence on the microeconomic response of manufacturing to trade liberalization in Chile indicates that those industries with the highest initial levels of nominal tariff protection in 1976 suffered the greatest declines in output by 1979 (De la Cuadra and Hachette 1991, 258), as shown in table 6.3. Several recent studies (Roberts 1996; Levinsohn 1999; Pavcnik 2002) have made use of plant-level data from 1979 to 1986 that was gathered by the Chilean National Statistics Institute. The data show weak evidence that the exportable manufacturing sector increased in importance relative to the import-competing and nontradables sectors between 1979 and 1986.

The growth of export industries in both the United States and Chile required time to build infrastructure and prepare land for export crops such as cotton and wheat in the United States and fruit and timber in Chile. As an example, between 1974 and 1989 Chilean fruit growers dramatically expanded land planted in apples and table grapes, as shown in table 6.4. At the

1. This statement is quoted in Taussig (1931, 117).

Table 6.4 Chilean Exports of Apples and Table Grapes

	1965	1974	1982	1989
Land planted (hectares)				
Apples	8,486	11,350	17,662	25,860
Table grapes	5,451	4,250	17,363	47,700
Exports (tons)				
Apples	12,264	11,526	101,641	316,800
Table grapes	6,816	12,698	83,185	693,000

Source: Chilean Development Corporation.

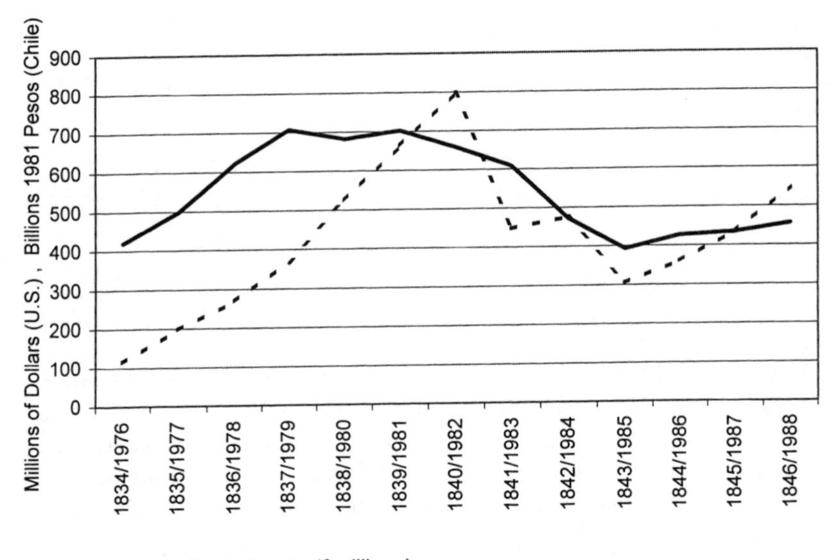

Fig. 6.1 Net asset growth of banks in United States and Chile

Sources: U.S. Bank Assets: U.S. Bureau of the Census (1975, 580–87). Chilean Deposit Bank Net Assets: International Monetary Fund, *International Financial Statistics.* Net assets are total end-of-year assets (the sum of lines 20 through 22f) minus credit from monetary authorities (line 26g); the nominal figures for each year are deflated by the December consumer price index deflator, which is taken from Banco Central de Chile (1989).

time of the 1982 crisis, much of the newly planted land was not yet producing.

Figure 6.1 shows the lending booms that took place in the United States and Chile during the periods following the trade liberalizations. In the United States bank assets rose at an annual rate of 19 percent between 1834 and 1837, whereas in Chile net bank assets rose at an annual rate of 29 percent between 1979 and 1982. Bank assets in the United States fell by 50 percent between 1839 and 1843, whereas net bank assets (i.e., assets minus cen-

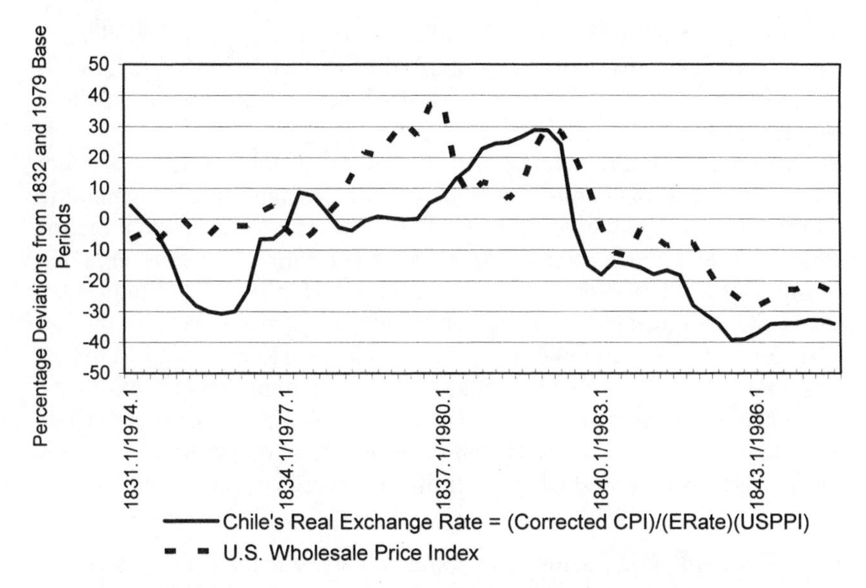

Fig. 6.2 Chile's real exchange rate (1974–87) and U.S. wholesale price index (1831–44)

tral bank "bailout" loans) in Chile fell by 60 percent between 1982 and 1985. The asset contraction in the United States was accompanied by the failure of about 200 banks (out of 900) at a cost paid by depositors, whereas in Chile the net asset contraction associated with the bailout of banks' bad loans created a future tax liability to Chilean taxpayers.

Simultaneous with the lending boom in each country was an appreciation of the real exchange rate, as shown in figure 6.2. In Chile the appreciation began in the second half of 1979 after the exchange rate was fixed at 39 pesos per dollar on June 30. In the two and one-half years between July 1979 and January 1982, the Chilean wholesale price index rose by 42 percent and the consumer price index rose by 68 percent. In the United States the appreciation began in the last quarter of 1834. In the two and one-half years between August 1834 and February 1837, the U.S. wholesale price index rose by 47 percent.

The end of Chile's real appreciation began with the devaluation of the exchange rate on 15 June 1982. The real depreciation hit an eighteen-month plateau in mid-1983 until a major devaluation in September 1984 initiated a final decline. The end of the U.S. real appreciation occurred simultaneously with suspension of bank convertibility during the panic of May 1837. Restoration of convertibility in early 1839 produced a secondary appreciation of the real exchange rate that ended in the last quarter of 1839 when the Second Bank of the United States closed amid widespread bank failures. The real depreciation took place by a fall in the price level rather than by a depreciation of the exchange rate. The price level hit a plateau for about eighteen months before the announced bankruptcy of the Second Bank set off a new wave of bank failures during the first half of 1842. During 1842 prices resumed their downward fall before reaching their nadir at the start of 1843.

There are obvious striking similarities in tariff policies, trade account movements, lending booms and busts, and real exchange rate movements in Chile and the United States. The most obvious difference is the manner by which the real depreciations took place (depreciation of the nominal exchange rate in Chile versus a fall in the price level in the United States). Are the similarities by chance, or are there common factors at work in the two episodes that produce similar outcomes? I next turn to explanations for the financial crises that have been offered by two different sets of economists: one set is composed of economists who have studied financial crises in Chile and other developing countries, and the other set is composed of economic historians who have studied nineteenth-century U.S. economic history.

6.4 Explanations of the Financial Crises in Chile and the United States

6.4.1 Two Inflations under Fixed Exchange Rates

When Chile fixed its exchange rate at 39 pesos to the dollar at the end of June 1979, monetary authorities had expected that the price level would quickly stabilize. This did not happen. In the next two years wholesale prices rose by 60 percent, and consumer prices rose by 67 percent. Even taking into account the 26 percent increase in the U.S. producer price index during the same period, Chile quickly developed a seemingly overvalued exchange rate. All accounts of the subsequent financial crisis must take into account the inflation under the fixed exchange rate, because the downward correction in the price level that began in the second half of 1981 raised real interest rates and put severe strains on the financial system.

A common explanation of the inflation in Chile under the fixed exchange rate is Chile's use of backward-looking wage indexation. Dornbusch, Goldfajn, and Valdés (1995, 228), along with many others, have expressed the belief that the real appreciation of Chile's exchange rate and subsequent rise in real interest rates in 1981 and 1982 can be explained by inertial real wages: "Disinflation was unsuccessful because of explicit indexation . . . Thus, as backward-looking indexation implied major wage increases, the fixed currency led almost automatically to overvaluation."

Wage indexation may have imparted inertia to the price level, but table 6.5 shows that actual wage increases outstripped mandated minimum increases throughout the period 1977–82, often by substantial amounts. Over the entire period between July 1976 and August 1981, nominal wage growth (938 percent) was over 60 percent greater than the mandated minimum increase (539 percent).

Harberger (1984) has pointed out that during 1979–81 unemployment

Table 6.5 **Nominal Wage Increases in Chile, 1976–81**

	Mandated Minimum Increase (%)	Actual Increase (%)
7/1/76–9/1/76	26	30.0
9/1/76–12/1/76	18	23.8
12/1/76–3/1/77	19	21.4
3/1/77–7/1/77	18	23.2
7/1/77–12/1/77	18	24.2
12/1/77–3/1/78	8	9.1
3/1/78–7/1/78	10	15.8
7/1/78–12/1/78	12	16.7
12/1/78–3/1/79	6	8.0
3/1/79–7/1/79	11	14.0
7/1/79–12/1/79	18	23.1
12/1/79–4/1/80	8	9.1
4/1/80–10/1/80	14	17.7
10/1/80–8/1/81	14	21.0
Cumulative (7/1/76–8/1/81)	539	938

Sources: Edwards and Edwards (1987, 148) for mandated minimum nominal wage increase; Banco Central de Chile (1989, 217–19) for actual nominal wage increase.

was falling at the same time that real wages were rising, so that the indexation of wages only became a binding constraint in the second half of 1981 as the economy's growth rate began to slow. By June 1982 the government had repealed the indexation of wages. Edwards (1986) and Morandé (1988) also express a more guarded assessment of the role of indexed wages in Chile's post-1979 inflation, placing greater emphasis on the capital inflows that followed the liberalization of the capital account during 1979 and 1980. Edwards suggests that the maintenance of a fixed exchange rate and wage indexation was only a mistake after the capital inflows began to dry up in late 1981.

Morandé (1988) makes an even stronger case that wage indexation did not lead to the real appreciation of the exchange rate in Chile. He finds that "virtually exogenous massive capital inflows" were primarily responsible for the peso's real appreciation between 1976 and the first half of 1982. Figure 6.3 shows the monthly inflows for banks (which represented about 80 percent of total private borrowing) approved by the central bank between 1978 and the end of 1982. Morandé finds that the sharp cessation of those capital inflows in late 1981 forced the real devaluation during the second half of 1982. This story of exogenous capital flows is also emphasized by Calvo, Leiderman, and Reinhart (1990) and in Calvo's (1998) model of herd behavior among international investors.

The explanation of an exogenous shock caused by the cessation of capital inflows is closely connected to the role played by other shocks to the Chilean economy. The price of copper halved between 1980 and 1982 at the same time that real international interest rates rose, compounding the

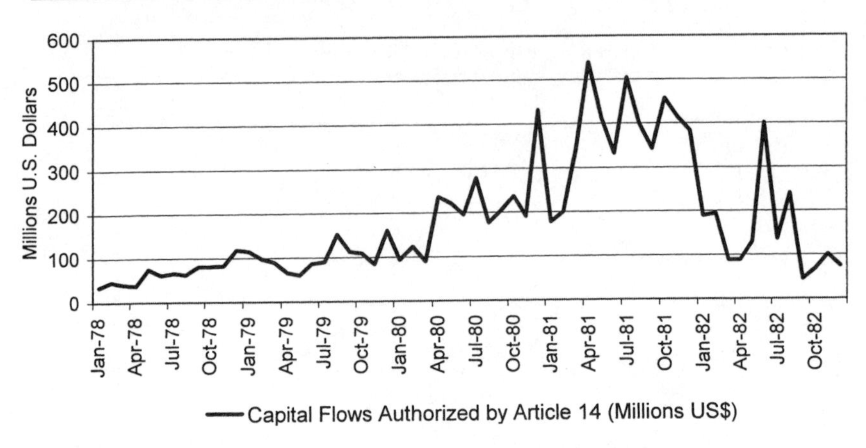

Fig. 6.3 Capital flows authorized each month by Chile's central bank

Chilean economy's adjustment to the higher oil prices caused by the second oil shock.

In August 1834, following approval by the U.S. Congress, the United States switched from a de facto silver standard to a de facto gold standard. The world relative price of silver to gold at that time was about 15.7:1. The U.S. mint ratio, which had previously been 15:1, was raised to 16:1. At the time of the change, no gold coins circulated in the United States, so the effective devaluation of the silver dollar was about 2 percent (from 15.7 to 16.0). By changing the mint ratio, the United States joined Great Britain on the gold standard.

At the time of the switch in the mint ratio the price level had been mildly declining. Beginning in August 1834 the U.S. wholesale price index rose by almost 40 percent over two years, as shown in figure 6.4. This price rise has been the subject of much debate among economic historians, the same way that Chile's inflation has been the subject of debate among economists. Temin (1969) has argued that the U.S. inflation was due to the retention of Mexican silver imports that had previously been exported to China. Between 1834 and 1837 the stock of specie in the U.S. rose by over 70 percent. Inflation accompanied the retention of the silver, but, as Temin noted, the retention depended on capital imports from the United Kingdom that made possible a level of spending consistent with the greater stock of specie. Temin summarizes his explanation as follows: "One can as easily say that the capital imports permitted the United States to retain the Mexican silver as that the cessation of silver shipments to China enabled the United States to import capital from Britain. The two events together produced the inflation" (1969, 88).

As with Chile, attention has also focused on the "exogenous" nature of the capital flows from Britain as a cause of the U.S. inflation of the 1830s. Smith and Cole (1935, 42) are among many who point out that following

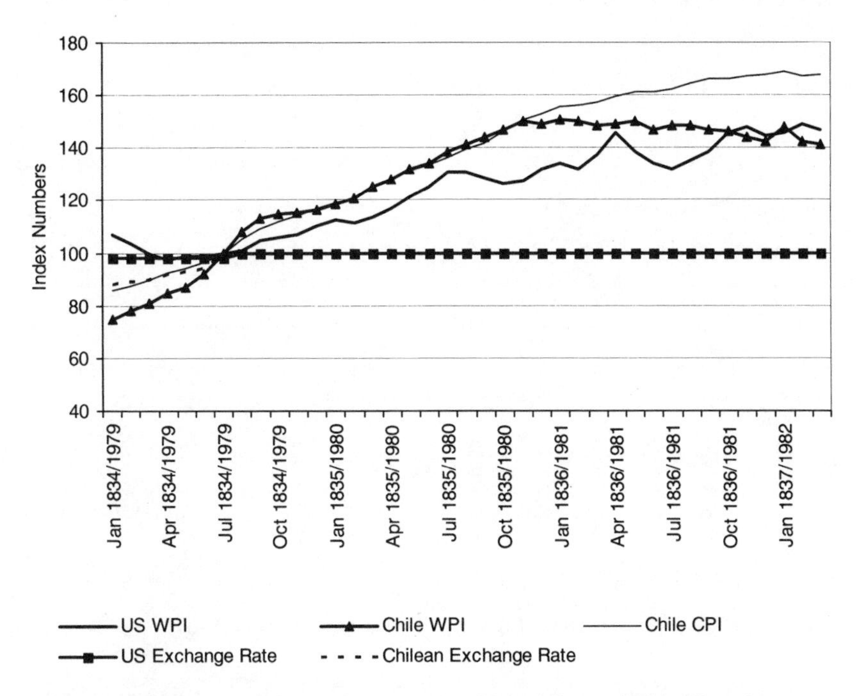

Fig. 6.4 Inflation under fixed exchange rates: United States (1834–37) and Chile (1979–82)

British disillusionment with South American loans in the 1820s, the United States of the early 1830s became attractive to British investors. The attraction was increased by the success of the Erie Canal and the potential for similarly high returns on other infrastructure projects. Smith and Cole as well as Macesich (1960), emphasize the capital inflows as the cause of the U.S. inflation:

> During the period of international borrowing by American states and business enterprises, the general level of domestic commodity prices rose relative to that of imported commodity values—the divergence being particularly great at the height of this borrowing movement in 1836–37. Subsequently, with the reversal of conditions and the apprehension by British investors of American securities . . . the level of domestic prices fell more sharply than that of imported goods. (Smith and Cole 1935, 68)

Unlike Chile, upward price inertia was not plausibly a factor in the U.S. inflation. As with Chile, the cessation of capital flows was closely correlated with a terms-of-trade shock and a rise in international interest rates. Figure 6.5 shows a comparison of the price of cotton in the 1830s with the price of copper in the late 1970s and early 1980s. Prior to each financial crisis, the price of the leading export fell by about 40 percent. In Chile's case, copper

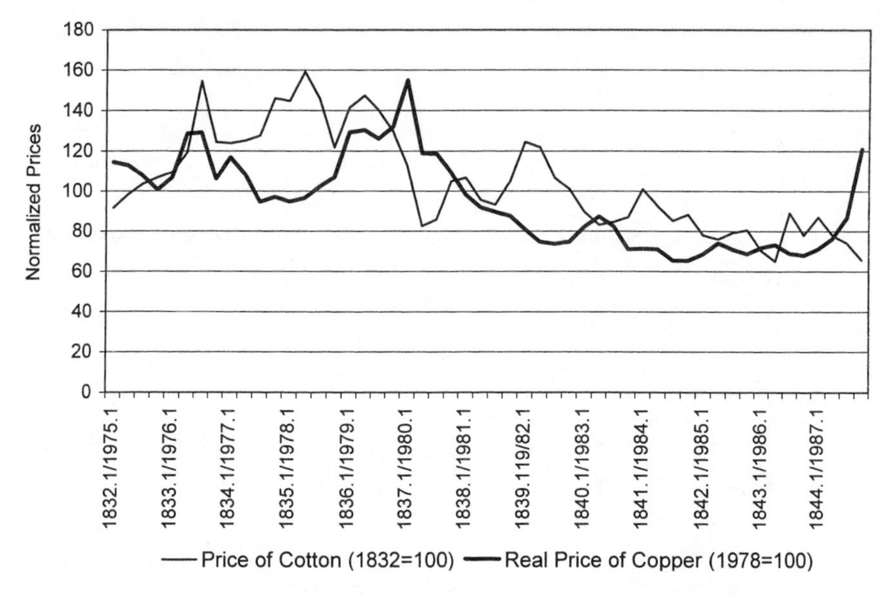

Fig. 6.5 Price of cotton (1832–44) and real price of copper (1975–87)

accounted for 46 percent of export earnings during 1979–81, whereas cotton accounted for 57 percent of U.S. export earnings during 1835–37.

In summary, large capital inflows can plausibly explain both inflations, and the U.S. price deflation and Chilean real exchange rate depreciation were caused by the cessation of the capital inflows. These capital inflows were closely related to the two lending booms shown in figure 6.1. Besides external causes of the lending booms, many economists have stressed internal causes related to moral hazard in banking. To these internal causes I now turn.

6.4.2 Moral Hazard and the Lending Booms

Central banks generally offer implicit or explicit guarantees on bank deposits and other financial system liabilities. These guarantees may cause banks to take on undue risks, including foreign exchange risk and asset risk, which make the banks prone to financial crisis. Moral hazard in banking is a common theme that has been explored in explanations of the financial crises in Chile and the United States.

Diaz Alejandro (1985), Edwards (1985), Arellano (1984), and Barandiarán (1983) all make the point that implicit state deposit insurance coupled with lack of supervision of lending activities created a problem of moral hazard in the Chilean banking system. All four of the above authors argue that the rescue in 1977 of all depositors and other creditors of Banco Osorno, a medium-sized bank that went bankrupt, provided a de facto guarantee of deposit insurance even when the government itself continued to claim that it would not rescue banks in the future. Harberger (1985) also argues that the financial crisis arose because banks, from the time of their privatization in 1975, carried with them a large portfolio of bad loans that gave rise to a false demand for credit that raised real interest rates, placing serious strains on other enterprises.

In the United States, the problem of moral hazard is generally associated with the actions of the Second Bank of the United States. Throughout the 1820s the Second Bank had developed a method of monitoring banks by using its position as the government's fiscal agent to accumulate large quantities of bank notes. It presented these bank notes to the issuing banks with the demand for payment in specie (silver or gold). The policy encouraged banks to remain liquid and prevented an overissuance of bank notes.

Following the passage of the 1833 Compromise Tariff Act, President Jackson announced his intention to withdraw all U.S. funds from the Second Bank. During the following two years, the government withdrew its funds from the Second Bank and deposited them with about eighty state deposit banks. At the termination of the so-called Bank War in 1834, Nicholas Biddle (the Second Bank's president) declared that the Second Bank would no longer monitor state banks by requiring specie in exchange for bank notes (Temin 1969, 60).

At the same time, the government had to create a new deposit bank system to handle fiscal revenues. In December 1834, Daniel Webster introduced congressional legislation to impose a 25 percent reserve requirement on all deposit banks (Timberlake 1978, 46). The bill was narrowly defeated by opponents, who argued that such a requirement would sabotage the new system. The Treasury secretary furthermore urged the deposit banks to lend with the public monies. By 1836 it appeared that specie reserve ratios of the deposit banks had fallen to low levels (Timberlake, 47). Many historians—including Schlesinger (1945), Meyers (1960), and Hammond (1957)—place the origins of the lending boom and inflation with the loose regulatory standards resulting from the Bank War.

The consequences of moral hazard in banking are limited by the credibility and extent of the government's guarantee to bank creditors. Dooley (2000) points out the importance of fiscal accounts for the credibility of the government's guarantee. Brock (1992) and Dooley both emphasize the size of the government's "bailout" funds for the potential costs of moral hazard.

Chile had run a primary fiscal surplus beginning in 1975 and continuing through 1981. Moreover, the government ran a significant total surplus (including debt service) during the three years of the credit boom and inflation (1979–81). The U.S. government had paid off its debt by 1833 and began to accumulate surplus revenue, which Congress voted to distribute to the states in 1836. According to Ratchford (1941, 85),

> When Congress finally voted to "loan" this surplus to the states, it added the climax to a long series of events that had raised the enthusiasm for borrowing and spending to a fever pitch. Even those states that did not wish to borrow were having funds thrust upon them; they could hardly be blamed if they regarded the federal funds as manna from heaven. Also, if Uncle Sam was so generous in prosperous times, surely he would not desert them if they incurred a debt and later found repayment difficult.

In addition, the United States had paid off the Revolutionary War debt of the states, so that there was precedent for assuming that the federal government would take responsibility for state debts incurred during the 1830s.

Finally, in both Chile and the United States the commitment to a fixed exchange rate with the major creditor country may have been an important signaling device by the government. Valdés (1994) believes that fixing the exchange rate in 1979 was an important financial guarantee by the government. Indeed, after the 1982 devaluation the government subsidized debt repayments by dollar debtors. Similarly, the 1834 change in the U.S. mint ratio served to integrate U.S. capital markets more closely with British capital markets by placing both currencies on the gold standard.

In essence, then, a strong case can be made that in both Chile and the United States moral hazard in banking was a significant problem. Implicit government guarantees permitted the moral hazard to take on a macroeconomic importance it would not otherwise have had. Moreover, it is likely that fiscal surpluses, combined with measures that fixed the exchange rates to the main creditor countries' currencies, also helped to create the lending booms in the two countries.

This head-to-head comparison of Chile and the United States has shown that the financial crises can plausibly be explained as the result of exogenous capital flows, changes in the terms of trade, poor financial regulation, and virtuous fiscal and exchange rate policy. Indeed, given that the intersection between economic historians studying the United States and economists studying Chile is the null set, the agreement of the two groups of economists on common explanations of the lending booms and financial crises is striking.

Is this all there is to the two crises? Are there other factors that play a role in the crises? In particular, is trade liberalization a pervasive background factor contributing to the crises, or is it merely of second-order importance to our understanding of the periods in question? The next section builds a conceptual framework in which time-to-build aspects of trade liberalizations combine with regulatory moral hazard to create financial fragility.

6.5 The Control of Moral Hazard by Weak Central Banks

Moral hazard exists on both sides of banks' balance sheets. The strength of the financial contracting models is in their characterization of financial contracts between lenders and borrowers. Financial intermediaries arise as a response to the moral hazard problem associated with providing funds to borrowers. Debt contracts with credit line features emerge from many of these models. On the other hand, the time-to-build financial contracting models ignore the problem of regulatory moral hazard.[2]

Nevertheless, liquidity risk and asset risk of banks are two main sources of regulatory moral hazard. First, banks can hold too few liquid assets to cover the liquidity shocks facing investments. Second, banks can invest in risky projects or fail to monitor those projects. In economies with weak supervisory agencies, these risks are primarily handled by two instruments. The first is the reliance on high reserve requirements to enforce bank liquidity. In Chile reserve requirements on demand deposits began at levels of 85 percent in 1976, whereas rates on time deposits were 55 percent. In the United States banks operated with reserve ratios (specie to bank notes plus deposits) of about 20 percent.

The second instrument is the imposition of credit ceilings. Chile employed credit ceilings on banks until May 1976 as a way of constraining credit growth. Credit ceilings act as a marginal 100 percent reserve requirement. That is, once the ceiling has been reached, any new deposit growth is turned into required reserves. Capital controls can play a similar role in limiting the growth rate of bank loans. After eliminating credit ceilings in 1976, the Chilean central bank relied on capital controls to limit the expansion of credit by the banking system.[3]

In the United States of the 1830s, both the Second Bank and the Suffolk Bank of Boston acted as clearinghouses for other banks. Both banks followed the practice of redeeming bank notes for specie at the issuing banks. In ways similar to a credit ceiling, specie redemption limited rapid loan growth. For example, a bank seeking to increase lending by issuing bank notes to borrowers would quickly have to pay specie to the Second Bank or the Suffolk Bank in exchange for the notes that ended up with the two clearinghouses.[4]

2. The problem is circumvented because, for example, demand deposits provide discipline in Diamond and Rajan (2001), a bank can only invest in one asset in Allen and Gale (1998, 2000), and a bank can costlessly provide liquidity in Holmström and Tirole (1998).

3. Another weak supervisory authority in the United States, the Federal Savings & Loans Insurance Corporation, attempted to limit the flow of brokered deposits to savings and loans organizations (S&Ls) in 1984, but was rebuffed by the U.S. Court of Appeals. Limits on the flow of brokered deposits, like capital controls, might have provided a crude method of controlling asset risk in the S&L industry. Figures taken from the balance sheets of S&Ls in 1984 indicate that fast-growing thrifts were more apt to hold riskier asset portfolios and to rely on more volatile sources of funding (White 1991).

4. Although it is common to view prudential regulation as being imposed on the banking system by supervisory agencies, in the United States of the early 1830s banks in New England voluntarily submitted to the specie redemption policy of the Suffolk Bank. Belonging to the Suffolk Bank clearinghouse was a commitment device that was of value to banks because it raised the value of their bank notes and increased the area of their circulation (see Calomiris and Kahn 1996).

To illustrate the changing nature of prudential regulation following a trade liberalization, suppose that an economy is initially growing slowly within the context of a protective trade regime. There are relatively few new investments compared to ongoing production, so liquidity demands on banks are small. Prudential regulation consists of reserve requirements and credit ceilings. Capital controls on external finance generally reinforce quantitative restrictions on imports.

Liberalization of the trade regime will create a new set of investments. Removal of quantitative import restrictions will allow agents to import at will, subject only to the availability of external finance. Credit ceilings, capital controls, or specie redemption policies will become onerous to those who wish to invest in the new economy. Political pressure will push for the removal of the crude, but effective, tools for prudential supervision. In the United States the strong political pressures working to cripple the Second Bank were closely allied with the Compromise Tariff and the westward expansion of the economy.

In Chile the central bank was weakened by its rescue of the savings and loan system in 1975. Credit expansion associated with the rescue effort accounted for roughly two-thirds of the central bank's total credit expansion between 1976 and 1978. The central bank did not have the resources or expertise to monitor banks. As De la Cuadra and Valdés (1992) document, it was not until 1980 that the Superintendency of Banks began to collect information on the largest debtors of the banking system. The central bank also did not have extensive resources to intervene in banks.

After the central bank eliminated credit ceilings in 1976, it gradually relaxed capital controls and reduced reserve requirements. Global limits on foreign indebtedness by banks were eliminated in June 1979, and monthly flow limits were eliminated in April 1980. Reserve requirements on demand deposits were lowered from 85 percent in 1976 to 10 percent by the end of 1980, and reserve requirements on short-term time deposits were lowered from 55 percent to 4 percent during the same time period. Regarding the political pressure on the central bank to loosen capital controls during this period, De la Cuadra and Valdés (1992, 20–21) write:

> The business community, in general, and some academic economists strongly attacked the central bank's policy. The business community blamed the policy for delaying a decline in the interest rate and for discriminating among borrowers, since those better connected to banks had access to cheaper financing. . . . Finding little support for its stance, the monetary authority eventually opened the capital account without restrictions—except for the prohibition of foreign loans with an average maturity of less than two years and the imposition of reserve requirements on foreign loans with maturities of between twenty-four and sixty-five months. This opening of the capital account occurred in April 1980

and was followed by large capital inflows during the remainder of the year and during 1981.

In both the United States of the 1830s and Chile, political pressures created partly by the opening of the economies led to the abandonment of crude tools for the control of moral hazard in banking. The abandonment was followed by large capital inflows, trade deficits, and diminished supplies of liquid assets by banks. During the period of large capital flows to the United States (1835–37, 1839) and Chile (1978–81) many investments were undertaken that fit into the time-to-build view of the adjustment to a trade liberalization. The problem for regulators was that traditional tools for controlling moral hazard—such as credit ceilings, capital controls, and bank notes for specie exchanges—were not compatible with a high-growth economy. In a political sense, the welfare gain from permitting fast credit growth to take advantage of new investments created by the opening of the economies exceeded the welfare loss from abandoning traditional tools of prudential oversight. Those same political factors pushed reserve ratios downward in the United States and Chile, thereby making banks less liquid. If most of the liquidity risk was nondiversifiable, then one could argue, à la Holmström and Tirole, that state-contingent aid to the banks was a more efficient use of government resources than imposing high reserve requirements.

In summary, credit ceilings, borrowing controls, and note redemption policies are crude but effective tools for controlling regulatory moral hazard. However, these tools all work by limiting the growth of banks. Credit ceilings and note redemption act as 100 percent marginal reserve requirements and thus, in addition, promote liquidity of the banks. In a time-to-build world, these tools are ill equipped to handle a rapid expansion of bank credit to finance new investments. Regulatory insistence on enforcing standards will be met by political pressure to drop the use of those tools. Without more sophisticated tools, the scrapping of the crude tools can easily lead to a lending boom with moral hazard showing up in the form of illiquid banks with overly risky loans. In the absence of more sophisticated bank supervision, the aftermath of a period of high growth and financial crisis will see a return to crude ways of controlling moral hazard by controlling growth.

6.6 Second-Generation Reforms

North (1961) has judged the years 1839–43 as a depressed period of economic activity whose only equal in U.S. history has been the Great Depression. Similarly, the years 1982–85 were a period of economic depression in Chile that were equaled in severity and duration in the twentieth century only by the Great Depression. Nonetheless, according to Gallman (1960) during the decade 1844–54 the United States had its highest rate of economic growth of the nineteenth century, averaging about 5.5 percent per year.[5] Similarly, Gallego and Loayza (2002) have characterized the years 1986–98 as the "golden period" for growth in Chile, with average growth rates exceeding 6 percent per year, among the highest in the world during this period.

Both countries engaged in similar reforms in the aftermath of the financial crisis. These second-generation reforms were instrumental for the creation of a financial system that would encourage the consolidation of free trade in each country. The first reform centered around the resolution of the debt problems arising from the financial crises. In the United States, nine states—Pennsylvania, Maryland, Illinois, Indiana, Michigan, Arkansas, Mississippi, Louisiana, and Florida (a territory)—defaulted on their debts, while many other states had difficulty servicing their debt (Ratchford 1941). A large fraction of state bonds were held in Europe, and in 1842 there were rumors of imminent war with Great Britain over the defaults. The federal government came under pressure to assume the state debts, but Congress tabled the proposal in 1843.

The debt crisis in the United States was resolved in two ways. First, five states negotiated adjustments in debt repayments, and others, principally New York, raised taxes and suspended construction on public works projects. In the end only four states defaulted outright. Second, beginning in 1842 virtually all states revised their constitutions to prohibit state borrowing beyond a nominal amount.[6] Sylla (2000, 523) makes the important observation that "Such limits, in context, may have had a paradoxical result. By making a state's ability to repay debt more certain, they likely increased its ability to borrow. That is one reason why the state debt crisis of the 1840s had minimal long-term effects on state credit."

The resolution of the Chilean debt crisis had two components. Most of the external debt had been contracted by banks and was not guaranteed by the government. Although the government temporarily guaranteed debt repayments during 1983–84, beginning in 1985 Chile's creditors agreed to the creation of debt buyback and debt-equity conversion mechanisms that resulted in a de facto downward adjustment in debt repayments during the period from 1985 to 1987 (Barandiarán and Hernández 1999; Brock 1999).

5. This rate of growth was equaled by the 1874–84 decade. All other nineteenth-century decadal growth rates were well below these figures.

6. The order of passage of these constitutional limitations on borrowing is as follows: Rhode Island (1842); Michigan (1843); New Jersey (1844); Louisiana and Texas (1845); Iowa and New York (1846); Illinois, Maine, and Wisconsin (1848); California (1849); Kentucky (1850); Indiana, Maryland, and Ohio (1851); Kansas (1857); Minnesota, Oregon, and Pennsylvania (1957).

The second component involved the repayment of central bank emergency loans that had been made to seventeen banks between 1982 and 1984. These loans were converted into subordinated debt of the central bank. By 1995 all but five banks (including the two largest) had extinguished their debt obligations. In 1996, the central bank was compensated for two-thirds of the remaining obligations and wrote off the remaining third as part of a final resolution of the problem.

In both the United States and Chile, external and internal debt obligations were not assumed by the national governments during the financial crises. The decade-long resolution of the subordinated debt matched the length of the passage of constitutional amendments to limit state borrowing. By imposing costs on banks and investors, the solutions in both countries made future lending booms less likely. Indeed, Ratchford (1941, 104) notes that if the U.S. federal government had assumed the states' debts in 1843 (as it had in 1790 with the states' Revolutionary War debts), "it would almost certainly have converted a precedent into a habit, the results of which are not pleasant to contemplate."

The next second-generation reforms in both countries were designed to eliminate special privilege from banking. In the United States this took two forms. First, virtually all states amended their constitutions to prohibit governments from investing in banks or other corporations. This kind of investment had been the source of much corruption in the 1830s and had led to the debt defaults by a number of state governments. Second, general incorporation laws were passed for banks (Wallich 2001). Under these laws, anyone with the specified minimum capital could establish a bank, subject to the state's requirement that bank notes be backed with approved securities and that other prudential regulations be observed. Bank note holders were generally protected by the bonds backing the notes, but deposits were subject to default risk.

These free banking laws were the first widely used general incorporation laws in the United States and minimized special privilege that had previously been associated with special incorporation laws for banks. This next generation of bank reform proved to be durable in the United States. The free banking period lasted until 1863, when the National Banking Act nationalized the issue of bank notes but preserved the general incorporation characteristics of free banking. Rockoff (2000, 679) attributes New York's rapid bank expansion in the 1840s to its initiation of free banking laws in 1838.

In Chile, second-generation banking reforms involved the 1986 Banking Reform Law and the 1989 Central Bank Law. The Banking Reform Law limited bank ownership of affiliated industrial companies, an important source of corruption prior to the financial crisis. The 1986 law also provided precise closure rules for banks and expressly ruled out bailouts from a deposit insurance fund. Later measures to open the banking system to foreign banks also encouraged a competitive banking system. The 1989 Central Bank Law reduced the potential for special government privilege by granting the central bank a large measure of autonomy in its conduct of monetary policy. Bank interventions, as well as other central bank policies, were shielded from government and political pressures, thus fostering credible regulatory policies.

The final second-generation reform in the United States and Chile was the establishment of a political consensus on trade policy. The U.S. trade liberalization in 1833 had been undertaken against the wishes of the Northern states in response to the threat of war from the South, whereas the Chilean trade liberalization was imposed in 1974 without popular support by a military government. The lack of political consensus in each country almost caused the trade liberalizations to unravel during the financial crises. Following the 1982 devaluation of the Chilean peso, protectionist pressures culminated in a 35 percent tariff in September 1984 that was combined with import surcharges and other financing restrictions (De la Cuadra and Hachette 1991; Edwards and Lederman 1998). In the United States, protectionist pressure during the height of the financial crisis resulted in the passage of the 1842 tariff, which imposed high duties on many items and generally reversed the Compromise Tariff's reductions.

Despite the return to protection, the resolution of the debt obligations incurred during the initial trade liberalizations and the creation of constitutional changes to separate banks from government set the groundwork for sustained outward-oriented expansions of each of the economies. Tariff reduction began again in Chile in 1985 and was pushed forward by the democratic governments of the 1990s. In the United States, a consensus among the political parties (the Whigs and the Democrats) resulted in the passage of a tariff reform bill in 1846 that initiated a period of liberal trade policies that lasted until the beginning of the Civil War in 1861.

6.7 Conclusion

In this paper I have put forward the thesis that trade liberalizations create the appropriate conditions for a financial crisis. Previous work has emphasized the role of moral hazard when a central bank guarantees financial system liabilities. This paper emphasizes the importance of time-to-build considerations that create financial fragility. A historical comparison of Chile (1970s and 1980s) and the United States (1830s and 1840s) has illustrated the empirical importance of time-to-build considerations as well as moral hazard in the creation of lending booms following a trade liberalization. In the aftermath of financial crises, second-generation reforms in both the United States and Chile focused on debt adjustment, the elimination of special privilege from banking, and constitutional reforms to limit state intervention in banking.

References

Allen, Franklin, and Douglas Gale. 1998. Optimal financial crises. *Journal of Finance* 53:1245–84.

———. 2000. Optimal currency crises. *Carnegie-Rochester Conference Series on Public Policy* 53:177–230.

Arellano, José Pablo. 1984. La dificil salida al problema del endeudamiento interno (The difficult exit from the internal debt problem). *Estudios CIEPLAN* 13:5–25.

Banco Central de Chile. 1989. *Indicadores económicos y sociales 1960–1988* (Economic and social indicators 1960–1988). Santiago, Chile: Banco Central de Chile.

Barandiarán, Edgardo. 1983. La crisis financiera chilena. *Documento de Trabajo* no. 6. Santiago, Chile: Centro de Estudios Públicos.

Barandiarán, Edgardo, and Leonardo Hernández. 1999. Origins and resolution of a banking crisis: Chile 1982–86. Working Paper no. 57. Santiago: Central Bank of Chile.

Bates, Robert, and Anne Krueger, eds. 1993. *Political and economic interactions in economic policy reform: Evidence from eight countries.* Cambridge, Mass.: Basil Blackwell.

Brock, Philip L. 1992. The macroeconomic consequences of loan-loss rollovers. In *If Texas Were Chile: A primer on banking reform,* ed. P. Brock, 351–68. San Francisco: ICS Press.

———. 1999. Emerging from crisis: Bank privatization and recapitalization in Chile. Washington, D.C.: World Bank, processed.

Caballero, Ricardo, and Arvind Krishnamurthy. 2000. International liquidity management: Sterilization policy in illiquid financial markets. Working Paper no. 00/04. MIT, Department of Economics.

———. 2001. International and domestic collateral constraints in a model of emerging market crises. *Journal of Monetary Economics* 48:513–48.

Calomiris, Charles, and Charles Kahn. 1996. The efficiency of self-regulated payments systems: Learning from the Suffolk system. *Journal of Money, Credit, and Banking* 28:766–97.

Calvo, Guillermo. 1987. On the costs of temporary policy. *Journal of Development Economics* 27:245–61.

———. 1998. Varieties of capital-market crises. In *The debt burden and its consequences for monetary policy,* ed. G. Calvo and M. King, 181–202. New York: St. Martin's.

Calvo, Guillermo, Leonardo Leiderman, and Carmen M. Reinhart. 1990. Capital inflows and real exchange rate appreciation in Latin America. *IMF Staff Papers* 40:108–51.

Calvo, Guillermo, and Enrique Mendoza. 1994. Trade reforms of uncertain duration and real uncertainty: A first approximation. *IMF Staff Papers* 41:555–86.

Chang, Roberto, and Andrés Velasco. 2000. Banks, debt maturity, and Financial Crises. *Journal of International Economics* 51:169–94.

Corbo, Vittorio. 1988. Problems, development theory, and strategies of Latin America. In *The state of development economics: Progress and perspectives*, ed. G. Ranis and T. P. Schultz, 145–86. New York: Basil Blackwell.

De la Cuadra, Sergio, and Dominique Hachette. 1991. Chile. In *Liberalizing foreign trade*. Vol. 1 *Argentina, Chile, and Uruguay,* ed. D. Papageorgiou, M. Michaely, and A. Choksi, 169–319. Cambridge, Mass.: Basil Blackwell.

De la Cuadra, Sergio, and Salvador Valdés. 1992. Myths and facts about financial liberalization in Chile: 1974–1983. In *If Texas were Chile: A primer on banking reform,* ed. P. Brock, San Francisco: ICS Press.

Diamond, Douglas W., and Philip H. Dybvig. 1983. Bank runs, deposit insurance, and liquidity. *Journal of Political Economy* 91:401–19.
Diamond, Douglas W., and Raghuram G. Rajan. 2001. Banks, short term debt, and financial crises: Theory, policy implications, and applications. *Carnegie-Rochester Conference Series on Public Policy* 54:37–71.
Diaz Alejandro, Carlos F. 1985. Good-bye financial repression, hello financial crash. *Journal of Development Economics* 19:1–24.
Dooley, Michael P. 2000. A model of crises in emerging markets. *Economic Journal* 100:256–72.
Dooley, Michael P., and Inseok Shin. 1999. Private inflows when crises are anticipated: A case study of Korea. Unpublished manuscript.
Dornbusch, Rudiger, Ilan Goldfajn, and Rodrigo O. Valdés. 1995. Currency crises and collapses. *Brookings Papers on Economic Activity,* issue no. 2:219–70.
Edwards, Sebastian. 1985. Stabilization with liberalization: An evaluation of ten years of Chile's experiment with free-market policies, 1973–1983. *Economic Development and Cultural Change* 33:223–54.
———. 1986. Monetarism in Chile, 1973–1983: Some economic puzzles. *Economic Development and Cultural Change* 34:535–59.
Edwards, Sebastian, and Alejandra Cox Edwards. 1987. *Monetarism and liberalization: The Chilean experiment.* Cambridge, Mass.: Ballinger.
Edwards, Sebastian, and Daniel Lederman. 1998. The political economy of unilateral trade liberalization: The case of Chile. NBER Working Paper no. 6510. Cambridge, Mass.: National Bureau of Economic Research.
Gale, Douglas, and Xavier Vives. 2002. Dollarization, bailouts, and the stability of the banking system. *Quarterly Journal of Economics* 117:467–502.
Gallego, Francisco, and Norman Loayza. 2002. The golden period for growth in Chile: Explanations and forecasts. Working Paper no. 146. Santiago: Central Bank of Chile.
Gallman, Robert. 1960. Commodity output, 1839–1899. In *Trends in the American economy in the nineteenth century,* ed. W. N. Parker, 13–67. Studies in Income and Wealth, vol. 24. Princeton: Princeton University Press.
Hammond, Bray. 1957. *Banks and politics in America, from the Revolution to the Civil War.* Princeton: Princeton University Press.
Harberger, Arnold. 1984. La crisis cambiara chilena de 1982 (The 1982 Chilean exchange rate crisis). *Cuadernos de Economia* 63:123–36.
———. 1985. Observations on the Chilean economy, 1973–83. *Economic Development and Cultural Change* 33:451–62.
Holmström, Bengt, and Jean Tirole. 1998. Private and public supply of liquidity. *Journal of Political Economy* 106:1–40.
Krueger, Anne O. 1978. *Liberalization attempts and consequences.* Cambridge, Mass.: Ballinger.
Krugman, Paul. 1998. What happened to Asia? Department of Economics, MIT. Unpublished manuscript.
Levinsohn, James. 1999. Employment responses to international liberalization in Chile. *Journal of International Economics* 47:321–44.
Little, Ian, Richard Cooper, Max Corden, and Sarath Rajapatirana. 1993. *Boom, crisis, and adjustment: The macroeconomic experience of developing countries.* New York: Oxford University Press.
Macesich, George. 1960. Sources of monetary disturbances in the United States, 1834–1845. *Journal of Economic History* 20:407–34.
McKinnon, Ronald I., and Huw Pill. 1996. Credible liberalizations and international capital flows: The "over-borrowing syndrome." In *Financial deregulation*

and integration in East Asia, ed. T. Ito and A. Krueger, 7–42. Chicago: University of Chicago Press.

Meyers, Marvin. 1960. *The Jacksonian persuasion.* Stanford, Calif.: Stanford University Press.

Morandé, Felipe. 1988. Domestic currency appreciation and foreign capital inflows: What comes first? Chile, 1977–82. *Journal of International Money and Finance* 7:447–66.

North, Douglass. 1961. *The economic growth of the United States 1790–1860.* Englewood Cliffs, N.J.: Prentice-Hall.

Pavcnik, Nina. 2002. Trade liberalization, exit, and productivity improvements: Evidence from Chilean plants. *Review of Economic Studies* 69:245–76.

Ratchford, B. U. 1941. *American state debts.* Durham, N.C.: Duke University Press.

Roberts, M. 1996. Employment flows and producer turnover. In *Industrial evolution in developing countries: Micro patterns of turnover, productivity, and market structure,* ed. M. Roberts and J. Tybout, 18–42. Oxford: Oxford University Press.

Rockoff, Hugh. 2000. Banking and finance, 1789–1914. *The Cambridge economic history of the United States.* Vol. 2, ed. Stanley Engerman and Robert Gallman, 643–84. Cambridge: Cambridge University Press.

Rodrik, Dani. 1994. The rush to free trade in the developing world: Why so late? Why now? Will it last? In *Voting for reform: Democracy, political liberalization, and economic adjustment,* ed. S. Haggard and S. Webb, 61–88. New York: Oxford University Press.

Schlesinger, Arthur M., Jr. 1945. *The age of Jackson.* Boston: Little, Brown.

Smith, Walter, and Arthur Cole. 1935. *Fluctuations in American business, 1790–1860.* Cambridge, Mass.: Harvard University Press.

Sylla, Richard. 2000. Experimental federalism: The economics of American government, 1789–1914. In *The Cambridge Economic History of the United States.* Vol. 2, ed. Stanley Engerman and Robert Gallman, 483–541. Cambridge: Cambridge University Press.

Taussig, Frank W. 1931. *The tariff history of the United States.* New York: Putnam.

Temin, Peter. 1969. *The Jacksonian economy.* New York: Norton.

Timberlake, Richard. 1978. *The origins of central banking in the United States.* Cambridge, Mass.: Harvard University Press.

Tornell, Aaron. 1995. Are economic crises necessary for trade liberalization and fiscal reform? The Mexican experience. In *Reform, recovery, and growth: Latin America and the Middle East,* ed. R. Dornbusch and S. Edwards, 53–73. Chicago: University of Chicago Press.

U.S. Bureau of the Census. 1975. *Historical statistics of the United States: Colonial times to 1970.* Washington, D.C.: GPO.

Valdés, Salvador. 1994. Financial liberalization and the capital account: Chile, 1974–84. In *Britain's economic performance,* ed. T. Buxton, P. Chapman, and P. Temple, 357–410. London: Routledge.

Wallich, John. 2001. State constitution reforms in the 1840s and 1850s and the relationship of American government and the economy. University of Maryland. Unpublished manuscript.

White, Lawrence J. 1991. *The S&L debacle: Public policy lessons for bank and thrift regulation.* New York: Oxford University Press.

7

Banks, Financial Markets, and Industrial Development

Lessons from the Economic Histories of Brazil and Mexico

Stephen Haber

The banking systems of most Latin American countries are small, concentrated, and inefficient. Financial markets do not serve as substitutes for banks: few firms can mobilize capital through the markets, and even the largest exchanges tend to be dominated by one or two issues. What effects do underdeveloped financial markets and banking systems have on the real economy? Do imperfections in capital markets serve as barriers to entry? If so, do financial barriers to entry have an effect on the competitive structure and performance of industry?

This paper addresses these questions by employing the historical record as a natural laboratory. I analyze the cases of Brazil and Mexico during their first major periods of banking and financial market reform: the years 1880 to 1930.

The use of history in a conference on financial market reforms in contemporary Latin America has disadvantages and advantages. The disadvantage is obvious: the reforms and outcomes analyzed took place in the past, sometimes a fairly distant past. The macroeconomic and political environments today are quite a bit different than they were 50 or 100 years ago.

The use of history does, however, provide a number of advantages in the empirical study of the economic outcomes of policy reforms. First, there is often a long lag between an institutional reform and a measurable response by firms or markets. The use of historical data allows us to measure the response of markets and firms over long time periods. In the cases under study here, we are able to take a forty-year view of the effect of a particular set of financial-market and banking reforms. Second, historical evidence allows

Stephen Haber is a professor of political science, a senior fellow at the Stanford Institute for Economic Policy and Research, and a senior fellow at the Hoover Institution.

the empirical investigation of questions that would be extremely difficult, if not impossible, to analyze with contemporary data because of confidentiality considerations. In the cases under study here, we are able to develop time-series, cross-sectional data sets on manufacturing firms. These data sets are enumerated at the firm level and include information about inputs, outputs, and sources of capital. In short, the use of historical data allows us to test hypotheses about the relationships among access to capital, industrial structure, and performance in ways that would not be possible through the analysis of contemporary data alone.

This paper focuses on the cases of Brazil and Mexico. I focus on these cases because they allow for a natural experiment of the effect of particular financial market reforms on the performance of manufacturing industry. That is, Brazil and Mexico were similar along a number of dimensions—except for the specific content of the financial-market and banking reforms that they carried out. Both countries had large economies (for Latin America). Both built national markets via the subsidizing of foreign-owned railroads during the period 1880–1914. Both, after 1890, were highly protectionist. Both were beneficiaries of foreign capital inflows in a broad range of sectors, but neither received much in the way of foreign direct investment in manufacturing.[1] Thus, foreign banks and securities markets could not serve as substitutes for domestic banks and markets. Finally, both countries had miniscule banking systems and financial markets until a series of reforms in the 1880s and 1890s completely rewrote the rules about banking and financial markets. In the content of those reforms, however, Brazil and Mexico strongly diverged.

In order to estimate the impact of financial-market and banking reforms on the real economy I look at a single industry: cotton textiles. I do so for both practical and theoretical reasons. First, the cotton goods manufacture was the most important industry in the countries under study. It surpassed all other industries in terms of capital invested, size of the work force, or percentage of value-added it contributed to total industrial output. Second, there are compelling reasons to focus on cotton textiles. In many industries it is extremely difficult to separate out the effects of capital constraints on the structure and performance of industry from other factors, such as economies of scale or barriers to entry created by advertising, patents, or the legal system.[2] In the cotton textile industry, however, these other factors

1. Brazil and Mexico were not exceptional in this regard. There was little in the way of foreign direct investment in manufacturing anywhere in the world in the years prior to 1940. This included even British India, where industrialization was accomplished almost entirely through local sources of capital.

2. Cement is a classic case. The high bulk-to-price ratio of cement means that it is economical to ship it only over short distances. In order to expand output and enter new markets, firms must erect new production facilities close to those markets. In order to keep out potential rivals, firms tend to erect more productive capacity than they require. The result is that the cement industry tends, almost everywhere in the world, to be characterized by local monopolies with excess capacity. See Johnson and Parkman (1983).

did not come into play: the capital equipment was easily divisible, the minimum efficient scale of production was small, and there were no barriers to entry created by patents, brands, or access to raw materials or other inputs.[3] The only important barrier to entry was access to finance. The textile industry therefore provides an excellent test case of the relationship between the development of the financial markets and banks that provide capital to an industry, and the development of the industry itself.[4]

The argument advanced runs in the following terms. The specific features of government regulation had a powerful effect on the size and structure of banking systems and financial markets. The size and structure of banking systems and financial markets, in turn, played a crucial role in determining the size, structure, and productivity of the textile industry. In Mexico, where government policies constrained the number of banks in any market, the distribution of bank loans among potential textile industrialists was narrow. In addition, financial markets did not serve as a substitute for the banking sector, except for a very limited number of well-connected financial capitalists, many of whom already had bank connections. In short, a small group of powerful financiers was able to obtain all the capital they needed, while everyone else was starved for funds. In Brazil, on the other hand, institutional reforms meant that securities markets were able to serve as a substitute for the banking system. The distribution of funds among potential textile industrialists was much broader than in Mexico. Access to institutional sources of finance did not serve as a barrier to entry. The outcomes were threefold: the Brazilian textile industry grew faster; it had a more competitive industrial structure; and its rate of productivity growth was twice that of the Mexican textile industry.

The first section of this paper compares the institutional history of financial intermediaries and textile mill financing in Brazil and Mexico. The second section assesses changes in the size and competitive structure of each country's textile industry in light of their histories of industrial finance. The third section presents estimates of total factor productivity growth. The fourth section concludes.

7.1 Banks, Financial Markets, and Textile Finance

7.1.1 Mexico

Modern banking arrived late to Mexico. The country's first chartered bank, a branch of the British Bank of London, Mexico, and South Amer-

3. The technology to produce cotton goods was easily available: British (and later American) machinery companies competed to provide machines and other inputs. There were also no barriers to entry created by advertising or branding: the wholesale purchasers of cotton cloth were expert judges of quality.

4. This does not mean that scale economies were insignificant in cotton textile production. Indeed, had economies of scale been negligible, access to capital could not have served as a

ica, was not opened until 1863. As late as 1884, only eight banks were in operation. This banking system developed on an ad hoc basis: special charters were granted either by the federal government or state legislatures.

The fact that the Mexican government was continually broke, however, created a strong incentive for the federal government to monopolize bank chartering as a means to provide itself with a ready source of credit. As Noel Maurer has shown, the federal government therefore engineered the merger of Mexico City's two largest banks in 1884, creating the Banco Nacional de México (Banamex). The intention of the government was to model Banamex on the early Bank of England, granting it a monopoly over the issuance of paper money in return for providing a credit line to the federal government. The bank would also act as the treasury's financial agent. At the same time, the federal government erected high barriers to entry for competing banks. The Commerce Code of 1884 required that they obtain the permission of congress and the secretary of the treasury to obtain a bank charter or increase their capital. They also had to pay a 5 percent tax on their issuance of bank notes. Banamex was exempted from the tax. Finally, Banamex was permitted to issue banknotes up to 3 times the amount of its reserves. Other banks had to maintain a 2:1 ratio.[5]

Mexico's already extant banks, particularly the Banco de Londres y México, realized that the commercial code and the special privileges of Banamex put them at a serious disadvantage. They therefore sued in federal court, and managed to obtain an injunction against the 1884 code. The ensuing legal and political battle wore on for thirteen years, until a compromise was finally hammered out by Secretary of Finance Limantour in 1897.[6]

There were four groups that pressured the federal government in the crafting of the 1897 General Credit Institutions and Banking Act: the stockholders of Banamex; the stockholders in the Banco de Londres y México; the stockholders in other, smaller, state-level banks; and the state governors (who wished to award cronies with bank charters). The resulting law could easily be predicted from knowledge of the players in the negotiations: Banamex shared many (although not all) of its special privileges with the Banco de Londres y México; the state banks were given local monopolies; and the state governors were able to award concessions to their cronies.[7]

barrier to entry. It does mean, however, that scale economies were exhausted in textiles at relatively small firm sizes compared to such industries as steel, cement, and chemicals.

5. For a detailed discussion of the original Banamex charter and the Commercial Code of 1884, see Maurer (2002, chap. 2).

6. Unlike English common law, in which any activity is legal unless it is specifically prohibited by law, Mexico's Spanish legal tradition held that all economic activities undertaken without authorization from either a general law or a specific concession were illegal. During the years from 1884 to 1897 Mexico possessed no body of banking law. Thus, bank charters had to be obtained by a special concession granted by the secretary of the treasury. Changes in the identity of the secretary had a direct effect on the ease with which a bank could obtain a charter.

7. In return, a state governor usually received a seat on the bank's board of directors, which entitled the governor to directors' fees and stock distributions. For a discussion, see Haber, Razo, and Maurer (forthcoming, chap. 4).

Holding the arrangement together was the fact that the federal government monopolized bank chartering. Legal barriers to entry into banking could not be eroded by competition among states for bank business, because states did not have the right to charter banks.[8]

The resulting competitive structure had the following features. Banamex and the Banco de Londres y México were granted a duopoly in the Mexico City market. In addition, only Banamex and the Banco de Londres y México had the right to branch across state lines. They were also permitted to hold lower ratios of reserves to banknotes than the state-level banks: 33 percent as opposed to 50 percent. Banamex was also granted the exclusive privilege of providing financial services to the government—collecting tax receipts, making payments, holding federal deposits, and underwriting all foreign and domestic federal debt issues.

State-level banks and their powerful patrons—the state governors—were also protected from competition. The law was written in such a way that, as a practical matter, only one bank could be established in each state, although existing banks were grandfathered in. The law specified that bank charters (and additions to capital) had to be approved by both the secretary of the treasury and the federal congress. In order to make this commitment credible beyond the tenure of Limantour as treasury secretary, the law also created three other barriers to entry. First, the law created very high minimum capital requirements, US$125,000 (later raised to US$250,000). Even the initial figure of $125,000 was more than twice the minimum capital required for a national bank charter in the United States, which was set at $50,000. Second, the law established a 2 percent annual tax on paid-in capital. The first banks granted a charter in each state, however, were granted an exemption from the tax. This gave the first banks into each market an insuperable advantage. Third, state banks were not allowed to branch outside their concession territories. This prevented banks chartered in one state from challenging the monopoly of a bank in an adjoining state. In short, the only threat to the monopoly of a state bank could come from a branch of Banamex or the Banco de Londres y México.[9]

The result was that Mexico had a very small and concentrated banking sector. In 1910, even if we include mortgage banks and count Banamex branches as independent banks, there were only forty-two formally incorporated banks in the entire country. The United States, for comparison purposes, had 25,151 banks and trust companies in that year (U.S. Department of Commerce 1997). The capital available to this banking system was also small: total assets in 1911 were approximately US$400 million (Secretaría de Hacienda, 255). For comparison purposes, total assets of the U.S. bank-

8. Had states had the right to charter banks, they would have been tempted to ratchet the minimum requirements for a bank charter downward as they competed against one another for bank business.

9. For discussions of the 1897 law see Haber (1991); Maurer (2002, chap. 3); Maurer and Haber (2002).

ing system were $22.9 billion (U.S. Department of Commerce). Finally, not only were Mexico's banks few in number and of small size, but the level of concentration was extremely high: Banamex and Banco de Londres y México accounted for more than 60 percent of all assets.[10] Estimates by Maurer (2002, chap. 3) put the Herfindahl index at .2, which is to say that even had there been interstate competition, the competitive structure of the industry would have been identical to that of an industry with only five equally sized banks.

The problems posed by a small and concentrated banking sector were compounded by the fact that banks had no way to assess the creditworthiness of potential borrowers, other than to rely on the personal connections of their directors. The result, as Maurer (2002, chap. 6) has shown, was that most lending went to insiders: bank directors, members of their families, or close friends. This was a common practice just about everywhere in the world in the nineteenth century—even in the United States (Lamoreaux 1994). There was a difference, however, between Mexico and the United States: Mexico had a few dozen banks, whereas the United States had tens of thousands. Thus, the potential number of entrepreneurs who could tap the banking system in Mexico was very small: some entrepreneurs were able to obtain bank loans, but most were not.

The financial markets did not fill the vacuum created by the banking system. Equity financing through the creation of a publicly held, joint stock company was also unknown in the Mexican textile industry until the late 1880s. It was not, in fact, until 1889 that Mexico passed a general incorporation law. Soon thereafter, the first limited-liability, joint stock companies began to appear. Yet, even after this institutional innovation, most entrepreneurs were unable to access outside capital from the markets. By 1908 only fourteen industrials were traded on the Mexico City Stock Exchange; no new firms joined their ranks until the late 1930s. Of those industrial companies only four were cotton manufacturers. Thus, of Mexico's 100 cotton textile firms in 1912 (controlling 148 mills), only 4 percent represented publicly traded joint stock companies.[11] These four firms, however, took a disproportionate share of total capital invested in the industry, accounting for 27 percent of all active spindles. Surprisingly, none of these four firms issued debentures.

The reason that the financial markets developed so slowly even after legal reforms should have encouraged the public ownership of corporations can largely be explained by the fact that it was not possible for outside in-

10. Calculated from data in Secretaría de Hacienda (236, 255).

11. The activity of the Mexico City stock exchange was followed by Mexico's major financial weeklies: *La Semana Mercantil,* 1894–1914; *El Economista Mexicano,* 1896–1914; *Boletín Financiero y Minero,* 1916–1938. The behavior of the shares of these firms is analyzed in Haber (1989, chap. 7). The total number of firms is from textile manuscript censuses in the *Archivo General de la Nación, Ramo de Trabajo,* box 5, file 4 (also see box 31, file 2).

vestors to monitor the activities of firms' directors and managers. Financial reporting requirements were not enforced. Although it was legally required, publicly traded manufacturing companies often failed to publish balance sheets in public documents (such as the *Diario Official* or the financial press) in many years. Moreover, even if balance sheets had been available, investors could not readily determine whether the founders (who served as firm directors) had divested themselves of their holdings in the firms. The result was that individuals tended to invest in only those enterprises controlled by important financial capitalists with proven track records. These tended to be the same individuals who owned the banks: the ability to obtain working capital from a bank allowed these individuals to borrow their way through downturns in the business cycle (Maurer and Haber 2002).

In short, when institutional innovations created opportunities for firms to obtain impersonal sources of finance, only a small group of entrepreneurs was able to benefit. The result was differential access to credit and capital—most entrepreneurs had to rely upon retained earnings and their informal networks of business associates for funds; a small group of entrepreneurs were able to obtain capital from the banks and the financial markets.

7.1.2 Brazil

Until the last decade of the nineteenth century, Brazilian textile entrepreneurs faced a banking system and securities markets similar to their Mexican counterparts. Beginning in the late 1880s, there was a short experiment with bank deregulation, and that experiment produced some lending to textile manufacturers. The experiment was cut short by the federal government in the late 1890s. Financial markets, however, substituted for the banking system. In fact, Brazil developed surprisingly active stock and bond markets in industrial securities in the 1890s. These remained active throughout the 1920s. The result was that impersonal sources of finance became widely available to Brazilian textile manufacturers.

Throughout most of the nineteenth century, institutions designed to mobilize impersonal sources of capital were largely absent in Brazil. An organized stock exchange had functioned in Rio de Janeiro since early in the century, but it was seldom used to finance industrial companies. During the period from 1850 to 1885 only one manufacturing company was listed on the exchange, and its shares traded hands in only three of those thirty-six years. Neither could Brazil's mill owners appeal to the banking system to provide them with capital. In fact, formal banks were so scarce as to be virtually nonexistent. As late as 1888 Brazil had but twenty-six banks, whose combined capital totaled only US$48 million. Only seven of the country's twenty states had any banks at all, and half of all deposits were held by a few banks in Rio de Janeiro (Topik 1987, 28; Peláez and Suzigan 1976, chaps. 2–5; Marques de Saes 1986, 73; Levy 1977, 109–12; Stein 1957, 25–27).

The slow development of these institutions can be traced in large part to public policies designed to restrict entry into banking. The imperial government, which held the right to charter banks, was primarily concerned with creating a small number of large superbanks that could serve as a source of government finance and that would prevent financial panics. The absence of banks not only restricted the amount of credit available to entrepreneurs, but it also meant that banks could not underwrite securities trading or finance securities speculation, the way they did in the United States and Western Europe (Sylla 1975, 52, 209). Finally, restrictive policies discouraged the spread of the corporate form of ownership: Founding a joint stock company required special government permission; shareholder liability was not limited; investors were not allowed to purchase stocks on margin; and banks were restricted from investing in corporate securities (Levy 1977, 117; Peláez and Suzigan 1976, 78–83, 96–97; Marques de Saes 1986, 22, 86).

In the last decades of the nineteenth century a dramatic reform of the regulations governing Brazil's capital markets took place. These changes began in 1882, when the government removed the requirement that joint stock companies obtain special charters from parliament. This reform also lowered, from 25 to 20 percent, the amount of paid-in capital required before the stock could be traded. In the case of insolvency, however, investors were still liable for the firm's debts, even if those shares had been traded away as long as five years before (Hanley 1995, 24, 27). As one might imagine, the lack of limited liability meant that these reforms had very little effect on the use of the stock and bond markets as sources of industrial investment.

The real impetus to regulatory reform did not get underway until 1888, when the imperial government abolished slavery. The end of slavery produced a series of unintended and unexpected outcomes that set in motion both the overthrow of the monarchy and the complete reform of banking and securities market regulation. Abolition drove a wedge between Brazil's planter class, which historically had been the mainstay of the monarchy, and the imperial government. In an effort to placate the planters by making credit more easily available, the imperial government awarded concessions to twelve banks of issue and provided seventeen banks with interest-free loans. The easy credit policies of 1888 were not enough, however, to stem the tide of Brazil's republican movement. In November of 1889 Dom Pedro II, Brazil's emperor, was overthrown and a federal republic was created.

The finance minister of the new republican government, Rui Barbosa, quickly pushed three crucial reforms through. First, the government deregulated the banking industry: banks could now engage in whatever kinds of financial transactions they wished, including the right to extend long-term loans and to invest in corporate securities. Second, the new general incorporation law limited liability to the face value of their shares. Third, the government instituted a set of mandatory disclosure laws that were highly unusual for the time. Brazil's publicly owned corporations were required to produce annual financial statements (many, in fact, produced them twice per year) and to reprint them in public documents, such as state or federal gazettes or the newspaper. In addition, their annual reports had to list the names of all shareholders and the numbers of shares they controlled. Finally, the annual report had to list the number of shares that had changed hands during the year, including information on the number of shares that traded in each transaction. Investors could thus obtain reasonably good information on the health of a firm, the potential liquidity of its shares, and the identities of its major shareholders.[12] Fifth, the government gave itself an incentive to enforce the reporting laws: it established a 5 percent tax on all corporate dividends.[13]

The results of these reforms were dramatic. The nominal capital of corporations listed on the Rio de Janeiro and São Paulo exchanges, which had stood at 410,000 contos (roughly $136 million) in May 1888, doubled to 963,965 contos by December 1889 under the new banking laws, and then doubled again by December 1890 when the use of the markets spread to other areas of economic activity. By December 1891, it reached 3,778,695 contos, roughly US$1 billion. Even accounting for inflation, the increase in the value of corporations listed on the São Paulo and Rio de Janeiro exchanges (in milreis terms) increased sixfold from 1888 to 1891.[14]

The *Encilhamento* financed large numbers of banks. In the short run these banks provided loans to Brazil's textile industry, and in some cases banks directly organized and ran textile companies.

Bank-financed industrial development was not, however, to be long-lasting in Brazil. The boom created by the *Encilhamento* created a speculative bubble that burst in 1892, bringing down many of the banks. The government therefore decided in 1896 once again to restrict the right to issue currency to a single bank acting as the agent of the treasury. These more restrictive regulations, coupled with the already shaky financial situation of many of the banks, produced a massive contraction of the banking sector. In 1891 there were sixty-eight banks operating in Brazil. By 1906 there were only ten, and their capital was only one-ninth that of the 1891 banks (Neuhaus 1975, 22).[15] The banking system then began to expand, led and controlled by a semiofficial superbank—the third Banco do

12. Shareholder lists were not always published in the abbreviated reports reprinted in the newspapers, but they were published in the original reports.

13. Significantly, the law did not establish a capital gains tax. This gave firms an incentive to reinvest profits and stockholders an incentive to take their earnings as capital gains, rather than as dividends.

14. 1888 data from Neuhaus (1975, 19 ff.). Data for 1889, 1890, and 1891 calculated from *O Estado de Sao Paulo* and *Jornal do Commercio,* consolidated stock tables (see table 7.1). A conto was equal to 1,000 milreis, the basic unit of Brazilian currency. There were roughly three milreis to the dollar in 1890.

15. For a discussion of bank portfolios see Hanley (1995); Triner (1994).

Brasil—which acted both as a commercial bank and as the treasury's financial agent.

After the contraction of the banking system in 1896, Brazil's banks appear to have lent very little money for long-term investment. Banks played an important role, however, in providing short-term, working capital to manufacturers by discounting commercial paper. In order to study the importance of such discounts in providing working capital I drew a sample of financial statements of fifteen publicly traded cotton textile manufacturing firms covering the years 1895 to 1940. These fifteen firms are not a random sample, but were chosen because it was possible to retrieve complete sets of their financial statements.[16] These fifteen firms controlled 42 percent of the industry's installed capacity in 1905 and 24 percent even as late as 1934. It is clear from comparing the financial data in the censuses to the financial data in these reports that these firms were more likely to have significant long-term bonded debt than was the norm, even for publicly traded, joint stock companies. These financial statements permit, however, the more detailed study of the structure of debt and equity than do manufacturing censuses, which measure only long-term debt. As table 7.1 shows, during the period 1895–1915 short-term debt accounted for 29 to 42 percent (depending on the year) of the total indebtedness of these fifteen firms.

The more important long-run effect of the *Encilhamento* was that the regulatory reforms of the securities markets gave rise to the widespread sale of equity and bonded debt to the investing public in order to mobilize long-term capital. The first reform was the establishment of limited liability. Limited liability overcame a fundamental asymmetry in incentives: Before 1890 the law created disincentives for entrepreneurs to issue debt and disincentives for investors to purchase equity because an investor was held to be

16. The fifteen firms are Companhia de Fiaçao e Tecidos Alliança, Companhia America Fabril, Companhia Brasil Industrial, Companhia de Fiaçao e Tecelagem Carioca, Companhia de Fiaçao e Tecidos Industrial Campista, Companhia de Fiaçao e Tecidos Cometa, Companhia de Fiaçao e Tecidos Confiança Industrial, Companhia de Fiaçao e Tecidos Corcovado, Companhia de Fiaçao e Tecidos Industrial Mineira, Companhia de Fiaçao e Tecidos Mageénse, Companhia Manufactora Fluminense, Companhia Petropolitana, Companhia Progresso Industrial do Brasil, Companhia de Fiaçao e Tecidos Santo Aleixo, and Companhia Fabrica de Tecidos Sao Pedro de Alcantara. Some of these reports were located in the Bibliotheca Nacional in Rio de Janeiro, filed erroneously in the periodicals section. Most were retrieved from the *Journal do Commercio* (Rio de Janeiro's major financial daily) and the *Diario Official* (Brazil's equivalent of the *Federal Register*). In theory, it would be possible to retrieve the reports of all publicly traded companies from these and similar sources—such as the *Diario Official* for each state and the major financial dailies of all the major cities, because under Brazilian law firms had to reprint abbreviated versions of their financial statements in public venues. In practice, however, this is a costly procedure because none of the relevant publications are indexed and each runs to roughly 20,000 pages per year. I therefore concentrated on the months of January, February, March, April, July, and August (when most firms produced their financial statements) for the *Jornal do Commercio* and the *Diario Official.* Even restricting analysis to these four publications and concentrating solely on the months listed above still requires the researcher to look at roughly 1 million frames of microfilm to cover the sixty years from 1880 to 1940.

Table 7.1 **Debt-Equity Ratios and Sources of New Capital for 15-Firm Sample, 1895–1940**

			Liabilities (millions of current milreis)			
Year	Paid in Capital	Retained Earnings	Short-Term Debt	Bond Debt	Total Liabilities	Debt-Equity Ratio
1895	10	1	2	5	19	0.68
1900	53	16	9	19	96	0.39
1905	61	30	7	16	115	0.26
1910	76	28	19	26	149	0.43
1915	81	30	26	38	175	0.57
1920	115	43	21	45	224	0.41
1925	145	118	54	39	357	0.35
1930	137	100	65	78	380	0.60
1935	135	124	66	64	389	0.50
1940	145	143	74	46	409	0.42

Sources: See footnote 16.

Notes: Large-scale, publicly traded Brazilian textile firms (estimated from balance sheets; includes short-term debt).

fully liable for a firm's debts in the case of insolvency, even if he had traded away the stock. From the point of view of founding groups of investors, the new limited liability law meant that they could go out to the debt markets and not be personally liable for those debts if the company failed. From the point of view of potential investors from outside the founding groups, limited liability meant that they could purchase equity shares in firms and not have to be concerned that they would be held personally liable for the firm's debts if it went bankrupt.[17]

The second crucial reform in securities markets were those related to mandatory disclosure. The 1890 regulatory law required firms to produce financial statements, reprint at least the balance sheets in public documents (such as a newspaper or state gazette), and include a statement in the report about the identity of each stockholder and the number of shares each stockholder owned. In the early stages of the use of the market it is likely the case that investors made decisions about which firms to invest in based on the reputations of the founding group of entrepreneurs. Over time, however, potential investors had far more information to go on: they knew who held controlling interest in the firm and they had a great deal of financial information available, including the firm's history of dividend payments, its

17. Limited liability eliminates the need for investors to monitor one another. In a situation in which liability is not limited, investors must create expensive covenants that restrict the transferability of ownership rights to individuals with sufficient wealth to cover their share of any liability resulting from insolvency. Alternatively, investors must engage in costly monitoring to verify the liquidity of their partners. See Carr and Mathewson (1988).

level of indebtedness, the size of its reserves, and the liquidity of their investment.

Essentially, corporate finance took the following form: a group of entrepreneurs tied through kinship or preexisting business relationships would come together and found a joint stock company. They would then issue a prospectus, find a broker or bank to act as an intermediary, and sell shares to the public. As a firm's capital requirements grew it would either issue new shares, which would be advertised in a public offering and handled by a broker, or issue bonds that would also be subscribed by the public through the services of a broker or a bank. Over time, therefore, stock ownership grew more diversified and individuals could choose between owning equity or owning debt. In the early stages of the development of the market this looked much like the Boston Stock Exchange: stocks tended to be closely held by the founding groups. Gradually, however, stock ownership became more diversified, particularly for the larger, more successful companies. By the 1920s, larger companies typically had more than 100 shareholders, and the rate of turnover of shares in the secondary markets was roughly 10 percent per year. It was also generally the case that no individual stockholder controlled more than 10 percent of a firm's shares. In fact, in the country's largest textile firm, the Companhia America Fabril, the minority shareholders actually banded together in the early 1920s and forced a reform of the board of directors, removing the founding group of entrepreneurs from their control of the firm (von der Weid and Rodrigues Bastos 1986).

In 1866 there were no joint stock companies in the Brazilian cotton textile industry. By the early 1880s there were two, accounting for 32 percent of the industry's installed capacity. By 1895, thirteen joint stock firms had been founded, and their capacity was seven times that of the joint stock companies in 1883. This mushroomed to sixty-six joint stock firms (accounting for 60 percent of industry capacity) by 1914, and to eighty joint stock firms (accounting for 70 percent of capacity) by 1925. This is especially impressive when one considers that total capacity was growing at an extremely rapid pace. Measuring capacity by the number of spindles in service (which gives lower-bound estimates because it does not capture increases in the speed of machines over time), total capacity increased more than threefold from 1881 to 1895, and then tripled again by 1905. It then doubled again by 1914, and then grew an additional 50 percent to 1925. At this point, total capacity was 2.4 million spindles, which is to say that capacity was roughly thirty times what it had been in the early 1880s (see table 7.2).

As important as the development of the equities markets in Brazil was the simultaneous development of markets for long-term debt. As was the case with equities, debt issues came in small denominations: virtually all had a par value of 200 milreis (about $50 in nominal terms at the 1900

Table 7.2 Size Estimates (in spindles) of the Cotton Textile Industries of Brazil, Mexico, India, and the United States, 1843–1934

Year	Mexico	Brazil	India	United States
1843	121,750			
1850	135,538[a]			
1865	154,822	14,875	285,524	
1875		45,830	886,098	
1878	323,176			
1880				10,653,435
1881		84,956		
1883		78,908		
1885			2,145,646	
1888	249,561[a]			
1891	277,784			
1893	370,570			14,384,180
1895	411,090	260,842[a]		
1896	430,868			
1898		279,666[a]		
1900	588,474		4,945,783	19,436,984
1905	678,058	778,224[a]		
1906	688,217			
1907	613,548	823,343		
1908	732,876			
1909	726,278			
1910	702,874			28,178,862
1911	725,297		6,357,460	
1912	762,149			
1913	752,804			
1914		1,634,449		
1915		1,598,568		
1918	689,173			
1919	735,308			
1920	753,837		6,763,036	34,603,471
1921	770,945	1,621,300[a]		
1923	802,363	1,700,000[a]		
1924	812,165	2,200,612		
1925	840,890	2,397,380		
1926	832,193	2,558,433		
1927	821,211	2,692,077		
1928	823,862			
1929	839,100			
1930	803,873		9,124,768	33,009,323
1931	838,223			
1933	862,303			
1934		2,507,126		

Sources: Mexico: Razo and Haber (1998). India: Report of the Bombay Millowners' Association (1900, 1911, 1920, 1930). United States: Haber (1991). Brazil (estimated from the following sources): Borja Castro (1869); Bibliotheca da Associacão Industrial (1882); Branner (1885); Commissão de Inquerito Industrial (1882); Ministerio da Industria (1896); Prefeitura do Distrito Federal (1908); Vasco (1905); Association of Cotton Textile Producers (1922, 1923, 1926a, 1928, 1935, and various years); Centro Industrial do Brasil (1909, 1915, 1917).

[a]Estimate based on partial census information.

dollar-milreis exchange rate), implying that they could be held by medium-sized savers. These debts took the form of general obligation bonds, were callable, carried nominal interest rates of 5 to 8 percent, and had terms of twenty years or more.

These debt issues raised significant amounts of capital. A comparison of the 1905 and 1915 textile manufacturing censuses indicates that firms located in Rio de Janeiro or the Distrito Federal, where the market was well developed, financed 69 percent of their increase in total capitalization through the sale of new long-term debt. For the country as a whole, 29 percent of new investment came in the form of long-term debt (see table 7.3). In 1915 the average (weighted) debt-equity ratio for firms in Rio de Janeiro or the Distrito Federal, not including bank loans, discounts, or other sources of short-term credit, was 0.43, three times its level in 1905. For the country as a whole, the debt-equity ratio in 1915 was 0.27, nearly twice its level in 1905 (see table 7.4).

This analysis based on census data significantly understates the importance of debt financing, because it does not include trade debt from suppliers, short-term liabilities (mostly commercial paper), and the small quantity of mortgage debt owed to banks. For that reason, I have estimated financial ratios for the fifteen-firm sample of publicly owned companies from their balance sheets. In 1915 the average (weighted) debt-equity ratio for these fifteen firms was 0.57 (see table 7.1). The balance sheet data also corroborate the census data in regard to the pattern of bond finance: The use of the bond market was most important during the periods 1905–10, when new bond debt accounted for 29 percent of all new investment, and 1910–15, when new bond debt accounted for 45 percent of all new investment (see table 7.1).

The use of long-term bond debt and the high percentages of capital coming from debt issues were quite remarkable by the standards of other countries. As late as 1910, the average debt-equity ratio of large-scale firms in the United States textile industry (those listed in *Moody's Manual of Investments*) was 0.40, roughly one-third lower than the debt-equity ratios for comparable Brazilian firms.[18] Even by 1920, when a few of the largest U.S. firms began to issue long-term bonds, the average debt-equity ratio of large-scale firms was only 0.29.[19] Most U.S. textile firms, of course, were unable to make use of the bond market and had to resort to the less optimal choice of

18. Low debt-equity ratios had characterized the development of the U.S. textile industry since the nineteenth century. In 1860 the large, integrated textile manufacturers of New England typically had debt-equity ratios of 0.20. All of this debt was short-term accounts payable and commercial paper. On the early industrial United States see Davis (1957); McGouldrick (1968).

19. These debt-equity ratios are probably upper-bound estimates because they do not represent the universe of U.S. cotton textile firms. If firms were privately held they would not have been listed in Moody's and thus would not enter this sample. See *Moody's Manual of Investments: American and Foreign* (1900, 1910, 1920).

Table 7.3 **Sources of New Capital for Brazilian Cotton Textile Firms, 1905–34**

Period	Location	Firms	Percentage Growth of Total Capital	Share of Total Growth, by Source (%)			
				New Paid Capital[a]	New Bond Debt	Retained Earnings[a]	New Paid Capital Plus New Retained Earnings
1905–15	All Brazil	174	88		29.2		70.8
	Firms located in RJ or DF	30	45		68.9		31.1
	Firms located in SP	43	272		14.4		85.6
	Joint stock firms in RJ	25	55		53.6		46.4
	Joint stock firms in SP	25	834		13.5		86.5
	Joint stock firms in other states	12	208		31.1		68.9
	Total joint stock firms	62	135		29.1		70.2
	Total private firms	112	35		29.8		70.2
1915–25	All Brazil	189	137	37.5	4.2	58.3	—
	Firms located in RJ or DF	28	118	36.1	3.5	60.4	—
	Firms located in SP	53	244	39.2	6.9	53.9	—
	Joint stock firms in RJ	25	136	35.9	6.5	57.6	—
	Joint stock firms in SP	33	270	37.9	7.0	55.1	—
	Joint stock firms in other states	20	109	33.9	1.1	65.0	—
	Total joint stock firms	78	181	36.9	6.4	56.7	—
	Total private firms	111	54	41.3	–10.2	68.9	—
1925–34	All Brazil	244	19	80.3	64.7	–45.1	—
	Firms located in RJ or DF	35	7	67.4	89.6	–56.9	—
	Firms located in SP	98	13	127.1	147.7	–174.7	—
	Joint stock firms in RJ	25	2	18.2	243.9	–162.1	—
	Joint stock firms in SP	31	1	578.4	2215.3	–2693.7	—
	Joint stock firms in other states	25	102	65.9	26.5	7.6	—
	Total joint stock firms	81	9	84.0	158.7	–142.7	—
	Total private firms	163	56	78.3	12.2	9.5	—

Sources: Estimated from Vasco (1905); Centro Industrial do Brasil (1915); Association of Cotton Textile Producers (1926b, 1935).

Notes: Share of total growth in liabilities, valued in current milreis. RJ = Rio de Janeiro; SP = São Paulo. Dash = not applicable for this year.

[a]In 1905, paid-in capital and retained earnings were not broken out separately in the census.

Table 7.4 Financial Structure of Brazilian Cotton Textile Firms, 1905–34

Year	Location	Firms	Paid Capital[a]	Long-Term Debt	Reserves[a]	Capital Plus Reserves	Total Capital	Debt-Equity Ratio
1905	All Brazil	90		28		177	205	0.16
	Firms located in RJ or DF	19		13		93	106	0.14
	Firms located in SP	17		4		24	28	0.16
	Joint stock firms in RJ	17		13		77	91	0.17
	Joint stock firms in SP	3		4		6	10	0.68
	Joint stock firms in other states	4				7	8	0.06
	Total joint stock firms	24		18		90	108	0.20
	Total private firms	66		11		87	97	0.12
	Joint stock firms as % Brazil			62.8		51.1	52.7	
1915	All Brazil	174	264	81	41	305	386	0.27
	Firms located in RJ or DF	30	87	46	21	108	154	0.43
	Firms located in SP	43	79	15	8	88	103	0.17
	Joint stock firms in RJ	25	79	40	21	100	140	0.40
	Joint stock firms in SP	25	67	15	8	75	90	0.20
	Joint stock firms in other states	12	17	6	2	19	24	0.30
	Total joint stock firms	62	163	60	31	194	255	0.31
	Total private firms	112	101	21	9	111	131	0.19
	Joint stock firms as % Brazil		61.6	74.5	76.8	63.7	65.9	

1925	All Brazil	189	463	103	350	813	916	0.13
	Firms located in RJ or DF	28	152	52	131	284	336	0.18
	Firms located in SP	53	178	32	143	321	353	0.10
	Joint stock firms in RJ	25	148	52	131	279	331	0.19
	Joint stock firms in SP	33	159	32	142	300	332	0.11
	Joint stock firms in other states	20	26	6	19	45	51	0.13
	Total joint stock firms	78	332	90	292	624	714	0.14
	Total private firms	111	130	14	58	188	202	0.07
	Joint stock firms as % Brazil		71.8	86.9	83.4	76.8	78.0	
1934	All Brazil	244	605	218	271	875	1093	0.25
	Firms located in RJ or DF	35	168	73	118	286	359	0.25
	Firms located in SP	98	235	98	65	300	398	0.33
	Joint stock firms in RJ	25	149	73	118	267	340	0.27
	Joint stock firms in SP	31	176	98	61	237	335	0.42
	Joint stock firms in other states	25	60	20	23	84	103	0.24
	Total joint stock firms	81	385	191	202	587	778	0.32
	Total private firms	163	219	27	69	288	315	0.10
	Joint stock firms as % Brazil		63.7	87.4	74.5	67.1	71.1	

Sources: See table 7.3.

Note: Does not include short-term debt. Paid capital and total capital reported in millions of current mil-reis. RJ = Rio de Janeiro. SP = São Paulo.

[a]The 1905 census did not report reserves and paid-in capital separately.

issuing preferred shares when they wanted to grow faster than was possible through the reinvestment of retained earnings.[20]

The development of the bond market appears to have been slowed by World War I. Between 1915 and 1925, new long-term bond issues accounted for only 4 percent of net new additions to invested capital. Thus, by 1925 debt-equity ratios fell to 0.13, less than half their 1915 levels (see tables 7.3 and 7.4) and roughly on par with Mexican debt-equity ratios circa 1910. In the 1920s the most important source of new investment capital for the Brazilian textile industry became retained earnings, which accounted for 58 percent of new additions to capital. The remainder of new capital spending was made up of new equity issues by already established companies and the founding of new firms, particularly in the state of São Paulo. In the latter part of the 1920s the debt market began to recover, although it appears that much of the debt issued was used to fund operating losses during the Great Depression. As table 7.3 indicates, the increase in debt almost exactly matches the contraction of retained earnings during the period 1927–34.

In short, Brazilian textile industrialists were limited in their sources of finance throughout most of the nineteenth century. Beginning in the late 1880s, however, regulatory reforms brought about important innovations in financial intermediation that made access to institutional sources of finance relatively easy for many entrepreneurs. Even though the development of these new sources of finance was slowed by WWI, it still produced an extraordinarily large and well-integrated capital market by the standards of developing economies at the time.

7.2 Finance and the Structure and Growth of the Textile Industry

What effects did these differences in the development of capital have on the development of the textile industry in the countries under study? One would expect at least four. First, Mexico's textile industry should have grown much more slowly than that of Brazil. Second, in Mexico, privileged access to capital should have served as a barrier to entry: capital market rigidities should have resulted in high levels of industrial concentration.

20. Preferred shares are less favorable for firms than bonds because, like bonds, they carry the requirement of guaranteed interest payments, but at the same time they afford the firm much less flexibility. Unlike bondholders, preferred shareholders have the right to make claims on profits beyond the guaranteed interest rate. In addition, bonds are amortized, whereas preferred shares are not. Unless repurchased from shareholders, preferred shares require the payment of guaranteed returns to their holders in perpetuity. Finally, any such repurchase must be done at the market value of the shares, unlike with callable bonds, which are repurchased at their par value. Since preferred shareholders have the right to a share of profits beyond the guaranteed interest rate, the profitability of the firm becomes capitalized in their market value. Thus, almost by definition, a firm that has the ability to buy back its preferred shares is going to have to pay a price significantly above the par value of the shares to do so.

Third, we would expect different trajectories of concentration: concentration should have fallen in Brazil, but not in Mexico. Fourth, one might expect differences in the rate of growth of productivity: Efficient Brazilian firms should have been able to expand rapidly because they would not have been liquidity constrained, as was the case with their Mexican counterparts. One would therefore expect that total factor productivity (TFP) growth would have been faster in Brazil than in Mexico. One would also expect that the firms with the fastest productivity growth in both countries would be those firms that were able to use banks or the securities markets to mobilize capital.

An examination of the data on the development of the textile industry in the two countries bears out these hypotheses. In regard to the rate of growth of the textile industry, the Brazilian textile industry, which had been virtually nonexistent in the first half of the nineteenth century, quickly outgrew Mexico's after its capital markets opened up. As late as 1883, the entire modern sector of the Brazilian cotton goods industry numbered only forty-four firms running just under 80,000 spindles, less than one-third the size of Mexico's cotton goods industry (see table 7.2). This relative size relationship continued into the mid-1890s, but over the following ten years widespread access to impersonal sources of capital in Brazil meant that its cotton textile industry was able to outgrow Mexico's by a factor of five, producing for the first time an absolute size difference in favor of Brazil. By the outbreak of WWI, Brazil's industry was roughly twice the size of Mexico's, a gap that grew to 3:1 by the onset of the Great Depression.

One might argue that capital immobilities had little to do with the rate of growth of the textile industry: demand factors were far more important in influencing industry growth. Mexico's industry was smaller and grew less quickly than that of Brazil because it had a smaller, poorer population. A comparison of Brazil and Mexico indicates, however, that demand factors cannot explain differences in observed industry size. First, both countries produced only for their own domestic consumption, because neither was efficient enough to compete against U.S. or British exports in international markets. Second, even though Brazil had a larger population than Mexico (because of Brazil's policy of subsidizing European immigration, its population was roughly 25 percent larger than Mexico's circa 1910), Mexican per capita incomes were roughly 40 percent higher than Brazil's. Given that the income elasticity of demand for textiles was very high, Mexico likely had a much higher per capita demand for textile products than the differences in per capita income would indicate.[21]

21. Contemporary observers noted this high income elasticity of demand for textile products. Their observations are reported in Haber (1989, 28–29). Accounting for imports would not overturn these results. Both countries were highly protectionist. Imports by 1910 therefore accounted for only 20 percent of consumption. This was almost entirely high-value, fine-weave goods.

As for the effects of capital immobilities on industrial concentration, the data are unequivocal: access to capital had a significant effect on the level of concentration. Table 7.5 presents estimates of four-firm concentration ratios and Herfindahl indexes.[22] For purposes of international comparison, I also present data on the United States and India.

There are a number of striking features of the data. The first is that Mexico's financial market reforms actually produced an *increase* in concentration. The trend in Mexico from the 1840s to the early 1880s was a gradual decrease in concentration—exactly the trend that one would expect in an expanding industry characterized by constant-returns-to-scale technology. As table 7.5 indicates, Mexico's four-firm ratio fell from a high of .579 in 1840 to a low of .158 in 1883, while the Herfindahl dropped from .114 to .019 over the same period. Beginning in the 1880s, the trend reversed, even though the industry was witnessing rapid growth. By 1902, both the four-firm ratio and the Herfindahl had dramatically increased, standing at .381 and .063, respectively. By international standards, Mexico's textile industry was extremely concentrated. To provide a comparison, the four-firm ratio in the U.S. textile industry in 1900 was .07, roughly one-sixth of the Mexican level. The Indian textile industry had a four-firm ratio of .19, roughly one-half the Mexican level.

Concentration in Brazil displays exactly the opposite pattern from Mexico. Prior to the 1890s, Brazil's relatively small textile industry displayed higher levels of concentration than Mexico's. By 1905, however, relatively widespread access to institutional sources of capital drove Brazil's four-firm ratio down to two-thirds that of Mexico, a ratio that was then maintained through the 1930s. The drop in the Herfindahl index was even more pronounced. During the period 1875–78, the Herfindahl index for Brazil was more than ten times that of Mexico. By 1905–06, Brazil's Herfindahl was 34 percent lower than Mexico's, and by 1912–14 it was 69 percent lower.[23]

One might argue that Mexico's higher concentration ratios had little to do with capital immobilities: Mexico had higher levels of concentration and a different trajectory of concentration because it had a smaller textile industry than Brazil. There are four problems with this line of argument.

22. These estimates of concentration are calculated at the firm level. This involved combining the market shares of all mills held by a single corporation, partnership, or sole proprietor. Market shares for Mexico and Brazil were calculated from estimates of the actual sales or value of output of mills. Market shares for India and the United States were calculated from data on installed capacity. Econometric work on the United States indicates that there was a 25 percent difference in output per spindle between average and best practice techniques. I therefore assumed that the largest firms in both countries were 25 percent more productive than the average and adjusted their market shares accordingly. On average and best-practice techniques, see Davis and Stettler (1966, 231).

23. One might argue that these differences in concentration would disappear if imports of foreign textiles were accounted for, but that argument does not stand up to the empirical evidence on textile imports. Indeed, both Brazil and Mexico followed highly protectionist policies after 1890, virtually eliminating imported cloth except for fine-weave, high-value goods.

Table 7.5 **Indices of Concentration in the Cotton Textile Industries of Brazil, Mexico, India, and the United States, 1840–1934**

	Four-Firm Ratio				Herfindahl Index		
Year	Brazil	Mexico	India	United States	Brazil	Mexico	India
1840		0.579				0.114	
1843		0.346				0.043	
1844		0.344				0.054	
1845		0.292				0.038	
1850		0.270		0.100		0.040	
1854		0.318				0.040	
1857		0.321				0.040	
1860				0.126			
1862		0.273				0.041	
1865		0.278				0.029	
1866	0.729				0.167		
1870				0.107			
1875	0.756				0.238		
1878		0.168				0.021	
1880				0.087			
1882	0.509				0.115		
1883	0.483	0.158			0.999	0.019	
1888		0.174				0.021	
1889		0.180				0.022	
1891		0.188				0.023	
1893		0.200		0.077		0.022	
1895		0.371				0.040	
1896		0.297				0.039	
1898		0.394				0.055	
1900		0.316	0.190	0.070		0.036	0.018
1902		0.381				0.063	
1904		0.328				0.041	
1905	0.215	0.315			0.027	0.041	
1906		0.338				0.048	
1907	0.217				0.027		
1909		0.337				0.047	
1910		0.255		0.075		0.028	
1911		0.328	0.190			0.049	0.018
1912		0.286				0.036	
1913		0.298				0.069	
1914	0.154	0.384			0.015	0.055	
1915	0.157	0.348			0.015	0.043	
1916		0.297				0.042	
1917		0.385				0.059	
1918		0.330				0.047	
1919		0.375				0.059	
1920		0.286	0.206	0.066		0.036	
1924	0.233	0.331			0.028	0.043	
1925	0.237	0.297			0.027	0.038	
1926	0.209				0.023		
1927	0.195				0.022		
1929		0.281				0.034	
1930			0.189	0.095			
1932		0.256				0.029	
1934	0.176				0.017		

Sources: See table 7.2.

Notes: Concentration by estimated capacity, measured at the firm level. A detailed discussion of the estimation procedures is available from the author.

The first is that this argument assumes that there is a direct link between industry size and industry structure: the larger a country's industry, the less concentrated it should be. In order to test this notion, I estimated four-firm concentration ratios and Herfindahl indexes for the Indian cotton textile industry. Since India's industry was roughly three times the size of Brazil's we should observe a lower level of concentration there. In fact, India's average level of concentration during the first three decades of the twentieth century was very close to that of Brazil, and during the 1920s exceeded Brazilian concentration (see table 7.5).

The second is that Mexico's industry leaders were tremendous operations in an absolute sense. Mexico's leading firms were not simply large relative to the small Mexican market, they were enormous operations even by U.S. and Indian standards. Mexico's largest firm in 1912, for example, the Compañía Industrial de Orizaba (CIDOSA), was a four-mill operation employing 4,284 workers running 92,708 spindles and 3,899 looms. Had it been located in the United States, it would have ranked among the twenty-five largest cotton textile enterprises. Had it been located in India it would have been among the top twelve textile enterprises.

The third problem with this argument is that it does not stand up to empirical evidence on the relationship between TFP and firm size. I have estimated Cobb-Douglas production functions for both the Mexican and Brazilian cotton industries, and these do not reveal positive scale economies. In fact, in the Mexican case, for the census years 1895, 1896, 1912, and 1913 the scale coefficient is negative, indicating that firms were suboptimally large (Razo and Haber 1998; Haber 1998). These production function results are buttressed by survivor analysis, which indicates that in both Brazil and Mexico the minimum efficient scale of production was a firm size that corresponded to a less than 1 percent market share (Haber).

The fourth problem with this hypothesis is that it cannot explain why Mexican concentration increased during a period when the industry was experiencing rapid growth, the years 1878–1902. Without some supply factor intervening during this period, Mexican concentration should have continued to decline, instead of jumping back up to its 1843 level.

In order to test this hypothesis in a formal manner, I estimated an ordinary least squares (OLS) regression that measures the elasticity of concentration with respect to industry size. The logic behind the estimation is the following: in an industry characterized by modest returns to scale, with no significant technological changes that would raise the minimum efficient scale of production in a discontinuous way, we should be able to predict the level of concentration simply by knowing the size of the industry. Similar regression results for Brazil and Mexico would indicate that concentration was simply a function of industry size. If, however, similar specifications of the regression for each country yield different results, then some interven-

Table 7.6 Alternate Specifications of Industrial Concentration Regressions

	Mexico		Brazil	
	Spec. 1	Spec. 2	Spec. 1	Spec. 2
A. Dependent Variable: ln (Herfindahl Index)				
Intercept	–3.933	–10.667	2.623	4.887
	(–3.332)	(–2.477)	(4.021)	(2.547)
ln(spindles) (proxy for industry size)	0.046	0.637	–0.447	–0.733
	(0.502)	(1.699)	(–9.288)	(–3.136)
Time		–0.017		0.0237
		(–1.621)		(1.250)
DW	0.82	1.11	0.07	0.13
Adjusted R^2	0.04	0.04	0.89	0.89
N	22	22	12	12
B. Dependent Variable: ln (Four-Firm Ratio)				
Intercept	–1.603	–5.349	2.295	4.346
	(–1.874)	(–1.667)	(5.318)	(3.716)
ln(spindles) (proxy for industry size)	0.024	0.353	–0.272	–0.531
	(0.365)	(1.264)	(–8.538)	(–3.727)
Time		–0.009		0.021
		(–1.210)		(1.858)
DW	0.85	1.03	0.06	0.14
Adjusted R^2	0.04	0.02	0.87	0.89
N	22	22	12	12

Source: Calculated from data in tables 7.2 and 7.5.
Notes: *T*-statistics in parentheses.

ing variable (like an imperfection in a factor market) must have been at work.[24]

Table 7.6 presents various regression specifications. All values are converted to natural logs in order to capture how changes in the size of the industry affect the change in concentration. Industry size is measured by the number of spindles.

The first section of table 7.6 measures concentration by the Herfindahl

24. The model makes the reasonable assumption that there were no discontinuous jumps in minimum efficient scales in either country, although it does allow for a gradual increase in minimum efficient scales. For this reason, it is unlikely that the elasticities of the size variables will sum to unity. Observations by contemporaries indicate that there were no discontinuous jumps in textile-manufacturing technology during the period that affected the Brazilian or Mexican industries. The only major innovation was the Northrup automatic loom, which was developed in the 1890s. However, the Northrup loom was not widely adopted in either country (there were only twenty-five of them in service in Mexico as late as 1910). Moreover, to the extent that there were technological jumps, these would be more pronounced in the Brazilian regressions than in those for Mexico, because of Brazil's faster purchase of new capacity. This would tend to bias the results against the hypothesis advanced here.

index. For Brazil we obtain unambiguous results: the parameter estimate for ln(spindles) is –0.447 with an R-squared of 0.89. The estimate is statistically significant at the 1 percent level of confidence. In short, in Brazil, the elasticity of concentration with respect to size was 44.7 percent (as industry size doubles, concentration decreased by 44.7 percent). For Mexico, however, the results are much less robust: the parameter estimate for ln(firms) is significantly lower (0.046), has the wrong sign (as industry size doubles, concentration increases by 4.6 percent), and is not statistically significant. Moreover, the R-squared is only 0.04, indicating that there is no correlation between industry structure and industry size.

Perhaps it is the case that these results are driven by differences in the distribution of observations over time. One might argue, for example, that technological change might have had an effect on the relationship between industry size and industry structure, and the first specification does not account for these changes because of differences in the frequency of the observations. I therefore added a time dummy to the regression in specification 2. The addition of this dummy, however, strengthens the qualitative results. As specification 2 of section A indicates, in Brazil, as industry size doubled, concentration *decreased* by 73 percent, whereas in Mexico, as industry size doubled, concentration *increased* by 64 percent. The adjusted R-squared for Brazil is 0.89 and for Mexico 0.04, indicating no correlation in Mexico between the two variables.

Section B repeats the procedures of section A, but substitutes the four-firm concentration ratio for the Herfindahl index as the dependent variable. The results are similar to those of section A. In Brazil, the relationship between industry size and industry structure is exactly what one would expect from an industry characterized by modest returns to scale: As the industry grows, concentration decreases. In Mexico, however, the expected relationship between industry size and industry structure, even accounting for technological change over time, does not hold: As the industry grew, concentration increased, suggesting that in Mexico an industry that was characterized by constant returns to scale was behaving like an industry characterized by sizable increasing returns to scale.

7.3 Total Factor Productivity Growth

One could argue that high levels of concentration were good for Mexico. Large firms might have been able to concentrate research and development (R&D), thereby affording Mexico faster rates of productivity growth. One might also argue, however, that high levels of concentration were bad for Mexico. Concentrated industry discourages competitive behavior, especially in an economy that was also highly protectionist.

Which way this cut is ultimately an empirical question. I therefore estimated levels and rates of growth of TFP for the Mexican and Brazilian textile industries. These estimates involved locating the textile censuses for Brazil and Mexico, putting them into machine-readable form, and then estimating TFP. Because the data were enumerated in the censuses at the firm level, I coded the data sets with dummy variables for age of firm, for location of firm, and perhaps most important, for the firm's source of capital.[25]

Following Kane's work on the United States, I employed the number of spindles as a proxy for the capital input of each company. Following Atack and Sokoloff on productivity in the United States, and Bernard and Jones on international productivity comparisons, I employed the number of workers as the measure of the labor input.[26] Output was proxied by the real value of production.

I employed multivariate regression analysis in order to estimate trend rates of growth of TFP and in order to decompose TFP by firm type, size, and access to capital from banks or securities markets. I used an unbalanced panel procedure to estimate basic pooled and fixed-effects specifications of regressions of the following type:

$$\mathbf{Y}_{it} = \alpha + \mathbf{B} \cdot \mathbf{X}_{it} + \mathbf{u}_{it}$$

where $\mathbf{Y}_{it}$ is the dependent variable of firm i at time t; α is the overall intercept term for all firms; $\mathbf{B}$ is a vector of coefficients corresponding to the $\mathbf{X}_{it}$ vector of independent variables, and $\boldsymbol{u}_{it}$ is a stochastic term.[27] I assume usual normality and independence conditions to obtain least-squares estimates of $\mathbf{B}$.[28]

I assume a Cobb-Douglas production function of the form $Y = A \cdot K^{\gamma} \cdot L^{1-\gamma}$ with constant returns to scale, where K and L represent the capital and labor inputs and A is a function that captures improvements in technology over time. In order to use linear estimation procedures, I take natural logarithms of a normalized production function of the form $y = k^{\alpha}$ where $y = Y/L$ and $k = K/L$ and add explanatory variables to arrive at the following model:

25. These TFP estimates follow earlier work done by Haber (1998), Maurer and Haber (2002), and Razo and Haber (1998).

26. This method of estimating inputs does not capture quality improvements in either labor or machinery over time. It will therefore tend to overestimate the unexplained residual output that cannot be attributed to capital or labor. See Atack (1985), Bernard and Jones (1996); Kane (1988); Sokoloff (1984).

27. For OLS estimates, this coefficient would be the same for all firms; for fixed effects, it was not estimated because it was allowed to vary freely among cross-sections. Both models—the basic pooled and fixed effects—produced the same qualitative results with minor differences in the magnitude of the estimated coefficients. In some cases, as with the time trend, the estimates were nearly identical. Thus, to avoid repetition, I report only results from the basic pooled model.

28. In the construction of time series for each observation unit, it is evident that plain OLS techniques would result in biased estimates because some of the variables in later periods could be predicted from earlier years (e.g., spindles at time t could very well be equal to spindles at time $t + 1$). The panel procedure individually identifies each company over time to correct for potential autocorrelation in its variables.

$$\ln y = \alpha + \beta_1 \cdot \ln k + \beta_2 \cdot \ln L + \beta_3 \cdot \text{Time Trend}$$

This specification allows us both to test for economies of scale and to obtain the rate of TFP growth, the coefficient on the time trend. I use variations of this equation to estimate the effects of other features of firms (location, traded status, vintage, and other relevant variables).[29]

Table 7.7 estimates TFP for Brazilian textile firms. Specification 1 indicates that, as predicted, there were negligible scale economies in the Brazilian cotton textile industry (the coefficient on firm size is negative, of small magnitude, and not statistically significant). The industry was, however, characterized by rapid productivity growth: the time trend was 6.1 percent per year. As expected, newer firms (those founded after 1905) had higher productivities than their older competitors (the coefficient translates into roughly an 8 percent TFP advantage for newer firms, everything else being equal). Perhaps most striking is the sizable impact of the joint stock corporate form. The coefficient of 0.226 on the joint stock dummy translates into a 25 percent TFP advantage over non–joint stock firms.

One might think that firms that were actively traded on an organized exchange might have been more efficient than joint stock firms that were not traded. The notion is that firms that were regularly traded were monitored more closely by large investors. Ideally, I would add a traded dummy to specification 1, to measure the marginal effect of being publicly traded. Traded firms were, however, a subset of joint stock firms, meaning that there is collinearity between the two variables. I therefore estimated the effect of being traded in specification 2 by substituting a traded dummy for the joint stock dummy. The hypothesis that traded status explains the advantage that joint stock firms had over their competitors can be rejected: the coefficient is large and statistically significant, but it is of a smaller magnitude than that on joint stock firms alone. It may have been the case that the secondary markets for equity were too thin to serve as efficient monitors; or, it may be the case that some of the most productive joint stock companies' shares were closely held by their original investors.

What effect did the ability to issue bonds have on the growth of TFP for

29. This specification provides a simple test for economies of scale, following the methodology of Atack (1985). The sign of β_2 would indicate whether, if negative, there are decreasing returns to scale or, if positive, increasing returns to scale. The magnitude of β_2 would indicate the level to which production deviates from the standard case of constant returns to scale. A coefficient of small magnitude, that is not statistically significant, would corroborate the hypothesis of constant returns to scale. The additional variables, dummies and interaction terms, are vectors of dummy explanatory variables (including limited liability status, trading in the stock market, and location in the central region, respectively); $\boldsymbol{\delta}$ and $\boldsymbol{\gamma}$ are correspondingly the coefficient vectors. These are used to further decompose the rate of growth (β_3) of TFP. I obtain the same results if I use a specification in which the variables were not normalized by the labor input, but in that case I would be unable to test for economies of scale. Regardless of whether I normalize by labor, β_3 remains the rate of TFP growth because in both cases, the contribution of the two inputs would have been accounted by the estimates of β_1 and β_2.

Table 7.7 **Alternate Specifications of Cobb-Douglas Production Functions, Brazilian Cotton Textile Industry, 1905–27**

	Dependent Variable: Log (Real Value of Production/Worker)[a]				
	Spec. 1	Spec. 2	Spec. 3	Spec. 4	Spec. 5
1. Intercept	6.502	6.389	6.268	6.154	6.256
	(39.678)	(38.909)	(38.652)	(40.351)	(37.689)
2. ln(spindles/worker) (proxy for capital)	0.316	0.331	0.348	0.304	0.298
	(8.765)	(9.100)	(9.603)	(8.607)	(8.336)
3. ln(workers) (proxy for firm size)	–0.012	0.002	0.018	0.034	0.019
	(–0.613)	(0.088)	(0.985)	(1.958)	(0.978)
4. Time	0.061	0.062	0.063	0.061	0.061
	(21.310)	(21.545)	(21.376)	(21.627)	(21.435)
5. Vintage (dummy for firms founded on or after 1905)	0.076	0.089	0.087	0.065	0.059
	(2.037)	(2.344)	(2.284)	(1.756)	(1.583)
6. Joint Stock (dummy for limited-liability joint stock company)	0.226				
	(5.770)				
a. Joint Stock Out (dummy for joint stock firm outside of competitive region)					0.285
					(2.248)
7. Traded (dummy for firms listed in stock exchange markets)		0.165			
		(3.872)			
8. Bonds (dummy for bonded debt)			0.093		
			(1.842)		
9. Region (dummy for firms in MG, RJ, DF, SP)				0.300	
				(8.281)	
a. Privately owned in MG, RJ, DF, SP					0.279
					(6.394)
b. Joint stock in MG, RJ, DF, SP					0.354
					(8.138)
N	1,017	1,017	1,017	1,017	1,017
Adjusted R^2	0.40	0.39	0.39	0.42	0.43

Sources: See table 7.2 Brazil sources.

Notes: MG = Minas Gerais; RJ = Rio de Janeiro; DF = Distrito Federal; SP = São Paulo.

[a]Sample runs from 1907 through 1927.

Brazilian firms? One view would hold that there should be a positive correlation between being able to sell debt and higher levels and rates of growth of productivity. In this view, firms that have established track records for being well managed will be the most likely to succeed in selling debt to the investing public. In turn, this reduces their cost of capital and further increases their growth of productivity. An alternative view, associated with Brander and Spencer (1989), is that if an owner-manager substitutes borrowed funds for equity, then the effort of the owner declines and the firm's output falls. The reason for this is that bondholders have less incentive than equity holders to monitor managers (Brander and Spencer). Specification 3 tests these hypotheses by introducing a dummy variable for firms whose bonds were traded on either the Rio de Janeiro or São Paulo exchanges. The magnitude of the coefficient is much smaller than that for being a joint stock company, indicating that while firms that issued bonds were roughly 10 percent more productive than the average firm, they were less efficient than joint stock firms as a group.

One might argue that the differences in TFP between joint stock and privately owned firms are due purely to regional productivity differences. Perhaps all of the low-TFP firms were located in isolated markets where transport barriers protected them from competition. Specifications 4 and 5 test this hypothesis. Specification 4 introduces a dummy variable for firms located in the highly integrated, rapidly growing, four-state market of Rio de Janeiro, the Distrito Federal, Minas Gerais, and São Paulo. The coefficient on region (0.300) indicates that there were in fact sizable regional productivity differences. Specification 5 decomposes the effects of region and joint stock status by introducing dummy variables for joint stock firms located outside the competitive region, joint stock firms located within the region, and all other firms in the region.[30] The results indicate that even if we control for regional effects, there was still a positive residual for firms that took the joint stock form (note that the coefficient in line 9b is of greater magnitude than that in line 9a, and both are significant at the 1 percent level). The regressions also indicate that joint stock firms outside the competitive region also had a sizable productivity advantage against their privately owned competitors. The coefficient of 0.285 (line 6a, specification 5) translates into a 33 percent productivity differential.

I estimated similar sets of regressions for Mexico. In the Mexican case it was not possible to estimate the marginal impact of being able to issue long-term bonds, because there was no bond market. It was possible, however, to estimate the marginal impact of access to bank capital, because I was able to code our textile data set for relationships between bankers and textile owners by looking at the interlock of bank and manufacturing firm directorates.[31]

Table 7.8 presents regression results on the rate of growth of output by firm type. The data are unambiguous. First, bank-connected firms grew roughly 50 percent faster than their competitors, but they were no larger

30. The fact that virtually all of the joint stock companies were located in the four-state region means that these variables are likely to be collinear. Thus, we cannot simultaneously introduce dummy variables for region and joint stock to measure the marginal effect of being traded, taking region into account.

31. Other measures of bank connection, based on internal bank data, produce similar qualitative results. For a complete discussion see Maurer and Haber (2002).

Table 7.8 **Output Growth Regression Results, Mexico**

	Spec. 1	Spec. 2	Spec. 3	Spec. 4	Spec. 5	Spec. 6	Spec. 7	Spec. 8
Constant	10.71	10.41	10.48	10.56	10.5	10.48	10.56	10.58
	(111.1)	(80.96)	(91.89)	(86.53)	(90.84)	(91.64)	(92.16)	(92.46)
Time	0.05	0.05	0.04	0.03	0.04	0.04	0.03	0.03
	(20.36)	(20.19)	(15.94)	(10.49)	(14.48)	(15.75)	(12.34)	(11.96)
Border		0.05	0.00	0.00	–0.01	0.00	0.00	0.00
		(0.2)	(0.02)	(0.01)	(0.04)	(0.03)	(0.01)	(0.01)
Central		0.55	0.53	0.53	0.53	0.53	0.53	0.53
		(3.8)	(4.19)	(4.2)	(4.17)	(4.19)	(4.20)	(4.17)
Bank			0.18	0	0.19	0.18		
			(3.23)	(0.03)	(3.32)	(3.23)		
Bank * time				0.01			0.01	0.01
				(1.8)			(3.72)	(3.68)
Limited			0.27	0.25	0.05	0.27	0.25	
			(3.26)	(2.9)	(0.26)	(3.27)	(2.9)	
Limited * time					0.01			0.01
					(1.21)			(2.85)
Traded			1.77	1.76	1.76	1.56	1.76	1.77
			(9.86)	(9.83)	(9.83)	(3.22)	(9.83)	(9.98)
Traded * time						0.01		
						(0.47)		
Obs.	1,488							
Adjusted R^2	0.1	0.14	0.32	0.32	0.32	0.32	0.32	0.32

Source: Maurer and Haber (2002).
Note: Dependent variable = value of output in 1900 pesos. *T*-statistics in parentheses.

than nonbank, privately owned firms when they were initially established. The few publicly traded companies were more than three times larger than their competitors at their founding, but grew no faster. Organization as a joint stock company (when combined with bank connection) produced an additional marginal effect on output, but the regression results did not allow any determination of whether this was a one-time-only or a dynamic advantage.

What effect did bank connection or being a publicly traded company have on TFP? The TFP estimates for Mexico are presented in table 7.9. The first specification indicates that the rate of growth of TFP was only half that of Brazil: 3 percent as opposed to 6 percent. This result is consistent with theory: The more concentrated structure of industry created lower incentives to compete, and the more difficult access to impersonal sources of capital made it more difficult for firms to purchase new plant and equipment quickly. Specification 1 also indicates that there were negligible scale economies in the Mexican textile industry.

The data also indicate that the marginal productivity of capital was much higher in Mexico than in Brazil. Regardless of the regression specification,

Table 7.9 **Mexican Total Factor Productivity Regressions**

	Spec. 1	Spec. 2	Spec. 3	Spec. 4	Spec. 5	Spec. 6
Constant	3.82	3.93	4.06	3.91	4.12	4.14
	(11.38)	(11.99)	(11.89)	(11.3)	(11.91)	(11.4)
ln(K/L ratio)	0.65	0.61	0.6	0.61	0.59	0.59
	(10.08)	(9.38)	(9.13)	(9.29)	(8.98)	(8.84)
ln(workers)	0.07	0.05	0.03	0.05	0.02	0.02
	(1.59)	(1.18)	(0.64)	(1.17)	(0.52)	(0.34)
Time	0.03	0.03	0.03	0.03	0.03	0.03
	(9.71)	(9.63)	(8.83)	(9.41)	(9.52)	(8.91)
Border		–0.04	–0.06	–0.04	–0.04	–0.02
		(0.29)	(0.41)	(0.25)	(0.26)	(0.13)
Central		0.24	0.25	0.24	0.24	0.23
		(2.46)	(2.55)	(2.41)	(2.44)	(2.28)
Bank			0.1			0.12
			(1.33)			(1.55)
Limited				–0.02		–0.14
				(0.19)		(1.25)
Traded					0.39	1.06
					(1.76)	(1.7)
Traded * time						–0.02
						(1.80)
Obs.	492					
Adjusted R^2	0.35	0.37	0.37	0.37	0.36	0.36

Source: Maurer and Haber (2002).
Notes: Dependent variable = value of output in 1900 pesos. *T*-statistics in parentheses.

the coefficient on the capital-labor ratio in Mexico is always twice that in Brazil (roughly 0.6 versus 0.3). This result is also consistent with theory. Mexican firms were, on the whole, more capital constrained than Brazilian firms. On the margin, additional units of capital in Mexico increased output much more than in Brazil.

Did Mexican firms that were bank connected or that were joint stock companies have a productivity advantage over their more liquidity constrained competitors? The results are clear: regardless of the specification used, I could find no significant difference in TFP between bank-connected and independent firms. In addition, firms that were joint stock companies did not enjoy higher TFP than their privately owned competitors. Being traded on the Mexico City exchange appears to have given firms a one-time productivity advantage, but the coefficient on traded is significant only at the 10 percent level of confidence (the *t*-statistic is 1.76). Whatever productivity advantage these firms did enjoy at the time of their incorporation dissipated over time: the interaction of traded status and time was negative. The only significant effect is a regional one: firms located in and around

Mexico City were roughly 25 percent more productive. In short, the results we obtained for Mexico stand in stark contrast to those for Brazil. The implication is that in Mexico the financial markets and the banks were not choosing winners, they were choosing insiders.

The vast differences between Brazil and Mexico in rates of growth of TFP indicate that there must also have been large absolute differences in the average productivity of capital and labor. I therefore draw a cross-sectional comparison of the average productivity of the Brazilian and Mexican textile industries in real U.S. dollars for 1912–14. I used capital-labor weights derived from a production function estimated on the Mexican data, in order to bias the TFP estimates in favor of Mexico. The results are as one would expect: average annual output (in 1929 U.S. dollars) per worker/spindle in 1912 in Mexico was $23,858. Average annual output per worker/spindle in Brazil was $31,850, 33 percent higher than in Mexico. Similar calculations for 1925 reveal even larger differences in average productivity.

7.4 Conclusions

What lessons are there to be drawn from this analysis of the effect of government regulation on banks, capital markets, and industrial development?

The first lesson concerns the number of banks that regulators may wish to have in the market. Most Latin American countries have small numbers of very large banks. Mexico is a classic case in point: It actually has fewer banks now than it did in 1911. One might argue that there are advantages to a concentrated banking system: There are economies of scale in financial services; large banks may be able to weather periods of volatility better than small banks; and it is easier for regulators to monitor the activities of a small number of large firms than to it is monitor the activities of a large number of small firms. There is, however, a disadvantage to a concentrated banking system. In an environment in which information is very costly, bankers face serious problems of information asymmetry. One way that they commonly overcome those information asymmetries is to lend to people whom they know personally—much in the same way as banks in the nineteenth-century United States. From the point of view of individual banks, such a strategy makes a good deal of sense. From the point of view of the economy as a whole, however, such a system is inefficient: only those individuals with personal ties to bankers can obtain credit; there are very few bankers; therefore only a very small number of individuals can get a loan. Absent institutional changes that reduce the cost of obtaining accurate financial information about potential borrowers, the most socially efficient policy might be to promote the formation of large numbers of small banks.

A second lesson is that there is nothing inevitable about the small size and concentrated structure of Latin America's securities markets. In the late nineteenth and early twentieth centuries, Brazil had well-developed markets for equity and long-term debt. Those markets were the product of a set of regulatory policies that allowed investors to monitor managers and to monitor each other. Both Brazil and Mexico had general incorporation laws that made the founding of a limited liability corporation an administrative affair. The difference was that Brazil had remarkably tough regulations for mandatory disclosure. Firms not only had to publish annual reports, they also had to disclose the identities and share positions of each of their investors. This allowed investors to know whether the founders of a firm, who usually dominated its board and its senior management, were liquidating their holdings in the firm.

Laws in and of themselves mean nothing if they are not enforced. Mexico also had mandatory disclosure laws. One crucial difference, however, was that Brazil enforced its (more stringent) laws, while Mexico did not. There are two lessons here. One lesson is obvious: If governments do not enforce their own laws, then legal reforms have little meaning. Another lesson is perhaps less obvious: governments must have incentives to enforce their own laws. The incentive for the Brazilian government to enforce its financial market laws was that limited liability companies were subject to a 5 percent tax on dividends. The Mexican government had no such incentive.

The existence of a dividend tax also had other, positive effects on the growth of the securities markets in Brazil and on industrial development, broadly speaking. First, a dividend tax gave firms an incentive to reinvest profits rather than pay them out as dividends. In the context of a capital-scarce country, this would have had a positive effect on industrial development. One consequence, perhaps unintended, of this tax was that it would have made shares more liquid than otherwise. Because a dividend tax encourages firms to reinvest rather than pay dividends, the value of additions to capital (in the form of increased cash balances, additional machinery, or increased inventories) would be capitalized in the market value of shares. Shareholders would still, therefore, have been the residual claimants on the profits made by the firm. In order to obtain income from their investment, however, they would have had to liquidate some of their shares. All other things being equal, this would have increased the number of shares traded. It also would have had the effect, over time, of encouraging a broad distribution of share ownership. The lesson is obvious: tax policies can play a role in encouraging the formation of securities markets. Specifically, a tax on dividends in the absence of a tax on capital gains will encourage firms to reinvest and will encourage shareholders to trade their holdings more actively.

Finally, there is a lesson about political systems and economic reforms. Just as there is a natural human tendency to barter, truck, and trade, there is also a natural human tendency to use politics to force others to transfer their wealth and sources of value. The Mexican government did not set out to write a set of laws that would make it difficult for most entrepreneurs to obtain bank credit or sell equity. The decisions to make it difficult to get a bank charter and not to enforce disclosure laws were driven by the demands of powerful constituents in the context of a highly centralized political system. It is quite unlikely that there will ever be a political system anywhere in which the politically powerful will not try to use their influence to produce economic benefits for themselves. One implication is that good policies require not only that policymakers be able to identify the right set of policies, but also that they have the political incentives to adopt and enforce those policies. Political systems that lack self-enforcing institutions designed to monitor and check opportunistic behavior by those who make and enforce policies are therefore less likely to be able to carry out successful financial market reforms.

References

Association of Cotton Textile Producers. 1922. Relatorio da Directoria, 1921–1922 (Report of the Directorate, 1921–1922). Trade association report. Rio de Janeiro: Centro Industrial de Fiaçao de Tecelagem de Algodão.

———. 1923. Exposição de tecidos de algodão (Exposition of cotton textiles). Trade association report. Rio de Janeiro: Centro Industrial de Fiaçao de Tecelagem de Algodão.

———. 1926a. Fabricas filiadas (Affiliated factories). Trade association report. Rio de Janeiro: Centro Industrial de Fiaçao de Tecelagem de Algodão.

———. 1926b. Relatorio da Directoria, 1921–1922 (Report of the Directorate, 1921–1922). Trade association report. Rio de Janeiro: Centro Industrial de Fiaçao de Tecelagem de Algodão.

———. 1928. Estatisticas da industria, commercio e lavoura de algodão relativos ao anno de 1927 (Statistics of the industry, commerce and growing of cotton for 1927). Trade association report. Rio de Janeiro: Centro Industrial de Fiaçao de Tecelagem de Algodão.

———. 1935. Fiaçao de tecelagem: Censo organizado pelo Centro Industrial de Fiaçao de Tecelagem de Algodão (Cotton textile production: Census organized by the Association of Cotton Textile Producers). Trade association report. Rio de Janeiro: Centro Industrial de Fiaçao de Tecelagem de Algodão.

———. Various years. Relatorio da Directoria. (Report of the Directorate). Trade association report. Rio de Janeiro: Centro Industrial de Fiaçao de Tecelagem de Algodão.

Atack, Jeremy. 1985. *Estimation of economies of scale in nineteenth century United States manufacturing.* New York: Garland.

Bernard, A. B., and C. I. Jones. 1996. Productivity across industries and countries: Time series theory and evidence. *Review of Economics and Statistics* 78 (1): 135–46.

Bibliotheca da Associação Industrial. 1882. *Archivo da Exposição da Industria Nacional de 1881* (Archive of the Expo of National Industry, 1881). Rio de Janeiro: Tipographia Nacional.

Borja Castro, Agostino Vioto de. 1869. Relatorio do Segundo grupo (Report of the second group). In *Relatorio da segunda Exposição Nacional de 1866,* ed. Antonio José de Souza Rego, 3–73. Rio de Janeiro. Monograph.

Brander, James A., and Barbara J. Spencer. 1989. Moral hazard and limited liability: Implications for the theory of the firm. *International Economic Review* 30 (4): 833–49.

Branner, John C. 1885. Cotton in the empire of Brazil. Miscellaneous Report no. 8. Washington, D.C.: U.S. Department of Agriculture.

Carr, Jack L., and G. Frank Mathewson. 1988. Unlimited liability as a barrier to entry. *Journal of Political Economy* 96 (4): 766–84.

Centro Industrial do Brasil. 1909. O Brasil: Suas riquezas naturaes, suas industrias (Brazil: Its natural wealth, its industries). Trade association report. Rio de Janeiro: Centro Industrial do Brasil.

———. 1915. Relatorio da Directoria para ser apresentado a Assemblea Geral Ordinaria do anno de 1915 (Report of the Directorate for presentation to the General Assembly, 1915). Trade association report. Rio de Janeiro: Centro Industrial do Brasil.

———. 1917. O centro industrial na Conferencia Aogodoeira (Industry association in the Cotton Conference). Trade association report. Rio de Janeiro: Centro Industrial do Brasil.

Commissão de Inquerito Industrial. 1882. Relatorio ao Ministerio da Fazenda (Report to the Ministry of Finance). Rio de Janeiro: Government of Brazil.

Davis, Lance. 1957. Sources of industrial finance: The American textile industry, a case study. *Explorations in Entrepreneurial History* 9:189–203.

Davis, Lance, and H. Louis Stettler III. 1966. The New England textile industry, 1825–1860: Trends and fluctuations. In *Output, employment, and productivity in the United States after 1800,* 213–42. New York: National Bureau of Economic Research.

Haber, Stephen. 1989. *Industry and underdevelopment: The industrialization of Mexico, 1890–1940.* Stanford, Calif.: Stanford University Press.

———. 1991. Industrial concentration and the capital markets: A comparative study of Brazil, Mexico, and the United States, 1830–1930. *Journal of Economic History* 51 (3): 559–80.

———. 1998. The efficiency consequences of institutional change: Financial market regulation and industrial productivity growth in Brazil, 1866–1934. In *Latin America and the world economy since 1800,* ed. John H. Coatsworth and Alan M. Taylor, 275–322. Cambridge: Harvard University Press.

Haber, Stephen, Armando Razo, and Noel Maurer. Forthcoming. *The politics of property rights: Political instability, credible commitments, and economic growth in Mexico, 1876–1929.* Cambridge: Cambridge University Press.

Hanley, Anne. 1995. Capital markets in the coffee economy: Financial institutions and economic change in São Paulo, Brazil, 1850–1905. Ph.D. diss. Stanford University.

Johnson, Ronald D., and Allen Parkman. 1983. Spatial monopoly, non-zero profits, and entry deterrence: The case of cement. *Review of Economics and Statistics* 65 (3): 431–39.

Kane, Nancy F. 1988. *Textiles in transition: Technology, wages, and industry relocation in the U.S. textile industry, 1880–1930.* New York: Greenwood Press.

Lamoreaux, Naomi. 1994. Insider lending: Banks, personal connections, and economic development in industrial New England. Cambridge: Cambridge University Press.

Levy, Maria Bárbara. 1977. *História da bolsa de valores do Rio de Janeiro.* Rio de Janeiro: Instituto Brasileiro de Mercados de Capitais.

Marques de Saes, Flávio Azevedo. 1986. Crédito e bancos no desenvolvimento da economia paulista, 1850–1930. São Paulo: Instituto de Pesquisas Econômicas.

Maurer, Noel. 2002. *The power and the money: The Mexican financial system, 1876–1928.* Stanford, Calif.: Stanford University Press.

Maurer, Noel, and Stephen Haber. 2002. Institutional change and economic growth: Banks, financial markets, and Mexican industrialization. In *The Mexican economy, 1870–1930: Essays on the economic history of institutions, revolution, and growth*, ed. Jeffrey Bortz and Stephen Haber. Stanford, Calif.: Stanford University Press.

McGouldrick, Paul F. 1968. *New England textiles in the nineteenth century.* Cambridge: Harvard University Press.

Ministerio da Industria, Viação, e Obras Publicas. 1896. Relatorio (Report). Rio de Janeiro: Government of Brazil.

Moody's manual of investments: American and foreign. 1900. New York: Moody's Investors Services.

———. 1910. New York: Moody's Investors Services.

———. 1920. New York: Moody's Investors Services.

Neuhaus, Paulo. 1975. *História monetária do Brasil, 1900–45.* Rio de Janeiro: Instituto Brasileiro de Mercado de Capitais.

Peláez, Carlos Manuel, and Wilson Suzigan. 1976. *História monetária do Brasil: Análise da política, comportamento e instituicões monetárias.* Brasilia: Instituto de Planejamento Economico e Social, Instituto de Pesquias.

Prefeitura do Distrito Federal. 1908. Noticia sobre o desenvolvimento da industria fabril no Distrito Federal e sua situação actual (Notice about the development of the textile industry in the Federal District and its current situation). Milano: Tipografia Fratelli Trevos.

Razo, Armando, and Stephen Haber. 1998. The rate of growth in productivity in Mexico, 1850–1933: Evidence from the cotton textile industry. *Journal of Latin American Studies* 30 (3): 481–517.

Report of the Bombay Millowner's Association. 1900. Bombay, India.

———. 1911. Bombay, India.

———. 1920. Bombay, India.

———. 1930. Bombay, India.

Secretaría de Hacienda, Mexico. *Anuario de estadística fiscal,* 1911–1912.

Sokoloff, Kenneth L. 1984. Was the transition from the artisanal shop to the nonmechanized factory associated with gains efficiency? Evidence from the U.S. manufacturing census of 1820 and 1850. *Explorations in Economic History* 21 (4): 351–82.

Stein, Stanley J. 1957. *The Brazilian cotton textile manufacture: Textile enterprise in an underdeveloped area.* Cambridge: Harvard University Press.

Sylla, Richard. 1975. *The American capital market, 1846–1914.* New York: Arno Press.

Topik, Steven. 1987. *The political economy of the Brazilian state, 1889–1930.* Austin: University of Texas Press.

Triner, Gail. 1994. Brazilian banks and economic development: 1906–1930. Ph.D. diss. Columbia University.

U.S. Department of Commerce, Bureau of the Census. 1997. *Historical statistics of the United States: Colonial times to 1970.* Series 10. New York: Cambridge University Press.

Vasco, Cunha. 1905. A industria do algodão: Boletim do Centro Industrial do Brasil (The cotton industry: Bulletin of the Brazilian Center for Industry). Trade association bulletin, 30 December.

von der Weid, Elisabeth, and Ana Marta Rodrigues Bastos. 1986. *O fio da meada: Estratégia de expansão de uma indústria têxtil: Companhia América fabril, 1878–1930.* Rio de Janeiro: Fundação Casa de Rui Barbara-Confederação Nacional de Indústria.

8

Toward a Liquidity Risk Management Strategy for Emerging Market Economies

Pablo E. Guidotti

8.1 Introduction

As emerging market economies recover from the period of extraordinary turbulence faced since the outbreak of the Asian crisis in 1997, it is important to set the agenda for noncrisis times. In periods of crisis it is the crisis itself that sets the policymakers' agenda.

Given the unquestionable link that exists between financial market conditions and economic growth and development, a central objective of this agenda should be how to restore *sustainable* capital flows to emerging markets while keeping open the capital account. In particular, policy should seek to produce a reduction in volatility not accompanied by a reduction in volume or an increase in costs. At the same time, it should recognize that industrial countries' official assistance bilaterally or through multilateral institutions is likely to be less forthcoming in the years ahead.

In this paper I want to focus on lessons we have learned from these past years of open but volatile capital flows, so as to identify domestic policies and international actions that are consistent with the above-mentioned objectives and the industrial countries' call to reduce the size of official financing packages based on moral-hazard considerations. In particular, I will argue that the best way in which emerging markets will obtain the strongest support from the official community in crisis times is by *helping themselves* during favorable times through the adoption of appropriate domestic policies.

The consultative process among Group of Seven (G7) economies and systemically important emerging market economies that led to the estab-

Pablo E. Guidotti is the director of the School of Government at Universidad Torcuato Di Tella in Buenos Aires, Argentina.

lishment of the so-called Group of Twenty-Two (G22), briefly followed by the Group of Thirty-Three (G33) and subsequently to the creation of a permanent Group of Twenty (G20), reflects the enormous interest that the international official community took in understanding and dealing with the volatility experienced by capital markets in the second half of the 1990s.

The rationale for having a multilateral discussion on what was called the "international financial architecture" stemmed from four main facts. First, crises in international capital markets appear to have become recurrent events. Second, the Russian default showed for the first time that crises in emerging markets have the ability to produce serious disruptions in liquid G7 asset markets. Third, the phenomenon of contagion showed that economic policies in one country could have significant externalities on other economies. Thus, it is not enough to focus on the quality of domestic economic policy; the quality of the policies of close as well as distant neighbors may turn out to be an important element affecting the investors' perception of country risk. Fourth, requirements for emergency assistance from the International Monetary Fund (IMF) have been increasing over time, raising a question about whether these could eventually threaten the institution's liquidity.

In response to these concerns, this process identified a number of useful recommendations that, if accompanied by widespread implementation, would reduce the likelihood of future crises. Most of these recommendations were included in the reports prepared by the G22 working groups on Transparency and Accountability, on Strengthening Financial Systems, and on International Financial Crises. Recently, the IMF and the Financial Stability Forum have done further work in these areas.

In my view, although the discussion on the international financial architecture has largely focused on the relevant issues, there are two areas where conclusions appear to be somewhat premature and have sparked significant controversy. The first one is the discussion on involving the private sector in crisis prevention and resolution.[1] The second is the discussion on exchange rate policy in emerging market economies. The analysis that follows in this paper identifies the main sources of concern, and attempts to provide additional suggestions to reach a better understanding of and consensus on the issues at stake.

The main message of this paper is that learning how to manage capital market disruptions in a world in which IMF lending is likely to be more limited than it was in the recent past remains one of the most pressing challenges that emerging market economies face. To handle this problem it is necessary to develop an economy-wide strategy to deal with liquidity risk.[2]

1. This general expression is used to encompass issues such as the modification of bond contracts to include so-called *collective action clauses,* burden sharing when default occurs, and the role of the IMF in relation to burden sharing.

2. This echoes Alan Greenspan's (1999a) call to develop a "liquidity at risk" approach for emerging market economies, in the same vein as Guidotti (1999).

Although development of better policies to manage the effects of capital market volatility may in turn be expected to help reduce it, the profession appears to be still at a considerable distance from understanding its systemic causes.

If a country manages the risks from capital flow volatility correctly, then it will be able to choose whether to have floating or a fixed-exchange rate regime, along traditional arguments in favor of one or the other. Hence, in principle, I find no presumption that exchange rate flexibility should be preferred when dealing with emerging market economies.

A country's risk management strategy to volatility should focus on three main areas: the financial system, public debt management, and the corporate sector. The task of the following sections is to articulate the main elements of a country's strategy to deal with liquidity (or rollover) risk. Rather than being comprehensive, I will focus on selected issues that in my experience proved crucial in dealing with market volatility in the 1990s, and whose importance has not been adequately emphasized or, in some cases, remains controversial. In the analysis, I will often refer to the recent experience of some emerging market economies, in particular that of Argentina during the 1990s, although in doing so I will identify lessons of more general applicability.[3] The strategy focuses on the financial system and on the financing policies in the public and the private sector. Once the main elements are presented, I will discuss the implications for exchange rate policy as well as for the role of the IMF.

8.2 Liquidity Risk Management in the Financial System

The financial system has been at the center of all major emerging market crises of the last decade. In many ways, it may be thought of as the "weak link" of economic performance precisely because, by its natural exposure to liquidity risk, it is closely monitored by investors and is in the front line of any sudden change in market sentiment about a country's economic performance.

Because of this fact, a banking system's health has always been the subject of attention by regulators. In recent years, the international official community has devoted particular attention to promoting the adoption by emerging-market countries of standards regarding capital adequacy, asset quality, and banking supervision. Little controversy exists today about the

3. Since the writing of this paper, Argentina suffered in late 2001 a crisis of enormous proportions that led to the abandonment of the convertibility regime that had served the country well during the previous decade. Although I will not attempt here to discuss in detail the current Argentine crisis, it is relevant to the issues analyzed in this paper to mention that a reversal of existing liquidity management policies, as well as the violation of the independence of the central bank, are central factors in explaining the financial collapse that preceded the devaluation of the peso in early 2002. Hence, an analysis of the current Argentine crisis will reinforce, rather than weaken, the arguments in favor of the development of sound liquidity management policies in emerging market economies.

importance of adopting the recommendations put forward by the Basel Committee on Banking Supervision, the Group of Ten (G10), and groupings such as the so-called G22. Some doubts, however, exist regarding the actual pace of implementation.[4]

This section focuses on three areas—transparency, liquidity requirements, and resolution of problem banks—that are central to the development of an effective strategy to deal with capital flows volatility and liquidity risk in the banking system. All of these are areas of considerable debate.

8.2.1 Transparency

Notwithstanding recent progress in reaching consensus on the role of market discipline in improving the quality of policy, the issue of how transparent central banks should be about their financial and reserve data remains controversial. On the one hand, some policymakers worry that disclosure of timely information on financial and monetary variables entails potential risks in terms of increasing the ability of markets to engage in potentially destabilizing speculation. On the other hand, there is mounting evidence that balance-of-payments crises have tended to occur in situations in which markets lacked timely information, rather than the opposite.[5]

As argued in the G22 (1998, the report of the Working Group on Transparency and Accountability), transparency is an essential element of any strategy to foster market confidence. By increasing accountability and market discipline, disclosure of timely information regarding variables such as international reserves, bank deposits, and asset quality may contribute significantly to avoiding the buildup of inconsistent policies as well as imprudent banking practices.

No matter how much we could theorize about the benefits of transparency, I find that the most compelling argument in favor of transparency comes from the pragmatic experience in Argentina during the Tequila, Asian, Russian, and Brazilian crises. *In all of these events I found that disclosure systematically played a stabilizing role in market behavior.*

The first direct evidence came at the start of the Tequila crisis. Right after the Mexican devaluation, the Argentine convertibility system came under pressure following the notion that a speculative attack would successfully lead to a devaluation of the peso and an exit from the monetary regime. This failing confidence in the peso was reflected in a significant differential between peso and dollar interest rates and by a persistent drain on international reserves. At that time, the public was informed on a weekly basis about the stock of international reserves along with the main items of the central bank's balance sheet. Of course, the lack of timely information

4. This prompted the Financial Stability Forum to establish a working group to report on implementation.

5. The Mexican crisis of 1994 and the Korean crisis of 1997 are clear examples of situations in which the market lacked information on the evolution of international reserves.

on the evolution of international reserves was keeping the market guessing about how much the central bank had intervened on any given day, setting the stage for the following day's market behavior. The fact that the market estimate of the bank's sales of reserves was systematically larger than the actual figure led us (the board of directors) at that time to decide to inform the public of the level of international reserves on a daily basis with the minimum possible lag of one day.[6]

The second piece of evidence came as the Tequila effect set in motion a bank run soon after the central bank was forced to close a small number of banks affected by heavy losses from bond trading. During this phase of the crisis a similar process occurred regarding the market's anxiety to know about the behavior of bank deposits. Data on bank deposits were published at that time on a monthly basis with a significant lag. Our reaction was again to counter anxiety with timely information. Despite the fact that a bank run was on, we decided to inform the public of the stock of deposits on a daily basis with the minimum possible lag of two days. Again, disclosure proved reassuring to markets.

Later, in the Asian, Russian, and Brazilian crises, financial variables such as international reserves, bank deposits, and interbank rates showed remarkable stability. Timely information to the market regarding such behavior turned out to be important in fostering confidence in the convertibility system at times of significant external turbulence.

Unfortunately, the policy of providing transparent international reserves data to the public was reversed in 2001. Interestingly, the perception by the public that reserve data were becoming less reliable contributed to the loss of confidence in the financial system that occurred that same year in Argentina.[7]

8.2.2 Liquidity Requirements

The discussion about the role of liquidity requirements on bank liabilities is central to the implementation of an adequate risk management policy for emerging market economies. Although this area has been the subject of analysis and debate during recent crises, a consensus comparable to that reached on capital adequacy or on the role of transparency remains elusive.

A frequent problem in analyzing bank liquidity in emerging markets is the problem of distinguishing between an individual's bank liquidity and the liquidity of the financial system. For instance, when looking at a single bank, government bonds are often considered liquid assets, but in systemic

6. Since then, central bank sales have been disclosed on the same day at the close of markets.

7. The loss of transparency took the form of utilizing foreign exchange reserves to finance the Argentine treasury through deposits made by the (no longer independent) central bank in the account of the Panamanian branch of the state-owned Banco de la Nación Argentina. Such deposits were double-counted as international reserves by the central bank, while the government had already used the funds to finance its budget deficit.

crises government bonds lose their liquidity as the country's credibility comes under scrutiny. Moreover, given that the return differentials between foreign assets and domestic government bonds and between the latter and other bank assets tend to be larger than in industrial countries, it is not surprising that banking institutions in emerging markets tend to hold significantly less liquidity than their industrial countries' counterparts.

Therefore, liquidity requirements provide a powerful tool for the central bank to manage liquidity in the financial system in a way that is not inconsistent with its objective of maintaining price stability for two reasons. First, it allows the central bank to use a channel through which it can expand or contract liquidity in the financial system *using bank rather than public funds.* This factor may be particularly important in reducing or eliminating any quasi-fiscal effects of central bank operations, as well as in dispelling concerns about the moral hazard typically associated with the lender-of-last-resort function of central banks.

When considering the appropriate level of liquidity requirements, a trade-off typically arises. On the one hand, higher bank liquidity implies lower bank-asset volatility in response to deposit volatility. On the other hand, to the extent that (internationally) liquid assets carry a lower rate of return relative to other assets, liquidity requirements on banks may imply higher intermediation costs and, therefore, higher average lending interest rates. The following stylized model illustrates this trade-off.

Consider an economy in which output is produced by use of a single variable input, working capital, which is lent to firms by banks in a competitive environment. Thus output, y, is produced according to the following (strictly concave) technology:

$$y = f(l) \equiv \frac{1}{\beta}\left(Z - \frac{l}{2}\right) l, \tag{1}$$

where l denotes bank loans, $f(.)$ is assumed to be quadratic, and Z and β are positive parameters.

At an optimum, working capital is used according to the following first-order condition:

$$I = f'(l), \tag{2}$$

where I denotes the lending interest rate. Equations (1) and (2) imply the following demand for loans:

$$l = Z - \beta I. \tag{3}$$

The representative bank's balance sheet is given by

$$l = (1 - e)(d + \varepsilon), \tag{4}$$

where e is the liquidity requirement, and the sum $d + \varepsilon$ denotes bank deposits. For simplicity, we assume that the liquidity requirement is not remunerated. Below, we show that all the qualitative implications are maintained when liquidity requirements are remunerated. Deposits are composed of a fixed amount, d, and a stochastic shock, ε, which is distributed with zero mean and a constant variance, σ. Hence, bank deposits are assumed to be subject to volatility, reflecting volatility of capital flows to the economy and, in particular, to the banking system. The shock ε may be thought of as the residual deposit volatility that cannot be absorbed by a limited discount-window facility.[8] Volatility in the banking system's funding is transmitted to the asset side of the balance sheet, inducing variability in bank credit and, therefore, in lending interest rates and output.

The representative bank is assumed to face a constant cost of funds, r, and to operate competitively with operating costs, ω, per unit of loans. Thus, the zero-expected-profits condition implies

$$EI = \frac{r}{(1-\delta)} + \omega, \tag{5}$$

where E denotes the expectations operator.

For given δ, equations (3)–(5) determine the distribution of I and l. Given the average (expected) cost of bank credit, equation (4) determines the average level of bank deposits, d, for which the banking system faces an infinitely elastic supply at the international interest rate, r.

The central bank chooses the liquidity requirement, e, in order to minimize volatility of output around a target (nonstochastic) level, y^*, obtained by setting $\delta = \varepsilon = 0$. By equation (5), the lending interest rate associated with y^* equals $I^* = r + \omega$. It can be easily shown that the loss function being minimized by the central bank, W, is given by

$$W = E(y - y^*)^2 = E(y - Ey)^2 + (Ey - y^*)^2. \tag{6}$$

Equation (6) shows that the loss function is composed of two terms. The first term on the right-hand side of the equation measures the volatility of output around its mean; the second term on the right-hand side measures the deviation of the expected output from the target level, y^*. By taking a Taylor expansion of y around y^*, and by equations (3)–(5), the loss function in equation (6) becomes:

$$W = (r + \omega)^2\left[(1 - e)^2\sigma + \left(\frac{e}{1-e}\right)^2\beta^2 r^2\right]. \tag{7}$$

The term in square brackets on the right-hand side of equation (7) captures the trade-off that results from the effects that liquidity requirements have on the above-mentioned two terms. On the one hand, a higher liquidity requirement reduces the volatility of credit, and hence the output around its

8. This would hold exactly if the central bank provided a deposit and a lending (discount-window) facility to banks at the international interest rate, r.

mean. On the other hand, a higher liquidity requirement increases the average level of lending interest rates, and hence results in a lower expected output relative to the target level. Thus, a trade-off emerges between the volatility of credit in response to shocks that affect the banking system, and the increase in the cost of credit that is associated with higher required liquidity.

Minimization of the loss function in equation (7) yields the optimum liquidity requirement. It is straightforward to show that the greater the volatility affecting the banking system, σ, the higher the optimum liquidity requirement. Also, the higher the deposit rate, r, and the higher the elasticity of the demand for bank credit (as implied by a higher value of β), the lower the optimum liquidity requirement. Interestingly, operating costs, ω, play no role in the determination of optimum e.

The qualitative implications of the model are maintained if liquidity requirements are remunerated, provided that the rate of remuneration is lower than the bank's cost of funding. This is typically the case if liquidity requirements are to be met with international assets. In this alternative framework, the banking system's funding cost, r, contains at a minimum the country-risk premium over the rate of return on internationally liquid assets, r^*. In this case, it can be shown that the loss function in equation (7) is given by

$$W = (r + \omega)^2 \left[(1 - e)^2 \sigma + \left(\frac{e}{1 - e} \right)^2 \beta^2 (r - r^*)^2 \right], \tag{8}$$

where the impact of the liquidity requirement on the interest spread is now linked to the country-risk premium rather than to the banks' funding cost.

The simple model above provides a rationalization for resorting to liquidity requirements when the volatility affecting the banking system cannot be fully absorbed by a limited use of the discount window. The focus on volatility is relevant for understanding why an important point is often missed by those who oppose requiring banks in emerging markets to hold more liquid assets than what would be privately desirable. What matters for economic development is not only the volume of credit but its sustainability over the length of the productive process being financed by banks. Volatile bank credit may often result in excessive projects' being cut off before maturity, with the consequent loss of efficiency.[9]

In sum, when governments do not enjoy stable access to international credit markets, credibility may require establishing clear limitations to the central bank's role as a lender of last resort. Hence, liquidity requirements

9. In their analysis of the effect of bank credit to the private sector on long-run growth, De Gregorio and Guidotti (1995) find strong evidence in support of this point of view. In particular, they find that, unlike in other regions of the world, bank credit is negatively associated with growth in Latin America. This puzzling result, which reflects a productivity rather than a volume effect, is explained in the context of the high volatility to which the region's financial systems were exposed during the sample period (1950–89).

on the banking system can be a useful element in the design of a strategy to manage capital flows volatility effectively.

To complete the argument it is necessary to show that the private sector alone will not adopt the adequate liquidity. This is relatively straightforward if we consider that banks typically believe that assistance from the central bank will be forthcoming when needed. If the problem is large enough, then such expectations may well be validated, putting price and economic stability at risk.

Therefore, banks tend to manage their individual liquidity without internalizing problems of a systemic nature. Moreover, because of this externality, banks tend to rely on domestic government bonds for the management of their individual liquidity. In the absence of regulation, the differential that typically exists in emerging economies between the rates of return on domestic vis-à-vis foreign assets generates few incentives for banks to hold foreign assets. Moreover, because prices of domestic government bonds are significantly more volatile in emerging economies than in industrial countries, banks in the former economies tend to hold a smaller share of their assets in liquid form.[10] To manage systemic crises, however, it is essential that liquidity be held in *international* assets that maintain their liquidity at times in which domestic government bonds lose theirs. Hence, the analysis here calls for adopting liquidity requirements that imply a larger share of assets' being held in liquid form (relative to what would be privately desirable), and a larger composition of those being held in the form of foreign rather than domestic assets.

Analysis of the response of the Argentine banking system to the Tequila effect shows precisely the importance of liquidity requirements as a shock absorber. Almost half of the 20 percent fall in the deposit base during the first quarter of 1995 was accommodated by a reduction in the liquidity requirement. Interestingly, liquidity requirements of the levels necessary to deal with potential falls in deposits on the order of 20 percent are not inconsistent with the levels of liquid assets held, for instance, by banks in industrial countries.[11]

As mentioned, the notion behind the adoption of liquidity requirements is that individual banks do not fully internalize the *systemic* liquidity risk associated with holding high-grade domestic assets, such as government bonds. The objective of having domestic banks hold foreign reserve assets

10. English and Reid (1995) report that U.S. banks hold between 15 and 30 percent of their assets in the form of government securities (investment account). In Argentina, bond holdings represented about 5 percent of bank assets in November 1994.

11. According to English and Reid (1995), medium- and small-sized banks—i.e., those with assets up to US$2 billion—at the end of 1994 held U.S. government securities in their investment accounts equivalent to 25–30 percent of net consolidated assets, and 40–45 percent of deposits. The fact that the levels of liquidity in the U.S. banking system fall with bank size is generally attributed to the reduced access of smaller banks to the Fed funds market. Banks in Germany, France, Italy, Spain, and the United Kingdom hold comparable levels of liquidity.

can be complemented with additional instruments. In particular, contingent credit lines or repurchase agreements with international banks may sometimes provide alternative ways of improving the quality of a financial system's liquidity position.[12]

Similarly, increasing the presence of international banks in the domestic financial system may contribute significantly to reducing its vulnerability. In a number of Latin American economies the significant consolidation process of the banking system since 1995 was led by foreign investment. This explains a significant part of the reason banking systems in the region exhibited a remarkable resilience to external conditions during the sequence of Asian, Russian, and Brazilian crises.

Liquidity requirements may play an additional positive role in the health of the financial system, because they impose a cost on holding nonperforming assets on bank balance sheets. This is so because a strategy of "evergreening" (whereby a bad asset is kept on the balance sheet and is financed by rolling over a deposit) requires the bank's ability to produce an increasing stream of foreign assets to meet the liquidity requirement. In emerging market economies, such a self-enforcing mechanism may be a useful complement to the task of bank supervisors.

Additionally, the level of liquidity requirements imposed on banks affects the capitalization of the financial system—by altering the cost of funding loans with capital relative to deposits, the liquidity requirement affects banks' financial structures. Therefore, from a regulator's point of view, the liquidity requirement can be used to enforce indirectly a desired capital-asset ratio in the banking system.[13] Although, of course, the capital requirement is the first best instrument to ensure an adequate minimum level of capitalization in the banking system, there are situations—common to developing countries and transition economies—in which effective enforcement of capital adequacy is not possible either because supervision is weak or because it is difficult to ascertain the value of bank assets.

The latter case, one in which it is difficult to know the value of bank assets, often reflects that there are no liquid secondary markets in which to obtain a market valuation of particular relevance. If the value of bank assets is unknown or, at best, is private information, it becomes impossible for the bank supervisor to obtain or to verify the true capital situation of the bank. As a result, the capital requirement would turn out to be simply unenforceable. Since bank assets and capital are private information, the bank would find it optimal to choose the desired capital-asset ratio while informing the supervisory authority of the (accounting) values of assets and capital that comply with the Basel standards.

To illustrate this point, consider the following simple model for a small,

12. Argentina, Mexico, and Indonesia have established contingent lines with foreign banks. Argentina, however, is the only example in which the mechanism in place was explicitly designed to provide liquidity to the banking system.

13. For an in-depth analysis of this issue, see Fernandez and Guidotti (1996).

open economy. Individuals hold three assets: international bonds, b, bank deposits (which also serve as money), M, and bank capital instruments (such as equity, and subordinated and convertible debt), K. It is assumed that bank equity, and hence ownership, is atomized. In equilibrium, arbitrage in the capital market ensures that (with no uncertainty) the return on bank capital is equated to the international interest rate, δ. The interest rate paid on bank deposits, however, is in equilibrium lower than δ, reflecting that money provides liquidity services in terms of (for instance) reduced transaction costs. In particular,

$$r = \delta - L(M), \tag{9}$$

where r is the interest rate on deposits, and $L(M)$ is the liquidity premium, which is a decreasing function of the level of bank deposits.[14] Hence, the equilibrium interest rate on deposits converges toward the international interest rate as the marginal gains, in terms of reduced transaction costs, fall when the level of deposits increases.

Banks provide loans, A, that firms use as input in their production processes. In equilibrium, the interest rate on bank loans, i, equals their marginal product, $P(A)$. Banks are price-takers in the loan market; hold liquid assets, R, required by the central bank; and finance their operations with deposits and capital. In addition, banks charge customers with service fees, F, in connection with the use of the payments system. It is assumed that service fees are collected in proportion to deposits, albeit at a decreasing rate. Hence $F'(M) > 0$, and $F''(M) < 0$. Management arranges bank operations so as to maximize profits and ensure a competitive return on equity. It maximizes

$$\pi = iA - rM - \delta K + F, \tag{10}$$

subject to the bank's balance sheet equation

$$A + L = K + M, \tag{11}$$

where L denotes the bank's holdings of (internationally) liquid assets, and the liquidity requirement, e, imposed by the central bank,

$$L \geq eM. \tag{12}$$

At an optimum, it can be shown that, with equation (12) binding,

$$i = \delta = \frac{r - F'(M)}{1 - e}. \tag{13}$$

By equation (13), the interest rate on loans equals the cost of capital and the interest on deposits net of service fees and the effect of the liquidity requirement. Defining by k the bank's choice of capital to loans (i.e., $k =$

14. See Fernandez and Guidotti (1996) for a derivation of the liquidity premium in a context in which money reduces transaction costs.

K/A), equations (9) and (13), and the equilibrium relation stating that $i = \delta = P(A)$, we obtain

$$k = 1 - (1 - e)\Omega(e), \tag{14}$$

where $\Omega(e)$ defines an inverse equilibrium relationship between the liquidity requirement and deposits. Equation (14) shows that, if $e = 1$, then the desired capital-asset ratio, k, also equals 1. Moreover, it can be shown that if $F'(M)$ tends to zero as M tends to infinity, then there exists a positive level of the liquidity requirement, $e(\text{min})$, such that the desired capital-asset ratio equals zero. More generally, for $e \in [e(\text{min}), 1]$, there is a positive equilibrium relationship between the level of the liquidity requirement and the equilibrium degree of capitalization chosen by the bank. Hence, by affecting the bank's financing structure, liquidity requirements can enforce a desired level of bank capital when the supervisor lacks adequate information about the value of bank assets.

8.2.3 Resolution of Problem Banks

No credible system of banking supervision and regulation can be enforced in emerging market economies without a strategy to deal with problem banks in place in a way that the market perceives is consistent with a manageable fiscal cost. Precisely because of the typically large difference that exists between industrial and emerging market countries in terms of their ability to finance fiscal deficits, the issue of dealing with problem banks is rather controversial and is one for which the practices of industrial countries may not be readily applicable to less developed economies.

The actual mechanism used to resolve problem banks sends a strong signal to the financial system in terms of their risk management policies. The less available are public funds during the resolution process, the stronger the market discipline imposed on the banking system will be. This, in turn, is likely to provide strong incentives to tighten risk management procedures in financial institutions.

As important as the design of the resolution process is, the most critical element for success in this area is implementation. Resolution of problem banks *during good times* may be the most effective way to transmit adequate incentives and market discipline to the financial system. Moreover, experience shows that resolution processes that do not rely on heavy use of public funds work much more efficiently in good times, when asset sales, mergers, and other bank-restructuring activities within the private sector are not hampered by the presence of systemic uncertainty. Therefore, resolution processes in emerging markets should be designed to be applicable when general economic conditions are favorable.

It is well established that vulnerability in the banking system is consistent with optimality. This simply reflects the fact that, by the nature of their business, banks are potentially exposed to situations of illiquidity that need not reflect insolvency. These situations are more likely to reflect systemic rather than individual illiquidity. Therefore, when the capacity to assist the banking system with public funds is limited, it is particularly important to design efficient resolution processes capable of distinguishing insolvency from systemic illiquidity.

Two important issues that arise when considering how best to deal with banking problems is how much discretion and ambiguity should be left to the supervisory authority, and to what extent it is desirable to develop a structured process of intervention. When the use of public funds is limited, it is desirable to develop a structured intervention process. This is important in order to avoid supervisory forbearance, and hence, to limit the probability of significant concentration of banking problems at specific times.

In what follows I attempt to identify basic elements of a consistent legal and regulatory framework that allows for the efficient handling of banking problems, recognizing explicitly the issue of scarcity of public funding.[15] For the sake of conceptual clarity, the discussion will focus on the case in which *no* lender-of-last resort exists at all. It is straightforward, however, to extend the ensuing analysis to the case in which the central bank plays a limited lender-of-last-resort role.

The first basic element to recognize is that, as a practical matter, it may be extremely difficult to distinguish illiquidity from insolvency ex ante. Hence, it is essential that the framework applying to the resolution of a liquidity problem be consistent with bankruptcy law. This follows from the requirement that actions taken to address illiquidity be immune from legal objection in the event that the institution later falls into insolvency.[16]

Therefore, the design of a resolution process involves working backward from the essentials of the bankruptcy proceedings, to the management of liquidity problems, and finally to the required corporate structure and prudential regulations of banking institutions.

Following this action plan, it is helpful to begin by establishing that a bank failure resolution process should be designed to

1. protect small depositors;
2. keep the bank in operation when possible;
3. allow for restructuring;
4. protect the asset side of the balance sheet, which is performing;
5. generate a market mechanism to revert runs; and
6. be stabilizing for expectations ex ante.

15. The ensuing analysis draws heavily on the legal framework currently in place in Argentina, and on the successful experience of Argentina in resolving bank problems after the Mexican crisis.

16. Most countries' legislation extends a "period of suspicion" on actions taken in the time that precedes bankruptcy. During this period, those actions, which affected net worth or the eventual seniority rankings of creditors, may be revised (or invalidated) by the courts during bankruptcy proceedings. For instance, according to Argentine law, the period of suspicion extends from the date on which, according to the judge's finding, default has occurred to the date on which bankruptcy is declared.

These objectives may be grouped according to three issues: item 1 deals with the issue of privileges among different liabilities; items 2–4 deal with maximizing bank net worth; and items 5 and 6 deal with the effect on expectations. These issues should not be thought of as separate because in some cases the overlap may be significant; for instance, maximizing bank value may call for providing seniority to specific liability holders.

Achieving objectives 1, 2, and 3 efficiently and, at the same time, making the resolution of an illiquidity problem consistent with one of (eventual) insolvency implies that, in the event of bankruptcy, small depositors and labor should be considered senior creditors with respect to holders of remaining liabilities. Moreover, for reasons that will become apparent below, I will argue that it is desirable to provide seniority to the remaining deposits over other bank liabilities.[17]

Protecting small depositors is often viewed as an instrument to reduce the social costs of resolving bank failures.[18] However, because small depositors comprise a constituency of a large number of creditors—typically uninformed and unsophisticated—their protection is desirable on efficiency grounds as well. Thus, introducing a mechanism that resolves their situation independently from that of other stakeholders contributes to the predictability and the efficiency of the overall failure-resolution process. As indicated earlier, consistency of the process implies that such seniority be explicitly granted by law.

In a similar vein, maximizing the value of a problem bank's assets (and, hence, its net worth) during the resolution process calls for establishing mechanisms that keep the resolved bank in operation while it is being restructured, transferred, or sold to new owners. This implies that available liquid assets may have to be used *during the resolution period* to pay labor obligations and minimal operating expenses. In particular, if the resolution process requires a restructuring, and the latter implies shedding of labor, then the bank's administrators should be able to meet labor obligations related with such restructuring *before and independently from the outcome of the process.* This requires that such actions be consistent with the disposal of assets in bankruptcy proceedings, and labor claims be granted seniority—along with small depositors.

Objectives 3 and 4 are closely related to the actual mechanics of the resolution process. Before turning to these it is essential to examine the way a bank's corporate structure should be designed to achieve the greatest effi-

17. Argentine banking law, for instance, makes all deposits senior with respect to other liabilities. However, the basic aspects of the analysis would remain unaffected if, alternatively, "large" deposits and other (nonsubordinated) bank liabilities are put on an equal footing vis-à-vis bankruptcy.

18. The protection of small depositors has also been rationalized in the banking literature as part of appropriate managerial incentives schemes—see, for instance, Dewatripoint and Tirole (1994).

ciency of such a process. In particular, this calls for adoption of a corporate structure for financial institutions that simplifies the separation between insolvency and illiquidity, and hence that allows a more efficient handling of each of these situations.

An attractive corporate structure for this purpose is constituted by a *bank holding company,* which fully owns, at a minimum, two distinct subsidiaries: a *payments bank* and a *financial subsidiary.*[19] Typically, to improve outside control, it may be helpful to require bank holding companies of a given size or larger to issue at least a minority share—ranging from 20 to 30 percent—of its equity in the stock market.

The payments bank's liabilities consist of checking and savings accounts—usually of overnight maturity—and deposits up to a maximum per depositor. These deposits typically would be insured; thus the maximum amount per depositor would be determined by the insurance coverage.[20] Hence, the liabilities of the payments bank are those directly related to the payment system, and those associated with small depositors.

On the asset side, the payments bank may hold only prime-quality assets, except for overdrafts of checking accounts and fixed assets linked to its operating structure.[21] Prime-quality assets include (1) foreign assets (government and high-grade corporate securities), (2) domestic government bonds, and (3) private domestic assets internationally rated as investment grade. The implications of different asset compositions for bank liquidity will be examined below.

Although the payments bank would not necessarily be subject to a capital requirement on a solo basis, the bank holding company would be required to maintain positive capital in the payments bank, with assets marked to market. (Notice that, to the extent that government bonds constitute a significant portion of assets, application of international capital-adequacy standards would yield a low requirement on the payments bank, thus covering mostly for market risk.)

As far as management is concerned, the proposed structure allows for a joint operation of the payments bank and the financial subsidiary in order to avoid costly duplications. However, the bank holding company would be required to identify at all times a self-contained managerial structure for the payments bank that would remain in place if the financial subsidiary were to be closed or sold, and to implement contracts accordingly. Hence, the branch network could be operated jointly between the financial sub-

19. One could think of more subsidiaries if, for instance, a bank could wish to split the financial subsidiary into a commercial subsidiary and an investment subsidiary. The aspect that is crucial to the analysis is the split between the payments bank and the remaining operations.

20. For the analysis it is immaterial whether deposit insurance is privately or publicly funded.

21. The emphasis here is on the transparency of asset valuation, rather than on liquidity. Of course, liquid assets are prime quality, by definition.

sidiary and the payments bank, but accounting books would be kept separate.

The financial subsidiary contains all remaining bank operations. Therefore, on the assets side, it would not differ significantly from a typical commercial bank. On the liabilities side, its main difference from a traditional commercial bank stems from its absence from the payments system—now handled through the payments bank—and the absence of small depositors. Thus, in principle, from a regulatory point of view the financial subsidiary would be subject to requirements similar to those for typical commercial banks.[22]

Consider next the mechanics of the problem-bank-resolution process. Such mechanics are essential for achieving objectives 2 to 4. Suppose a bank faces a run on its deposits. By the corporate structure described above, illiquidity will show up in all likelihood at the financial subsidiary.[23] The relevant case to examine is one in which illiquidity cannot be overcome with limited recourse to the discount window. Hence, this is a situation in which illiquidity would, in the absence of a resolution mechanism, lead to bankruptcy.

When illiquidity is strong enough to force the financial subsidiary into default, the bank holding company requests the supervisory authorities to place it under "suspension"—i.e., to freeze all operations except for those that are essential to preserve capital.[24] This implies suspension of convertibility of deposits into cash, but allows bank to continue to collect on their assets. At this stage, to the extent that it can operate normally, the payments bank may not be placed under suspension.

During the suspension period, bank assets are audited and marked at liquidation value. Equity and (if necessary) subordinated debt are written off to zero. In order to implement a resolution that is consistent with bankruptcy law, assets and remaining liabilities of the financial subsidiary are set to constitute a voluntary mutual fund, provided agreement is reached among a sufficiently large group of creditors. The majority required for such an agreement should be, in principle, consistent with those required by law under bankruptcy proceedings.[25] In the mutual fund, deposits are ex-

22. A central issue, which goes beyond the scope of this paper, is to determine the extent to which prudential regulations—in particular, capital requirements—in emerging markets should be more stringent than the Bank for International Settlements' recommendations. For a discussion, see Guidotti (1996) and Fernandez and Guidotti (1996).

23. This occurs for two reasons. First, unlike the financial subsidiary, the payments bank holds the most liquid assets. Second, empirical evidence shows that small-size deposits, as well as checking and savings accounts, tend to be much more stable during a bank run than larger-size deposits and other bank liabilities.

24. The mechanism of suspension—part of Argentina's financial legislation—has been used successfully in the bank-restructuring process that occurred during and after the Mexican crisis.

25. These majorities may imply the agreement of a certain minimum number of creditors, or a minimum share of capital. For instance, according to Argentine bankruptcy law, agreement is required to reach at least 51 percent of creditors and 66 percent of capital.

changed into senior shares, while other liabilities are transformed into junior shares. Finally, conditional on its materialization, the administration of the mutual fund is auctioned off to a third company. To define the terms of the auction, however, we need to understand what happens with the payments bank in the resolution process.

The main advantage of the proposed corporate structure is that, through isolation of a set of banking operations from the resolution process, the latter can be made more efficient. However, since all bank capital is lost in the process, the bank holding company cannot be expected to maintain operation of the payments bank. Thus, the above-mentioned auction should also encompass the sale of the payments bank.

Although the sale of the payments bank can be viewed as independent from auctioning the administration of the mutual fund, there may be economies of scale in concentrating both on a single acquirer. This is particularly evident in the case in which the assets going to the mutual fund are administered from the payments bank's branch network.

Thus, following the latter structure, the auction would imply the sale of the payments bank with its operating structure, plus the administration of the mutual fund. In this process, an important practical issue arises when determining what administrative structure should be included with the mutual fund. Typically, the process of acquisition implies a significant restructuring of the former financial subsidiary's administrative structure. Therefore, any layoff of employees of the former financial subsidiary would be funded by the proceeds from the sale of the payments bank or, alternatively, by sale of the assets of the financial subsidiary prior to the constitution of the mutual fund. (This, however, is consistent with the seniority provided to labor claims.)

Proceeds from the sale of the payments bank that are not used to pay labor obligations go to repay *pari passu* deposits of the financial subsidiary. Hence, only the portion of deposits that exceeds the proceeds from the sale of the payments bank need to be ultimately converted into senior shares of the mutual fund.

Finally, although the present framework is flexible enough to allow for a variety of auction strategies to maximize value, a simple example is one in which the acquirer offers a price of the payments bank plus a remunerative scheme for the administration of the mutual fund that increases by tranches, as a function of the assets recovered.[26]

To exemplify the benefits of the resolution process just described, it is useful to translate it into the implicit contract that would be perceived ex-ante by the various bank stakeholders. In particular, it is important to examine whether objectives 5 and 6 are achieved.

26. For incentive schemes of this type used by the Federal Deposit Insurance Corporation in the United States, see Ludwig (1994).

First, consider small depositors. Compared to traditional commercial banks, the above corporate structure clearly provides greater protection to small depositors as well as to the payments system. Consequently, such a structure should result in lower funding costs from those liabilities.

Next, consider the effect on holders of remaining deposits and other liabilities. In these cases, the above structure and resolution process imply making the privileges granted by bankruptcy law explicit in the respective financial contracts. This is because the resolution process is to be applied *only in the event a bank defaults.* Thus, by making the resolution of bank problems more efficient without altering seniority rights, all liability holders should find themselves better off. This follows from the fact that net worth is maximized. Hence, establishing state-contingent mechanisms for problem-bank resolution of the type outlined here can only be stabilizing for expectations ex ante, and results in lower funding costs for financial institutions.

Compared to that of a typical commercial bank, the corporate structure examined in this section may (although not necessarily) imply a somewhat higher level of liquid assets. This follows primarily from the fact that the payments bank holds only prime-quality assets. However, it is worth noting that although it may imply higher holding of domestic government bonds, the proposed structure does not imply more stringent liquidity or capital requirements. Indeed, as argued earlier, the financial subsidiary would be subject to regulatory requirements that do not differ significantly from those adequate for traditional commercial banks. Thus, as regards bank profitability, the requirements imposed on asset quality by the proposed structure may have to be balanced against the likely reduction in funding costs derived from a more stable financial system.

8.3 Financing Strategies in the Public and Private Sectors

The experience of emerging market economies during recent periods of turbulence in international capital markets has shown that the debt management strategy that country follows during the years preceding the crisis is a key element in determining the success or failure of dealing with an external shock. In particular, a relevant variable in determining the success of dealing with external vulnerability has been the choice of maturity structure of the economy's net debt, resulting from the financing policies adopted both privately and publicly.[27]

This section will examine the role of debt management policies in reducing the risks associated with capital flows volatility. Before turning to this issue in detail, however, it is useful to review some apparently conflicting results and policy implications from the theoretical literature on public debt

27. See the recent IMF (2000) study, "Debt and Reserve-Related Indicators of External Vulnerability."

management. In essence, these conflicting views follow from two main lines of research that have approached similar issues from quite separate perspectives.

On the one hand, what I would call the *conventional view*—following Tobin's (1971) pioneering work—has cast the choice of the maturity structure of the public debt in terms of the objective of minimizing the cost to the treasury of the public debt. In a similar vein, some have emphasized the role government can play in promoting the development of liquid markets for private financial instruments. This, in turn, would induce a fall in the funding cost to the public and private sectors. When translated into explicit policy recommendations, these arguments have tended to promote the buildup of short-maturity public debt. In some countries, notably Mexico before the Tequila crisis, a reduction in the average maturity of the public debt has been further induced by the government's use of short-term bonds to sterilize capital inflows.

Another strand of literature, on the other hand, emphasized the role of the maturity of the public debt in situations in which government policies lack credibility. In this line of work, Calvo and Guidotti (1990, 1992) examined the implications of time-inconsistency or lack of credibility regarding inflation for the management of the public debt and, in particular, the choice of maturity structure and indexation of domestic public debt. Giavazzi and Pagano (1991) and Alesina, Prati, and Tabellini (1991) focused on the role of debt maturity and, more generally, on the role of the profile of debt payments in preventing credibility crises. They underscore the risks of having significant levels of public debt rollover in situations in which capital markets may be subject to high volatility. In sum, the policy implication that follows from this literature is that governments should strive to lengthen the maturity of public debt and achieve a smooth profile of amortization and interest payments.

What, then, explains these apparently conflicting policy recommendations regarding the maturity structure of the public debt? An answer to this question lies in determining whether the choice of the maturity structure of the public debt can be effectively analyzed in isolation from the private sector's choice of the maturity structure of its obligations. In this respect, a central issue is whether the public sector retains access to capital markets in situations in which the liquidity of the private sector might be squeezed. If the public sector is able to borrow abroad in large amounts under such circumstances, it can always provide the liquidity needed to compensate for any maturity mismatch between assets and liabilities in the private sector. The most typical case in point is provided by the central bank's perceived ability to be a lender of last resort during systemic tests—then the choice of debt maturity can be effectively analyzed in isolation from that of the private debt. This is essentially the scenario that applies to the analysis of debt management policies in industrial countries and is implicit in the conventional view.

The literature focusing on credibility issues, however, brings to the forefront the point that debt management may be a key element in determining the capital markets' attitude towards the private sector, and therefore in explaining why the economy can be subject to crises. Hence, as will be argued below, the choice of the optimal maturity structure of the public debt may well not be independent from the structure of assets and liabilities of the private sector.

The debt crisis of the 1980s and the episodes of capital flow volatility of the 1990s left a clear lesson in terms of the importance capital markets assign to the intertemporal solvency of the public sector. As emphasized in a number of studies, there is evidence that, rather than focusing on the fiscal accounts of any given year or month, capital markets tend to look at the concept of (intertemporal) fiscal solvency in order to determine the market value of the public debt. Hence, stock concepts—such as constructs of government net worth—appear to have higher explanatory power than flow concepts (e.g., fiscal deficits).[28]

To explore this issue in greater depth, consider a simple balance sheet approach proposed by Guidotti and Kumar (1991), applied both to the private and the public sectors. A summarized government balance sheet is given by

$$EA^* + FS = C + R + B^G + EB^{*G} + NW^G, \tag{15}$$

where A^*, FS, C, R, B^G, B^{*G}, and E denote the stock of foreign exchange reserves, the present discounted value of present and expected future fiscal surpluses, currency in circulation, bank reserve accounts with the central bank, the outstanding domestic and foreign public debt, and the exchange rate, respectively. NW^G denotes government net worth. For simplicity, and to abstain from discussing the role of exchange rate changes, it will be assumed henceforth that the exchange rate is fixed and equal to 1. Similarly, for illustrative purposes, it is assumed that the domestic public debt is denominated in domestic currency, and foreign debt in foreign currency.[29]

Equation (15) simply states that the perceived fiscal solvency of the public sector—as measured by NW^G—depends on stock concepts. Moreover, equation (15) consolidates the accounts of the treasury with those of the central bank. Thus, the monetary base—i.e., $C + R$—is accounted in the balance sheet as non-interest-bearing public debt. In the absence of domestic credit by the central bank, the monetary balance sheet can be thought of as being given by $EA^* = C + R$.[30]

28. As regards the 1980s debt crisis, for instance, Guidotti and Kumar (1991) find a significant correlation between measures of intertemporal government solvency and secondary market prices of the external public debt of highly externally indebted countries.

29. As will be seen later, this simplification may be relevant on practical grounds.

30. This would hold exactly under a currency board arrangement. Fixed exchange rate regimes or quasi–currency boards (such as Argentina's) typically allow for domestic credit by the monetary authority. To maintain focus and to economize on notation, this possibility is ignored in the present discussion. However, doing so loses no substantive issue.

Consider next the typical balance sheet of the main sectors of the economy: firms, banks, and households. Firms' assets and liabilities are given by

(16) $$\Pi = B^F + EB^{*F} + L^F + NW^F,$$

where Π, B^F, B^{*F}, L^F, and NW^F denote the present discounted value of expected profits, the stocks of domestic and foreign debt issued by firms, the outstanding stock of bank loans to firms, and firms' net worth, respectively.

Banks' assets and liabilities are given by

(17) $$L^F + L^H + R + B^G = D + ED^* + NW^B,$$

where L^H, D, D^*, and NW^B denote the stock of bank loans to the household sector, the stocks of domestic and foreign bank deposits and liabilities, and the banking system's net worth, respectively.[31]

Finally, the balance sheet of the household sector is given by

(18) $$EA^{*H} + W + C + D + B^F + NW^B + NW^F = L^H + FS + NW^H,$$

where EA^{*H}, W, and NW^H denote foreign assets held by households, the present discounted value of current plus expected future household wage-income streams, and the private sector's net worth, respectively.[32] Equation (18) shows that current and expected future fiscal surpluses should be computed as a liability for the private sector in applying a balance sheet approach to households.

Combining equations (15)–(18), the economy's balance sheet obtains

(19) $$\text{GDP} + EA^* + EA^{*H} = ED^* + EB^{*F} + EB^{*G} + NW^G + NW^G,$$

where GDP ($= \Pi + W$) denotes the present discounted value of current and expected future output. In our simple framework, it is given by the present discounted value of the sum of two income streams: firms' profits and wages.

Equation (19) illustrates a number of important and basic issues. First, *the economy's perceived (intertemporal) solvency depends on the perceived consolidated net worth of the public and private sectors.* Thus, in principle, at any given point in time, the market response to variations in the perceived solvency of either individual sector should matter only to the extent to which it affects the solvency of the consolidated.[33] However, since in emerg-

31. Although D and D^* can be thought of as only bank deposits, they also include longer term obligations typically issued by the banking system, such as commercial paper, negotiable obligations, external lines of credit, etc. Subordinated debt instruments would be considered part of NW^B, following standard definitions of bank capital.

32. The reader is reminded that, in order to economize on notation, it is assumed that only banks hold domestic government bonds. Typically, households are major holders of public debt.

33. Interestingly, this observation may help resolve the puzzle posed by the apparent failure of capital markets in assessing weak (intertemporal) fiscal positions in a number of highly indebted industrial countries.

ing markets government net worth is typically easier to assess than that of the private sector, the former is taken as a proxy for the latter. Hence, the requirement that government be intertemporally solvent (i.e., that $NW^G > 0$) is generally imposed in addition to the requirement of solvency of the consolidated sectors.[34]

Second, equation (19) clearly illustrates that "liquidity" *crises can occur even when economic policies are in place to ensure intertemporal solvency; hence the importance of the maturity structure of the economy's debt.* As shown by equation (5), the economy's assets are in large part (e.g., GDP) illiquid. Moreover, the size of the private sector's foreign assets, EA^{*H}, is typically difficult to determine, and its availability to respond to obligations or to be tapped by government is uncertain.[35] Thus, the traditional analysis of a country's ability to service its external debt obligations tends to focus largely on the size of international reserves, EA^*.

However, it follows clearly from equation (19) *that the maturity structure of the public debt may play an important role in preventing liquidity crises.* To analyze this issue in more detail it is important to understand how the private and public sectors interact, and what instruments are available to government to deal with liquidity problems.

Equation (19) shows that, by being involved in production and investment, the private sector is typically illiquid—i.e., the maturity of its assets is longer than that of its liabilities. Hence, the private sector may be subject to liquidity problems that may not necessarily reflect insolvency. Such maturity mismatch tends to be particularly acute in the banking system, as shown by equation (17).

What, then, is the role of the public sector? The public sector contributes to the economy's liquidity through policies that affect the stock of international reserves and through the choice of the maturity structure of its obligations. As argued earlier, a crucial issue is to determine whether the public sector retains its market access during times when the liquidity of the private sector is being tested.

If the public sector retains its market access, then it can use it to provide liquidity and hence to compensate for any private maturity mismatch. This implies, by equation (19), the obtaining of liquid funds, EA^*, in exchange for longer maturity debt, EB^{*G}. This is the framework that applies to in-

34. The difficulty in assessing the solvency of the private sector as well as the ability of the government to reestablish its own solvency by strengthening its fiscal position often stems from the perception that the stock of the private sector's financial wealth is difficult to determine and is, from the standpoint of taxation, outside the government's reach.

35. The issue of the Argentina bond at the worst point of the 1995 financial crisis is a rare example of the government's being able to tap the private sector's external assets. In my view, this was possible because the financing provided through the Argentina bond was part of a critical mass of external funds—provided by international banks and multilateral organizations—equal to one year's worth of public debt amortization and interest payments. In this context, the repatriation of funds by residents (i.e., domestic banks and firms) turned out to be a good investment, since it was followed by a sharp increase in the value of domestic assets.

dustrial countries for which policies regarding public debt management can thus be effectively analyzed in isolation from considerations regarding private-sector liquidity.

In emerging markets, however, the relevant framework is the polar opposite of the one just described. Hence, the choice of the maturity structure of government bonds needs to be analyzed in conjunction with the liquidity policies followed by the private sector. Furthermore, since part of the liquidity held by the banking system may reflect regulatory requirements—such as liquidity requirements—then *public debt management policies may have to be analyzed in close connection with the design of the regulatory framework applied to the banking system.*[36]

The above observations suggest that public debt management and banking regulations in emerging markets should be designed to compensate the natural maturity mismatch present in the private sector. This suggests lengthening the maturity of the public debt and adopting liquidity requirements in the banking system that directly relate to the maturity mismatch of private bank and nonbank liabilities. It also suggests avoiding the use of short-term debt to sterilize capital inflows, and not choosing the maturity structure of the public debt solely on the basis of minimizing the (nominal) cost to the treasury or for developing liquid domestic money markets. These objectives, while relevant in the market-access case, may well turn out to be less important in situations in which the public sector is subject to a liquidity test along with the private sector.

Since only external assets and liabilities enter equation (19), one may wonder whether the above policy implications may have to be qualified as regards the composition of the public debt. In particular, it may be argued that these considerations should apply only to foreign debt and not necessarily to domestic debt.[37] Two issues are important here. First, equations (16)–(18) show that the maturity structure of the domestic debt may affect the transmission of the liquidity crisis across the different sectors of the economy. Also, as a practical matter, it may not be possible to separate residents from nonresidents in terms of the maturity structure of the instruments they hold.[38] Nevertheless, it may still be desirable to have short-term debt instruments denominated in domestic rather than in foreign currency.

Although the analysis focused mostly on the banking system as the po-

36. The term *liquidity requirement* refers to the requirement that a bank hold a proportion of its liabilities (usually deposits) in liquid assets designated by the regulatory authority. In some cases, liquidity requirements do not pass through the central bank's accounts. Hence, they are not part of the standard definition of international reserves.

37. In fact, most of the official discussion on liquidity risk focuses on external assets and liabilities. See, for instance, the Group of Twenty-Two (1998) "Reports on the International Financial Architecture," Greenspan (1999a,b), and the IMF's report on "Debt and Reserve-Related Indicators of External Vulnerability" (2000).

38. In particular, in countries such as Argentina where a significant portion of the private and public debt is issued in foreign currency, both domestic and foreign residents end up holding both foreign and domestic currency debt in their portfolios.

tentially most vulnerable area in the private sector, the corporate sector should also be taken into account in the analysis of the economy's exposure to liquidity risk. It is important for the design of the public-financing strategy to collect timely information on the sources of liquidity risk in the corporate sector: the maturity profile of domestic and external corporate liabilities, and the ownership structures of issuers.[39] The latter element points to foreign ownership and credit ratings, which are relevant in evaluating a firm's exposure to rollover risk and its capacity to obtain lines of credit from abroad.

8.3.1 Elements of Public Debt Management

The design of a public debt management strategy involves the choice of various characteristics of debt instruments—such as the maturity profile, the currency denomination, and composition between floating- and fixed-rate bonds—for a given level of the outstanding public debt stock, which is typically thought of as being determined by a separate set of fiscal policy considerations.

Although the evolution of the public debt stock is generally seen as reflecting tax-smoothing and fiscal-sustainability considerations, situations of imperfect credibility may imply that the structure and composition of the public debt, itself, may influence decisions regarding the optimal evolution of the public debt. For instance, Calvo and Guidotti (1991, 1992) show that imperfect credibility associated with the currency denomination of the public debt may give rise to the phenomenon of *debt aversion,* a situation in which even if the interest rate equals the rate-of-time preference (and in the absence of shocks), it is optimal to progressively repay the public debt in full. Of course, when the presence of shocks is taken into account the actual optimal evolution of the public debt would result from the interaction between the principles of tax smoothing and debt aversion (see Calvo and Guidotti 1992). When the probability of default is taken into account, the debt-aversion principle can be easily shown to carry over to foreign currency debt.

Furthermore, Guidotti (1999) argues that, if the standard concept of fiscal sustainability is complemented with the notion that, as a practical matter, the market imposes an upper bound on the borrowing requirement that a country may finance in a given year, then a relationship among the budget deficit, the stock of public debt, and the debt maturity structure is obtained.

39. An element that may have been important in explaining the ability of Argentina's corporate sector in navigating through the Asian and Russian crises without significant disruptions can be found in the ownership structures of the issuers of private external debt. In particular, about 80 percent of Argentina's corporate external debt is issued by multinational companies or banks, which maintained access to external financing even under volatile conditions.

The following example illustrates the relationship. Consider the following equation describing the evolution over time of the ratio of public debt to GDP, b:

$$\dot{b} \equiv d - nb, \tag{20}$$

where d and n denote the budget deficit as a proportion to GDP and the (assumed constant) growth rate, respectively. Sustainability implies the following relationship between long-run growth and the budget deficit (holding with inequality when debt aversion exists):

$$d \leq nb. \tag{21}$$

For a given long-run (potential) output growth rate, equation (21) characterizes a relationship between the stock of debt and the maximum (structural) budget deficit, consistent with a nongrowing or declining debt-to-GDP ratio.

We can define the yearly borrowing requirement (net of any prefunding) as a proportion to GDP, x, in the following way:

$$x = d + \frac{b}{m}, \tag{22}$$

where m denotes the average maturity of the public debt. (It is assumed for the example's sake that amortizations are uniformly distributed over time.) Equation (22) states simply that the yearly borrowing requirement is the sum of the deficit plus amortizations.

Suppose we are interested in a measure of the sustainable deficit that, in addition, is consistent with not exceeding a target yearly borrowing requirement. Equations (21) and (22) imply the following relationship between sustainable budget deficit and average debt maturity:

$$d = x \frac{1}{1 + \frac{1}{nm}}. \tag{23}$$

For given x and n, equations (21) and (23) provide fiscal sustainability criteria that relate the budget-deficit and public-debt objectives to the maturity structure of the public debt. In particular, to ensure that a country has an adequate liquidity position vis-à-vis capital markets, as measured by the yearly borrowing requirement (net of any prefunding), there is an inverse relationship between average debt maturity on the one hand, and the sustainable budget deficit and long-run debt-to-GDP ratio on the other. The shorter the maturity of the public debt, the smaller the maximum allowable deficit and long-run debt-to-GDP ratio. Hence, this example shows that in many cases the design of a debt management strategy cannot be studied in isolation from the overall framework of fiscal policy.

The public sector can play a very important role in improving the economy's debt management policies, in particular when the private-sector capital market is still relatively underdeveloped—sometimes as a result of a history of high inflation or the presence of capital account restrictions—and firms have limited access to international financial markets. In these cases, the government may find itself in a privileged position to facilitate access of the private sector to longer term financing by providing liquid benchmarks that can then be used to price private issues at reasonable cost.

This suggests that public-sector financial policy should limit short-term debt. Since central banks in many cases are the principal issuers of short-term notes to conduct monetary policy, this analysis would provide an argument in favor of undertaking open market operations through repurchase agreements with banks using treasury bonds of longer maturity.

The report of the Working Group on Strengthening Financial Systems (in G22 1998) suggested a number of useful principles regarding the public sector's role in developing domestic capital markets. Notably, the creation by the public sector of a yield curve with liquid benchmarks issued at the relevant maturities can help the private sector price its own issues, and hence to obtain adequate measures of country- and foreign-exchange risk.[40]

The experience of emerging market countries in Latin America and Asia during recent capital market crises suggests a number of observations that could be useful in formulating a sound government-debt policy.

First, wherever possible, public debt management policy decisions should be concentrated at the treasury, which should be the sole issuer of public debt. Central bank operations for monetary policy objectives could then be undertaken through open market operations or repurchase agreements using existing public debt instruments. This organization allows for better coordination and formulation of the government's debt strategy.

Second, a central objective of debt management policy should be to limit rollover risk by avoiding the concentration of payments—of interest and principal—in any given year. In most emerging market economies that start with a relatively short average maturity on their public debt, this could imply that new issues should have longer maturities than outstanding debt.

However, aiming at lengthening the maturity structure of the public debt may sometimes be costly because the interest rate required by the market increases as we move along the yield curve. Experiences of some Latin American economies such as Argentina, Brazil and Mexico suggest that in the absence of well-developed domestic markets, the government may find it advantageous first to build a yield curve in foreign currency debt, and only then to move on to develop the yield curve in domestic currency. In the case of Argentina, for instance, the government was able to achieve a well-

40. This characteristic can also be found in theoretical analysis on the optimal maturity structure of the public debt. See, for instance, Calvo and Guidotti (1992, 1993).

balanced amortization schedule for its public debt, with an average maturity of about eight years, by issuing a significant portion of its debt in the major currencies (U.S. dollars, euros, and yen). As the yield curve in foreign currency was established, Argentina was able in 1997 to issue fixed-rate domestic currency bonds of up to ten-year maturity at reasonable terms. The recent successful experience of Mexico in developing a long-term market for domestic currency bonds at fixed rates also points to a similar process, whereby the country starts by creating long-term benchmarks in foreign currency and then proceeds to issuing local-currency, long-term bonds at favorable terms.

Of course, issuing foreign currency debt in significant amounts carries risk exposures that must be managed. These risk exposures arise not only from the fact that debt is denominated in foreign currency but from the fact that foreign debt may in turn be denominated in different foreign currencies. At minimum, it would appear that governments should limit drastically the issue of short-term debt in foreign currency, reserving those markets for longer term instruments.[41] Furthermore, as the cases of Russia and Brazil have eloquently shown, the buildup of short-term debt in domestic currency can also be destabilizing for expectations and may lead to loss of monetary control.[42]

A complementary factor in reducing risk and volatility in capital markets is the development of institutional investors such as pension funds, insurance companies, money market funds, and banks. Developing legislation that ensures stable development of institutional investors may be a key element in the design of a government's financing strategy.

A third useful observation relates to generating a liquidity cushion at the treasury or the central bank in order to provide flexibility in the timing of transactions and to avoid the need to issue debt at times of increased volatility or high interest rates.[43] This important element has been used successfully by Argentina in its financing strategy during the Asian and Russian crises. Ideally, the optimal amount of precautionary liquidity would depend on the costs and on the external vulnerability of the economy, as perceived by the marketplace. As a rule of thumb, Guidotti (1999) has suggested that countries manage their reserves and liabilities so as to be able to avoid borrowing for up to one year. Greenspan (1999a,b) and the IMF (2000) have further elaborated on this rule (see also Bussiere and Mulder 2000).

Finally, an essential element of a sound debt management strategy in both the public and private sectors is the diversification of potential buyers of fixed-income instruments. The higher the number of domestic and for-

41. Mexico and Korea are examples of countries where the buildup of short-term debt in foreign currency has been central to their external vulnerability.

42. For a theoretical analysis of the role of domestic debt in the formation of expectations, see Calvo (1988) and Guidotti and Kumar (1991).

43. For an in-depth analysis, see Guidotti (1999).

eign investors that hold a country's debt, the more stable market access and financing costs will be. The diversification of the investor base requires establishing a regular dialogue with market participants (even at times when no immediate plans to tap that market exist) and developing a team devoted to the task of providing the market with timely information about the country's economy and policies in place.

Diversification of the investor base also requires understanding the needs of particular classes of investors. For instance, pension funds usually prefer long-duration instruments, whereas money market funds are more likely buyers of short-term instruments, and banks tend to lean toward floating-rate instruments. Sometimes tension exists between a desire to tailor instruments to the specific needs of institutional investors, on the one hand, and the need to rely on standard (easier to price) types of instruments, on the other.

8.4 Implications for Exchange Rate Policy and the Role of the IMF

The recent periods of volatility in international capital markets have prompted many to examine what role was played by the exchange rate regime in the various crises. More generally, the fact that a number of emerging market economies chose to introduce more flexibility into their exchange rate policies in response to financial turmoil opened a debate on what exchange rate regime is better for emerging markets. In the international official community there has been a tendency to conclude that exchange rate flexibility was preferred over other alternatives, while the academic debate remains considerably more cautious on this same issue (see, e.g., Calvo and Reinhart 2000).

The purpose of this section is not to enter into the debate on which exchange rate regime is better for emerging market economies, but rather to examine how the previous considerations of liquidity risk and the design of policies regarding the financial system and debt management relate to the monetary policy framework and, in particular, to the exchange rate system in place.

When examining how policy should be designed to manage risks associated with capital flow volatility, the discussion about the exchange rate system should come last, not first. Moreover, I would argue that, to the extent there is an adequate risk management strategy in place and there is a commitment to maintain price stability, then the choice of exchange rate regime becomes less relevant.

Take, for instance, the case of the banking system. It may be argued that, although the ability of the central bank to assist the banking system under a liquidity crunch is effectively limited to the stock of international reserves under a fixed exchange rate system, under a flexible exchange rate regime the central bank has no limit on the discount-window facility that would be available to the banking system. However, to the extent that any commitment to price stability exists at all, the above-mentioned difference seems rather irrelevant from a policy perspective because the limit imposed by the stock of international reserves—the only liquid asset of the public-sector—would be binding under both exchange rate regimes. A need for liquidity assistance to the banking system that exceeds the stock of international reserves will be consistent with credibility of price stability only if it does not endanger the perceived solvency of the public sector. This would imply, however, the issue of public debt (or a tax hike) to finance the assistance to the banking system, a solution that—if credible—is available independently of the exchange rate regime in place.

Having said this, however, it is reasonable to establish that, in the context of previous analysis, a fixed exchange rate regime may in practice require more (international) liquidity than a flexible exchange rate regime. On the contrary, a flexible exchange rate regime may require more *institutional strength* to attain credibility, and deeper financial markets for the public and private sectors to be able to issue long-term bonds at manageable costs. In fact, lack of long-term domestic markets is a powerful element in support of the argument that emerging market economies would benefit significantly from adopting a major reserve currency (such as the U.S. dollar or the euro) as their own.[44]

Finally, the adoption of an economy-wide strategy to deal with liquidity risk in emerging markets has obvious implications for the role of multilateral organizations such as the IMF. After a sequence of crises in which IMF packages have increased in size, there is a sense that national policies in emerging market economies carry significantly larger external effects today than in earlier periods, when capital markets were less integrated globally (see De Gregorio et al. 1999).

The tension between the risk of moral hazard and the genuine role of the IMF in limiting the presence of rational contagion and multiplicity of equilibria produces a world in which it is increasingly important to ensure that official financing is both *limited* and *effective.*

The IMF's Contingent Credit Line (CCL) is an institution that will serve to protect emerging market economies from financial contagion. However, access to the CCL is limited to no more than 500 percent of a member's IMF quota.[45] How, then, is effectiveness ensured? Many thought of complementing official financing with what has been called *private-sector involvement,* namely ex post burden sharing in crisis resolution. Although it is productive to examine and elaborate rules for the resolution of international crises, very much in the spirit of this paper's analysis, it is certainly the case that emerging market economies should put the emphasis on which

44. This issue is central to the dollarization proposal. See Guidotti and Powell (2001).
45. In practice, access may be even lower.

risk management policies should be in place ex ante in order to avoid the difficult process of involving private creditors ex post. Hence, the issues discussed in this paper should be viewed as essential components of a strategy to produce a stronger international financial system, in a world in which an individual country's ability to receive official funding will be more limited.

8.5 Concluding Remarks

This paper has focused on the importance of developing an economy-wide risk management strategy for emerging market economies. Systematically looking at the various aspects of such strategy implies connecting a number of decisions that are often examined in isolation from each other. In particular, the analysis shows the importance of looking at liquidity management in the banking system, and the management of debt in the public and private sectors as a whole. Also, reflecting the forward-looking nature of economic decisions, the design of the banking crisis resolution process is an essential element of the overall risk management strategy.

Liquidity risk is ultimately the reflection of the market's reaction to a country's credibility in honoring its commitments and obligations. Hence, it is not possible to conceive a successful strategy to deal with liquidity risk unless sound fiscal policies are followed. Furthermore, an evaluation of fiscal sustainability often depends crucially on what the level of the country-risk premium is. In turn, country risk is significantly affected by financial conditions.

At the same time, for emerging market economies to succeed in reducing the country-risk premium it is essential to invest in developing *institutional strength.* In this regard, improving the quality of spending programs and strengthening the capacity and independence of the judicial system should top the public policy agenda.

References

Alesina, A., A. Prati, and G. Tabellini. 1991. Public confidence and debt management: A model and a case study of Italy. In *Public debt management: Theory and history,* ed. R. Dornbusch and M. Draghi, 94–118. Cambridge: Cambridge University Press.

Bussiere, M., and C. Mulder. 2000. Which short-term debt over reserve ratio works best: Operationalizing the Greenspan/Guidotti rule. IMF Working Paper. Washington, D.C.: International Monetary Fund.

Calvo, G. 1988. Serving the public debt: The role of expectations. *American Economic Review* 78 (4): 647–61.

Calvo, G., and P. E. Guidotti. 1990. Indexation and maturity of government bonds: A simple model. In *Public debt management: Theory and history,* ed. R. Dornbusch and M. Draghi, 51–82. Cambridge: Cambridge University Press.

———. 1992. Optimal maturity of nominal government bonds: An infinite-horizon model. *International Economic Review* 33 (4): 895–919.
———. 1993. Management of the nominal public debt: Theory and applications. In *The political economy of government debt,* ed. H. A. Verbon and F. A. A. M. van Widen, 207–32. Amsterdam: Elsevier Science.
Calvo, G., and C. Reinhart. 2000. Fear of floating. *Quarterly Journal of Economics* 17 (2): 379–408.
De Gregorio, J., B. Eichengreen, T. Ito, and C. Wyplosz. 1999. *An independent and accountable IMF.* London: Centre for Economic Policy Research.
De Gregorio, J., and P. E. Guidotti. 1995. Financial development and economic growth. *World Development* 23 (3): 433–48.
Dewatripoint, M., and J. Tirole. 1994. *The prudential regulation of banks.* Cambridge: MIT Press.
English, W., and B. Reid. 1995. Profits and balance sheet development at U.S. commercial banks in 1994. *Federal Reserve Bank of New York Bulletin.*
Fernandez, R., and P. Guidotti. 1996. Regulating the banking industry in transition economies: Exploring interactions between capital and reserve requirements. *Journal of Policy Reform* 1 (May): 109–34.
Giavazzi, F., and M. Pagano. 1991. Confidence crises and public debt management. In *Public debt management: Theory and history,* ed. R. Dornbusch and M. Draghi, 125–42. Cambridge: Cambridge University Press.
Greenspan, A. 1999a. Currency reserves and debt. Remarks before the World Bank Conference on Recent Trends in Reserve Management, 29 April, Washington, D.C.
———. 1999b. Efforts to improve the "architecture" of the international financial system. Testimony before the Committee on Banking and Financial Services, U.S. House of Representatives. 20 May.
Group of Twenty-Two. 1998. Reports on the international financial architecture, October. Available online at [http://www.bis.org].
Guidotti, P. E. 1996. Supervisory, regulatory, and banking practice issues in avoiding crises. Banking Crises in Latin America, IDB and The Group of Thirty.
———. 1999. On debt management and collective action clause. In *Reforming the international monetary and financial system,* ed. P. Kenen and A. Swoboda, 265–76. Washington, D.C.: International Monetary Fund.
Guidotti, P. E., and M. Kumar. 1991. Domestic public debt of externally indebted countries. *IMF Occasional Paper* no. 90. Washington, D.C.: International Monetary Fund, June.
Guidotti, P. E., and A. Powell. 2002. Dollarization in Argentina and Latin America. In *International financial markets: The challenge of globalization,* ed. L. Auernheimer. University of Chicago Press: Forthcoming.
International Monetary Fund. 2000. Debt and reserve-related indicators of external vulnerability. Washington, D.C.: IMF.
Ludwig, E. 1994. Resolving failed banks. Working paper presented at the International Conference of Bank Supervisors meeting, 23–27 May, Vienna, Austria.
Tobin, J. 1971. An essay on the principles of debt management. In *J. Tobin: Essays in economics,* vol. 1. Amsterdam: North-Holland. Originally published in *Fiscal and debt management policies,* Englewood Cliffs, N.J.: Prentice Hall, 1963.

III
Fiscal Policies

9

Taxation Reform in Latin America in the Last Decade

Vito Tanzi

9.1 Introduction

Next to the weather, taxes must rank universally as one of the most discussed topics of conversation. This is especially true for Latin America, which, in the last decade, has experienced a high degree of tax activism and several attempts aimed at reforming the countries' tax systems. Most governments have come into office promising to improve the tax systems to make them simpler to administer, easier to comply with, and more equitable. Most governments, however, have quickly resigned themselves to tinkering with the tax systems rather than truly reforming them. Administrative difficulties and strong political opposition to reform have been obstacles that governments have found difficult or even impossible to remove. Yet, as this paper shall show, gradually some important changes have taken place so that the tax systems of today are significantly different from those of a decade or more ago.

Many of the Latin American countries that have faced macroeconomic difficulties and that have chosen to go to the International Monetary Fund (IMF) for fund-supported programs have given particular importance to the objective of raising revenue. However, at times, this objective has been pursued or achieved at the cost of simplification or of equity improvement. Several Latin American countries have been only partially successful in

Vito Tanzi is an undersecretary in the economic ministry in Italy. He wrote this paper while he was director of the fiscal affairs department at the International Monetary Fund, and a senior associate with the Carnegie Endowment's Economic Reform Project.

Valuable advice and assistance received from Carlos Silvani, Juan Toro, and Howell Zee was much appreciated. Asegedech Woldemariam was helpful in collecting some of the statistical information.

raising the level of taxation in neutral and equitable ways. However, as we shall show, many countries succeeded in raising their tax levels.

This paper will survey some of the major developments in taxation that occurred in Latin America over the last decade. Given the number of countries involved and the many changes that have taken place, only the most important changes can be discussed. Furthermore, more attention will be given to developments in larger countries. Section 9.2 identifies the major factors that have influenced tax developments in Latin America. Section 9.3 identifies major developments in tax systems, section 9.4 discusses distinctive features of the Latin American tax reform efforts, and section 9.5 discusses some developments in tax administration. Section 9.6 draws some conclusions.

9.2 Main Influences on Tax Developments

Although most governments inherit tax systems that do not fully conform with their desires or goals, and that they would thus like to change, there are often more immediate or fundamental influences that at times force governments to take action. This section identifies the most important among these for the Latin American countries, although undoubtedly there were additional factors or influences that, in particular countries, might have been as important.

9.2.1 The Debt Crisis of the 1980s

Perhaps the first influence worth mentioning is the debt crisis that began in Mexico in 1982 and spread to most other Latin American countries. The debt crisis reduced the ability of these countries to finance their public spending through foreign borrowing and, because of the increase in the cost of servicing the debt, forced most Latin American countries to cut public spending or to increase their levels of taxation. These countries were faced with the need to increase their primary surpluses (the difference between ordinary revenues and noninterest expenditures) in order to service their debts. This situation, per se, would have created strong incentives for governments to increase taxation levels especially when, for political or legal reasons, noninterest spending could not be reduced. As it was, capital spending was often reduced, thus contributing in part to the reduction of the rate of growth through the 1980s and (more immediately) increasing the primary surpluses of these countries.

The fact that many of these countries negotiated adjustment programs with the IMF exposed them to additional pressures to improve their fiscal accounts. The fund often provided technical assistance in the tax area, assistance that aimed at strengthening tax systems so that they would become more efficient. It is important to stress two points in this context. First, fund or no fund, the fiscal situation needed to be strengthened because of the macroeconomic situation. Thus, the often-heard argument that these countries were forced by the fund to cut spending or increase taxes ignores reality. Second, whenever possible the fund's advice was to strengthen tax administrations and widen tax bases, rather than simply to increase rates or cut expenditures as some fund critics have argued.

9.2.2 The Inflationary Context

The debt crisis was accompanied by economic developments that had strong influences on the tax systems of these countries. One such development was inflation. Many factors contributed to inflation, but inflationary financing of public spending (i.e., recourse to monetary expansion) must surely have been the most important. Throughout the 1980s and until the mid-1990s Latin America experienced strong inflationary pressures that in some countries reached very high levels. In 1990, the average increase in the cost-of-living index for the Western Hemisphere reached 461.1 percent per year. In Argentina it reached 3,080 percent in 1989. In Bolivia it reached almost 12,000 percent in 1985. In Brazil it reached almost 13,000 percent in 1990 and around 2,000 percent in 1993–94. In Mexico it reached 58 percent in 1985. The period after 1995 has seen much lower rates of inflation for most countries.

When inflation reaches very high levels and the collection lags are significant, the positive effect of the fiscal drag on tax revenue is overwhelmed by the negative impact of what came to be called the *Tanzi effect*.[1] This effect stipulates that the longer the collection lag and the higher the rate of inflation, the larger will be the proportional, negative effect on tax revenue. However, the absolute effect depends also on the initial level of the average tax ratio. The higher the initial average tax ration, the greater will be the absolute fall in tax revenue given the average collection lag for the whole tax system and the rate of inflation.[2] Because income taxes generally have longer lags than other taxes, their relative contribution to total tax revenue generally falls during the period of inflation.

The countries tried to react to the effect of inflation on their tax revenue by (1) attempting to reduce the collection lags through administrative changes;[3] (2) relying more on taxes with shorter collection lags such as value-added taxes and excises; (3) anticipating tax payments through withholding; and in extreme cases (Brazil and Chile), (4) indexing the tax liabilities for the period of the lag. The indexation factor was supposed to reflect the rate of inflation over the period of the delay. Through this latter mecha-

1. The *collection lag* is the time that elapses between an event that creates a tax liability and the time when the government receives the payment.

2. For the technical details the reader is referred to Tanzi (1977, 1989).

3. These included increased penalties on delays in payment because high inflation with low penalties encourages taxpayers to delay the timing of their payments.

nism Brazil significantly reduced, but did not completely neutralize, the negative effect of inflation on its tax revenue (see Gianbiagi 1987).

The effect of inflation on the tax system was especially important for high-inflation countries. Whereas the acceleration of inflation until the early 1990s reduced the average tax ratios, the deceleration of inflation in the latter part of the 1990s increased them and thus contributed to improvement in the fiscal accounts in more recent years. This reverse Tanzi effect was especially important in Argentina, Bolivia, Nicaragua, Peru, and some other countries. However, inflation is likely to have had a more permanent effect on the tax systems by changing their structures in permanent ways. For example, by distorting the incomes from capital sources (interest rates, profits, capital gains) it led to policy measures aimed at reducing taxes on these incomes.

9.2.3 Trade Liberalization

The spreading of the so-called Washington consensus encouraged many developing countries to reduce restrictions on trade. Chile, Mexico, Bolivia, Argentina, and other Latin American countries endorsed this trend and some of them significantly reduced both quantitative restrictions on trade and nominal tariffs. Export duties, which in earlier years had played an important role in several Latin American countries, including Argentina, almost disappeared. Import duties fell, thus reducing the share of tax revenue that had been coming from that source. This was a significant change in the tax structure of these countries. It made the tax systems less distortional but, at the same time, it created the need for compensatory revenue sources. In any case, this was an important development for the tax systems of the region.

The servicing of the foreign debt required that some of the foreign currency earned from exports had to be used to pay interest and principal on the debt. The result of this use of foreign currency earnings was a reduction in imports, which also directly (and indirectly, through its effect on economic activities), reduced the tax base.[4]

9.2.4 Globalization and Capital Account Liberalization

The period that we are analyzing witnessed an acceleration of the globalization of economic systems and the gradual liberalization of capital movements. As a result of these trends, there was growing pressure on Latin American countries to reduce the tax rates, particularly on enterprises but also on individuals. As we shall see below, most of the countries joined the worldwide movement toward lower marginal tax rates on individuals and on enterprises.

4. For a discussion of the link between imports and total tax revenue, see Tanzi (1989).

9.2.5 Simplification of Tax Systems

Perhaps one final trend worth mentioning is the movement toward simplification of the tax systems to reduce the compliance costs for taxpayers and the collection costs for tax administrations. Both of these costs had been particularly high in Latin American countries. Although progress in this direction has been only partial, there has been some. For example, although in the early 1980s many of these countries were characterized by the existence of a large number of taxes, there has been a process of tax pruning that has significantly reduced the number of taxes used to collect revenue. For example, in the early 1980s there were as many as 96 taxes used by Argentina and some 300 taxes used by Costa Rica to generate revenue. In both cases there has been a substantial reduction of these numbers. Also, the growing use of banks to accept tax payments has reduced compliance costs.[5]

9.3 A Panoramic View of Major Tax Developments

Table 9.1 provides information on tax revenues as shares of gross domestic product (GDP) for nineteen Latin American countries during the 1980–99 period. It should be noted that the table is limited to tax revenue of central governments and thus it excludes taxes imposed by subnational governments. These local governments can be important in countries that have federal structures, especially Brazil and Argentina. For these two countries more comprehensive data for general rather than just central government are provided in tables 9.2 and 9.3.

Table 9.1 shows that for most countries the share of central-government tax revenue in GDP increased significantly in recent years, especially in the postinflationary period. Large increases are shown, for example, by Argentina, Bolivia, Brazil, Peru, and a few other countries.[6] The tables also show the considerable range in these tax ratios, with Brazil collecting around 30 percent of GDP while several other countries collect only around 10 percent.

The tax burden of a country can, of course, be too high or too low in relation to various objectives including macroeconomic stability, economic efficiency, need for social spending, and so on. Although it is impossible to establish, even theoretically, what an optimal tax ratio should be, economic

5. In the past, and in some countries, taxpayers needed to stand in line (at times, for days) in front of tax offices to make payments. In particular cases, such as Brazil, this compliance cost had led to demonstrations against the government.

6. In Brazil the level of taxation of general government increased significantly during the 1950s and 1960s. During this period it grew from about 14 percent of GDP in 1950 to about 26 percent of GDP in 1970. In the most recent years it has increased again (see Varsano et al. 1998). In Argentina the level of taxation has grown significantly over the 1990s.

Table 9.1 **Total Tax Revenues of the Central Governments (as % of GDP)**

Country	1980	1981	1982	1983	1984	1985	1986	1987	1988	1989	1990	1991	1992	1993	1994	1995	1996	1997	1998	1999
Argentina	9.1	12.0	10.1	9.1	8.4	10.0	9.5	9.4	7.2	9.6	12.4	14.2	16.5	17.9	17.7	17.3	16.0	17.3	17.6	17.6
Bolivia	8.5	9.2	4.9	2.9	2.1	7.9	7.9	8.1	8.4	7.9	8.2	8.7	10.7	11.4	12.4	12.4	12.3	14.5	16.3	18.1
Brazil	7.7	7.6	7.5	8.0	6.6	6.4	6.5	6.0	6.0	5.7	10.2	10.0	9.4	10.6	13.2	12.6	11.8	12.6	14.5	15.0
Chile	17.4	19.2	18.3	17.7	19.6	19.1	18.4	18.1	15.5	15.1	14.5	16.7	17.3	18.0	17.5	17.0	18.2	17.6	17.8	16.9
Colombia	7.6	7.2	7.3	6.7	6.8	8.6	9.0	9.5	9.4	9.3	9.3	10.7	11.2	11.6	11.8	11.4	11.5	12.2	10.5	10.8
Costa Rica	11.2	12.0	12.5	15.6	15.3	15.2	13.8	14.5	14.4	14.4	14.0	11.4	12.0	12.1	11.7	12.5	12.7	12.6	12.8	12.5
Dominican Republic	7.1	6.6	5.6	5.4	5.9	6.4	8.1	7.9	7.5	8.0	7.6	7.6	7.2	7.4	7.7	8.0	7.2	9.3	9.9	9.8
Ecuador	7.1	6.6	5.6	5.4	5.9	6.4	8.1	7.9	7.5	8.0	7.6	7.6	7.2	7.4	7.7	8.0	7.2	9.3	9.9	9.8
El Salvador	11.1	11.4	10.6	10.6	11.6	11.6	13.1	10.9	9.3	7.6	9.1	9.5	9.6	10.3	10.9	12.0	11.3	11.1	10.3	10.5
Guatemala	8.6	7.6	7.2	6.3	5.3	6.1	7.0	8.1	8.7	7.8	6.8	7.3	8.2	7.8	6.7	8.0	8.8	9.4	9.6	10.0
Haiti	7.2	10.1	10.9	11.6	11.7	12.5	10.2	10.4	10.6	10.4	8.7	9.5	6.1	5.5	2.6	6.4	7.5	9.2	8.9	9.1
Honduras	14.2	12.7	12.7	11.8	13.5	14.0	13.5	14.0	11.7	11.8	14.1	14.5	15.4	14.8	14.3	15.7	14.4	14.1	17.0	17.7
Mexico	15.8	11.4	10.6	11.1	11.0	10.9	11.5	10.8	12.2	12.1	11.5	12.0	12.4	11.4	11.3	9.2	9.0	9.8	10.5	11.2
Nicaragua	22.2	19.5	21.5	25.9	30.6	27.7	27.8	24.8	19.2	21.7	13.5	17.7	19.2	18.7	19.3	20.6	20.7	23.0	24.1	23.0
Panama	13.9	14.3	13.7	14.4	13.8	13.8	14.5	14.7	9.6	8.2	11.7	12.5	12.5	12.1	11.8	12.5	12.1	12.5	12.1	12.6
Paraguay	8.4	7.5	8.2	6.4	6.6	6.9	6.8	7.0	6.9	8.8	9.5	9.4	9.3	9.4	10.7	12.2	11.5	11.8	11.6	10.8
Peru	15.8	13.2	13.0	10.7	11.6	13.4	11.3	8.4	7.7	6.1	7.7	8.9	10.0	10.1	11.2	11.6	12.1	12.1	12.1	11.4
Uruguay	15.5	16.1	13.6	14.0	12.5	13.6	14.7	15.0	15.4	14.3	14.4	14.3	14.9	14.7	13.1	14.6	14.9	15.8	16.1	15.4
Venezuela	5.9	9.9	9.2	9.6	9.9	11.0	12.9	8.6	7.7	4.5	3.7	4.4	5.5	7.2	8.7	8.2	7.9	9.8	10.3	10.3

Source: ECLAC (Economic Commission for Latin America and the Caribbean) based on official data.

Table 9.2 **Brazil: Tax Revenue of General Government (as % of GDP)**

Year (PIB)	1990	1991	1992	1993	1994	1995	1996	1997	1998	1999
Union	20.53	16.72	17.50	18.47	20.46	20.01	19.35	19.80	20.73	21.38
Main budget	9.25	6.99	7.43	7.78	8.55	8.24	7.60	7.49	8.28	8.39
Income tax	4.83	3.64	3.95	3.98	4.07	4.82	4.65	4.48	5.30	5.47
Individuals	0.36	0.15	0.15	0.21	0.27	0.32	0.30	0.31	0.31	0.30
Enterprises	1.65	0.86	1.39	1.03	1.23	1.40	1.60	1.41	1.34	1.27
Withholding	2.82	2.63	2.42	2.74	2.56	3.10	2.75	2.76	3.65	3.89
Tax on production	2.55	2.23	2.39	2.44	2.18	2.08	1.96	1.92	1.79	1.61
Tax on financial transactions	1.41	0.62	0.64	0.81	0.69	0.50	0.36	0.44	0.39	0.48
Foreign trade taxes	0.42	0.44	0.41	0.45	0.52	0.76	0.54	0.59	0.72	0.78
Land taxes	0.00	0.02	0.00	0.01	0.00	0.02	0.03	0.03	0.02	0.02
Bank debits tax (IPMF)				0.07	1.06	0.02	0.00	0.00	0.00	0.00
Fees	0.04	0.04	0.04	0.04	0.04	0.05	0.05	0.04	0.05	0.03
Social security budget	9.17	7.88	8.19	8.94	9.76	9.45	9.51	10.08	9.93	10.58
Payroll deductions	5.36	4.71	4.78	5.42	4.96	4.98	5.18	5.11	5.18	4.70
COFINS (a sales tax)	1.61	1.35	1.01	1.34	2.47	2.27	2.20	2.12	1.96	3.06
Bank debits tax (CPMF)								0.80	0.90	0.79
Tax on liquid profit	0.57	0.29	0.73	0.77	0.93	0.87	0.80	0.83	0.73	0.67
PIS, PASEP (a sales tax)	1.20	1.07	1.09	1.14	1.08	0.91	0.92	0.84	0.79	0.82
Civil servants contributions	0.11	0.12	0.07	0.08	0.22	0.33	0.33	0.30	0.28	0.31
Other	0.33	0.35	0.51	0.19	0.10	0.10	0.08	0.07	0.09	0.24
Other	2.11	1.84	1.88	1.75	2.15	2.32	2.24	2.23	2.51	2.41
PGTS severance contribution	1.54	1.34	1.32	1.25	1.41	1.51	1.50	1.50	1.87	1.72
Regulatory fees	0.10	0.13	0.16	0.11	0.11	0.13	0.11	0.11	0.10	0.12
Education payroll fee	0.22	0.16	0.17	0.13	0.35	0.37	0.35	0.32	0.27	0.23
Sistema "S" (2) (a payroll fee)	0.24	0.21	0.23	0.26	0.28	0.31	0.27	0.31	0.27	0.33

(*continued*)

Table 9.2 (continued)

Year (PIB)	1990	1991	1992	1993	1994	1995	1996	1997	1998	1999
States	9.04	7.31	7.37	6.48	8.00	8.34	8.21	7.95	7.89	7.74
GST/VAT (ICMS)	8.47	6.87	6.91	6.11	7.37	7.31	7.15	6.89	6.77	6.72
Tax on automobiles (IPVA)	0.19	0.08	0.14	0.13	0.17	0.38	0.40	0.44	0.49	0.44
Stamp duty (IJCD)	0.02	0.01	0.02	0.02	0.02	0.03	0.03	0.03	0.04	0.03
Fees	0.10	0.12	0.12	0.08	0.11	0.16	0.16	0.16	0.16	0.13
State social security	0.14	0.16	0.09	0.11	0.29	0.42	0.43	0.39	0.40	0.37
Other	0.11	0.07	0.10	0.03	0.04	0.04	0.04	0.04	0.03	0.05
Municipalities	0.94	1.19	0.99	0.78	1.00	1.39	1.40	1.34	1.28	1.20
Tax on services (ISS)	0.34	0.34	0.32	0.35	0.42	0.51	0.56	0.52	0.50	0.48
Real estate property tax (IPJU)	0.24	0.46	0.32	0.15	0.21	0.43	0.43	0.42	0.39	0.36
Tax on real estate transfers (IJBI)	0.07	0.13	0.09	0.06	0.08	0.10	0.09	0.09	0.09	0.08
Fees	0.16	0.19	0.18	0.13	0.17	0.26	0.26	0.25	0.23	0.23
Local social security	0.01	0.02	0.01	0.01	0.03	0.04	0.05	0.04	0.04	0.04
Other taxes (3)	0.12	0.06	0.07	0.09	0.07	0.05	0.02	0.02	0.02	0.01
Total	30.51	25.22	25.86	25.73	29.46	29.74	28.96	29.09	29.90	30.32

Table 9.3 **Argentina: Tax Income (as % of GDP)**

Concept	1993	1994	1995	1996	1997	1998	1999[a]
Income and capital gains	1.86	2.32	2.48	2.56	2.91	3.24	3.31
Earnings	1.81	2.26	2.42	2.50	2.85	3.18	3.26
Movements in prices of capital, gambling, and sport income	0.03	0.03	0.04	0.04	0.04	0.03	0.03
Other	0.02	0.03	0.02	0.02	0.02	0.02	0.02
Estates	0.26	0.22	0.18	0.28	0.19	0.28	0.60
Assets	0.19	0.15	0.05	0.03	0.02	0.01	0.00
Personal assets	0.06	0.06	0.12	0.24	0.17	0.26	0.19
Other	0.01	0.01	0.01	0.01	0.01	0.01	0.40
Income from goods and services and transactions	8.97	6.71	8.56	8.75	9.24	9.19	9.17
Gross value-added tax (VAT)	6.88	6.75	6.76	6.92	6.99	7.00	6.61
Unified internal	0.99	0.93	0.90	0.71	0.65	0.65	0.64
Liquid fuels	0.87	0.80	0.69	0.86	1.34	1.24	1.26
Electricity consumption	0.06	0.07	0.07	0.07	0.06	0.06	0.06
Stamps	0.06	0.04	0.02	0.02	0.02	0.02	0.02
Other	0.11	0.12	0.12	0.18	0.19	0.22	0.58
Trade and international transactions	1.07	1.12	0.81	0.86	0.99	0.96	0.83
Import duties	0.54	0.61	0.68	0.70	0.83	0.90	0.78
Import statistics	0.49	0.47	0.08	0.12	0.13	0.03	0.02
Export duties	0.01	0.01	0.01	0.01	0.00	0.01	0.01
Other	0.02	0.03	0.03	0.03	0.02	0.02	0.02
Other[b]	0.52	0.37	0.37	0.01	0.01	(0.01)	0.00
Tax regularizations	0.52	0.37	0.37	0.01	0.01	(0.01)	0.00
Social security contributions[c]	5.58	5.40	4.75	3.95	3.78	3.64	3.49
Employees	—	—	1.24	1.03	0.91	0.81	0.77
Employers	—	—	2.92	2.26	2.34	2.38	2.34
Self-employed	0.30	0.59	0.58	0.67	0.53	–0.45	0.38
Nonidentified employees and employers	5.28	4.81	—	—	—	—	—
Gross tax revenue	18.25	18.13	17.15	16.41	17.11	17.30	17.41
Reimbursements	0.35	0.44	0.44	0.27	0.22	0.17	0.20
Export reimbursements	0.33	0.34	0.36	0.22	0.20	0.17	0.20
Other	0.02	0.10	0.08	0.04	0.02	0.00	0.00
Net tax revenue	17.90	17.69	16.71	16.14	16.89	17.13	17.21
Provincial taxes	3.70	3.74	3.54	3.56	3.68	3.91	3.81
Gross total tax revenue	21.60	21.43	20.25	19.68	20.79	21.21	21.22

(*continued*)

Table 9.3 (continued)

			Provincial Taxes (as % of GDP)			
Year	Total	Gross Income	Real Estate	Auto	Stamps	Other
1980	3.60	1.68	0.70	0.29	0.58	0.26
1981	2.95	1.48	0.67	0.26	0.42	0.14
1982	2.44	1.28	0.58	0.21	0.29	0.12
1983	1.82	1.00	0.40	0.17	0.21	0.03
1984	2.33	1.21	0.62	0.28	0.20	0.04
1985	2.76	1.41	0.69	0.33	0.28	0.06
1986	3.10	1.69	0.70	0.28	0.37	0.06
1987	2.70	1.55	0.52	0.23	0.33	0.07
1988	2.38	1.30	0.54	0.22	0.23	0.07
1989	2.09	1.13	0.52	0.21	0.18	0.05
1990	2.52	1.25	0.58	0.26	0.20	0.12
1991	2.82	1.51	0.66	0.29	0.31	0.06
1992	3.53	1.95	0.68	0.30	0.38	0.24
1993	3.71	2.07	0.63	0.30	0.40	0.32
1994	3.74	2.12	0.66	0.32	0.39	0.23
1995	3.54	2.01	0.63	0.31	0.36	0.23
1996	3.56	2.02	0.60	0.30	0.35	0.29
1997	3.68	2.05	0.62	0.31	0.32	0.38
1998[d]	3.88	2.17	0.67	0.33	0.32	0.40

Source: National Direction of Fiscal Coordination data.
Notes: Dashes indicate the information is not available.
[a]Preliminary data.
[b]Includes quasi taxes and other minor taxes.
[c]Includes national taxes not collected for the Administrators of Pension Funds.
[d]Estimates.

initiative and activity, and ultimately growth are likely to be discouraged by a high level of taxation, especially if accompanied by an unproductive use of the tax revenue. It should be added, however, that it is very difficult to isolate the effects of high taxation on the rate of growth. Therefore, there are remarkably few empirical studies that have tried to link the level of taxation to economic performance.[7] Mutatis mutandi, it can be argued that taxes should be raised when they are so low that the government is unable to finance essential public spending.[8] This low level of taxation can be a major obstacle to the growth of a country's economy.

Obviously, the quality of the tax system and of the tax administration, the

7. For a theoretical discussion of some of these points, see Tanzi and Zee (1998). The difficulty is that when the level of taxation changes, several other important variables also change. Establishing a counterfactual, or isolating econometrically the impact of taxation, is almost impossible.

8. However, it begs the question of whether more revenue would be spent for essential public spending. It also ignores the distortional nature of the tax increase.

quality of the expenditure policy, and the quality of the management of public spending have much to do with establishing an optimal level for tax revenue. In spite of all these qualifications, one may venture a view that in Latin America, taxes may be too high in Brazil, at about 30 percent of GDP, and too low in Guatemala, Haiti, and other countries, at about 10 percent of GDP. Obviously, countries that receive public revenue from the export of publicly owned commodities (oil, copper, gold) do not need to raise as much in tax revenue as countries that do not have such incomes. This is the case in Venezuela, Mexico, Ecuador, and a few of the other countries that show relatively low average tax revenue.

The rest of this section provides a broad-brush review of major structural developments in Latin American taxation.

9.3.1 Decreasing Importance of Foreign Trade Taxes

An important change in Latin American tax systems has been the declining importance of foreign trade taxes. In addition to the fall in "disposable" foreign exchange earnings mentioned earlier, this change reflects a reaction on the part of the Latin American policymakers against the policies of import substitution that had been popular until the 1970s. The fall in revenue from foreign trade taxes was a consequence of decisions to reduce tariffs on imports and exports and to replace the lost revenue with taxes on domestic consumption. The substitution of import duties with domestic taxes on consumption had been a standard recommendation by tax experts.

Table 9.4 provides data on the relationship between revenue from import duties and the value of imports for sixteen Latin American countries. This relationship can be defined as the *effective tariff rate* or the *collected tariff rate*. The table shows the fall in the effective tariff rate between 1985 and the most recent available year. With a few exceptions, the fall characterizes many countries, particularly Ecuador, Peru, and Uruguay. However, if in the past a country forbade the importation of many products but allowed a few essential goods to come in duty free, it would not have shown any revenue from import duties. Therefore, if this country relaxed its restriction on trade and allowed previously forbidden goods to be imported subject to some tariff, it would show (an increase in) revenue. Therefore, the figures in table 9.4 must be interpreted with some caution because an increase in the collected tariff rate does not necessarily imply that restrictions on trade have increased.

Table 9.5 shows, for a selected group of countries, the fall in international trade taxes over a decade. A longer period would probably show greater falls. Substantial falls are shown by Argentina, Chile, Colombia, and Peru, with each losing around 1 percent of GDP in revenue. Trade taxes have become a progressively smaller share of all tax revenue. This is likely to be a desirable development.

Before moving to the next issue, it may be worthwhile to mention that a

Table 9.4 **Latin America: Collected Tariff Rates (tariff revenue as % of value of imports)**

Country	1985	1990	Most Recent Available Year[a]
Argentina[b]	16.18	10.40	9.74
Bolivia	7.85	4.75	5.01
Brazil	6.59	10.53	8.88
Chile	16.69	10.37	10.56
Colombia	14.82	18.54	9.06
Costa Rica	10.64	10.29	8.26
Dominican Republic[b]	14.58	10.60	12.80
Ecuador	24.26	13.14	8.27
El Salvador	4.25	4.69	5.88
Guatemala	11.89	7.03	8.42
Nicaragua	6.44	8.61	13.45
Panama	10.90	11.38	9.59
Paraguay	5.14	5.88	7.95
Peru	28.18	11.01	11.77
Uruguay	13.50	12.72	6.07
Venezuela	11.44	9.99	9.65

Sources: IMF (1997); IMF (various issues); OECD (various issues, except as noted specifically).

Note: Data are unweighted averages.

[a]Last year for which data are available in 1995 for most countries and an earlier year or 1996 for some countries.

[b]Data provided by the country authorities and IMF staff estimates.

Table 9.5 **Selected Latin American Countries: Taxes on International Trade, 1985–98 (as % of GDP)**

Country	1985–89	1990–94	1995–98
Argentina	1.8	0.9	0.8
Bolivia	1.9	1.4	1.4
Brazil	0.5	0.4	0.6
Chile	3.2	2.2	2.1
Colombia	2.2	1.4	1.0
Costa Rica	2.9	2.8	2.6
Mexico	1.1	1.0	0.6
Peru	2.2	1.3	1.5
Venezuela	1.9	1.8	1.6
Unweighted average	2.0	1.5	1.3

Sources: Country documents and IMF staff estimates.

bad feature of Latin American taxation—one that loomed large in the 1960s and 1970s—has almost disappeared, namely export taxes. These taxes are likely to be among the most distortional taxes. Especially in Argentina these taxes played a major role in earlier years.

9.3.2 Increasing Importance of the Value-added Tax

In the past two decades, one trend that has been of fundamental importance in the tax systems of Latin American countries has been the introduction of the value-added tax (VAT). Without a doubt, this development has been the most important change in Latin America's taxation in a long time. The VAT landed first in Brazil in January 1967, having been imported from Europe where it had been recently introduced. In the 1970s it spread to other Latin American countries and, during the 1980s and 1990s, it was introduced in all the Latin American countries. In fact, in the Americas today the United States is the only country without a VAT.

Table 9.6 provides essential information on the VAT for nineteen Latin American countries. It gives the date the VAT was introduced, the rate (or rates) at the time of introduction, and the rate (or rates) for selected periods up to July 2000. It will be seen that the nominal rates have generally gone up since the introduction of the VAT. Several countries apply single rates on the taxable base; several others apply differentiated rates on different categories of goods.

The issue of whether the VAT should be applied with one or more rates is an important one from efficiency, political, and administrative angles, and is an issue that continues to attract a lot of attention on the part of policymakers and tax experts in Latin America and elsewhere. Optimal taxation theory would suggest that rates should vary depending on the price elasticity of the specific goods taxed. Thus, prevailing (academic) taxation theory would recommend differentiated rates based on elasticity considerations. The lower the price elasticity of a product, the higher the rate should be.[9] Political or equity considerations would also favor differentiated rates but differentiation based on the degree of necessity of the particular good in the households or in the households of the poorer taxpayers. Thus, goods of basic necessity, or those bought predominantly by lower-income families, should be exempt or taxed at low rates regardless of their elasticity. This political approach is obviously based not on efficiency but on social considerations. In fact, it conflicts with optimal taxation theory. The approach has received strong backing in France and through that country has influenced the VATs of several African countries. It is also the approach endorsed by the European Union, although in the European countries the rate differentiation is normally limited to two rates. Politicians favor this approach because it makes them appear sensitive to equity considerations.

9. For a strong defense of single rates see Harberger (1990).

Table 9.6 **Cross-Country Comparisons: Value-added Tax Rates (%)**

Country	Date VAT Introduced or Proposed	At Introduction	July 1992	October 1993	March 1994	September 1995	July 1996	June 1997	March 1999	July 2000
Argentina	Jan. 1975	**16**	**18,** 26, 27	**18,** 26, 27	**18,** 26, 27[a]	**21,** 27	**21,** 27	**21,** 27	10.5, **21,** 27	10.5, **21,** 27
Bolivia	Oct. 1973	5, **10,** 15	**14.92**[b]	**14.92**[b]	**14.92**[b]	**14.92**[b]	**14.92**[b]	**14.92**[b]	**14.92**[b]	**14.92**[b]
Brazil	Jan. 1967	**15**	9.89, 12.36, **20.48**[c,d]	9.89, 12.36, **20.48**[c,d]	9.89, 12.36, **20.48**[c,d]	9.89, 12.36, **20.48**[c,d]	.89, 12.36, **20.48**[c,d]	9.89, 12.36, **20.48**[c,d]	9.89, 12.36, **20.48**[c,d]	9.89, 12.36, **20.48**[c,d]
Chile	Mar. 1975	8, **20**	**18**	**18**	**18**	**18**	**18**	**18**	**18**	**18**
Colombia	Jan. 1975	4, 6, **10**	8, **12,** 20, 35, 45	8, **14,** 20, 35, 45	8, **14,** 20, 35, 4	8, **14,** 15, 20, 35, 45[e]	8, 15, **16,** 20, 35, 45, 60[e]	8, 15, **16,** 20, 35, 45, 60[e]	8, 15, **16,** 20, 35, 45, 60[e]	8, 10, **15,** 20, 35, 45[e]
Costa Rica	Jan. 1975	**10**	**8**	**8**	**8**	**10**	**15**	**15**	**13**	**13**
Dominican Republic	Jan. 1983	**6**	**6**	**6**	**6**	**8**	**8**	**8**	**8**	**8**
Ecuador	July 1970	4, **10**	**10**	**10**	**10**	**10**	**10**	**10**	**10**	**12**
El Salvador	Sept. 1992	**10**	**10**	**10**	**10**	**13**	**13**	**13**	**13**	**13**
Guatemala	Aug. 1983	7	7	7	7	7	7	**10**	**10**	**10**
Haiti	Nov. 1982	7	**10**	**10**	**10**	**10**	**10**	**10**	**10**	**10**
Honduras	Jan. 1976	**3**	7, 10	7, 10	7, 10	7, 10	7, 10	7, 10	**12,** 15	**12,** 15
Mexico	Jan. 1980	**10**	**10**	**12.5**	**12.5**	**12.5**	**12.5**	**15**	12.5, **15**	12.5, **15**
Nicaragua	Jan. 1975	**6**	5, 6, **10**	5, 6, **10**	5, 6, **10**	5, 6, 10, **15**	5, 6, 10, **15**	5, 6, 10, **15**	5, 6, 10, **15**	5, 6, **15**
Panama	Mar. 1977	5	5, 10	5, 10	5, 10	5, 10	5, 10	5,10	5, 10	5,10
Paraguay	July 1993	**12**	**10**	**10**	**10**	**10**	**10**	**10**	**10**	**10**
Peru	July 1976	**3, 20, 40**	**18**	**18**[f]	**18**[f]	**18**[f]	**18**[f]	**18**[f]	**18**[f]	**18**[f]
Venezuela	Oct. 1993	**10**	n.a.	**10**	**10**	**10**	**10**	**16.5**	**16.5**[h]	**15.5**[i]
Unweighted average		10.37	11.36	14.88	14.88	15.68	15.93	14.74	15.24	15.17

Source: IMF, Fiscal Affairs Department

Notes: n.a. = not available.

Rates shown in bold type are so-called *effective standard rates* (tax exclusive) applied to goods and services not covered by other especially high or low rates. Some countries use a zero rate for a few goods, and tax exports.

[a]Supplementary VAT rates of 8 percent and 9 percent on noncapital goods imports; through "catch-up," these can revert to 18 percent retail.

[b]Tax-exclusive rate (legislated tax-inclusive rate is 13 percent).

[c]Tax-exclusive rate (legislated tax-inclusive rates are 9, 11, and 17 percent, respectively).

[d]On interstate transactions the tax-exclusive rates are 9.89 and 12.36 percent, depending on the region. The VAT for intrastate transactions varies from state to state, from a rate of 17–18 percent (standard rate) to 25 percent.

[e]As of November 1999 the general rate will be decreased to 15 percent. Vehicles with a value over US$35,000 will be taxed at a rate of 45 percent rather than 60 percent.

[f]Starting on 1 April 1995, the general rate is maintained at 10 percent in the border areas, except in the sale of real estate, which is subject to 15 percent.

[g]The 18 percent rate includes 2 percent of the Municipal Promotion Tax.

[h]Venezuela applies additional rates of 10 percent and 20 percent on specified luxury goods.

[i]A special 8 percent rate applies to imports and supplies in the tax-free port of Margarita Island.

While theoretical or efficiency considerations, on one hand, and equity or political considerations, on the other, favor the use of multiple rates, administrative and practical considerations as well as public choice arguments favor single rates on wide bases. Administrative difficulties and compliance costs for taxpayers grow exponentially with the increase in the number of rates because it is more difficult for tax administrations to control tax evasion and more costly for taxpayers to keep accounts when there are multiple rates and the same producers or distributors sell products taxed at different rates. Practical difficulties arise because estimates of elasticities for products or groups of products—elasticities that are necessary to follow optimal taxation principles—are normally not available. For these reasons most practicing tax experts and tax administrators favor single-rate VATs applied on bases that are as wide as possible.

Narrow tax bases introduce difficulties similar to those of multiple rates because the exempt part of the tax base must be either zero-rated or exempt. *Zero-rating* implies that those who sell these products not only should not pay taxes on their sales, but should be reimbursed for the taxes levied at earlier stages of the productive process that are contained in the final products. This obviously introduces major administrative and compliance difficulties. When the products sold are exempt rather than zero-rated, there is no requirement for compensation for taxes paid at earlier stages so that the prices of the products continue to include some taxation.[10]

To the extent that VATs have replaced foreign trade taxes or (cascading) turnover taxes as they have done in many Latin American countries, they have removed distortions in the prices of the products. The VATs zero-rate exports so that the importing country can impose its own VAT rates on the imported product. This removes distortions on trade. Zero-rating of exports is essential to remove the taxes already incorporated in the previous stages of production in the export prices. Exempting exports would be insufficient to achieve this result.

However, zero-rating of exports generates administrative difficulties for many tax administrations, including those of Latin American countries. First, it creates incentive for faking exports or faking invoices of domestic purchases in order to claim refunds from the tax administrations. Second, the timing of the refunds is also a problem. Often exporters have to wait a long time (in some cases several years) before they get the refunds to which they are entitled.[11] In some cases, this delay has been a cheap source of credit for governments that are short of revenue and a great irritant to taxpayers. Although there are no systematic statistics to back this conclusion,

10. In addition to the arguments made above, single rates are preferable because they do not create pressures for similar favorable treatment by those who sell products that are fully taxed, as happens with multiple rates.

11. This has been such an issue in Argentina that recently there have been proposals to abolish the VAT and replace it with a retail sales tax.

anecdotal evidence indicates that the greater the fiscal difficulties of a country, the longer it takes for exporters to be compensated for the taxes contained in the costs of their exports. When interest rates are high and the accumulated arrears are large, this can impose high costs on exporters and to some extent can neutralize or reduce the advantage of using a VAT. This is an area where tax administration can become tax policy.

Value-added taxes have become the workhorse of the Latin American tax systems. With the passing of time their importance in the revenue structures of these countries has increased greatly, either because the rates have generally been raised over time, as shown in table 9.6; because the tax bases have been widened; or because the quality of the tax administration has improved. The results of these changes, for a selected group of Latin American countries, are shown in table 9.7. It shows that revenues from VATs have grown significantly over the past decade. For example, Argentina has almost tripled its revenue from this tax. Brazil, Argentina, and Chile collect large shares of their total tax revenues from VATs. For these countries VATs are generating revenue levels comparable to those of European countries. On the other hand, because of significant erosion of the tax base, Mexico collects relatively little from this source: with a 15 percent tax rate, it collects only about 2.5 percent of GDP. A large share of the implicit VAT subsidies for Mexico go to the highest income deciles (see Dalsgaard 2000).

The average revenue productivity of the VAT can be defined as the amount of revenue expressed as a share of GDP that each unit of the nominal rate generates. For example, a 10 percent rate that generates 5 percent of GDP in tax revenue has a productivity of 0.5. The revenue productivity is obviously an important characteristic. If all countries used the same tax

Table 9.7 **Selected Latin American Countries: Domestic Taxes on Goods and Services, 1985–98 (as % of GDP)**

	1985–89			1990–94			1995–98		
Country	Total	VAT	Excises	Total	VAT	Excises	Total	VAT	Excises
Argentina	2.2	2.2	—	6.6	4.8	1.8	8.4	6.6	1.8
Bolivia	2.9	2.4	0.5	5.0	4.1	0.9	6.6	5.4	1.2
Brazil	—	—	0.5	10.6	9.8	0.8	9.4	9.0	0.4
Chile	12.5	9.1	2.7	10.9	8.4	1.9	11.7	8.9	2.0
Colombia	3.4	2.7	0.7	4.5	3.8	0.7	5.1	4.5	0.6
Costa Rica	8.9[a]	3.7	3.2	10.6[a]	5.1	2.8	12.2[a]	6.4	3.1
Mexico	5.9	3.3	2.5	4.6	3.0	1.6	4.0	2.5	1.5
Panama	4.4	1.4	2.2	4.6	1.8	2.0	4.3	1.9	1.7
Peru	5.6	1.6	2.9	6.2	3.2	2.9	7.8	5.9	1.9
Venezuela	1.4	0.1	1.4	1.5	0.5	1.0	5.0	3.9	1.0

Source: Country documents and IMF staff estimates.

Note: Dashes indicate information is not available.

[a]Includes taxes on import duties.

base for the VAT and had comparably efficient tax administrations, there would be a direct relationship between revenue and tax rate. In practice, the revenue productivity of the VAT tends to be high in some countries and low in others. For example, it is as high as 0.5 for Chile and only 0.2 for Mexico. Chile, with a rate of 18 percent, collects almost 9 percent of GDP in tax revenue; Mexico, with a rate of 15 percent, collects less than 3 percent of GDP. In Argentina, Peru, and Uruguay the average productivity is around 0.35. The performance of Chile in this context stands out.[12] This result depends on both the efficiency of the tax administration and the inclusiveness of the tax base. Chile has the most inclusive tax base of any Latin American country.

The size of the VAT base is obviously an important question of tax policy. Some countries have used a fairly comprehensive base while others have used a much narrower base, which, for political, social, or administrative considerations, has left out many products or sectors. These exclusions have often complicated the design of this tax. This has surely happened in Peru and Ecuador. However, apart from the legal definition of the base, the quality of the tax administration is also important.

Studies of tax evasion related to the VAT for several Latin American countries have shown widely divergent rates of tax evasion among countries and, for example, between Chile and Mexico.[13] As indicated earlier, however, the quality of the tax administration is also affected by the legal definition of the base. A wide base, taxed with one rate, is likely to generate far fewer problems for the tax administration than a narrow base with more than one rate. In the early 1990s Argentina dramatically increased its revenue from the VAT by widening the tax base. The new Mexican administration will need to widen the Mexican tax base for the VAT if it wishes to raise tax revenue.

In conclusion, to the extent that VATs have replaced foreign trade taxes and cascading domestic sales taxes, they have made the Latin American tax systems much more neutral and possibly more productive than the earlier systems. In some countries, and especially in Chile, the preference for a broad-based VAT has been based on the belief that a VAT favors saving and that taxes do not help much with income distribution (see Engel, Galetovic, and Raddatz 1997).

9.3.3 Stagnation of Income Taxes

With very few exceptions, Latin American countries continue to be allergic to income taxes. Thus, most Latin American countries continue to collect relatively little from taxes on income, especially as compared to in-

12. Brazil also collects a lot of revenue from the VAT. However, it does it with three different VATs imposed at three different levels of government.

13. For Mexico, see Aguirre and Shome (1988); for Chile, Serra (1994). See also Silvani and Brondolo (1993).

dustrial countries. The reasons for this outcome are several: (1) very large personal exemptions that often wipe out much of the legal tax base; (2) large legal deductions often for expenses that are disallowed in other parts of the world; (3) reluctance to tax financial incomes out of fear that savings would be reduced or would escape to income tax–free countries or to tax-free accounts in the United States or elsewhere; (4) falling statutory tax rates; and (5) tax administrations that still make tax evasion possible, or even easy.

Given that income distributions in Latin America are quite uneven and are becoming more so, and given the buildup of pressure to have more equitable social policies and more progressive tax systems, the low contributions of income taxes to tax revenue should be considered one of the major shortcoming of Latin American tax systems.[14] In general, total taxes on incomes generate less than 5 percent of GDP and in several Latin American countries much less than that. As far as taxes on enterprises are concerned, in terms of revenue generation, they are not too far out of line from those of Organization for Economic Cooperation and Development (OECD) countries. Thus, the basic difference comes from the taxes on individuals. These represent the greatest undeveloped part of the tax systems of Latin American countries and the major source of potential new tax revenue for governments in need of additional resources.

In a recent paper Shome (1999) has calculated personal exemption levels and limits on upper income brackets as multiples of countries' per capita GDPs. He has shown that, on average, for South America the personal exemptions levels as shares of per capita GDP rose from 0.46 in 1985 or 1986 to 1.36 in 1997. For the Latin American countries of Central and North America the increase was from 0.83 to 2.74. For the upper income bracket limits, the trend was in the other direction. Shome's paper makes it clear why income taxes produce so little in many of these countries.[15] As an extreme example, in Honduras in 1991, a taxpayer would need to have an income 687 times the per capita income of the country before being subject to the highest marginal tax rate. By 1997, this multiple had been reduced substantially but was still at the remarkable level of 104 times the per capita income. Obviously those who have such high taxable incomes are very few and their incomes probably come from sources that are either not taxed or that are difficult to identify.

The effect of international trends or of globalization on the income taxes of the Latin American countries is shown in tables 9.8 and 9.9. The first table refers to personal income taxes and the second to corporate income taxes. The tables show the tax rates on the first bracket and the rates on the highest marginal bracket. The starting year for these tables is around 1986,

14. For Latin America as a whole the Gini coefficient has been estimated at 0.50 for the decade of the 1990s. See Deininger and Squire (1998, 263).

15. It shows that tax evasion may be just a small part of the story.

Table 9.8 **Personal Income Tax Rates, 1985–2000 (% of taxable income)**

Country	1985 or 1986[a]	1992	1997	1998	1999 or 2000
Argentina	16.5–45.0	15.0–30.0	6.0–33.0	6.0–35.0	9.0–35.0
Bolivia	. . . –30.0	10% flat rate	13% flat rate	13% flat rate	13% flat rate
Brazil	0.0–60.0	10.0–25.0	15.0–25.0	15.0–25.0	15.0–27.5
Chile	0.0–57.0	5.0–5.0	5.0–45.0	5.0–45.0	5.0–45.0
Colombia	. . . –49.0	5.0–30.0	35% flat rate	35% flat rate	35% flat rate
Costa Rica	5.0–50.0	10.0–25.0	10.0–25.0	10.0–25.0	10.0–25.0
Dominican Republic	2.0–73.0	3.0–70.0	3.9–70.0	0.0–25.0	0.0–25.0
Ecuador	19.0–40.0	10.0–25.0	10.0–5.0	10.0–25.0	0.0–15.0
El Salvador	3.0–60.0	10.0–30.0	10.0–30.0	10.0–30.0	10.0–30.0
Guatemala	11.0–48.0	4.0–34.0	15.0–30.0	15.0–25.0	15.0–25.0
Honduras	3.0–40.0	12.0–40.0	9.0–40.0	10.0–30.0	10.0–25.0
Mexico	3.0–55.0	3.0–35.0	3.0–35.0	3.0–40.0	3.0–40.0
Nicaragua	15.0–50.0	8.0–35.5	10.0–30.0	10.0–30.0	10.0–30.0
Panama	13.0–56.0	3.5–56.0	4.0–30.0	4.0–30.0	2.0–30.0
Paraguay	5.0–30.0	5.0–30.0	3.0–30.0	3.0–30.0	3.0–30.0
Peru	2.0–56.0	6.0–37.0	15.0–30.0	15.0–30.0	15.0–30.0
Venezuela	12.0–45.0	10.0–30.0	6.0–34.0	6.0–34.0	6.0–34.0
Simple average	7.3–49.6	7.1–33.1	8.1–32.4	8.0–29.2	7.1–27.8

Sources: Secondary published sources such as publications of tax summaries by Price Waterhouse, Coopers and Lybrand, International Bureau of Fiscal Documentation, and other similar sources.

[a]The average shown is a joint average of the two years.

Table 9.9 **Corporate Income Tax Rates, 1986–2000 (% of taxable income)**

Country	1986	1992	1997	1998	1999 or 2000
Argentina	0.0–33.0	20.0	33.0	35.0	35.0
Bolivia	0.0–30.0	0.0	25.0	25.0	25.0
Brazil	29.0–50.0	25.0–40.0	15.0–25.0	15.0–25.0	15.0
Chile	10.0–37.0	15.0	15.0	15.0	15.0
Colombia	40.0	30.0	35.0	35.0	35.0
Costa Rica	0.0–50.0	30.0	30.0	30.0	30.0
Dominican Republic	0.0–49.3	0.0–49.3	25.0	25.0	25.0
Ecuador	0.0–59.0	0.0–44.4	25.0	25.0	15.0–25.0
El Salvador	0.0–30.0	0.0–25.0	25.0	25.0	25.0
Guatemala	0.0–42.0	12.0–34.0	25.0	30.0	30.0
Honduras	0.0–55.0	0.0–40.2	15.0–30.0	15.0–35.0	15.0–35.0
Mexico	5.0–42.0	0.0–35.0	34.0	34.0	35.0
Nicaragua	0.0–45.0	0.0–35.5	30.0	30.0	30.0
Panama	0.0–50.0	2.5–45.0	30.0–34.0	30.0–34.0	30.0
Paraguay	0.0–30.0	0.0–30.0	25.0–30.0	25.0–30.0	25.0–30.0
Peru	0.0–40.0	0.0–30.0	30.0	30.0	30.0
Uruguay	0.0–30.0	0.0–30.0	30.0	30.0	30.0
Venezuela	18.0–67.7	20.0–67.7	15.0–34.0	15.0–34.0	15.0–34.0
Simple average	3.6–43.3	5.3–36.5	19.2–29.7	19.2–30.4	17.5–28.6

Sources: Secondary published sources such as publications of tax summaries by Price Waterhouse, Coopers and Lybrand, International Bureau of Fiscal Documentation, and other similar sources.

which, as may be recalled, was the year of the major tax reform in the United States during the Reagan administration.[16]

Table 9.8 shows the rather sharp fall in the highest, or marginal, tax rates for the income of individuals. Between 1986 and 2000 the highest rate fell by more than 20 percentage points on the average. In 2000, Chile and Mexico are the only two countries with marginal tax rates reaching (Mexico) or exceeding (Chile) 40 percent. For most countries the marginal tax rates are equal to, or less than, 30 percent. When these low rates are set next to the very high personal exemptions and deductions, and when it is recalled that many Latin American countries tax capital gains and incomes from financial sources very little, if at all, it is easy to see why personal income taxes generate so little revenue or why the progressivity of these taxes does almost nothing for the progressivity of the tax system. This is true even for a country such as Chile (see Engel, Galetovic, and Raddatz 1997). Incidentally, the nominal rates of the personal income taxes in Latin American countries have fallen much more than the nominal rates of the OECD countries.

Table 9.9 provides information on the corporate income tax rates for the 1986–2000 period. These rates have also fallen significantly, but less than the personal income tax rates. Also, in comparison to the rates of the OECD countries, they have fallen more rapidly but by a smaller difference than for the personal income taxes. It is worth pointing out that although Chile has the highest rate on the income of individuals it now has the lowest rate on the income of corporations. This is consistent with its philosophy that only individuals—not corporations—should be taxed.[17]

In spite of the above trends and of the reluctance to collect large amounts of revenue from income taxes, there is evidence of some increases in revenue from these taxes. For example Argentina, Brazil, Bolivia, and, until recently, Peru had increased the share of income taxes into GDP in recent years. On the other hand, revenue from these taxes have fallen in Colombia and Mexico.

9.4 Some Distinctive Features of Latin American Taxation

The inability or unwillingness to raise more revenue from income taxes, coupled with the pressing need in many of these countries for additional tax revenue, has contributed to some interesting experimentation with new taxes or with new approaches to taxation. Not all of these experiments are desirable but they are all interesting. It would require too much space to address this issue in detail; however, one can get a taste of it by referring to

16. It should be mentioned that these rates are only indicative, because they ignore particular features that may make actual payments differ from the levels indicated by the rates in the tables.

17. In fact, for distributed profits the taxes paid at the enterprise level are credited against the taxes paid by the individuals.

three initiatives pursued in the 1990s: gross assets taxes; taxes on bank debits; and minimum taxes.

9.4.1 Gross Assets Taxes

Table 9.10 provides some basic information on gross assets taxes and on other types of taxes on net worth or assets. A description and analysis of gross assets taxes is contained in Sadka and Tanzi (1993). The original idea for such a tax originated with Maurice Allais in a book published in French in 1967. The tax, which is applied at rates of 1–2 percent of the gross assets of enterprises, is essentially a minimum tax to force enterprises to use their assets productively and to make sure they do not fully avoid contributing to tax revenue through tax gimmicks or through outright tax evasion.[18] This tax was first introduced in Mexico a decade ago and was subsequently used in Argentina, Costa Rica, Guatemala, and Venezuela. It has been or is being considered by other countries. This tax has a lot of merit on economic grounds but remains controversial with the owners or managers of enterprises. It remains to be seen whether it will spread or disappear. It generally generates more revenue than taxes on net worth, which often end up being taxes on very small bases because of the mismatch in the assessment of assets and liabilities.

9.4.2 Financial Transactions or Bank Debit Taxes

A less attractive innovation is the tax on bank debit. As table 9.11 shows, this tax is now in existence in Brazil, Colombia, Ecuador, and Venezuela. In earlier years it was also used in Argentina and Peru and last year it was considered in Mexico (which eventually decided against its introduction). In Colombia the tax was introduced to make up for revenues lost by lowering the VAT rate. In Ecuador it replaced income taxes. When this tax was first introduced in Argentina and Peru in the early 1990s the results were not good. The initial revenue contribution quickly eroded and various problems appeared.

In its more recent versions the tax seems to have generated fewer difficulties, at least in the short run, and more revenue than in the earlier years and the tax has acquired some strong supporters.[19] There is very little popular opposition to it, it is relatively easy to administer,[20] and it generates significant revenue. It has even been argued by the Brazilian director of taxation that the tax provides information that facilitates the fight against evasion. If

18. Initially if enterprises did report an income, the gross assets tax was rebated against the corporate income tax. However, it is now the reverse, so that the corporate income tax is rebated against the gross asset tax. This change was made to allow U.S. firms to use as tax credit in the United States the full amount paid for the income tax. Before the change the United States limited the tax credit to the net amount paid for the income tax.

19. A couple of years ago the president of Colombia almost convinced the president of Mexico to introduce this tax.

20. Actually, the banks do all the collecting.

Table 9.10 **Net Worth or Assets Tax, 1986, 1992, 1997, and 2000 (%)**

Country	1986	1992	1997	1998	2000
Argentina	1.5 on net worth[a]	2.0 on gross assets	1.0 on assets	1.0 on assets	1.0 on assets
Brazil	—	—	—	—	—
Chile	—	—	—	—	—
Colombia	8.0 on net worth	7.0 on net worth	—	—	—
Costa Rica	0.36–1.17 on fixed assets	0.36–1.17 on fixed assets	1.0 on assets	1.0 on assets	1.0 on assets
Dominican Republic	—	—	—	—	—
Ecuador	0.15 on assets	0.15 on net worth[b]	0.15 on net worth[b]	0.15 on net worth[b]	0.15 on net worth[b]
El Salvador	0.1–1.4 on net worth	0.9–2.0 on assets	—	—	—
Guatemala	0.3–0.8 on real estate[c]	0.3–0.9 on real estate[c]	0.2–0.9 on real estate	1.5 on assets	1.5 on assets
Honduras	—	—	—	1.0 on assets	0.75 on assets
Mexico	—	2.0 on gross assets[a]	1.8 on assets[a]	1.8 on assets[a]	1.8 on assets[a]
Nicaragua	1.0 on real estate[c]	1.5–2.5 on net worth	1.0 on real estate	1.0 on real estate	1.0 on real estate
Panama	1.0 on net worth[d]	1.0 on net worth[d]	1.0 on net worth[d]	1.0 on net worth[d]	1.0 on net worth[d]
Paraguay	1.0 on real estate[c]	1.0 on real estate[c]	1.0 on real estate[c]	1.0 on real estate[c]	1.0 on real estate[c]
Peru	1.0–2.5 on net worth	2.0 on net worth	0.5 on net worth	0.5 on net worth	—
Uruguay	2.8 on net worth	2.8 on net worth	1.5–3.5 on net worth	1.5–3.5 on net worth	1.5–3.5 on net worth
Venezuela	—	—	—	1.0 on assets[a]	1.0 on assets[a]

Sources: Secondary published sources such as publications of tax summaries by Price Waterhouse, Coopers and Lybrand, International Bureau of Fiscal Documentation, and other similar sources.

Note: Dashes indicate information is not available.

[a]Minimum corporate income tax; can be credited against normal corporate tax. The income tax can be credited against the gross assets tax in order to avoid the foreign investors' problem of crediting against tax liability in the home country.

[b]1 percent of assets as income tax advance payment.

[c]The base is real estate. The tax, however, is conceived not as a property tax but as an additional corporate tax.

[d]This tax has the form of a license to do business. The maximum tax amount is 20,000 colones per year.

Table 9.11 **Gross Revenue from Bank Debit Taxes**

Country	Year	Tax Rate	Gross Revenue: In % of GDP	Gross Revenue: In % of Tax Revenue	Productivity[a]
		Countries Where Tax Is Being Enforced			
Brazil	1994	0.25	1.06	3.6	4.24
	1997	0.20	0.80	2.8	4.00
	1998	0.20	0.90	3.0	4.50
	1999	0.22[b]	0.79	2.6	3.61
Colombia	1999	0.20	0.77	4.3	3.85
Ecuador	1999	1.00	3.50	26.7	3.50[c]
		Countries Where Tax Was Discontinued			
Argentina	1989	0.70	0.66	4.3	0.94
	1990	0.30	0.30	2.0	0.99
	1991	1.05[b]	0.91	5.4	0.86
	1992	0.60[b]	0.29	1.5	0.97[d]
Peru	1990	1.41[b]	0.59	6.4	0.42
	1991	0.81[b]	0.46	5.0	0.57
Venezuela	1994	0.75	1.30	7.7	2.60[d]
	1999	0.50	0.60	4.9	1.80[d]

Source: Country documents and staff estimates.

[a]Revenue in percent of GDP divided by average statutory rate.

[b]Average effective rate during the year, taking into account a lapse in the tax in early 1999 followed by its reinstatement at a 0.38 percent rate later in the year.

[c]Not adjusted for the fact that the tax base includes both debits and credits.

[d]Adjusted for the period during which the tax was in effect.

it is applied at a very low rate, it may conform with a kind of "honeybee" approach to taxation whereby each collection is so small that it does not elicit a response on the part of the taxpayer. However, at higher rates and especially over a longer time frame this tax is likely to have higher costs.

The bank debit tax is essentially an excise tax imposed on a specific activity or tax base, namely the use of bank checks. If the tax rate is small and the elasticity of demand for bank checks is low, as it is likely to be in the short run and especially if certain transactions are not taxed, the tax may generate few attempts at tax avoidance. However, if the rate goes up, individuals will realize that there are ways of avoiding this tax. Some of these ways may be costly; some may be less so. Use of cash instead of checks would be one such way.[21] Use of dollars instead of local currency would be another. Arranging to make payments through foreign accounts would be still another, and bartering would be a further one. If, in time, the tax leads

21. Such use would promote underground economic activities, which would encourage tax evasion. See Tanzi (1980).

to a reduction in financial transactions, it will inevitably affect the efficiency of the economy.[22] However, it must be recognized that all taxes have costs. Therefore, the choice must be made among second- or even third-best options. If the bank debit taxes are used at low rates and only for periods of transition to better revenue sources, then maybe they deserve a less negative reaction than most tax experts would have toward them. However, they should not become permanent features of tax systems, especially at high rates.

9.4.3 Simplified Taxes for Small Taxpayers

While in industrial countries a large share of the total sales or of the total incomes originate in relatively few enterprises, developing countries are characterized by high degrees of informality. For example, the International Labor Organization (ILO) has estimated that informal-sector employment, as a percentage of nonagricultural employment, in the mid-1990s was 57 percent in Mexico, 53 percent in Argentina, 56 percent in Brazil, and 51 percent in Chile (see ILO 1997). Small activities create major problems for tax administrations in all countries but especially in developing countries where accounting standards are low and these activities are more prevalent. Various countries such as France, Italy, Israel, and others have developed highly sophisticated methods that "presumptively" tax these activities. The Italian *studi di settore* probably represents the most sophisticated current attempt at using these methods for taxing small-business activities.

During the past two decades most Latin American countries have introduced some presumptive (simplified) forms of taxation for small taxpayers. However, a few countries (Argentina, Bolivia, Brazil, and Peru) have established a single, comprehensive tax that substitutes for more than one of the major taxes (VATs, income taxes, and social security taxes). Other countries, such as Costa Rica, the Dominican Republic, Guatemala, Mexico, Nicaragua, and Paraguay have presumptive (simplified) taxes for small taxpayers, but these taxes substitute only for either the VAT or the income tax. The *monotributo* of Argentina and the Simples tax of Brazil are particularly interesting recent examples of simplified taxes aimed at replacing several taxes. These taxes deserve particular studies.[23] It is still too early to tell whether they will prove to be good taxes.

9.5 Developments in Tax Administration

Important changes have taken place in tax administration but some needed reforms are still pending. This section briefly discusses these two aspects.

22. For an analysis of bank debit taxes in Latin America, see IMF (2000).
23. See, for example, Brazil, Secretariat of Federal Revenues (2000).

9.5.1 Achievements

At least four significant achievements merit mention:

- *Computerization.* Significant progress has been made in this area. The successful introduction of computerization has allowed tax administrations to process tax returns and payments more efficiently. As a consequence, the control of stop-filers and delinquent accounts has improved in most Latin American countries.
- *Control of large taxpayers.* Special units for controlling large taxpayers have been successfully established in many countries. These large-taxpayer units allow better monitoring of taxpayers who often account for large proportions of total revenue. They also permit the introduction of new systems that are first adopted for large taxpayers and then applied more broadly.
- *Widespread use of withholding systems.* The wider use of withholding systems has allowed a reduction in tax evasion, especially for small and medium taxpayers. For example, customs agencies now typically withhold some estimated income taxes at time of import, and large taxpayers withhold VAT when they purchase goods from small taxpayers. Even in industrial countries, withholding at the source is a very useful tool for tax compliance. Statistics indicate that tax evasion is much higher in sectors where withholding at the source does not occur.
- *Growing public awareness of the need to improve tax administration.* Gradually, the public has recognized the importance of improving tax compliance in order to reduce the tax burden on good taxpayers and to promote fair competition. As a consequence, political support for reforming tax administrations has gained momentum.

Reforms to be Completed

Although much progress has been made in tax administrations, there is still scope for additional progress especially in improving basic procedures such as registration of taxpayers, modernization of procedures for filing and payment, and for many other procedures. In addition, we list below some other important tasks to be completed:

Professionalizing tax administration management. In most Latin American countries, tax administrations are still highly influenced by political circumstances and pressures. To carry out a successful tax-administration reform process, reformers need to be independent of, and isolated from, political interference. In some countries, top officials of the tax administration are considered part of the political team of the government in power. Thus they change frequently, making long-range planning difficult. Tax administrations should acquire a degree of independence that would make them similar to central banks. Peru tried to do this in the early 1990s when it created a new and presumably independent tax administration with salaries similar to those of the central bank. However, with the passing of time, the earlier independence may have been reduced.

Putting firewalls between political and administrative decisions. There are still too many pressures on tax administrators to deal politically with some important taxpayers or categories of taxpayers. Tax commissioners are often pressured by politicians to go easy on some taxpayers and, perhaps, to be severe with others, and senior tax administrators still spend too much time negotiating with specific taxpayers. Only in very few Latin American countries are tax administrators immune from these kinds of pressures so that they are able to apply the tax laws in a fair and objective way. The combination of political pressures and still-too-wide discretion over the application of tax laws remains a central problem for Latin American countries. In some cases, it corrupts the administrative process.

Need for stronger political commitment to the reform of tax administrations. In many countries there is still too much attention paid to tax *policy* and not enough to tax *administration*, without the realization that when tax administration is not good it becomes "tax policy" because it distorts the policy decisions away from their intended effects. Thus, tax administration needs to receive at least as much attention as tax policy.

Reduction of corrupt practices for employees of the tax administrations. Corruption is still a problem in the tax administrations of many Latin American countries, and frequent contacts between tax administrators and taxpayers, coupled with administrative discretion in many decisions, creates many situations in which some employees abuse their power. The weakness of the judiciary and the opacity of laws and regulations often make corruption a relatively risk-free activity for those who engage into it. More progress in this area is needed to make those who work in tax administrations conform to higher standards. Administrations must have more capacity to get rid of questionable employees. They should not be prevented from doing so by labor laws or corrupt or inefficient legal systems.

Increasing the risk for noncompliant taxpayers. In many Latin American countries only a small number of noncompliant taxpayers are effectively punished.[24] The reasons are several: first, the audit function is weak; second, audit coverage and staff devoted to audits are too low; third, tax codes allow taxpayers to easily challenge the tax administration and to postpone

24. Almost none go to jail.

for a long time the imposition of penalties that, in any case, are generally low; and finally, the weaknesses of the legal system reduce the ability of the tax administrations to use that system to uphold the laws.

9.6 Concluding Remarks

This paper has described some of the important changes that have taken place in the tax systems of Latin American countries. These changes have been important such that, in significant ways, the tax systems of these countries at the end of the decade of the 1990s were different from and better than those that prevailed ten or twenty years earlier.

Major changes were the introduction and the spreading of the VAT, the reduction of trade-related taxes, the reduction in the number of taxes used to raise revenue, the increase in the level of taxation in many countries, and important improvements in tax administration. There is no question that in terms of criteria such as efficiency and facility of collection today's tax systems are better than those of the past. They are generally less distortive and less arbitrary. However, they still fall short in some important ways.

First, although tax revenue has increased, some of the most important countries (e.g., Argentina, Brazil, Mexico, Colombia, Peru, and Venezuela) and many of the others are still experiencing significant fiscal deficits. In theory, one could argue that the problem could be solved by reducing public spending. However, given pressing social needs and the fact that some of these countries want to have social programs similar to those of the European countries, the need to increase revenue further is likely to remain. Thus, new revenue sources must be found.

Second, and related to the first point, are major questions of equity in the tax systems. As mentioned earlier, the Latin American countries have shown great reluctance or inability to make the personal income tax contribute more to total revenue. This tax, which is of overwhelming importance in industrial countries, plays a very marginal role in Latin America.[25] Furthermore, property taxes, which could also contribute to the equity of the tax system, have been almost insignificant. Given the worsening situation in the distribution of income and the growing political awareness of this trend, it would be helpful if both the income tax and the taxes on property played larger roles both in contributing more revenue and in improving the progressivity of the tax systems. Efficiency concerns about this desirable change are often exaggerated.

Third, as has been mentioned, there have been major administrative improvements, but directors of taxations are still subject to many pressures to

25. It is interesting to note that during the Peron years, in the late 1940s and early 1950s, the taxes on income generated revenue that was a greater share of GDP than they do today.

adjust the tax payments of particular taxpayers who are politically powerful. These political influences, which occasionally make tax payments dependent on political connections, must come to an end.

Fourth, an issue of great importance (especially for Argentina and Brazil) that has not been discussed in this paper is the effect of fiscal federalism on the tax systems. In the two countries just mentioned, fiscal federalism has been a major obstacle to tax reform.

Finally, and again especially in some specific countries, social security taxes have been very high, thus perhaps contributing to unemployment. The reduction of these taxes in connection with the privatization of pension systems is also a topic of major importance in some Latin American countries.

References

Aguirre, Carlos, and Parthasarathi Shome. 1988. The Mexican value-added tax (VAT): Methodology for calculating the base. *National Tax Journal* 41:543–54.

Allias, Maurice. 1967. *Les conditions de l'efficacite dans l'économie*. Paris: Nationale Superieure des Mines de Paris.

Brazil, Secretariat of Federal Revenue. 2000. The simplified taxation, filing, and payment systems for small taxpayers. Paper presented at CIAT meeting, 2–5 October, Taormina, Italy.

Dalsgaard, Thomas. 2000. The tax system in Mexico: A need for strengthening the revenue-raising capacity. Economics Department Working Paper no. 233. Washington, D.C.: Organization for Economic Cooperation and Development.

Deininger, K., and Lyn Squire. 1998. New ways of looking at old issues: Inequality and growth. *Journal of Development Economics* (2): 259–87.

Engel, Eduardo, Alexander Galetovic, and Claudio Raddatz. 1998. Taxes and income distribution in Chile: Some unpleasant redistributive arithmetic. NBER Working Paper no. 6828. Cambridge, Mass.: National Bureau of Economic Research, December.

Gianbiagi, Fabio. 1987. O Efeito-Tanzi e o Imposto de Renda da Pessoa Fisica: Um Caso de Indexaçao Imperfeita (The Tanzi effect on the personal income tax: A case of imperfect indexation). *Revista de Finanças Públicas* (Brasilia) 47 (July/August/September).

Harberger, Arnold. 1990. The uniform-tax controversy. In *Public finance, trade, and development*, ed. Vito Tanzi, 3–17. Detroit, Mich.: Wayne State University Press.

International Labor Organization. 1997. *World labour report 1997–98: Industrial relations, democracy, and social stability*. Switzerland: ILO.

International Monetary Fund. 1997. *World economic outlook*. Washington, D.C.: IMF.

———. 2000. Bank debit taxes in Latin America: An analysis of recent trends. Fiscal Affairs Department. Mimeograph.

———. Various issues. *Government finance statistics*. Washington, D.C.: IMF. Organization for Economic Cooperation and Development. Various issues. *Revenue Statistics*. Paris: OECD.

Organization for Economic Cooperation and Development. Various issues. *Revenue statistics.* Paris: OECD.

Sadka, Efraim, and Vito Tanzi. 1993. A tax on gross assets. *Bulletin of International Bureau of Fiscal Documentation* 47 (2): 66–73.

Serra, Pablo. 1994. Es eficiente el sistema tributario Chileno? (Is the Chilean tax system efficient?). *Cuadernos de Economía* 31 (December).

Shome, Parthasarathi. 1999. Taxation in Latin America: Structural trends and impact of administration. IMF Working Paper no. 99/19. Washington, D.C.: International Monetary Fund, February.

Silvani, Carlos, and John Brondolo. 1993. An analysis of VAT compliance. In *Combating tax abuse and fraud: Technical papers and reports of the CIAT technical conference*. Venice, Italy: CIAT.

Tanzi, Vito. 1977. Inflation, lags in collection, and the real value of tax revenue. *IMF Staff Papers* 24 (March): 154–67.

———. 1978.Inflation, real tax revenue, and the case for inflationary finance: Theory with an application to Argentina. *IMF Staff Papers* 25 (3): 417–51.

———. 1980. The underground economy in the United States: Estimates and implications. *Banca Nazionale del Lavoro Quarterly Review* 135 (December): 427–53.

———. 1989. The impact of macroeconomic policies on the level of taxation and the fiscal balance of developing countries. *IMF Staff Papers* 36 (3): 633–56.

Tanzi, Vito, and Howell H. Zee. 1998. Fiscal policy and long-run growth. *IMF Staff Papers* 44 (2): 179–209.

Varsano, Ricardo, José R. Afonso, Erika A. Araújo, Elisa de Paula Pessôa, Júlio C. Ramundo, and Napoleão L. da Silva. 1998. A carga tributária Brasileira (The Brazilian tax burden). *Boletim Conjuntural* 40 (January): 37–44.

10

Taxing for Equity
A Proposal to Reform Mexico's Value-Added Tax

Enrique Dávila and Santiago Levy

10.1 Introduction

After the 1994–95 economic crisis, the Mexican economy is showing signs of stability and renewed economic growth. Although real gross domestic product (GDP) fell by 6 percent in 1995, the annual average growth rate for the next five years is expected to be 5.4 percent. The recovery of stability and growth derives from a wide variety of factors, among them an effective monetary policy, the positive impact of economic growth in the United States, and the favorable effects of the North American Free Trade Agreement (NAFTA). Another instrumental element has been fiscal discipline, reflected in the fact that in the preceding five years the average budget deficit has been 0.8 percent of GDP.

Fiscal discipline can be achieved by strengthening revenues or limiting expenditures. In the case of Mexico, during the 1996–2000 period, the latter has played a major role. As figure 10.1 shows, programmable expenditure will total, on average, 15.9 percent of GDP between 1995 and 2000, below the 17.7 percent average registered between 1985 and 1994. The contraction is still larger if we consider the cost of the social security reform.[1]

The authors are officials at the Mexican Ministry of Finance (Secretaría de Hacienda y Crédito Público) and the Mexican Social Security Institute (Instituto Mexicano del Seguro Social), respectively.

The opinions expressed here do not necessarily coincide with those of the institutions with which the authors are affiliated.

1. A new social security law came into effect in July 1997, establishing individual retirement accounts for workers, as opposed to the prior "pay as you go" system. As part of this reform, the federal government must meet the cost of retired workers' pensions under the previous law, which accounts for annual expenditures above 1 percent of GDP. Thus, in order to compare programmable expenditure series for the period 1980–2000, the data must exclude the cost of the reform.

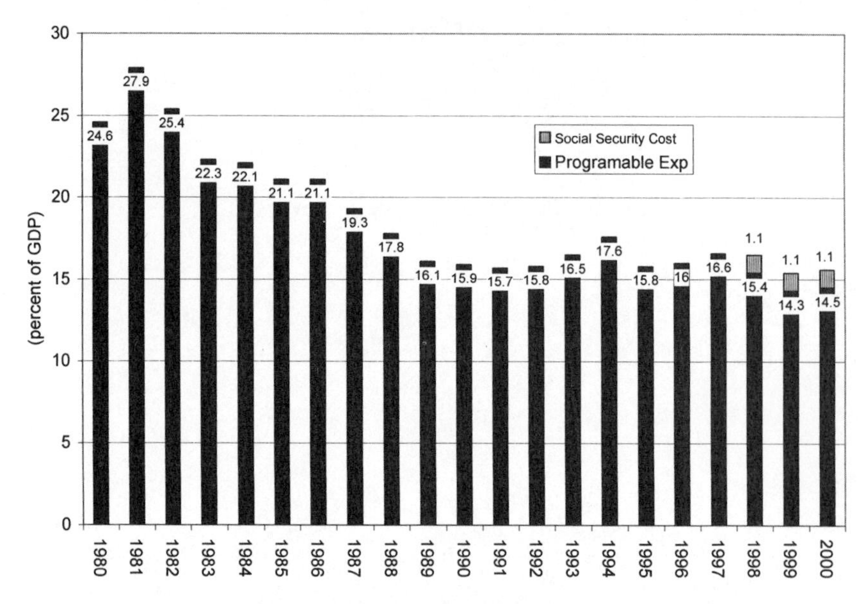

Fig. 10.1 Programmable expenditure, 1980–2000 (percentage of GDP)

Limiting public expenditures, although inevitable in a context of a weak tax base,[2] gives rise to significant social and economic costs, particularly in a society whose demographic dynamics require increasingly complex programs in education and health.[3] This is compounded by substantial shortages of physical infrastructure that constrain the country's growth and hinder a balanced regional development.[4]

These arguments have led policymakers and, more generally, public opinion, to put fiscal reform on the agenda. In the current Mexican context, such reform should have multiple objectives: broadening the tax base; simplifying compliance; finding more effective mechanisms to distribute tax and expenditure responsibilities among the three levels of government; and aligning incentives in order to reduce informal employment and foster investment. Each of these objectives represents substantial challenges. There is, however, an additional objective that must be emphasized for the reasons explained above: increasing revenues.

2. Mexico's ratio of fiscal revenues to GDP is among the world's lowest. In 1996 this ratio was well below that of Sweden, France, Italy, the United Kingdom, the United States, and Canada, and even that of Korea, Chile, Turkey, Brazil, Nicaragua, and Costa Rica. Moreover, if the contributions paid by Petróleos Mexicanos are excluded, this ratio would be lower than in Peru, Colombia, and Panama; see OECD (1999) and CEPAL (1997).

3. In a preliminary estimation undertaken by the Mexican Ministry of Finance (SHCP), unmet public expenditure needs were calculated at nearly 3 percent of GDP; see Ministry of Finance (1998).

4. Dávila, Kessel, and Levy (2002) argue that NAFTA will worsen the differences between Mexico's north and south, which is why a special investment effort in productive infrastructure and transportation is called for in Mexico's southern region.

A measure that would greatly contribute to achieving this last objective is to modify consumption taxes, and particularly the value added tax (VAT). This is because the current multirate regime generates considerable costs,[5] fosters evasion, and significantly limits its revenue-raising potential. Nevertheless, proposals to modify the VAT regime, particularly those intended to establish a uniform 15 percent rate, are confronted with an almost insurmountable obstacle: the negative impact that such a measure would have on low-income groups, which makes the proposal unacceptable to an important number of legislators (a position that, from our point of view, is correct).

This situation presents a strong paradox, to which this paper intends to find a possible solution: consolidating economic stability and increasing social spending to favor low-income groups is not feasible without a fiscal reform; however, a fiscal reform seems, in principle, harmful to low-income groups. The solution we propose here is, basically, very simple: to separate redistributive considerations from the VAT regime, using other instruments to compensate (or even overcompensate) low-income households for the undesirable redistributive effects of such a measure.

This paper analyzes the incidence of the VAT in Mexico. We first argue that the current VAT regimes (zero-rates and exemptions for various categories of goods) are ineffective and inefficient tools with which to combat poverty, which is why they must be eliminated (sections 10.2 to 10.4). However, it is essential that part of the population be compensated for the impact of adjusting VAT rates (section 10.5). We establish that some proportion of the country's population (low-income groups) are eligible for compensation and that individuals belonging to such groups each receive either a Slutsky transfer or a uniform compensation for all members of the target population (section 10.6). Next we analyze, at a conceptual level and concretely for Mexico, the type of instruments and incentives that can be used to carry out these compensations (section 10.7). Section 10.8 summarizes the conclusions of the analysis and makes some brief remarks on the political economy implications of our proposal.

10.2 General Analysis

A well-known empirical regularity is the systematic differences among household consumption patterns of different income levels (even control-

5. Efficiency costs referred to here are transaction costs, which increase exponentially with the number of rates applied. In a Walrasian world, where perfect information is available, there are no transaction costs and individuals voluntarily comply with the contracts they subscribe (and, presumably, also comply with their fiscal obligations), it would be optimal, under different scenarios, to apply different tax rates to different products (e.g., depending on the share represented by payments to labor in added value). However, abandoning such simplifying assumptions means that, in practice, fiscal experts tend to prefer a single VAT rate. This stance may be justifiable based on analytical proposals similar to those expressed by Holmström and Milgrom (1987) with regard to the optimal contracts needed to solve the principal/agent question.

ling for demographic effects; see, e.g., Theil 1980, 10; Deaton and Muellbauer 1984, 24). For microeconomists this implies that it is convenient to postulate that individuals' preferences are not homothetic (and therefore Engel curves are not, in general, straight lines departing from the origin) in order to build models whose predictions will not be easily refuted by empirical observations. The specific form of the Engel curves will depend on the level of aggregation: If only a few generic categories of goods and services are considered (such as food, clothing, transportation, etc.), Engel curves will depart from the origin and will be strictly increasing, and each category will absorb a significant share of total spending. On the other hand, if goods and services are specified in great detail (for instance, bottled soft drinks, polyester shirts, taxi rides, etc.) Engel curves will frequently not depart from the origin and will show decreasing sections (to the extent that, in certain cases, consumption may again be nil at certain income levels), and each good or service will absorb a small share of total spending (see Mas Colell, Whinston, and Green 1995, 25).

For policymakers, differences in consumption patterns associated with different income levels give a certain appeal to the subsidizing of goods and services (or consumption categories) whose share in household expenditures increase as income levels decrease. On this basis, different countries have justified subsidizing the following items (in the broad sense of the term, which includes granting preferential tax treatments):

- basic grains (wheat, corn, or rice, depending on the country) and their main consumption derivatives (such as bread or tortillas);
- edible vegetable oils;
- food in general, based on Engel's Law;[6] and
- current consumption in general, based on the hypothesis that average and marginal propensities to consume are decreasing functions of income levels.[7]

In this paper, however, we argue that, at least in the case of countries with highly concentrated income distributions, such as Mexico, subsidizing consumption is both ineffective and inefficient as a redistributive instrument. Its ineffectiveness, on the one hand, derives from two reasons. First, even if the subsidy is complete—that is, if the good or service is free—the quantity consumed is finite, limiting the size of the subsidy received by the poorer households. Second, if the subsidy is not complete—that is, if the good or service has a positive price—the size of the subsidy poorer households are

6. Stated by Engel in 1857. In 1957, Houthakker published a bibliographical survey to commemorate this paper's centennial. A quick review of Mexican households' spending patterns (INEGI 2000) confirms the current validity of this empirical regularity.

7. This is the famous "fundamental psychological law" discussed by Keynes in chapter 8 of his *General Theory of Employment, Interest, and Money* (1943).

likely to receive is seriously limited by their income (as well as by the need to spend in other goods or services).

Its inefficiency, on the other hand, derives from the fact that a small share of spending in the subsidized product by a high-income household may exceed, in absolute terms, a large share of spending in the same product by a low-income household. Income concentration translates into a concentration of spending, and even in concentration of consumption in goods and services considered as basic. Under these circumstances, a large share of the subsidy will be captured by middle- and high-income groups.

Even if consumption of a good or service were identical at every income level, it would mean that half of the total subsidy would be captured by the less poor half of the population. Hence, in order to concentrate a consumption subsidy in the poorer population, broad consumption categories should not be subsidized. Instead, it is necessary to identify specific goods and services consumed only by the poorer households. This requires making a careful distinction between "luxury" and "popular" presentations of the same category of goods or services, which normally imposes large administrative costs and induces simulations, or even corruption, both of which are very difficult to fight. In any case, as stated in the previous paragraphs, these carefully defined goods or services will usually absorb a small share of household spending, highlighting the ineffectiveness of this instrument.

More generally, any attempt to transfer income to poor households by means of *consumption* subsidies (either explicit or implicit) will reflect the existing inequality in income distribution. Consequently, as long as such inequality is present, general subsidies for certain groups of products, whether explicit through budgetary resources, or implicit by means of tax deductions or exemptions, will have limited redistributive effects and, from a certain perspective, may even have adverse consequences.

In the case of Mexico, the government has traditionally subsidized consumption of certain goods and services such as tortillas, electricity, passenger railroad services, and local telephone fees, as well as food, medicines, medical examinations, and educational services, the latter by means of special regimes in the payment of the VAT (zero-rates and exemptions). These dispersed efforts and, sometimes, the use of relatively ineffective instruments (in terms of their redistributive impact) have generated efficiency costs that eventually limit the country's growth potential. This, in turn, has a negative effect on the poor by reducing their employment opportunities and the fiscal resources available to fund social programs.

Despite these negative effects, this situation was justified to the extent that there were no alternative instruments to reduce inequalities, because not trying to correct the sharp concentration of income certainly could not be considered as an option. Nevertheless, during the last few years there has been some progress in Mexico in designing and using mechanisms that allow the following practices:

- carrying out *direct* income transfers to well-identified population groups, which significantly increases the efficiency of such transfers, as opposed to the alternative of generalized subsidies;
- using *monetary* transfers, which brings greater flexibility in terms of the amounts to be transferred, as opposed to the alternative of in-kind subsidies by means of free delivery or subsidized availability of a particular product, such as milk or tortillas, thus achieving greater effectiveness; and
- in some cases, conditioning these income transfers on specific behavior by the targeted households, helping them to permanently increase their income levels through investments in their human capital.

Consequently, one must assess the convenience of concentrating redistributive efforts in a set of highly effective and efficient instruments that simultaneously reduce income inequalities and separate redistributive considerations from the relative price structure, and, particularly, from the consumption tax regime.[8] Such an approach leaves the possibility of assessing the price and tax structure strictly in terms of effectiveness and efficiency, which would, for instance, prevent cross-subsidies in telephone services or eliminate subsidies to electricity rates, significantly improving competition and efficiency in those sectors. More precisely, this would also allow taxes to fully perform their core function, which consists in guaranteeing the sustainable financing of public expenditures, particularly for social programs.

10.3 Mexico's VAT Regime

The VAT is a good instrument, since individuals are taxed in accordance with their spending, independently of the source of their income. Even an individual who has evaded a significant amount of income tax will eventually pay VAT on such income when he or she spends it acquiring goods and services. Nonetheless, in the case of Mexico, these advantages are limited by the presence of two special VAT regimes: zero-rates and exemptions.

In the zero-rate regime, a good or service is not taxed in any of its production stages; this is achieved by means of a tax reimbursement scheme that returns the VAT paid on inputs to the producer. Goods such as food, medicines, books, magazines, and newspapers are under this regime. On the other hand, in the exemption regime the good or service is not taxed only on its last sage of production, making a reimbursement scheme unneces-

8. Distributive considerations should certainly be an essential part of other economic policies, for instance, education, regional development, labor training, and so on. In any case, the tax system cannot be based exclusively on consumption taxes because these are usually not progressive; progressiveness in the tax structure may be achieved by means of the income tax (*impuesto sobre la renta* [ISR]), reforming it in order to increase its efficiency and equity.

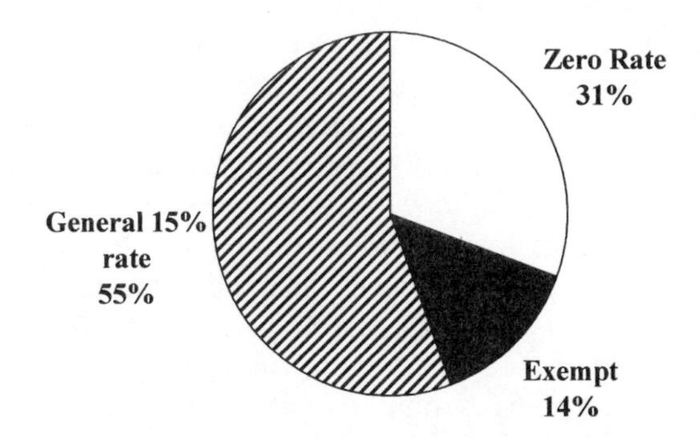

Fig. 10.2 Composition of current monetary expenditures by VAT regimes (%)

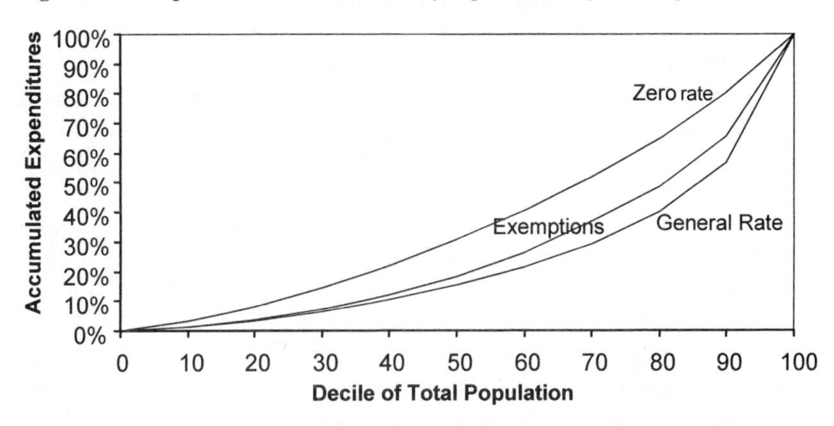

Fig. 10.3 Distribution of current monetary expenditures by VAT regime

sary. Medical examinations and education, among other services, are currently under this regime. As figure 10.2 shows, these two special VAT regimes account for 45 percent of households' current monetary expenditures, according to the 1998 National Household Income and Expenditure Survey (*Encuesta Nacional de Ingresos y Gastos de los Hogares de 1998* [ENIGH-98]).

Figure 10.3 shows the Lorenz curve for current monetary expenditures for all goods classified in these VAT regimes (zero-rate, exemption, and general rate), ordering individuals according to the total current per capita income of the households in which they live.[9]

9. This measure is more refined than the one presented in the (printed) tables of the 1998 ENIGH (INEGI 2000), which employs household deciles according to their current monetary income. Total current income takes nonmonetary income into account (such as self-consumption, payments in kind, and the imputed rent of owned housing, either borrowed or received as fringe benefit), and the expression in per capita terms corrects for differences in household size. From here on, decile distribution will refer to deciles of individuals according to total per capita current income of the households they inhabit.

One can gather from these two figures that, although goods and services under the zero-rate regime show a smaller concentration than the rest, 35.1 percent of the implicit subsidy is captured by the last two deciles, 69.2 percent by the last five, and only 8.1 percent by the first two. This means that, for every peso of revenue forgone due to the zero-rate regime, only around thirty cents reach the poorest half of the population. In the case of exempt goods and services, the distribution of the implicit subsidy is still more unfavorable: 51.3 percent goes to the last two deciles, 81.7 percent to the last five, and only 3.6 percent to the first two. This means that, for every peso of revenue forgone due to the exemption regime, less than twenty cents reach the poorest half of the population.

These results may be analyzed from a different perspective, considering the impact of a decrease in the VAT's general rate: given the distribution of expenditures on goods and services under the general regime (15 percent rate), the distribution of the implicit subsidy associated with a rate decrease would be equally unfavorable: 59.8 percent of the revenue forgone would benefit the last two deciles, 84.7 percent the last five, and only 1.5 percent the first two.

Based on these findings, we conclude that the VAT's special regimes (or any decrease in the general rate) are neither efficient nor effective mechanisms to transfer income to the poor population. As was pointed out earlier, this results from the fact that a high concentration of wealth and income determines a high concentration of consumption, including items considered basic, such as food. Therefore, the implicit subsidy or revenue loss stemming from the special regimes goes, to a great extent, to high-income groups (or, at least, to the population that is not poor).

10.4 A VAT Reform That Eliminates Special Regimes

10.4.1 Slutsky Compensations

Following the previous discussion, it would be desirable to eliminate the VAT special regimes, as long as low-income households are compensated for the loss of the implicit subsidies received through them. We propose a Slutsky compensation, to be achieved by direct transfers of monetary income to poor households.[10] To model this, we assume a market economy in

10. As is well known, the Slutsky compensation of a price increase is calculated to allow the consumer to acquire, if he so wishes, the same basket than before the change in prices. Conversely, the Hicks compensation is calculated so that the basket acquired by the consumer under the new situation remains indifferent with regard to the original basket. In differential terms, both approaches are equivalent (and mention is made only of the Slutsky, and not the Hicks, matrix), but if the variations are discrete, the Slutsky compensation may bring about an improvement in the consumer's welfare (if preferences are strictly convex). See Mas Colell, Whinston, and Green (1995, 29–30).

which individuals are confronted with a given price vector ($\mathbf{p} = [p_j]$),[11] which increases to ($\mathbf{p}' = [p'_j]$)[12] as a result of the disappearance of the VAT special regimes, so that

$$(1) \qquad \Delta\mathbf{p} = \mathbf{p}' - \mathbf{p}.$$

We assume that every individual has (not strictly) monotonous and convex (but not homothetic) preferences. The hth individual initially has a given income level, y_h, which increases as a result of a compensation by Δy_h, to reach y'_h. The consumption basket originally chosen by the hth individual is $\mathbf{x_h} = (x_j^{[h]})$, and after the VAT reform and the compensation it is $\boldsymbol{x}'_h = (x_j'^{[h]})$, whereas, in the absence of compensations, it would have been $\boldsymbol{x}''_h = (x_j''^{[h]})$, y_h would have remained unchanged.[13] Compensation to the hth individual is determined according to Slutsky's criterion:

$$(2) \qquad y'_h - y_h = \Delta y_h = \Delta\mathbf{p}\mathbf{x_h},$$

so that, under to the previous assumptions, $\mathbf{x}'_\mathbf{h}$ is preferred or indifferent to $\mathbf{x_h}$. Moreover, if strictly convex preferences are assumed, $\mathbf{x}'_\mathbf{h}$ is strictly preferred to $\mathbf{x_h}$. Notice that in order to calculate the amount of the compensation for each individual it is only necessary to have information on his or her consumption basket before the reform, as well as the reform's impact on prices.[14]

10.4.2 Impact on Tax Revenues

The reform we analyze is setting a 15 percent single VAT rate for all goods and services and eliminating special regimes (zero-rates and exemptions).[15] Consider a vector of (integrated) increases in VAT rates ($\Delta\mathbf{t} = [\Delta t_j]$), whose jth component is

- zero, if j is a product already under the general regime;
- 15 percent, if j is a product under the zero-rate regime; and

11. Under the convention that price vectors are row vectors and quantity vectors are column vectors.

12. This assumption allows simplifying the study of the impacts resulting from the adjustment in VAT rates. Nevertheless, in his comments to a previous version of this paper, Vito Tanzi indicated that, if a restrictive monetary policy is maintained, the rise in VAT rates would not be a reason to increase the general price level. This would imply that the impacts would appear by means of factors' real earnings and would require a much more elaborate analysis.

13. We assume in particular that the wage vector ($\mathbf{w} = w_k$], where $k = 1, \ldots, q$ indicates the specific type of labor) remains constant. In a general equilibrium context, the reform's impact on the labor market would require modeling; however, for the reasons to be stated, this is not the approach taken here.

14. It is assumed that consumption decisions are made directly by the individuals, although in practice many of them are made at the household level, which expresses, in a smaller scale, the problems related with Arrow's General Possibility Theorem and would lead us to household decisions. These complications are ignored in this paper.

15. We also assess a possible decrease in the general rate to 13 percent. The corresponding calculations are omitted in order to simplify the presentation, but are available for interested readers to analyze.

- a percentage based on the value added share in the final stage of production in the price of product j, if j was under the exemption regime.

The economy's consumption vector before the VAT reform ($\mathbf{x} = [x_j]$) is the sum of the individual consumption demands:

$$\mathbf{x} = \sum_{\mathbf{h}} \mathbf{x_h} \tag{3}$$

By analogy,

$$\mathbf{x}' = \sum_{\mathbf{h}} \mathbf{x}'_{\mathbf{h}} \tag{4}$$

$$\mathbf{x}'' = \sum_{\mathbf{h}} \mathbf{x}''_{\mathbf{h}}. \tag{5}$$

Based on the above, the impact on tax revenues (ΔR) of eliminating the special VAT regimes, in the absence of any compensation, would be

$$\Delta R = \sum_j (\Delta t_j) p_j x''_j. \tag{6}$$

This impact, expressed in pesos of December 2000,[16] is estimated at 81.3 billion pesos.[17] Note that this calculation excludes revenues obtained from taxing the remaining components of final demand.[18] In principle, estimates of ΔR's must take into account a certain degree of tax evasion. On the other hand, however, the presence of a single rate, constant through time, significantly simplifies auditing and, therefore, tends to reduce evasion and increase revenues. We ignore both considerations and set a value for ΔR that, on balance, could be considered conservative.

The VAT in Mexico is a federal tax subject to revenue-sharing with local governments (states and municipalities) as set in the *Ley de Coordinación Fiscal* (Fiscal Coordination Law). If λ is the share of revenues transferred to states and municipalities, then

$$\Delta R_F = (1 - \lambda)\Delta R \tag{7}$$

$$\Delta R_L = \lambda \Delta R, \tag{8}$$

where subindexes F and L refer to the federal and local (states and municipalities together) levels of government, respectively.

We assume that compensation to consumers is paid by the federal gov-

16. Every monetary figure is expressed in December 2000 pesos.

17. In fact, for lack of sufficient information, the calculations were carried out using vector $\mathbf{x}$ and not $\mathbf{x}''$, which may imply a certain overestimate—which, nevertheless, is countered by two significant underestimations. First, employing ENIGH-98 data ignores income and consumption-level improvements between 1998 and 2000; second, the national accounts data are not made compatible, and the correction of the underestimation that may exist in the ENIGH-98 is omitted (the latter is discussed in section 10.5).

18. Such omission is justified, in part, because taxing government consumption would not represent any additional net revenues for the public sector, and exports are exempt from VAT.

ernment, so that ΔR_F is the upper bound on resources available for that purpose. Since currently $\lambda = 0.33$, ΔR is divided into 54.5 billion pesos for the federal government and 26.5 billion for states and municipalities. We take λ as constant, although it might be possible that it could change as part of the VAT reform.

10.4.3 Impact on Prices

We assume that, for the jth product, only a fraction $\alpha_j \in [0, 1]$ of the increase in the VAT rate is transferred to the price paid by consumers, so that

$$\Delta p_j = \alpha_j(\Delta t_j)p_j, \tag{9}$$

and substituting equation (9) in equation (2):

$$\Delta y_h = \sum_j \alpha_j(\Delta t_j)p_j x_j^{(h)}, \tag{10}$$

so that the values of α_j play a crucial role in determining individuals' compensations.[19]

In perfectly competitive markets $\alpha_j = 1$, and the entire change in the VAT rate is transferred to final consumers. This may be the case, for example, of perfectly tradable goods, or goods produced under constant returns to scale. Nevertheless, it is also possible that $\alpha_j < 1$, as may be the case, for example, of imperfectly tradable goods for which the law of one price does not hold (if there is some trading, transportation, or local distribution component). Alternatively, there may be imperfect competition in some markets (e.g., medicines) that prevents the entire transfer of the VAT increase into the price faced by consumers, resulting instead in a compression of price-cost margins.

In cases where $\alpha_j < 1$, it is clear that price-cost margins are income for certain households, so that, to the extent these margins contract as a result of a change in the VAT regime, these households' incomes will decrease. In addition, the VAT reform in principle should also affect the wage vector $\mathbf{w}$, with subsequent impacts on price-cost margins.

To formally capture these phenomena, it would be necessary to model the VAT reform in a general equilibrium context. The cost of this, however, is to introduce a large number of quantitative parameters that are highly difficult to estimate, reducing the reliability of the numerical calculations, which are one of the core interests of this paper. Therefore, we set out two solutions. First, we assume that owners of productive assets in sectors featuring imperfect competition—where reductions in the price-cost margins would occur—are individuals in the last two and one-half deciles of the income distribution, who are not considered for compensations in any of the scenarios contemplated below. Therefore, the whole weight of the VAT re-

19. The analysis of the monetary theory aspects discussed in note 12 is omitted in the following paragraphs.

form would fall on such individuals, both in their role as consumers and as receivers of monopolistic rents.

Second, and given the practical relevance of price impacts (Δp_j), we propose a simple mechanism that takes advantage, if the reform was carried out, of the actual information about the path followed by prices after the reform and that, ex post, guarantees the target population that compensations according to equation (10) entirely reflect price increases generated by the reform. In order to do that,

- Set a fixed time period, $\Delta\tau$, for the VAT reform to fully affect prices, beginning at the moment the reform is carried out, τ_0.
- Estimate the price vector ($\hat{\mathbf{p}} = [\hat{p}_j]$[20]) at the date $\tau_1 = \tau_0 + \Delta\tau$ under the assumption that there is no VAT reform, so that $\hat{p}$ only reflects inflation expectations.
- At the date τ_1, use observed prices after the reform ($\hat{\mathbf{p}}' = [p_j']$[21]) to determine the vector[22]

$$\Delta\mathbf{p} = \mathbf{p}' - \hat{\mathbf{p}}, \tag{11}$$

which serves as basis to grant compensations.[23]

Figure 10.4 exemplifies this for the *j*th good or service. The continuous line shows the path actually followed by the price of the *j*th product up to the moment τ_0, that is, before the reform, and the dotted line signals the expected price path after τ_0 in the absence of VAT reforms. The continuous line to the right of τ_0 would, if applicable, represent the actual path after the reform has been carried out. Therefore, once the period $\Delta\tau$ has elapsed after the reform, there is a difference between the actual price (p_j') and the price estimated in the absence of reform ($\hat{p}_j$), which helps determine the amount of compensation to grant.

We can, ex post, calculate the α_j implicit in the price paths. Taking equations (9) and (11) results in

$$\alpha_j = \frac{p_j' - \hat{p}_j}{(\Delta t_j)\hat{p}_j} \tag{12}$$

and may be aggregated into an α index,

$$\alpha = \sum_{j=1}^{n} \alpha_j \theta_j, \tag{13}$$

20. To simplify notation, the index indicating the date the price vector (τ_1) is omitted.

21. Likewise, the date index is omitted.

22. So that equation (11) substitutes, in practice, equation (1).

23. It is assumed above that compensations are paid ex post (on date τ_1). If they were to be paid ex ante (on date τ_1) it would require estimating the expected price increase as a result of the reform ($\Delta\hat{p}$), from estimated coefficients $\hat{\alpha}_j$: $\Delta\hat{p}_j = \hat{\alpha}_j (\Delta t_j)\hat{p}_j$, in order to obtain the expected prices after the reform: $\hat{\mathbf{p}}' = \hat{\mathbf{p}} + \Delta\hat{\mathbf{p}}$, which would serve as basis to grant the (initial) compensations. If $p' > \hat{p}'$, complementary compensations would be granted ex post.

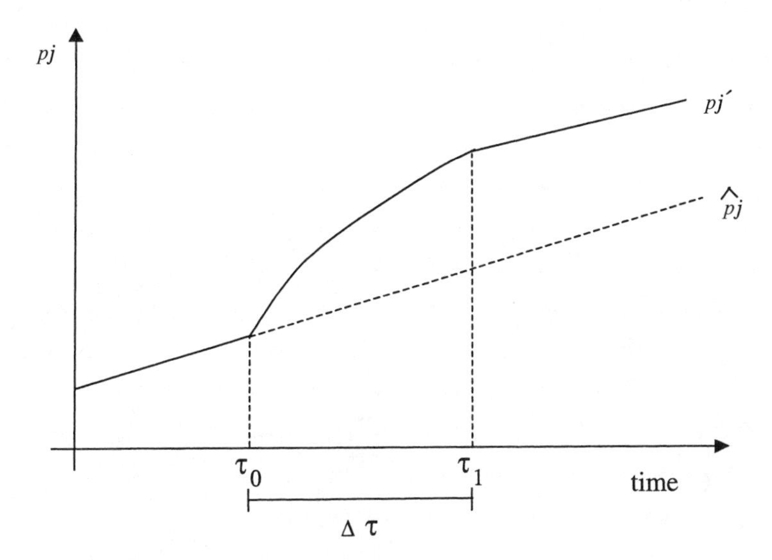

Fig. 10.4 Path followed by the price of the *j*th good or service

where θ_j is the weight of the *j*th good or service in the consumer price index (henceforth INPC, from the Spanish *Índice Nacional de Precios al Consumidor*).[24]

In the rest of this paper we present simulations for four different values of α, namely, 0.25, 0.50, 0.75, and 1.00. On this basis, table 10.1 shows the reform's impact on the INPC and on the cost of the basic food basket (CCBA, from the Spanish *Costo de la Canasta Básica Alimentaria*).

As can be seen from table 10.1, when $\alpha = 1.00$, the impact on the CCBA is 15 percent, which derives from the fact that the basic food basket is currently subject to the zero-rate regime and would become part of the general regime at a rate of 15 percent. The impact on the INPC would be much lower because, as shown in figure 10.2, more than half of households' spending goes to goods and services subject to the general regime, and due to the fact that eliminating the exemption regime would have an impact of less than 15 percent, because the additional tax only affects the added value in the last stage of production.

10.4.4 Relative Impacts on Household Spending

Figure 10.5 shows the estimated percentage impact of the VAT reform on the current monetary spending of different households for various values of

24. For consistency purposes, weights based on the ENIGH-98 were employed in the simulations instead of the weights used by Banco de México that are modified with large intervals. The econometric estimations carried out by the Ministry of Finance (Secretaría de Hacienda y Crédito Público) in 1997 suggest a $\alpha = 0.50$ value based on the experience of the VAT general rate change carried out in 1991.

Table 10.1 Impact of the VAT Reform on Price Indexes (%)

	α			
Index	0.25	0.50	0.75	1.00
CCBA	3.8	7.5	11.3	15.0
INPC	1.6	3.2	4.7	6.3

Note: See text for abbreviations.

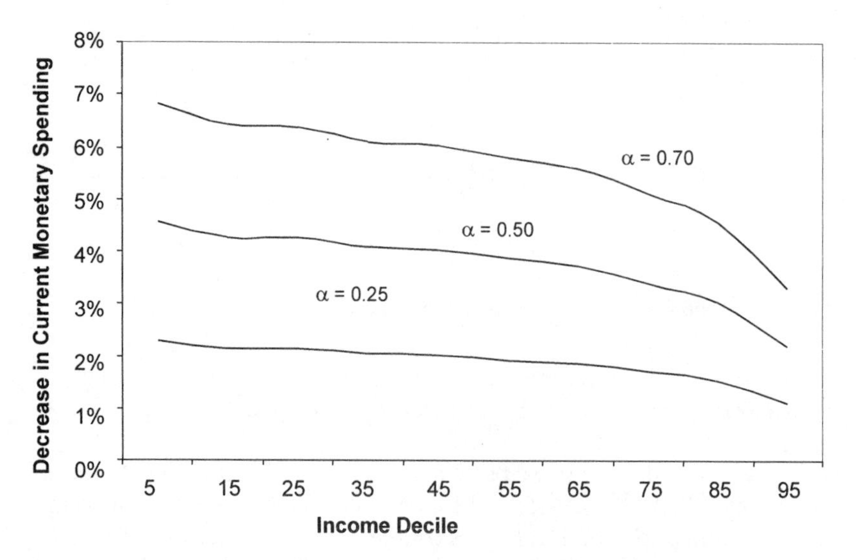

Fig. 10.5 Impact of VAT reform on current monetary spending (%)

α.[25] Clearly, the percentage impact on the 1st decile is much larger than on the 10th. Even in the intermediate case in which $\alpha = 0.50$, eliminating special regimes would be equal to an almost 5 percent decrease in consumption for households in the first two deciles. Therefore, it is essential that changes in the VAT be complemented by compensating measures that are clearly redistributive.

10.5 Target Image for Compensations

This section presents a target image for compensations, which we translate, in later sections, into operational strategies given the heterogeneous

25. Calculating these impacts evidently requires knowledge of vector $\mathbf{a} = [\alpha_j]$. The extreme assumption that $\forall j$: $\alpha_j = \alpha$ was employed in these exercises, but, if additional information is available, it is possible to recalculate the impacts for α_j differing among themselves. This applies for every numerical exercise to be presented.

features of the population to be compensated. The target image contemplates two basic aspects: the set of people for whom compensation is desirable (target population), and the desirable size of compensation to grant to each individual.

10.5.1 Target Population

Assume there are m individuals in the country, ordered by an increasing function of their income:

$$y_h \leq y_{h+1} \quad h = 1, \ldots, m-1, \tag{14}$$

so that y_1 and y_m, respectively, represent the income level of the poorest and the richest individual in the country. Let $y^* \in [y_1, y_m]$ be the income level that separates the population M into two sets:

$$M_a = \{h \mid y_h \leq y^*\} \tag{15}$$

$$M_b = \{h \mid y_h > y^*\}, \tag{16}$$

where M_a is the population set that should be compensated for the VAT reform, and M_b (its complement) is the population set that would pay fully for the reform. Recalling that # is the operator that counts the elements on the set formed by the operand, we have

$$m_a = \#(M_a) \tag{17}$$

$$m_b = \#(M_b) = m - m_a \tag{18}$$

so that

$$\beta = \frac{m_a}{m} \tag{19}$$

is the share of the total population that will be compensated.

Notice that, under the assumption that equation (14) describes a strictly increasing function, there is a one-to-one relationship between y^* and β. Therefore, we can either set an income level y^* to divide the population into low- and high-income groups, or alternatively set a share β of the population to be compensated, which implicitly defines a y^* income level that partitions the population into two subsets.[26] The value of y^* could, for example, stand for a line of the extreme poverty (so that M_a would be the extremely poor population). However, this is not the only possibility, because M_a could also include those in moderate poverty, by setting a higher value for y^*. Since discussing the specific value of y^* would stray from the purposes of this paper, from here on the discussion will focus on the value of β, which

26. Although only the β such that $\beta m \in \mathbb{N}$, the set of natural numbers, would be strictly admissible, and that each would correspond with an *interval* of possible values $y^* : y^* \in [y_{\beta m}, y_{\beta m+1})$, where $\beta m = m_a$.

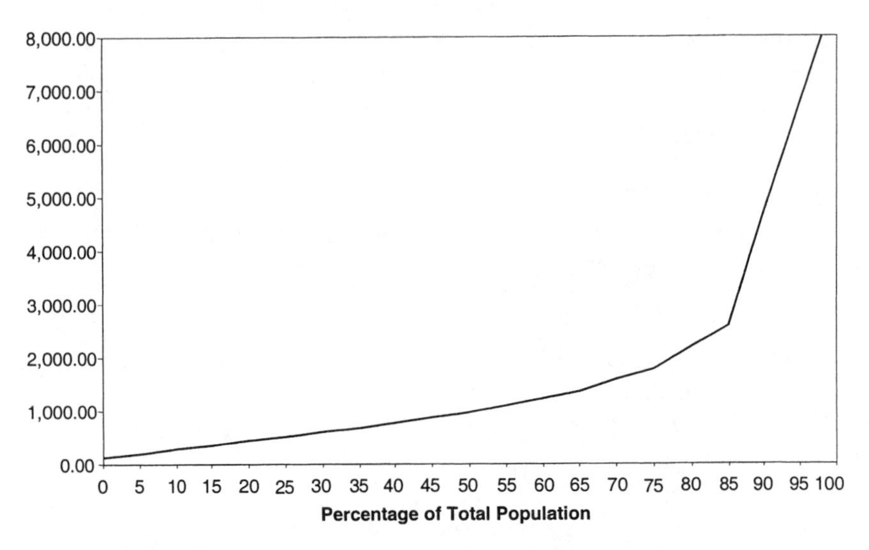

Fig. 10.6 Total per capita monthly current income, 1998 (pesos)

has a clear intuitive interpretation, and we will make calculations for four values of this parameter: 0.25, 0.50, 0.75, and 1.00 (the last one in order to assess the consistency of such calculations).

Total per capita monthly current income for all household members (y_h) in 1998 is shown in figure 10.6.

In principle, the area under the curve should equal aggregate household income, as reported in the National Accounts System (*Sistema de Cuentas Nacionales de México* [SCNM]) for 1998, but this is not the case because aggregate income in the 1998 ENIGH is significantly below that reported in the SCNM.[27] However, we did not carry out any adjustments to reconcile the data, because, first, the discrepancy with the SNCM is most likely attributed to the fact that the 1998 ENIGH does not fully capture (due to differentiated nonanswering) higher-income households,[28] which is why the adjustment does not affect the middle- and low-income households, which are the ones of interest for the compensation strategy. Second, underdeclaring is concentrated in the last deciles of income distribution, and thus it has little practical relevance in terms of defining the potential target population to be compensated when considering instances where $\beta \leq 0.75$.

In any case, income differences captured by the 1998 ENIGH are suffi-

27. According to the SCNM for 1998, households' net disposable income is twice the total household current income registered in the ENIGH-98.

28. That is, although the richest households in the country are sometimes part of the ENIGH, the probability that they answer a survey is very low (much lower than for the middle- and low-income households).

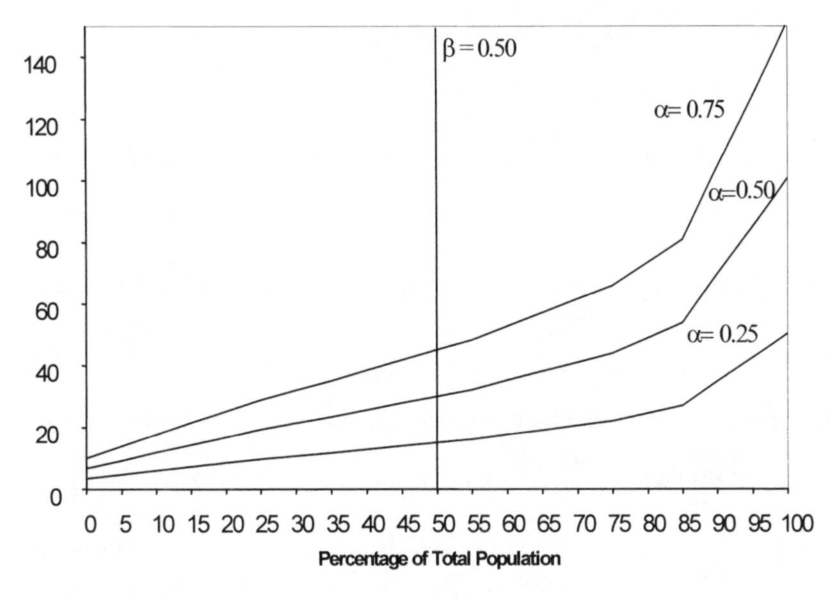

Fig. 10.7 Slutsky compensations (monthly pesos)

ciently large to make compensating the whole population unadvisable, which is why we work with values for β that are strictly less than 1.

10.5.2 Exact Compensations

Figure 10.7 shows the monthly amounts of the Slutsky compensation for the average households in each income decile, that is, the values of Δy_h according to equation (10).[29] As one can see, the Slutsky compensation (for a given value of α) is an increasing function of income.[30] The area under such function, up to a given value of β (arbitrarily fixed at 0.50 in figure 10.7), stands for the total fiscal cost of the exact compensations granted to all individuals, which we will designate as CE (an increasing function of m, α, and β):

$$\text{CE}(m, \alpha, \beta) = \sum_{h=1}^{\beta m} \Delta y_h \quad (20)$$

29. The ENIGH-98 database was used to disaggregate each household's expenditure for goods and services considered under the general regime and those under special regimes: zero-rate (aggregate) and exemption (disaggregated, in order to take into account the differences in value added percentages in the last stage). Nevertheless, with the purpose of lessening the effect of buying pattern irregularities (as well as of sample variations), impact estimates were carried out for the average individual in each decile.

30. It should be noted that it does not necessarily have to be so. If goods and services subject to special regimes, taken together, behaved as an inferior good from a certain income level, the Slutsky compensation curve would decrease from that income level. However, for the Mexican case, the goods and services subject to special regimes, taken together, behave as normal goods, so that the Slutsky compensation monotonously increases with income levels.

Table 10.2 Fiscal Cost of Exact Compensations (billions of pesos)

α/β	0.25	0.50	0.75	1.00
0.25	1.9	3.8	5.7	7.6
0.50	5.5	11.0	16.5	22.0
0.75	10.8	21.7	32.5	43.4
1.00	20.3	40.7	61.0	81.3

On the other hand, the total cost of the exact compensations, CE(.), must satisfy the following budget constraint:

$$\text{(21)} \qquad CE(m, \alpha, \beta) \leq (1 - \lambda)\Delta R = \Delta R_F,$$

that is, the total cost cannot exceed the additional resources available to the federal government as a result of the VAT reform. Table 10.2 presents estimates of CE for selected values of α and β and for an m equivalent to 97.4 million individuals.[31]

Because, as was indicated earlier, ΔR_F is equal to 54.5 billion pesos, it is clear that, even under the most pessimistic assumptions of the impact of the reform on prices ($\alpha = 1.00$), it is possible to compensate up to 75 percent of the population ($\beta = 0.75$) and still have resources left over. This, in the end, is a reflection of Mexico's sharp income concentration.[32]

10.5.3 Uniform Compensations

Although, in principle, every individual should receive his or her exact compensation (which would differ among individuals, given the assumption in equation (14) that $y_h < y_{h+1}$), this may not be feasible in practice, due to the difficulty of having information on each individual's consumption basket, $\boldsymbol{x}_h$, as well as mechanisms to transfer income to each individual.

Thus, alternatively, we may consider a uniform compensation (Δy) for the whole target population.[33] To consider this, we introduce a new parameter, $\gamma \in [0, 1]$, that measures the share of the target population that is overcompensated: that is, the population receiving a compensation Δy, which is greater than Δy_h, the Slutsky compensation. Consequently, $(1 - \gamma)$ is the share of the target population that is undercompensated (for which $\Delta y < \Delta y_h$). The uniform compensation is set (for a given value of α) in terms of the individual that is nearest to $\gamma\beta m$, that is:

$$\text{(22)} \qquad \Delta y = \Delta y_{R(\gamma\beta m)},$$

31. According to the 12th General Population and Housing Census (*XII Censo General de Población y Vivienda*), 2000.

32. Notice that for $\alpha = \beta = 1$ the fiscal cost of exact compensations equals ΔR (i.e., the total additional revenues). The consistency in this derives from the fact that we also used ENIGH-98 consumption data to calculate additional revenue.

33. This clearly represents the other extreme instance. According to the available tools, uniform compensations for target population subsets may also be considered.

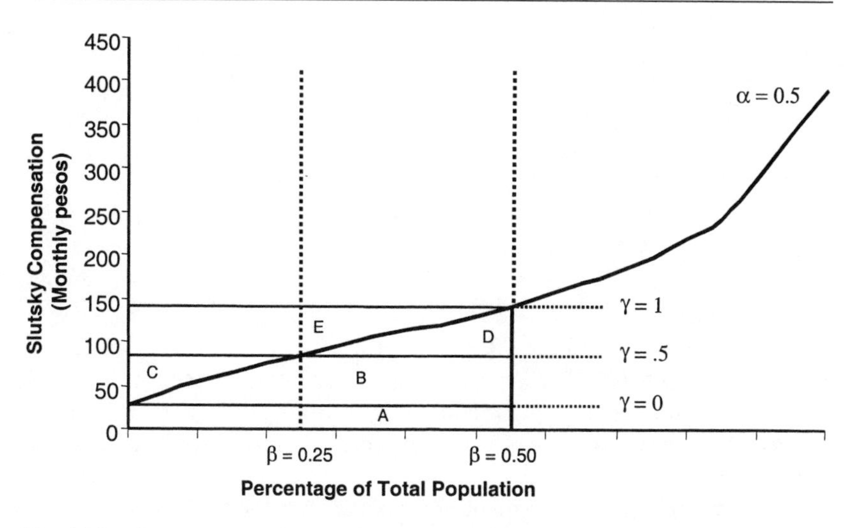

Fig. 10.8 Overcompensation and undercompensation

where $R(.)$ is the round-off function to the nearest positive integer, so that $\Delta y = \Delta y_h$, for the h nearest to $\gamma\beta m$.[34] Therefore, if $\gamma = 0$, the poorest individual will be taken as reference point and the entire target population, with the exception of this individual, will be undercompensated. On the other end, when $\gamma = 1$, the compensation is established in terms of the marginal individual of the target population (the least poor), so that the rest of the target population is overcompensated. Lastly, if $\gamma = 0.5$, the compensation is set for the individual in the middle of the target population, with half overcompensated (those with the lowest incomes) and the other half undercompensated.

The fiscal cost of a uniform compensation to every individual in the target population is designated as CU, an increasing function of m, α, β, and γ:

$$\text{CU}(m, \alpha, \beta, \gamma) = m\beta\Delta y \tag{23}$$

The uniform compensation is shown in figure 10.8, where, to simplify, we only graph the Slutsky function (Δy_h) for $\alpha = 0.50$ and set $\beta = 0.50$.

When $\gamma = 0$, the total cost of a uniform compensation for the entire target population is A and we undercompensate, vis-à-vis the exact compensation, every individual in the target population—except the poorest—by a total amount $B + D$. When $\gamma = 0.5$, the total cost of a uniform compensation is $C + B + A$, overcompensating, vis-à-vis the exact compensation, the poorest 25 percent of the population by C, and undercompensating the next poorest 25 percent by D. When $\gamma = 1$, the total cost of a uniform compen-

34. Because the exact value of this expression might not be a positive integer, as happens, in particular, if $\gamma = 0$.

Table 10.3 Annual Fiscal Cost of Uniform Compensations (billions of pesos)

	0.00				0.50				1.00			
$\gamma/\alpha/\beta$	0.25	0.50	0.75	1.00	0.25	0.50	0.75	1.00	0.25	0.50	0.75	1.00
0.25	1.0	1.9	2.9	3.9	1.9	3.8	5.7	7.6	2.8	5.6	8.5	11.3
0.50	1.9	3.9	5.8	7.7	5.6	11.3	16.9	22.6	8.8	17.5	26.3	35.1
0.75	2.9	5.8	8.7	11.6	10.7	21.5	32.2	43.0	19.3	38.5	57.8	77.1
1.00	3.9	7.7	11.6	15.4	17.5	35.1	52.6	70.2	52.9	105.9	158.8	211.7

sation is $A + B + C + E + D$, overcompensating the entire target population, except for the marginal individual, by a total amount $C + E$.

Table 10.3 shows the fiscal cost of uniform compensations for selected values of α, β, and γ.[35]

Uniform compensations also need to meet a budget constraint analogous to equation (21). Since ΔR_F amounts to 54.5 billion pesos, it is clear that for $\alpha \geq 0.75$ and $\beta \geq 0.75$, overcompensating the entire target population is not feasible (i.e., $\gamma = 1.00$).[36] What is surprising, however, is that it would still be feasible to do so for the remaining cases, which illustrates the wide room to maneuver generated by the VAT reform. In particular, if $\alpha = 0.50$[37] and $\beta = 0.75$, it is possible to overcompensate the entire target population and still obtain surplus revenues for the federal government.

As noted before, uniform compensations either under- or overcompensate part of the target population, depending on γ's value. When $\gamma = 1.00$, the entire target population is overcompensated, except for the last individual, and the total cost of a uniform compensation will exceed the total cost of the exact compensation. Intuitively the difference can be seen as a measure of the *redistributive effort* (beyond Slutsky's compensation) associated with the VAT reform; that is, a measure of the *additional income* received by the lowest-income households.

Table 10.4 shows, for $\gamma = 1.00$, the differences between the exact and uniform compensations for selected values of α and β. Clearly, the redistributive effort is an increasing function of β because, as β increases, not only does the target population increase, but also—given the population ordering in equation (14)—the marginal individual taken as reference for compensation has a higher income, and we have empirically found that the Slutsky compensation is an increasing function of income. Therefore, when β increases, the amount of the uniform compensation increases as well, which, in turn, broadens the gap between it and the exact compensation,

35. For the reasons set forth in note 22, data for $\gamma = 0.00$ and $\gamma = 1.00$ are obtained by interpolating, despite the fact that data for the poorest and the richest individual are available in ENIGH-98.

36. Neither would it be feasible for $\alpha = 0.50$ and $\beta = 1.00$.

37. A value that, as expressed in note 24, is consistent with the econometric estimations available.

Table 10.4 Redistributive Effort (billions of pesos)

α/β	0.25	0.50	0.75	1.00
0.25	0.9	1.8	2.8	3.7
0.50	3.3	6.6	9.8	13.1
0.75	8.4	16.8	25.2	33.7
1.00	32.6	65.2	97.8	130.4

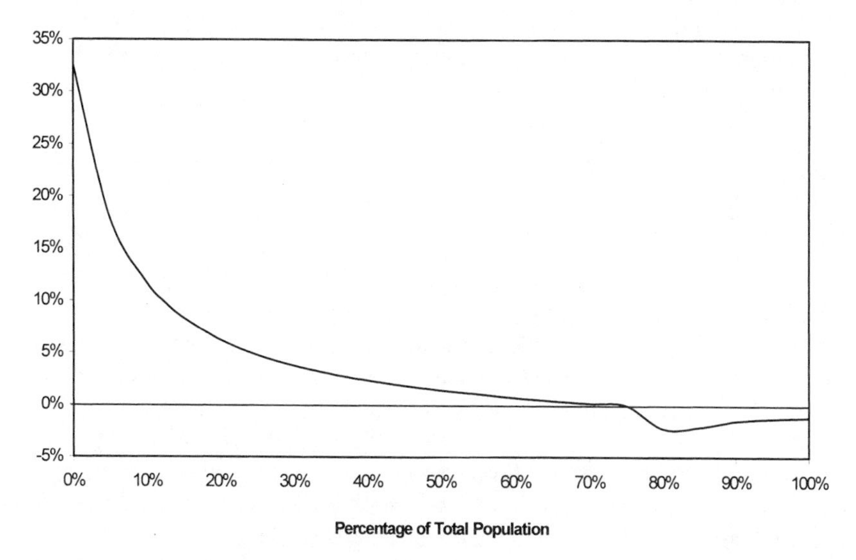

Fig. 10.9 Redistributive impact by income decile (%)

particularly benefiting lower-income individuals. Figure 10.9 shows the gap between the exact and the uniform compensation, by income levels, for $\gamma = 1$ as a function of α and β.

Clearly, the VAT reform accompanied by the proposed compensations has a clear redistributive effect, since lower-income households in the target population obtain an additional transfer equal to the gap (for $\gamma = 1.00$) between the uniform and the exact compensation. When $\beta = 0.75$, this additional income is equivalent to 33 percent for the poorest individual in the population and to 5 percent for the marginal individual in the first quartile.[38] Conversely, the high-income individuals must absorb a reduction in their income equivalent to the Slutsky compensation. When $\beta = 0.75$, this effect is confined to the last quartile of the population, the point where incomes increase substantially according to figure 10.6. We can translate all this in terms of Gini indexes. In the absence of the reform, this index stands

38. The marginal individual in the extremely poor population, as will be made clear in the next section, when the Education, Health, and Food Program, Progresa, is examined.

at 51.4. With the VAT reform, but in the absence of compensations, it increases to 51.8. However, with the VAT reform and with a uniform compensation it is equal to 50.2 (50.8) when $\beta = 0.75$ (0.50).[39]

In sum, in a country with an extremely skewed income distribution like Mexico, it is feasible to overcompensate the lower-income population for a change in the VAT rate, transferring *additional* resources to this population, improving income distribution as a result of the reform and, at the same time, to experience a significant rise in tax revenues, net of compensations. Therefore, in these circumstances, the distributive problem associated with a change in VAT rates is not a budgetary matter but, as is made clear in the following section, a matter of tools.

10.6 Compensation Tools

10.6.1 General Introduction

The compensations set out in the previous section may be carried out by means of several tools. For the reasons expressed before, these tools should allow monetary transfers to be made to individual households. In this way, families may receive a benefit at least equivalent to (or greater than) the monetary sacrifice implicit in the VAT reform.

Assume there are l tools with such features, indexed by $i(i = 1 \ldots, l)$. Each tool has a well-defined target population (set M_i^*), although the population it actually reaches (set M_i) may be different, due to inclusion (set I_i) and exclusion (set E_i) errors specific to each tool. Then

$$E_i = M_i^* - M_i \tag{24}$$

$$I_i = M_i - M_i^* \tag{25}$$

Also, let m_i^* represent the size of the target population of the ith tool and m_i the size of the population actually reached by it, that is,

$$m_i^* = \#(M_i^*) \tag{26}$$

$$m_i = \#(M_i), \tag{27}$$

so that the target population is the population actually reached plus the exclusion errors, minus the inclusion errors:

$$m_i^* = m_i + \#(E_i) - \#(I_i) \tag{28}$$

Following the discussion in the previous section, we assume that, due to operational constraints, individuals with different income levels in a population reached by the same tool cannot be distinguished, so that all individuals in that population receive the same income transfer, delivered by the ith

39. Given, as noted before, $\alpha = 0.50$ and $\gamma = 1.00$.

tool, of an amount Δy_i.[40] Therefore, the fiscal cost of feasible compensations (CF) will be

$$\text{CF} = \sum_{i=1}^{1} m_i \Delta y_i, \tag{29}$$

which is the total population reached by each tool, with the corresponding compensation. We assume that, given the population reached by each tool, $\Delta y_i s$ are set in such a way that a budget constraint like equation (21) is maintained.

The family of sets $\{M_i\}$ should ideally constitute a partition of set M_a, that is, of the target population set according to equation (15), such that the entire target population is covered by compensations:

$$M_a = \cup_{i=1}^{l} M_i, \tag{30}$$

that is, that each individual in the target population is reached by at least one tool. In addition, each individual would be reached by only one tool:

$$i \neq s\colon M_i \cap M_s = \phi, \tag{31}$$

where ϕ is the empty set, so that belonging to a population reached by one tool would exclude belonging to a population reached by another tool.

This situation represents a theoretical ideal only for compensation purposes. Nonetheless, this is not likely at all, and the following will usually exist, for the tool set:

- exclusion errors given by set E:

$$E = M - \cup_{i=1}^{l} M_i, \tag{32}$$

  formed by those individuals who are eligible for compensation but do not belong to any of the populations reached by the available tools;
- inclusion errors, given by set I:

$$I = M_b \cap (\cup_{i=1}^{l} M_i), \tag{33}$$

  formed by those individuals not eligible for compensation (since they have an income above y^*) but who will nonetheless receive it because they belong to the population reached by one of the tools; and
- duplication errors, formed by the family of sets: $\{D_{is} \mid i = 1, \ldots 1; s = i + 1, \ldots 1\}$, where

$$D_{is} = M_i \cap M_s, \tag{34}$$

  since it is possible that some individuals simultaneously belong to two or more populations reached by different tools and may therefore re-

40. In fact, even if there is information available on individuals' incomes, it may be convenient not to employ it and maintain a uniform transfer, in order not to distort incentives.

ceive more than one compensation; such duplication errors are summarized in the set[41]

(35) $$D = \cup_{s=i+1}^{l} \cup_{i+1}^{l} D_{is}.$$

Note that inclusion and exclusion errors thus defined refer to all tools taken together and cannot be obtained mechanically by aggregating inclusion and exclusion errors of each tool.

The fiscal cost of feasible compensations is the cost of the uniform compensation, plus the cost of the compensations given to the population erroneously included, minus the cost of the compensations that should have been given to the population erroneously excluded, plus the cost of duplication errors. For the simple case when $\forall i$: $\Delta y_i = \Delta y$, this is

(36) $$\text{CF} = \text{CU} + \Delta y[\#(I) - \#(E) + \sum_{s=i+1}^{1} \sum_{i=1}^{1} \#(D_{is})].$$

10.6.2 Specific Instruments

In Mexico there is a limited number of tools available to carry out direct monetary income transfers; here we focus on three:

1. The Education, Health, and Nutrition Program (*Programa de Educación, Salud, y Alimentación,* or Progresa)
2. Government contributions to individual retirement accounts created with the Social Security Law[42]
3. Pensions paid by social security[43]

To simplify, we assume that the compensation granted through each tool is the same: that is, $\Delta y_1 = \Delta y_2 = \Delta y_3 = \Delta y$. As discussed, the specific amount of Δy corresponding to the uniform compensation depends on α, β, and γ, as shown in table 10.5.

Education, Health, and Nutrition Program (Progresa)

The first tool to consider ($i = 1$) is the Education, Health, and Nutrition Program, Progresa, focused on the extremely poor population. Progresa's target population (M_1^*) is about 25 percent of the entire population, or approximately 25 million individuals (m_1^*). It thus covers the first two and one-

41. However, evidently the data of tripling (or quadrupling, etc.) observed when analyzing the entire family of sets D_{is} are lost.

42. Complemented by rises in the monetary benefits received by public-sector workers.

43. The Direct Agricultural Support Program (*Programa de Apoyos Directos al Campo* [Procampo]) grants direct monetary transfers to agricultural producers, but only those who prove that they grew a selected group of products before trade opening (the products most affected by such an opening). This restriction makes it difficult to employ it for general compensation purposes, which is why it is not considered among the tools under analysis.

Table 10.5 **Uniform per-capita Compensation (pesos per month)**

	0.00				0.50				1.00			
γ/α/β	0.25	0.50	0.75	1.00	0.25	0.50	0.75	1.00	0.25	0.50	0.75	1.00
0.25	3.31	6.61	9.92	13.22	6.54	13.08	19.61	26.15	9.66	19.31	28.97	38.62
0.50	3.31	6.61	9.92	13.22	9.66	19.31	28.97	38.62	15.02	30.04	45.06	60.08
0.75	3.31	6.61	9.92	13.22	12.26	24.51	36.77	49.03	21.98	43.97	65.95	87.93
1.00	3.31	6.61	9.92	13.22	15.02	30.04	45.06	60.08	45.31	90.61	135.92	181.23

half of the 3rd decile and matches the target population for compensation when $\beta = 0.25$.

Nevertheless, Progresa currently operates only in rural areas (those with less than 2,500 inhabitants) and in smaller urban areas (2,500 to 14,999 inhabitants),[44] so its current coverage (M_1) only reaches 14 million persons (m_1). Furthermore, approximately 2 million people belonging to the target population live in areas without the education and health services required for Progresa to operate. Thus, its potential coverage (which we designate as M'_1) reaches 23 million persons (m'_1). Therefore, there is a margin of 9 million people ($m'_1 - m_1$) to increase Progresa's coverage. Current coverage only represents 60 percent of potential coverage and 55 percent of the target population.

The fact that Progresa has not yet fully reached its potential coverage generates, by itself, a significant exclusion error, both for the program as such (in terms of its target population) and for the compensation strategy in the case of a VAT reform (in terms of the target population for compensation purposes). Consequently, the following analysis will assume that Progresa reaches its potential coverage. This still leaves the problem of those living in areas with no access to education and health services that are not part of Progresa's potential coverage. This, together with errors of the eligibility system,[45] makes Progresa's potential coverage, by income deciles, look as in figure 10.10. As shown, Progresa's potential coverage decreases with income levels, but there are significant exclusion (E'_1) and inclusion (I'_1) errors equal, respectively, to 35 percent of the target population and 32 percent of potential coverage. Their relevance to the compensation strategy, in particular their contribution to I according to equation (34), depends on the value of the β selected: if $\beta = 0.75$, Progresa practically would not generate inclusion errors, and for $\beta = 0.50$, the inclusion error would be small.

Progresa's monetary transfers consist of

44. As long as areas with very high, high, and medium-high marginality levels are concerned, according to the National Population Council's (*Consejo Nacional de Población* [Conapo]) indicators.

45. That is, per capita income of household members.

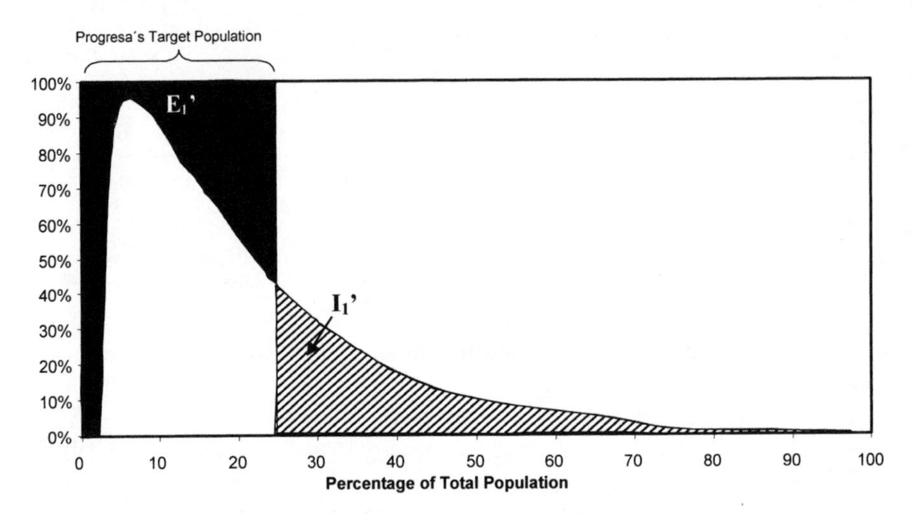

Fig. 10.10 Progresa's potential coverage (% of population)

- a basic monthly transfer of 135 pesos per household, conditioned upon its regular attendance to medical units;
- scholarships linked to school attendance, from third grade of elementary school (90 pesos) through the third year of secondary education (290 pesos for boys and 335 pesos for girls[46]); and
- resources for school supplies, from the first grade of elementary school until the third grade of secondary education.[47]

Individual Retirement Accounts

The new social security law, in effect since 1997, created individual retirement accounts (CIAs) for every worker enrolled in the Mexican Social Security Institute (*Instituto Mexicano del Seguro Social* [IMSS]), that is, for each salaried worker employed in the formal private sector. This account has two subaccounts: one for retirement and one for voluntary contributions.

The retirement account CIA receives contributions from the workers, the employers, and the federal government, the last of these contributions independent of wage levels and indexed to the INPC, amounting to 67.91 pesos per month. When workers reach sixty-five years of age, they can dispose of the balance on the retirement subaccount to acquire a pension for both themselves and their spouse and minor children. On the other hand, the voluntary subaccount may receive contributions from worker and employer

46. Gender differentiation begins in the first year of secondary education.

47. Monetary supports have an upper limit of 820 pesos per month (not taking school supplies into account). Moreover, Progresa grants in-kind support, including a basic health kit and nourishment supplements for pregnant and lactating women, as well as for every child from four months to five years of age showing signs of undernourishment.

alike, and the worker may draw on it once every six months. Therefore, deposits from the federal government into the voluntary subaccounts would represent a direct monetary transfer to workers.[48] Consequently, this would be an adequate tool to compensate salaried workers in the formal private sector, that is, the IMSS-enrolled workers and their families. Monetary fringe benefits could complementarily be increased for public-sector workers enrolled in the Institute of Security and Social Services for State Workers (*Instituto de Seguridad y Servicios Sociales de los Trabajadores del Estado* [ISSSTE]), the Social Security Institute of the Armed Forces (*Instituto de Seguridad Social de las Fuerzas Armadas* [ISSFAM]), and Petróleos Mexicanos' (PEMEX) social security scheme.

Government deposits in the voluntary subaccount, together with an increase in monetary benefits for the public-sector workers, would (jointly) constitute the second compensation tool ($i = 2$).[49] The target population of this tool consists of households with salaried members, since, according to current legislation, every salaried worker must be enrolled in a social security institution. Consequently, the exclusion error (E_2) would consist of the population living in households where there are only uninsured salaried workers, which derives from the evasion, on the part of employers, of social security obligations. On the other hand, the inclusion error (I_2) is scarcely relevant in conceptual and practical terms.[50]

Figure 10.11 shows the share of the population living in households with insured members (M_2) and with salaried, but uninsured, workers (E_2), by income decile:

Clearly the probability that an individual belongs to a household where insured workers live rises with income levels, so that compensating insured workers may give way to significant inclusion errors (I), even when applying a high β value (such as $\beta = 0.75$).

The tool's exclusion error (E_2), generated by employers' evasion of their social security duties, is significant. However, even if the coverage were to be entirely eliminated, it would remain considerably below 100 percent, which indirectly reflects the significance of self-employment in the Mexican economy as well as the intrinsic limitation of social security coverage, since salaried workers are the only ones entitled to it.[51]

48. If the VAT reform proposed here were to be carried out, it would be desirable to contemplate the possibility of modifying the social security law in order to allow more frequent—maybe even monthly—disposals, as well as to establish the possibility that the federal government can credit these accounts.

49. With the rise experienced by revenue sharing and contributions, compensating state and municipality workers would be perfectly financiable.

50. It deals with families of individuals who are nonsalaried but pretending to be salaried in order to have access to social security benefits.

51. The social security reform created the Family Health Insurance (*Seguro de Salud para la Familia* [SSF]), allowing for a voluntary kind of insurance with the same in-kind benefits granted by IMSS's Illness and Maternity Insurance (*Seguro de Enfermedades y Maternidad* [SEM]) in the compulsory regime. However, the attention mechanisms offered to the open population are still attractive, so this insurance currently covers only 0.2 million families.

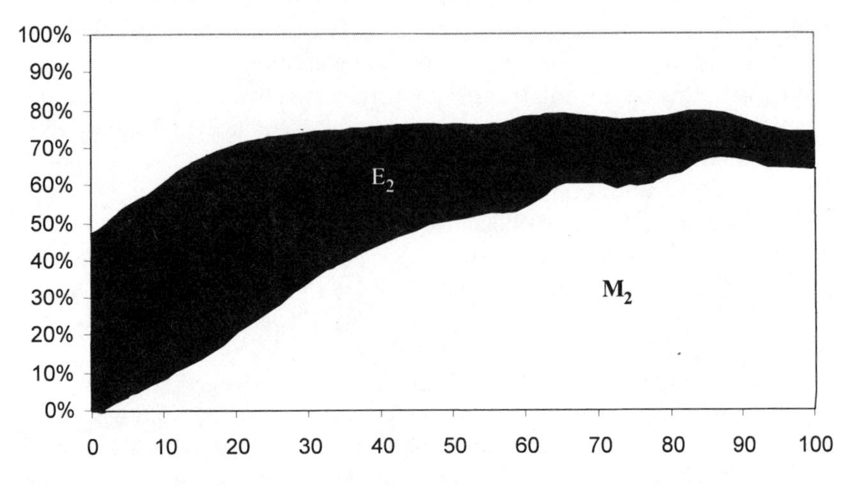

Fig. 10.11 Population living in households with salaried workers, insured and uninsured (% of population)

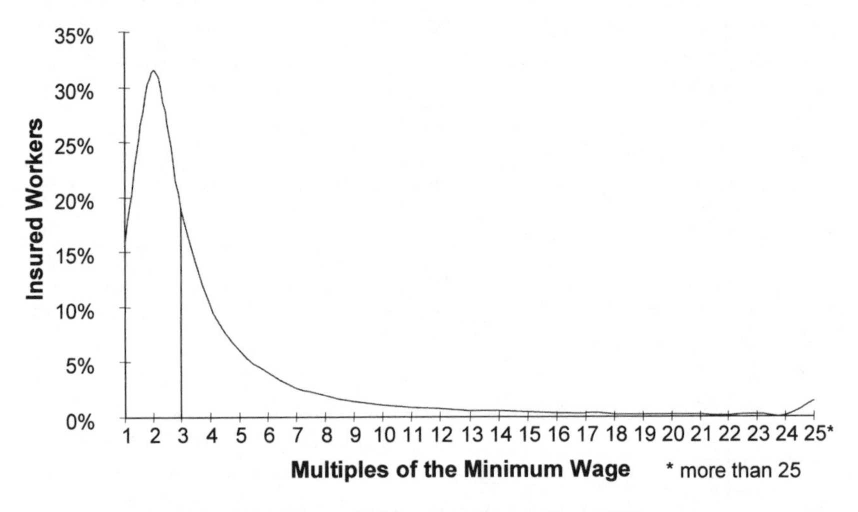

Fig. 10.12 Income of IMSS-enrolled workers (times the smDF)

It should be noted that the dispersion observed in the population linked to the formal sector among the different deciles is fundamentally due to sociodemographic factors (such as household size, number of wage-earners working in the household, and income similarities among them) and the relative slowness with which per capita income rises in deciles 2 through 4 (as it gathers from figure 10.6).

To illustrate this point, figure 10.12 presents IMSS-enrolled workers' income distribution, in multiples of Mexico City's minimum wage (smDF), according to the institution's data. Salaried workers in the formal private sector are highly concentrated around 1 to 3 smDF, which makes it unad-

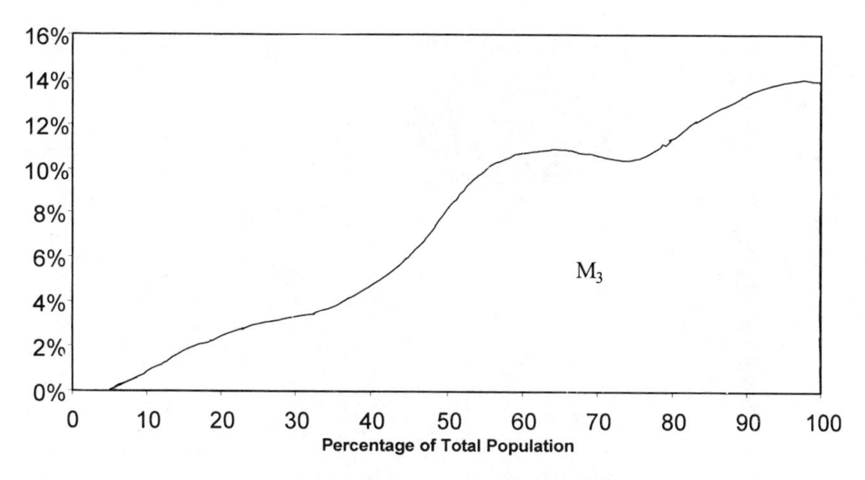

Fig. 10.13 Population with retired workers in the household (%)

visable to constrain the compensation to enrolled workers in a certain level of income. Furthermore, such a measure would create incentives to underdeclare, of the kind intended to be eliminated with the social security reforms (see section 10.8).

Adjusting Social Security Pensions

The third compensation tool ($i = 3$) is retirement pensions granted by the social security institutions, which benefit households with retired workers (the population dealt with by means of this tool, M_3).[52] Figure 10.13 shows the share of households with retired workers in the total population by income decile.

As can be seen (and contrary to expectations), the population living in households with retired workers is concentrated around the last five deciles, so that using this tool tends to increase the inclusion error, at least for relatively low values of β. Nonetheless, we keep this tool in the selected set because retired workers are unable to increase their income by participating in the labor market.

10.6.3 Duplication, Inclusion, and Exclusion Errors

We turn now to an analysis of duplication, inclusion, and exclusion errors when compensations are granted simultaneously via the three tools mentioned above, assuming that Progresa attains its potential coverage.[53] Figure 10.14 depicts, for each decile, the union of the populations consid-

52. In this case, the target population does not differ from the population dealt with, which is why neither the exclusion (E_3) nor inclusion (I_3) errors specific to this tool are defined.

53. Current coverage of this program, M_1, is not considered, because, as has been noted previously, it is quite below their potential coverage (M'_1) and still lower than the target population (M^*_1).

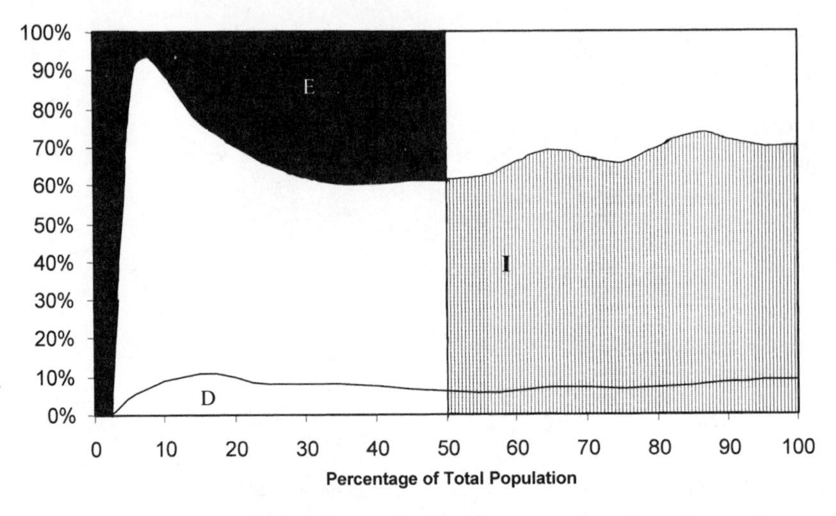

Fig. 10.14 Population in households with insured and pensioned members and Progresa's potential coverage (% of population)

Table 10.6 Exclusion and Inclusion Errors

β	Exclusion Error (%)[a]	Inclusion Error (%)[b]
0.25	28.01	73.28
0.50	33.28	50.48
0.75	33.68	26.16

[a]Percentage of target population for compensation purposes.
[b]Percentage of dealt-with population.

ered in the three tools, as well as inclusion (I), exclusion (E), and duplication (D) errors for $\beta = 0.50$.

As can be seen, duplication errors never exceed 11 percent and are on average 7 percent of the total population, and nearly 11 percent of the population reached (since it represents 67 percent of the total population). Therefore, joint use of compensations via Progresa and payments to insured and retired workers does not generate any serious duplication problems. However, the union of the populations reached by the three tools remains well below the target, since between the 3rd and the 8th deciles it covers only between 60 percent and 69 percent. Table 10.6 shows average coverage and inclusion and exclusion errors for selected values of β:

Clearly, there is a significant exclusion error, which only serves to stress the urgency of creating additional tools for transferring income to the moderately poor population not linked to the formal sector, which, in practice, consists of mainly the urban informal sector. Lastly, note that the inclusion

Table 10.7 Annual Fiscal Cost of Feasible Compensations (billions of pesos)

	0.00				0.50				1.00			
γ/α/β	0.25	0.50	0.75	1.00	0.25	0.50	0.75	1.00	0.25	0.50	0.75	1.00
0.25	2.9	5.8	8.7	11.5	5.7	11.4	17.1	22.8	8.4	16.8	25.3	33.7
0.50	3.9	5.8	8.7	11.5	8.4	16.8	25.3	33.7	13.1	26.2	39.3	52.4
0.75	2.9	5.8	8.7	11.5	10.7	21.4	32.1	42.8	19.2	38.3	57.5	76.7
1.00	2.9	5.8	8.7	11.5	13.1	26.2	39.3	52.4	39.5	79.0	118.5	158.1

error is also high, since it reaches 50 percent of the population dealt with, for β = 0.50 (although it falls to 26 percent for β = 0.75).

10.6.4 Fiscal Cost

Table 10.7 summarizes the fiscal cost of the feasible compensations for selected values of α, β, and γ, assuming that Progresa covers its target population[54] and that per capita transfers are the same for each tool, corresponding to the parameters' selected values:

Note that even under the pessimistic assumption that α = 1.00, the entire target population may be overcompensated (γ = 1.00) for β = 0.50, although this leaves the federal government with practically no net revenue (since ΔR_F equals 54.5 billion pesos). Alternatively, assuming that α = 0.50, the entire target population may be overcompensated for β = 0.75 and additional resources may still be left for the federal government.

10.7 Some Comments on Incentives

This section briefly comments on the incentives associated with the proposed compensation strategy. First, note that Progresa and the social security institutions offer an adequate incentive system to the populations they deal with (M_1 and M_2). Progresa motivates health care and regular school attendance by children; moreover, monetary transfers allow households to improve the quality and quantity of their nourishment (see IFPRI 2000) and allow them to take advantage of local food supply.

Households covered by social security may confront health-disrupting events at a very low marginal cost, since they receive medical attention (including highly specialized medical attention) without having to pay deductible amounts or copayments; also, monetary fringe benefits absorb the implicit cost of not working (see Dávila and Guijarro 2000). On the other hand, IMSS's new pension system (based, as previously noted, on the CIA)

54. Attaining Progresa's potential coverage means a fiscal cost amounting to 7.8 million pesos, which is not, however, included in the table's calculations because it is not attributable to the compensation strategy.

and the gradual evolution (throughout ten years, since 1997) toward a practically uniform contribution in order to finance in-kind benefits granted by SEM eliminated many of the elements distorting the link between contributions to social security and their expected benefits, which substantially improved the incentive system (see Dávila 1997).

Second, the compensation strategy proposed here would strengthen already existing incentives for the population dealt with by Progresa and in order to have a formal salaried employment.[55] Note that in the case of Progresa, this would increase the pressure on the eligibility system while the coverage is increased, which (if such effect is considered relevant) could make it advisable to augment it *before* announcing the increase in Progresa's transfers.

Concerning social security, the additional incentive toward formalization is considered socially desirable, but it may not suffice to counter existing disincentives generated by social security contributions that are basically perceived as taxes (such as IMSS's day care center and social benefit insurance), and by the fact that public-sector health services freely offered to the open (uninsured) population operate, in practice, as a subsidy to informality. This last effect is also a determinant to disincentive self-employed workers' enrollment to the SSF. In any case, it cannot be ignored that, in different contexts, self-employment is highly efficient and is perceived by workers as desirable (e.g., see Maloney 1996), which is why its disappearance cannot, and should not, be forced. Conversely, its incorporation into the compulsory social security regime should be proposed at least with regard to health services as well as for these workers to comply with their legal obligation to cooperate in the raising of consumption tax revenues (and particularly VAT). In order to grant an effective incentive for this formalization process, a proposal may be made to extend the right to a negative income tax to low-income self-employed workers, although such an extension would take the form of a virtual payment applicable toward the SSF acquisition.

10.8 Conclusions

This paper builds a simple analytical framework to determine the redistributive impact of a VAT reform. The framework does not capture the general equilibrium effects of the reform, which is why we cannot measure the efficiency gains obtainable from eliminating the differentiated regime or the effects of the reform on the labor market. Our aim has been more modest: on the one hand, to concentrate on the possible measures to compensate (or even overcompensate) for the adverse redistributive effects of a VAT reform

55. The advantages of being a security pensioner would also rise, but this would have no practical consequences in the short term, since this is a closed population.

and, on the other, to obtain relatively reliable numerical estimates of these effects.

The analytical framework allows to assess the redistributive impact as well as the fiscal costs of compensating the target population, in terms of three key parameters: the percentage increase in VAT rates transferred to final consumers, α; the share of the total population considered low-income subject to compensation, β; and the share of the target population eligible for overcompensation, γ. Our numerical estimates are based on the 1998 National Household Income-Expenditure Survey (*Encuesta Nacional de Ingresos y Gastos de los Hogares para* 1998). We conclude that, paradoxically, the sharp inequality in Mexico's income distribution offers, in principle, an opportunity to implement a VAT reform that simultaneously raises revenues and redistributes income. Specifically, if $\alpha = 0.50$, it is financially possible to overcompensate three-quarters of the population with a redistributive effort of 25.2 billion (representing net transfers toward the first 3 quartiles of income distribution) and still obtain surplus revenue for the federal government of nearly 16.0 billion, as well as 26.5 billion pesos' worth of additional revenues for states and municipalities.

We considered three tools available to the federal government to undertake, in practice, these compensations, and developed a conceptual framework to identify exclusion, inclusion, and duplication errors. In the numerical applications we find that, for the case where the target population consists of the first 3 quartiles of income distribution ($\beta = 0.75$), it is operationally[56] possible to compensate or overcompensate 66 percent of such population, with the population in the urban informal sector being the most difficult to reach, translating into a 34 percent exclusion error. At the same time, and for the same case, the inclusion error would be 26 percent of the population reached, and the possible duplication error would be 11 percent of such population.

We think that the previous results are interesting, although clearly more work needs to be done on the impact of the VAT reform on individuals' incentives, particularly concerning their participation in the formal labor market. From the point of view of policymakers, however, the results only present a partial solution to the problem set out in the introduction, as often happens in the design of economic policy. A uniform 15 percent VAT rate would significantly increase fiscal revenues and allow[57] an improvement in income levels for 67 percent of the low-income population (for $\beta = 0.5$), although there would be a negative impact on the remaining 33 percent, posing in turn a serious dilemma. (Note, however, that income improvements would reach 72 percent of the extremely poor.) This percentage could be substantially increased by improving Progresa's eligibility system

56. And also financially if $\alpha = 0.50$.
57. As shown in table 10.7.

and designing strategies to reach the population without access to education or health services.

In any case, the question that remains to be analyzed is whether, with the resources made available by the reform, net of compensations, it is feasible to design other programs and measures to assist the population not covered by the tools studied here. We think this is feasible to the extent that the additional fiscal resources are channeled toward social expenditures.[58] This would contribute to the elimination of the current dilemma posed by a reform of the VAT, creating conditions such that a vote in favor of the reform is also a vote in favor of equity.

More generally, we believe that the approach introduced in this paper may be applied to an analysis of situations in which efficiency and equity conflict. As mentioned in the introductory paragraphs, the absence in the past of direct redistribution tools led to the use of prices and rates (such as electricity, phone services, water, etc.) for publicly produced goods with redistributive purposes, with high efficiency costs;[59] the same objective was also pursued through price controls or fiscal subsidies for selected products, generally food. The significant inequity in income distribution was the motivation to establish these measures and, paradoxically, is what made them ineffective and inefficient. To the extent that we are able to replace such income transfers with tools that are similar to the ones set forth in this paper, we are convinced that achieving higher equity and higher efficiency simultaneously is feasible. We should stress that from the point of view of low-income households, what matters is not what instrument of economic policy is used but, rather, whether the goal is achieved.

We conclude with some political economy considerations associated with the feasibility of our proposals. The key point to note, of course, is that the reform of the VAT is a permanent change. Therefore, if the compensating mechanisms are to be accepted by the target population (and, in principle, by their representatives in congress), they must also be permanent and have the same binding force that the tax reform has—that is, they must be incorporated in a law.

In the case of pensions, this is not much of a problem, because these are already set by law. However, the same is not true of other instruments proposed here to compensate part of the target population, particularly with Progresa, which, as shown, plays a central role in compensating those in extreme poverty. Because resources for Progresa are voted annually in the fed-

58. An option would be to create a national system of scholarships to encompass half the population (since the families belonging to the first 5 deciles confront economic problems for their children to complete junior high school without delays). Another option is the previously discussed possibility of expanding the application of the negative income tax to low-income self-employed workers as a virtual payment applicable to the SSF contribution.

59. Throughout 2000, household consumption subsidies implicit in electricity rates amounted to nearly 22.4 billion pesos, of which it is estimated that only 44 percent is captured by the first 5 deciles of income distribution.

eral budget (as, indeed, is the program itself), there is no mechanism on the part of the government to make credible its commitment to permanently compensate the poor. Clearly a "tax me, I trust you" attitude on the part of those affected by the reform toward the government will not be acceptable. On the one hand, people in poverty have already experienced that income transfers (in cash or in kind) are extremely volatile. On the other hand, political parties—particularly those in opposition—realize that at least in some cases in the past, transfer programs to the poor have been subject to short-run electoral manipulations by the party in power, and they will certainly be reluctant to run the risk that these situations might repeat themselves.

Hence, putting aside the technical issues on which this paper has mostly centered, a proposal for a VAT reform along the lines suggested here faces an equally large challenge in the design of the institutional mechanisms that can make the compensation strategy acceptable both to the target population and to opposition parties in congress—a task that is made more difficult given the deviations observed in the past, at least in the judgment of some.

Legislating income transfers to the poor as part of a broader concept of social security may provide part of the answer.[60] However, an equally important part of the answer may be that the institutions to carry out these income transfers work well, both in the sense that the transfers reach the target population, and in the sense that society in general, and political parties in particular, perceive these transfers to be the result of a legal obligation of the Mexican State and not the expression of the goodwill of the government currently in power.

A formal modeling of these issues is beyond the scope of this paper. Some may argue that those laws and institutions do not yet exist in Mexico and that, therefore, technical issues aside, a proposal like the one ventured here will not prosper. Even if that is the case, it is important to underline the large costs of not having an adequate institutional framework, because the reform of the VAT regime is only one of many cases in which equity and efficiency can be greatly improved through the use of direct income transfers.

References

Comisión Económica para América Latina (CEPAL). 1997. Series macroeconómicas del istmo Centroamericano, 1950–1996. Mexico.

60. Income transfers associated with "traditional" social security have been limited to those workers and their families who work in the formal sector. This is a large limitation in Mexico, and one can speculate whether programs like Progresa, which also provide income transfers contingent upon some behavior, could be thought of as a limited form of social security.

Dávila, E. 1997. Mexico: The evolution and reform of the labor market. In *Labor Markets in Latin America,* ed. S. Edwards and N. Lustig, 292–327. Washington, D.C.: Brookings Institution.
Dávila, E., and M. Guijarro. 2000. Evolución y reforma del sistema de salud en México (Evolution and reform of the health system in Mexico). Santiago, Chile: CEPAL.
Dávila, E., G. Kessel, and S. Levy. 2002. El Sur también existe: Un ensayo sobre el desarrollo regional de México (The South also exits: An essay on the regional development of Mexico). *Economía Mexicano* 11 (2).
Deaton, A., and J. Muellbauer. 1984. *Economics and consumer behavior*. New York: Cambridge University Press.
International Food Policies Research Institute (IFPRI). 2000. Progresa (report).
INEGI. 2000. *Encuesta nacional de ingresos y gastos de los hogares de 1998.* Mexico.
Holmström, B., and P. Milgrom. 1987. Aggregation and linearity in the provision of intertemporal incentives. *Econometrica* 55 (2):
Keynes, J. M. 1943. *Teoría general de la ocupación, el interés y el dinero.* Mexico: Fondo de Cultura Económica.
Maloney, William F. 1996. Dualism and the unprotected or informal labor market in Mexico: A dynamic approach.
Mas Colell, A., M. Whinston, and J. Green. 1995. *Microeconomic theory.* New York: Oxford University Press.
Ministry of Finance. 1998. Algunos aspectos del gasto público en México.
Organization for Economic Cooperation and Development. 1999. *Economic surveys,* no. 10, Paris: OECD.
Theil, H. 1980. *The system-wide approach to microeconomics.* Chicago: University of Chicago Press.

Comment Ricardo Fenochietto

The paper by Dávila and Levy is interesting, with important policy implications for Latin America. Although this paper refers to the particular case of Mexico, the problem is more universal: the VAT is the most applied consumption tax internationally. One hundred five countries, many of them underdeveloped or developing, have a VAT; most of them exempt basic necessities from the base and give direct subsidies to the poor if their budget permits.

Problems with Exemptions

This paper shows the problem of alleviating poverty through exemptions in consumption taxes, in particular in the VAT, of goods and services that are supposedly a large part of the basic consumption basket of the poor.

The authors are right in pinpointing the inefficiencies and difficulties of VAT exemptions, and I think they are benevolent, because there are more

Ricardo Fenochietto is a private consultant and teaches graduate classes in taxation in Buenos Aires, Argentina.

problems than the ones shown in the work. They propose to lift these exemptions and give a Slutsky type of compensation to the poorest households. These compensations are based on the previous income of the household, a basis that presents problems of targeting, as noted by the authors, but also problems of work disincentives and moral hazard. These problems can make the compensations larger than calculated by the authors.

Both poverty alleviation programs analyzed in this paper, exemptions in consumption taxes and direct subsidies, present inconveniences (some clearly noted by the authors and some not). The case of exemptions of goods and services in the VAT presents the following problems: they are limited (a) by the income of the households, which presents the paradox that when the income is lower, the consumption is less and the subsidy also decreases—and, in the extreme, the indigent without income do not receive a subsidy; or they are limited (b) when the good is not taxed at zero rate (or totally exempted). This total exemption is very difficult to attain without an efficient tax administration.

Table 10C.1 explains which is the procedure to be followed to tax a good like bread at zero rate, reimbursing the tax paid in previous stages to the final stage when the good is sold to final consumers. The implicit assumption is that the bread is produced in five stages, and that all except the last are taxed at a rate of 21 percent.

For the exemption to be broad and for the good to be taxed at zero rate, it is necessary to devise some mechanism to pay back the baker the tax paid in the previous stages, which amounted to $52,50.

The usual mechanisms are to allow the computation of that fiscal credit against the fiscal debit one has over taxed goods, or its compensation against the payment of other taxes, or the total reimbursement in cash or bonds. However, any of those mechanisms requires an efficient tax administration (TA): it requires the bakeries to send all their invoices to the TA,

Table 10C.1 Example of an Exemption in the Last Stage ($)

	Amount of Purchases	Fiscal Credit	Amount of Sales	Fiscal Debit	Tax Collected
Wheat	0	0	100	21	21
Cereals market	100	21	150	31.5	10.5
Flour	150	31.5	180	37.8	6.3
Wholesale distribution of bread	180	37.8	250	52.5	14.7
Baker	302.5	0	352.5	0	0
Total tax collected					52.5
Tax collected with exemption in the last stage:			$52.50		
Tax collected with zero tax rate:			(63.00)		
Difference:			50 × 21% = $10.50		

and these in turn must be controlled and paid back in case they qualify for the exemption.

High-income households consume many of these goods and services. To prevent the subsidy from benefiting them, it is necessary to establish fine categories within goods. However, this introduces additional serious problems in the tax administration.

In the particular case of Mexico and Argentina, certain components of the basic food basket are exempt. In Argentina, for example, bread and milk are exempted—but not all types of bread or all types of milk, only the types supposedly consumed by the poor. Hence, white, french, and ordinary bread are exempted, but not German, *criollo*, sandwich, and hot-dog bread, among others. It is very difficult for the tax administration to control all the invoices, so it is possible to disguise German bread as French bread, and evade the tax.

The exemptions for the poor also cause the potential inclusion of other goods and services not consumed by the poor, but whose manufacturers have engaged in rent seeking to obtain the exemption. This is the case in Mexico and Argentina with newspapers and magazines, among other products, and even in Argentina with services, like cable television, that the poor do not consume.

Even if the exemptions do not constitute evasion, they encourage or cause evasion in at least two ways: nonpayment (induced by the irritation provoked in compliant taxpayers), and the forgery of taxed operations as exempted.

The following excerpt from the Bible (Matt. 17:24–27) explains the first of these exemption problems. Jesus recommends that one of his disciples (Peter) pay taxes, even though they were exempted, so as not to irritate those who are paying:

> And when they were come to Capernaum, they that received tribute [money] came to Peter, and said, Doth not your master pay tribute? He saith, Yes. And when he was come into the house, Jesus prevented him, saying, What thinkest thou, Simon? of whom do the kings of the earth take custom or tribute? of their own children, or of strangers? Peter saith unto him, of strangers. Jesus saith unto him, Then are the children free. Notwithstanding, lest we should offend them, go thou to the sea, and cast an hook, and take up the fish that first cometh up; and when thou hast opened his mouth, thou shalt find a piece of money: that take, and give unto them for me and thee.

I pinpointed the problem of tax evasion because it is serious in Argentina and in many LACs (see table 10C.2). In Argentina the level of evasion in the VAT is around 40 percent. (GDP is 300 billion, consumption is 240, base is 158, taxable consumption is 180, and a 21 percent rate should collect 31 billion. Instead, the VAT collects a little more than 19 billion pesos.)

Table 10C.2 Tax Evasion in Argentina, Estimated by Different Methods

	Year	Level
Monetary method	1995	42% of potential tax revenue
Monetary method	1996	40% of potential tax revenue
Monetary method	1997	39% of potential tax revenue
Current accounts	1996	41% of potential tax revenue
Current accounts	1997	39% of potential tax revenue
Survey	1999	55% of taxpayers do not file taxes

Source: Fenochietto (1999).

Problems with Direct Subsidies

The case of direct transfers also presents several problems. It is necessary, and not easy in LACs, to target the poor and to devise procedures to distribute the subsidy. Moreover, most social protection and social security programs present incentive costs and moral hazard. One consequence is that, when income targeting is employed, more people will "appear" as poor, and hence the total amount spent on direct subsidies will be greater than initially calculated. In addition, programs that try to motivate human capital acquisition do not recognize the role of families and firms in that regard and tend to promote scholarships, such as in the PROGRESA program. Previous papers (see Heckman et al. 1997; Heckman et al. 1999) showed that in the United States and Argentina politicians tend to promote formal schooling and high school instead of early school programs and vocational training, which help the poor more.

The paper presents an important and classical dilemma. Subsidizing the poor through exemptions creates more contradictions than the ones described by the authors. The direct transfers analyzed in this paper also have more problems than the ones mentioned by the authors. We should take into account, both theoretically and empirically, the pros and cons of both schemes.

References

Fenochietto, Ricardo. 1999. Economía informal y evasión impositiva en Argentina: Distintos mecanismos de medición, sus objectivos. Consejo de Profesionales en Ciencias Económicas de la Capital Federal (CPCECF) *Séptimo Congreso Tributario,* 121. Buenos Aires, Argentina: CPCECF.

Heckman, J., R. Cossa, L. Lochner, and C. Pessino. 1999. A budget for skill formulation in Argentina. University of Chicago and University Torcuato Di Tella. Unpublished manuscript.

Heckman, J., L. Lochner, J. Smith, and C. Taber. 1997. The effects of government policy on human capital investment and wage inequality. *Chicago Policy Review* 1 (2): 1–40.

11

Tax Reform in Brazil
Small Achievements and Great Challenges

Rogério L. F. Werneck

11.1 Introduction

In the late 1980s, as it became evident that the Brazilian economy would have to go through a serious fiscal-adjustment effort, the possibility of meeting a sizable part of the required adjustment from the revenue side was seen with skepticism. Over the previous twenty years, the aggregate tax burden had remained remarkably stable, fluctuating around one-fourth of gross domestic product (GDP). In fact, the evolution of the tax revenue in the early 1980s would lend force to that skepticism. Although the tax burden was hiked up in 1990, as a result of a once-and-for-all federal revenue increase produced by the Collor stabilization plan, it was brought back to an average of roughly 25 percent of GDP over the 1991–93 period. It was quite difficult to envisage by then that, at the end of the 1990s, the tax burden would have reached 32 percent of GDP, more than 6 percentage points above the 1991–93 average, as may be seen in table 11.1.

It seems almost incredible that such an impressive increase in the aggregate tax revenue could after all be obtained in such a short period. It is that raise in the tax burden that explains most of the remarkable fiscal adjustment that has been allowing the consolidation of the stabilization effort that has been carried out in the country since 1993. The feasible fiscal adjustment ended up being very different from what would be desirable. A strong political coalition prevented the advancement of reforms that could

Rogério L. F. Werneck is a professor in the Department of Economics at the Catholic University of Rio de Janeiro.

This paper benefited from comments from José Antonio Gonzalez and participants of the Latin American Conference on Fiscal and Financial Reforms, organized by the Center for Research on Economic Development and Policy Reform, held at Stanford University in November 2000.

Table 11.1 **Brazil, Gross Tax Burden (1968–99)**

Period	Tax Revenue of All Government Levels (in % of GDP)
1968–80	25.1
1981–89	24.8
1990	28.8
1991–93	25.3
1994–98	29.6
1999	31.7

Sources: 1968–98, Secretaria para Assuntos Fiscais, National Bank for Economic and Social Development (BNDES); 1999, Brazilian Institute of Geography and Statistics (IBGE).

open the way to a deeper cutback in expenditure programs that remain protected by the constitution, and most of the adjustment had to stem from the revenue side. In order to keep public accounts under a reasonable degree of control, with public indebtedness in a sustainable path, it became necessary to extract from society almost one-third of GDP in taxes. By all means an overexertion, given the stage of development of the Brazilian economy.

However, the three levels of government in Brazil are not only collecting 32 percent of GDP in taxes: they are also doing it in a very clumsy way, raising a large and increasing part by means of the worst kind of taxes. Nevertheless, despite all the public outcry and the significant mobilization of both the executive office and congress with the goal of a tax reform, so far there is no effective headway to be seen.

This paper is an attempt to assess what has happened and why progress has been so disappointing. It starts with a very short section on the deterioration of the Brazilian tax system, followed by a section analyzing tax reform initiatives since 1997 and showing how they recently ended in deadlock. Section 11.4 raises a number of important points that one has to take into account to fully grasp the difficulties that are to be faced by the reform, from an aggregate point of view. In order to analyze those points more carefully, a very simple consistency model is presented in section 11.5 and is used for simulations. The final section calls attention to how fiscal federalism difficulties have considerably amplified the complexity of the reform.

11.2 The Deterioration of the Brazilian Tax System

Back in the mid-1960s, a very commendable tax reform, including a pioneering value added taxation scheme, was successfully implemented in Brazil (see Guérard 1973). However, over the last thirty years much of what was achieved by that refurbishment was lost, as the quality of the Brazilian tax system went through a clear and worrisome deterioration process, at least in what concerns the taxation of goods and services.

It is impossible to understand what happened to the tax system since the 1960s without keeping in mind the economic and political difficulties faced by the country over the last two decades. The first half of the 1980s was marked by the end of the military regime and the enormous resistance of public opinion to the idea that a forty-year period of rapid economic growth had finally come to an end, in the wake of a combination of adverse external conditions and major blunders in economic policy, particularly in 1979 and 1980. In early 1985, the military would walk away, leaving behind an economy in disarray with an unsolved annual 200 percent inflation problem, which was bound to snowball into an even bigger problem that would haunt the country for the next ten years.

Fighting high inflation would become the dominant public policy issue of the reborn democratic regime. The pressing need to deal with this problem and the early failures of the new civilian government to implement a successful stabilization plan would greatly aggravate the difficulties the country would have to face in the coming years. Actually, it should be remembered that the redemocratization process had suffered a major blow at the very moment of its inception. Unluckily, Tancredo Neves, an able and influential politician, who had been elected the first president of the civilian regime by an impressive coalition of political forces, died before taking office, opening the way to a considerably less endowed and less influential vice president. During the first three years of his government, congress was drafting a new constitution, which was finally promulgated in late 1988.

Unfortunately, the long and delicate political negotiations that brought about the new constitution took place exactly when the central government had become notably feeble, due to the shortcomings of President Sarney, who had been accidentally inducted into office, and remained continuously mobilized by the quest for a higher degree of legitimacy. In fact, the central government became even feebler after the failure of two stabilization shocks, in 1986 and 1987. Those politically costly fiascoes would open the way for the major constitution reform blunder of 1988. A long-lasting and powerful vicious circle was set in motion and gathered strength, rapidly amplifying the complexity of the challenges to be faced by the country in the following years.

Drafted without minimum consistency guidelines, which the politically crippled executive branch was unable to press for at that moment, the new constitution failed to endow the state with a coherent mechanism to protect the interests of the majority of the population against the multiple pressures of an emerging mass democracy. Instead, it amplified the scope for the historically widespread rent-seeking behavior of many segments of the Brazilian society, imposing upon the federal budget a considerable additional burden, exactly when the union's fiscal resources were being reduced in favor of state and local governments, in the wake of a newly introduced but basically inconsistent fiscal federalism arrangement.

Table 11.2 **Brazil: Composition of the Tax Revenue (1989–99)**

	1989		1999	
Revenue Source	% of GDP	Share (%)	% of GDP	Share (%)
Taxes on imports	0.4	1.8	0.8	2.6
Taxes on goods and services	10.9	45.3	14.8	46.8
Property taxes	0.1	0.5	1.0	3.0
Taxes on personal income and profit	5.2	21.4	5.4	17.0
Payroll taxes	6.6	27.1	7.9	25.1
Other	0.9	3.9	1.8	5.5
Total	24.1	100.0	31.6	100.0

Source: BNDES, Secretaria para Assuntos Fiscais.

As the new tax system designed in 1988 was phased in during the early 1990s, the central government faced growing financial difficulties. Soon, however, as could be expected, it started an unrelenting reaction to evade the pincer movement of shrinking revenues and swelling expenditures that had been imposed on the union by the new constitution. As often happens, increasing revenues proved to be much easier than cutting back expenditures, especially when a large part of the federal spending could not be reduced unless politically costly constitutional amendments were duly approved by congress.

Although there was a very sharp increase in the gross tax burden over the 1990s, there was not any striking change in the broad composition of the aggregate tax revenue over the period, as may be seen in table 11.2. Taxation of goods and services continued to be the mainstay of the tax system, generating almost half of the aggregate collected revenue. The share of the total revenue stemming from the taxation of personal income and profits was reduced from 21.4 percent to 17 percent. The share of payroll taxes was also brought down from 27.1 percent to one-fourth of the total revenue.

Although there was a remarkable increase in the importance of property taxes, in the wake of the modernization of the tax collection apparatus of the largest municipalities in the country, property taxes were still responsible for only 3 percent of the total tax burden in the end of the period. The local government sphere has been particularly benefited by the generous revenue-sharing scheme that was introduced in the 1988 constitution. As may be seen in table 11.3, the pass-through of federal and state tax revenue allowed municipal governments to multiply their collected revenue by a factor of 3.5 in 1999.

Actually, the union's consistent effort to increase its tax revenue over the period—in order both to recover what had been lost to state and local gov-

Table 11.3 **Brazil: Distribution of the Total Tax Revenue and Revenue-Sharing Pass-through, 1999 (R$ billions)**

	Collected Revenue	Pass-through of Federal Revenue to State and Municipalities	Pass-through of State Revenue to Municipalities	Final Revenue Distribution
Union	215.9	–25.1		190.8
States	78.2	13.3	–19.2	72.3
Municipalities	12.2	11.8	19.2	43.2
Total	306.3			306.3

Source: Secretaria de Receita Federal.

Table 11.4 **Importance of Cascading Taxes: Share of Turnover Taxes in the Total Tax Revenue Managed by the Federal Revenue Service**

Period	Share of Cascading Taxes (period average, %)[a]
1986–88	7.3
1989–93	22.2
1994–98	29.6
1999	35.1
2000	39.7

Source: Secretaria da Receita Federal.

[a]Includes revenues from IPMF/CPMF, FINSOCIAL/COFINS, and PIS/PASEP.

ernments and to be able to properly finance its much-enlarged spending responsibilities—would prove to be a tremendous success, were it not for a big problem that the broad tax classification adopted in table 11.2 concealed. As the central government devised every kind of exotic taxation scheme that could raise revenues that would not be shared with lower-level governments, most of the substantial increase in the federal tax burden achieved over the last decade stemmed from very low-quality taxes. Most often that meant various forms of cascading turnover taxes, which, back in the mid-1960s, seemed to have been definitely eliminated from the Brazilian tax system.

The figures presented in table 11.4 are particularly striking. They show the marked deterioration in the quality of the tax burden imposed by the union that was observed since the early 1990s, especially since 1993. The share of the combined revenue of three cascading taxes in the total tax revenue managed by the Federal Revenue Service jumped from an average of 7.3 percent in 1986–88 to an average of 29.6 percent in 1994–98, only to jump again to 35.1 percent in 1999 and to almost 40 percent in 2000.

At the state level, distortions of a different kind accumulated over the last three decades. Part of the difficulties also stemmed from the 1988 constitution, which granted the states a much freer hand to introduce changes in their value added taxes (VATs). Because most of the uncoordinated changes were in fact for the worse, they slowly transformed the pioneering, reasonably well designed value added taxation scheme that had been introduced by the 1967 reform into a confusing, disharmonious collection of twenty-seven highly complex state-tax codes, forming an unmanageable crazy quilt of VAT arrangements.

Although most states are still facing severe fiscal stringency, they have been using their freer hand in tax matters to fight a fierce fiscal war, competing among themselves to see which one offers the most generous tax breaks and succeeds in attracting the flashier big industrial investment projects. The cutthroat competition has been particularly pathetic in the case of the car plants. As a result, the country is lavishly favoring auto makers with an enormous amount of tax expenditures, merely in order to have something it could probably get for free.[1] The collective irrationality of that fiscal war has been a source of increasing resentment among governors and has come to be perceived by a growing number of them as the swan song of the present state-VAT arrangement.

It is easy to understand, therefore, why there has been a growing outcry in favor of a deep change in the way goods and services are being taxed in the country. Because that has become the focal point of the discussion, the term "tax reform" will be used throughout the paper to mean indirect-taxation reform. In all fairness, however it should be noted that in what concerns taxes on profits and personal income, although the tax base is far from being properly exploited, there have been increasing rationality and significant improvements over the last few years. Also, the tax collection apparatus has become much more effective, because it is being rapidly modernized, particularly at the federal level. Although the analysis of such achievements is beyond the scope of the present paper, they should not go unnoticed.

11.3 Tax Reform: Public Outcry and Government Response

Tax reform is always bound to be a very controversial issue. However, that seems to be particularly true in today's Brazil, given the extent of the required changes in the tax system and the complexity of the country's fiscal federalism arrangement. The 1967 reform, which molded a large part of the present tax system, was both designed and implemented in the shadow of the authoritarian regime that had taken power in 1964. Moreover, although the 1988 reform took place when the military had already walked away, it was negotiated in a climate of very little concern with fiscal consistency. In both 1967 and 1988, therefore, even if for widely different reasons, the real proportions of the conflicts of interests involved in a tax reform

1. See "Brazil Shows How Much It Loves Carmakers," *Business Week: Latin American Edition,* 23 October 2000.

were much less clear than they are now bound to be, as has been conspicuously shown by the discussion of tax reform issues in the country over the last few years.

The widespread dissatisfaction with the clumsy and complex way the three levels of government have been extracting more than 30 percent of GDP in taxes from the economy has turned the country into a hotbed of exotic wonder-working tax reform proposals. In fact, two of those proposals became fairly popular among some segments of the business community in the mid-1990s. According to one of these proposals, all taxes would be eliminated and replaced by a single and unique tax on all financial transactions. The other proposal envisaged a new system in which all forms of taxation requiring the filing of tax returns would be replaced by "automatic and easy-to-collect" taxes imposed on financial transactions and on a short list of goods and services. This list would include oil, electricity, telecommunications services, tobacco, beverages, and cars.[2]

In spite of all the outcry over the tax system, the Cardoso government, which took office in early 1995, remained too busy to have a clear stance about the tax reform, at least until late 1997. Of course, lip service continued to be paid to the importance of carrying on a deep tax reform, which had been defended since the president's electoral campaign. However, the new government had first to deal with the difficulties imposed by the Mexican crisis—and, in fact, during its first months it was deeply divided on how to react to the crisis. When it pulled itself together, as the effects of the external turmoil on Brazil proved to be less strong than anticipated, the executive office was able to extract from congress important constitutional reforms that would open the way to the privatization of state-owned enterprises in mining, telecommunications, and electricity supply industries. However, that proved to be the relatively easy part of the constitutional reform program. Typically, those reforms involved no more than changing or eliminating a couple of words in the constitution. However, there were many other, much more complex, reforms ahead, such as the tax reform, the social security reform, and the public administration reform, which required a detailed and complex redesign of the existing arrangements. In fact, in 1995, the new government had no articulate or detailed plans for those far more complicated reforms. It simply did not know what it really wanted from congress.

It seemed that 1996 should be the year to push forward the pending reforms, especially when it became clear that 1995 had been marked by a very serious deterioration of the public accounts. However, the government would be completely mobilized with something else. The vast political capital amassed in the wake of the success of the inflation-fighting program

2. Short descriptions of such proposals may be found in Confederação Nacional da Indústria (1998).

would be mainly allocated to extracting from congress a constitutional amendment that would allow the reelection of the president. The executive office played a tough game and finally got the amendment approved in early 1997. Precious time had been lost, however, because the economy was becoming increasingly vulnerable to a less favorable external environment.

The more optimistic analysts believed that, having assured himself of the possibility of being reelected, and having therefore reinforced his political capital, the president would finally be ready to press congress to move forward the required constitutional reform program. However, nothing of the sort happened. Quite to the contrary, in the second quarter of 1997, the government started to publicly discuss whether the pending reforms were in fact needed and even considered the possibility of launching an ambitious public investment program. Soon, however, the government would be shaken back to reality with the sudden change in the international environment caused by the Asian crisis.

In late 1997, hastily preparing an emergency fiscal adjustment package that had to be announced in the wake of the external crisis, the federal government decided that it was about time to show a more active role in the mostly nonsensical debate on tax reform that was taking place in congress and within the business community. At an already troubled moment, the uproar over taxes was bringing much additional bad press. Although far from prepared to present a detailed tax reform proposal, the government was able to announce a sensible outline of what it considered to be the required reform.

According to that outline, the envisaged reform should concentrate on straightening out the way goods and services were taxed in the country. The idea was to eliminate all forms of turnover and cascading taxes, to discard the existing federal tax on manufactured goods, to dismantle the inconsistent and distorting set of state VATs, and to dispense with the service tax, which had been so poorly exploited by local governments.[3] Those taxes would be replaced by three new ones: a consistent broad-based nationally managed VAT, a new federal excise tax on a small number of goods and services, and a local retail sales tax. A new set of revenue-sharing and compensation rules would be designed in such a way as to preserve federal, state, and local governments from revenue losses.

3. It should be not only mentioned but stressed that the government never admitted the possibility of parting with the federal tax on financial transactions. It was not included among the cascading taxes that would be eliminated. Distorting as it could certainly be, the tax would be confined to a small rate, it was argued. Being very hard to evade, it could be a source of invaluable information to tax collectors in their effort to curb evasion of other taxes, if only congress could pass the required legislation allowing tax authorities full access to detailed tax revenue data, compiled by the financial system, that could reveal the annual amount of tax on financial transactions charged to each taxpayer. Such legislation was finally approved by congress in early December 2000.

The announcement that, based on such an outline, the government was preparing a detailed tax reform proposal to be eventually submitted to congress produced a clear turnaround in the ongoing debate. The government had established a new focal point. During the next few months the federal tax authorities seemed mobilized by the challenge of transforming that simple sketch of far-reaching changes in the tax system into a minutely consistent and implementable reform project. However, such mobilization would soon lose momentum. The fiscal adjustment package that had been announced in late 1997 had given the economy some leeway to face the shock waves of the worst part of the Asian crisis. In the second quarter of 1998, however, as soon as the external environment became less unfavorable again, the government proved to be confident enough to suspend a sizable part of the fiscal adjustment measures it had so hastily announced some months before. In the wake of that fallback, the seeming urgency of the tax reform disappeared. Top priority was given to assuring victory in the coming presidential election.

It was not a very wise move. A few months after, in August 1998—still two months before the election—the Brazilian economy would be caught in a very vulnerable position by the shock wave of the Russian crisis. This time it was a major shock wave, but the adoption of all relevant reacting measures had to wait for the election. When the measures were finally adopted, tough as they were, given the circumstances, they proved to be far from sufficient to prevent the economy from plunging into the serious foreign exchange crisis of early 1999.

However, the most traumatic part of the crisis was soon over. Restoration of confidence was rapid, and the overshooting of the exchange rate was surprisingly short-lived. By mid-1999, it was already perfectly clear that the impact of the devaluation would be much less costly than anticipated, in terms of both the inflationary shock and the initial depressing effects on the level of activity. In March, the government itself had announced that it was expecting a contraction of 3.5 to 4 percent in the level of activity in 1999. It was certainly a happy surprise after all that such a troubled year brought no fall at all in GDP but a positive growth rate of almost 1 percent.

Short as it was, however, the fright of the foreign-exchange crisis of early 1999 seems to have inculcated a surprising degree of conviction in the reelected government about the need to maintain and consolidate the fiscal adjustment measures adopted since the Russian crisis. However, in what concerned the tax reform, the government emerged from the crisis extremely skeptical about the possibility of going ahead with the proposal outlined in late 1997. In a landmark interview with a major newspaper in mid-March 1999, the president was particularly candid on the matter, leaving no doubts whatsoever about how he was assessing the odds. He simply said that the tax reform was too complex and that he thought the country still "lacked the required consciousness" of the involved issues and interests. Pushing the reform forward would simply paralyze the parliament, so heavy were the required political negotiations.[4]

Crystal-clear as that position may have seemed, it would soon prove to be politically untenable. Having put off the tax reform for his whole first term in office, the president suddenly found out that there was no political room left for *explicitly* putting off the reform for still another term. After all, if the tax reform was considered to be too complex to be negotiated in congress when the president was just beginning his second term, it was hard to believe that it would be seen as an easier task in 2000, when the local elections campaign would naturally lead to a much hotter discussion of the involved issues. Of course, it was even harder to believe that the reform would be perceived as a simpler challenge during the second half of the presidential term, when congressmen and governors would be involved in a complex redeployment of political forces in preparation for the general elections of 2002. Postponing the reform to a more convenient moment would therefore almost certainly mean leaving the whole issue for the next presidential term.

In congress, it was immediately perceived that the president's position was in fact untenable. Given the unyielding public outcry over the inadequacy of the tax system, it would be very difficult to continue to evade the whole issue, particularly in such an overt manner. Almost simultaneously, the presiding officers of both the senate and the chamber of deputies made incisive declarations to the media, disagreeing with the president's stance and strongly stressing how urgent they thought a tax reform really was. Given the impending possibility of losing initiative in such an important matter to congress, the executive office was forced to back off and declare that the reform was in fact a top-priority issue. Having been obviously dragged into a battle it would rather evade, and, worse, in the uncomfortable position of follower of the congress, the executive branch seemed in late March 1999 not only unprepared for the coming action in this area but also dangerously tempted to resort to improvisation (see R. L. F. Werneck, "Reforma o Contragosto" (Unwilling Reform) in *O Estado de S. Paulo,* 2 April 1999, p. 32).

However, with the benefit of hindsight, one may say that, from then on, the government would deal with the tax reform as if it had decided to follow a different course of action. More precisely, perhaps one should say a course of inaction. This certainly does not mean that nothing happened: in fact, over the following eighteen months the tax reform issue would involve a convoluted and far from uneventful game between congress and the executive office. However, at the end of that game, the latter's strategy proved to have simply focused on a firm adherence to the stance the president had so

4. See "Reforma política é a prioridade, anuncia FHC (Political reform is the priority)," *O Estado de S. Paulo,* 14 March 1999.

clearly expressed before having been forced, back in March 1999, to unwillingly play such a game with congress.

Although the end of that meandering story is somewhat melancholic, its thread certainly deserves attention. A tax reform with a scope as wide as that outlined by the executive office in late 1997 involves a very delicate operation in which a substantial part of the tax system is replaced by a new one. In principle, that should be done in such a way as to assure that the adopted changes form a viable, organic, and consistent new arrangement. A brand-new incongruous patchwork may end up being even worse than the present arrangement, deplorable as it undeniably is. To avoid that kind of botched outcome, the executive office has to be able to negotiate with congress the reform as whole. That does not mean that the basic proposal should be seen as immutable: it may well be extensively modified in congress. However, changes have to be introduced in such a way as to preserve the reform's consistency.

That only stresses how complex the required negotiations are. They are no easy task. However, there seems to be little hope of success if the executive office is not able to start the whole political bargaining process from a very clear and convincing basic proposal. That is exactly what the late 1997 outline seemed to be. The essence of that outline was even revived in October 1999, when the executive office announced a somewhat different tax reform proposal. Where the proposal concerned taxes to be eliminated there was not any major change. The difference was in the taxes to be created. The 1997 idea of a loosely defined "nationally managed" VAT was turned into a plain federal VAT with a clearly established revenue-sharing scheme with state and local governments. Additionally, the new federal excise tax on goods and services proposed in 1997 was converted into a new *state* excise tax.

The clear-cut definition of the proposed VAT as a federal tax triggered immediate strong opposition to the government's new proposal in congress and among state governors. Such fierce resistance made the government even more skeptical about the possibility of going ahead with a consistent tax reform. Since then, the executive office has been trying to dissociate itself from the kind of reform that it had outlined in late 1997 and, again, in late 1999. In fact, that withdrawal was far from easy, because the essence of the proposal that the government was trying to abandon was in the meantime being adopted by congress. Ironically, in March 2000 the Chamber of Deputies' Special Committee for Tax Reform approved a proposal that in many ways resembled what seemed to have been initially envisaged by the executive office.

In agreement with the main idea that pervaded the 1997 outline, the Special Committee proposed the elimination of all forms of turnover and cascading taxes, the discarding of the existing federal tax on manufactured goods, the dismantling of the inconsistent set of state VATs, and the discarding of the service tax charged by local governments. According to the proposal approved by the committee, the combined revenue generated by all those taxes would be raised by a new broad-based dual VAT—involving the supposedly harmonic coexistence of separate federal and state VATs—and a new municipal retail sales tax.[5]

As a matter of fact, a variant of that proposal, defended by the Special Committee's rapporteur but not voted on by the committee, also gained some importance in the recent tax reform debate.[6] In the proposed alternative, the dual VAT would only be required to generate enough revenue to compensate for the combined revenue that would be lost with the elimination of the existing federal tax on manufactured goods, the state VAT, and the local-government service tax. The remaining and substantial revenue loss that would stem from the elimination of all turnover and cascading taxes would be recouped by a new loosely defined "noncumulative" tax on goods and services (see Afonso et al. 2000).

Confronted with those two proposals, the government did not hide its strong resistance to both of them. At the end of a noisy five-month public quarrel over the reform, in which state governors played a key role, the executive office announced that still another proposal would be submitted to congress. When the proposal was finally disclosed in early August 2000, however, it was found out that the executive office had abandoned altogether the original idea of eliminating turnover and cascading taxes. The main proposed change, a new destination-based VAT, still imposed by the states but under nationally mandated uniform rules, was fiercely objected to by some governors. A few days later, the presiding officer of the Chamber of Deputies, supported by all party leaders, simply declared that the proposal had been considered a nonstarter, because it failed to address the main tax reform issues. After almost three years, negotiations had ended in deadlock, but the executive office did not seem to be particularly disappointed.

11.4 Unraveling the Deadlock: A Partial Assessment of the Difficulties

Looking back on what has happened since late 1997, one may be tempted to explain the tax reform deadlock by resorting to the usual handy scapegoat: lack of required political will in Brasília. President Cardoso's penchant for procrastination during his first term in office makes jumping to such conclusion even more tempting. However, doing so would mean evading a deeper understanding of the difficulties and uncertainties that turn the idea of implementing a sound tax reform in Brazil today into a challenge of extreme complexity. Of course, one may always say that, confronted with

5. For a good description of the Special Committee's approved proposal, see Afonso et al. (2000).

6. The committee's rapporteur is the congressman in charge of drafting the discussed legislation.

such challenge, the government simply shied away. However, even though that is partly true, it is still interesting to find out in more detail why the tax reform challenge has come to be perceived as some kind of Herculean task in Brasília.

Table 11.5 allows a comparison of the main features of the five tax reform proposals defended in the country since 1997, as discussed in section 11.3. Except for the last proposal, which seems to have been designed in part to bring down the curtain, all the other four have important common ele-

Table 11.5 Tax-Reform Proposals Comparison of Main Features

Proposal	Taxes to be Eliminated	Taxes to be Created
Executive's late-1997 proposal (October)	• All turnover and cascading taxes (Cofins, PIS-Pasep), except tax on financial transactions • Federal tax on manufactured products (IPI) • State VAT (ICMS) • Service tax charged by local governments (ISS)	• Nationally managed VAT • Federal excise tax on goods and services • Retail sales tax (IVV)
Executive's late-1999 proposal (October)	• All turnover and cascading taxes (Cofins, PIS-Pasep), except tax on financial transactions • Federal tax on manufactured products (IPI) • State VAT (ICMS) • Service tax charged by local governments (ISS)	• Federal VAT • State excise tax on goods and services • Municipal retail sales tax (IVV)
Special committee's proposal (March 2000)	• All turnover and cascading taxes • Federal tax on manufactured products (IPI) • State VAT (ICMS) • Service tax charged by local governments (ISS)	• Dual VAT (coexisting federal and state VATs) • Municipal retail sales tax (IVV)
Nonvoted rapporteurs' proposal (March 2000)	• All turnover and cascading taxes • Federal tax on manufactured products (IPI) • State VAT (ICMS) • Service tax charged by local governments (ISS)	• Dual VAT (coexisting federal and state VATs) • Noncumulative excise tax
Executive's proposal (August 2000)	• Federal tax on manufactured products (IPI) • State VAT (ICMS) • Service tax charged by local governments (ISS)	• Federal tax on goods and services (IBS) • Nationally uniformed state VAT • Municipal retail sales tax (IVV)

ments. They seem to share the same basic diagnosis of what is wrong with indirect taxation in the country. They are strikingly similar where they discuss taxes to be eliminated and are not very dissimilar where they discuss taxes to be created. Considering that two of those proposals stemmed from the executive office and two from congress, that seems to point to a surprising degree of agreement on the main line of the required reform.

The guiding idea is the reconstruction of value added taxation on broader and more rational grounds in such a way as to allow the elimination of the turnover and cascading taxes that have gained so much importance over the last decade. The big question is how that switching of tax base should be brought about. The difficulties involved are certainly amplified by the complexity of the Brazilian fiscal federalism, especially because value added taxation has traditionally been the mainstay of revenue at the state level. However, without trying in any way to underestimate the involved fiscal federalism problems, it may be worthwhile to postpone the discussion of those difficulties to section 11.7 and to concentrate first on problems of a different kind that seem to have received less attention, but that will have to be duly faced by a tax reform that follows the common line pervading the first four proposals of table 11.5.

In principle, the reform should be implemented in such a way as to avoid any loss of aggregate tax revenue, no matter how the revenue is shared among the three levels of government. It is therefore easy to conclude that it will only be possible to part with the cascading taxes, and the substantial revenue that has been raised by them, if the new value added taxation scheme is able to generate a revenue far greater than the combined revenue that today stems from the state VAT (ICMS), the federal tax on manufactured goods (IPI), and the service tax imposed by local governments (ISS). In 1999, as shown in table 11.6, the total revenue generated by those three taxes reached BR$88.9 billion (9.2 percent of GDP). The new value added taxation scheme should be able to raise much more than that in order to

Table 11.6 **Revenue from Taxes To Be Eliminated (1997 and 1999)**

	1997		1999	
Taxes	Revenue (R$ billions)	Revenue (as % of GDP)	Revenue (R$ billions)	Revenue (as % of GDP)
COFINS (federal turnover tax)	19.1	2.2	32.2	3.4
PIS-PASEP (federal turnover tax)	7.6	0.9	9.8	1.0
IPI (federal tax on manufactured goods)	16.8	1.9	16.5	1.7
ICMS (state value-added tax)	59.6	6.8	67.7	7.0
ISS (service tax imposed by local governments)	4.8	0.5	4.7	0.5
Total	107.9	12.4	130.9	13.6

allow the removal of the turnover taxes. Even if one leaves aside the tax on financial transactions (CPMF), from which the federal government refuses to part, one has to have in mind that the remaining turnover taxes (COFINS and PIS-PASEP) raised R$42 billion (4.4 percent of GDP) in 1999. Therefore, the new set of taxes introduced by the reform should be able to generate a total revenue of R$130.9 billion, corresponding to 13.6 percent of GDP. As may be also seen in the bottom line of the same table, that revenue target has been moving up very rapidly in the wake of the growing importance of federal cascading taxes. In 1997, it corresponded to only 12.4 percent of GDP.

Raising such impressive revenue will require a very broad-based value added taxation scheme. Although, in principle, there is no problem in devising a legal definition of the VAT base that is as broad as possible, there should not be any doubt about the intensity of the opposition such a proposal will have to face in congress. The existing base of the current state VAT (ICMS) would have to be substantially broadened, particularly in such a way as to include most services, which so far have been basically sheltered from explicit taxation. That kind of change is bound to meet with strong resistance in congress. On the other hand, the broadening of the value added tax base may well require a heavier taxation of a considerable number of goods and services whose consumption has been usually classified as either essential or meritorious, and that will also spur serious opposition in Congress.

Any tax reform proposal strengthening the importance of value added taxation should therefore take into account the powerful coalition that, in many different ways, will be pressing for the erosion of the potential base of the new tax. The resulting political pressure could easily push the reform to an unreasonably high required VAT rate. One must also keep in mind that, no matter how broad the legal tax base that may eventually be extracted from congress, there is still uncertainty about the extent to which such a base will be effectively exploited, given the limitations of the tax-collecting apparatus. Actually, there is a well-known two-way relationship to be taken into account. On one hand, the VAT base has to be broad enough to allow the required tax rate to be reasonably low. On the other hand, with a high VAT rate, it will be unwise to count on an effective broad base, even if, legally, the base seems to be broadly defined.

11.5 Simulations and Reform Uncertainty

From an aggregate point of view, the first four reform proposals outlined in table 11.5, which have so much in common, could be seen as special cases of a more general proposal that could be stylized as follows. All taxes listed in table 11.6 (COFINS, PIS-PASEP, IPI, ICMS, and ISS) would be eliminated. Their combined revenue would be generated by three new taxes: a

Table 11.7 **Total Revenue from Taxes to be Eliminated and Revenue-Sharing Pass-through, 1999 (R$ billions)**

	Collected Revenue	Pass-through of Federal Revenue to State and Municipalities	Pass-through of State Revenue to Municipalities	Final Revenue Distribution
Union	58.5	–7.8		50.7
IPI	16.5			
COFINS	32.2			
PIS/PASEP	9.8			
States	67.7	4.1	–16.9	54.9
ICMS	67.7			
Municipalities	4.7	3.7	16.9	25.3
ISS	4.7			
Total	130.9			130.9

Source: Secretaria da Receita Federal.

value added tax, an excise tax, and a retail sales tax. The differences among the four proposals have to do mostly with the design of the value added taxation scheme and the excise tax. There is no doubt that, from the viewpoint of fiscal federalism, those are certainly very big differences, but they are not as big when seen from an aggregate perspective. If one sticks to that perspective—for a while, at least—the stylized proposal just outlined may be very useful, because it allows a clearer discussion of some of the consistency problems that have to be taken into account.

The involved problems may be analyzed with a very simple consistency model.[7] The basic aggregate constraint is that the total revenue will be preserved. The new taxes would have to be able to generate as much revenue as is being generated by the taxes that are to be removed. Being such combined revenue given by R, defined as

$$R = \text{ICMS} + \text{IPI} + \text{ISS} + \text{COFINS} + \text{PIS-PASEP}, \quad (1)$$

the total-revenue preservation constraint may be written as

$$\text{EXC} + \text{VAT} + \text{ST} = R, \quad (2)$$

where EXC, VAT, and ST are, respectively, the revenues stemming from the excise tax, the value added tax, and the retail sales tax.

The value and decomposition of the total revenue that stemmed in 1999 from the taxes that are supposed to be eliminated are presented in table 11.7. In the same table, one may also see the involved revenue-sharing pass-

7. Werneck (2000) presents a complete consistency model developed especially to analyze the late 1997 tax reform proposal, based on data available in early 1998. In this section, a simplified version of that model will be used in a more limited way, just to shed some light, from an aggregate point of view, on difficulties and uncertainties involved in the stylized reform proposal depicted above. A full exploitation of the model's possibilities may be found in Werneck.

throughs, as well as the resulting final distribution of resources among the three government levels, shown on the right-hand column. The new taxes would have to be able to raise a total revenue of BR$130.9 billion.

The most important of those taxes would be the VAT. What has been envisaged—in fact, by all of the reform proposals presented in table 11.5—is a destination-based consumption-type VAT. Aggregate consumption in 1999 has probably topped R$600 billion.[8] However, that estimate supposedly includes indirect taxes on consumption, whereas the model assumes a tax-exclusive VAT rate. On the other hand, the official national-accounts GDP figure probably underestimates the true value of the aggregate output by a considerable margin. Moreover, keeping in mind the residual treatment given to consumption in the national accounts, it is reasonable to assume that a disproportional part of the GDP underestimation falls upon aggregate consumption.

All qualifications being taken into account, the R$600 billion figure was considered an acceptable upper bound for the potential VAT base. However, roughly one-fifth of that corresponds to residential housing services, and it is hard to believe that it will be politically feasible to define a VAT base broad enough to embrace explicit and implicit residential rents. Again, that only stresses the need to consider the possibility of having an effective VAT base much narrower than the potential one, as was underlined in section 11.4.

One may write the VAT revenue as

$$\text{VAT} = t_{\text{VAT}}\, a_{\text{VAT}}\, B_{\text{VAT}}, \tag{3}$$

where B_{VAT} is the potential tax base, t_{VAT} is the tax rate, and a_{VAT} is the base exploitation coefficient, measured by a positive number not greater than 1. That coefficient, which gauges the broadness of the VAT base, will deserve a close attention.

Before considering more elaborate simulation exercises, it may be useful to establish a basic benchmark by asking a very simple question. What would be the required VAT tax rate if the total revenue now stemming from the taxes that are to be eliminated were to be entirely generated by the VAT? Assuming both EXC and ST in equation (2) to be zero and using equation (3), one gets a very simple expression for the required VAT tax rate,

$$t^*_{\text{VAT}} = \frac{R}{a_{\text{VAT}} B_{\text{VAT}}}, \tag{4}$$

which leads to a straightforward back-of-an-envelope calculation. If one overoptimistically assumes the a_{VAT} coefficient to be equal to 1 and, there-

8. Estimate based on the available detailed 1998 national accounts and the preliminary estimate of the 1999 nominal GDP, assuming that aggregate personal consumption remained constant as a proportion of GDP.

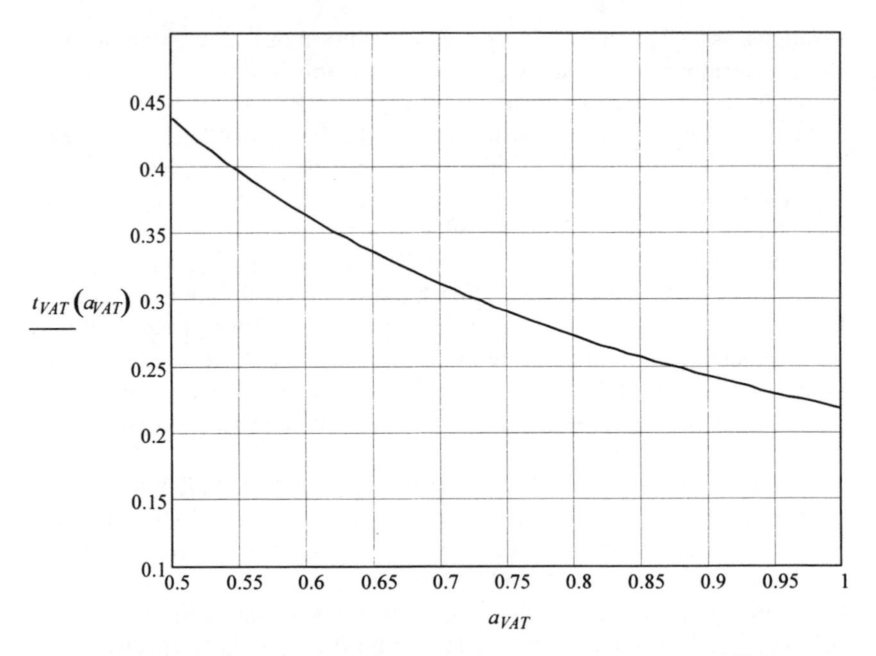

Fig. 11.1 Required VAT rate for different values of the base-broadness coefficient a_{VAT}
Note: Benchmark case: revenue of all eliminated taxes entirely generated by the VAT.

fore, the effective VAT base to coincide with the potential R$600 billion base, the VAT rate would have to be equal to approximately 21.8 percent in order to generate the R$130.9 billion, currently collected by the taxes that are to be eliminated. Allowing for the narrowing of the tax base that would stem from the exclusion of residential housing services would mean assuming a_{VAT} to be roughly equal to 0.8 instead of 1. Under that assumption, the required VAT rate would leap to around 27.3 percent. Of course, an even narrower tax base, as could be reasonably expected, would lead to quite immoderate rates, as may be seen in figure 11.1.[9]

The possibility of exorbitant rates' being required after all calls attention to a logical pitfall that may be involved in treating the effective broadness of the VAT base, measured by a_{VAT}, as an exogenous variable independent of the tax rate. Given a legal definition of how broad the base is supposed to be and the degree of efficacy that may be expected from the tax-collecting

9. The average revenue productivity of the VAT is defined as the revenue, as a percentage of GDP, generated by each percentage point of the nominal tax rate. Among Latin American countries, Chile, with 0.5, has the highest VAT revenue productivity. A tax rate of 18 percent allows the collection of 9 percent of GDP in revenue. It is curious to notice that, if the new Brazilian VAT could attain such a high productivity, the generation of revenue corresponding to 13.6 percent of GDP would require a rate of 27.2 percent, which is strikingly close to the rate calculated above. See Tanzi (2000) for recent data on VAT productivity in Latin America.

apparatus, it may be far more reasonable to assume that the effective broadness of the base depends on how high the imposed VAT rate is. The higher the tax rate, the stronger the evasion incentives and the narrower the effective base.

One could incorporate that assumption into the model, supposing that the effective broadness of the VAT base may be written as

$$h = h(a_{VAT}, t_{VAT}, v), \tag{5}$$

a constant elasticity function that simply corrects the legally determined value of a_{VAT}, taking into account the tax rate t_{VAT} and the elasticity v. So far, the model was implicitly assuming that v was simply equal to zero. That means, for example, that if the legally defined base broadness corresponded to 70 percent of the potential base, one could supposedly count on such broadness, no matter how high the tax rate is. Undoubtedly, this is a very unrealistic assumption.

When equation (5) is introduced into the model, equation (3), which establishes the VAT revenue, must be rewritten as

$$\text{VAT} = t_{VAT}\, h(a_{VAT}, t_{VAT}, v) B_{VAT}. \tag{6}$$

According to that equation, what would the required VAT tax rate be, if the total revenue now stemming from the taxes that are to be eliminated were to be entirely generated by the VAT? Under such extreme assumption, one could have

$$t_{VAT}\, h(a_{VAT}, t_{VAT}, v) B_{VAT} = R. \tag{7}$$

Attributing plausible values to the involved parameters and exogenous variables, one may obtain the required VAT rate as the root of the above equation. Assuming again the potential base B_{VAT} to be R$600 billion, one may attribute different sets of values to a_{VAT} and to the elasticity v and obtain for each of those sets the corresponding root value that determines the required VAT tax rate t^*_{VAT}. Results of such simulations are presented in figure 11.2, for different values of a_{VAT} and v.

When the elasticity is assumed to be zero, one gets the lowest curve, which is identical to the one shown in figure 11.1. The other three curves of figure 11.2 were obtained by making v equal to 0.1, 0.25, and 0.33, respectively. It may be seen that, as one makes more pessimistic assumptions on the base narrowing that may stem from an increase in the tax rate, the involved trade-off between base broadness and the required rate becomes considerably more adverse.

To what extent could the trade-off be eased by bringing the excise tax and the retail sales tax back to the scene? As a matter of fact, it is hard to see how the retail sales tax could help much, at least from an aggregate viewpoint. The idea of introducing a sales tax has basically stemmed from fiscal federalism concerns. It is much more a form of giving the lower-level govern-

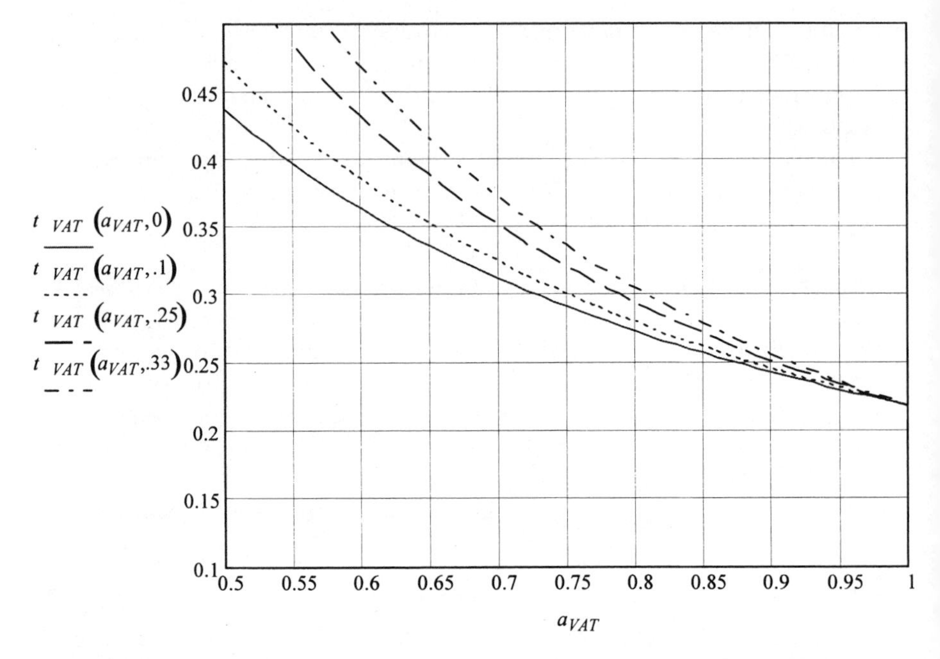

Fig. 11.2 Required VAT rate for different values of the base-broadness coefficient a_{VAT} and the elasticity v

Note: Benchmark case: total revenue of eliminated taxes entirely generated by the VAT.

ments a tax revenue to collect than an attempt to ease the pressure on value added taxation. In fact, because the sales tax and the VAT constitute a rather odd combination, there has even been a proposal to reduce this strangeness by piggybacking the retail sales tax onto the VAT. States or municipalities would collect an additional percentage on top of the VAT rate. Even if such a solution is not adopted, one should not miss the point that the sales tax, as has been envisaged in the various reform proposals, seems to be simply a way to redistribute the power to tax the VAT base within the federation.[10]

Would the excise tax do the trick? Of course, it all depends on how much revenue could be expected from it. As a matter of fact, all tax reform proposals that envisaged the creation of an excise tax, collected either at federal or state level, were marked by a rather loose definition of what would be the tax base—and were much looser yet where they concerned tax rates and revenue to be expected. However, in the discussion of the late 1997 proposal, a reasonable estimate of the value that could be raised by the excise

10. It goes without saying that the same point becomes still more forceful in the case of a dual VAT arrangement.

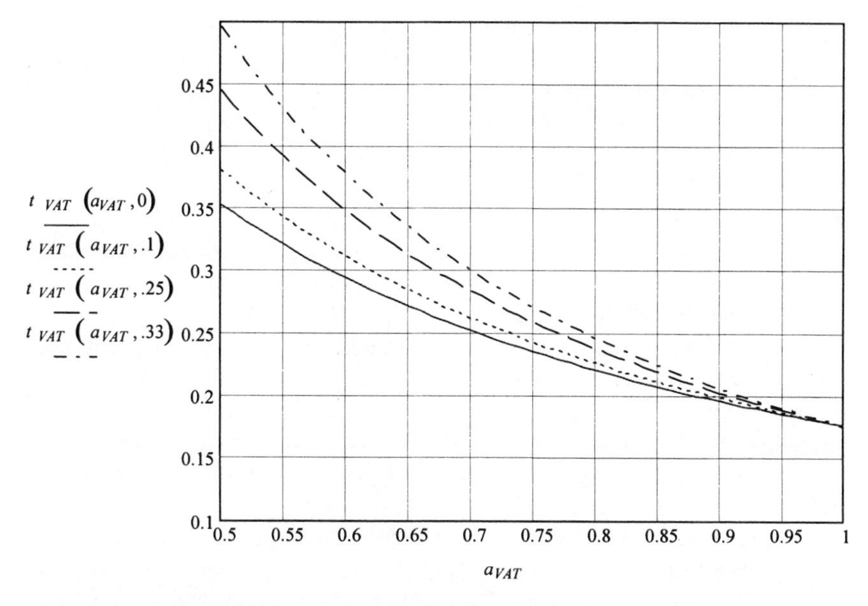

Fig. 11.3 Required VAT rate for different values of the base-broadness coefficient a_{VAT} and the elasticity v

Note: Total revenue of eliminated taxes generated by the VAT, complemented by R$25 billion of excise-tax revenue

tax was considered to be between 2 and 2.5 percent of GDP. In 1999, that meant something on the order of R$20 to R$25 billion. Even if one takes the upper limit, there would still be a revenue of R$105.9 billion left to be generated by the VAT-cum-sales-tax arrangement, if the R$130.9 billion target were to be reached.

How much lower would the required VAT tax rate be? In order to answer that question, the simulations that led to the results presented in figure 11.2 were repeated, under the assumption that the targeted VAT revenue was only BR$105.9 billion. The results are presented in figure 11.3, for different values of a_{VAT} and v.

If a_{VAT} could be made equal to 1, the R$25 billion of excise tax revenue would allow a reduction in the required VAT rate from 21.8 percent, as was shown in figure 11.2, to 17.7 percent, as may be seen in figure 11.3. Roughly, it would take R$6 billion of excise tax revenue for each percentage point of reduction in the required VAT rate. However, as one attributes lower and more realistic values to a_{VAT}, assuming a narrower effective base, the required VAT rate increases very quickly. For a_{VAT} equal to 0.7, the required rate would lie between 25 and 30 percent, depending on which value is attributed to the elasticity v, in a range that goes from zero to 0.33. It should be noticed, however, that the narrower the effective VAT base, the stronger the sensitivity of the required VAT rate to an increase in the excise tax revenue.[11] When a_{VAT} is made equal to 0.7 and the elasticity v is assumed to be zero, it takes only R$4.2 billion of excise tax revenue to reduce the required VAT rate in 1 percentage point, from roughly 25 to 24 percent. When a_{VAT} is kept at 0.7 but the elasticity is assumed to be 0.33, it takes much less—only R$2.4 billion. However, the rate reduction is from approximately 30 to 29 percent.

The big question is how broad the VAT tax base finally extracted from congress could be. As seen above, about one-fifth of the potential base corresponds to residential housing services. As discussed in section 11.4, congress is bound to show great resistance to the inclusion of such services in the base and, also, to broadening the base as much as is needed in order to let it embrace most other services. Furthermore, arguments based on the idea of labeling the consumption of certain goods and services as either essential or meritorious should bring additional erosion to the tax base finally approved by congress. All things considered, in the end the feasible base may be excessively narrow and require an unreasonably high VAT rate. One may see, therefore, that there are considerable political and legislative risks to be taken into account, even if the involved difficulties are merely seen from an aggregate point of view.[12] Those risks are much amplified however when the difficulties that stem from fiscal federalism are brought to the scene.

11.6 The Fiscal Federalism Conundrum

It is impossible to fully understand the present deadlock in the tax reform negotiations without having in mind the complexity of the Brazilian fiscal federalism. If there is any hope of breaking the deadlock, that task is bound to require a much clearer analysis of interests, apprehensions, reasons, and motivations of the main actors involved. Today, nobody in the country seems to be satisfied with the present tax system. Cutting across the whole political spectrum in congress, there is an impressive consensus on the urgent need of a bold reform. However, as often happens, the consensus disappears as soon as the generic idea of the reform is left behind and the discussion starts to be a bit more detailed.

As seen in the previous sections, the main line of the reform proposals that have been discussed since 1997 involves a deep change in the way goods and services are taxed in the country. What has been envisaged is a reconstruction of value added taxation on broader and more rational grounds, in such a way as to allow the elimination of the turnover and cascading taxes

11. That may be easily checked in equation (4), which implicitly assumes the elasticity v to be zero. In that equation, the derivative of the required VAT rate with respect to R increases when a_{VAT} decreases.

12. See Werneck (2000) for an attempt to take those risks into account in the evaluation of the late 1997 proposal using an analytical framework based on Monte Carlo simulations.

that have gained so much importance over the last decade. However, because the combined revenue raised by taxes to be eliminated corresponds to 13.6 percent of GDP, that means a gigantic operation of extraordinary complexity and rife with uncertainties—particularly when seen from the point of view of fiscal federalism.

Since the late 1997 proposal, the federal government was careful enough to assure that there was no intention of imposing any kind of loss to any of the three government tiers. Neither the union nor any state or municipality would have to cope with shrinking fiscal resources. Commendable as that stated intention certainly was, it is widely known that in a reform of such scope it is practically impossible to prevent significant losses. Although it has been proposed that resources from a national compensation fund would be available to offset any losses, potential losers thought they had good reasons to be skeptical about the possibility of relying on the promised compensation scheme.

As seen in section 11.3, such skepticism lent force to proposals of abandoning the idea of a nationally managed VAT and adopting instead a dual VAT, involving the harmonic coexistence of separate but integrated federal and state value added taxes. That was the distinctive mark of the third and fourth proposals listed in table 11.5 (see Afonso et al. 2000). However, the federal government has remained unconvinced about the dual VAT arrangement.[13]

Because the three levels of government have been engaged for a long time in a very wearisome fiscal-adjustment effort, uneasiness about the possibility of losing revenue has been exacerbated. Initially, when the first reform proposal was outlined in 1997, apprehension about possible losses imposed by the reform was found primarily among governors and mayors. More recently, however, the federal government itself started to show its own misgivings, fearing that the reform could in some way reverse the spectacular increase in federal tax revenue observed since 1993, putting in jeopardy the consolidation of the whole stabilization effort.

The tax reform debate has become a noisy clash of conflicting views, increasingly marked by strong risk aversion toward revenue losses. There is fear on all sides. Initially agreed-upon compensation rules might not be respected and could be altered in the future. The tax base of the new VAT might have a totally different regional distribution, as the current origin-based value added tax is converted into a destination-based one. The total revenue collected might shrink. Introducing radical changes in consolidated tax legislation might open the way for unending litigations. For whatever reason, there could be revenue losses.

13. A full analysis of the possibilities of the dual VAT arrangement goes beyond the scope of the present paper. See Varsano (1995; 1999), Bird (1999), Bird and Gendron (1997), Keen (2000), and McLure (1999a,b).

Although there is an increasingly clear perception that the "fiscal war" among states is leading nowhere, governors fear a tax reform might tie their hands and put an end to the practice of using tax breaks to attract industrial investors. Also, governors of states situated in regions currently benefited by federal tax incentives fear that a reform might mean the final wiping out of those privileges.

As all those apprehensions interact, the result has been an escalating noncooperative game, marked by increasing mistrust—a game that seems to have pushed some of the involved parties into totally unreasonable positions. Federal tax authorities started to heartily defend the idea that cascading taxes are not so bad after all. At the state level, some governors seem entrenched to the point of defending as something sacred their right to continue to impose on some services, such as telecommunications, a 40 percent state VAT.

Even if there were a cooperative game within the federation, the reform would still be a rather complex operation—and, of course, such complexity has been much amplified by the conflicted way the reform has been discussed. As the difficult negotiations have dragged on over the years, relationships between some key interlocutors have become obviously overstrained, and some of the contending positions are becoming unreasonably crystallized.

Given the undeniable urgency of the reform, it is important to know how to start again, from scratch, if needed. There is no possible justification for prolonging the brutally irrational way the three levels of government have been extracting 32 percent of GDP in taxes from the economy. The powerful tax policy mobilization that was required to stage the stabilization battle has now to be reversed, opening the way to less primitive taxation forms that may enhance competitiveness and economic growth. There is no sense in putting off the whole reform issue to the other side of the 2002 elections. The present deadlock can only be broken by the federal government. In order to dispel the widespread mistrust that brought negotiations to a halt, the government has to show a credible commitment to a new tax reform proposal much bolder than the one announced in August 2000.

Concern with assuring the overall consistency of the new tax system that will stem from the reform should not be taken to the point of assuming that all changes will have to take place at the same moment. That would make the involved challenge seem more formidable than it actually is. A wiser move would be to try to decompose the envisaged reconstruction of the tax system into modules that would allow less complex political negotiations, easier implementation, and some degree of experimentation as the reform is phased in. This would also allow some leeway to correct unforeseen effects on the distribution of the tax revenue within the federation and to devise ways to offset revenue losses as the reform is pushed forward. Abandoning the idea of a sudden drastic reform that involves a sharp discontinuity and contemplating, instead, a sequence of relatively small changes that follow a careful and coherent plan seems to be a better way to assure less defensive and more cooperative stances from all those involved. That seems to be the key to overcoming the current deadlock.

On the other hand, it seems that too much stress has been put on indirect taxation in Brazil. The problem could become more tractable if part of that stress could be shifted onto the issue of direct taxes, because there seems to be ample room for a more intelligent exploitation of the personal income tax base in the country.[14]

References

Afonso, J. R., E. A. Araújo, F. Rezende, and R. Varsano. 2000. A tributação brasileira e o novo ambiente econômico (The Brazilian tax system and the new economic environment). *Revista do BNDES* 13 (June): 137–70.

Bird, R. 1999. Rethinking subnational taxes: A new look at tax assignment. IMF Working Paper no. WP/99/165. Washington, D.C.: International Monetary Fund, October.

Bird, R., and P. P. Gendron. 1997. Dual VATs and cross border: Two problems and one solution. University of Toronto, International Center for Tax Studies. Manuscript.

Confederação Nacional da Indústria. 1998. *Anais do seminário de reforma tributária* (Annals of the tax reform seminar). Rio de Janeiro: CNI, Unidade de Política Econômica.

Guérard, M. 1973. The Brazilian value-added tax. *IMF Staff Papers* 20 (July): 318–78.

Keen, M. 2000. VIVAT, CVAT, and all that: New forms of value-added tax for federal systems. IMF Working Paper no. WP/00/83. Washington, D.C.: International Monetary Fund, October.

McLure, C. E., Jr. 1999a. Implementing a state VAT: Breaking the logjam in tax assignment. Stanford University, Hoover Institution. Mimeograph.

———. 1999b. Protecting dual VATs from evasion on cross-border trade: An addendum to Bird and Gendron. Stanford University, Hoover Institution. Mimeograph.

Tanzi, V. 2000. Taxation in Latin America in the last decade. Paper prepared for the Conference on Fiscal and Financial Reforms in Latin America. 9–10 November, Stanford University.

Varsano, R. 1995. A tributação do comércio interestadual: ICMS atual versus ICMS partilhado (The taxation of interstate trade: ICMS versus shared ICMS).

14. A recent study conducted by the federal tax authorities concluded that the total revenue currently being generated by the still highly complex income tax system, which involves a top rate of 27.5 percent, could also be raised by a simple flat tax arrangement, which would keep the present US$5,000 per year basic exemption level and impose a tax rate of only 7.7 percent. That seems to be a good measure of the inefficacy of personal income taxation in the country. See "Alíquota única para IR esbarra em resistência política e jurídica," *Valor Econômico,* 18 October 2000.

Texto para Discussão no. 382. Brasília, Brasil: Instituto de Pesquisa Ecônomica Aplicada, September.
———. 1999. Subnational taxation and treatment of interstate trade in Brazil: Problems and a proposed solution. Paper presented at the World Bank Conference. Valdívia, Chile.
Werneck, R. L. F. 2000. A nova proposta de reforma tributária do governo: Limites do possível e incertezas envolvidas (The government's new tax reform proposal: Limits of the possible and uncertainties involved). *Revista de Economia Política* 20 (1): 92–118.

Comment Carola Pessino

Tax reform is a topic of extreme relevance both in Latin American countries and in other countries trying to reach a higher degree of fiscal federalism. Besides, it is also a key issue as regards growth and competitiveness in this region. I will comment on three matters that I consider important, and that, in my opinion, are not sufficiently stressed in this paper. I will also compare them with the executive's power proposal that came forward in Argentina in 1999; that has not been passed yet either, but shares many aspects with the Brazilian one.

My three comments will be (1) on the need to introduce in the reform ways to solve the problem of the vertical fiscal imbalance present in many federal countries, (2) to claim that the ideal tax to replace the ICMS (the Brazilian state VAT) and other turnover taxes is not vacuous, and that the best is the shared value-added tax (SVAT), a dual VAT; and (3) that the political difficulty of replacing origin taxation with destination taxation can be partially solved through a Canadian-like equalization transfer.

On the Need to Solve the Vertical Fiscal Imbalance Problem

It is important to stress the fact that both Brazil and Argentina need tax reform, but they need first a consistent and incentive-compatible tax-sharing revenue reform. I cannot see one without the other, and if I had to choose one, I would prefer the shared-revenue reform rather than the tax reform. Why? Because without reforming coparticipation, either level of government can revert the tax reform to its previous or even a worse state of events. On the other hand, even if the author correctly claims he is only trying to deal with the revenue-neutral operation of doing an efficient tax reform, the main point is that it is impossible and even useless to achieve it, unless the fiscal incentives of both the states and the federal government are improved.

Carola Pessino is professor of economics at Universidad Torcuato di Tella in Buenos Aires, Argentina.

I am referring to the vertical fiscal imbalance that pervades governments in Argentina, Brazil, and other federal countries. These countries are called *federal* because they are autonomous in the expenditure (but not in tax-rate) setting, base, and so on—that is, not in deciding the amount of taxes they want to have, and the size of public expenditure they would prefer.

Werneck mentions an example of this in the federal government of Brazil's having to invent very bad and inefficient cascading new taxes to circumvent the fact that it had to share revenue with the provinces; without doing so it would have been unable to diminish the fiscal deficit of the nation.

Another example is seen in the case of Argentina. The provinces promised, back in 1993, to gradually eliminate the gross receipts tax (*ingresos brutos*) and *sellos* (both of them cascading, turnover, and kafkian taxes). In fact, the provinces eliminated these taxes only for their own products, but left them in place for identical products made in other provinces, thus creating unconstitutional interior customs.

As figure 11C.1 shows, one of the most dramatic facts in Argentina today is the vertical fiscal imbalance. Although the provinces and municipalities spend 47 percent of total expenditure, they collect only 24 percent of the total revenues. As figure 11C.2 shows, there are enormous differences among provinces: While some collect more than 50 percent of total provincial revenue, others collect less than 10 percent.

In Brazil, if the ICMS is BR$67.7 billion and is one of the principal state taxes, and total Brazilian tax collection is 32 percent of GDP (i.e., around BR$800 billion), then ICMS is only 8–9 percent of GDP, leaving for the central government the bulk of tax collection but not the responsibilities of expenditure, as happens in Argentina. We should take into account that this imbalance can also be due to the following facts:

1. In Brazil, since the ICMS is an origin-VAT, and since there is fiscal vertical imbalance, it has caused the famous tax war between the states (or at least between some of them). Why? Because lowering tax rates of an origin consumption tax or a production tax leads to better conditions for investment to localize in the places where taxes were lowered. On the other hand, given the revenue-sharing agreement, states that lower rates are waiting for the helpful hand of the federal government, in (the likely) case they enter into fiscal problems.

2. A similar thing happens in Argentina, not only with the above-mentioned state gross receipts tax, but also with federal taxes such as the VAT and the income tax. Since provinces get a fixed percentage of these taxes, their total tax collection is of less concern; add to this the fact that the national government has agreed to give them at least a minimum amount, no matter how much is collected. One consequence of this was the creation of the so-called *industrial promotion* in the 1970s—a device to artificially attract investment, allowing some provinces to defer or not pay the payment

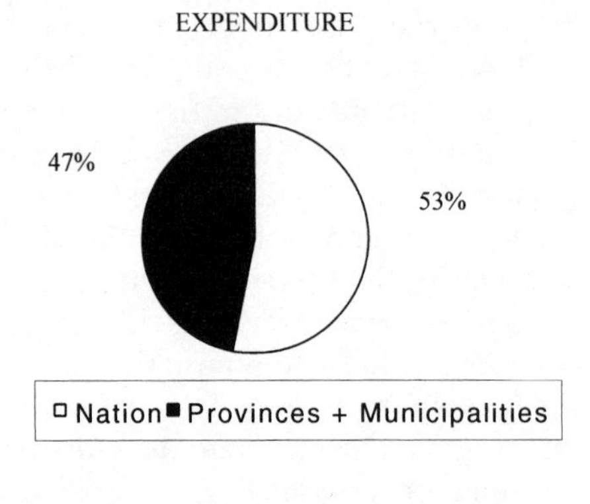

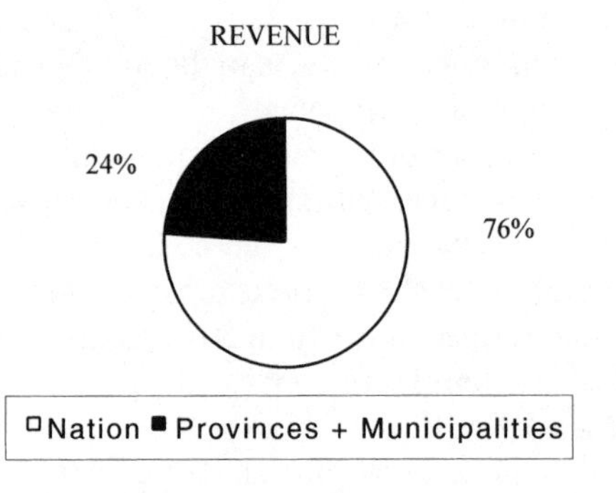

Expenditure and Revenue of Total Consolidated Government

By levels of Government In millions of $ Year 1997

	EXPENDITURE		**REVENUE**	
Nation	$41 175.00	53.4%	$54 573.00	76.1%
Provinces	$28 579.00	37.0%	$13 455.00	18.8%
Municipalities	$7 385.00	9.6%	$3 708.00	5.2%
TOTAL	$77 139.00	100.0%	$71 736.00	100.0%

Fig. 11C.1 Vertical fiscal imbalance: Argentina, 1997
Source: Minister of the economy, fiscal bulletin 1997 (fourth quarter).

of the national taxes for industries locating in their territories. Today, this costs Argentina $800 million a year. Given that it is an exemption, with the ensuing cheating and rent seeking, its total cost is estimated at least to double that amount.

Hence, I think it is important to stress that current sharing arrangements between states and the federal government can and do lead to bad taxes and bad exemptions, and—as has been the history in Argentina and Brazil—has helped things get worse as time goes by. Thus tax reform cannot be discussed before these federal arrangements.

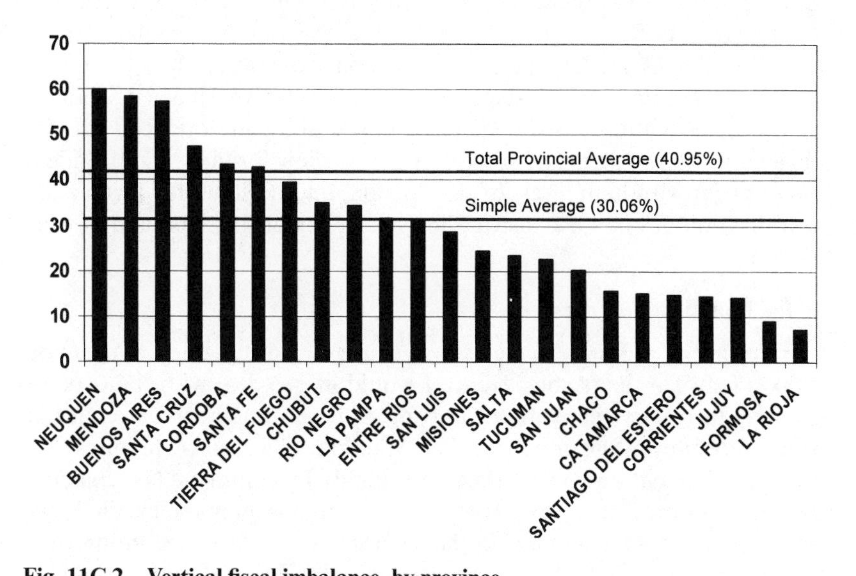

Fig. 11C.2 Vertical fiscal imbalance, by province
Source: Minister of the economy, projection of budget execution (1998).

The Best Tax to Replace Cascading and Production Taxes: The SVAT

My second point deals with the ideal tax or taxes to replace the ICMS and turnover taxes in Brazil, and gross receipts taxes in Argentina, while taking into account that the provinces need more fiscal responsibility (allowing them a higher tax base and to set their own tax rates).

In addition to this, given the facts of a concentration (both geographically and in amount) of income distribution, a high share of consumption and production taxes on total revenue, and, finally, high rates of tax evasion, Argentina's executive power arrived to the conclusion in 1999 that the SVAT was the best tool to replace the inefficient state taxes. On top of this, it would also allow for the decentralization of taxes. A team of national and international experts under my coordination put forward the reform, which, although has not yet been passed, is being considered by Argentina's current government.[1]

The positive aspect of the SVAT is that it is both a federal and a provincial tax, and given the federal participation, it does not require the compli-

1. See Varsano (1995); Fenochietto (1998); Courchene (1998); McLure (1999); Bird (1999); Secretary of Fiscal Equity (1999). Fenochietto learned about the Varsano proposal of the *barquinho* in Brazil, adapted it to the Argentine context, and commended it to McLure, who was hired by the Argentine government. He was surprised that a proposal of a provincial VAT could be practically implemented. In short, a new literature was developed on the subject.

cated administrative procedures, as discussed in Europe, with the clearing-house method or the deferred payment of the tax in interprovincial sales. In the SVAT, there is a federal perception rate on those sales, which is later on refunded to the states as the stages of production evolve. Hence it is practical; it is a destination-based consumption tax, and therefore does not distort localization of firms. Besides, it does not allow for tax wars. It is ideal for countries with high levels of tax evasion, and it allows for further decentralization of taxes because it allows for a flexible tax base and flexible tax rates.

On the Equalization Transfer

The problem, as Werneck mentions, remains the distribution of the mass of taxes between the parties. Hence I would like to deal with the issue of changing the tax system without hurting, at least initially, the revenues of the nation or any of the provinces. The Argentine constitution requires that the initial distribution be left intact. To sum up, I recommend (1) replacing the inefficient provincial taxes with an SVAT and keeping the original revenue initially intact; (2) reducing the federal VAT rate and accordingly increasing the provincial VAT rates, allowing for tax decentralization; and (3) distributing the remaining coparticipation mass according to the equalization transfer, which is the subject of this section.[2]

We worked with a team of Canadian experts (which included Thomas Courchene) and, without going into many details, arrived at the conclusion that the equalization transfer (similar to the Canadian) would still allow some part of the federal revenue to be shared with the provinces, satisfying the constitutional principle of equity; would not lead to the rescue of badly managed provinces; and would allow (partial) compensation of the producing provinces.

Hence, we added to the SVAT the equalization transfer, which consists of calculating the tax base for each province and the average tax rate, and then computing the difference between the potential provincial tax collection and this average in per capita terms. If the potential provincial tax collection is lower than the average, those provinces would be compensated in the difference calculated above. This equalization transfer (derived from the now lower coparticipation mass of the nation) would provide an incentive for the provinces to collect taxes because it is calculated over the *tax base,* not the taxes actually collected. Hence, a province will receive the same transfer, based on its potential to collect taxes, regardless of whether the province chooses to fulfill its collection potential.[3] It is important to notice

2. The actual proposal for reform in Argentina contemplated additional important considerations, such as decentralization of other taxes, a time frame that would allow for gradually achieving the new tax rates, etc. For more on it see note 1.

3. The equalization formula in per capita terms can be written simply as $E_i/N_i = \text{Max}(0, t^*[C/N - C_i/N_i])$ where i indexes provinces, E is the equalization transfer, N is the population,

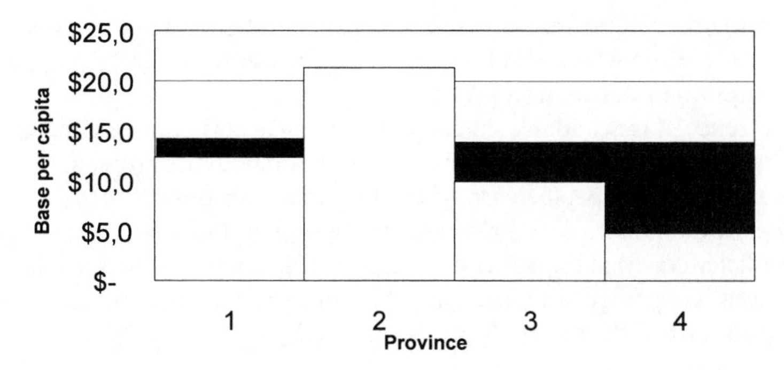

Fig. 11C.3 Equalization transfers

that this transfer would be recalculated periodically (every one or two years) and does not stay fixed, as actual coparticipation rates do. Figure 11C.3 shows the workings of the equalization transfer assuming there are only four provinces. The darker shaded areas indicate the average provincial collections and the amount of transfer is shown by the lighter shaded area. If one province decided to be a bad tax collector, its transfer would not change because it is based on the potential revenue; hence the transfer would not benefit an inefficient province, but would motivate the efficient ones. In short,

1. The transfer rewards good tax collection, because it remains the same whether the province collects more or less, or claims more or less exemption (this is the opposite of what is going on in Brazil and Argentina these days).
2. It helps the truly poor provinces according to their tax base per capita, and hence it gives citizens at least the average of per capita public spending.
3. As shown in Fenochietto and Pessino (2000),[4] the transfer deals with at least some of the greatest political opponents to this reform: the self-described "producing provinces."

In short, Werneck's paper deals with one of the most important problems in Latin American countries today. However, I have sought to emphasize the following: (1) consideration of the vertical fiscal imbalance created by current coparticipation agreements; (2) choice and implementation of the SVAT, given that imbalance; and (3) use of the equalization transfer, which

C is consumption, and t^* is the average provincial tax rate. Hence, province i receives a per capita equalization transfer E_i/N_i to compensate for its lower potential tax collection in comparison to the average (for all provinces) per capita potential tax collection.

4. Fenochietto and Pessino (2000). Basically, they show that replacing the provincial production taxes by a provincial destination VAT while keeping total revenues constant and provincial tax rates equal, the producing provinces either would collect less revenues or would need higher tax rates to collect the same revenue as before. This loss in revenue is positively related to the value of exports of the province. On the other hand, the equalization transfer is higher, other things constant, the higher the provincial exports are.

gives provinces good incentives, is equitable, and compensates provinces that lose revenue when switching from production or origin VAT taxes to consumption or destination VAT taxes.

In essence, it is my advice that any tax reform of this kind should include the three points mentioned above that have to do with the problem of fiscal federalism. In the specific case of the tax reform in Brazil, in the first instance, I would discard the national VAT to replace the ICMS. Although it is an efficient tax that replaces a cascading inefficient tax, it worsens the vertical fiscal imbalance, and hence it is bound to end up in some years to be worse than when the reform was implemented.

References

Bird, Richard. 1999. Rethinking tax assignment: The need for better subnational taxes. IMF Working Paper no. 99/165. Washington, D.C.: International Monetary Fund.

Courchene, Thomas. 1998. Fiscal federalism in Argentina: Towards a nation-province covenant. Manuscript prepared for the World Bank and for the Secretary of Fiscal Equity, Argentina.

Fenochietto, Ricardo. 1998. El IVA compartido: Una herramienta útil para el reemplazo del impuesto sobre los ingresos brutos y la descentralización de tributos (The shared value-added tax: A useful tool to replace the gross receipts tax and for tax decentralization). *Jornadas de Finanzas Públicas* 31:151.

Fenochietto, Ricardo, and Carola Pessino. 2000. The shared value added tax: How it works and why it is the best tool for optimal fiscal federalism in countries with consumption based taxes. *Documento de Trabajo* no. 176. Buenos Aires: Universidad del Cema, September. Available online at [http://www.cema.edu.ar/publicaciones/].

McLure, Charles. 1999. Implementing subnational VATs on internal trade: The compensating VAT (CVAT). *International Tax and Public Finance* 7 (6): 723–40.

Secretary of Fiscal Equity. 1999. Proposal of reform to the federal coparticipation regime in Argentina. Buenos Aires: Chief of Cabinet of Ministers of the Argentine Government.

Varsano, Ricardo. 1995. A tributação do comércio interestadual: ICMS atual versus ICMS partilhado (Taxation of interprovincial trade: Current ICMS versus shared ICMS). *Texto para Discussão* no. 382. Brasilia: Instituto de Pesquisa Ecônomica Aplicada, September.

Comment Michael Michaely

One of the papers' primary contributions is the construction of a model to analyze the feasibility of replacing one set of taxes (for goods and services) by another set; in the concrete case, by (exclusively, or mostly) a federal-

Michael Michaely is the Aron and Michael Chilewich Professor Emeritus of International Trade at the Hebrew University of Jerusalem.

level VAT. Simulation exercises using this model then show alternative levels of required tax rates.

Without subtracting from the value of this analysis—and certainly not in any way suggesting a substitute for it—it appears to me that presenting some of its basic ideas in a diagrammatic form may help bring the system's essential elements into focus. Specifically, this could easily address the issue, raised by Werneck and incorporated in his model, of the "effectiveness" of a tax base (or the degree of tax evasion) being dependent on the tax rate; that is, its being endogenously determined. I thus propose such presentation as a supplement to the analysis; this is done in figure 11C2.1.

Let

t = tax rate (in this instance, VAT rate);
r = ratio of tax base to GDP;
a = isorevenue curve (T = tax revenue, specified either in money or as proportion of GDP);
b = response of tax base to tax rate; and
T_1, T_2 = (alternative) desired levels of tax revenue.

With T_1, the tax rate should be fixed at t_1, yielding the tax-base ratio r_1. As the diagram is drawn, this is the only tax rate compatible with the desired level of tax revenue. At a higher tax, the revenue would be higher than desired; and it would be below target with a lower tax rate. This specific outcome is due to b being drawn as steeper than a. Were it the other way around, the conclusion would stay the same, except for actual revenue being below target at a tax rate above t_1, and vice versa.

It is also conceivable that b would cut a twice (or logically even more). In

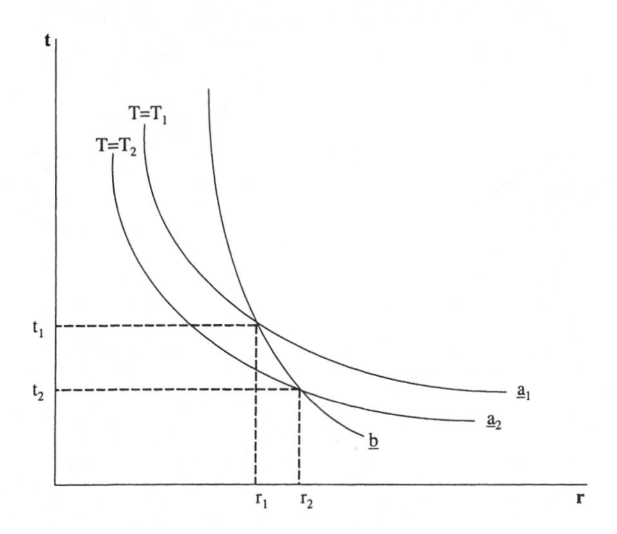

Fig. 11C2.1 Compatibility of the tax rate with revenue targets

this case, there would be not one but two (or more) tax rates that are compatible with the desired revenue target. On conventional taxing principles, the lower of these tax rates (combined with the higher tax-base ratio) should then be selected.

Turning back to the case of a single compatible rate, suppose t_1 is considered too high (for conventional reasons—economic or political). The target tax revenue must then be lowered, to a level such as T_2: the tax rate would be fixed at t_2, with a tax-base ratio of r_2. This inference depends again on slopes. Were *b* to be drawn as flatter than *a*, a lower tax ratio would yield a higher revenue. This is analogous to a position of unstable equilibrium. It is one often assumed in policy debates.

The last inference does not depend on an assumed effect of the tax rate on GDP—the latter is taken here as a given, as it is in Werneck's analysis. Allowing such an effect would require a three-dimensional analysis. Curves like a_1, a_2 would then be derived from slices of a three-dimensional body.

Contributors

Philip L. Brock
Department of Economics
University of Washington
M-230 Savery Hall
P.O. Box 353330
Seattle, WA 98195

Ricardo J. Caballero
Department of Economics
Massachusetts Institute of Technology
E52-252A50 Memorial Drive
Cambridge, MA 02142

Vittorio Corbo
Pontificia Catholic University of Chile
Casilla 76, Correo 17
Santiago
Chile

Enrique Dávila
Public Policy Unit
Mexican President Staff
Constituyentes 1001 Edificio A, Piso 6
Colonia Belen de las Flores
C.P. 01110
Mexico D.F.

Francisco Gil Díaz
Minister of Treasury and Public Credit
Pimer Patio Mariano 3er Piso
Palacio Nacional
Col Centro
Mexico D.F. 06000

Tatiana Didier
The World Bank
Department of Macroeconomic Development and Growth
1825 R Street NW
Washington, DC 20009

Ricardo Fenochietto
Virrey Arrendondo 2225 Piso 1
Buenos Aires 1426
Argentina

Gustavo H. B. Franco
Rio Bravo Investimentos Ltda
Av. Nilo pecanha 50-22, salas 2201-2202
Centro
Rio de Jeneiro, RJ 20020-100
Brazil

Márcio G. P. Garcia
Pontificia Universidade Catolica do Rio de Janeiro
Rua Marques de Sao Vicente, 225
Rio de Janeiro, RJ
2245-900

José Antonio González
General Director for Insurance and Securities
Ministry of Treasury and Public Credit
Tercer Patio Mariano 4o Piso
Palacio Nacional
Col Centro
Mexico D.F. 06000

Pablo E. Guidotti
Universidad Torcuato Di Tella
Minones 2159/77
1428 Buenos Aires
Argentina

Stephen Haber
Department of Political Science
Stanford University
Stanford, CA 94305

Anne O. Krueger
Suite 12-300F
International Monetary Fund
700 19th Street NW
Washington, DC 20431

Santiago Levy
General Director
Mexican Social Security Institute
Reforma 476, 1er Piso
Col Juarez
Mexico D.F.

Michael Michaely
Hebrew University of Jerusalem
32 Arbel St.
P.O.B 84488
Mevasseret-Zion 90805
Israel

Carola Pessino
Universidad del CEMA
Cordoba 374
1045 Capital Federal
Argentina

Klaus Schmidt-Hebbel
director, Economic Research
Central Bank of Chile
Augustinas 1180, Casilla 967
Santiago
Chile

Vito Tanzi
Sottosegretari
Italian Ministry of Economy and Finance
Rome, Italy

Aaron Tornell
Department of Economics
University of California, Los Angeles
Bunche Hall 8387
Box 951477
Los Angeles, CA 90095-1477

Rogério L. F. Werneck
Department of Economics
Pontifical Catholic University (PUC-Rio)
Rua Marques de Sao Vicente, 225
Rio de Janeiro, RJ
22453-900
Brazil

Alejandro Werner
Director of Economic Studies
Bank of Mexico
5 de mayo 18, piso 4
Col Centro
Mexico D. F. 06059

Roberto Zahler
Fromer Central Bank Governor
Zahler y Compañia
Ave Ricardo Lyon 222
Oficina 1701
Providencia
Santiago de Chile

Author Index

Subject Index